TANAK

TANAK

A THEOLOGICAL AND CRITICAL INTRODUCTION
TO THE JEWISH BIBLE

MARVIN A. SWEENEY

Fortress Press
Minneapolis

TANAK
A Theological and Critical Introduction to the Jewish Bible

Cover image from: Bezalel Narkiss, *Hebrew Manuscripts in the British Isles: Spanish and Portuguese Manuscripts*. [Oxford]: Oxford University Press, [1982]. 1st edition. 2 Volumes.
Cover design: Laurie Ingram
Book design: Duncan Burns, Forthcoming Publications

Library of Congress Cataloging-in-Publication Data
Sweeney, Marvin A. (Marvin Alan), 1953-
  Tanak : a theological and critical introduction to the Jewish Bible / Marvin A. Sweeney.
    p. cm.
  Includes bibliographical references and index.
  ISBN 978-0-8006-3743-9 (alk. paper)
  1. Bible. O.T.--Theology. 2. Bible. O.T.--Criticism, interpretation, etc. I. Title.
  BS1192.5.S94 2011
  221'.6--dc22
                        2011015058

The paper used in this publication meets the minimum requirements of American National Standard for Information Sciences — Permanence of Paper for Printed Library Materials, ANSI Z329.48-1984.

Manufactured in the U.S.A.

15   14   13   12   1   2   3   4   5   6   7   8   9   10

For Rolf and Hildegard Knierim

Contents

b.   The Exodus from Egypt   85

c.   From Raamses to Sukkot:
     Consecration of the First-Born   91

d.   From Sukkot to Etham: The Pillar of Fire and Cloud   92

e.   From Etham to the Sea: Deliverance at the Reed Sea   92

f.   From the Reed Sea to the Wilderness of Shur/Elim:
     Water in the Wilderness   93

g.   From Elim to the Wilderness of Sin:
     Quails and Manna   94

h.   From Sin to Rephidim: Amalek and Jethro   95

i.   From Rephidim to Sinai: Revelation of Torah   96

     1)   Arrival at Sinai   96

     2)   Revelation from the Mountain   97

     3)   Revelation from the Tabernacle   107

     4)   Census and Organization of the People
          around the Tabernacle   121

12. The Generations of Aaron and Moses: Israel under
     the Guidance of the Levites   123

     a.   Sanctification of the People at Sinai Led by the Levites   127

     b.   From Sinai to the Wilderness of Paran:
          Rebellion in the Wilderness   131

     c.   Moses' Final Addresses to Israel,
          Transfer of Leadership, and Death in Moab   145

          1)   The Account of Moses' Speeches to Israel
               in Moab   148

               a)   Moses' First Speech to Israel:
                    Exhortational Summary of Israel's Journey
                    from Horeb/Sinai to Moab   148

               b)   Moses' Second Speech to Israel:
                    Exhortational Summary of Divine Torah   150

               c)   Moses' Third Speech to Israel:
                    Blessings and Curses   161

               d)   Moses' Fourth Speech to Israel:
                    Final Exhortation to Observe the Covenant   163

          2)   The Account of Moses' Transfer of Leadership,
               Death, and Burial in Moab   164

PART IIIA. THE FORMER PROPHETS

PART IIIB. THE LATTER PROPHETS

PART IV. THE KETUVIM/WRITINGS

PART V. CONCLUSION

ACKNOWLEDGMENTS

This volume is the product of a lifetime of study of the Tanak and Jewish tradition from the time of my childhood education, Bar Mitzvah, and Confirmation in Judaism at Temple B'nai Abraham, Decatur, Illinois (1958–71); my undergraduate education in Religious Studies and Political Science at the University of Illinois, Urbana-Champaign (1971–75); my year as the first full-time Jewish (non-degree) student at the Princeton Theological Seminary (1975–76); my Ph.D. program at the Claremont Graduate School (1976–83); and postdoctoral study at the Hebrew University of Jerusalem (1988–90). It is also the product of my years of professional engagement in Bible and Jewish Studies as Jewish Studies Teacher at the Jewish Center, Princeton, New Jersey (1975–76); Hebrew Teacher at Congregation Emanuel, San Bernardino, California (1980–82); Assistant and Associate Professor of Religious Studies at the University of Miami (1983–94); Yad HaNadiv Barechah Foundation Fellow in Jewish Studies at the Hebrew University of Jerusalem (1989–90); Dorot Research Professor at the W. F. Albright Institute, Jerusalem, Israel (1993–94); Adult Education Teacher at Temple Israel of Greater Miami (1984–93); Visiting Professor of Bible at the Hebrew Union College—Jewish Institute for Religion, Los Angeles (1994–95; 1999; 2003–4); Lilly Research Professor (1997–98); Professor of Hebrew Bible at the Claremont School of Theology (1994–present); Professor of Religion at the Claremont Graduate University (1994–present); Taus Lecturer at Congregation Beth El in San Pedro, California (1996–present); Lecturer at the Har-El Institute, Palm Desert, California (2003–present); and Professor of Tanak at the Academy for Jewish Religion California (2001–present). During these years I have learned much from a multitude of teachers, colleagues, and friends, both at the institutions where I have taught and studied and through the various scholarly and community organizations in which I have had the pleasure to be involved. I am blessed by a multitude of students as well, including undergraduate, graduate, ministerial, rabbinical, cantorial, chaplaincy, and lay students from a wide variety of religious backgrounds.

I am indebted to my wife, Muna, and our daughter, Leah, for their love, support, and understanding throughout the course of writing this book—and many others, both finished and yet to come! Were it not for them, I could accomplish nothing.

I would like to thank my Ph.D. student, Ms. Soo Jung Kim, for her careful reading of the manuscript; her sharp eye has saved me from many errors.

I also wish to thank Dr. Duncan Burns, of Forthcoming Publications, who did the final copy-editing of the volume. Any errors that remain are my own responsibility.

I dedicate this volume to Rolf and Hildegard Knierim. Rolf was my Ph.D. advisor. He guided my initial dissertation, trained me to be a biblical scholar and theologian, and continues to teach me so much about the fields of biblical theology and biblical studies in general. Hildegard, his wife, guides him and his students through life with matchless good humor and hospitality!

NOTE TO THE READER

In keeping with some streams of Jewish tradition, in the following pages I do not spell out the name of G-d but use terms such as YHWH, G-d, the L-RD, Eloqim, Eloqeinu, and so on, so as not to desecrate the Holy Name of G-d.

ABBREVIATIONS

AB	Anchor Bible
ABD	*Anchor Bible Dictionary*. Edited by D. N. Freedman. 6 vols. New York, 1992
AnBib	Analecta biblica
ANEP	*The Ancient Near East in Pictures Relating to the Old Testament*. Edited by J. B. Pritchard. Princeton, 1954
ANET	*Ancient Near Eastern Texts Relating to the Old Testament*. Edited by J. B. Pritchard. 3d ed. Princeton, 1969
AOAT	Alter Orient und Altes Testament
AOTC	Abingdon Old Testament Commentaries
AThANT	Abhandlungen zur Theologie des Alten und Neuen Testaments
BBB	Bonner Biblische Beiträge
BEATAJ	Beiträge zur Erforschung des Alten Testaments und des antiken Judentum
BETL	Bibliotheca Ephemeridum Theologicarum Lovaniensium
Bib	*Biblica*
BibInt	*Biblical Interpretation*
BibOr	Biblica et orientalia
BibSem	The Biblical Seminar
BJS	Brown and Judaic Studies
BKAT	Biblischer Kommentar Altes Testament
BO	Berit Olam
BWANT	Beiträge zur Wissenschaft vom Alten und Neuen Testament
BZAW	Beihefte zur Zeitschrift für die Alttestamentliche Wissenschaft
CBQ	*The Catholic Biblical Quarterly*
CBQMS	Catholic Biblical Quarterly Monograph Series
CCAR	Central Conference of America Rabbis
ChrH	The Chronicler's History
ConBibOT	Coniectanea biblica: Old Testament Series
ContCom	Continental Commentaries
CR:BS	*Currents in Research: Biblical Studies*
CRIANT	Compendia rerum Iudaicarum ad Novum Testamentum
DJD	Discoveries in the Judean Desert
DtrH	Deuteronomistic History
EncJud	*Encyclopaedia Judaica*. 16 vols. Jerusalem, 1972

FAT	Forschungen zum Alten Testament
FOTL	Forms of the Old Testament Literature
FRLANT	Forschungen zur Religionen und Literatur des Alten und Neuen Testaments
HALOT	*Hebrew and Aramaic Lexicon of the Old Testament.* Edited L. Koehler and W. Baumgartner. 5 vols. Leiden, 1994–99
HAT	Handbuch zum Alten Testament
HBT	*Horizons in Biblical Theology*
HKAT	Handkommentar zum Alten Testament
HS	*Hebrew Studies*
HSM	Harvard Semitic Monographs
HSS	Harvard Semitic Studies
HUCA	*Hebrew Union College Annual*
IBT	Interpreting Biblical Texts
ICC	International Critical Commentary
IDB[S]	*The Interpreter's Dictionary of the Bible Supplementary Volume*
IEJ	*Israel Exploration Journal*
Int	*Interpretation*
JAOS	*Journal of the American Oriental Society*
JBibTh	*Jahrbuch für Biblische Theologie*
JBL	*Journal of Biblical Literature*
JPS	Jewish Publication Society
JR	*Journal of Religion*
JSJSup	Journal for the Study of Judaism Supplement Series
JSOT	*Journal for the Study of the Old Testament*
JSOTSup	Journal for the Study of the Old Testament Supplement Series
JSS	*Journal of Semitic Studies*
KAT	Kommentar zum Alten Testament
LBT	Library of Biblical Theology
LHBOTS	Library of Hebrew Bible/Old Testament Studies
NCenB	New Century Bible Commentary
NEAEHL	*New Encyclopaedia of Archaeological Excavations in the Holy Land.* Edited by E. Stern et al. 4 vols. Jerusalem, 1993
NICOT	New International Commentary on the Old Testament
OBO	Orbis Biblicus et Orientalis
OBT	Overtures to Biblical Theology
OT Guides	Old Testament Guides
OTL	Old Testament Library
POS	Pretoria Oriental Studies
ResBibSt	Resources for Biblical Studys
SAC	Studies in Antiquity and Christianity
SBL	Society of Biblical Literature
SBLDS	Society of Biblical Literature Dissertation Series
SBLMS	Society of Biblical Literature Monograph Series

SBLSymS	Society of Biblical Literature Symposium Series
SBS	Stuttgarter Bibelstudien
SBT	Studies in Biblical Theology
SBTS	Sources for Biblical and Theological Study
SOTSMS	Society for Old Testament Study Monograph Series
TDNT	*Theological Dictionary of the New Testament.* Edited by G. Kittel et al. 10 vols. Grand Rapids, 1964–76
ThLZ	*Theologische Literaturzeitung*
TSAJ	Texte und Studien zum antiken Judentum
VTSup	Vetus Testamentum Supplements
WBC	Word Biblical Commentary
WMANT	Wissenschaftliche Monographien zum Alten und Neuen Testament
ZAW	*Zeitschrift für die alttestamentliche Wissenschaft*

Part I

Introduction

A. The Tanak as the Foundation of Judaism

THE TANAK, OR THE JEWISH BIBLE, stands as the quintessential foundation for Jewish life, identity, practice, and thought from antiquity through contemporary times. The five books of the Torah, or the Instruction of G-d to the Jewish people and the world at large, constitute the foundation of the Tanak. According to Jewish tradition (Exod 19—Num 10), the Torah was revealed to the nation Israel at Mount Sinai while the people were journeying from Egypt through the wilderness of Sinai on their way to return to the land of Israel to take up residence in the land promised by G-d to their ancestors, Abraham and Sarah; Isaac and Rebecca; Jacob, Rachel and Leah; and the twelve sons of Jacob. The four books of the Nevi'im Rishonim, or the Former Prophets, provide an account of Israel's life in the land from the time of the conquest under Joshua until the time of the Babylonian exile, when Jerusalem and the Temple were destroyed and Jews were exiled to Babylonia and elsewhere in the world. The four books of the Nevi'im Ahronim, or the Latter Prophets, provide an assessment of the reasons why G-d chose to exile Jews from the land of Israel and the scenarios by which G-d would choose to restore Jews to the land of Israel once the exile was completed. The eleven books of the Ketuvim, or the Writings, include a variety of books of different form and purpose that address various aspects of Jewish worship, critical thought, future expectations, history, and life in the world, both in the land of Israel and beyond.

The Torah and the other books of the Tanak hardly stand as the exclusive foundation for Judaism. The Torah is read in continuous conversation with the other books of the Prophets and the Writings, and the Tanak as a whole is read in continuous conversation with the other writings of Judaism, such as the Rabbinic literature of the Talmuds, the Midrashim, the Targums, and the speculative or mystical literature; the medieval and modern works of Jewish liturgy, halakhah, commentary, philosophy, Kabbalah, and Hasidism. With regard to the books of the Tanak, it is not clear that all of them were intentionally composed for the purpose of intertextual dialogue among them, but their inclusion in the Tanak requires that they be read as such in Jewish tradition. With regard to the Tanak and the rest of Jewish tradition, it is not clear that the Tanak was composed to be in intentional dialogue with the later works, but it is clear that most of the later writings were intentionally composed to be in dialogue with the Torah and the rest of the Tanak to some degree. In order to understand that dialogue fully, it is essential to understand the literature of the Torah and the rest of the Tanak in and of itself, recognizing that the Tanak cannot function as a complete and self-contained revelation analogous to the manner in which the Old and New Testaments are read in much of Protestant Christianity. The Torah and the rest of the Tanak are the foundation of Jewish tradition, but the Tanak cannot be viewed as complete in Judaism without ongoing dialogue with the rest of the tradition that constitutes Judaism throughout its history and into the future.

In an effort to interpret the Tanak as the foundational sacred scriptures of Judaism, this volume proposes a systematic critical and theological study of the Jewish Bible. It draws upon the Christian discipline of biblical or Old Testament theology, although its aims and presuppositions are very different, in large measure due to the different aims and presuppositions of Judaism and Christianity. It is critical insofar as it draws heavily on modern critical study of the Bible, although throughout the volume it will be clear that the critical foundations must themselves be self-critically examined at every point in order to provide a secure basis for theological assessment of the biblical works. The reason for such self-critical analysis lies in the fact that modern interpreters are so frequently influenced by their own religious and cultural traditions in reading the Bible and making claims for what the Bible has to say. It is theological insofar as it attempts to discern the theological viewpoints articulated by the biblical texts by close attention to its formal linguistic features and modes of expression, its historical and cultural contexts, and its willingness to grapple with the major theological, hermeneutical, and historical questions of its time. At the same time, this work recognizes that the process of reading biblical literature necessarily entails construction of the biblical text by readers who bring their own worldviews and presuppositions to the interpretative task. It is also theological insofar as it includes dialogue with the Jewish tradition at large. Such an interpretative stance recognizes that the interpretations offered in this work are nothing more than that. They are interpretations of the Bible that may or may not withstand the test of critical scrutiny and that may or may not be accepted as correct, useful, insightful, or even complete. As such, they are part of the ongoing dialogue that has taken place among the Jewish people—and among all interpreters of the Tanak at large—from the time that the books of the Tanak were first written and read. On that basis, a systematic critical and theological assessment of the Tanak provides foundations for dialogue with the rest of the Jewish tradition and perhaps also for dialogue with other Jewish and non-Jewish interpreters of the Bible.

B. CHRISTIAN OLD TESTAMENT THEOLOGY

Jon Levenson argues that Jews are not interested in biblical theology because the field is inherently Christian and because so much of its teaching is antithetical to that of Judaism if not outright anti-Jewish.[1] To a certain degree, he is correct. Biblical and Old Testament theology are quintessentially Christian theological disciplines designed to address questions of Christian theological thought, particularly the interrelationship between the biblical text as read in Christianity and the formulation of dogmatic or systematic Christian theological teachings that play such an important role in Christian life and thought. Judaism does not rely on systematic theology or doctrines in quite the way that Christianity does. Instead, Jewish interpreters pay close attention to the details of the biblical text in an effort to discern the various aspects of its meaning and its impact on Jewish life and thought. Nevertheless, Christian biblical and Old Testament theology provide a model of systematic interpretation of the Bible from which Jewish biblical interpretation may benefit. Although Christian efforts at such systematic interpretation of the whole of the Christian Bible or the Old Testament are not always successful, the question raised by the field—viz., to what degree can the Old Testament as a whole be interpreted?—is a valid question that may be asked by Jews of the Tanak. Biblical theology provides a synthetic overview of the interpretation of the Bible that aids interpreters in understanding the Bible at its most general and overarching levels. That is not to say that detailed exegesis of individual passages is no longer necessary; rather, biblical theology is ideally based on the detailed exegesis of individual passages that contribute to the overall interpretation of the biblical text. For Jews, biblical theology provides the means to incorporate the interpretation of the individual passages of the Tanak into an overarching scheme that will facilitate fuller understanding of the interpretation of the Tanak at large. Such an effort has the potential to provide Judaism with a fuller reading of its foundational scriptures. It also has the potential to provide similar insight to non-Jewish readers via a Jewish reading of the biblical text that is frequently quite distinct from Christian (or Muslim) readings of the same.

A brief and selective survey of the field of Christian biblical or Old Testament theology illustrates both Levenson's concerns about the field and the possibilities that a Jewish biblical theology might offer.[2]

The origins of biblical theology appear in the 1787 inaugural lecture of Johan P. Gabler, "An Oration on the Proper Distinction between Biblical and Dogmatic Theology and the Specific Objectives of Each," which celebrated Gabler's appointment to the faculty of the University of Altdorf.³ Gabler took up a problem faced by Protestant theologians concerning the interrelationship between interpretation of the biblical text and dogmatic theology as the foundations for Christian thought and practice. Although the Protestant Reformation, initiated by Martin Luther in the early sixteenth century, asserted the principle of *sola scriptura,* "scripture alone," as the foundation for Christian thought, dogmatic theology, derived from a combination of scriptural interpretation and human reason, actually governed the formation of Protestant theology, often confusing the boundaries between the two fields and giving ascendancy to dogmatic theology. The issue was exacerbated by the question of the interrelationship between the New Testament and the Old Testament, particularly because the New Testament so frequently overrode the Old Testament in Christian thought, thereby undermining the status of the Old Testament as sacred scripture. Gabler argued that interpreters must distinguish between historical and universal concerns or between human and divine concerns. In Gabler's understanding, the Bible provided a combination of historical/human and universal/divine concerns that must be considered in the development of Christian dogmatic theology. That is, the Bible would have to be analyzed to determine which of its elements were historical/human and which were universal/divine and therefore fit for the development of dogmatic theology. Of course, Christian doctrines concerning G-d, Christ, sin, and salvation would be considered universal/divine in Gabler's reckoning; other aspects, such as Esther's portrayal of divine absence at a time of threat to the Jewish people, would be considered historical or human and therefore less influential in the development of Christian doctrine. Gabler did not offer further writings on the field of biblical theology, but his essay nevertheless inaugurated the field and defined its basic parameters for well over a century.

Throughout much of the nineteenth and early twentieth centuries, the field of biblical theology focused especially on Gabler's distinction between the historical and the universal, as well as the interrelationship between the Old Testament and the New Testament. The New Testament was generally given theological priority since it spoke directly of Christ as the foundation for Christianity, and the Old Testament tended to be treated as a historical document that paved the way forward for the New Testament. The historically oriented source-critical research of the time, identified especially with Julius Wellhausen, and the prevailing anti-Semitism of the period played important roles delegitimizing major portions of the Old Testament as historical.⁴ Wellhausen's schema for the formation of the Pentateuch and the development of Israelite religion posited a progressive decline in which the early J source of the Pentateuch presented face-to-face encounters between human beings and G-d, much like the Prophets, whereas the later E, D, and P sources displayed increasing distance between G-d and humanity, culminating in the Priestly source which, in Wellhausen's view, focused on issues of ritual, law, and the self-interests of the priesthood at the expense of an authentic relationship between G-d and human beings. Thus, the priesthood represented the particularism of Judaism, which ultimately produced Rabbinic Judaism, while works such as Deutero-Isaiah represented the universalism of Judaism, which would culminate in the development of Christianity as the true fulfillment of the Old Testament. Wellhausen viewed himself as a historian, but his work and that of his followers had tremendous impact on the field of biblical theology, which increasingly set aside historical elements of the particularistic Old Testament in favor of the so-called universal elements that would be found in the New Testament. Many biblical theologians would therefore focus on "universal" categories, such as "G-d, Man, and Salvation" or the like, which of course are central to the New Testament, to organize their theologies.[5] Such efforts highlight the universal elements that tied the Old and New Testaments together and that showed how the Old Testament paved the way for the New Testament.

Nevertheless, such efforts also played a role in raising questions concerning the revelatory character or authority of scripture within Christianity. If some aspects of the Old Testament and perhaps also the New were only historical, they could not be viewed as authoritative sacred scripture, and yet such texts and perspectives were part of the Christian Bible. This led, in the early twentieth century, to intense discussion concerning the interrelationship between the history of Israelite religion and the field of Old Testament theology in an effort to clarify the status of historical material in the Bible and to justify the enterprise of Old Testament theology in principle. As an advocate of the field of Old Testament theology who also recognized the historical character of the Bible, Walter Eichrodt published a three-volume Old Testament theology in 1933–39 which attempted to interpret the entire Hebrew Bible around the theme of covenant, while recognizing the historical nature of the conceptualization of covenant throughout.[6] Eichrodt's work is still in print today and remains highly influential. It has the advantage of attempting to account for the entirety of the Hebrew Bible, but it also displays major problems. One is Eichrodt's own anti-Semitism, which comes to expression in his characterization of Judaism's "torso-like appearance . . . in separation from Christianity."[7] A second is the fact that not all of the Hebrew Bible can be interpreted in relation to the theological concept of covenant: for example, Esther and Song of Songs do not even mention G-d, and the wisdom literature frequently expresses skepticism about such notions. Neither is successfully incorporated into Eichrodt's schema. A third is the disintegration of the notion of covenant in the Pentateuch and beyond. Because of the prevailing source-critical models of the time, texts in the Pentateuch that mention covenant were frequently relegated to different historical sources and considered as different covenants, viz., the Noachic covenant (Gen 9), the J account of the covenant with Abram (Gen 15), the P account of the covenant with Abraham (Gen 17), and so on. The use of historical perspective thereby undermined the crucial role played by covenant texts in tying the Pentateuch together and in providing the foundations for a literary-theological history of G-d's covenant with Israel. A final issue is the selection of the theme, "covenant," which was intended to facilitate discussion of the interrelationship between the Old Testament and the New Testament, insofar as the term "testament" is a classical English term for the word covenant, which of course would facilitate tracing the evolution of Israelite notions of covenant into the new covenant of Christianity.

With the end of World War II, the recognition of Nazi atrocities during the war, and the failure of the churches to speak out effectively against the German government, German Protestant theologians began to rethink Christianity's theological perspectives and moral worldview. Karl Barth focused on a theology of the divine word in which Jesus Christ as divine word embodies both G-d's election of humanity at large for salvation and G-d's rejection of human sin.[8] Dietrich Bonhoeffer, who was murdered by the Nazis late in the war, argued that Jesus Christ represented G-d's suffering in the world and served as a call for human beings to act within the world at large to bring about justice. Although both were influenced by the Shoah or Holocaust, neither developed a major theological reassessment of the church's relationship with Judaism and both continued to view Judaism in classical supersessionist terms. Nevertheless, both influenced the field of Old Testament theology by viewing scripture as an expression of the divine word that called for human moral and religious response.

Perhaps the most important Old Testament theology written after the war was that of Gerhard von Rad.[9] Heavily influenced by Barthian hermeneutics and his own pre-war attempts to trace the literary and theological coherence of the J stratum of the Pentateuch, von Rad argues that the Old Testament is based on the concept of *Heilsgeschichte*, or "sacred history," in which the Bible proclaims G-d's acts of salvation on behalf of Israel and the world throughout history. Although von Rad's work was heavily influenced by contemporary historical and source-critical research, his tradition-historical approach went a long way in overcoming the very fragmented readings of the Bible prompted by Wellhausenian source analysis. Basically, von Rad's analysis emphasized the tradents of the Bible who collected and wrote down the oral traditions of ancient Israel to form the literary works of the Pentateuch, Deuteronomistic History, Prophets, and so on. These works presented theological constructions of historical events that would serve as the foundations for ancient Israel's understanding of G-d as Israel's saving agent throughout history, from creation through the eschatological realization of YHWH's saving grace. Von Rad's scheme, of course, culminated in the New Testament and had little to say about post-biblical Judaism. Furthermore, his work did not account adequately for non-historical works such as the wisdom books, prompting him to write a third volume on wisdom literature after the initial publication of his Old Testament theology. Nevertheless, his focus on the theological and literary coherence of the Old Testament constituted an important step forward.

Von Rad's work pointed out the discrepancies between the historical events that informed biblical literature and the Bible portrayal of those events: for example, the portrayal of the conquest of the land of Israel in the book of Joshua did not actually take place; Israel emerged in the land over a long period of time from the earlier Canaanite population and from tribal groups who settled amongst the Canaanite population. But Christianity (and Judaism) did not depend upon reconstructed history as a basis for theology; rather, the Bible's portrayal of events stood as the foundation for later Christian (and Jewish) theology and perceptions of G-d and the world. Consequently, Brevard Childs began to call for a biblical theology that was based on the final or canonical form of the biblical text, rather than on a historical reconstruction of the events presented in the Bible or even on a reconstructed biblical text.[10] Neither the pentateuchal sources nor the reconstructed First, Second, or Third Isaiah could form the foundation for a biblical theology. Instead, the final forms of the books of Genesis or Isaiah must stand as the foundation for biblical theology. Further-more, biblical theology did not have the luxury of concentrating only on the historical or the prophetic books, as von Rad's theology had done—it must take up all of the biblical books, including the priestly literature of the Pentateuch, such as Leviticus, the wisdom literature, such as Proverbs and Job, and previously overlooked narrative works, such as Esther and Song of Songs. Yet Childs's concept of canon was not limited only to the Hebrew Bible. The Christian Bible included the New Testament as well, and so his understanding of a proper biblical theology called for a canonical theology of both the Old and New Testaments in which the respective testaments would be put into dialogue with each other. In this way, Genesis, for example, might be read in relation to Matthew and Matthew in relation to Genesis. Childs did not eschew the historical work of his time and incorporated historical perspective into his overall analysis of each biblical book. His view of canon proved to be very limited insofar as he simply presumed the final form of the Hebrew Bible to be the definitive form of the biblical text, while the Christian Bible must account for a variety of canonical forms, such as the Septuagint, the Vulgate, the Peshitta, and others. Nevertheless, Childs' work laid the foundations for holistic readings of those texts and dialogic readings of biblical texts in conversation with each other.

Although Christian biblical theology was relatively slow in recognizing the problem of the Shoah or Holocaust and the role that Christianity had played over the course of nearly two millennia in laying the foundations for modern anti-Semitism, theologians of various types raised the issue and ultimately began to influence biblical theology. Jules Isaac's penetrating study of the New Testament and early church demonstrated how early Christianity had fomented anti-Jewish attitudes.[11] Rosemary Radford Ruether provided a similar perspective based on her study of early patristic literature.[12] Paul Van Buren argued that Christians must learn to recognize the Old Testament as Jewish literature that is also read in the context of Christianity.[13] Clark Williamson called upon Christian thinkers to rethink classic supersessionist and anti-Jewish readings in the biblical interpre-tation and systematic theology.[14] Katharina von Kellenbach pointed to the emer-gence of anti-Semitism in modern feminist theology, where Judaism frequently emerges as a paradigm for patriarchy.[15] Erich Zenger called upon Christian interpreters to read the Bible differently in the aftermath of the Shoah.[16] The theological discussion of the impact of the Shoah on modern biblical exegesis and theology had a major impact on the field of Old Testament Theology in the later twentieth century and beyond. Influenced also by rhetorical criticism, which studies the means of communication and persuasion in the Bible, Walter Brueggemann produced a magisterial study that focused on the Hebrew Bible's discourse and dialogue about G-d.[17] He recognized the challenges posed by the Shoah, particularly the role that the vilification of Judaism had played in Christian theology throughout the centuries. Although he argued that the Shoah could not stand as the center of an Old Testament theology, Old Testament theology cannot proceed without recognition of the continuing problem of evil in the world represented by the Shoah. Biblical theology was not simply an ivory tower occupation of academics and clerics; rather, it was a field that had extraordinary influence in shaping attitudes, meaning that it must be pursued with an appropriate eye to the practical impact that theological statements might have in the world in which we live. The Shoah constitutes a major and unanswerable challenge to claims about YHWH's sovereignty and fidelity. Such a challenge likewise has implications for Christian claims about Jesus Christ and his relationship to the world at large. Furthermore, Brueggemann's interests in the discursive and dialogical aspects of the Bible prompted him to recognize how the Bible's various perspectives enter into an intertextual dialogue about G-d, Israel, and other issues that appear among the various books of the Bible.

Recognition of the problems posed by the Shoah and Christianity's vilification of Judaism had a major impact on German Old Testament theology as well. Rolf Rendtorff's massive theology of the Old Testament calls for a common Jewish and Christian reading of the Hebrew Bible.[18] Rendtorff's work is informed by his interaction with Jewish scholars, particularly Moshe Greenberg, who calls for a holistic reading of the Bible. Consequently, Rendtorff is very interested in reading the final forms of biblical books, although like Childs he does not take full account of the various versions in which the Bible appears in Christianity. Rendtorff's call is based on the recognition that Judaism and Christianity share the same basic scriptures, but it is also based on the historical paradigms regnant in the field throughout much of the twentieth century that posit one dimension of meaning in the interpretation of biblical literature. Although well-motivated by an appropriate concern to rectify the wrongs of Christian anti-Jewish attitudes in exegesis, Rendtorff's work suffers from the presupposition that a shared or common reading of scripture is necessary to mend the rifts between Judaism and Christianity. Ultimately, Rendtorff's model collapses the distinctions between Judaism and Christianity into a common theological perspective. But it is precisely the notion that Judaism must conform to the beliefs and perspectives of Christianity that created the problem of Christian anti-Semitism in the first place.

In order to promote a constructive relationship between the two traditions, they must learn to accept the differences between them and nevertheless view each other as a valid form of theological perspective and practice, even though they do not share in the same perspectives and practices. Acceptance of the other—and of the right of the other to hold differing views—is the true key for a harmonious relationship between the two traditions.

Levenson is correct to observe that the field of biblical theology is a Christian field that addresses Christian concerns, but the above survey also demonstrates that Christian Old Testament theology has learned to take up Jewish concerns as well, particularly in the aftermath of the Shoah, and that Christians are very interested in dialogue with Jews, especially concerning the interpretation of the Bible. Furthermore, although the field is constructed to address the interrelationship between biblical exegesis and systematic theology in Christian thought, it has also produced some important advances, such as the capacity to address the interpretation of entire biblical books, the interrelationship between historical events and the different presentation of the same events in the Bible, the inability to reduce the Hebrew Bible to a single theme or concern, the communicative and dialogical functions of scripture, and the need to read the Hebrew Bible or Old Testament as sacred scripture in its own right apart from the concerns of the New Testament.

C. JEWISH BIBLICAL THEOLOGY

Although biblical theology has been a Christian theological discipline throughout its history, Jews have participated in the field in various capacities from the Age of Enlightenment on.[19] One may trace the beginnings of Jewish participation in the field to the work of Moses Mendelssohn, who argued in his 1783 volume, *Jerusalem, or On Religious Power and Judaism*, that Judaism must be regarded alongside Christianity as a valid religion of reason insofar as it held to three basic points: (1) the existence of one G-d, (2) divine providence, and (3) immortality of the soul.[20] In Mendelssohn's understanding, Torah constituted the particular dogma of Judaism that gave it a distinctive identity and enabled it to carry out its mission to bring teachings of divine justice and holiness to the nations. His Torah translation and commentary was designed to teach Jews how to participate as Jews in modern German society as well as to provide access to the Jewish tradition. Leopold Zunz's 1832 volume, *Die Gottesdienstliche Vorträge der Juden*, employed historical scholarship in an attempt to demonstrate that the practice of preaching sermons (Hebrew, *divrê tôrâ*) was a central act of Rabbinic Judaism that had foundations in the biblical period.[21] The work was instigated by the attempt of the Prussian government to deny clerical licensing to Rabbis, but it also proved to be a ground-breaking study in the theological worldview and practices of Judaism from the biblical period on.

The early twentieth century saw a number of works that would have an impact on the conceptualization of a Jewish biblical theology. Among the earliest were works by Franz Rosenzweig and Martin Buber, who collaborated in their efforts to reconnect modern Jews with the Jewish tradition by means of a university-level educational program known as the *Jüdische Lehrhaus*, as well as their unique translation of the Bible that was designed to acquaint German-speaking Jews with the dynamics and meaning of the Hebrew text.

Rosenzweig's 1921 book, *Der Stern der Erlösung*, examined Jewish liturgical life and its sense of encounter with G-d as a basis for demonstrating that Judaism embodies a life of religious faith in which Jews encounter the sacred in the world of creation.[22] In contrast to the largely historical or linear paradigms of escha-tologically oriented religious life that were so common in Christian thought, Rosenzweig argued that Jewish prayer is fundamentally cyclical in which Jews encounter a recurring pattern of liturgical celebration as part of their efforts to recognize the holy presence of G-d in the world and its impact on human life. Such a meta-historical life of holiness embodies eschatological promise during the course of history and not at its end, and so Judaism serves as a source of inspi-ration to Gentiles, whose historically oriented models of eschatology strive to achieve such encounter with the holy.

Buber's 1923 book, *Ich und Du*, builds upon his experience with Hasidic Judaism to develop a model of encounter and dialogue between human beings and G-d in the world.[23] G-d, the eternal "Thou" (German, *Du*), addresses human beings through the various experiences of life in the world. It then becomes the human task to recognize the divine address in the larger world of creation and to respond to that address, recognizing the presence of the divine that permeates all of creation and experience in keeping with the teachings of Hasidism and earlier Lurianic Kabbalah. Because Jews had been exiled from the land of Israel, Jews living in the diaspora had lost the foundational dialogical dimensions of recog-nizing G-d in the world of creation. For Buber, the model of dialogue, in which each participant recognizes the quintessential integrity of the other, whether G-d, human, text, nature, or others, constitutes the core of Jewish experience and knowledge. Buber's later writings probed Hasidic tradition in an attempt to pro-vide a fuller background for the model initially laid out in *Ich und Du* as well as the question of the absence of G-d in the aftermath of the Shoah or Holocaust.[24]

Abraham Joshua Heschel's writings began with his 1936 Ph.D. dissertation, *Die Prophetie*, in which he examined the notion of divine pathos in a study that focused especially on eighth- and seventh-century prophets, such as Amos, Hosea, Isaiah, and Jeremiah.[25] Heschel had been born into a Hasidic dynasty and was educated to become a Rebbe, but sought out secular learning as a young man and ultimately earned a Ph.D. in Bible and esthetics at the University of Berlin under Max Dessoir, Alfred Bertholet, and others.[26] Heschel's work was hardly the typical source-critical dissertation of the time. Heavily influenced by Hasidic and Lurianic notions of the interrelationship between the divine and the human, Heschel focused instead on the prophet's experience of G-d and G-d's experience of the human in times of crisis. Heschel's theory of divine pathos was an attempt to describe the impact that human beings had upon G-d, particularly when they acted in a manner that brought about divine punishment and death. Heschel's study demonstrated the degree to which G-d is vulnerable to pain and pathos as well as G-d's need for relationship with human beings. His later writings continued to focus on the divine need for encounter with humans as well as explorations of the holiness of Jewish tradition, such as Shabbat observance, the revelatory character of Rabbinic literature, and the central importance of the land of Israel to Judaism.[27]

Yehezkel Kaufmann was one of the first modern Jewish Bible scholars to write systematically on ancient Israelite religion. His eight-volume Hebrew work on the history of Israelite religion, published from 1937 through 1956 (and abridged in English in 1970 and 1972), was an attempt to study the emergence and development of universal monotheism from its earliest expressions in ancient Israelite society.[28] Contrary to the Wellhausenian-based scholarship of his time, Kaufmann argued that the Temple and priesthood were the central religious institutions of ancient Israel from the beginning, and that both articulated universal divine monotheism from the beginning of Israel's history. Kaufmann was heavily influenced by modern Zionist thought, particularly the work of Ahad Ha-Am, and posited that the national spirit of biblical Israel provided the foundations for Israel's unique concept of monotheism as the hallmark of its religious worldview.

The experience of the Holocaust, or Shoah as it is more properly known, in which some six million Jews were deliberately murdered by the German government and its supporters during World War II, provided a particularly important stimulus to Jewish theology in general as well as in relation to theological discussion concerning the Jewish Bible in particular. Biblical scholars were generally not involved in the discussion, as contemporary Jewish Bible scholars tended to be very historically and philologically oriented, but Jewish philosophers and theologians began a far-ranging discussion with important consequences for the theological interpretation of the Bible, particularly the questions concerning divine power, presence, and justice, which are generally articulated in the Bible. Already in the 1950s, the above-mentioned works by Martin Buber and Abraham Joshua Heschel had broached the question of the absence of G-d. Ignaz Maybaum, a German Reform scholar who escaped the Shoah, argued in 1965 that the murder of six million Jews must be viewed as a vicarious sacrifice meant to provoke the revulsion of humankind and therefore to instigate efforts to bring an end to such injustice.[29] His work was met with widespread criticism, especially since its implicit sanction of the murder of so many people as an act of G-d could not be defended morally.

Richard Rubenstein's 1966 study, *After Auschwitz: Radical Theology and Contemporary Judaism*, shook the foundations of Jewish (and Christian!) thought with its claim that the experience of the Shoah demonstrated that G-d was dead and that Judaism would have to rethink and reject the fundamental theological foundations of its identity.[30] Rubenstein, a Conservative Rabbi and academic, argued that the deliberate murder of six million Jews completely undermined the moral foundations of Judaism and any claim of divine justice, morality, or even existence. In Rubenstein's view, a moral, omniscient, and omnipotent G-d could not allow the Shoah to take place; the fact that it had taken place demonstrated that the classical notions of a just, all-powerful, and active G-d who rewarded the righteous and punished the sinful were not true. There was no divine covenant at Sinai; the Jewish people was not the chosen people of G-d; and human beings were left to themselves to devise systems of moral order and practice in the world. The consequences also extended to Christianity (and Islam) insofar as Christianity was dependent upon Judaism for its theological claims to represent the new or true Israel. Rubenstein's later works have focused on the themes of the absence of G-d in modern secular society.

Emil Fackenheim, a German Reform Rabbi who escaped the Shoah to become a Jewish philosopher in Toronto, responded to Rubenstein with his 1970 volume, *G-d's Presence in History*, with its calls to affirm divine presence in the world despite the experience of evil.[31] Fackenheim argued that modern Jews are called to believe in G-d as the 614th commandment (note, Rabbinic Judaism holds that 613 commandments are required for full Jewish observance): that is, to deny Hitler a posthumous victory by allowing Judaism to die out because of the Shoah. Fackenheim looked back in history to argue that previous disasters that might be seen as analogous to the Shoah, such as the destructions of the First and Second Temples respectively by the Babylonians in 587–586 BCE and by the Romans in 70 CE, prompted Jews to reaffirm their faith in G-d and to reconstitute Judaism in the aftermath of the disaster. Following the Babylonian exile, Judaism emerged as a religious movement under foreign rule, and following the Roman destruction, Rabbinic Judaism emerged as the classical form of Jewish observance. Fackenheim's later work focused on the theme of *Tikkun Olam*, "repair of the world," or the human obligation to work as partners with G-d to complete the creation and sanctification of the world, and on his efforts to probe the theological ramifications of the Shoah in biblical tradition.[32] Fackenheim studies the implications of the deaths of Job's ten children as well as the theme of the absence of G-d in the book of Esther as unanswered questions from the Bible that continue to demand our attention.

Eliezer Berkovits, an Orthodox Rabbi and scholar, examined the theme of the hidden face of G-d (Hebrew, *hestēr pānîm*) in both the Bible and Rabbinic literature in an effort to highlight the question of human responsibility in the aftermath of the Shoah.[33] The Shoah is devoid of moral explanation or justification, but it points to the realities of human existence in the aftermath of disaster, viz., the need to accept responsibility for the future rather than allowing the evils of the past to overwhelm human life. In this respect, Berkovits builds on Fackenheim's earlier arguments that Jews are partners with G-d in creation and that our task is to help to complete and sanctify creation at large. In his view, such an approach that calls for the acceptance of responsibility even in the face of evil is a means by which human beings strive to reach moral maturity in the world. Berkovits's earlier 1969 work, *Man and G-d: Studies in Biblical Theology*, laid the foundations for his discussion of theology after the Shoah by focusing on the knowledge, spirit, and name of G-d, as well as dealing with concerns of divine holiness, justice, truth, and Sedaqah, "charity" (or "righteousness"), that human beings must emulate in order to lead a righteous and holy life.[34]

Discussion concerning the theological significance of the Shoah by these scholars and others has continued unabated through the present, but it also had an impact on the field of biblical studies as Jewish biblical scholars began to ask theological questions of the Bible itself. Moshe Goshen-Gottstein was an early advocate of Jewish biblical theology. Although he was especially well-known for his philological work in Syriac and other Semitic languages, Goshen-Gottstein was well-versed in the fields of Old Testament Theology and Israelite Religion and began to call for a Tanak Theology that would give expression to the religious ideas of ancient Israel.[35] Mattitiahu Tsevat likewise called for the development of a Jewish biblical theology based on careful philological, grammatical, and historical analysis of biblical texts that gave expression to Israel's religious ideas.[36] Moshe Weinfeld had already begun such work with his study of the Deuteronomic school that focused on the religious ideas of Deuteronomy and the so-called Deuteronomistic History, with a special emphasis on the understanding of covenant in relation to the ideas of national identity and social justice.[37] Harry Orlinsky likewise took up the understanding of covenant throughout the Pentateuch and the rest of the Bible as the foundation for Israelite national and religious identity, focused on G-d's grant of the land of Israel as the foundational aspect of the covenant between G-d and the nation of Israel.[38] David Blumenthal examined the book of Psalms in an effort to study the problem of divine responsibility for the Shoah.[39] As in the case of an abusive parent, Blumenthal argued, Jews must both acknowledge divine complicity in the Shoah and learn to forgive G-d's evil, much as the victims of child abuse must learn to forgive the abusive parent so that they may go on to lead meaningful and productive lives.

One of the most influential figures in the field of Jewish biblical theology is Jon Levenson, who argues that Jews should not be interested in biblical theology because of its inherently Protestant Christian character and its anti-Jewish bias.[40] Levenson has nevertheless gone on to make substantive contributions to the field, despite the fact that he views his work as the history of Israelite religion, not biblical theology.[41] Levenson's Ph.D. dissertation on Ezek 40–48 challenged the reigning Wellhausenian view that Ezekiel and his vision of the restored Temple in Ezek 40–48 must be viewed as late priestly expressions of the decline of Israelite religion.[42] Instead, his work employed the standard tools of historical-critical scholarship to probe the dimensions of holiness in Ezekiel's vision in an effort to demonstrate that the vision was central to Ezekiel's religious worldview. Throughout the study, Levenson focused on the role of the Temple as the holy center of creation, the locus of the Garden of Eden, and the institutional foundation for the revelation of G-d to Israel and creation at large. A later monograph employed a comparative study of Sinai and Zion to demonstrate that the Pentateuch's portrayal of divine revelation at Mt. Sinai was based on the understanding of the role of the Jerusalem Temple on Mt. Zion as the locus for divine revelation to Israel and the world at large.[43]

A third study took up the question of theodicy, insofar as the Temple, as the holy center of creation, served as the foundation for order in the world.[44] Levenson demonstrated that YHWH's defeat of chaos, expressed throughout liturgical texts as YHWH's defeat of chaos monsters identified with the sea, such as Leviathan and Behemoth, takes place at every morning service in the Temple, when light illumines the interior of the Temple and drives away the darkness (which symbolizes chaos) to form a new order in creation for the day at hand. The Temple thereby symbolizes divine order in the world, which comes to expression in the natural world of agriculture and life, the human world of politics and protection from enemies, and the moral world of human ethical and ritual action that renders the world of creation as holy. Key to his argument is a rereading of Gen 1:1—2:3 in which Levenson employs Rashi's exegesis of the passage to show that it does not present the notion of *creatio ex nihilo*, "creation out of nothing." Instead, he demonstrates that in Genesis, G-d brings a preexisting chaos into order. This notion is consistent with other texts, such as Ps 74 or Job 38, which portray G-d's defeat of sea-based chaos monsters as part of the divine effort to bring order to the world. A fourth study on *The Death and Resurrection of the Beloved Son* provides a basis for distinguishing fundamental differences in the theological worldviews of Judaism and Christianity.[45] Levenson focuses on the understanding of child sacrifice in the Bible, particularly in Gen 22, which presents the binding of Isaac. Judaism employs the narrative as a basis for its own identity as the chosen people of G-d: that is, just as G-d redeemed Isaac from death as a sacrifice, so G-d redeemed Israel from death in Egyptian bondage and other threats. Christianity employs the narrative as a foundation for its understanding of the crucifixion or sacrifice of Christ, which then functions in Christianity as a means to assert its claims to be recognized as the true people of G-d.

Levenson's 1997 commentary on the book of Esther enables him to examine a text that has frequently been labeled as a non-theological work and largely excluded from discussions of biblical theology.[46] The book of Esther does not mention the name of G-d, but it portrays the problem of divine absence at a time when a foreign government threatens to destroy the entire Jewish people. No better biblical analog to the modern experience of the Shoah can be found. Again,

Levenson employs the tools of modern historical-critical research to counter claims that Esther is fundamentally interested in fomenting violence against gentiles and to demonstrate its religious importance as a book fundamentally concerned with the question of the absence of G-d in a time of crisis. His 2006 study, *Resurrection and the Restoration of Israel*, revisits his earlier concern with biblical conceptions of resurrection and death in an effort to demonstrate that these themes point to a larger concern with the restoration of the nation of Israel in the aftermath of crisis.[47] Of course, such a concern is also relevant for the modern world in which Judaism must rebuild the Jewish people, both in the diaspora and in the modern state of Israel, in the aftermath of the Shoah.

Another major figure in the field is Michael Fishbane, who focuses especially on the hermeneutics of reading the biblical text in the context of Jewish tradition. Fishbane's work presents a challenge to the historical-critical models that have dominated modern scholarship. Ironically, such models have served a modern Protestant theological agenda by emphasizing the Bible and its historical context alone as a source for divine revelation, rather than the context of either the Jewish or Roman Catholic traditions in which the Bible has been read. Fishbane's early work, *Biblical Interpretation in Ancient Israel*, focused on tracing the lines of inner-biblical exegesis in an effort to show that the reading of scripture and reflection on its meaning in relation to the needs of the present is a quintessentially Jewish model that begins in the Bible itself and continues through the Rabbinic midrashic tradition and beyond.[48] He distinguishes the *traditum*, "tradition," and the *traditio*, "traditioning," of the exegetical process, and identifies four major exegetical categories: (1) scribal exegesis, which focuses on how scribes reworked and corrected earlier biblical texts; (2) legal exegesis, which focuses on law as a living tradition that adapts to meet the needs of ancient Israelite society; (3) aggadic exegesis, which takes up moral, didactic, and non-halakhic issues as a means to affirm the past, present, and future in the Jewish imagination; and (4) mantological exegesis, which focuses on the interpretation of prophetic oracles, dreams, visions, omens, and so on.

Fishbane's later writings attempt to trace the exegetical process from its origins in the Bible into the Rabbinic, Kabbalistic, Hasidic, and other movements in the history of Judaism. His 1994 study, *The Kiss of G-d*, traces the interpretation of Song 1:2, "let him kiss me with the kisses of his mouth," in Kabbalistic and Hasidic tradition as a means to develop an understanding of the depths of the divine–human relationship.[49] Fishbane's 1998 study, *The Exegetical Imagination*, rejects the notion that Judaism gave up mythological thinking in its reading of texts, and instead emphasizes the *poesis* of midrashic exegesis in the Bible's mythological portrayal of the dimensions of G-d, Israel, creation, the Exodus, messianic ideals, and so on, in the literature of the Midrashim and the Zohar.[50] His 2002 commentary on the *Haftarot*, the prophetic texts read as part of the weekly and holiday liturgy of the synagogue, provides a modern commentary on the prophetic readings that places them in their ancient contexts as well as their contexts throughout the course of Jewish tradition.[51] His 2003 study, *Biblical Myth and Rabbinic Mythmaking*, presents a comprehensive treatment of mythopoeic thought from the Bible through the Midrash and the Zohar.[52]

A number of Fishbane's students have made significant contributions to the field as well. Bernard Levinson focuses on the hermeneutics of reading legal texts in an effort to demonstrate the process by which ancient Israel reflects upon its law codes and rewrites them to address the problems faced by a living society interested in doing justice for its constituents.[53] The continual rethinking and updating of law anticipates Rabbinic halakhic exegesis and discussion. Marc Brettler focuses especially on the interpretation of historical narratives.[54] With a background in modern Hebrew literature as well as in Bible, Brettler emphasizes the literary and theological issues prompted by historical literature in which readers must understand the hermeneutical principles and perspectives by which such texts depict the past. Benjamin Sommer focuses especially on the dynamics of intertextual reading, both within the Bible and between the Bible and other elements of Jewish tradition. His 1998 monograph, *A Prophet Reads Scripture*, examines the dynamics of Second Isaiah's reading of earlier prophetic tradition in anticipation of the period of restoration that would follow the end of the Babylonian exile.[55] His 1999 study, "Revelation at Sinai in the Hebrew Bible and in Jewish Theology," examines the dialogical give and take between Exod 19–24 and other biblical texts and their later readers, such as the Talmud, Maimonides, modern Jewish scholars, and others.[56] His 2009 essay, "Dialogical Biblical Theology," presents a very useful survey of the field that moves Jewish readings of the Bible from a view that the Bible constitutes artifacts by which we may reconstruct the past to a view in which the Bible constitutes scriptures by which we may draw upon the past to address the present and future.[57]

My own work has addressed the field of Jewish biblical theology for a decade and a half. My 2000 and 2008 surveys of the field provide essential overviews of issues pertaining to Jewish biblical theology.[58] My 1996 commentary on Isa 1–39 focused especially on the ideological influence of the Davidic/Zion tradition on the works of Isaiah ben Amoz and his tradents.[59] My 1997 study, "Tanak versus Old Testament," lays out an understanding of the distinctive perspectives inherent in the differing organizations of the Jewish and Christian Bibles: that is, while the Christian Bible presents a linear understanding of history from creation through the ultimate revelation of Christ, the Tanak presents a cyclical understanding of history from the ideals of the Torah, the disruption of those ideals in the Prophets, and through the attempt to reconstruct and realize those ideals in the Writings.[60] My 1998/2000 paper on "Reconceiving the Paradigms of Old Testament Theology in the Post-Shoah Period" argues that modern biblical theology must take account of the realities of the Shoah and the national character of the Jewish people as an ongoing theological reality from ancient through modern times.[61] My 2000 study, "Isaiah and Theodicy after the Shoah," challenges Isaiah's theology of teleological redemption for the people of Israel in Babylonian exile by asking about the justice rendered to those who suffered the Assyrian and Babylonian invasions of Israel and Judah.[62] My 2000 study, "Absence of G-d and Human Responsibility in the Book of Esther," examines a text which presents the problem of divine absence at a time when a foreign government has determined to murder the entire Jewish people, arguing that the most unlikely human being, in this case Esther, must be prepared to rise to the occasion because she is the only one who can do so.[63] My 2000 commentary on the Twelve Prophets examines the distinctive theological worldviews of each of the Twelve as well as the two major versions of the Book of the Twelve.[64] My 2001 study, *King Josiah of Judah: The Lost Messiah of Israel*, examines the historical, literary, and theological dimensions of King Josiah's attempt to restore the Jewish nation in the aftermath of Assyrian invasion and conquest.[65] My 2003 commentary on Zephaniah provides a detailed study of the theological foundations of the prophet and of King Josiah's reforms.[66] My 2005 survey of the Prophetic Literature focuses on the various theological dimensions of reading the prophetic books, such as Isaiah's adherence to Davidic/Zion tradition, Jeremiah's identity as a priest from Anathoth who teaches Mosaic Torah, or Ezekiel's identity as a Zadokite priest in exile.[67] My 2005 study, "The Democratization of Messianism in Modern Jewish Thought," reads the reconceptualization of the Davidic promise in Isa 55 in relation to later Jewish thinkers, such as Moses Mendelssohn, Isaac Luria, and Ahad Ha-Am.[68] My 2007 commentary on Kings focuses especially on the theological dimensions of that work's reading of Israel's and Judah's histories.[69] My 2008 study, *Reading the Hebrew Bible after the Shoah*, examines the impact of the Shoah on modern readings of the Bible and particularly emphasizes the debate that takes place among the biblical books on questions of theodicy.[70]

A variety of scholars take up various important issues relevant to Jewish biblical theology. Sara Japhet examines the theological worldview of Chronicles, which portrays the interrelationship between a just and holy deity and the nation Israel, with its moral and ritual obligations to sanctify itself before G-d.[71] Moshe Greenberg takes up the theological problems of the book of Job, recognizing that Job ends up a wiser man by better seeing G-d's work in the world.[72] Jacob Milgrom examines the spatial, ritual, and ethical dimensions of holiness in his three-volume commentary on Leviticus.[73] Benjamin Uffenheimer takes up the differing theologies of the prophets Isaiah and Micah, pointing to the diversity of viewpoints expressed by the prophets.[74] Israel Knohl studies the interrelationship between ritual and ethical action in the Holiness Code of Lev 16–27, and later argues that the many voices evident in the Bible indicate that it is a pluralistic work in which the many voices engage in debate with one another if only by virtue of their inclusion in the Bible.[75] Isaac Kalimi maintains that the Bible cannot be reduced to a single theme, arguing that theology must take account of the Bible's authors, redactors, and later tradents.[76] Tikva Frymer-Kensky argues that the Bible presents an alternative voice by which to engage in dialogue with Rabbinic and subsequent Jewish tradition. Esther Fuchs calls for a fundamental rethinking of patriarchal authority and assumptions, both within the Bible and among its interpreters.[77] Yair Hoffman takes up the question of theodicy in a study of Jeremiah's oracle against Babylon insofar as Jer 50–51 views the downfall of Babylon as an expression of divine justice.[78] Dalit Rom Shiloni focuses on the intertextual relationship between biblical works in an effort to demonstrate how exilic prophets, such as Jeremiah and Ezekiel, reflect on earlier tradition in an effort to address the theological questions posed by the exile.[79] Edward Greenstein argues that Lamentations charges G-d with going too far in destroying Jerusalem.[80] Ziony Zevit's survey of the field of Jewish Bible theology raises problems such as the relationship between the Bible and later tradition, the Christian character of the field of biblical theology, and the prescriptive versus the descriptive nature of the field.[81] Frederick Greenspahn traces the history of Jewish ambivalence towards the Bible as he prepares a larger study on the reception of the Bible in Judaism from antiquity to the present.[82] Joel Kaminsky examines the concept of election in the Bible, rejecting calls to give up the notion of election and instead calling upon Jews and Christians to recognize their distinctive self-understandings as a basis for dialogue.[83] And most recently, Benjamin Sommer investigates the notion of G-d's body in the Bible as a basis for developing notions of divine fluidity of representation in the Kabbalistic literature and other streams of Jewish (and Christian) thought.[84]

Altogether, Jewish biblical scholars demonstrate a lively interest in the field that promises to provide a foundation for thinking about the theological worldview of the Bible itself and its importance for contemporary Judaism.

D. THE TASK OF JEWISH BIBLICAL THEOLOGY

The task of a Jewish biblical theology cannot be the same as that of a Christian Old Testament theology or a Christian biblical theology.[85] Fundamentally, Judaism is committed to a relationship with G-d as defined through divine Torah whereas Christianity is committed to the notion that its relationship with G-d is defined through Jesus Christ. Because of their differing characters, the Bible is formed and read differently within the respective contexts of Judaism and Christianity, and those differences must be taken into account when undertaking Jewish (or Christian) biblical theology. There are of course a number of major dimensions in which these differences must be recognized in order to lay the foundations for a Jewish biblical theology.

One major dimension is the distinctive forms of the Jewish Tanak and the Christian Old Testament.[86] Although the Tanak and the Old Testament share largely the same books, they appear in fundamentally different forms that are shaped by the cultural background, the theological viewpoints, the literary contexts, and the interpretative perspectives of their respective communities and traditions. Because the Tanak is situated among the Jewish people, it appears exclusively in Hebrew and Aramaic, the primary languages spoken by the Jewish people in antiquity and adopted for sacred use. Furthermore, the Tanak is ordered according to a standard three-part structure that includes the Torah or Instruction of YHWH, the Nevi'im or Prophets, including both the Former and the Latter Prophets, and the Ketuvim or Writings. This order presupposes the Jewish commitment to divine Torah as the ideal foundation of Jewish tradition, accounts of the disruption of that ideal in the Nevi'im or Prophets, and expressions of attempts to restore that ideal in the Ketuvim or Writings. Because the Christian Bible is situated among Gentiles, it appears in a variety of languages and versions, such as Hebrew, Greek, Latin, Aramaic, Syriac, Ethiopic, and others. Its overall structure invariably includes both the Old Testament and the New Testament, which expresses the fundamental Christian belief that Jesus fulfills the Old Testament. Within this framework, the structure of the Christian Old Testament differs widely, depending on a variety of factors, such as the cultural context, the manuscript tradition, the historical context, the canonical context, and others. Nevertheless, the advent of modern printing has resulted in a relatively standardized order, including the Pentateuch, the Historical Books, the Wisdom and Poetic Books, and the Prophets.

The first segment of the Jewish Bible is the Torah, which includes the books of Genesis or Bereshit (*běrē'šît*), Exodus or Shemot (*šěmôt*), Leviticus or Vayiqra' (*wayyiqrā'*), Numbers or Bamidbar (*bammidbār*), and Deuteronomy or Devarim (*děbārîm*). Although the Hebrew term *tôrâ* is frequently translated as "law," this is incorrect since the term is derived philologically from the verb root, *yrh*, which in Hiphil conjugation means "to guide" or "to instruct," rendering the proper translation of *tôrâ* as "guidance" or "instruction." A brief survey of the books of the Torah indicates that although they do contain elements of law, they contain much else as well. Indeed, the Torah recounts the ideals of Israel and its relationship with G-d, including recognition of YHWH as the one G-d, author of creation and partner in covenant with the nation Israel; Israelite identity and history as a living nation and society in relation to G-d; the divine promises of the land of Israel and protection from enemies; the legal instructions revealed to Israel by G-d so that the nation might form a living and just society in the land of Israel; and Israel's pledge to observe those instructions. Thus Genesis recounts the history of the world from creation through G-d's selection of Abraham and Sarah and their descendants through Isaac and Rebekah, Jacob, Leah, and Rachel, and the twelve sons of Jacob, as partners in a divine covenant to complete the creation of the world. Exodus includes the narrative of G-d's redemption of the people of Israel from Egyptian bondage, divine guidance of the people from Egypt into the wilderness, and the revelation of divine Torah as the foundations by which Israel might construct a just and living society in the land of Israel in keeping with divine expectations. Leviticus recounts instruction in holy matters of the Temple and Temple service that pertains especially to the priesthood. Numbers recounts Israel's journey through the wilderness from Sinai to the promised land together with a great deal of legal instruction pertaining to life in the land. Finally, Deuteronomy presents Moses' last speeches to the people of Israel immediately prior to their crossing the Jordan River to take possession of the land of Israel in which he reiterates the legal instruction of Exodus, Leviticus, and Numbers. Close attention to the laws of Deuteronomy, however, indicates that Deuteronomy frequently revises older laws or presents new ones that give greater rights to the poor and women in Israelite society, demonstrating the principle that the law in the Torah is not an absolute category but a living legal system that is subject to change or modification in order to ensure that justice is done and that the needs of Israelite society are met.[87]

The second segment of the Tanak is the Prophets or Nevi'im, so named because the authors of the books of the Prophets are believed to be prophets. Nevi'im comprises two major portions, the Former Prophets or Nevi'im Rishonim, which includes the books of Joshua, Judges, Samuel, and Kings, and the Latter Prophets or Nevi'im Aḥronim, which includes the books of Isaiah, Jeremiah, Ezekiel, and the Book of the Twelve Prophets, although the Babylonian Talmud notes the order, Jeremiah, Ezekiel, Isaiah, and the Twelve. The two segments differ in genre, the Nevi'im Rishonim are largely narrative-historical works whereas the Nevi'im Aḥronim are largely prophetic literature including a combination of oracular material and narrative. The two sections are largely concerned with interpreting the failure of Israel and Judah to achieve the ideals laid out in the Torah. Both segments of the Prophets are fundamentally concerned with the question of the Babylonian Exile, in which Israel and Judah were exiled from the land promised to them in the Torah, and both are fundamentally committed to the principle that the cause of the exile was Israel's and Judah's failure to live in accordance with divine Torah. Thus, the Prophets are fundamentally concerned with the question of theodicy, viz., defending the righteousness and power of G-d against claims that G-d was somehow unjust or powerless in allowing Israel and Judah to be cast into exile. Instead, both segments of the Prophets maintain that G-d judged Israel and Judah for failure to live by divine Torah and decreed exile as the punishment for that failure.

The Former Prophets recount Israel's history in the land of Israel from the time of Israel's entry into the land under the leadership of Joshua through the Babylonian Exile.[88] The book of Joshua recounts how G-d fulfilled the covenant with Israel by enabling the people to conquer the land of Israel in a series of three swift campaigns characterized by divine miracles that resulted in the complete collapse of the Canaanites and the loss of relatively few Israelite lives. The book of Judges recounts the early history of Israel under the leadership of the Judges which posits a repetitive cycle in which the people would turn to foreign gods, YHWH would bring an enemy to punish the people, the people would return to

G-d and cry out for help, and then G-d would send a Judge to deliver the people. Overall, the book shows a steady decline in which the people become increasingly Canaanite and unruly, culminating in the rape and murder of the Levite's concubine in the Benjaminite city of Gibeah and the near destruction of the tribe of Benjamin. The book of Samuel recounts the origins of kingship in Israel, beginning with the failed kingship of Saul ben Kish and focusing especially on the rise of David ben Jesse as the founder of the royal house of David that would rule Israel and Judah for some four hundred years. Finally, the book of Kings recounts the history of the kings of Israel and Judah from the time of Solomon ben David through that of Jehoiachin ben Jehoiakim who was exiled to Babylonia. The narrative recounts Solomon's building of the Temple, the division of the kingdom into northern Israel and southern Judah, the destruction of northern Israel by the Assyrians, the destruction of Jerusalem and the temple by the Babylonians, and the exile of Judah to Babylonia. At all points, the history maintains that the suffering of the people was due to their failure to observe divine Torah.

The Latter Prophets present the books of the Prophets of Israel, each of which is concerned with explaining the suffering of the people of Israel and Judah, culminating in the Babylonian Exile and the divine plans for the restoration of the nation once the exile was completed.[89] Each of the Latter Prophets is rooted in a distinctive institutional identity that influences his understanding of Israel's or Judah's relationship with G-d and the nature of the prophetic message. Isaiah ben Amoz is a royal counselor heavily influenced by the Davidic/Zion tradition, which posits an eternal covenant between YHWH, the sovereign deity of all creation, and Israel. In the Davidic/Zion tradition YHWH will defend David and Jerusalem/Zion, and Israel will maintain faith in YHWH. The book of Isaiah presents the punishment of Israel and Judah by the Assyrians and Babylonians as the result of the people's and monarch's failure to have faith in YHWH during the times of crisis, but it also projects YHWH's actions to return the exiled people to Jerusalem once the Babylonian Exile is over. Jeremiah is a priest of the line of Ithamar ben Aaron heavily influenced by the Mosaic ideal of observance of divine Torah as the basis for the relationship between YHWH and Israel/Judah. The book of Jeremiah recounts Jeremiah's struggles in Jerusalem with the house of David, the Temple, and the people. The prophet charges that the failure to observe Mosaic Torah, including Jerusalem's alliance with Egypt, the villain of the Torah narrative concerning the Exodus, is the fundamental cause of Jerusalem's fall to the Babylonians. Once the Exile is completed, Jeremiah posits a return to Jerusalem. Ezekiel is a Zadokite priest exiled to Babylonia who holds that the sanctity of the Jerusalem Temple, recognized as the holy center of creation, is key to Israel's and creation's welfare and stability in the world. The book of Ezekiel therefore interprets the Babylonian Exile as the result of the desecration of the Jerusalem Temple. The prophet calls for a purge of Jerusalem and creation at large that will result in the construction of a new Temple in Jerusalem together with the restoration of Israel at the center of a new creation. Finally, the Book of the Twelve Prophets includes the works of twelve individual prophetic figures, each of whom has a distinctive viewpoint and set of concerns. When read as a whole, the Twelve interprets Israel's history from the time of the northern kingdom of Israel through the Babylonian Exile and the Persian-period restoration. Overall, the Book of the Twelve takes issue with the book of Isaiah, which posits punishment for Israel and the nations by G-d, positing that both G-d and a Davidic messiah will lead Israel against the aggressor nations in an ultimately successful effort to force them to submit to G-d at the restored Jerusalem Temple.

The Ketuvim or Writings include the books of Psalms, Proverbs, Job, the Five Megillot/Scrolls, including Song of Songs, Ruth, Lamentations, Qoheleth/Ecclesiastes, and Esther, Daniel, Ezra–Nehemiah, and Chronicles.[90] The Babylonian Talmud (*b. Baba Batra* 14b) employs a roughly historical order in stipulating that the order is Ruth, Psalms, Job, Proverbs, Qoheleth, Song of Songs, Lamentations, Daniel, Esther, Ezra–Nehemiah, and Chronicles. The Ketuvim collectively anticipate the restoration of the ideals of Israel that were earlier articulated in the Torah. Psalms presents the address of Israel's worshippers to G-d, asking for deliverance from enemies and anticipating the time when G-d will respond to those pleas. Proverbs articulates an ideal world of creation in which wisdom may be learned by observing the patterns of creation and society insofar as G-d consulted Wisdom in creating the world. Job argues that the attainment of wisdom is not so easy since G-d may act in ways that humans find difficult to understand, but it calls upon humans nevertheless to adhere to G-d while continuing to ask critical questions of G-d. The Five Megillot are each read in relation to one of the holidays of Judaism to illustrate its teachings, viz., Song of Songs is read on Passover to portray the intimate relationship between G-d and Israel, Ruth is read on Shavuot insofar as Ruth's conversion to Judaism represents revelation of divine Torah, Lamentations is read on Tisha b'Av to lament over the loss of the Temples and other tragedies in Jewish history, Qoheleth is read on Sukkot to explore the transitory nature of human life while affirming commitment to G-d, and Esther is read on Purim to remember how Esther and Mordecai acted to protect Jews from annihilation by Haman's decree. Daniel is read as a projection of the time when G-d will act to deliver Israel from its mortal enemies. Ezra–Nehemiah recounts the reconstruction of Jewish life in Jerusalem and the land of Israel as well as the reconstruction of the Temple. Chronicles presents a history of the world from the time of creation through Cyrus's decree enabling Jews to return to Jerusalem to rebuild the Temple in an effort to recount the Temple's role as the holy center of creation and of Jewish life.

Whereas the Tanak is structured according to a cyclical pattern of the institution of ideal Jewish life, the disruption of Jewish life, and the restoration of that ideal, the Christian Old Testament is structured according to a linear principle that posits the revelation of Christ as the culmination of human history. Thus, the Pentateuch recounts the early history of the world from the time of creation through the time of Israel's ancestors. The Historical Books recount Israel's later history in the land and in exile from the time of Joshua through the time of Esther and the Persian empire. The Wisdom and Poetic Books address an eternal present in which the questions of the meaning of life and worship of the divine are addressed. Finally, the Prophets recount the punishment of Israel and look forward to the time of redemption. Insofar as the Old Testament is read in relation to the New Testament, the time of redemption is of course inaugurated with the revelation of Jesus Christ. The New Testament exhibits a similar structure. The Gospels recount the earliest history of the lifetime and crucifixion of Jesus. The book of Acts recounts the later history of the early Christian movement that begins in Jerusalem but moves on to Rome as the center for divine action in the world. The Epistles again address the timeless issues of Christian theology, organization, and practice. And finally, the book of Revelation anticipates the second coming of Christ as the culmination of world history.

A second dimension is the context of Jewish tradition, which of course differs markedly from Christian tradition. Whereas the Christian Old Testament is read first in relation to the New Testament and then in relation to subsequent Christian tradition with an eye to defining the dogmatic or systematic theological principles that define Christian faith and practice, the Tanak is read in relation to the entirety of Jewish tradition with an eye to defining both the identity of Jews as a distinctive and holy people and the halakhic practices and religious perspectives that are pertinent to Judaism. Because of the overwhelming role of the New Testament in defining Christian faith and practice, the New Testament's well-recognized dependence upon the Old Testament frequently results in readings in which the Old Testament is subordinated to the New and in which the Old Testament is read piecemeal in an effort to bring Christ or the Gentiles to the forefront of Old Testament interpretation. Insofar as Christ as portrayed in the New Testament results from a combination of perspectives from the Old Testament and from Greco-Roman culture and religion, Christ represents a foreign element that is not directly mentioned in the Old Testament and yet is read back into it. Although the nations are mentioned throughout the Old Testament, Christianity identifies with the Gentiles and places them at center stage in its understanding of the relationship between G-d and humankind so that the people of Israel are ultimately displaced in Christianity as the people of G-d. Although Jewish readings of the Tanak show a similar tendency to allow later tradition to control the reading of the Tanak, later Jewish tradition grows primarily out of the Tanak itself and does not introduce such a markedly foreign element, such as Christ, nor does it give emphasis over the people of Israel to a secondary group, such as the Gentiles, from the outset of the reading process. Rather, the relationship between the Tanak and subsequent Jewish tradition represents an organic and integrated process of development from the Tanak in which biblical concepts of G-d and the Jewish people stand as the bases for the development of Jewish thought in post-biblical Jewish tradition. New and foreign elements do appear in subsequent Jewish tradition, but they do not fundamentally alter the under-standing of G-d or the depiction of the Jewish people as the central divine and human characters in Jewish thought.

The term biblical theology denotes properly a concern with the construction of G-d as presented in the Bible. In this respect, biblical theology is differentiated from biblical anthropology, which is fundamentally concerned with the construc-tion of human beings in the Bible. Biblical theology and biblical anthropology are generally considered to be two distinct fields of concern, but they are intimately related in a Jewish biblical theology. Although Judaism is concerned with G-d as the one true creator and sovereign divinity of the universe, it discourages attempts to delimit or define G-d in any way. Such delimitation or definition of G-d is considered as idolatry in Judaism insofar as it suggests that G-d is some-how limited or finite and thereby subject to outside control by human beings or perhaps other entities or factors. Although G-d is beyond human definition and comprehension, human beings nevertheless stand in relation to G-d by means of the covenant made between G-d and Judaism, within the context of all creation, and therefore Jews must come to some understanding of G-d and attempt to engage G-d within the context of that relationship. The Bible is read as G-d's address to the Jewish people, here defined as Israel and Judah, but it also portrays the attempts by the Jewish people to understand and engage G-d.

When reading the Bible in relation to the larger context of Judaism, Jewish biblical theology must consider the relationship between the Bible and post-biblical Jewish tradition and literature. Like Christianity, Judaism tends to read later literature and tradition back into the Bible. Although such a reading strategy is legitimate insofar as it promotes full integration of the Bible into the tradition as a whole and recognizes the role of readers in the construction of literature, it blurs the distinctive character of the Torah and the rest of the Bible as the foun-dation of Jewish tradition and compromises a full understanding of the historical development of Judaism. Such a strategy was employed in Christianity to weaken the connection between the Jewish people and the Bible and thereby to open the way for Christianity to be viewed as the true Israel, the true heirs of the Hebrew Bible, and even as the true addressees of the Hebrew Bible. Although such dis-placement is hardly a concern within Judaism, a full understanding the historical development of Judaism calls for an understanding of the Bible in and of itself in a manner that each of the major branches of Judaism can affirm. The various branches of Orthodox Judaism maintain that all of the Torah, both written and oral, was revealed at Mt. Sinai and that the task of Jews is to learn progressively the entirety of Torah that then comes to expression in post-biblical Jewish literature and practice. Conservative Judaism maintains that Torah is revealed throughout history as the Jewish people collectively determine the understanding of Judaism in each generation. Reform Judaism maintains that all Torah was revealed at Mt. Sinai, but that the revelation included the principles of change or evolution that would take place in relation to the needs of later times. Each branch of Judaism in its own way therefore sees the Torah and Bible as foundational stages in a continually evolving Judaism, whether that evolution takes place as part of a process of learning the whole or adapting to the needs of later time. In all cases, the Torah and the rest of the Bible function as the foundations of Judaism and need to be read in their own right as sacred scripture that can then enter into dialog with the rest of the Jewish tradition. By reading the Bible as a foundational and distinctive expression of Jewish thought, Jewish biblical theology points both to the change or evolution in Jewish thought and practice that has taken place in the past and to the change and evolution that may take place in the future, whether such change is understood as the continued learning of Torah, the consensus of the Jewish people in each generation, or a deliberate change or evolution in keeping with the needs of modern times.

Jewish biblical theology must therefore assert that the Bible be read as the foundational sacred scriptures of Judaism. In considering such a proposition, interpreters must recognize the nature of Judaism, viz., it is a synthesis of two essential elements, religion and nationhood. On the one hand, Judaism is a religious tradition that is characterized by a distinctive set of beliefs and practices. On the other hand, Judaism is a distinctive people or nation that has lived in its own land and which also lives in the larger Gentile world. Judaism is a nation that is bound by a religious relationship with YHWH. Judaism maintains adherence to YHWH, the one true G-d of the universe, the one true creator of the universe, and the one true sovereign of the universe who enters into an eternal covenant with the Jewish people. That covenant entails obligations on the part of both parties. G-d is enjoined to show ḥesed or "fidelity" to the Jewish people, to protect them from threats, to ensure their life in the land of Israel and the world, and to serve as the source of justice, righteousness, and mercy in the world. The Jewish people for their part are enjoined to show ḥesed or fidelity to YHWH, to live in accordance with the will of YHWH, acknowledging YHWH as the one true G-d of the universe and observing the sacred teachings of divine Torah or instruction that YHWH has revealed to the Jewish people.

YHWH's relationship with the Jewish people is set within the larger context of YHWH's relationship with creation and the nations at large, so that the Jewish people function as a distinctive, priestly, or chosen people within that larger relationship. As a result of its distinctive relationship with YHWH, Judaism also has a distinctive relationship with the rest of the world as a holy people that is enjoined with the task of teaching or demonstrating to the world knowledge of G-d and knowledge of practices of holiness, justice, and mercy that G-d expects of the world at large. That does not mean converting the rest of the world to Judaism. But it does mean that Judaism serves as a catalyst to the nations of the world who must come to their own understandings of G-d, holiness, justice, and mercy in the world. Such a task calls for the Jewish people to develop its own sacred and national traditions to maintain its distinctive sense of identity in the world and not to collapse that identity into that of the nations and world at large. Within the

Jewish tradition, the Bible serves as the foundation. As such, it enters into dialog with the other elements of Jewish tradition, viz., the subsequent sacred literature, practices, and socio-political and cultural expressions of the Jewish people throughout history, including Jewish life in the land of Israel and in the Diaspora.

A third dimension is close attention to the entirety of the biblical text in Jewish interpretation.[91] Whereas Christian Old Testament theology can be selective in its treatment of the Old Testament, Jewish biblical theology must take into account the entirety of the Tanak and the Hebrew or Aramaic text which stands as its basis. To a degree, this issue is a product of Christianity's penchant for reading the Old Testament through the lens of the New Testament and thereby giving privilege to those books or texts that support Christological readings of the Bible. The result has been the phenomenon of "a Bible within the Bible" in Christianity's reading of the Old Testament in which books such as Genesis, Samuel, Psalms, or Isaiah are privileged whereas books such as Leviticus, Joshua, Esther, or Ezekiel are neglected or even vilified. To be fair, Christian biblical theology has recognized this issue and has begun to address it by promoting canonical models for doing biblical theology. And certainly Judaism has its own issues with the privileging of books, such as the Torah, Prophets, and Megillot that are regularly read in the context of Jewish worship whereas books from the Writings and many elements of the Prophets are not. Nevertheless, Jewish exegetical tradition has consistently called for close attention to the biblical text, and it has seen its task as the interpretation of the entirety of the biblical text, focusing especially on a detailed analysis of the Hebrew text through the Targums or the work of the medieval Bible commentators rather than the piecemeal or typological interpretations offered by Christian commentators. Rabbi Akiva, for example, was known for calling for the interpretation of every feature of the Torah text no matter how insignificant because, as a basis for the revelation of the divine will at Sinai, every feature of the Torah text is significant and subject to interpretation.

The first element in a Jewish reading of the Tanak is adherence to the Masoretic text. Although scholarship has recognized significant and differing versions of the text of the Hebrew Bible, such as the biblical texts of the Dead Sea Scrolls, the Septuagint, the Peshitta, the Vulgate, and others,[92] the Masoretic Hebrew and Aramaic text of the Bible functions as the foundational sacred scriptures of Judaism. This is not to say that the Masoretic text is the earliest or even the most coherent text of the Bible currently known, but it is the text that has served as the basis for Jewish Bibles for at least eleven hundred years and probably more.[93] There are, of course, complications. For one, extant manuscripts of the Masoretic text date only to the mid-ninth century or so and not earlier. Modern scholarship has no clear idea as to the shape or form of the Masoretic text prior to this period because no copies of the Masoretic Bible are extant. It is known that the Ben Asher family of scribes played the major role in defining and supplying the vowel pointing and accents of the Masoretic text, but scholars have little idea as to the shape or form of that text prior to the work of the Masoretes, principally the Ben

Asher family, who shaped the Masoretic text into its final form. Given the Masoretic traditions of the *qĕrē'/kĕtîb*, marginal notes in which the Masoretes note textual emendations and alternative readings by providing an alternative vowel pointing to the consonantal text, and the tradition of the *tiqqûnê sôpĕrîm*, the emendations of the scribes, generally for theological reasons, it is clear that Masoretic text contains disputed readings which likely go back to alternative versions of the proto-Masoretic Hebrew text or to differences of viewpoint as to how the proto-Masoretic text should be read. Indeed, the Dead Sea Scrolls demonstrate that alternative versions of the Hebrew Bible were extant in the late Second Temple period. Jeremiah, for example, appears in two different versions at Qumran, most of which represent a proto-Masoretic text not that different from the text in use today and one which represents a shorter and differently arranged text of Jeremiah that appears to underlie the Greek Septuagint version of the book.[94] Despite the textual variety evident in the Hebrew biblical manuscripts at Qumran, there is evidence of a proto-Masoretic text, such as the Murabbaʿat Scroll of the Twelve Prophets or the Naḥal Ḥever Greek Twelve Prophets scroll which appears to have been translated from a proto-Masoretic text.[95]

Scholars have generally recognized that the Masoretic text may not be the earliest known text form of the Bible. Many argue that the Greek Septuagint provides a primary witness to the Old Greek version of the text which may represent the oldest known version of the Hebrew Bible. In the case of the above-mentioned Jeremiah, the shorter text included in the Septuagint and extant in a Hebrew version at Qumran may well represent the earliest known version of Jeremiah. Others, however, such as the Septuagint versions of Daniel and Esther, display an expanded text; Daniel includes the apocryphal works, Susanna, Bel and the Dragon, and the Prayer of the Three Young Jews, that are not found in the Masoretic version of the text, and Esther includes references to G-d that are also not found in the Masoretic version.

Apart from the question of the priority of Septuagint or Masoretic forms of biblical books, modern scholarship has become accustomed to emending the Masoretic text based on readings from the Septuagint and other versions that are deemed to be original. In general, such decisions are based in favor of readings that make more sense, presupposing that the scribes who transmitted the proto-Masoretic text made errors that introduced corruptions into the Hebrew text. There are indeed examples of textual corruption—1 Sam 13:1 is a primary case in point—but such a principle of textual corruption misses some important points. Scribes tend to correct their work in an effort to produce a coherent reading; indeed, the Septuagint text displays an interest in creating an esthetically pleasing and meaningful text designed to make sense to an educated Hellenistic reader. It makes more sense to posit that the difficult text is earlier and that the smoother text is the result of an effort to render a text that is meaningful to the reading audience, particularly when it is a text translated from an original language to a second language. Furthermore, the various text traditions demonstrate an interest in introducing midrashic or interpretative elements into their texts, such as the alternative versions of the Jeroboam narratives in the Septuagint version of 1 Kgs 12:24; the Qumran sect's modification of Isa 2:2-4 in 1QIsaiah^a to refer to themselves as the transmitters of divine Torah to the nations; or Jerome's introduction of a reference to the resurrection of Jesus in Zeph 3:8. Although the case may be made that selected books or readings in the Septuagint, Qumran scrolls, or the other versions may be original, the case for the priority of other textual witnesses is not always clear. Alternative readings in the other textual traditions may indicate the history of the development of the Hebrew text and the hermeneutics by which it was read, but in the end the question of textual priority is irrelevant in a Jewish biblical theology. The Masoretic text is accepted as sacred scripture in Judaism, and it must therefore stand as the subject of interpretation in a Jewish biblical theology.

The exegetical method by which the Masoretic text of the Bible is read must also be considered. Traditional Jewish scholarship identified four basic levels of interpretation expressed through the Hebrew term *pardēs*, "garden (of Eden)," which serves as an acronym for the four exegetical strategies.[96] The first is *pěšāṭ*, the "simple" or "plain" meaning of the text. The second is *remez*, the "allegorical" or "alluded" meaning of the text, often involving Gematria or Notarikon or other allusionary techniques. The third is *děrāšâ*, the homiletical or midrashic interpretation of texts, sometimes in relation to other biblical texts, sometimes in relation to other Jewish texts, and sometimes in relation to other issues. And the fourth is *sôd*, the "secret" or "mystical" meaning of the text, generally related to Kabbalah. The last three techniques are classically Jewish forms of textual interpretation that are designed to relate the biblical text to later forms of Jewish literature and thought and thereby to impose later meanings on texts that were not written for such purpose. The first technique, *pěšāṭ*, however, is designed to interpret the plain meaning of the text and to enable it to speak on its own terms without reference to later forms of Jewish literature. Insofar as the purpose of Jewish biblical theology is to interpret the Bible in its own right as sacred literature designed to give expression to concerns contemporary with its composition and then to put the Bible in dialog with later Jewish tradition, *pěšāṭ* emerges as the basis for exegetical method in Jewish biblical theology. The use of *pěšāṭ* enables the Bible to speak on its own terms as the foundational dialog partner of Jewish tradition.

The development of *pěšāṭ* exegetical method is evident within the Bible itself in comments that are designed to explain a statement or term to the reader, such as 1 Sam 9:9, which explains the use of the Hebrew term, *rō'eh*, "seer," with the comment, "Formerly in Israel when a man would go to inquire of G-d, he would say, 'Come, let us go to the seer,' for in former times a prophet (*nābî'*) was called a seer." The *pěšāṭ* method is also extensively employed in the early translations of the Bible, including both the earliest forms of the Septuagint and the Targums, insofar as translation is a form of interpretation. The Old Greek of the Septuagint,

Targum Onkelos to the Torah, and Targum Jonathan to the Prophets demonstrate interests in rendering the Hebrew text as accurately as possible, although a
certain element of translation is inevitable when translating from one language to
another. Later manifestations of pĕšāṭ exegesis appear in the early halakhic
midrashim, such as the Mekhilta' de-Rabbi Ishmael or Siphre Devarim, both of
which are intended to explain the meaning of the legal codes in Exod 20–23 and
Deut 12–26 respectively. The pĕšāṭ technique comes to full expression in the
medieval commentators, such as Rashi, Radaq, Abraham Ibn Ezra, and others
who sought to interpret the plain meaning of the biblical text as a result of
challenges to Judaism by both Islam and Christianity that Jews had misinter-
preted their scriptures, thereby failing to see the truth of Islam or Christianity. By
focusing on the plain meaning of the text, particularly through the use of
philology and grammar, the medieval interpreters demonstrated that the biblical
text had a coherent message of its own that did not need the recognition of non-
Jewish movements of Islam and Christianity to demonstrate a foreign meaning
beyond that expressed by the text itself.

Although modern historical-critical exegesis was developed in Protestant
scholarly circles beginning in the period of the Enlightenment, it is the successor
to a certain degree of the medieval Jewish interpreters. The use of philological
and grammatical principles for interpretation was honed by the medieval Jewish
biblical scholars and developed further in modern times by source-, text-, redac-
tion-, form-, and tradition-criticism as well as by archeology and the comparative
study of ancient Near Eastern literature. Although early critical exegesis was often
designed to serve the Protestant principle of *sola scriptura*, or "scripture alone," as
the basis of Christian thought—and frequently with an eye to undercutting Jewish
and Roman Catholic claims to the text—critical exegesis is designed like pĕšāṭ to
enable the Bible to speak on its own terms. Like their medieval forebears, modern
Jewish biblical scholars have learned to employ methods introduced by non-
Jews—and to reject the excesses of those methods—to elucidate the meaning of
biblical texts. Many of the excesses of source-, text-, redaction-, and tradition-
criticism have been tempered by the introduction of literary-, rhetorical-,
linguistic-, and even reader-response criticism that calls for recognition of textual
coherence, elements of plot and character development, the persuasive and communicative aspects of a text, and even the role of the reader instead of exclusively
the author in constructing the meaning of a text. This is not to deny the historical
dimensions of texts that early historical critics emphasized. Rather, it is a recognition that a text must be read in both its synchronic and diachronic dimensions.
Synchronic refers to the purely literary and expressive character of the full or final
form of a text apart from factors of composition, such as authorship, authorial
intention, and the historical settings of composition. Diachronic refers to the
historical character of a text, such as the postulated authorship of a text, its historical setting and development, and its reception in defined historical contexts.
Analysis of both aspects of a text is necessary for its full interpretation.

A fourth dimension is the dialogical character of the Jewish Bible. Prior work in Christian biblical theology has demonstrated that there is no theological center to the Old Testament, viz., no single thematic or theological principle has been identified that binds the entirety of the Bible together. Early attempts to organize a theology around G-d, Man, and Salvation fail because not all of the books are concerned with G-d (i.e. Esther, Song of Songs) or salvation, a foreign concept brought in by the New Testament. Von Rad's efforts to make *Heilsgeschichte* the unifying theme of the Old Testament fail due to its overemphasis on historical narrative and its inability to account adequate for wisdom and other books that are not primarily concerned with history. Eichrodt's emphasis on covenant fails because the theme of covenant does not come to expression in every book of the Bible. Childs' focus on canonical criticism fails because he is unable to account for the variety of texts and canonical forms that appear within Christianity. Rendtorff's theology fails because it does not account for the contexts of Judaism and Christianity in which the Bible is read, thereby giving it a distinctive function in each tradition. Gerstenberger's theology fails because it is based on the premise that there is no theological unity in the Old Testament, which means that only individual themes are treated in isolation. Brueggemann's theology is very intriguing, but ultimately, it cannot account for the entire Bible.

But in fact, the diversity of concerns raised within the various books of the Bible provides a basis for thinking about the Tanak as a whole, not as a work concerned with a single theme, but as a canonical work in which the full variety of books, concerns, and viewpoints are represented therein. Indeed, many books differ markedly from each other and sometimes even flatly contradict each other. Deuteronomy updates the laws of Exodus with greater concern for the rights of the poor and women. Chronicles gives an alternative account of Israelite and Judean history from that presented in Joshua, Judges, Samuel, and Kings with a distinctive theological viewpoint. Jeremiah frequently challenges the views of his senior colleague, Isaiah, and Ezekiel in turn challenges Jeremiah. Job directly challenges the theological worldview of Proverbs; Lamentations challenges the worldview of the Prophets; and Daniel draws upon Isaiah, Jeremiah, and Ezekiel in an effort to work out a new and different understanding of divine purpose in world events. When readers observe that the books of the Tanak differ so markedly among themselves, the task becomes not one of attempting to reconcile the differences as past interpreters have unsuccessfully attempted to do, but one of recognizing that the differing viewpoints in the Bible is intentional and therefore a subject of concern in a Jewish (or a Christian) biblical theology.

The variety of viewpoints expressed in the Bible represents a dialog on major issues that takes place both among the books of the Bible and with the readers of those books, in whatever historical and cultural context in which they might reside. Such a model of dialog is a classic Jewish form. It is well represented in the Rabbinic Kallah, the meetings of the Rabbis in Talmudic times to discuss points of halakhah and to make their decisions.[97] Because of the dialogical nature of the

Rabbinic Kallah and commitment to the notion that the study of Torah is an ongoing process of revelation, the Rabbis preserved both the majority opinions on points of discussion in the Talmud as well as the minority positions in case future discussion might indicate defects in the reasoning of the majority or important insights in the decisions of the minority. Thus Judaism does not find itself based in dogmatic or systematic theological principles as Christianity attempts to do; instead, Judaism emerges as a religion of continuous dialog, both with the traditions and among contemporaries through time, as it seeks to understand the divine will as expressed in Torah and subsequent Jewish tradition.

Recognition of the dialogical character of the Bible calls for a methodological approach based in intertextuality that complements the concern with pĕšāṭ or the plain meaning of the text outlined above. The purpose of such an approach is to recognize the interrelationships among the biblical books, whether intentional or not, as well as efforts to expound upon them, both by other biblical books and by the readers or interpreters of biblical books, as a fundamental aspect of the inter-pretation of biblical literature. Indeed, such an approach echoes the Rabbinic concern with dĕrāšâ, the homiletical approach noted above that employs mid-rashic intertextual dialog as an essential foundation for its homiletical exposition. Such an approach is well-rooted in the Bible itself as the above-noted examples of inner biblical exegesis among the biblical books, either to disagree with them or to elaborate, expound upon, and extend the meaning of the earlier text, so clearly represent. It is also well represented by later interpreters of biblical books who likewise seek to elaborate, expound upon, and extend the meaning of biblical texts and sometimes to disagree with them as well. Such an approach appears in the Targums, such as Targum Jonathan on the Torah in Exod 19 which notes how G-d held Mt. Sinai over the heads of the people of Israel, threatening to drop it on them if they declined to observe divine Torah. It is also well represented in the various midrashim and Talmudic texts that expound upon the books of the Bible, as exemplified by the discussion of the *Lex Talionis* in Exod 21:22-25; Lev 24:10-22; and Deut 19:15-21 (see *m. Baba Kamma* 8:1; *b. Baba Kamma* 83b–84a).

Recent advances in intertextual methodology or reading strategies come into play, particularly the work of Mikhail Bakhtin who explores the intertextual character of literary texts. Intertextuality includes a number of dimensions.[98] One is the overriding role of the reader of a text who constructs its meaning or interpretation based not on the intentions of the author but on the perceptions of the reader in relation to textual world that the reader inhabits. Here, the inten-tions of the author are irrelevant, both because the author may not be known or alive any longer to explain his or her work, and because a literary work takes on a life of its own once it leaves the hand of its author. In such an instance, the reader becomes the arbiter of textual construction and meaning, not the author who is no longer present. Indeed, biblical literature is perhaps the foremost example of such reading strategy, insofar as the authors of biblical texts are rarely known. But the lack of an author has not deterred later readers from interpreting biblical literature in relation to their own respective religious traditions and worldviews. Does the Bible point to modern diaspora Jewish life or to the modern state of Israel? Does it point to Jesus or even to the establishment of the Christian church in all of its various forms? Probably not in both instances, but one can trace the thread of interpretation through the traditions of Judaism and Christianity to arrive at phenomena noted. Indeed, such adaptability enables scripture to address unforeseen developments and nevertheless stand as the foundation for later forms of religious expression.

A second dimension is the inherent coherence of literature, whether it is deliberately written as a coherent text or not. Placement in a literary context demands that a text be read in relation to that literary context in an effort to construct how the various elements of the text function together in the mind of the reader. It does not matter if a text was written to be coherent or if it was composed in stages, edited, or even placed randomly together. Again, texts take on a life of their own once they leave the hands of their authors, and they are then able to address unforeseen circumstances and realities, as indicated above. At this point, the interpreter must ask how a unit of text fits in or relates to the preceding and following material or material that is grouped together with the text under consideration in a larger literary or canonical framework. Simply by being placed together with other text, a text under consideration enters a literary context and that context then becomes an element of its interpretation. It does not matter, for example, if Isa 1–39 was written to give expression to the words and activities of the eighth-century prophet Isaiah ben Amoz, if Isa 40–55 was written by an anonymous exilic prophet at the end of the Babylonian exile, and if Isa 56–66 was written by one or more anonymous prophets working in the early Persian period. Isaiah 1–66 functions as a single book that gives expression to the words of Isaiah ben Amoz even if the eighth-century prophet did not write the book in its entirety or even one word of it. Interpreters must account for both the unity of its expression as well as the disunity of its composition to come to a full understanding of a book which is in dialog with its readers and whose segments are in dialog with each other.

A third dimension is the inherent intertextual interrelationship between texts, whether they are placed together within the same immediate literary context or not. In the case of biblical texts, their placement together within a biblical canon establishes an intertextual relationship among all of the texts of that canon and thereby calls for reading each of the texts within that biblical canon, however defined, in relation to the other texts of that canon. In such an instance, the books within a canon must be considered to be in dialog with each other insofar as they each articulate a set of ideas within the framework of their literary context. Thus, the book of Jeremiah is in dialog with all of the books of the Torah, insofar as Jeremiah calls for observance of divine Torah as a fundamental principle of his worldview. But Jeremiah is also in dialog with Job, not because Jeremiah cites Job or Job cites Jeremiah, but because both take up the question of suffering, warranted or not, imposed by G-d. Likewise, Jeremiah is in dialog with the

Psalms, in part because he employs the psalmic genre of lament to give expression to his suffering, and Jeremiah is in dialog with Kings and Chronicles because of the book's construction of the history of the last years of the kingdom of Judah much as Kings and Chronicles undertake the same task with differing results. But interpreters must also consider the larger literary world of texts beyond the immediate context of a defined literary canon, such as the Bible. When read in relation to the larger literary framework of Judaism, the intertextuality of the Bible includes the entire body of literature included in Judaism, such as the Targum, Midrashim, Talmuds, commentaries, mystical literature, Zionist literature, and so on. And when read in relation to the worlds of Christianity, Islam, and the cultures of America, the Middle East, Europe, Africa, Asia, and beyond, the circle of intertextual relations within which the Bible functions widens accordingly in relation to the literary world of the reader.

A final dimension is the deliberate intertextual relationship between works of literature, most commonly referring to those cases when one work deliberately cites or alludes to another. The Bible is filled with such examples of inner-biblical exegesis, in which later writers attempt to explain, elaborate upon, disagree with, or otherwise interpret and react to other biblical texts. Instances occur within biblical books, as indicated by the redactional expansion and reworking of biblical texts. The placement of superscriptions at the head of prophetic books is a case in point, insofar as the superscription identifies the following material as the word of the prophet in question or pertaining to the prophet, and thereby contextualizes the book. The placement of Deuteronomy following Genesis—Numbers is another case in point, insofar as Deuteronomy revises the laws of the earlier books, as exemplified by the slave law in Deut 15 which gives greater rights to the poor and to women than Exod 21. Another example is the citation of Proverbs' maxim, "the fear of YHWH is wisdom," in Job 28:28 as part of a text that challenges the contention in Proverbs that wisdom is readily discerned by observing nature. A further example is Chronicles' recasting of the historical texts of Samuel and Kings in an effort to challenge Kings' principle that disaster occurs as a result of the sins of the ancestors, and to argue instead that it comes as a result of the sins of the current generation. And Esther enters the dialog to assert that G-d does not enter into history in the way that either Kings or Chronicles asserts, but that human beings must fend for themselves.

Fundamentally, the Tanak is an intertextual and dialogical book. It enters into dialog with its readers, it engages dialog among its constituent texts, and it engages dialog beyond its own confines with the larger bodies of literature in Judaism and the world beyond. All of these dimensions of intertextuality enter into the exegetical discussion of the Tanak and play their roles in defining the interrelationships among the various texts that comprise the Tanak.

In sum, a Jewish biblical theology must engage the text of the Bible firsthand, grappling with the interpretation of the Hebrew and Aramaic text; discerning the diachronic dimensions of its literary form, compositional history, generic and linguistic features, communicative features, socio-historical setting, and the potential intentions of its authors; and grappling with the synchronic dimensions again of its literary coherence, plot and character development, and its inter-textual relationships. A Jewish biblical theology therefore points to the founda-tions for an ongoing dialog concerning the identity and character of G-d, the Jewish people, the world of creation, the nations at large, and their interrelations with each other. It is on the basis of this dialog begun in the Bible that Judaism is formed.

NOTES

[1] Jon D. Levenson, "Why Jews Are Not Interested in Biblical Theology," in *Judaic Perspectives on Ancient Israel*, ed. J. Neusner et al. (Philadelphia: Fortress 1987), 287–307, reprinted in Levenson, *The Hebrew Bible, the Old Testament, and Historical Criticism: Jews and Christians in Biblical Studies* (Louisville: Westminster John Knox, 1993), 33–61, 165–70. See my "Why Jews Should Be Interested in Biblical Theology," *CCAR Journal* 44, no. 1 (1997): 67–75.

[2] Cf. my "Jewish Biblical Theology and Christian Old Testament Theology," *ThLZ* 134, no. 4 (2009): 397–410. For surveys of the field of Biblical or Old Testament Theology, see Hans-Joachim Kraus, *Die biblische Theologie. Ihre Geschichte und Problematik* (Neukirchen–Vluyn: Neukirchener, 1970); James Barr, *The Concept of Biblical Theology: An Old Testament Perspective* (Minneapolis: Fortress Press, 1999); Leo Perdue, *Reconstructing Old Testament Theology: After the Collapse of History* (Minneapolis: Fortress Press, 2005); as well as my "Biblical Theology. I. Hebrew Bible/Old Testament," in *Encyclopedia of the Bible and its Reception*, vol. 3, ed. H. J. Klauck et al. (Berlin: de Gruyter, forthcoming); idem, "Jewish Biblical Theology," in *The Hebrew Bible: New Insights and Scholarship*, ed. F. E. Greenspahn (New York: New York University Press, 2008), 191–208; idem, "The Emerging Field of Jewish Biblical Theology," in *Academic Approaches to Teaching Jewish Studies*, ed. Z. Garber (Lanham, MD: University Press of America, 2000), 84–105; Benjamin D. Sommer, "Dialogical Biblical Theology: A Jewish Approach to Reading Scripture Theologically," in *Biblical Theology: Introducing the Conversation*, ed. L. G. Perdue et al. (LBT; Nashville: Abingdon, 2009), 1–53.

[3] Johann P. Gabler, "An Oration on the Proper Distinction between Biblical and Dogmatic Theology and the Specific Objectives of Each," in *Old Testament Theology: Flowering and Future*, ed. B. C. Ollenburger (SBTS 1; Winona Lake, IN: Eisenbrauns, 2004), 497–506.

[4] Julius Wellhausen, *Die Composition des Hexateuch und der Historischen Bücher des Alten Testaments* (Berlin: Reimer, 1889); idem, *Prolegomena to the History of Ancient Israel* (Gloucester, MA: Smith, 1973). For discussion of anti-Semitism in Germany, see Paul Lawrence Rose, *Revolutionary Antisemitism in Germany from Kant to Wagner* (Princeton: Princeton University Press, 1990), and in France, see Arthur Hertzberg, *The French Enlighten-ment and the Jews* (New York: Columbia University Press, 1968).

[5] For example, Ludwig Köhler, *Old Testament Theology* (Philadelphia: Westminster, 1957).

[6] The English version of Eichrodt's study is *Theology of the Old Testament* (2 vols.; OTL; Philadelphia: Westminster, 1961–67).

[7] Eichrodt, *Theology*, 1:26.

[8] For discussion of Barth and Bonhoeffer, see Clark Williamson, *A Guest in the House of Israel: Post-Holocaust Church Theology* (Louisville: Westminster John Knox, 1993), 119–22; Stephen R. Haynes, *The Bonhoeffer Legacy: Post Holocaust Perspectives* (Minneapolis: Fortress Press, 2006).

[9] Gerhard von Rad, *Old Testament Theology* (2 vols.; New York: Harper & Row, 1962–65).

[10] Brevard S. Childs, *Biblical Theology of the Old and New Testaments: Theological Reflection on the Christian Bible* (Minneapolis: Fortress Press, 1993).

[11] Jules Isaac, *The Teaching of Contempt: The Theological Roots of Anti-Semitism* (New York: Holt, Rinholt & Winston, 1964).

[12] Rosemary Radford Ruether, *Faith and Fratricide: The Theological Roots of Anti-Semitism* (Eugene, OR: Wipf & Stock, 1997). Regretfully, her study of modern Israel, *The Wrath of Jonah: The Crisis of Religious Nationalism in the Israeli–Palestinian Conflict* (New York: Harper & Row, 1989), co-authored with her husband Herman J. Ruether, was so hopelessly biased against Israel that it undermines her credibility.

[13] Paul Van Buren, "On Reading Someone Else's Mail: The Church and Israel's Scriptures," in *Die Hebräische Bibel und ihre Zweifache Nachgeschichte. Festschrift für Rolf Rendtorff*, ed. E. Blum et al. (Neukirchen–Vluyn: Neukirchener, 1990), 595–606.

[14] Williamson, *A Guest*, passim.

[15] Katharina von Kellenbach, *Anti-Judaism in Feminist Religious Writings* (Atlanta: Scholars Press, 1994).

[16] Erich Zenger, *Das erste Testament. Die jüdische Bibel und die Christen* (Düsseldorf: Patmos, 1993), 12.

[17] Walter Brueggemann, *Theology of the Old Testament: Testimony, Dispute, Advocacy* (Minneapolis: Fortress Press, 1997).

[18] Rolf Rendtorff, *The Canonical Hebrew Bible: A Theology of the Old Testament* (Leiden: DEO, 2005).

[19] Cf. my "Jewish Biblical Theology and Christian Old Testament Theology."

[20] Moses Mendelssohn, *Jerusalem, or On Religious Power and Judaism* (Hanover, NH: University Press of New England, 1983); see my "The Democratization of Messianism in Modern Jewish Theology," in *Biblical Interpretation: History, Context, and Reality*, ed. C. Helmer (SBLSymS 26; Atlanta: Society of Biblical Literature, 2005), 87–101, especially 94–97, for discussion of Mendelssohn.

[21] Leopold Zunz, *Die Gottesdienstlichen Vorträge der Juden* (Hildesheim: Olms, 1966).

[22] Franz Rosenzweig, *The Star of Redemption* (Notre Dame, IN: University of Notre Dame Press, 1985).

[23] Martin Buber, *I and Thou* (New York: Charles Scribner's, 1970).

[24] For example, *The Eclipse of G-d: Studies in the Relation between Religion and Philosophy* (New York: Harper & Row, 1952).

[25] Abraham Heschel, *Die Prophetie* (Krakow: Nakladem Polskiej Akademi Umiejetmpco, 1936); English ed., *The Prophets* (Philadelphia: Jewish Publication Society, 1962).

[26] For discussion of Heschel, see especially Edward K. Kaplan and Samuel H. Dresner, *Abraham Joshua Heschel: Prophetic Witness* (New Haven: Yale University Press, 1998); Edward K. Kaplan, *Spiritual Radical: Abraham Joshua Heschel in America* (New Haven: Yale University Press, 2007).

[27] Abraham Heschel, *Man is Not Alone* (Philadelphia: Jewish Publication Society, 1951); idem, *G-d in Search of Man: A Philosophy of Judaism* (New York: Meridian & Jewish Publication Society, 1955); idem, *The Sabbath: Its Meaning for Modern Man* (New York: Farrar, Straus & Giroux, 1951; idem, *Israel: Echo of an Eternity* (New York: Farrar, Straus & Giroux, 1969).

[28] Yehezkel Kaufmann, *A History of Israelite Religion from Antiquity to the End of the Second Temple* (8 vols.; Tel Aviv: Mosad Bialik, 1937–56 [Hebrew]); idem, *The Religion of Israel from its Beginnings through the Babylonian Exile* (New York: Schocken, 1972); idem, *The Babylonian Captivity and Deutero-Isaiah: History of the Religion of Israel* (New York: Union of

38 I N T R O D U C T I O N

American Hebrew Congregations, 1970); see also Thomas Krapf, *Yehezkel Kaufmann. Ein Lebens- und erkenntnisweg zur theologie der Hebräischen Bibel* (Berlin: Insitut Kirche & Judentum, 1990); idem, *Die Priesterschrift und die vorexilische Zeit*. *Yehezkel Kaufmanns vernachlässigter Beitrag zu Geschichte der biblischen Religion* (OBO 119; Freiburg: Üniversitätsverlag, 1992).

[29] Ignaz Maybaum, *The Face of G-d after Auschwitz* (Amsterdam: Polak & Van Glennep, 1965).

[30] Richard Rubenstein, *After Auschwitz: Radical Theology and Contemporary Judaism* (Indianapolis: Bobbs-Merrill, 1966).

[31] Emil Fackenheim, *G-d's Presence in History: Jewish Affirmations and Philosophical Reflections* (New York: New York University Press, 1970).

[32] Emil Fackenheim, *To Mend the World: Foundations of Jewish Thought* (New York: Schocken, 1982); idem, *The Jewish Bible after the Holocaust: A Rereading* (Bloomington: Indiana University Press, 1990).

[33] Eliezer Berkovits, *Faith after the Holocaust* (New York: Ktav, 1973).

[34] Eliezer Berkovits, *Man and G-d: Studies in Biblical Theology* (Detroit: Wayne State University Press, 1969).

[35] Moshe Goshen-Gottstein, "Christianity, Judaism, and Modern Study," in *Congress Volume: Edinburgh, 1974*, ed. J. A. Emerton (VTSup 28; Leiden: Brill, 1975), 69–88; idem, "Jewish Biblical Theology and the Science of the Bible," *Tarbiz* 50 (1980–81): 37–64 (Hebrew); idem, "Tanakh Theology: The Religion of the Old Testament and the Place of Jewish Biblical Theology," in *Ancient Israelite Religion: Essays in Honor of Frank Moore Cross, Jr.*, ed. P. D. Miller et al. (Philadelphia: Fortress Press, 1987), 587–644.

[36] Mattitiahu Tsevat, "Theology of the Old Testament: A Jewish View," *HBT* 8 (1986): 33–49.

[37] Moshe Weinfeld, *Deuteronomy and the Deuteronomic School* (Winona Lake, IN; Eisenbrauns, 1992); idem, *Social Justice in Ancient Israel and the Ancient Near East* (Jerusalem: Magnes, 1995).

[38] Harry M. Orlinsky, "The Biblical Concept of the Land of Israel: Cornerstone of the Covenant Between G-d and Israel," in *The Land of Israel: Jewish Perspectives*, ed. L. Hoffman (Notre Dame: University of Notre Dame Press, 1986), 27–64.

[39] David Blumenthal, *Facing the Abusing G-d: A Theology of Protest* (Louisville: Westminster John Knox, 1993).

[40] Levenson, "Why Jews," passim.

[41] See my assessment of Levenson's work, "Why Jews are Interested in Biblical Theology: A Retrospective on the Work of Jon D. Levenson," in *Jewish Book Annual* 55–56, ed. A. Bernstein-Nahar (1997–99/5758–59): 134–68.

[42] Jon D. Levenson, *Theology of the Program of Restoration in Ezekiel 40–48* (HSM 10; Missoula: Scholars Press, 1976).

[43] Jon D. Levenson, *Sinai and Zion: An Entry into the Jewish Bible* (Minneapolis: Winston, 1985).

[44] Jon D. Levenson, *Creation and the Persistence of Evil: The Jewish Drama of Divine Impotence* (Princeton: Princeton University Press, 1988).

[45] Jon D. Levenson, *Death and the Resurrection of the Beloved Son: The Transformation of Child Sacrifice in Judaism and Christianity* (New Haven: Yale University Press, 1993).

[46] Jon D. Levenson, *Esther: A Commentary* (OTL; Louisville: Westminster John Knox, 1997).

[47] Jon D. Levenson, *Resurrection and the Restoration of Israel: The Ultimate Victory of the G-d of Life* (New Haven: Yale University Press, 2006).

[48] Michael Fishbane, *Biblical Interpretation in Ancient Israel* (Oxford: Oxford University Press, 1985).

[49] Michael Fishbane, *The Kiss of G-d: Spiritual and Mystical Death in Judaism* (Seattle: University of Washington, 1994).

[50] Michael Fishbane, *The Exegetical Imagination: On Jewish Thought and Theology* (Cambridge: Harvard University Press, 1998).

[51] Michael Fishbane, *Haftarot: The JPS Bible Commentary* (Philadelphia: Jewish Publication Society, 2002/5762).

[52] Michael Fishbane, *Biblical Myth and Rabbinic Mythmaking* (Oxford: Oxford University Press, 2003).

[53] Bernard M. Levinson, *Deuteronomy and the Hermeneutics of Legal Innovation* (Oxford: Oxford University Press, 1997).

[54] Marc Brettler "Biblical History and Jewish Biblical Theology," *JR* (1997): 563–83; cf. his *How to Read the Bible* (Philadelphia: Jewish Publication Society, 2005).

[55] Benjamin D. Sommer, *A Prophet Reads Scripture: Allusion in Isaiah 40–66* (Stanford: Stanford University Press, 1998).

[56] Benjamin D. Sommer, "Revelation at Sinai in the Hebrew Bible and in Jewish Theology," *JR* 79 (1999): 422–51.

[57] Sommer, "Dialogical Biblical Theology," passim.

[58] See my "The Emerging Field" and "Jewish Biblical Theology."

[59] *Isaiah 1–39, with an Introduction to Prophetic Literature* (FOTL 16; Grand Rapids: Eerdmans, 1996).

[60] "Tanak versus Old Testament: Concerning the Foundation for a Jewish Theology of the Bible," in *Problems in Biblical Theology: Essays in Honor of Rolf Knierim*, ed. H. T. C. Sun et al. (Grand Rapids: Eerdmans, 1997), 353–72.

[61] "Reconceiving the Paradigms of Old Testament Theology in the Post-Shoah Period," *BibInt* 6 (1998): 142–61; reprinted in A. O. Bellis and J. S. Kaminsky, eds., *Jews, Christians, and the Theology of the Hebrew Scriptures* (SBLSymS 8; Atlanta: Society of Biblical Literature, 2000), 155–72.

[62] "Isaiah and Theodicy after the Shoah," in *Strange Fire: Reading the Bible after the Holocaust*, ed. T. Linafeldt (BibSem 71; Sheffield: Sheffield Academic, 2000), 208–19.

[63] "Absence of G-d and Human Responsibility in the Book of Esther," in *Reading the Hebrew Bible for a New Millennium: Form, Concept, and Theological Perspective*. Vol. 2, *Exegetical and Theological Studies*, ed. W. Kim et al. (SAC; Harrisburg, PA: Trinity Press International, 2000), 264–75.

[64] *The Twelve Prophets* (2 vols.; BO; Collegeville, MN: Liturgical, 2000).

[65] *King Josiah of Judah: The Lost Messiah of Israel* (Oxford: Oxford University Press, 2001).

[66] *Zephaniah* (Hermeneia; Minneapolis: Fortress Press, 2003).

[67] *The Prophetic Literature* (IBT; Nashville: Abingdon, 2005).

[68] See "The Democratization."

[69] *1 and 2 Kings: A Commentary* (OTL; Louisville: Westminster John Knox, 2007).

[70] *Reading the Hebrew Bible after the Shoah: Engaging Holocaust Theology* (Minneapolis: Fortress Press, 2008).

[71] Sara Japhet, *The Ideology of the Book of Chronicles and its Place in Biblical Thought* (Frankfurt: Lang, 1989); idem, *I and II Chronicles: A Commentary* (OTL; Louisville: Westminster John Knox, 2002).

[72] Moshe Greenberg, "Reflections on Job's Theology," in *Studies in the Bible and Jewish Thought* (Philadelphia: Jewish Publication Society, 1995), 327–33.

[73] Jacob Milgrom, *Leviticus* (3 vols.; AB 3, 3A, 3B; Garden City: Doubleday, 1991–2000).

[74] Benjamin Uffenheimer, "Isaiah's and Micah's Approaches to Policy and History," in *Politics and Theopolitics in the Bible and Postbiblical Literature*, ed. H. Graf Reventlow et al. (JSOTSup 27; Sheffield: Sheffield Academic, 1994), 176–88.

[75] Israel Knohl, *The Sanctuary of Silence: The Priestly Torah and the Holiness School* (Minneapolis: Fortress Press, 1995); idem, *The Divine Symphony: the Bible's Many Voices* (Philadelphia: Jewish Publication Society, 2003/5763).

[76] Isaac Kalimi, "Religionsgeschichte Israels oder Theologie des Alten Testaments," *JBibTh* 10 (1995): 45–68; and "History of Israelite religion or Hebrew Bible/Old Testament Theology? Jewish Interest in Biblical Theology," in *Early Jewish Exegesis and Theological Controversies: Studies in Scripture in the Shadow of Internal and External Controversies* (Assen: Van Gorcum, 2002), 107–34.

[77] Tikva Frymer-Kensky, "The Emergence of Biblical Theologies," in Bellis and Kaminsky, eds., *Jews, Christians*, 109–21.

[78] Yair Hoffman, "Jeremiah 50–51 and the Concept of Divine Evil in the Hebrew Bible," in H. Graf Reventlow and Y. Hoffman, eds., *The Problem of Evil and its Symbols in Jewish and Christian Tradition* (JSOTSup 366; London and New York: Continuum, 2004), 14–28.

[79] Dalit Rom Shiloni, "Ezekiel as the Voice of the Exiles and Constructor of Exilic Identity," *HUCA* 76 (2005): 1–75; idem, "Facing Destruction and Exile: Inner-Biblical Exegesis in Jeremiah and Ezekiel," *ZAW* 117 (2002): 189–205.

[80] Edward Greenstein, "The Wrath of G-d in the Book of Lamentations," in Graf Reventlow and Hoffman, eds., *The Problem of Evil*, 29–42.

[81] Ziony Zevit, "Jewish Biblical Theology: Whence? Why? And Whither?," *HUCA* 49 (2005): 289–340.

[82] Frederick Greenspahn, "Jewish Ambivalence towards the Bible," *HS* 49 (2007): 7–21.

[83] Joel Kaminsky, *Yet I Loved Jacob: Reclaiming the Biblical Concept of Election* (Nashville: Abingdon, 2007).

[84] Benjamin D. Sommer, *The Bodies of G-d and the World of Ancient Israel* (Cambridge: Cambridge University Press, 2009).

[85] See my essay, "Reconceiving the Paradigms of Old Testament Theology."

[86] For full discussion of this issue, see my essay, "Tanak versus Old Testament."

[87] Levinson, *Deuteronomy and the Hermeneutics of Legal Innovation*.

[88] For discussion of the Former Prophets, generally identified in scholarly circles as the Deuteronomistic History, see my *King Josiah of Judah*, 21–177; and *1 and 2 Kings*, 1–44.

[89] See my *The Prophetic Literature*.

[90] See my *Reading the Hebrew Bible after the Shoah*, 167–227.

[91] See "Bible, Exegesis and Study," *EncJud* 4:889–915; and M. Sæbø, ed., *Hebrew Bible/Old Testament: The History of its Interpretation*. I/1, *Antiquity* (Göttingen: Vandenhoeck & Ruprecht, 1996).

[92] See especially Emanuel Tov, *Textual Criticism of the Hebrew Bible* (2d ed.; Minneapolis: Fortress Press, 2001).

[93] See Christian D. Ginsburg, *Introduction to the Massoretico-Critical Edition of the Hebrew Bible* (New York: Ktav, 1966).

[94] See Emanuel Tov, "Jeremiah," in E. Ulrich et al., eds., *Qumran Cave 4. X. The Prophets* (DJD 15; Oxford: Clarendon, 1997), 145–207.

[95] P. Benoit et al., *Les Grottes de Murabbaʻat* (DJD 2; Oxford: Clarendon, 1961); Emanuel Tov et al., *The Greek Minor Prophets Scroll from Naḥal Ḥever (8ḤevXIIgr)* (DJD 8; Oxford: Clarendon, 1990).

[96] "Bible, Exegesis and Study," *EncJud* 4:890.

[97] "Kallah, Months of," *EndJud* 10:710–12.
[98] See especially Mikhail Bakhtin, *The Dialogic Imagination* (Austin: University of Texas, 1981); Barbara Green, *Mikhail Bakhtin and Biblical Scholarship: An Introduction* (SemSt 38; Atlanta: Society of Biblical Literature, 2000).

Part II

The Torah

A. OVERVIEW

The Torah, also known as the Pentateuch or the Five Books of Moses, constitutes the foundational work of both the Tanak in particular and all forms of Judaism in general. Indeed, the Hebrew term *tôrâ* means "instruction," insofar as it is a noun derived from the *hiphil* form of the Hebrew verb root *yrh*, which means "to guide, instruct," and it is employed especially in reference to divine instruction of Israel throughout the Tanak.[1] Such divine instruction includes the individual civil and ritual laws that appear throughout the Torah in order to provide the foundations for a just and stable society and a viable sacred religious establishment, but it also includes the metanarrative of Israel's origins within the context of world history from the time of creation that provides identity for the people of Israel and the rationale for the creation of a just and holy society within that world.

The Torah presents an account of Israel's origins and its relationship with YHWH, from the time of the creation of the world through the early history and development of humankind, the history of Israel's earliest ancestors, the formation of the nation Israel through the Exodus from Egyptian bondage under the leadership of Moses, the revelation of divine Torah at Mt. Sinai, the period of wilderness wandering, and finally, Moses' last addresses to Israel on the eve of its entry into the Promised Land of Israel. Although the Torah appears as five sequential yet discrete narrative books—Genesis, Exodus, Leviticus, Numbers, and Deuteronomy—analysis of the literary features of the Torah narrative indicates that the five books do not constitute the synchronic literary structure of the work. Instead, the so-called *toledoth*, "generations," formulae, a series of formulae based on variations of the phrase, *wĕ'ēlleh tôlĕdōt PN*, "and these are the generations of PN," in Gen 2:4; 5:1; 6:9; 10:1; 11:10; 11:27; 25:12; 25:19; 36:1; 37:2; and Num 3:1 constitute the synchronic literary structure of the work. The *toledoth* formulae introduce successive segments of the Torah narrative that trace Israel's history from "the generations of heaven and earth" in Gen 2:4, that is, humankind as descended from Adam and Eve, through "the generations of Moses and Aaron" in Num 3:1, that is, Israel under the leadership of its Levitical priesthood acting on behalf of YHWH.

Identification of the *toledoth* formulas as the structural markers of the Torah in its present form begins with the work of Frank Moore Cross, Jr. In his foundational study of the P stratum of the Pentateuch, Cross argues that P is not a self-standing source, but must be recognized as the final redactional stratum that edited and arranged the final form of the Pentateuch and wrote substantial sections of the work. The P stratum of the Pentateuch employed the *toledoth* formulae to organize the literary structure of the book of Genesis and itinerary notices concerning the movement of Israel from Egypt through Sinai and the Wilderness to organize the literary structure of the narrative in Exodus, Leviticus, and Numbers.[2] For Cross, the *toledoth* formulae refer to the above-noted instances in Genesis in which variations of the formulaic phrase, *wĕ'ēlleh tôlĕdōt (terah /PN)*, "and these are the generations of (Terah/PN)" (Gen 11:27), introduce narratives that feature the lifetimes and activities of the descendants of the figure in question. The itinerary formulas refer to the notices concerning the locations of Israel's encampment during its journey from Egypt to Moab prior to its entry into the Promised Land of Israel, for example, *wayyis'û bĕnê yiśrā'ēl mēra'mĕsēs sukkōtāh*, "and the people of Israel journeyed from Rameses to Sukkot" (Exod 12:37).

Cross's hypothesis raises two important questions. The first question is the role of the initial *toledoth* formula in Gen 2:4a, *'ēlleh tôlĕdōt haššāmayim wĕhā'āres bĕhibārĕ'ām*, "these are the generations of the heavens and the earth when they were created." Interpreters have been divided concerning the function of this statement. Some argue that it functions as a summation of the narrative concerning the creation of heaven and earth in Gen 1:1—2:3, whereas others point to its introductory role in relation to the following narratives concerning human origins beginning in Gen 2:4b.[3] Although the references to "heaven and earth" and the use of the term *bĕhibārĕ'ām*, "when they were created," suggest a retrospective viewpoint that would support the former interpretation, several indicators point to a prospective viewpoint. First is the use of the term *tôlĕdôt*, based on the verb root, *yld*, "to give birth," which indicates what is generated *from* or *by* the heavens and the earth, that is, the human beings that are noted in Gen 1:26-28. Second is the literary function of the other *toledoth* formulae, which note the generations of an ancestral figure, and then proceed to discuss that figure's descendants, for example, the notice concerning Adam in Gen 5:1 introduces a genealogy of Adam's descendants in Gen 5:1—6:8; the notice concerning Noah in Gen 6:9 introduces the narrative concerning Noah and his sons in Gen 6:9—9:29; the notice concerning the sons of Noah in Gen 10:1 introduces genealogies of Noah's sons in Gen 10:1—11:9; the notice concerning Shem in Gen 11:10 introduces a genealogy of Shem's descendants in Gen 11:10-26; the notice concerning Terah in Gen 11:27 introduces the Abraham narratives in Gen 11:27—25:11; the notice concerning Ishmael in Gen 25:12 introduces a genealogy of Ishmael's descendants in Gen 25:12-18; the notice concerning Isaac in Gen 25:19 introduces the Jacob narratives in Gen 25:19—35:29; the notice concerning Esau in Gen 36:1

introduces Esau's genealogy in Gen 36:1—37:1; and the notice concerning Jacob
in Gen 37:2 introduces the Joseph narratives in Gen 37:2—50:26. As these examples indicate, Gen 2:4a may have somewhat of retrospective function in relation
to Gen 1:1—2:3, but it also points forward to the accounts of Adam (and Eve) as
the beginning of a sequence of accounts that take up early human history from
the time of creation through the time of Joseph. In the case of the longer narratives, for example, Adam (Eve), Noah (sons), Terah (Abraham), Isaac (Jacob),
and Jacob (Joseph), the narrative points to the key figures in the development of
the people Israel. In the case of the shorter narratives, for example, Ham and
Japhet, Ishmael, and Esau, the narrative points to those lines that spin off from
the main characters to develop humankind at large. The resulting structure of
Genesis therefore emerges as an introductory narrative concerning the creation of
heaven and earth in Gen 1:1—2:3 followed by a sequence of narratives in Gen
2:4—50:26, each introduced by an example of the *toledoth* formula, that takes up
the development of Israel within the context of humankind.

The second question takes up the role of the itinerary formulae in the literary
structure of Exodus, Leviticus, and Numbers. Here, the structural role of the
itinerary formulae is rather straightforward, insofar as the formulae point to the
movements of Israel from Egypt to Moab as a basic plot element in the pentateuchal narrative. Thus, the narrative begins in Exod 1:1—12:36 with Israel in
Egypt as the site for the initial enslavement and the encounter between YHWH
(represented by Moses and Aaron) and Pharaoh that leads to the Israelite slaves'
release at Rameses. Itinerary formulae, each of which introduces a narrative block
that recounts a successive stage in the journey, then follow. Thus, the notice in
Exod 12:37 introduces Israel's journey from Rameses to Sukkot in Exod 12:37—
13:19 sees the redemption of the first-born; Exod 13:20 introduces the journey
from Sukkot to Etam in Exod 13:20-22 that highlights YHWH's representation as
a pillar of fire and cloud, replicating the image of a Temple altar in operation;
Exod 14:1 introduces the journey from Etam to the Red/Reed Sea in Exod 14:1—
15:21 that focuses on Israel's deliverance at the Sea; Exod 15:22 introduces the
journey from the Sea to the Wilderness of Shur/Elim in Exod 15:22-27 that
focuses on water in the wilderness; Exod 16:1 introduces the journey from Elim to
the Wilderness of Sin in Exod 16:1-36 that focuses on quails and manna; Exod
17:1 introduces the journey from Sin to Rephidim in Exod 17:1—18:27 that takes
up Amalek and Jethro; Exod 19:1 introduces the journey from Rephidim to Sinai
in Exod 19:1—Num 10:10 that takes up the lengthy narrative concerning the
revelation at Sinai; Num 10:11 introduces the journey from Sinai to the Wilderness of Paran in Num 10:11—19:22 that takes up the motif of rebellion in the
wilderness; Num 20:1 notes the journey from Paran to the Wilderness of Zin/
Kadesh in Num 20:1-21 that again notes water from the rock; Num 20:22 introduces the journey from Zin/Kadesh to Mt. Hor in Num 20:22—21:3 that takes up
the death of Aaron; Num 21:4 introduces the journey from Hor to Edom/Moab in
Num 21:4-35 that sees the defeat of Sihon and Og; and Num 22:1 introduces the

arrival at Moab in Num 22:1—36:13 that sees census and organization of the people prior to their entry into the Promised Land.

Two questions remain open when considering the *toledoth* organization of Genesis and the itinerary organization of Exodus—Numbers. First, what is the relation of Deuteronomy to the preceding material, particularly since Deuteronomy continues to portray the people of Israel in Moab prior to their entry into the land of Israel? Second, what is the relationship between the two textual blocks in Genesis and Exodus—Numbers that are organized according to such different principles?[4]

The first question is easily answered. Because Deuteronomy portrays the people of Israel in Moab in keeping with their arrival in Moab in Num 22:1—36:13, Deuteronomy must be subsumed into the structural organization of the itinerary pattern identified in Exodus—Numbers. It is clear that Deuteronomy is not written with this structural pattern in mind; indeed, diachronic research on Deuteronomy points to its compositional origins as an independent D source or literary composition that is quite distinct from the JEP material in Exodus—Numbers.[5] Nevertheless, a synchronic reading of Deuteronomy in relation to Exodus—Numbers demands that Deuteronomy be subsumed into the structural organization of Exodus—Deuteronomy insofar as it presents Moses' final addresses to Israel following their arrival in Moab and prior to their entry into the land of Israel. Deuteronomy thereby presents an account of Moses' rehearsal of YHWH's Torah or expectations of Israel as the people take possession of the land.

The second question is far more difficult until one observes the presence of a previously unnoticed *toledoth* formula in Num 3:1, *wě'ēlleh tôlědōt 'ahǎrōn ûmōšeh běyôm dibber yhwh 'et mōšeh běhar sînāy,* "and these are the generations of Aaron and Moses on the day that YHWH spoke with Moses on Mt. Sinai."[6] Although this example of the *toledoth* formula falls outside of Genesis, it is tied to the examples from Genesis by its similar formulation and by its increasingly narrow focus on Aaron and Moses as a group within the twelve tribes of Israel (see Gen 37:2), viz., the key Levitical figures who will provide leadership for Israel during the Exodus period (Moses) and as high priests once Israel is settled in the land (the descendants of Aaron; see Num 17–18). Whereas interpreters would see little relationship between Num 3:1 and the *toledoth* formulae in Genesis due to the role that diachronic reading strategies play in fragmenting readings of texts, a synchronic reading of this formula in relation to the others demands that it be viewed as a continuation of the sequence begun in Genesis. Thus, it points to the role that the *toledoth* formulae play in delineating the full literary structure of the final synchronic form of the Pentateuch. Although the itinerary notices clearly play an important structural role in Exodus—Deuteronomy, that structure is subsumed to that of the *toledoth* formula. Indeed, the different organizational patterns point to a diachronic literary history that must have led to the formation of the present form of the text, but once that text is formed, synchronic literary patterns then govern its overall structure. Thus, the *toledoth* formulae point to a progression of textual blocks in the Pentateuch that traces the development of Israel within humankind from Adam through Moses and Aaron as the Levitical or priestly leadership of Israel within humanity. The itinerary notices trace the journey of Israel from Egypt through the lifetime of Moses, first as the twelve tribes of Israel (Exod 1:1—Num 2:34) and then under the leadership of Aaron and Moses (Num 3:1—Deut 34:12). The literary structure of the Pentateuch may be presented as follows:

Synchronic Literary Structure of the Pentateuch:
History of Creation/Formation of People Israel

I.	Creation of Heaven and Earth	Gen 1:1—2:3
II.	Human Origins	2:4—4:26
III.	Human Development/Problems	5:1—6:8
IV.	Noah and the Flood	6:9—9:29
V.	Spread of Humans over the Earth	10:1—11:9
VI.	History of the Semites	11:10-26
VII.	History of Abraham (Isaac)	11:27—25:11
VIII.	History of Ishmael	25:12-18
IX.	History of Jacob (Isaac)	25:19—35:29
X.	History of Esau	36:1—37:1
XI.	History of the Twelve Tribes of Israel	Gen 37:2—Num 2:34
	A. Joseph and his brothers in Egypt	Gen 37:2—50:26
	B. deliverance from Egyptian bondage: Rameses	Exod 1:1—12:36
	C. from Rameses to Sukkot: consecration of first-born	12:37—13:19
	D. from Sukkot to Etam: pillar of fire and cloud	13:20-22
	E. from Etam to the sea (Pihahirot/Baal Zephon): deliverance at sea	14:1—15:21
	F. from Reed Sea to Wilderness of Shur/Elim: water in wilderness	15:22-27
	G. from Elim to Wilderness of Sin: quails and manna	16:1-36
	H. from Sin to Rephidim: Amalek and Jethro	Exod 17:1—18:27
	I. from Rephidim to Sinai: revelation of Torah	Exod 19:1—Num 10:10
	1. arrival at Sinai	Exod 19:1-2
	2. revelation from mountain: ten commandments; covenant code; building of the tabernacle	Exod 19:3—40:38
	3. revelation from tabernacle: laws of sacrifice and holiness code	Lev 1–27
	4. census and organization of people around tabernacle	Num 1:1—2:34

XII.	History of Israel under the Guidance of the Levites	Num 3:1—Deut 34:12
A.	sanctification of the people led by the Levites	Num 3:1—10:10
B.	from Sinai to Wilderness of Paran/Kibroth Hattaavah: rebellion in the wilderness	10:11—11:35a
C.	from Kibroth Hattaavah to Hazeroth	11:35b—12:15
D.	from Hazeroth to the Wilderness of Paran	12:16—19:22
E.	from Paran to Wilderness of Zin/Kadesh: water from rock	20:1-21
F.	from Zin/Kadesh to Mt. Hor: death of Aaron	20:22—21:3
G.	from Mt. Hor to Edom/Moab: defeat of Sihon and Og	Num 21:4-35
H.	arrival at Moab: Balaam; census and organization of the people	22:1—36:13
I.	Moses' final address to Israel: repetition of the Torah	Deut 1:1—34:12

Having delineated the synchronic literary structure of the Torah, discussion must now turn to its diachronic dimensions. From the Talmudic period on when Joshua was identified as the author of the account of Moses' death and burial in Deut 34:5-12 (*b. Baba Batra* 15a), interpreters have been concerned with the question of the composition of the Pentateuch.[7] Indeed, the question is crucial within Jewish thought because it points to the ongoing process of revelation throughout history as Jewish interpreters have read earlier texts and attempted to discern their meaning in relation to divine intention by updating and editing earlier compositions as well as by writing commentary upon them. In modern times, Christian interpreters have played a key role in developing models for the composition of the Pentateuch, notably the Graf–Wellhausen hypothesis which posited a four-stage process of growth, beginning with the J source, which employed the divine name (JHWH) and derived from the earliest periods of the Davidic monarchy in the tenth and ninth centuries BCE; the E source, which employed the divine designation ELOQIM until the time of Moses and derived from the northern kingdom of Israel in the eighth century BCE; the D source, which comprised Deuteronomy and derived from the late seventh-century reign of King Josiah of Judah; and the P source, which likewise employed the divine designation ELOQIM until the time of Moses, focused on priestly law and ritual, and derived from the late exilic or early post-exilic periods in which Ezra and Nehemiah emerged as the leadership of Israel following the fall of the house of David.

Problems have emerged in the Graf–Wellhausen hypothesis from its inception. A full history of discussion is hardly possible here,[8] but several glaring issues are noteworthy. First is the inherent anti-Semitism in the proposal to identify priestly and ritual concerns with the late emergence of Judaism as a degeneration of the ideal religious models identified in the earlier J source, particularly since temple and priesthood constituted the foundation of ancient Israel's religious establishment from well before the period of the monarchy. Indeed, Wellhausen attempted to privilege his own understanding of Protestant Christianity as a prophetic ideal of a direct human relationship with G-d in the J source and to identify priestly mediation as an obstacle to the divine–human relationship that would be identified with Judaism, the Roman Catholic Church, and his own Protestant theological opponents in the church of his day. Readers may also note the degree to which Wellhausen argues the case for source differentiation in his treatment of the primeval history and the Abraham–Sarah narratives in his foundational work, *Die Composition des Hexateuchs*,[9] but simply presupposes and applies his earlier conclusions as he works through the balance of the material from the Jacob narratives on.

Second is the appearance of features in the J material that are identified with the later interaction between Israel/Judah and Assyria/Babylon in the eighth to sixth centuries BCE,[10] such as the Tower of Babel narrative that presupposes the ziggurat of Babylon in the J narrative of Gen 11:1-9; the reference to "Ur of the Chaldeans" in the J statement of Gen 11:28, a designation identified only with the Neo-Babylonian empire of the late seventh and early sixth centuries BCE; the identification of Assyrian *palu* campaigns in which the Assyrian king would march through his land each year to assert his authority with Abram's march the length of the land of Canaan in the J narrative of Gen 12:1-9; the influence of Assyrian treaty rituals the ceremony of passing through the halves of sacrificed animals in the J material of Gen 15:7-11; the identification of Pithom and Rameses as the cities of Egypt where Israelite resided in the J statement in Exod 1:11 although the name Pithom (*pr 'itm*, "House of Atum") is known only from the end of the Saite period in 525 BCE;[11] the influence of Assyrian vassal treaty language, particularly the apodictic statements, throughout the corpus of biblical law in the early Covenant Code in Exod 20–23; the seventh-century law code of Deut 5; 12–26; and elsewhere.

Third is the evidence that comes from redaction-critical study, such as the long-standing insight that J, E, and P cannot stand as independent sources, but must be viewed as strata that successively take up, update, and reinterpret earlier layers of material. Likewise, scholars continue to note the role that D appears to play in Genesis—Numbers and both thematic and historical differentiation within the purportedly monolithic P source.[12] Noteworthy examples of redaction-critical observations that challenge aspects of classical source theory include the placement of the narratives concerning the Judean-oriented patriarch, Abraham, at the head of a sequence in which the northern Israelite figures, Jacob and Joseph, follow; the relatively ideal characterization of the Judean-oriented Abraham in relation to the more flawed characters of the northern-oriented Jacob and Joseph; the role that Judah plays as moral agent and protector, displacing Reuben as the brother who would spare Joseph's life in Gen 37 and protect Benjamin in Gen 42–43; the concern to avoid intermarriage with Egypt and Canaan in Gen 12; 20; 26; 34; and 38 in contrast to Joseph's marriage to Asenath daughter of the Egyptian priest Potiphera and the birth of their sons Manasseh and Ephraim, the two chief tribes of Israel, in Gen 41 and 48; the influence of D materials in the characterization of Israel's sins in worshipping a golden calf at Sinai as those of the later northern kingdom of Israel in Exod 32–34; and the identification of the fearful spies with the northern Israelite tribes in contrast to the faithful Judean Caleb in the JP narratives of Num 13–14.

These observations do not negate the fundamental enterprise of reconstructing the compositional history of the pentateuchal narrative as many have argued.[13] Instead, they point to the need to reconceive the fundamental conceptualization of the JEDP model advocated in the Graf–Wellhausen hypothesis with a model that avoids the anti-Semitic theological presuppositions inherent in Wellhausen's work; the extensive evidence of eighth- to sixth-century Assyrian and Babylonian influence in the J stratum of the Pentateuch; and redaction-critical evidence that points to J redaction of earlier E material, D redaction of earlier E and J material, P redaction of earlier JED material and differentiation within the P material itself. Such a model would presuppose a foundational northern Israelite E stratum from the early eighth-century BCE materials now found in Genesis, Exodus, and Numbers; a J stratum that would redactionally expand and rework E in the late eighth through the seventh century BCE in Genesis, Exodus, Leviticus, and Numbers; a Judean D source from the late seventh century BCE that was redactionally worked into the earlier framework of Genesis—Numbers; and the final P stratum from the early Persian period that would organize and give shape to the final form of the Pentateuch. Specific aspects of this model will be addressed as discussion turns to the individual structural sub-units of the Torah narrative at large.

NOTES

[1] Though the Hebrew term *tôrâ* is frequently rendered as "law," this is an erroneous translation derived from the New Testament Epistles of Paul, who translates *tôrâ* with the Greek term, *nomos*, "law," in an attempt to characterize Torah polemically as a static, monolithic, unbending, and ultimately useless obstacle to human salvation in contrast to Christ. See "*Nomos*," *TDNT*, 1022–85; cf. *HALOT*, 1710–12 "Torah," *EncJud* 15:1235–46.
[2] Frank Moore Cross, Jr., "The Priestly Work," in *Canaanite Myth and Hebrew Epic* (Cambridge, MA: Harvard University Press, 1973), 293–325.
[3] See the discussion in David M. Carr, *Reading the Fractures in Genesis: Historical and Literary Approaches* (Louisville: Westminster John Knox, 1996), 73–75, 93–101, 120–25.
[4] For discussion of the relationship between Genesis and Exodus—Numbers, see the essays published in Thomas B. Dozeman and Konrad Schmid, eds., *A Farewell to the Y-hwist? The Composition of the Pentateuch in Recent European Interpretation* (SBLSymS 34; Atlanta: Society of Biblical Literature, 2006).

[5] See now Moshe Weinfeld, "Deuteronomy, Book of," *ABD* 2:168–83; idem, *Deuteronomy 1–11* (AB 5; New York: Doubleday, 1991), 1–122; Marvin A. Sweeney, *King Josiah of Judah: The Lost Messiah of Israel* (Oxford: Oxford University Press, 2001), 137–69.

[6] I am indebted to Matthew Thomas, former Ph.D. student in Hebrew Bible at Claremont Graduate University, who pointed out the significance of Num 3:1 (see his Claremont dissertation, "These are the Generations: Identity, Promise, and the Toledoth Formulae" [Ph.D. diss., Claremont Graduate University, 2006]); see also Sven Tengström, *Die Toledotformel und die literarische Struktur der priesterlichen Erweiterungsschicht im Pentateuch* (ConBibOT 17; Uppsala: Gleerup, 1981), 54–59.

[7] For discussion of the history of research on the Pentateuch, see "Pentateuch," *EncJud* 13:231–62; Albert de Pury and Thomas Römer, "Le Pentateuch en question. Position du problem et brève historie de la recherché," in A. de Pury, ed., *Le Pentateuch en Question* (Geneva: Labor et Fides, 1989), 9–80; Joseph Blenkinsopp, *The Pentateuch: An Introduction to the First Five Books of the Bible* (New York: Doubleday, 1992), 1–30; Ernst Nicholson, *The Pentateuch in the Twentieth Century: The Legacy of Julius Wellhausen* (Oxford: Oxford University Press, 1998); Jean-Louis Ska, *Introduction to Reading the Pentateuch* (Winona Lake, IN: Eisenbrauns, 2006), 96–164. For an overview and discussion of the Pentateuchal sources, see Antony F. Campbell and Mark A. O'Brien, *Sources of the Pentateuch: Texts, Introductions, Annotations* (Minneapolis: Fortress Press, 1993).

[8] For discussion of the problems with the Graf–Wellhausen hypothesis, see especially Nicholson, *The Pentateuch*, 95–268; Ska, *Introduction*, 127–64.

[9] *Die Composition des Hexateuch* (Berlin: Reimer, 1889).

[10] See, for example, Thomas L. Thompson, *The Historicity of the Patriarchal Narratives. The Quest for the Historical Abraham* (BZAW 133; Berlin: de Gruyter, 1974); John Van Seters, *Abraham in History and Tradition* (New Haven: Yale University Press, 1975); idem, *Prologue to History: The Y-hwist as Historian in Genesis* (Louisville: Westminster John Knox, 1992); idem, *The Life of Moses: The Y-hwist as Historian in Exodus—Numbers* (Louisville: Westminster John Knox, 1994); for an overview discussion, see Nicholson, *The Pentateuch*, 132–60.

[11] Tom F. Wei, "Pithom," *ABD* 5:376–77.

[12] See, especially, H. H. Schmid, *Der sogenannte J-hwist. Beobachtungen und Fragen zur Pentateuchforschung* (Zurich: Theologischer Verlag, 1976); Erhard Blum, *Die Komposition der Vätergeschichte* (WMANT 57; Neukirchen–Vluyn: Neukirchener, 1984); idem, *Studien zur Komposition des Pentateuch* (BZAW 189; Berlin: de Gruyter, 1990); Christoph Levin, *Der J-hwist* (FRLANT 157; Göttingen: Vandenhoeck & Ruprecht, 1993); Nicholson, *The Pentateuch*, 161–221.

[13] See Nicholson, *The Pentateuch*, 222–48.

B. The Toledoth/Generations Sequence in the Torah

1. The Creation of Heaven and Earth

The Torah—and indeed the Bible as a whole—begins its synchronic narrative presentation of the origins of Israel with an account of the creation of the world at large in Gen 1:1—2:3. By tying Israel's origins to the creation of the world, the Pentateuchal narrative aims to demonstrate that Israel occupies a central role in the world of creation. Insofar as that role includes the obligation to observe divine Torah and to establish the holy sanctuary by which G-d's presence is recognized in the world, Israel emerges in the Torah narrative as a holy nation—chosen by G-d—whose task is to act as partners with G-d in completing and sanctifying creation at large. Although other nations are not obligated to observe the full provisions of the divine Torah revealed to Israel in the Pentateuchal narrative, they are portrayed as witnesses to divine acts on behalf of Israel (for example, the exodus from Egypt); as parties that interact with Israel and its ancestors, sometimes in opposition and sometimes in cooperation; and as exemplars of human action, either righteous (for example, Jethro's instructions to Moses to set up a judiciary in Exod 18) or wicked (for example, the sins of Sodom and Gomorrah in Gen 18–19), from which Israel is enjoined to learn proper conduct. The Torah prescribes no specific obligation for Israel to teach the nations about G-d or divine expectations. Therefore, the holy role defined for Israel in the midst of creation indicates that Israel is to serve an exemplary role of holy conduct in accordance with divine Torah from which the nations will learn to recognize G-d as the author of creation and the judge of holy and righteous conduct and to conduct themselves accordingly.

The Torah's account of creation begins with an introductory statement in Gen 1:1-2 of the chaotic character of the heavens and earth at the beginning of the sequence of creation. The Western world is accustomed to reading these verses as a programmatic statement of G-d's creation of the world *ex nihilo*, that is, out of nothing, viz., "in the beginning, G-d created the heavens and the earth, and the earth was formless and void. . . ." Yet Rashi's grammatical and philological analysis of these verses demonstrates that the passage is to be read as a statement of G-d's bringing order out of a pre-existing chaos, viz., "when G-d began to create the heavens and the earth, the earth was formless and void. . . ."[1] This understanding is consistent with other biblical traditions that presuppose G-d's subduing of chaos monsters, such as Leviathan (Isa 27:1; Ps 74; Job 40:25-32, respectively), Rahab (Isa 51:9-11); or Behemeth (Job 40:15-24), or creating wisdom as the first act of ordering a chaotic world (Prov 8:22-36; cf. Isa 40:12-31).[2] Such a portrayal of divine action provides an important model for human action as well, that is, the obligation to create order and holiness in an otherwise chaotic world. Indeed, the model of G-d's creating order out of chaos comes to expression every day in the morning liturgy of the Jerusalem Temple when the sun first shines into the open doors of the Temple at daybreak, illuminating the interior of the Temple and exposing the various Temple furnishings that symbolize the holy order of G-d's house at the center of creation. Insofar as the priests and people play a role in the morning liturgy, the daily liturgical re-enactment of creation provides an important reminder of the human obligation to emulate G-d by acting to bring order and holiness to the world.

The six-day sequence of creation then follows in Gen 1:3-31 in a well-ordered narrative presentation of the basic elements of the created world. Indeed, the six days of creation are paired into two groups of three, insofar as the first element of the pair presents the creation of the basic structures of order that are followed by the second element of each pair that presents details as to how that basic principle comes to expression. Thus, the creation of light out of darkness on the first day in Gen 1:3-5 is paired with the account in Gen 1:14-19 of the creation of heavenly lights on the fourth day and their role in reckoning time, that is, days and years, as an aspect of the holy order of creation; the creation of a firmament to separate the heavens from the earth on the second day in Gen 1:6-8 is paired with the account of the fifth day of creation in Gen 1:20-23 of the sea creatures and birds who will inhabit the two spheres; and the creation on the third day of the earth and sea as well as vegetation in Gen 1:9-13 is paired with the account in Gen 1:24-31 of the creation of living creatures and human beings as well as the provision of plants for food on the sixth day. In all cases, G-d declares the creation to be good, including the emphatic declaration in Gen 1:31 that all creation, including the human beings, is very good. Indeed, the creation of human beings in the image of G-d entails a human obligation to emulate G-d in carrying out the responsibility to "rule" the created world on G-d's behalf to ensure its continuing order and sanctity. That task is underlined by the command to "be fruitful and multiply," generally considered the first of the 613 commandments incumbent upon Jews.

The final segment of the creation narrative in Gen 2:1-3 includes a statement that creation is complete and an account of G-d's instituting the Shabbat (Sabbath) on the seventh day as a holy day of rest. By sanctifying time within the order of creation, the Torah narrative indicates the holy character of creation at large and the obligation of human beings to emulate G-d's rest on the seventh day as an act that upholds and maintains the holiness of creation.[3] Weekly observance of the Shabbat thereby becomes the fundamental reminder of the place of human beings in the world of divine creation and the obligation to act as partners with G-d in maintaining the sanctity and order of the created world, not only in relation to Shabbat but in relation to the entire body of divine instruction as well. The obligation to observe Shabbat is identified as a běrît ʿôlām, "eternal covenant," in Exod 31:16, which underscores the human obligation to maintain the sanctity of creation.

Diachronically speaking, Gen 1:1—2:3 is the product of the P stratum of the Pentateuch. The passage therefore represents a conceptualization of creation and the observance of the Shabbat associated with priestly circles in the latter stages of the Babylonian Exile or the early Persian period when Ezra and Nehemiah called for observance of the Shabbat as a fundamental expression of Jewish religiosity (see Neh 9:6-37; 10:31-34; 13:15-22; cf. Isa 56:1-8; 58:13-14; 66:23). Interpreters recognize how the Genesis creation account appears deliberately to contrast with the Babylonian creation account, the Enuma Elish, in which Marduk, the city god of Babylon defeats the chaos monster, Tiamat, and establishes order in both the natural world of creation and the socio-political world of the nations by establishing his own rule over the world.[4] Insofar as Marduk's temple, the ziggurat Entemenankhi, is located at the center of the city of Babylon, Marduk's victory signifies Babylon's role as ruler of the nations in Babylonian thought. Whereas Marduk must fight Tiamat and her allies to establish order in the world, G-d has only to speak and order emerges from the primeval chaotic "deep" (Hebrew, těhôm, a cognate of Akkadian, tiʿamatu, "Tiamat"). Jerusalem then emerges as the holy center of all creation and the nations in Judean thought.

Although some modern scholars have attempted to claim that the Shabbat is a late, priestly, cultic innovation, perhaps derived from Babylonian practice, ample attestation for the observance of Shabbat in both Israel and Judah appears in eighth-century prophetic texts, such as Amos 8:5; Hos 2:13; and Isa 1:13 (see also 2 Kgs 4:22-23, which relates Shabbat to the time of the ninth-century prophet Elisha; 2 Kgs 16:17-18, which refers to the king's Shabbat passage from the royal palace to the Jerusalem Temple in the time of the late eighth-century King Ahaz).[5] Insofar as these references appear in some of the earliest known writings of the Hebrew Bible, it would appear that Shabbat was already observed in Israel and Judah at least as early as the ninth or eighth century BCE. The historical origins of the observance must remain unknown.

2. The Generations of Heaven and Earth: Human Beings

The formulaic notice in Gen 2:4a, "these are the generations of the heavens and the earth when they were created," introduces the synchronic accounts concerning the creation and character of human beings in Gen 2:4—4:26. Although modern critical scholarship identifies these narratives as an alternative account of creation according to the J source, their placement immediately following Gen 1:1—2:3 in a synchronic reading of the text signifies an interest in focusing on the origins and character of human beings within the context of creation at large. Following the introductory formula in Gen 2:4a, the narrative proceeds with three basic episodes.

The first episode in Gen 2:4b-25 presents the basic account of the creation of human beings in the Garden of Eden. Although Gen 1:26-28 has already noted the creation of humans as the culmination of the six days of creation, the present narrative notes G-d's creation of the primal human being first followed by efforts to create a world in which the human live. The primal human is called hā'ādām, in Hebrew, which means simply, "the human." At this point, there is no gender differentiation other than the grammatical necessity in Hebrew to identity hā'ādām as male. Having created hā'ādām, G-d then turns to the creation of the Garden of Eden as an ideal place for hā'ādām to live, with fruit trees and vegetation for food, the tree of life, the tree of knowledge of good and evil, the four rivers, including the Pishon (perhaps the Nile),[6] Gihon (the spring under the Temple Mount in Jerusalem), the Tigris, and the Euphrates, that define and water the Garden of Eden. Insofar as the Gihon is identified as the central river between the Pishon and the Tigris/Euphrates, the Garden of Eden may be identified with the site of the future Jerusalem Temple, under which the Gihon flows and whose iconography includes images of plants, trees, animals, and cherubim identified with the Garden. G-d places hā'ādām in the midst of the Garden to till it, but warns him against eating from the tree of the knowledge of good and evil lest he die. Noting that hā'ādām is lonely, G-d first creates animals and birds, which hā'ādām names. When this fails to provide suitable companionship, G-d casts a "deep sleep" on hā'ādām, takes one of his "sides" (Hebrew ṣelaʿ, often translated as "rib," means "side," which indicates the division of the primeval hā'ādām into male and female). This episode concludes with a brief etiology of marriage and relations between the sexes, that is, the man clings to his wife so that they become one flesh, and a notice that the two were naked (Hebrew, ʿārûmmîm) and yet not ashamed. These notices prepare the reader for the next episode in which the man and the woman will be expelled from the Garden.

The second episode in Gen 3:1-24 focuses on the character of human beings with an emphasis on their knowledge of good and evil and their mortality. The episode is based on an initial encounter between the woman and the snake in the Garden who persuades her to eat from the tree of the knowledge of good and evil.

The snake is identified as the most "crafty" (Hebrew, '*ārûm*) of all the animals of the Garden, a pun intended to highlight the nakedness ('*ărûmmîm*) of the humans noted in Gen 2:25. Although both the snake and the woman are frequently characterized as sinful by interpreters, they in fact engage in a dialog that demonstrates a basic principle of human existence, viz., humans must employ their knowledge of good and evil to analyze a given situation and make decisions about a proper course of action, even when they are not possession of all of the facts. The snake raises points that are ambiguous. The snake's question, "Did G-d really say you shall not eat from any tree in the Garden?" is designed to evoke reflection, particularly from the woman, who was created only after G-d gave the commands prohibiting the eating from the tree of knowledge. Her answers indicate that she does not have a full grasp of the commands initially given to *hā'ādām*. Furthermore, Adam is apparently there with her according to v. 6, but he says nothing and thereby must take a share of responsibility for the debacle that follows. The snake's statements, that the humans will not die but will become like G-d, knowing good and evil if they eat the fruit, are true to a degree and suggest that G-d is keeping something from the humans. Faced with such ambiguity, the woman acts in a manner that sets the pattern for all humanity, viz., she analyzes the situation and then acts on the basis of her analysis of the information before her. In doing so, she and the man gain wisdom, and the first thing they realize is that they are naked and must cover up.

The recognition of human nakedness then sets the stage for the confrontation with G-d and the judgment meted out to each party. The man, who failed to exercise responsibility by speaking up in this matter, is expelled from the Garden, is condemned to mortality, and is forced to work by the sweat of his brow to produce food. (The woman, who in fact made the wrong choice, is forced to endure the pain of childbirth and nevertheless desire her husband.) Adam subsequently names her *ḥavvâ*, or Eve, a term that means "life," to signify her role as the mother of all human life. The snake is cursed to crawl on his belly and to endure the enmity of human beings. In order to prevent the humans from re-entering the Garden, G-d posts cherubim with a flaming sword, which anticipates the cherubim engraved on the doors of the Holy of Holies in the Jerusalem Temple (1 Kgs 6:31-36). Insofar as the priest approaches the Holy of Holies during worship at the Temple, he represents Adam attempting to re-enter the Garden where the Presence of G-d is manifested.[7] The tree remains present at the Temple as well in the form of the ten Menorot or lamp stands that are shaped as seven-branched trees to give light in the Temple.

The concluding episode in Gen 4:1-26 focuses once again on the character of human beings, but emphasizes the violence that breaks out among them. The sons of Adam and Eve are Cain and Abel. Whereas Abel is a shepherd, Cain is a farmer. When G-d accepts Abel's offering of animals from his flock but refuses Cain's offering of produce, Cain becomes despondent. This provides the opportunity for the narrative to stress the human obligation to act righteously even in times of adversity. Cain of course ignores this advice and kills his brother. When questioned by G-d, he retorts, "Am I my brother's keeper?" which functions as a rhetorical question in the narrative to assert that of course he is. Cain is forced into a life of wandering as punishment, but is marked by G-d to protect him. Violence continues among subsequent descendants of Adam and Eve when Lamech brags to his wives that he has killed a man who wounded him. Yet, together with the violence, human progress in the forms of music, metal working, and recognition of YHWH, continues to develop. These motifs of human violence and progress prepare the reader for what is to come. On the one hand, the violence will be punished with the flood, but the progress made by humans also signals a capacity to learn and create, thereby demonstrating the need for divine guidance so that humans might learn to employ their knowledge of good and evil to live righteously and constructively.

All three episodes in this textual block are examples of the J narrative, which was written in Jerusalemite circles during the late monarchic period from the late eighth through the seventh centuries BCE. The Jerusalemite perspective is particularly clear insofar as the narrative continually highlights features of the Jerusalem Temple, viz., the identification of the Garden of Eden with the Holy of Holies of the Jerusalem Temple, the identification of the tree of knowledge in the Garden with the Menorot or lamp stands of the Temple, and human need for divine instruction or Torah which is of course the primary role of the Jerusalem Temple. Jerusalemite polemics are also evident, such as the prohibition against the worship of female fertility deities, such as Astarte, Qadeshah, or Hathor, who are generally portrayed as naked women with snakes and fruit-bearing tree branches in hand, surrounded by gods of life and death, and mounted or standing on top of a lion or other powerful animals.[8] In the Genesis narrative, all of these elements are turned against the woman, viz., her nakedness becomes a source of shame and her capacity to bear children is a punishment; the snake and the tree, normally symbols of fertility, life, and fruitfulness, become elements that lead her to punishment and exclusion from the Garden; and life and death remain as the poles around which her life and the life of humanity revolve. Nevertheless, Eve is responsible for the introduction of wisdom to humanity, much like ancient Near Eastern goddesses, such as the Mesopotamian Ishtar and the Egyptian Maat, who are frequently identified with wisdom and order in the world of creation. Her capacity to give birth and thus to create human beings like G-d would play a role in associating her with wisdom, although the narrative carefully avoids having her eat from the tree of life and death and thus attain immortality like G-d. The narrative thereby stands in stark contrast with ancient Near Eastern mythology, such as the Mesopotamian Gilgamesh epic, which holds that humans can attain immortality (for example, the flood hero Utnapishtim) even if such attainment is rare.

There is some evidence to indicate that women played roles in the liturgical life of northern Israel. For instance, Miriam leads women in worship in Exod 15;

Jephthah's daughter engages in mourning rituals in Judg 12; the maidens dance in the vineyards at Shiloh in Judg 21; Hannah prays at the Shiloh sanctuary in 1 Sam 1; and the Kuntillat Ajrud inscriptions indicate that the consort of YHWH of Samaria was Asherah.[9] Women play no such roles in the Jerusalem Temple, however, for reasons that are not entirely clear, although popular Judean religiosity suggests involvement of women similar to that of the north. Judean sacrifice calls for the presentation of male animals as required offerings; female animals are only presented as votive offerings. Perhaps the obligation of the Levites, who replace the first-born sons as priests in the service of YHWH (see Num 3; 4; 8), is considered as analogous to the required offerings at the Temple. As for the Cain and Abel story, one sees the eternal conflict between shepherds, who require large tracts of untouched land for grazing, and farmers, who require large tracts of land for cultivation. Such conflict would have appeared in both Israel and Judah, although Judah was more mountainous, less agriculturally developed, and its economy more focused on animal husbandry than that of its northern neighbor.

3. The Generations of Adam: Problems in Human Development

This brief section in Gen 5:1—6:8 traces the generations of Adam in an effort to prepare the reader for the crisis of the flood, first by tracing the human line through Noah, the hero of the following narrative, and his sons, Shem, Ham, and Japhet, and then by describing a major breakdown in the order of creation when "the sons of G-d" mate with human women. The passage is quasi-mythological insofar as it describes fantastic life spans for human beings—for example, 969 years for Methuselah—and the possibility that a human being, such as Enoch, might walk with "G-d." Such a statement suggests a lapse in the boundaries between the heavens and the earth, and thus a lapse in the order of creation insofar as Enoch appears to enter the divine realm. Such a breakdown is further reinforced by the brief narrative which recounts the mating of "the sons of G-d," apparently angelic figures from the heavenly court of G-d, who mate with human women to produce the giants or Nephilim who once lived in the land of Canaan (Num 13:31-33). Although the initiative for such union comes from "the sons of G-d," G-d determines that the wickedness of human beings is great and decides to destroy creation, although Noah finds favor with G-d and will subsequently serve as the figure who saves a remnant of life in the world to begin again.

The formulaic character of Gen 5:1—6:8 identifies it as a product of the P stratum of the Pentateuch. Classical priestly concerns appear in the construction of human genealogy as well as the concern for establishing and maintaining boundaries between the heavens and the earth or the divine and the human spheres of creation.

4. The Generations of Noah: The Flood

The account of the flood in Gen 6:9—9:29 focuses on the breakdown of creation that resulted from G-d's dissatisfaction with the increasing violence and wickedness of human beings and the eternal covenant that is established between G-d and humanity at the conclusion of the narrative to the provide means to resolve the problems in their relationship. The narrative sets the natural seasonal order of the world, and it sets the stage for the proliferation of human beings throughout the earth.

Fundamentally, the flood narrative depicts the complete reversal of creation as a result of G-d's dissatisfaction with the actions of human beings in the world. Just as the natural order of creation emerges from the water of the deep in Gen 1:1—2:3, so the fountains of the deep and the floodgates of heaven open up to inundate the world once again and return it to its primordial state prior to creation. G-d views Noah as a righteous man, and therefore informs Noah of the divine intention to strike a covenant with him while destroying creation. G-d therefore instructs Noah in the building of a ship and the collection of pairs of all animals so that he might save himself, his family, and all types of animal life, including pairs of all clean and unclean animals, to begin creation once again.

The duration of the flood is described as a period of forty days of rain and one hundred and fifty days of water inundating the earth, although the narrative notes that the rains began on the seventeenth day of the second month in Noah's six hundredth year and that the land was dry on the twenty-seventh day of the second month of Noah's six hundred and first year.

At the conclusion of the flood, Noah's offerings to G-d prompted G-d to swear never again to destroy the earth and to maintain the order of creation through the seasonal and daily cycles of seedtime and harvest, cold and heat, summer and winter, and day and night. After renewing the command to "be fruitful and multiply (Gen 9:1; cf. 1:28), G-d strikes a *běrît ʿôlām*, "eternal covenant," with Noah and humankind that is designed to deal with the problem of human violence. Insofar as the shedding of blood had been such a problem from the time of Cain and Abel on, G-d grants human beings the right to eat animals for food. Because blood is associated with the life of every living being, it is holy and therefore unfit for human consumption. Furthermore, G-d prohibits the shedding of human blood and requires punishment for anyone who commits such an act. Indeed, the holiness of blood is a key consideration in the Judean sacrificial system. Because blood is holy, it is drained from sacrificial animals and returned to the earth when offerings are made at the Temple (Lev 17), and kosher dietary laws emulate sacrificial practice in the Temple by requiring that human beings drain the blood of an animal before eating its meat (Lev 11; Deut 14). Likewise, the shedding of human blood defiles the killer and the nation at large requiring that such defilement be purged from the midst of Israel to restore its sanctity before G-d (Exod 21:12-14; Num 35:30-35; Deut 19:10). The rainbow then serves as a reminder for G-d's eternal covenant with humankind.

The narrative concludes with an episode in which Noah's son Ham is cursed for an impropriety committed against Noah while he was asleep from drinking. Insofar as Ham is the ancestor of Canaan, this segment of the narrative prepares the reader for the charge that the Canaanites committed sins and polluted their land, prompting G-d to reassign it to Israel.

Diachronic analysis identifies the flood narratives as the product of a P reworking in an earlier J narrative.[10] P elements of the narrative include the eternal covenant between G-d and humanity, particularly with its focus on the sanctity of blood, the 150-day duration of the flood, and the gathering of animals in pairs. J elements of the narrative include the forty-day duration of the flood, the gathering of seven pairs of clean animals and one pair of unclean animals, and the setting of seasonal patterns. Although J is concerned with matters of sacrifice and stability in the world of creation, P reworks the narrative so that it becomes an expression of the eternal covenant by which G-d vows to maintain the natural order of the world (Gen 9:16), the covenant with the ancestors of Israel (Gen 17:7, 13, 19), the sanctity of Shabbat (Exod 31:16), the priestly offering of bread/challah before G-d at the Temple (Lev 24:8), and the priesthood of Israel/Judah through the line of Pinhas ben Elazar ben Aaron (Num 18:9; 25:13).

The flood tradition is well known in Mesopotamia, where it comes to expression in the Sumerian Ziusudra myth, the Gilgamesh epic which recounts how Utnapsihtim and his wife attain immortality by surviving the flood, and the Atra Hasis myth which explains the origins of death, disease, still birth, and so on, as means to protect the gods from the noise caused by increasing numbers of human beings.[11] Whereas the Mesopotamian flood traditions posit a flood caused by divine attempts to limit the human population for their own comfort, both the P and J accounts posit that the flood was caused by human wrongdoing. Again, both P and J maintain that human beings bear responsibility for maintaining the order of creation.

5. The Generations of Noah:
The Spread of Humans over the Earth

The brief narrative in Gen 10:1—11:9 focuses on Shem, Ham, and Japhet, the sons of Noah, as their descendants spread throughout the earth. Each son represents one of the basic elements of the human population—that is, Shem is the ancestor of the Semitic peoples identified with western Asia, Ham is the ancestor of the African peoples associated with Africa and extending into Canaan, and Japhet is associated with the peoples of Asia Minor and Europe. In general, this section prepares the reader for the focus on the generations of Shem, the ancestor Abram—and therefore of Israel—who will become the central concern of the Pentateuchal narrative.

In addition to its genealogical framework, this sub-unit includes the Tower of Babel narrative to explain how the various peoples who spread throughout the world were differentiated by language as well as by geographical location. Again, a concern to maintain boundaries between the heavens and the earth together with an interest in polemicizing against the Babylonian empire and its religious establishment determines the course of the narrative. Because all nations of the earth speak the same language, they are able to gather at the land Shinar, the site of ancient Babylon, to build a city and a tower that would reach to the heavens. The city, of course, is Babylon, capital of an empire that incorporated many nations in the ancient world, and the tower is the ziggurat Entemenanki, the Temple of Marduk, which symbolizes both Marduk's rule over all creation and Babylon's rule over the nations. Because G-d feels threatened by the Babylonian attempt to reach the heavens, G-d confuses the speech of the nations and scatters them across the world so that they will be unable to unite in their efforts to attain heaven. The name of Babylon, Hebrew *bābēl*, is then explained as a derivation of the verb, *bālal*, "to confuse," to demonstrate that Babylon is not a source of power and unity in the world, but a source of confusion and division before YHWH.[12] The narrative thereby provides background to the following accounts of YHWH's choice of Abraham and Sarah, ancestors of Israel, to found a nation that would serve as the basis for YHWH's revelation to the world as the true source of power and unity.

When viewed diachronically, Gen 10:1—11:9 emerges as a combination of P and J narrative strata.[13] Whereas J focuses on the ancestors of Babylon, Canaan, and the Semites together with the tower of Babel narrative, P fills out the genealogy as a means to contextualize these materials and tie them into the overall narrative framework of the Torah. The polemics against Babylon fit well within the context of the late monarchical period, which saw concern with the alliance between the house of David and Babylon (cf. Isa 39). They would also have functioned in relation to the exilic and post-exilic periods when Babylon became the enemy nation responsible for the destruction of the Jerusalem Temple and the Babylonian exile. Indeed, the human attempt to ascend to heaven comes to expression in the Babylonian Adapa myth, in which Adapa is invited to ascend through the seven levels of heaven to appear before Anu, the primordial Mesopotamian god of heaven.[14] When offered the bread and water of life, however, Adapa refuses—based on the advice of Enki/Ea—and thereby consigns human beings to mortality.

6. The Generations of Shem: History of the Semites

The account of the generations of Shem in Gen 11:10-26 provides a brief genealogy of the sons of Shem from the time of the flood through the birth of Abram, Nahor, and Haran, the sons of Terah. This brief sub-unit, derived entirely from P, thereby introduces the reader to Abram/Abraham, the ancestor of Israel, as the focus of the balance of the pentateuchal narrative.

7. The Generations of Terah: Abraham and Sarah, Ancestors of Israel

The account of the generations of Terah in Gen 11:27—25:11 focuses on Abraham and Sarah as the ancestors of Israel within the overall synchronic structure of the Torah, but a close narrative analysis of this material indicates an interest in examining the character and role of G-d in relation to Abraham and Sarah.[15] Throughout this narrative block, Abraham appears as a very idealized, righteous, and magnanimous figure, one who serves as the platform from which G-d is introduced to the Jewish people and to the world at large. The text raises questions of divine righteousness and divine fidelity: Will G-d keep the promises made to Abraham? Or not? Ultimately, Genesis demonstrates that G-d is righteous, but it keeps readers in suspense for some eleven chapters as it seeks to answer these questions.[16]

Genesis 11:27-32 states that Abram is the son of Terah, who lived in the city of Ur of the Chaldeans, that Abram married Sarai, and that Sarai did not bear a child. Indeed, Sarai's/Sarah's barrenness emerges as the leitmotif upon which the narrative bases its examination of G-d's character. The narrative proceeds by stating that Terah moved his family from Ur to the city of Haran in upper Syria and that Terah died in Haran.

Genesis 12–14 then provides a detailed picture of Abram and his interaction with G-d. With the possible exception of his actions in Egypt, where he tells the Egyptians that Sarah is his sister rather than his wife, Abram emerges as an exemplary character, whereas G-d emerges as a figure that makes unfulfilled promises and continuous demands. Despite the promises and demands, G-d places Abram and Sarah in danger at every turn.

Genesis 12:1-9 begins with G-d's commands to Abram to leave his native land and his father's house, to go to the land that G-d will show him, and promises that G-d will make him a great nation, that G-d will bless him and make his name great, and that G-d will make Abram a blessing for all the families of the earth. This is a remarkable set of demands and promises, and yet Abram does not question or resist G-d. Instead, he shows complete faithfulness in G-d, who sends

him into the unknown, and shows himself to be an obedient servant of G-d when
he follows G-d's instructions to move his wife and household to the land of
Canaan.[17]

The portrayal of Abram's (and G-d's) character becomes all the more
remarkable in Gen 12:10-20, in which a famine brought about by G-d afflicts the
land of Canaan to which Abram has just moved his family.[18] Having been placed
by G-d under threat, Abram commits an act that many condemn when he
declares in Egypt that Sarai is his sister rather than his wife because he is afraid
that the Egyptians will kill him to take his beautiful wife. Many interpreters contend that the designation of the wife as sister is a common ancient Near Eastern
language convention that expresses the intimacy of the relationship.[19] But such an
observation misses the point of the narrative that Abram feels threatened in a
foreign land and allows his wife to be taken into the harem of the Pharaoh, who is
best able to protect Sarai. Abram's act demonstrates his own weakness and
vulnerability in a patriarchal society.[20] After Pharaoh takes Sarai into his harem,
he ultimately learns the truth, returns Sarai to Abram, and allows Abram to leave
unharmed. Interpreters generally overlook an important point of the narrative,
viz., Sarah's descendants could have been Egyptians. The question of Egyptian
offspring for the ancestors will appear again in Genesis,[21] but more importantly,
the question concerning G-d's actions in putting Abram and his family under
threat lingers.

Abram next appears in Gen 13 tending sheep in the Negev wilderness with his
nephew Lot. As the flocks grow numerous, the shepherds of Abram and the
shepherds of Lot begin to fight among themselves as they compete for pasture-
land. In order to avoid further conflict, Abram tells Lot to choose which part of
the land he would like. Lot chooses the well-watered and greener land of Sodom
and the Jordan Valley, and leaves Abram to live on the land that was left over.
This is a very remarkable and unselfish act by Abram when considered in the
context of an ancient patriarchal society in which Abram as the senior male had
the right to choose the best land for himself.

The ideal portrayal of Abram's character continues in Gen 14. When Sodom is
attacked and Lot is carried off captive by the raiding Mesopotamians, Abram does
not hesitate to raise an army and rescue Lot and the other captives. When the
King of Sodom offers a reward, Abram turns it down, and instead worships G-d
at the site of Salem, that is, Jerusalem (cf. Ps 76:3). Indeed, Gen 14:18 identifies
Melchizedek as the priest of El Elyon at Salem (cf. Ps 110, in which YHWH
informs David that he is a priest after the order of Melchizedek). In addition, Gen
14:20 notes that Abram paid a tithe at Salem, in keeping with later requirements
that Israelite men pay a tenth of a tithe of their annual income to support the
Temple and monarchy (Lev 27:30-33; Num 18:21-32; Deut 14:22-29; cf. Gen
28:22; 1 Sam 8:15, 17; *m. Ma'aserot* 1:1).[22] In doing so, Abram already exhibits the
piety and observance of later generations of Jews who would worship G-d at the
Jerusalem Temple.

Having portrayed Abram in generous and idealistic terms, Genesis then turns to the question of G-d's fidelity in chapters 15–17 by portraying the covenant with Abram/Abraham. Genesis 15 opens with G-d's repeated promises to Abram, "Fear not Abram, I am a shield to you; your reward shall be very great."[23] At this juncture, the narrator takes the opportunity to remind readers of Sarah's barrenness. Without a son to serve as Abram's heir, all of Abram's wealth, standing, and special relationship with G-d are meaningless. When Abram points this out to G-d, G-d reiterates the promises that Abram will become the father of great nation that will possess the land of Canaan/Israel. G-d even signs the agreement in the manner of ancient treaties by symbolically passing between the pieces of sacrificed animals, which signifies that one who violates the terms of the treaty will suffer the same fate as the sacrificial animals (cf. Jer 34:18).[24] Yet, by raising the question of the next generation, Abram raises the question of divine fidelity. Thus far, Abram has done all that is asked of him; but G-d has not yet fulfilled the promises.

This tension in the portrayal of G-d is reinforced with the birth of Ishmael in Gen 16. Sarah continues to remain barren, and ultimately, she exercises the legal right of women in the ancient Near East to provide her husband with offspring through a maidservant.[25] In this case, the maidservant is Hagar, an Egyptian woman, who bears Ishmael to Abram. The birth of the half-Egyptian Ishmael presents an ironic question, viz., will Abram's covenant continue through an Egyptian, the very people who threatened Abram in Gen 12 and the people who would enslave Abram's descendants in Exodus? Although Ishmael is granted his own set of promises from G-d, Gen 17 continues by articulating the covenant between G-d and Abram. The covenant is sealed by circumcision in which Abram symbolically signs the agreement by circumcising himself and his house. Again, Abraham does what he is asked, but G-d makes promises that are not yet fulfilled.

The presentation of the Abraham tradition in the Bible reaches its climax in Gen 18–22, which focuses ever more closely on the character of G-d. Although Abraham plays a major role in these chapters, the narrative raises questions concerning G-d's righteousness and fidelity. The Sodom and Gomorrah narratives in Gen 18–19 raise these questions in a very pointed manner. After repeating the still-unfulfilled promise that Sarah will bear a son and that Abraham's descendants will become a great nation, G-d informs Abraham of the decision to destroy the purportedly wicked cities. Ironically, it is Abraham and not G-d who raises the moral question of the destruction of an entire population—"Far be it from you! Shall the judge of all the earth not do justice?"—and Abraham ultimately persuades G-d not to carry out the destruction if there are ten righteous people in the cities. Despite the portrayal of Sodom as an entirely wicked city in Gen 19, readers are left with a very uncomfortable question concerning G-d's proposal to destroy entire cities. What would G-d have done if Abraham had not spoken up?

Finally, Gen 21 presents the birth of Isaac to Sarah and Abraham, resolving the literary tensions surrounding Sarah's barrenness and G-d's unfulfilled promises of a son. Furthermore, Hagar and Ishmael are expelled with divine acquiescence. And yet G-d demands even more of Abraham. Having given him the son that has been promised, G-d tests Abraham in Gen 22 by demanding that he offer Isaac as a burnt offering on Mt. Moriah, traditionally understood to be the site of the future Temple in Jerusalem (2 Chr 3:1). Ironically, Abraham has never disobeyed G-d throughout the entire narrative sequence of Gen 11–22, but G-d's integrity is once again subject to question. If Isaac is to die, the covenant potentially comes to an end; even if Sarah bears another son, the morality of Isaac's death is still in question. Although G-d stops Abraham from sacrificing Isaac, the reader is left to wonder whether Abraham—or G-d—is tested in this narrative.[26]

The balance of the narrative in Gen 23–25 traces the rest of Abraham's life, including the death and burial of Sarah, the marriage of Rebekah to Isaac, and Abraham's subsequent marriages and children, but the critical examination of Abraham and G-d is now complete. G-d finally emerges as a righteous figure who shows fidelity in relationship with Abraham even if questions might be raised concerning G-d.

Diachronic consideration of the Abraham/Sarah narratives indicates that their final form is the product of P redaction and composition. The bulk of the P material appears in the genealogical materials of Gen 11:27, 31, 32; the covenant narrative of Gen 17:1-27; the birth of Isaac in Gen 21:1b-5; the death and burial of Sarah in Gen 23:1-20; and the death of Abraham and genealogy of Ishmael in Gen 25:7-11a, 12-17.[27] These materials indicate P's interests in working Abraham/ Sarah material into its overall genealogical framework for the history of Israel and its presentation of covenant with the context of creation.[28] Such an agenda is crucial to establishing the eternal covenant of YHWH with creation and Abraham/Sarah in particular as a foundation for the restoration of Jerusalem, Judah, and the Temple in the early Persian period. The critical examination of YHWH's fidelity would be particularly appropriate in the context of the early Persian period as well given the recent experience of the Babylonian exile and questions concerning divine commitment to the restoration. It would also be pertinent in relation to other experience of exile and challenge, for example, the destruction of the Second Temple by Rome in 70 CE, the failure of the Bar Kochba revolt in 135 CE, the massacres of Jews along the Rhine by the Crusader armies in the late eleventh century, the expulsion of Jews from Spain in 1492, the Chmielnitzki massacres of Jews in the mid-seventeenth century, and others.

Setting aside the P framework, the bulk of the Abraham–Sarah narratives emerge as the product of the EJ stratum of the Pentateuch.[29] While interpreters cannot be certain that the order of the underlying EJ stratum corresponds to the present order of the text, the Judean orientation of this material is quite clear.[30] The placement of narratives concerning the ancestors most closely associated with Judah prior to those associated with northern Israel (Jacob, Joseph) and the relatively ideal presentation of Abraham's character when compared with Jacob and Joseph is a very clear indicator of Judean interests in claiming the founding ancestors of the entire people of Israel as their own. The association of Abraham and Sarah with Hebron, the capital of the tribe of Judah and David's first capital during the period of his rule over Judah alone, as well as the burials of subsequent ancestors, viz., Isaac and Jacob, in the cave of Machpelah together with Abraham and Sarah, likewise points to a Judean interest in claiming priority among the ancestors. Other indications of Judean interests include Abraham's traversing all of Canaan, including major northern sites such as Shechem, Beth El, and Ai (Gen 12:1-9), much as Assyrian kings would traverse their realms in an annual *palu* campaign designed to demonstrate and assert sovereignty throughout their kingdoms; the overriding concern for the birth of a son to inherit Abraham's house, much as the house of David was concerned with the birth of a son to secure the future of the dynasty (Gen 15); the correspondence between the land granted by YHWH to Abraham in Gen 15 and that ruled by David in 2 Sam 8; the association of Abraham with the future site of the Jerusalem Temple, identified as Salem in Gen 14 and Moriah in Gen 22 (cf. 2 Chr 3:1); the association of Abraham with the region of the Dead Sea bordering Judah in Gen 13 and 18–19; the association of Abraham with Philistia and the Negev regions bordering Judah in Gen 20; and the granting of a covenant to Abraham in Gen 15 much like that granted to David in 2 Sam 7. When read in the context of the late eighth and seventh centuries BCE, the EJ Abraham–Sarah narratives indicate Judah's self-understanding as the remnant or heir of all Israel and its role in restoring the original unity of the twelve tribes of Israel in the aftermath of the Assyrian destruction of the north. Again, the critical examination of YHWH's fidelity toward Abraham and Sarah would be particularly pertinent in the aftermath of the destruction of northern Israel.

The E material pertaining to Abraham and Sarah appears within Gen 20–22, chapters which are concerned with Abraham's sojourns in Philistia and the Negeb as well as his relations with these regions. Some attention is given to the covenant in elements of Gen 15 and the binding of Isaac as well.[31] The paucity of material devoted to Abraham in the E tradition and its focus on outlying border regions suggest that Abraham may have been viewed as more of a peripheral figure in the north when compared to major ancestors so clearly associated with the north, such as Jacob and Joseph. If Abraham remains the founding ancestor in E (much like Isaac), perhaps the tradition recognizes a period of Judean rule under David and Solomon that was later set aside as northern Israel becomes the dominant power in relation to the much smaller Judah. The narrative concerning the binding of Isaac, in which Sarah's first-born is redeemed for holy service to YHWH, may well reflect a northern practice of designating first-born sons as priests rather than the tribe of Levi.[32]

Finally, historical scholars have been at a loss when attempting to reconstruct the historical setting for the life of Abraham and Sarah that might be represented in the Genesis narratives. Although attempts have been made to place Abraham in the Amorite period (ca. 2300–1800 BCE) and the Amarna period (ca. 1400 BCE) or the Late Bronze period (1550–1200 BCE), none has proved satisfactory.[33] The Abraham–Sarah narratives display too much awareness of concerns from the period of Israel's life in the land (ca. 1200–587 BCE), such as interactions with the Philistines, who also arrived in Canaan ca. 1200 BCE, much like Israel, and the influence of the Assyrians and Babylonians.[34] Given the inability to reconstruct a convincing pre-Israelite historical setting for either Abraham and Sarah or the narratives about them, interpreters must accept that the Genesis narratives concerning Abraham and Sarah represent Israel's or Judah's memories of their ancestors and reflection upon them.[35]

8. The Generations of Ishmael

Genesis 25:12-18 presents a brief genealogy of Ishmael, son of Abraham and Hagar as part of the overall P genealogical framework of the Pentateuch. Its function, however, is to close off the line of Ishmael so that the following narrative can concentrate on the line of Isaac as the heir to the covenant between YHWH and Abraham and Sarah, and as an ancestor of the nation Israel.

9. The Generations of Isaac: Jacob/Israel and Neighbors

The account of the generations of Isaac in Gen 25:19—35:29 focuses on Jacob as the son of Isaac and Rebekah who will become the heir of the covenant and the father of the tribes of Israel. Although the narrative focuses on the characterization and interrelationships of its major characters, Isaac, Rebekah, Jacob, Esau, Laban, Leah, Rachel, as individuals, the narrative is fundamentally concerned with examining the tribal structure of the nation of Israel and its relationships with neighboring nations, such as Edom and Aram.[36] Each of the major male characters is identified in the narrative as the eponymous ancestor of their respective nation, viz., Jacob is the ancestor of Israel (Gen 32:28; 35:10); Esau is the ancestor of Edom (Gen 25:30); and Laban is the ancestor of Aram (Gen 31:24). Likewise, each of the twelve sons of Jacob is the eponymous ancestor of a tribal group within the larger structure of the nation Israel, and the status of their respective mothers aids in explaining the status of the tribe within Israel. Thus the sons of Leah, Jacob's first wife, include Reuben, Simeon, Levi, and Judah, all of whom are displaced in one form or another within Israel. The sons of Bilhah, the handmaid of Rachel, are Dan and Naphtali, who are peripheral tribes in the northernmost Galilee region. The sons of Zilpah, the handmaid of Leah, are Gad and Asher, who are peripheral tribes located near Phoenicia and the Trans-Jordan respectively. The later sons of Leah, Issachar and Zebulun, are likewise peripheral tribes located in the Galilee region. The sons of Rachel, Jacob's favored wife, are Joseph and Benjamin, who are the two key eponymous ancestors among the tribes of Israel. Joseph becomes the father of Ephraim and Manasseh, the two major tribes of northern Israel, and Benjamin becomes the ancestor of Israel's first royal dynasty, the house of Saul, into which David was married. The importance of each of these eponymous ancestors is highlighted by a series of puns associated with their names that highlight the geographical significance of the territory with which each figure is associated or characteristics which each nation or tribe represents.

By examining the identities and interrelationships of its primary characters in this fashion, the narrative attempts to demonstrate that Jacob/Israel is indeed the heir to the covenant of YHWH, but it also points to tensions within the tribal structure of Israel and to tensions between Israel on the one hand and Edom and Aram on the other. Jacob is hardly the ideal figure like Abraham. Throughout the narrative, Jacob is often self-serving in his dealings with others and he also suffers the consequences when other characters best him, afflict him with their own problems, or even suffer themselves on his account or at his expense. Indeed, Jacob is ultimately a tragic figure in this narrative (and in the following Joseph narratives), insofar as he suffers conflict among his wives and children, conflict with his neighbors, long periods of exile in a foreign land, conflict with G-d, and the early death of his beloved Rachel. Nevertheless, the presentation of Jacob with all of his problems and flaws serves as a means to facilitate reflection and introspection on the part of its readers, viz., how does one cope with both the opportunities and the tensions and reverses that Jacob must face during the course of his lifetime? To what extent is he responsible for his own problems? To what extent does Jacob learn to take action to address or to overcome the problematic scenarios that he faces throughout?

The Jacob narratives make heavy use of the motifs of national identity, conflict among the characters, particularly sibling rivalry, and ironic reversal in order to make its points.[37] Indeed, the narrative begins in Gen 25:19-26 with a portrayal of Jacob and his fraternal twin brother Esau struggling with each other even before birth while both were still in Rebekah's womb. YHWH's oracle to Rebekah makes it very clear that her sons are two separate nations, that one will be mightier than the other, and that the older will serve the younger. Although Esau is born first, Jacob (*ya'ăqōb*) emerges holding on to the heel (Hebrew, *'āqēb*) of his brother in an attempt to be born first and thus inherit the rights of the first-born. Already, the pun of the term for heel with the name Jacob highlights the conflict between the two sons. Likewise, the identification of Esau as red (Hebrew, *'admônî*) and like a hairy (Hebrew, *śē'ār*) mantle highlights Esau identification with Edom (Hebrew, *'ĕdôm*) located in the land of Seir (Hebrew, *śē'îr*).

The following narrative in Gen 25:27-34 continues to highlight the differences and conflicts between the two brothers. Esau is a hunter, and Jacob is a mild man who stays by the tents. Esau is loved by his father, Isaac, and Jacob is loved by his mother, Rebekah. When Esau returns famished from hunting without success one day to find Jacob cooking a stew identified only as "that red stuff" (Hebrew, *hā'ādōm*), Jacob agrees to Esau's demand to give him some on condition that Esau give up his birthright as first-born. Not only does the pun again reinforce Esau's identity as Edom, but the narrative also takes the opportunity to demonstrate Esau's dismissive attitude toward his status as first-born.

Genesis 27 brings the conflict between the two brothers to a head when Rebekah prompts Jacob to deceive his father into granting him Esau's blessing as the first-born son. Her motivation for doing so is not only her favor for Jacob, but Esau's marriage to Canaanite and Hittite women (cf. Gen 26:34-35). Because Isaac's eyesight is so poor, Rebekah is able to achieve the deception by disguising Jacob with lambskins to make him seem hairy and Esau's clothing so that he might bring the food that his father requested from Esau prior to giving his blessing. Insofar as Jacob is "smooth-skinned" (Hebrew, *ḥālāq*), the narrative provides another opportunity for readers to discern the national significance of the characters insofar as the Judean town of Halaq marked the Israelite border with Edom in the region of Seir (Hebrew, *śē'îr*). Although Jacob succeeded in deceiving his father and obtaining the blessing that anticipates his dominance over nations and his brothers, the blessing later given to Esau foresees that he will break Jacob's yoke from his neck after a period of service. Esau's anger at the deception is such that Rebekah prompts Jacob to flee to Haran in order to find a wife from the family of Rebekah and more immediately to save his own life.

Jacob's journey to Haran takes him through Beth El, later to become the chief sanctuary for YHWH in the northern kingdom of Israel. While spending the night, Jacob experiences a vision of YHWH, who grants him the covenant earlier granted to Abraham and Isaac.

Jacob's arrival at Haran introduces him to his uncle Laban (Hebrew, *lābān*, which means "white" and signifies the snow-capped peaks of the Lebanon mountain range), who proves to be a more formidable challenge than Esau. His arrival also provides the opportunity to reverse the sibling rival motif, insofar as Jacob immediately falls in love with Rachel, the younger daughter of Laban. Jacob arranges a marriage with Laban by contracting for a seven-year period of service to pay the bride price, but belatedly discovers that he has in fact married Leah, Laban's older daughter. In order to marry Rachel he must contract for an additional seven years of service to Laban. The sibling rivalry motif immediately emerges as the wives/sisters compete for their husband's affection, but this time the conflict results in distress for Jacob. As the unloved wife, Leah immediately has four children, Reuben, Simeon, Levi, and Judah, while Rachel remain barren. Rachel provides her hand maid, Bilhah, who gives birth to Dan and Naphtali.

Leah counters with her own hand maid, Zilpah, who bears Gad and Asher. After Rachel obtains some mandrakes, regarded as a fertility drug in the ancient world, by promising Leah extra nights with Jacob, Leah gives birth to Issachar, Zebulun, and Dinah, but Rachel finally gives birth to Joseph. When Jacob prepares to leave Laban to return home, he is tricked into serving Laban for another six years to provide the means to support his family. Even upon leaving Haran, Laban has cause to pursue Jacob when he learns that his household gods have been stolen. Unknown to Jacob, Rachel was the culprit, and when Jacob declares that whoever is in possession of Laban's gods is subject to death, he unwittingly seals the fate of Rachel, who will later die giving birth to Benjamin. Unable to find his gods, Laban and Jacob make a treaty that defines their respective territories. The boundary between Aram and Israel is called "a heap of witness," Hebrew, *gal'ēd*, which is a pun on the regional name, Gilead (Hebrew, *gil'ād*), which marks Israel's frontier with Aram.

Jacob's return to the land of Israel provides an opportunity to return to the matter of his relationship with Esau, but Gen 32 makes sure to provide readers with important signs of his ties to the Trans-Jordan and northern Israel and his identity as the eponymous ancestor of Israel. He camps at Mahanaim, an important Israelite city in the Trans-Jordan throughout the monarchic period. He wrestles (Hebrew, *yē'ābēq*) with a divine figure at Penuel (*pĕnû'ēl*), another Israelite city in the Trans-Jordan along the Jabbok (*yabbōq*) River, whose name is explained in relation to Jacob's face to face (*pānîm 'el pānîm*) encounter with G-d. Insofar as Jacob walks away limping, his injury explains the Israelite practice of not eating the thigh portions of a sacrificial animal, but offering this part of the animal entirely to G-d. The divine figure names Jacob, Israel (Hebrew, *yiśrā'ēl*), explaining that Jacob has struggled (Hebrew, *śārîtā*, "you have struggled") with G-d and humans and prevailed, although the name Israel actually means, "G-d rules."

Jacob faces more obstacles as he placates Esau, who approaches with an army of four hundred men, but each is able to go his own way. Jacob settles first in Shechem, a key city in northern Israel, where his daughter Dinah is raped, in a narrative (Gen 34) that is tied together with other narratives concerned with the question of intermarriage with the Egyptians and Canaanites in the larger framework of Genesis.[38] He finally returns to Beth El, the site of northern Israel's sanctuary, where he is named Israel once again, blessed by YHWH, and granted the land of Israel. But after departing Beth El, Rachel tragically dies giving birth to Benjamin. At the close of the narrative, a summation of Jacob's sons/Israel's tribes appears, followed by a notice of the death and burial of Isaac.

Although the Jacob narratives now function as part of the general P narrative within the Pentateuch, very little P material appears within these narratives, indicating that P plays a largely redactional role in editing an earlier text into the larger literary context.[39] The bulk of the narrative is therefore an underlying EJ composition. Although much material is attributed to J, a number of factors indicate that the extent of J influence is not as extensive as past scholarship suggests, so that the Jacob cycle is fundamentally an E or northern Israelite layer.[40] As noted above, Jacob is identified as the eponymous ancestor of Israel, but he is associated primarily with key northern Israelite sites throughout the narrative, for example, Beth El, the royal sanctuary of the northern kingdom of Israel and the location where he is granted the covenant by YHWH (Gen 28:10-22; 35:1-15; cf. 1 Kgs 12:29); Mahanaim, a key Manassite/Israelite city in the Trans-Jordan during the reigns of the house of Saul and the early house of David (Gen 32:1-22; 33:1-16; cf. 2 Sam 2:8-9; 17:24—19:8; 1 Kgs 4:14); Penuel, an administrative center in the Trans-Jordan fortified by the first northern Israelite King Jeroboam, ben Nebat (Gen 32:23-33; cf. 1 Kgs 12:25); Sukkot, another key Trans-Jordanian city in the territory of Gad (Gen 33:17; cf. Josh 13:27); and Shechem, the central city of northern Israel where the northern Israelite kingdom was founded (Gen 33:18; cf. 1 Kgs 12:1-24). When Jacob is located in the south, he is in or on his way to his father's spheres of influence, that is, Philistia and the region of Beer Sheba (Gen 25:19—28:9); Beth Lehem when Rachel dies (Gen 35:16-21); Kiriath Arba/Hebron where Isaac dies and is buried (Gen 35:27-29). Indeed, the narratives concerning the births of his sons indicate the primary roles of Joseph and Benjamin, the ancestors respectively of the key northern Israelite tribes, Ephraim and Manasseh, and the first royal tribe. Although Judah is included among the first four sons born to Jacob by Leah, all are peripheral, viz., Reuben is located in the Trans-Jordan and is displaced when he has relations with Bilhah (Gen 35:22), Simeon and Levi are both discredited for their slaughter of the men of Shechem (Gen 34:30-31), and Judah, although ruler of all Israel during the reigns of David and Solomon, became a vassal of northern Israel throughout most of northern Israel's history, that is, during the reigns of the Omride and Jehu dynasties until the Assyrians defeated the Syro-Ephraimitic coalition that attempted to force Judah into an alliance against Assyria (see 1 Kgs 16:23—2 Kgs 16:20).

The northern orientation of the Jacob narratives also appears in the portrayal of Jacob's conflicts with Laban and Esau, particularly since each is the eponymous ancestor of Aram and Edom respectively, the two key nations with which northern Israel was in conflict throughout the Omride and Jehu periods. Northern Israel fought an extended war with Aram from the mid-ninth through the early eighth centuries BCE. The Omride King Ahab (869–850) was killed by Arameans at Ramoth Gilead (1 Kgs 22); King Jehu (842–815 BCE) overthrew the house of Omri for its failures against the Arameans, but was himself contained by Aram who stripped Israel of its Trans-Jordanian territories (2 Kgs 10:32-33); Joash (802–786 BCE) finally defeated the Arameans and restored Israel's territory (2 Kgs 22–25), setting the stage for the long peaceful reign of Jeroboam ben Joash (786–746 BCE) who ruled over a kingdom like that of Solomon (2 Kgs 14:23-39). Jacob's long period of servitude to Laban and the final settlement of their border appear to reflect the period of Israel's subjugation to Aram and its subsequent reversal of fortune. Jacob's interrelationship with Esau has similar implications, particularly since Esau initially serves his younger brother but then will break away. Biblical accounts indicate that Edom was subjugated to Judah as early as the reign of David (2 Sam 8:13-15). Edom reportedly revolted unsuccessfully against Judah late in Solomon's reign (1 Kgs 11:14-22), and finally succeeded during the reign of Joram (849–842 BCE; 2 Kgs 8:20-22). Although Edom is nominally ruled by Judah, Judah itself is a vassal of northern Israel throughout this period, as indicated by Jehoshaphat's (873–849 BCE) association with the house of Omri, including accompanying both Ahab and Ahaziah to war (1 Kgs 22, especially vv. 44, 47-49) and marrying his son to Athaliah, described both as the daughter of Omri (2 Kgs 8:26), which would make her Ahab's sister, and daughter of Ahab (2 Kgs 8:18). When the Omride King Jehoram (849–843 BCE) went to war against King Mesha of Moab (2 Kgs 3), he is accompanied by King Jehoshaphat of Judah and the unnamed king of Edom, an obligation of vassals to a suzerain. When Amaziah of Judah (800–783 BCE) attempted a revolt against Israel following his own victory over the Edomites, King Jehoash (Joash) attacked Beth Shemesh and breached the walls of Jerusalem to bring his Judean vassal back into line (2 Kgs 14:1-22).

All of these factors indicate that the Jacob narratives were written as a reflection on northern Israel's experiences of both loss and defeat and later restoration vis-à-vis Aram and Edom during the late ninth through the early eighth centuries BCE, culminating in the reign of Jeroboam ben Joash, who ruled peacefully over a kingdom roughly equivalent to that of Solomon during the mid-eighth century BCE. As the eponymous ancestor of Israel, Jacob's experiences of defeat, restoration, and reconciliation vis-à-vis Laban and Esau reflect Israel's experiences of defeat at the hands of both Aram and Edom as well as its ability to reassert its standing relative to both nations during the reign of Jeroboam ben Joash. Likewise, the tensions between Jacob's wives reflect the tensions among the constituent tribes of Israel during this period, which saw the loss of the Trans-Jordan, including Reuben, Gad, and part of Manasseh, during this period, as well as the loss of Edom and tensions with Judah. Nevertheless, the narrative is clear: Joseph, the father of Ephraim and Manasseh, and Benjamin, the first royal tribe (and not Judah!), are the favorites of Jacob among all the tribes of Israel. Such a scenario suggests that the reign of Jeroboam ben Joash was the setting for the composition of the E stratum of the Pentateuch.

When the Jacob narratives were taken up by the J tradition during the late eighth through the seventh centuries BCE, they are placed in a framework that points to the priority of the Judean- (and Davidic-)oriented Abraham in the history of Israel and its covenant with YHWH. Indeed, Jacob's contentious character contrasts with that of the far more ideal Abraham. Likewise, the P tradition reinforces Jacob's later status among the ancestors of Israel within its own genealogical presentation.

10. The Generations of Esau/Edom

The presentation of the lengthy genealogy of Esau in Gen 36:1—37:1 plays a similar role to that of Ishmael in Gen 25:12-18, that is, it is designed to close off the line of Esau within the larger structure of the Pentateuchal narrative so that the subsequent presentation may focus on Jacob and his sons. P's interests in Esau may be explained by the fact that Esau is the fraternal twin brother of Jacob, Edom's alleged role in the destruction of the Jerusalem Temple (see Obadiah; Psalm 137), and continuing conflict with Edom and the Idumeans in the Persian period.

11. The Generations of Jacob/Israel

The presentation of the generations of Jacob/Israel in Gen 37:2—Num 2:34 is a lengthy narrative concerning the Israel's sojourn in Egypt from the time of Joseph through the Exodus from Egypt and the revelation of Torah at Sinai. It includes a number of large subunits that take up various stages of Israel's movement from one location to another, defined particularly by the itinerary formulae in Exod 1:1—Num 2:34 and beyond, viz., the journey from Canaan to Egypt in the time of Joseph (Gen 37:2—50:26); deliverance from Egyptian bondage at Rameses (Exod 1:1—12:36); the journey from Rameses to Sukkot and the consecration of the first-born (Exod 12:37—13:19); the journey from Sukkot to Etam and the pillar of fire and cloud (Exod 13:20-22); the journey from Etam to the sea and deliverance at the sea (Exod 14:1—15:21); the journey from the Reed Sea to the Wilderness of Shur and the issue of water in the wilderness (Exod 15:22-27); the journey from Elim to the Wilderness of Sin and the quails and manna (Exod 16:1-36); the journey from Sin to Rephidim and the encounters with Amalek and Jethro (Exod 17:1—18:27); and the journey from Rephidim to Sinai with the revelation of Torah at Sinai (Exod 19:1—Num 2:34). The Sinai revelation pericope of course divides further into its own constituent sub-units which will be discussed below.

The present text is the product of the P stratum of the Pentateuch, but the appearance of the Toledoth formula concerning Moses and Aaron in Num 3:1 suggests that the P genealogical structure has been overlaid on an earlier narrative Exodus—Numbers that was defined by its itinerary formulae. Each of the constitutive narratives nevertheless displays P influence as well, a feature which will be discussed in the treatment of each sub-unit below. Likewise, a combined EJ narrative underlies the entire P redaction.

a. Joseph and His Brothers in Egypt

The Joseph narrative in Gen 37:1—50:26 follows closely upon the Jacob narratives, but shifts its concerns from Jacob's relations with his neighbors and his wives to Joseph's relations with his brothers and his role as the favored or leading son of Jacob. Just as Jacob and the other major characters of the Jacob narrative were eponymous figures who represented nations or tribal groups in Israel, so Joseph and his brothers are also eponymous ancestors who represent the twelve tribes of Israel. Likewise, just as Jacob's character undergoes development as he interacts with the other major figures of the narrative, so Joseph's character develops as he meets the various challenges of his life to rise to a position of authority in Egypt and in relation to his father and brothers. There is a difference, however, in that Jacob never becomes a full ideal figure—indeed, Jacob's favoritism to Joseph and Benjamin is the root cause of many of the problems that develop between Joseph and his brothers, but Joseph ultimately emerges as an ideal character—and leader of the sons of Jacob/tribes of Israel—who is able to learn from and to overcome his faults to a degree that Jacob can never attain. In short, the Joseph narrative is a study in the development of character and leadership as Joseph's abilities to overcome adversity, to learn from his own mistakes, and as a result to develop his own capacities for leadership, place him in a position to deliver his entire family/nation from famine in the land of Canaan. Insofar as Joseph is the father of Ephraim and Manasseh, the two chief tribes of Israel, it becomes apparent that the character study of Joseph is a narrative that is concerned ultimately with the roles of Ephraim and Manasseh as the leading tribes among Israel.

The Joseph narrative begins very inauspiciously with the portrayal of the seventeen-year-old Joseph as the favored, spoiled, and arrogant son of Jacob who very early in life lets his brothers and parents know of his destiny to rule over them all. Of course, when Joseph relates his grandiose dreams of his brothers and parents bowing down to him, he provokes the hatred on behalf of his brothers that will result in an attempt by the brothers to murder their arrogant younger sibling. Although Reuben, as the oldest son of Jacob, attempts to spare Joseph's life, the delay prompted by the brother's debate as to how to dispose of Joseph only results in his being sold into slavery in Egypt. To cover their actions, the brothers report to their father that Joseph has been killed by a wild animal, prompting Jacob to mourn without comfort for the loss of his favored son.

The narrative concerning Tamar and Judah in Gen 38 provides a brief interlude that functions much like other narratives concerning the prospect of intermarriage with the Egyptians, the Philistines, or the Canaanites, such as the three instances of the endangered matriarch in Gen 12; 20; and 26; and the rape of Dinah in Gen 34. Whereas Judah had sons as a result of his marriage to a Canaanite woman, his daughter-in-law, Tamar, takes action after the death of her husband and his brothers to ensure the continuity of Judah as an Israelite line that will lead ultimately to the origins of the house of David. This will have important implications for the birth of Ephraim and Manasseh to Asenath, Joseph's Egyptian wife, later in the narrative.

The refinement of Joseph's character is the subject of Gen 39–41 as he finds himself as a slave in the house of Potiphar, chief steward of Pharaoh, who purchased Joseph from the Ishmaelites. Joseph demonstrates his talents for leadership early on as he takes charge of Potiphar's house and makes him prosperous. But he also encounters adversity when he refuses the advances of Potiphar's wife, who then claims that Joseph attempted to rape her. But Joseph's leadership talents continue to emerge, even when he is imprisoned on the basis of this false charge. Joseph makes friends in prison and develops a reputation as a wise man and dream interpreter. After correctly interpreting the dreams of two fellow prisoners, he is brought to the attention of Pharaoh, who has had his own puzzling dreams. When Joseph correctly interprets the Pharaoh's dreams as signs of prosperity followed by famine, he advises Pharaoh on how to prepare for the famine by buying and storing grain during the period of prosperity and then selling it to the people during the time of famine. As a result, Pharaoh appoints Joseph to high office—second only to Pharaoh—and assigns him with the job of preparing for the famine as he advised. Joseph is also assimilated into Egyptian culture, taking on the Egyptian name Zaphenath Paneah, and marrying Asenath, the daughter of the Egyptian priest, Potiphera. His sons, Manasseh and Ephraim, are therefore half-Egyptian.

Joseph's reunion with his brothers when they come to Egypt looking for food in Gen 42–45 provides the key opportunity for Joseph to overcome his own faults and demonstrate his character and capacity for leadership among his brothers. Facing famine in Canaan, Jacob sends ten sons to Egypt to obtain food, but he continues to show favoritism towards his sons by refusing to send Benjamin, Joseph's only full brother born to Rachel. Joseph recognizes his brothers, but they do not recognize him, and he demands that they leave one of their number as a hostage to ensure that they will bring their youngest brother Benjamin to appear before Joseph in order to prove their own honesty. As the oldest, Reuben is the spokesman, and decides to leave Simeon as the hostage. As for Joseph, he takes care of his brothers by filling their sacks with grain, but also by surreptitiously placing their money in their sacks so that the food they needed was free. When the famine persists and the brothers must return to Egypt for more grain, Reuben again acts as spokesman and swears to his father that Jacob may take Reuben's own sons if Benjamin does not return alive. On seeing Benjamin in court when the brothers return to Egypt, Joseph nearly breaks down, but hides his feelings. He nevertheless engineers a trick to ensure his brother's return by placing a silver goblet in Benjamin's bag so that he might accuse him of theft. The episode introduces narrative tension: Will Joseph take revenge on his brothers? Or not? But when the brothers return, Judah emerges as the spokesman in place of Reuben to plead for mercy and recognition of their innocence. At this point

Joseph can no longer hide his feelings, and identifies himself in a very emotional scene, stating, "I am Joseph. Is my father still well?" But rather than take vengeance on his brothers, which he had all power to do, Joseph reconciles with his brothers and claims that although the brothers meant to do him evil, G-d meant their actions for good as Joseph became the means by which Israel was saved from famine in the land. As a result, Gen 46–47 relates how Joseph's high position in Egypt enables Jacob and all of his family to move to Egypt and thereby to escape the famine in Canaan.

The Joseph narrative concludes with several key scenes that speak to the status of Joseph's sons, Manasseh and Ephraim, in relation to Israel at large. When Jacob is about to die in Gen 48, he summons Joseph and his sons to give them his blessing. During the course of the blessing, Jacob formally adopts Manasseh and Ephraim as his own sons, which gives them full status as tribes in Israel, though he designates Ephraim as first-born in place of the older Manasseh. But when he blesses all of his sons in Gen 49, he grants Judah the right to rule in Gen 49:8-12, after displacing the older Reuben, Simeon, and Levi. Finally, Gen 50 relates the deaths of both Jacob and Joseph, and it concludes the narrative by reiterating YHWH's promises to return Israel to the land of Canaan as promised to Abraham, Isaac, and Jacob.

Diachronic analysis of the Joseph narratives indicates that the final form is the product of P redaction, but this stratum only represents a relatively light redactional layer.[41] Otherwise, the bulk of the narrative is the product of EJ strata.[42] Although scholars are accustomed to think of the J material as the earlier layer, a number of factors suggest that J is in fact a redactional stratum that has reworked an earlier E narrative.

First is the fact that Joseph, the primary subject of the narrative, is the ancestor of Manasseh and Ephraim, the two leading tribes of the northern kingdom of Israel. Judah plays a visible but relatively minor role in the narrative. Joseph matures throughout the narrative and ultimately emerges as an ideal ruler in Egypt and an ideal leader among his brothers. He consistently projects a moral character in the narrative, even when tempted by Potiphar's wife. He shows the Egyptians, both Potiphar and even Pharaoh, how to rule their respective realms. He saves his entire family from famine, including his father, who caused the problems in the family by playing favorites, and his brothers, who sold him into slavery. He emerges as the true protector of his younger brother Benjamin. And he shows wisdom and magnanimity throughout. By characterizing Joseph in these terms, the narrative makes the case that the Joseph tribes must be recognized as the central and ruling tribes of all Israel. Judean readers would hardly look to Joseph as an ideal figure, particularly when Solomon fills that role in the south.

Second is the role played by Judah in the narrative. Source-critical scholars consistently point to the doublets in the narrative, such as the role of the Midianites or the Ishmaelites in taking Joseph down to Egypt or the shifting roles of Reuben and Judah as the leading spokesmen among the brothers before Jacob and Joseph, as a means to distinguish between the J and E strata of the Joseph narratives. Reuben makes sense as the spokesman since he is after all the oldest of Jacob's sons. But the role of Judah calls for comment, particularly because he supplants Reuben as spokesman for the brothers before both Jacob and Joseph. Scholars are well aware that Reuben ultimately disappears as a coherent tribe in Israelite history, but there is little reason for him to disappear in the narrative. Judah, however, emerges as the brother who offers to protect Benjamin, which is particularly striking because of Benjamin's role as the first royal tribe in Israel and Judah's role as the tribe that supplanted Benjamin with the establishment of the ruling house of David, first in Israel and later in Judah alone. But Judah ultimately does not and cannot protect Benjamin. That role is accomplished by Joseph alone, the ideal, magnanimous ruler among the brothers. Judah may try, but he is inadequate before Joseph.

But the figure of Judah emerges as ever more important in narratives that are clearly redactional in relation to the larger Joseph narrative. The Judah and Tamar narrative is generally regarded as a J insert into the underlying Joseph story, but it plays a key role in the overall plot of the whole. Although Judah's sons were born to a Canaanite mother, all died, and Tamar's relations with Judah, even though she was forced to disguise herself as a prostitute, ensured that her late husband and her father-in-law had Judean descendants. Such a concern relates to the portrayal of Joseph's sons in the larger Joseph narrative who are born to Joseph by his Egyptian wife Asenath. Although the narrative gives little indication that this is an issue, it does make sure to portray Jacob's adoption of the two boys and the designation of Ephraim as the first-born to ensure that they have full standing in the family and among the tribes of Israel. Insofar as the Tamar episode appears as a redactional insertion into the narrative, its purpose becomes clear in relation to the question of Joseph's sons, viz., whereas Judah's descendants are Israelite, Joseph's are half-Egyptian, which raises questions about the status of Ephraim and Manasseh in Israel that best serves Judean—not northern Israelite—interests. Judean interests are further underscored in Jacob's blessing of his sons in Gen 49—again an inserted text—that portrays Judah and not Joseph (or Ephraim and Manasseh) as the ruling tribe of Israel.

Finally, the concluding notices about the burial of Jacob at Machpelah in Judah indicates a Judean interest in subsuming the patriarch most closely identified with the north to Judah as well.

It would appear that a J redaction reworked an underlying E narrative about Joseph to suit Judean interests. Whereas Joseph emerges as an ideal ruler in the E layers, his ideal role is subject to question in the J reworking of the narrative, particularly since he assimilates into Egyptian culture by marrying the daughter of an Egyptian priest, in contrast to Judah whose descendants—including the house of David—are traced back to Tamar. Joseph's association with Egypt of course has its consequences, as Egypt becomes the nation that enslaves Israel in the following Exodus narrative. Such a Judean redaction of the Joseph narrative is easily set in the eighth and seventh centuries BCE following the collapse of northern Israel when the house of David, first under Hezekiah and later under Josiah, unsuccessfully attempted to reassert control over the north. The E stratum is easily set in the northern kingdom of Israel during the later rule of the Jehu kings when Israel emerged secure after a long history of threat and turmoil, first under the rule of the house of David which imposed forced slavery on the north during the reign of Solomon and later under Arameans who subjugated Israel during the late ninth and early eighth centuries BCE. Indeed, interpreters have noted the parallels between Joseph and Jeroboam ben Nebat, the founding king of northern Israel, who overthrew oppressive Judean rule under the house of David and led Ephraim and Manasseh to become the central tribes of the powerful Israelite kingdom.[43] Insofar as Joseph shows magnanimity toward his wayward brothers, led by Judah, he emerges as an ideal contrast to Solomon when seen from a northern Israelite perspective.

NOTES

[1] See Harry M. Orlinsky, *Notes on the New Translation of the Torah* (Philadelphia: Jewish Publication Society, 1969), 49–52; Nahum Sarna, *Genesis* (JPS Torah Commentary; Philadelphia: Jewish Publication Society, 1989/5749); John Skinner, *Genesis* (ICC; Edinburgh: T. & T. Clark, 1969), 12–13, n. 1; Claus Westermann, *Genesis 1–11* (ContCom; Minneapolis: Augsburg, 1984), 78.

[2] See Jon D. Levenson, *Creation and the Persistence of Evil: The Jewish Drama of Divine Impotence* (New York: Harper & Row, 1988).

[3] See Abraham Joshua Heschel, *The Sabbath: Its Meaning for Modern Man* (New York: Farrar, Straus & Young, 1951).

[4] For discussion of the *Enuma Elish*, see W. G. Lambert, "Enuma Elish," *ABD* 2:526–28.

[5] In addition, Assyrian records from the late eighth century may refer to Sennacherib's attack against Lachish on the Shabbat; see G. F. Hasel, "Sabbath," *ABD* 5:849–56, especially 853.

[6] Cf. Gen 25:18. See Sarna, *Genesis*, 19–20; W. W. Müller, "Pishon," *ABD* 5:374.

[7] For texts from the Second Temple period that emphasize this role for the high priest, see C. T. R. Hayward, *The Jewish Temple: A Non-Biblical Sourcebook* (London: Routledge, 1996).

[8] For pictorial representation of the goddess figures, see especially *ANEP*, 464, 465, 469, 470–74.

[9] Zev Meshel, "Kuntillat 'Ajrud," *ABD* 4:103–9.

[10] See Antony F. Campbell and Mark A. O'Brien, *Sources of the Pentateuch: Texts, Introductions, Annotations* (Minneapolis: Fortress Press, 1993), 25–27, 95–97, for the P and J versions of this narrative.

[11] For texts and discussion of the Mesopotamian flood traditions, see *ANET*, 42–44 (Ziusudra), 72–99 (Gilgamesh), 104–106 (Atra Hasis); W. G. Lambert and A. R. Millard, *Atra Hasis: The Babylonian Story of the Flood* (Oxford: Clarendon, 1969).

[12] The Akkadian word for Babylon, *bab ilu*, actually means "Gateway of the gods."

[13] See Campbell and O'Brien, *Sources of the Pentateuch*, 27, 97–98.

[14] For the Adapa myth, see *ANET*, 101–3.

[15] For analysis of the character of G-d in Genesis, see also W. Lee Humphreys, *The Character of G-d in the Book of Genesis: A Narrative Appraisal* (Louisville: Westminster John Knox, 2001).

[16] See my analysis of the Abraham/Sarah narratives in *Reading the Hebrew Bible after the Shoah: Engaging Holocaust Theology* (Minneapolis: Fortress Press, 2008), 23–41.

[17] For discussion of the promise of land to the patriarchs, see Claus Westermann, *The Promises to the Fathers: Studies on the Patriarchal Narratives* (Philadelphia: Fortress Press, 1980); see also Harry M. Orlinsky, "The Biblical Concept of the Land of Israel: Cornerstone of the Covenant Between G-d and Israel," in *The Land of Israel: Jewish Perspectives*, ed. L. Hoffman (Notre Dame: University of Notre Dame Press, 1986), 27–64.

[18] For discussion of the role played by narratives concerned with threats to matriarchal figures in the Genesis narrative, see my "Form Criticism: The Question of the Endangered Matriarchs in Genesis," in *Method Matters: Essays on the Interpretation of the Hebrew Bible in Honor of David L. Petersen*, ed. J. M. LeMon and K. H. Richards (ResBibSt 56; Atlanta: Society of Biblical Literature, 2009), 17–38.

[19] See Nahum Sarna, *Understanding Genesis: The Heritage of Biblical Israel* (New York: Schocken, 1970), 102–3; Ephraim A. Speiser, *Genesis* (AB 1; New York: Doubleday, 1964), 91–94.

[20] Note especially that Gen 20:12 later explains that Sarah is Abraham's half-sister, meaning that his statement is not a lie.

[21] See Gen 16, which relates the birth of Abram's son, Ishmael, to Sarah's Egyptian handmaiden, Hagar. Note also that the Abraham–Sarah narratives ultimately pass the covenant on to Isaac and not to the Egyptian-born Ishmael. This stands in contrast to the birth of Joseph's two sons, Manasseh and Ephraim, to his Egyptian wife, Asenath, in Gen 41:50-52. Both sons are eventually adopted by Jacob in Gen 48. It is striking that Abraham, who is often identified in relation to Judean interests (see Ronald E. Clements, *Abraham and David: Genesis 15 and its Meaning for Israelite Tradition* [SBT 2/5; London: SCM, 1967]), avoids passing his inheritance on to Egyptian-born offspring, whereas Joseph, the ancestor of the major tribes of the northern kingdom of Israel, does not.

[22] See Moshe Weinfeld, "Tithe," *EncJud* 15:1156–62.

[23] For detailed discussion of Gen 15, see my "Form Criticism," in *To Each its Own Meaning: Biblical Criticism and their Application*, ed. S. L. McKenzie and S. R. Haynes (Louisville: Westminster John Knox, 1999), 58–89.

[24] For discussion of sacrifices in relation to ancient Near Eastern treaties, see Moshe Weinfeld, "The Covenant of Grant in the OT and in the Ancient Near East," *JAOS* 90 (1970): 184–203.

[25] Sarna, *Understanding Genesis*, 127–29; Speiser, *Genesis*, 119–21.

[26] Rabbinic tradition notes that Isaac never comes home to Sarah following this incident, and that Sarah dies thinking that her son is dead (*Leviticus Rabbah* 20:2; *Pirke Rabbi Eliezer* 32).

[27] See Campbell and O'Brien, *Sources of the Pentateuch*, 28–31.

[28] See Tammi J. Schneider, *Sarah: Mother of Nations* (London: Continuum, 2004), who argues that the covenant includes Sarah as well as Abraham.

[29] For identification of the J and E material, see Campbell and O'Brien, *Sources of the Pentateuch*, 98–108, 166–70.

[30] For discussion of the Judean orientation of this material, see especially Clements, *Abraham and David*, passim.

[31] For delineation of the E material, see Campbell and O'Brien, *Sources of the Pentateuch*, 166–70.

[32] For example, Samuel, the first-born son of Hannah and Elkanah, is deposited in the Shiloh temple to be raised as a priest in Levi in 1 Sam 1–3. Note also YHWH's statement in Num 3 that the first-born served as priests prior to the designation of Levi in Num 17–18 and Jeroboam's practice of allowing anyone to be a priest rather than Levites (1 Kgs 12:31).

[33] See especially Thomas L. Thompson, *The Historicity of the Patriarchal Traditions: The Quest for the Historical Abraham* (BZAW 133; Berlin: de Gruyter, 1974); John Van Seters, *Abraham in History and Tradition* (New Haven: Yale University Press, 1975).

[34] See also Erhard Blum, *Die Komposition der Vätergeschichte* (WMANT 57; Neukirchen–Vluyn: Neukirchener, 1984); David M. Carr, *Reading the Fractures of Genesis: Literary and Historical Approaches* (Louisville: Westminster John Knox, 1996).

[35] See Mark S. Smith, *The Memoirs of G-d: History, Memory, and the Experience of the Divine in Ancient Israel* (Minneapolis: Fortress Press, 2004).

[36] For discussion of the geo-political significance of the Jacob narratives, including its use of puns, see my study, "Puns, Politics, and Perushim in the Jacob Cycle: A Case Study in Teaching the English Hebrew Bible," *Shofar* 9 (1991): 103–18; cf. Stanley Gevirtz, "Of Patriarchs and Puns: Joseph at the Fountain, Jacob at the Ford," *HUCA* 46 (1975): 33–54.

[37] For a discussion of the motif of sibling rivalry, see especially Michael Fishbane, "Composition and Structure in the Jacob Cycles (Gen 25:19–35:22)," in *Text and Texture: Close Readings of Selected Biblical Texts* (New York: Schocken, 1979), 40–62.

[38] See also Gen 12; 20; 26; 38.

[39] For identification of the P material, see Campbell and O'Brien, *Sources of the Pentateuch*, 31–33.

[40] For identification of the J and E material in the Jacob cycle, see Campbell and O'Brien, *Sources of the Pentateuch*, 108–19, 170–75.

[41] For the P materials in the Joseph narratives, see Campbell and O'Brien, *Sources of the Pentateuch*, 34–35.

[42] For identification of the E and J strata of the Joseph narratives, see Campbell and O'Brien, *Sources of the Pentateuch*, 175–83, 120–31, respectively.

[43] See especially James L. Kugel, *In Potiphar's House: The Interpretive Life of Biblical Texts* (San Francisco: HarperSanFrancisco, 1990), who traces the interpretation of the Joseph narratives in Rabbinic Judaism, early Christianity, and early Islam, and notes particularly the parallels drawn between Joseph and Jeroboam.

b. The Exodus from Egypt

A major transition takes place in the Torah with the shift from Genesis to Exodus, Leviticus, and Numbers. Whereas the Genesis narratives focus on G-d's relationship with the ancestors of Israel as individuals and family groups, Exodus, Leviticus, and Numbers focus on Israel as a nation that experiences G-d's actions on Israel's behalf in the Exodus from Egypt, the Revelation at Sinai, and the Wilderness Wanderings prior to entry into the promised land. Whereas the literary structure of Genesis is defined by the appearance of the *toledoth* formulas that introduce the sequence of generations in the history of creation, apart from the reference to the *toledoth* of Aaron and Moses in Num 3:1, the literary structure of Exodus, Leviticus, and Numbers is defined by the itinerary formulas that mark the stages of Israel's journey from Egypt to Sinai and through the wilderness to the promised land of Israel.

Nevertheless, the signs of continuity are clear in the synchronic presentation of the Pentateuchal narrative. The 600,000 strong nation of Israel in Exodus— Numbers grows out of the family units constituted by the twelve sons of Jacob in the Genesis narratives. The reference to the *toledoth* of Aaron and Moses in Num 3:1 works the Exodus—Numbers (Deuteronomy) narratives into the overall literary structure of the Pentateuch. The references to the *běrît ʿôlām*, "the eternal covenant," between G-d and the world noted in Gen 9 (Noah) and Gen 17 (Abraham) appear again in reference to the Shabbat (Exod 31), the presentation of bread/challah before the Holy of Holies (Lev 2), and the priestly line of Pinhas ben Elazer ben Aaron (Num 25). G-d's promises to the ancestors continue in G-d's promises to the nation Israel. And finally, G-d's role as creator is manifested as creation plays a role in delivering and sustaining Israel during the entire period of the Exodus, revelation at Sinai, and the wilderness wanderings.

Exodus 1:1—12:26 is the first major component of the narrative that focuses on Israel as a nation in relation to the Exodus from Egypt. It begins by marking the transition of Israel from a clan-based grouping of family units that came down to Egypt from Canaan to a nation based on tribal units that is about to depart from Egypt on its journey through the wilderness to the promised land. It continues by introducing the figure of Moses, who will serve as G-d's agent for leading Israel through the Exodus, the revelation at Sinai, and the wilderness period, and by relating G-d's confrontation with Pharaoh in the form of the ten plagues. Throughout the unit, Israel is located in Egypt, particularly at the store cities of

Pithom and Raamses, until the outset of the next unit in Exod 12:37—13:19, which sees Israel journey from Raamses to Sukkot.

Exodus 1:1—12:36 presents the Exodus from Egypt as an account of the confrontation between YHWH and the Egyptian Pharaoh. Although the Pharaoh appears throughout the narrative as the human monarch of Egypt, the Pharaoh was considered by the Egyptians to be the embodiment of the falcon or sky god, Horus, who protects his manifestation as Pharaoh. As Horus, Pharaoh is also the son of the great sun god, Re, and when the Pharaoh dies, he becomes the god Osiris, who rules the underworld. The absence of overt divine associations with Pharaoh in the Exodus narrative is deliberate, insofar as the narrative attempts to demonstrate that YHWH alone must be recognized as G-d of all creation, including both the natural world and the world of human events. By redeeming Israel from Pharaoh's control, YHWH demonstrates to Israel and to the nations of the world, beginning with Egypt and including all the nations that witness YHWH's acts in the narrative, that YHWH is the one true G-d. In addition to the premise of the divine character of Pharaoh in Egyptian thought, the narrative also presupposes aspects of the Canaanite fertility god, Baal, in its characterization of Pharaoh. As a result of YHWH's initial victory over Pharaoh, the narrative instructs its readers to observe the festival of Pesach (Passover) to commemorate the Exodus from Egypt and YHWH's role as the true G-d of all creation.

The narrative employs a number of features of the natural world in both Egypt and the land of Israel, the fundamental concerns of life, fertility, and death, and even some well-known folklore motifs to portray YHWH's victory over the Egyptian Pharaoh in delivering Israel from his control.

The first is the mention in Exod 1 of the increasing numbers of the Israelites, even after they are enslaved by the Egyptians, and the Egyptians' fear of Israel. This motif presupposes the roles of Pharaoh and Baal as guarantors of fertility in creation, but the increasing numbers of the Israelites function as a direct challenge to these roles by YHWH, who ensures the fertility of Israel despite the efforts of the Egyptians to oppress them. It also presupposes the early command of G-d to human beings in Gen 1:28 to "be fruitful and multiply." The motif continues with the Pharaoh's commands to the Israelite midwives to kill any male baby born to the Israelite women, but the midwives of course disobey this unjust and murderous command, which makes Pharaoh appear immoral, desperate, and impotent before G-d. The explanation given by the midwives to Pharaoh for their failure to carry out the command, viz., the Israelites are so vigorous that they give birth before the midwives arrive, reinforces the unfavorable portrayal of Pharaoh in relation to YHWH. His subsequent command to murder every male baby born to Israel reinforces this characterization.

The presentation of Moses' birth, upbringing in the royal household of Egypt, and escape to the wilderness employs elements of irony, Israelite religious identity, and folklore to advance the portrayal of YHWH's victory over Pharaoh.

Moses is YHWH's agent for delivering Israel from Egyptian bondage. The narrative makes it clear that he is born to Levitical parents, which means he is born to the tribe that will emerge as Israel's priesthood, dedicated to the worship of YHWH and the teaching of YHWH's Torah. Although Moses clearly comes under Pharaoh's decree to murder male Israelite babies, his mother and sister take action to save his life by placing him in a sealed wicker basket that floats him down the Nile River until he is discovered, taken in, and raised by the daughter of Pharaoh. The folklore motif of divine intervention to save the life of an infant who will eventually become ruler of a great nation is well-known in the ancient world. Sargon of Akkad is likewise floated down a river and saved to become ruler of his nation. Others saved by the gods include Cyrus of Persia and Romulus and Remus of Rome. Elements of irony include the raising of Moses in Pharaoh's own house by Pharaoh's own daughter, her defiance of her father when she recognizes the infant as a Hebrew, and the employment of Moses' true mother to serve as his wet nurse. The ultimate irony, of course, is that Moses is raised as a prince in the royal house of Egypt, which prepares him for his future role as leader of Israel.

Moses' identity with his own people, whether known to him or not, and his moral perspective become clear as he grows up. On seeing an Egyptian taskmaster beating a Hebrew slave, he kills the taskmaster and thereby delivers the slave. Although the act is committed to save the Israelite from unjust punishment, it does leave Moses with blood on his hands, much like David, who was later unable to build the Temple for the same reason (see 1 Chr 28:3), which may have implications for Moses' later life. When Moses flees to the wilderness to escape Pharaoh's death sentence, he arrives at a well, which generally portends marriage (cf. Gen 29:1-20), Moses defends the seven daughters of Reuel, also known as Jethro, priest of Midian. Moses' chance encounter sets the course for his future insofar as Reuel/Jethro becomes the means by which Moses encounters YHWH and Reuel's daughter Zipporah becomes his wife and bears him a son, Gershom.

YHWH's role as creator is highlighted in the narrative concerning Moses' initial encounter with YHWH in Exod 3–4. His vision of YHWH's angel on Mt. Horeb, also known as Mt. Sinai, appears in the form of a burning bush that is not consumed by fire. The vision presupposes the *rubus sanctus*, a prickly bush with small roses and raspberry-like fruit that turns black when ripe,[1] that would appear to be on fire when viewed from a distance. Angels are frequently portrayed as flaming or gleaming beings, and the Hebrew word for bush, *sĕneh*, forms a pun with *sînāy*, Sinai. But liturgical concerns also inform the narrative as Moses must remove his shoes because he stands on holy ground. YHWH's commission of Moses to deliver Israel from Egyptian oppression establishes continuity with the ancestral narratives when YHWH identifies the divine Self as the G-d of Abraham, Isaac, and Jacob. Most notably, YHWH's statement of the divine name, *'ehyeh 'ăšer 'ehyeh*, "I am who I am," is a rhetorical device, the idem per idem, that identifies a subject in relation only to itself and therefore provides absolutely no information. This is a deliberate ploy to assert and protect the holiness of the divine name by declining to state it to Moses. Knowledge of a divine name in ancient Egypt and elsewhere gave a human being power over the deity in question, and the Exodus narrative deliberately avoids granting such power to Moses until Moses fully understands the holy nature of G-d and his role in carrying out the task at hand. Furthermore, YHWH's response, 'ehyeh 'ăšer 'ehyeh, "I am who I am," provides an interpretation of the divine name YHWH, which is formulated in Hebrew much like the Hiphil or causative imperfect form of the verb, hyh, "to be," viz., "he is," or "he brings into being." In this respect, the narrative provides an interpretation of the divine name that highlights the reality of YHWH and YHWH's role as creator.

Moses' reluctance to speak, claiming that he is a man of uncircumcised lips, highlights his role as a typical ancient Near Eastern oracle diviner who speaks on behalf of a god (sometimes in a state of ecstasy), and provides the opportunity to introduce Moses' older brother Aaron as the spokesman on behalf of Moses. Insofar as Aaron will later become the priest, he already assumes the role of communicator, interpreter, and teacher of the divine word spoken through Moses, which is of course a primary role of the priest in ancient Israel. The use of Aaron's and Moses' staff establishes the role of the Levitical rod as a symbol of Levitical priestly authority, and it provides the occasion to demonstrate YHWH's mastery over both nature and Egypt where snake charming was a well-known art.

The confrontation with Pharaoh commences with Exod 5, in which Moses and Aaron appear before Pharaoh to demand that he let the people of Israel go to celebrate a festival for YHWH in the wilderness. The challenge highlights the liturgical aspects of the narrative, the concern with creation insofar as the celebration is in the wilderness, and the power of YHWH insofar as they mention a threat that YHWH may strike them. The confrontation is highlighted by Pharaoh's leading question in Exod 5:2, "who is YHWH that I should heed him and let Israel go? I do not know YHWH." The rest of the narrative will focus on informing Pharaoh—and Israel—just who YHWH is. The tension of the narrative is further highlighted by Pharaoh's imposition of additional labor on Israel and the people's resistance to Moses and Aaron.

Following this initial setback, YHWH's confrontation with Pharaoh enters its main stage in Exod 6:1—12:36. YHWH begins this stage by finally revealing the divine name, YHWH, to Moses and by reiterating the covenant with Israel's ancestors to grant them the land of Israel and to deliver them from Egyptian oppression. YHWH's instruction to Moses to inform the people of YHWH's identity and to instruct them in YHWH's promises, includes the statement in Exod 6:7, "And I will take you to be my people, and I will be your G-d," a formulaic statement of the covenantal relationship between YHWH and the people of Israel.[2]

YHWH's further instructions to Moses and Aaron stipulate that Moses will speak to Pharaoh on G-d's behalf and that Aaron will act as Moses' prophet, which sets the pattern of priests and prophets as interpreters of the divine. A problematic aspect of YHWH's instructions is the claim that YHWH will harden Pharaoh's heart to ensure that Pharaoh will refuse to accede to YHWH's demand to free Israel. Pharaoh's refusal would then ensure that the punishments against Egypt would be witnessed by Egypt (and Israel) so that all would know YHWH's identity and power. Although this motif functions as a means to reveal YHWH in the narrative, it raises a problematic moral question as to whether or not Pharaoh should be allowed to exercise his own free will, perhaps to accept YHWH's demands and to avoid the punishments that he and his nation will suffer. The issue becomes even more pointed when the people of Israel are treated in similar fashion for the same purpose in Isaiah.[3]

Of the ten plagues unleashed against Egypt in Exod 7–12, the first nine represent natural features of the land of Egypt or the land of Canaan.[4] The Nile River turning to blood reflects the rising waters of the late summer when the Nile carries red earth from its headwaters in the south of the Nile Delta region in the north. The frogs naturally are carried by the rising waters as well, and the gnats and flies appear when the waters recede and the frogs begin to die. Cattle disease and boils are a natural result of the inundation of the land by the gnats and flies. Hail and thunder are rare, but nevertheless occur in Egypt and Canaan. Locusts are likewise a well-known feature of both lands, generally every seven years. Darkness may be explained by an eclipse of the sun or by the Sharav or Hamsin, the dry desert sirocco wind that appears at the change of seasons in the spring and fall and frequently blocks the sun and the moon with blowing dust and sand. The Exodus narrative thereby explains the origins of all of these natural features of the land as acts of YHWH at the time of the Exodus, which of course further identifies YHWH as the author of all creation in keeping with Gen 1.

But the narrative also includes liturgical dimensions. Throughout the narrative, the plagues are initiated when Moses commands Aaron to extend his hand and rod over the land so that the plague might commence. Such a portrayal explains the origins and power of the Levitical rod carried by the Levitical priests as a means of identifying their holy roles and employed in oracular inquiry of YHWH. Likewise, the tenth plague, the death of the first-born, has important liturgical dimensions related to the conceptualization of Israel's priesthood and the observance of Passover, which commemorates the exodus from Egypt. Whereas all the first-born of Egypt, both animal and human, will perish in this plague, the first-born of Israel are redeemed by the smearing of the blood of a sacrificial lamb on the doorposts of Israelite households. The use of the blood from the sacrificial lamb then explains the origins of the Passover sacrifice, a central act in the Temple observance of Passover as explained in Exod 12 (see also Lev 23:4-8; Num 28:16-25; Deut 16:1-8; cf. Exod 23:14-19; 34:18-20). The redemption of the Israelite first-born also emerges as a means to establish the origins of the priesthood and to designate Israel as a priestly people (see Exod 9:6) dedicated to the service of YHWH and the observance of divine Torah. Exodus 34:18-20 categorically states that all that breaks the womb, that is, the first-born to the mother, belongs to YHWH. Such a statement calls for the sacrificial offering of first-born animals of flock or herd to YHWH, but the first-born of human beings are redeemed so that they might instead be employed in the service of YHWH. Statements by YHWH to Moses in Num 3:11-13, 40-51 make it clear that first-born males were to serve as priests for YHWH until they were later replaced by the tribe of Levi. Although the current form of the Bible presupposes the role of the Levites as priests (cf. Gen 22, which relates the redemption of Isaac, the first-born of Sarah, for service to YHWH as heir to Abraham's covenant), examples such as Samuel, first-born son to Hannah, wife of Elkanah of the tribe of Ephraim, indicate an early practice of dedicating first-born sons to serve as priests.

Although scholars have attempted to find the historical background of the Exodus narratives in the reign of Pharaoh Rameses II (1290–1224 BCE), no evidence has ever been identified for a massive movement of Hebrew slaves from Egypt to the wilderness and beyond. The Egyptians were known to hold *apiru/ habiru* slaves, particularly after the period of Hyksos rule in 1800–1550 BCE, but these slaves cannot be identified with the events of the book of Exodus. By the reign of Rameses's son, Merneptah (1224–1216 BCE), Israel is a recognized semi-nomadic group in the land of Canaan.

The narrative is composed to make theological assertions concerning YHWH and the people of Israel. It does not constitute a verifiable account of Israel's history; rather, it is remembered history that explains YHWH's acts on behalf of Israel, YHWH's role in bringing about various elements of creation, and important aspects of Israel's obligations to worship YHWH and to remember YHWH's deliverance of Israel from Egypt.

The P elements of the Exodus narrative emphasize the liturgical dimensions of YHWH's actions and the construction of Israel;[5] indeed, the instructions concerning the observance of Passover is a key dimension of the P stratum. Likewise, the P identification of the divine name in Exod 6 finally identifies YHWH to Moses as the G-d of Israel who made the covenant with Israel's ancestors in Genesis (cf. Exod 3).

Insofar as the divine name is revealed in Exod 3 and 6, differentiation of the E and J strata becomes far more difficult beginning in Exod 1–12 because a primary criterion in differentiating these sources is now removed. The J stratum includes most of the basic elements of the Moses and plague narratives, and may well be responsible for identifying Moses as a Levite in keeping with the role played by the Levites as priests and the celebration of Passover in the Jerusalem Temple.[6] Although J has extensively reworked the underlying E narrative to portray Judean elements of religiosity and the understanding of YHWH in the Exodus, vestiges of the E narrative nevertheless appear at various points, such as the burning bush episode in Exod 3, which portrays Moses' encounter with YHWH through an angel. E concerns may also underlie the motifs of creation, particularly since northern Israel shared with Judah an understanding of YHWH as creator of the natural world, and the redemption of the first-born, which would explain the origins of northern Israel's understanding of priesthood.[7]

c. From Raamses to Sukkot: Consecration of the First-Born

Exodus 12:37—13:19 recounts Israel's journey from Raamses to Sukkot, which constitutes the first stage of the Exodus from Egypt. The site of Sukkot remains uncertain, although many identify it with the Egyptian city or region of Tjeku (Tel Maskhuta) located on the eastern edge of the Nile Delta region.[8]

This unit marks the formal departure of Israel from Egypt and the beginning of its journey into the wilderness and on into the promised land following 430 years of slavery. It numbers Israel at 600,000 men, apart from women and children, and an unspecified mixed multitude that travelled with them. The mixed multitude appears to be foreigners who joined Israel, and sometimes they function as a source of tension and apostasy among the people. The passage adds descriptions of the unleavened bread that the Israelites took with them in their haste to depart, which both explains the use of Matzot (unleavened bread) at Passover as well as the practice of offering unleavened bread at the sacrificial altar of the Temple. The all-night vigil likewise highlights an observance of Passover.

The bulk of the passage takes up instructions concerning the observance of Passover. The first set of instructions in Exod 12:43-51 takes up the Passover sacrifice. All Israel is commanded to eat the Passover sacrifice, but foreigners may eat of it only after they have been circumcised, which would constitute an ancient and formal ceremony of conversion to Judaism. The second set of instructions takes up the first-born. In keeping with the laws of Exod 34:18-20, Exod 13:1-16 calls for the consecration of first-born humans and animals to G-d, and it provides additional instruction concerning the observance of Passover, including the seven days of eating Matzot or unleavened bread to remember the Exodus from Egypt, the obligation to teach one's children about the significance of Passover as YHWH's deliverance of Israel from Egypt, the obligation to make this teaching a sign on the hand and forehead, and the obligation to devote the first-born to YHWH. Although first-born clean animals are to be offered to YHWH, first-born asses and human beings are redeemed.

Altogether, the passage emphasizes the observance of Passover as a means to commemorate YHWH's actions in delivering Israel from Egypt.

Diachronic reading of this passage indicates that it is a combination of various sources. Some have argued that it is D,[9] although most consider it to be a combination of P, E, J, and perhaps an unknown source.[10] The P stratum focuses on defining the observance of Passover by Israel alone, but it specifies the means by which foreigners might become a part of Israel by circumcision (conversion) and thus join in the observance. The underlying E material provides basic instruction concerning the observance of the seven days of Matzot, which accompany the one day of Passover, and the dedication of the first-born to G-d. Such dedication would explain the practice of offering the first-born of the flocks and herds to YHWH at the Temple, and the practice of dedicating the first-born sons as priests to officiate over the offerings to YHWH (cf. 1 Sam 1–3). Insofar as Passover is a spring festival, it celebrates new life in the world of creation and human beings as well as the Exodus from Egypt.

d. From Sukkot to Etham: The Pillar of Fire and Cloud

The brief notice in Exod 13:20-22 of Israel's journey from Sukkot to Etham highlights YHWH's guidance of the people in the form of a pillar of cloud by day and a pillar of fire by night. Generally assigned to the J stratum,[11] the image of cloud and fire identifies YHWH's presence among Israel with the imagery of the altar of the Jerusalem—or any—Temple. When offerings are burned on the Temple altar, the rising pillar of smoke, fire, and cloud can be seen from miles around and become a visible means to portray YHWH's holy presence.

e. From Etham to the Sea: Deliverance at the Reed Sea

Exodus 14:1—15:21 presents the culminating event of YHWH's deliverance of Israel from Egypt at the Reed (Red) Sea.[12] The narrative combines interests in the depiction of G-d as the creator of all the world and as deliverer of Israel, the liturgical worship of YHWH in the Temple and the depiction of the divine presence as a pillar of fire and cloud, and the theological motif of the hardening of Pharaoh's heart. Altogether, the passage continues in its focus on laying the foundations for Israel's identity as a nation delivered by YHWH once it enters the promised land.

The narrative essentially functions as a mythological portrayal of combat between YHWH and Pharaoh at the Reed Sea, although it is clear from the outset that Pharaoh is little more than a foil to YHWH with little capacity to act independently and no possibility to triumph. Although Pharaoh had earlier agreed to let Israel go free, YHWH hardens Pharaoh's heart once again so that the miraculous nature of the deliverance—and thus YHWH's power—may be recognized.

YHWH's role as deliverer is clear when the pillar of fire and cloud—now identified as the angel of G-d—moves to a position between Israel and the sea, on the one hand, and the approaching Egyptian chariots, on the other hand. As instructed by YHWH, Moses extends his hand and rod over the sea. The motifs of YHWH as creator come to the forefront as the east wind, that is, the Sharav/ Hamsin or sirocco, blows to divide the waters of the sea, allowing dry land to emerge in the midst of the waters. Such a scenario is a reprise of the creation account in Gen 1, in which dry land likewise emerges from the waters. As the pillar of fire and cloud holds back the Egyptians, Israel crosses the sea to the safety of the opposite shore. Although the Egyptian army attempts to flee, YHWH hurls them into the sea, which closes over and drowns them when Moses extends his rod once again.

Israel's witness of YHWH's power in delivering them from Egypt prompts the liturgical singing of the Song of the Sea in Exod 15. The song is cast in the form of a classical hymn of song of praise which celebrates YHWH's great acts in delivering Israel from Egypt.[13] In presenting the song of the sea, the narrative sets the paradigm for liturgical worship of G-d in Israel's temples once they are settled into the promised land. It is noteworthy that while Moses and Israel sing the song in Exod 15:1-19, Miriam and the women likewise sing the song in Exod 15:20-21, which suggests the participation of women in liturgical worship.

Interpreters generally consider the Song of the Sea in Exod 15:1-19 as a non-source text, although it appears in the context of the P and EJ framework.[14] Such a contention indicates that the Song of the Sea was a part of northern Israelite worship that was taken up by the E stratum and later contextualized by both J and P into a narrative that would also inform Judean liturgy.

The mythological character of the narrative and the Song of the Sea are crucial, insofar as they depict YHWH's use of the sea to defeat Egypt, a very human enemy. The hymn takes up motifs that are well known from Ugaritic mythology, viz., the defeat of the sea god, Yamm, by the Canaanite storm god, Baal, who then emerges as the head of the Ugaritic pantheon. It likewise calls to mind the defeat of the sea monster Tiamat by the Babylonian city god, Marduk, who likewise becomes creator and head of the Babylonian pantheon as Babylon becomes capital of an empire. The Song of the Sea challenges these notions by depicting YHWH's absolute power over both nature and human events, viz., the sea is not an agent that challenges YHWH, but only functions as a tool under YHWH's control to defeat the Pharaoh of Egypt as the very human protagonist of the narrative. In contrast to YHWH, Baal and Marduk must struggle to overcome and subdue the elements of nature. Not only does Israel witness YHWH's power at the sea, the nations also watch as YHWH leads Israel through the sea to YHWH's holy sanctuary (Exod 15:13-18) to confirm to both Israel and the nations of the world that YHWH is the ruler of all creation.

f. From the Reed Sea to the Wilderness of Shur/Elim: Water in the Wilderness

The brief narrative in Exod 15:22-27 reiterates the depiction of YHWH as master of creation and as healer. When Israel comes to the bitter and undrinkable waters at Marah, G-d shows Moses a type of tree or bush that could be used to sweeten and purify the water. But this narrative also sets the theme for the wilderness rebellion motif that will emerge as a major theological problem throughout the wilderness narratives. YHWH states the terms for the relationship with Israel, that is, if the people observe YHWH's commandments, YHWH will not bring plagues against like those that afflicted the Egyptians.

This narrative is a combination of P, J, and non-source elements.[15] Insofar as the wilderness traditions depict Israel's wilderness rebellion in relation to northern Israelite practice, they appear to represent a Judean polemic against the north that is designed to explain the theological problem of northern Israel's demise by charging northern Israel with rebellion against YHWH. The P and J character of this narrative would then serve such an effort by emphasizing that observance of YHWH's will is key to Israel's welfare in the wilderness.

g. From Elim to the Wilderness of Sin: Quails and Manna

Exodus 16:1-36 begins to focus more intently on the wilderness rebellion motif as Israel sets out on its way to Mt. Sinai. Such a portrayal enables the narrative to reiterate YHWH's roles as master of creation and deliverer of Israel, but it also provides an opportunity to demonstrate that the Shabbat, the holy seventh day of rest (Gen 2:1-3), is inherent in the natural order of creation. These motifs allow the narrative to contrast YHWH's mercy and patience with Israel's ingratitude and impatience. When faced with a lack of food, the people complain that they would have been better off dead in Egypt than out in the wilderness, which must be recognized as a caricature of Israel designed to highlight the growing tension between the people and G-d and the roles that Moses and Aaron—the Levites— must play in mediating the relationship between them. YHWH's provision of food is also a caricature as YHWH employs creation to rain down bread (Manna) and quails for the people to eat, covering the camp. In portraying YHWH's mercy, however, the narrative is careful to tie in the question of the observance of YHWH's commandments, in this case, observance of Shabbat, insofar as no one is to gather food on Shabbat and a double portion of food is provided on the sixth day so that no work will be necessary on the seventh. Of course, some in the camp gather on the seventh day, which provides the opportunity for YHWH to chastise the people for their behavior. At this early point in the wilderness rebellion traditions, there is little in the way of retribution for the violation of YHWH's commands, although as tensions build during the course of the later narratives, G-d's impatience with Israel will grow, leading to disastrous consequences.

Again, the narrative is the product of the P and J strata which signals the role of Judean interests in presenting Israel's rebellion in the wilderness as a means to chastise northern Israel and to explain the theological problem of northern Israel's demise. Insofar as the narrative would be read by Judeans following the Babylonian exile, it also provides the opportunity for Judean introspection when Judah suffered the same consequences as its northern neighbor.

h. From Sin to Rephidim: Amalek and Jethro

Exodus 17:1—18:27 takes up two sets of concerns. The first is YHWH's sustenance and protection of Israel in the wilderness, and the second is Jethro's advice to Moses to set up a judicial system in Israel to assist him in administering a large and often contentious nation. As priest of Midian, Jethro serves as a representative of the divine, and his statements in the narrative indicate his adherence to YHWH.

The lack of water at Rephidim provides the occasion once again to stress YHWH's role as creator as the basis for YHWH's sustenance of Israel, but it also presents the people's complaining to Moses about his role in leading them from Egypt to the wilderness. The people's complaint and longing for secure lives in Egypt are once again a caricature, but the purpose is to highlight tensions within the community and to contrast the people's attitude with YHWH's deliverance of them from Egyptian bondage and care for them in the wilderness. YHWH instructs Moses to use his rod to produce water from the rock, but the narrative emphasizes that this is the same rod that Moses used to strike the Nile to produce the plagues against Egypt. Such a notice highlights the character of YHWH as a potential threat to the people as well as their deliverer, and again aids in building toward the conflict that will erupt between YHWH and the people later in the wilderness.

The narrative concerning the attack against Israel launched by Amalek likewise highlights YHWH's protection of Israel in the wilderness as well as the role of the rod of Moses in symbolizing that protection. As long as Moses' hands with the rod of G-d were stretched out, Israel would prevail over Amalek, but if his hands tired, Amalek would prevail. Because Aaron and Hur stepped in to support Moses' arms, Joshua was able to defeat Amalek. The basis for the curse leveled against Amalek by YHWH promising to blot out the name of Amalek is not entirely evident in the immediate context. The attack is unprovoked, but Deut 25:18 makes it clear that the Amalekites attacked defenseless stragglers at the end of Israel's column in a bid to wipe out Israel entirely. The command to blot out Amalek is applied in general to those who would destroy Israel, such as Haman, who is a descendant of the Amalekite King Agag in the book of Esther (Esth 3:1; 1 Sam 15:32).[16]

The narrative concerning Jethro is only loosely tied to the portrayal of YHWH as creator—and only because Moses first encountered Jethro in the wilderness of Sinai. Instead, it is an attempt to shift the emphasis on the motif of YHWH's care for Israel in the wilderness from the provision of water and protection to the provision of a court system as a means to resolve conflict in Israel and aid in creating a stable and productive society. In this respect, the narrative anticipates the revelation of divine law at Sinai which is soon to follow.

The narrative first establishes Jethro's identification with YHWH. Jethro comes to see Moses in order to return his wife, Zipporah, and their two sons, Gershom and Eliezer, whom Moses had sent away. Many contend that Moses divorced Zipporah, and later references in Num 12 to Moses' Cushite wife, perhaps a woman other than Zipporah, and the portrayal of Midianite woman in Num 25 as leading Israelite men into apostasy aids in reinforcing such a perception. Jethro's recounting of YHWH's acts on behalf of Israel aids in building the motif of the nations' witness of YHWH, but Jethro's statement in Exod 18:10-11 that YHWH is blessed for delivering Israel from Egypt and that YHWH is greater than all gods indicate that Jethro is an adherent of YHWH. Such a contention of course builds on the portrayal of Jethro's presumed ancestor, Cain, in Gen 4 and the statement in Gen 4:26 that people began to invoke the name of YHWH in the time of Cain. Rabbinic tradition reads his statement as an indication that Jethro converted to Judaism.[17] The second portion of the Jethro narrative focuses on Jethro's advice to Moses to establish a judicial system to assist him in arbitrating disputes among Israel. The appointment of honest, just, and G-d-fearing judges from among the people of Israel recognizes the need to establish an institutional judicial system to serve the needs of a large nation rather than the model of a tribal chieftain who decides all matters himself. The role of the chieftain remains in place, however, insofar as Moses—as Levite—becomes the chief magistrate, a role that is reserved for the Levites in Deut 16:8-13.

The diachronic dimensions of this narrative emerge in relation to the identification of its compositional strata.[18] Although the narrative is placed within a P framework, it is largely an EJ production. J elements appear in Exod 17 as a means to contrast Israel's complaints against YHWH with YHWH's care for the people. Nevertheless, the appearance of the elders of Israel, a northern Israelite institution, in the narrative suggests that J has reworked underlying E material to highlight polemics against the north. The Jethro narrative is an E production that has been placed in the J framework to anticipate the revelation of law. Moses is not clearly identified as a Levite in this narrative, and the appointment of non-levitical judges suggests a practice of northern Israel as well.

i. From Rephidim to Sinai: Revelation of Torah

The lengthy narrative concerning the revelation to Israel of YHWH's Torah at Mt. Sinai comprises Exod 19:1—Num 2:34 and serves as the centerpiece of the entire Torah narrative. Its components include the arrival at Sinai in Exod 19:1-2, revelation from the mountain in Exod 19:3—40:48, revelation from the Tabernacle in Lev 1:1—27:34, and the census and organization of the people around the Tabernacle in Num 1:1—2:34.

1) Arrival at Sinai

Exodus 19:1-2 provides an introduction to the Sinai narrative with a brief notice of Israel's arrival at Sinai. The date of the arrival—on the third new moon following Israel's departure from Egypt—establishes the date of the festival of Shavuot, "Weeks," which commemorates the revelation of Torah together with the conclusion of the grain harvest. As a P composition, the notice functions as part of the P framework for the Torah.[19]

2) Revelation from the Mountain

The narrative in Exod 3:3—30:38 concerning the revelation of YHWH's Torah from Mt. Sinai begins with the portrayal of the people gathered at Mt. Sinai in Exod 19:3-25. The narrative deliberately correlates the roles of Mt. Sinai and the Jerusalem Temple as the central loci for the revelation of YHWH's Torah in an effort to correlate YHWH's roles as creator of the universe and deliverer of Israel.[20] The Jerusalem Temple after all is conceived as the holy center of creation in ancient Judean thought.[21] In this case, YHWH's role as deliverer of Israel does not take the form of combat against an enemy, but as the teacher of the laws that will provide the foundation of a just, holy, and stable society once the nation is established in the promised land of Israel.

Several dimensions of the narrative indicate that Mt. Sinai is stylized as the Temple. First is the command that the people are to be considered as a kingdom of priests, a holy nation, and a treasured people for YHWH, insofar as they are expected to express their holiness by observing YHWH's covenant and teaching their children what YHWH did for them in delivering them from Egypt. In this respect, Israel serves as a priestly nation among all the nations of the world. Second is the portrayal of YHWH in thick cloud, which symbolizes the thick smoke of the Temple incense burners that fill the Temple when YHWH is manifested in the Holy of Holies. The later references to lightning and thunder reflect the ten Menorot or lamp stands that flash light in the midst of the incense smoke and the sound of the shofars or ram's horns that are sounded in the Temple at times of worship. The third is the setting of boundaries at the base of the mountain beyond which Israel must not step, which symbolizes the holy boundaries of the Temple courts and the fact that only the priests may enter the Temple. The fourth is the need for the men to purify themselves by washing themselves and their clothing and avoiding sexual contact with women before appearing at the mountain, much as they would be expected to do before appearing at the Temple. Finally, the need for the priest to remain pure as he represents the people before G-d symbolizes the role of the high priest during Temple worship in later times.

G-d's revelation of Torah to the people commences with the Ten Commandments in Exod 20. Although they are frequently viewed as the basic law of ancient Israel, the Ten Commandments are not law per se because their forms as categorical imperatives and prohibitions render them impossible to adjudicate in a court of law. Instead, they must be viewed as statements of the ideal principles, both religious and civil, that underlie the ancient Israelite and Judean legal systems. The first command appears in vv. 2-3, which include YHWH's statement of self-identification followed by the prohibition against having other gods besides YHWH. The command establishes YHWH's fundamental identity for Israel as sole G-d and deliverer from Egypt, and thereby becomes a principle that Israel must recognize forever. The second command in vv. 4-6 reinforces the first by prohibiting the manufacture and worship of images in any form to represent YHWH. YHWH's following promise to punish those who reject YHWH to the third and fourth generations or to show fidelity to those who love YHWH to the thousandth generation becomes the subject of debate in biblical tradition. Ezekiel (Ezek 18) and 1-2 Chronicles (2 Chr 36), for example, maintain that each generation is not punished or rewarded based on the actions of its forbears, but is solely responsible for its own fate. The third command demands that the people not swear falsely in the name of YHWH, which aids in maintaining justice in the Israelite/Judean judicial system and rejects the notion that YHWH can be controlled in any fashion by one who utters the divine name.[22] Jewish tradition understands this command to be a prohibition against uttering the holy name of G-d at any time, except when the high priest enters the Holy of Holies of the Jerusalem Temple at Yom Kippur. The fourth command in vv. 8-11 demands that Israel remember and sanctify the Shabbat by forgoing all work on the seventh day. The basis for this command appears in creation itself insofar as YHWH rested on the seventh day after having created the world during the preceding six days. This command differs from its corresponding form in Deut 5:14-15, which calls upon Israel to observe the Shabbat and states that YHWH's deliverance from Egyptian bondage is the basis for Shabbat observance. The two versions are generally understood to provide a comprehensive basis for Shabbat observance in pentateuchal tradition. The fifth command in v. 12 calls upon the people to honor their fathers and mothers, which aids in establishing respect for the authority of older generations as a means to create social stability in Israelite/Judean society. The sixth command is a prohibition against murder. Although the command is often incorrectly understood as a categorical prohibition of killing in general, it is directed specifically against illegal killing. The seventh command prohibiting adultery protects the integrity and sanctity of the marriage relationship and thereby aids in promoting social stability. The eighth command prohibits stealing, which likewise promotes social stability with respect to the ownership of property or rights of any kind. The ninth command prohibits bearing false witness, which protects the integrity of the Israelite/Judean court system. Finally, the tenth command prohibits coveting a neighbor's house, wife, slaves, animals, and any property in an attempt to address one of the fundamental causes of societal discord and illegal acts.

The following passage in Exod 20:15-23 establishes Moses as the intermediary between YHWH and the people, which sets the pattern for the role of the priesthood in Israelite and Judean temples. Not only will the priests serve as intermediaries, their duties include the teaching of divine Torah, its implementation, and its adjudication. The command to build an altar for YHWH establishes the institutional context in which the people will relate to YHWH at the temples by means of liturgy and offerings. The instruction is careful to differentiate Israelite/Judean practice from that of other nations, and the altar or temple site then becomes the place associated with YHWH and the revelation, teaching, and implementation of divine Torah.

The first major body of law appears in Exod 21–23, which includes a comprehensive and basic set of civil and religious law for ancient Israel and Judah. Exodus 21:1—22:26; 23:1-9 contain the civil laws that are designed to implement justice in the life of the people and thereby to constitute an ideal society. Topics include all the basic laws that would lead to social stability and the resolution of problems in Israel's social life. The initial slave law sets the terms by which men and women serve a term of service to repay debt, although women are sold into a marriage that cannot be terminated unless the husband fails to meet his responsibilities whereas the man goes free if he so chooses after a period of six years of service. Issues of murder and manslaughter are addressed; whereas murder is punishable by death, manslaughter calls for the provision of refuge. Kidnapping and reviling one's parents are capital crimes. Issues of assault, battery, accidental injury, and property damage are all assigned their respective penalties and means of compensation. The principle of *Lex Talionis*, in which an attempt is made to set a principle of reciprocity for the resolution of death, injury, and property damage appears in Exod 21:23-24 (cf. Lev 24:17-21; Deut 19:21), although later rabbinic tradition sees in this statement a principle of compensation for such acts rather than one of inflicting a similar punishment on the perpetrator. The ox-goring laws are commonly employed both in Israel and ancient Near Eastern law as examples for the adjudication of issues of death, bodily injury, property damage, and liability under various sets of circumstances. Other issues of theft, property, and sexual or marriage issues are also treated. Various statements of principle appear, for example, sorcery, bestiality, sacrifice to foreign gods, oppression of foreigners, oppression of widows and orphans, mistreatment of the poor and employees, and the overturning of justice in the courtroom are not tolerated. Religious laws appear in Exod 22:27-30; 23:10-19, such as the prohibition against reviling G-d or rulers among the people as well as the commands to bring offerings from the first fruits, first-born sons, and first-born cattle to G-d. The basis of such religious commands, including the proper use of meat for food (and thus the treatment of living creatures; cf. Gen 9), is to ensure the sanctity of the people before G-d. The religious commands include observance of every seventh year as a time to allow land to lie fallow, observance of Shabbat, and the three major festivals, Matzot or Unleavened Bread in the spring (Passover), the Harvest (of grain; Shavuot), and the Ingathering (of fruit; Sukkot) at the end of the year. Each of these festivals marks the stages of the Israelite agricultural season in the natural cycle of the year, and all Israelite men are required to bring the first fruits of the harvest, herd, and flock associated with each festival as offerings to YHWH. Each festival is later identified with historical events as remembered in Jewish tradition, that is, Passover and the Exodus from Egypt, Shavuot and the Revelation of Torah at Sinai, and Sukkot or the period of Wilderness Wandering.

The concluding material in Exod 23:20-33 emphasizes the role of YHWH's angel to protect Israel, to drive out foreigners from the land promised to Israel, and to turn against Israel should the nation fail to observe YHWH's will. In addition to the concern with prohibiting worship of foreign gods, YHWH's role as creator enters into the picture as even the wild animals of the land will turn against Israel should the people fail to adhere to YHWH. The ideal boundaries of the land extend from the Sea of Reeds (Red Sea) and Sea of Philistia (Mediterranean) to the Euphrates River in Mesopotamia.

Exodus 24 depicts the sealing of the covenant between YHWH and Israel. Together with Moses, Israel's key institutional leaders, Aaron and his sons, representing the future priesthood, and the seventy elders, representing the civil leadership of the nation, ascend the mountain to conclude the covenant. The visionary portrayal of YHWH depicts YHWH enthroned in the heavenly court. The sapphire pavement for YHWH's feet would represent the firmament of the heavens or sky (Gen 1:6-8). The meal eaten by the participants represents the sacrificial meals to be eaten at the temples at times of worship. But only Moses would ascend into the clouds at the top of the mountain to receive the balance of the Torah, much as the high priest would later enter into the Holy of Holies of the Temple to appear before YHWH.

Scholars have had difficulty pinpointing the compositional origins of Exod 19–24 in relation to the major pentateuchal strata. Exodus 19 and 24 are generally attributed to a J reworking of earlier E material, with some editing by the P stratum.[23] The Ten Commandments in Exod 20 are generally assigned to the E stratum,[24] although the Covenant Code has proved resistant to source assignment.[25] Nevertheless, the many allusions to the Covenant Code in Amos's oracle against northern Israel in Amos 2:6-16 indicate that the Covenant Code was set in northern Israel at least by the mid-seventh century BCE,[26] which coincides with the time when most[27] interpreters believe that the E stratum was composed. Such a scenario suggests that northern legal instruction in Exod 19–24 was reworked into a J narrative stratum and later adapted to the context of the P Sinai Pericope. The E stratum of this material would have presented the Ten Commandments and Covenant Code as revelation by YHWH so that these materials would function as basic legal instruction in northern Israel. The J redaction of this material would have been part of an effort to lay the basis for the resumption of Davidic rule over the north in the time of Josiah by identifying Sinai revelation with revelation in the Jerusalem Temple.[28] The P edition of this work would have presented it as divine revelation to be identified with the restored Jerusalem Temple in the early Persian period.

Exodus 25–31 presents the concluding segment of YHWH's initial instructions to Moses concerning the construction of the Tabernacle and its furnishings, the establishment of the priesthood, and observance of Shabbat in the midst of Israel. Although the Tabernacle is a temporary structure, housed in a tent and designed to travel with the people of Israel through the wilderness, it quite clearly sets the pattern for the later construction of the Temple once the people have settled in the land of Israel. Like the later Temple, the Tabernacle functions as the holy center of creation and Israel insofar as it provides a visible and tangible foundation for the manifestation of divine presence and the revelation of divine instruction in the world.[29]

The construction of the Tabernacle is conceived as a tĕrûmâ, "offering," by the people of the raw materials from which the Tabernacle and its equipment will be manufactured. A tĕrûmâ refers to various offerings (Num 15:19; Deut 12:6), especially those made to support the priesthood (Lev 7:14; 22:12; Num 1:8; Ezek 44:30; Neh 10:38; 2 Chr 31:10), such as the thigh portion offered at the priestly ordination ceremony (Exod 29:27; Lev 7:34; 10:14; Num 6:1), the half-shekel tax for maintaining the sanctuary (Exod 30:13), the tithe of the Levites (Num 18:24), and the designation of land for the holy Temple (Ezek 45:1 6; 48:8, 10).

YHWH's instruction concerning the construction of the various holy items includes: the ark in which the tablets of the covenant are to be placed (Exod 25:10-16); the cover for the ark including the two cherubim, which symbolize the throne of YHWH (Exod 17–22); the table and its equipment for the presentation of the bread/challah before YHWH (Exod 25:22-30); the lamp stand and its seven lamps, which illuminate the sanctuary and symbolize the light at creation, the tree in the garden, and divine instruction (Exod 25:31-40); the Tabernacle structure per se, which includes a Holy of Holies where the Ark will reside as well as a courtyard area before the Holy of Holies (Exod 26:1-37); the sacrificial altar that will reside in the courtyard (Exod 27:1-8); and the enclosures that will define the sacred boundaries of the Tent of Meeting which houses the entire sacred structure (Exod 27:9-19). Altogether, the Tabernacle constitutes a portable sanctuary in the midst of Israel during the wilderness period, and it represents a model for the construction of the Temple once the people are settled in the land of Israel.

Instructions concerning the institution of the priesthood and the liturgy include: the production of pure olive oil to be used for the continuous lighting the sanctuary (Exod 27:20-21); the manufacture of the priestly vestments to indicate the sanctity of the priests who will serve before YHWH in the Tabernacle and later in the Temple (Exod 28:1-43); the ordination ceremony for the consecration of the priests for holy service before YHWH and to serve as intermediaries between YHWH and the people (Exod 29:46); the construction of the incense altar for the continuous offering of incense before YHWH (Exod 30:1-10); the census of the people and the obligation to pay the Temple tax for the support of the sanctuary (Exod 30:11-16); the construction of the laver or wash basin for the purification of the priests who will serve in the sanctuary (Exod 30:17-21); the manufacture of aromatic anointing oil for the consecration of the priests (Exod 30:22-33); the manufacture of the incense to be offered before YHWH (Exod 30:34-38); the designation of Bezalel ben Uri ben Hur of the tribe of Judah to serve as master craftsman for the construction of the Tabernacle and its equipment and Oholiab ben Ahisamach of the tribe of Dan to assist Bezalel (Exod 31:1-11); and finally the instruction to observe the holy Shabbat as a sign of the *běrît 'ôlām*, "eternal covenant" between YHWH and Israel to consecrate Israel as a holy nation (cf. Exod 19:6) in the midst of creation (Exod 31:12-17). At the conclusion of the instruction narrative, YHWH gives Moses the two tablets of the covenant to take to the people waiting below (Exod 31:18).

Although the account of Israel's compliance with YHWH's instructions concerning the building of the Tabernacle will follow in Exod 35–40, the Exodus narrative first turns to an account in Exod 32–34 of Israel's apostasy against YHWH by constructing and worshipping the golden calf at the base of Mt. Sinai. While Moses was on the mountain with YHWH receiving the divine Torah for forty days, the people waiting at the base of the mountain were growing anxious when he did not return. As a result, they collected gold from their own possessions and brought it to Aaron, who fashioned it into a golden calf for the people to worship. Having been warned by YHWH of the people's apostasy, Moses first convinces YHWH not to destroy the people lest YHWH's own divine integrity come into questions. He then descends from the mountain with the tablets of the covenant in his hands to find the people engaged in the illicit worship of the golden calf. He shatters the tablets, destroys the golden calf, and calls for those who are for YHWH to stand with him. When the Levites respond to his call, Moses commands them to kill all who had sinned against YHWH by taking part in the worship of the golden calf.

Following the slaughter of the guilty by the Levites and a plague by YHWH that further decimated the people, the narrative takes the opportunity to reflect on this episode by portraying a dialog in the Tent of Meeting between Moses and YHWH in which Moses asks YHWH to let him know YHWH's ways and to continue to lead the people through the wilderness. In essence, Moses asks YHWH to maintain the relationship between YHWH and Israel. As a result of this encounter, YHWH instructs Moses to prepare two new tablets for the covenant, and then YHWH reveals the divine presence to Moses on Mt. Sinai. The revelation comes in an enumeration of the divine qualities in Exod 34:6-7, which define the divine name in relation to the fundamental attributes of mercy and justice that YHWH's name represents. On the one hand, YHWH's compassion is described at length, but on the other hand, YHWH's capacity to do justice and to punish wrongdoing is also described at length. By defining both sides of the holy personality, the narrative presents a deity who shows mercy and compassion by creating the world and by delivering Israel from Egyptian oppression, together with the divine capacity to punish not only the Egyptians when it suits the divine purpose to do so, but Israel as well when Israel turns against YHWH. In this respect, the narrative addresses the human experience of both mercy and judgment in the world.

During the course of this encounter, YHWH instructs Moses to write a new set of tablets. The resulting laws in Exod 34:10-26 reiterate much of what has already been said in the Covenant Code of Exod 21–23, but it reorganizes and adds new material so that the new law code begins with prohibitions against making covenants and marriages with the pagan peoples of the land as well as the worship of their gods. On the basis of this encounter, Moses is changed, insofar as his face is radiant when he descended from the mountain with the new set of tablets in hand. As a result, he would wear a veil when he was among the people, but would remove it when he entered the Tent of Meeting to appear before YHWH.

At the synchronic level, Exod 32–34 clearly functions as a means to address problems in the relationship between YHWH and Israel, particularly Israel's experience of evil in the world—for example, foreign invasion, exile from the land, the destruction of the Temple, and son on.—despite YHWH's promises of fidelity to the covenant.[30] Although the narrative notes the problems in YHWH's holy character, viz., YHWH is both a beneficent and a dangerous presence, it deliberately focuses on Israel's apostasy as the cause for the disruption of the relationship. In doing so, it defends YHWH as ultimately righteous and justified in the actions taken here, and instead emphasizes the responsibility that human beings have in maintaining the relationship with YHWH. To a large degree, such claims redefine the notion of covenant insofar as YHWH's failure to protect the people in times of crisis is blamed on the people themselves in an effort to exhort them to greater efforts to adhere to their own requirements in the covenant relationship. Indeed, the question is debated elsewhere in the Bible as well, viz., whereas much of biblical literature accepts the notion that YHWH righteously judges the people, works such as Psalms, Job, Esther, Lamentations, and Song of Songs, and pericopes such as Gen 18, 1 Kgs 22, and Jer 20 probe the questions of divine capriciousness and absence so that biblical literature effectively engages in dialog with itself by presenting a variety of viewpoints on the issue. In the present case, the issue is not resolved, insofar as tensions between YHWH and Israel— and YHWH's own impatience—become major issues throughout the rest of the wilderness narratives, culminating in YHWH's decision to destroy the wilderness generation—and Moses—prior to their entry into the promised land of Israel.

Exodus 32–34 must also be considered in relation to its diachronic dimensions.[31] Although the bulk of the Sinai pericope is P stratum material, Exod 32–34 is largely a J narrative that has reworked underlying E material. It is striking therefore that it employs models of northern religiosity to convey the sins of the Israelites in the wilderness, viz., the golden calf is the icon placed by King Jeroboam ben Nebat, the first king of northern Israel, in the sanctuaries at Dan and Beth El and northern Israel was known for not having a Levitical priesthood (1 Kgs 12:25-33). Although readers of 1 Kgs 12–13 are accustomed to think of northern worship and practice as idolatrous, they must recognize that the golden calves functioned only as mounts above which YHWH was conceived to be enthroned, much as the Cherubim of the Ark of the Covenant functioned in the Jerusalem Temple. The J form of the narrative is designed to explain the fall of the northern kingdom of Israel as a consequence of sin and thereby to exhort southern Judean readers to redouble their adherence to YHWH through the Jerusalem Temple during the period of the late monarchy. Insofar as the narrative draws heavily on several key intertexts—that is, the Covenant Code in Exod 21–23, the command against marrying the Canaanite nations in Deut 7:1-6, Elijah's experience of YHWH at Mt. Horeb in 1 Kgs 19—the narrative was written as part of an effort by King Josiah to justify his program of religious reform and national restoration, in part by pointing to the example of northern Israel and by redoubling efforts to revere YHWH in the Jerusalem Temple under the supervision of the Levitical priesthood. Exodus 32–33 was easily picked by P and incorporated into the priestly narrative of the revelation at Mt. Sinai as a means to explain the reality of exile and the need to adhere to YHWH in the late- and post-exilic periods.

The segment of the Sinai pericope concerning YHWH's revelation from the mountain concludes with the account of Israel's compliance with the instructions to build the Tabernacle in Exod 35–40. The passage largely reiterates the elements laid out in Exod 25–31, although it takes special care to note the role that the people play both in offering the materials necessary for construction, as well as in carrying out the work of construction under the supervision of Bezalel and Oholiab. In this respect, the Tabernacle is indeed a *tĕrûmâ* or offering by the people (cf. Exod 25:2). Key dimensions of this narrative appear in Exod 35:2-3, which calls once again for observance of the Holy Shabbat as a means to sanctify both creation and the people in Exod 40:34-38 when YHWH's presence fills the Tabernacle after the work of construction and sanctification was completed. In this manner, YHWH's holy presence would be manifested among the people in the Tabernacle throughout the rest of the wilderness period and in the temples once Israel had settled in the land. Indeed, interpreters have noted that the completion of the Tabernacle and YHWH's identification with it constitute a stage in the completion of creation that began in Gen 1:1—2:3, particularly since various statements from Gen 1:1—2:3 are reiterated or echoed in Exod 39:43 (cf. Gen 1:31); Exod 39:32 (cf. Gen 2:1); Exod 40:33b-34 (cf. Gen 2:2); Exod 39:43 (cf. Gen 2:2); and Exod 39:43 (Gen 2:3).[32] Because the Temple is the Holy Center or the Microcosm of Creation, the manifestation of YHWH's presence in the Temple and the observance of Shabbat both complete and sanctify creation as anticipated in Gen 2:1-3.

NOTES

[1] Nahum Sarna, *Exploring Exodus: The Heritage of Biblical Israel* (New York: Schocken, 1986), 39.

[2] For analysis of this formula and its variations, see Rolf Rendtorff, *Die "Bundesformel." Eine exegetisch-theologische Untersuchung* (SBS 160; Stuttgart: Katholisches Bibelwerk, 1995).

[3] See Isa 6, in which Isaiah is commanded to make Israel blind, deaf, and dumb so that YHWH's power might be revealed.

[4] For discussion of the natural background of the plagues, see especially Sarna, *Exploring Exodus*, 68–73.

[5] For the P elements of the narrative, see Antony F. Campbell and Mark A. O'Brien, *Sources of the Pentateuch: Texts, Introductions, Annotations* (Minneapolis: Fortress Press, 1993), 35–30.

[6] For the J stratum of the narrative, see Campbell and O'Brien, *Sources of the Pentateuch*, 131–42.

[7] For the E elements of the narrative, see Campbell and O'Brien, *Sources of the Pentateuch*, 183–85.

[8] Jo Ann H. Seely, "Succoth," *ABD* 6:217–18.

[9] Martin Noth, *Exodus: A Commentary* (OTL; Philadelphia: Westminster, 1962), 101.

[10] Campbell and O'Brien, *Sources of the Pentateuch*, 40, 142, 185, 198, but cf. William H. C. Propp, *Exodus 1–18* (AB 2; Garden City; Doubleday, 1999), 373–80, who considers the passage to be largely a P reworking of an underlying E stratum.

[11] Campbell and O'Brien, *Sources of the Pentateuch*, 143.

[12] Hebrew *yam sûp* means "sea of reeds," apparently in reference to the marshes that mark the transition from the Nile delta region to the wilderness. Later traditions, such as the Septuagint, understand the term as a reference to the Red Sea.

[13] George W. Coats, *Exodus 1–18* (FOTL 2A; Grand Rapids: Eerdmans, 1999), 117–20.

[14] Campbell and O'Brien, *Sources of the Pentateuch*, 40–41, 143–44, 185–86, 198.

[15] Campbell and O'Brien, *Sources of the Pentateuch*, 41, 144, 198.

[16] See Zev Garber, "Reconstructing Theodicy and Amalekut: A Personal Apologia," in *Shoah: The Paradigmatic Genocide. Essays in Exegesis and Eisegesis* (Studies in the Shoah 8; Lanham: University Press of America, 1994), 119–36.

[17] See Judith Baskin, *Pharaoh's Counselors* (BJS 47; Chico: Scholars Press, 1983), 45–74.

[18] Campbell and O'Brien, *Sources of the Pentateuch*, 43, 144–45, 186–87.

[19] Campbell and O'Brien, *Sources of the Pentateuch*, 43.

[20] See Jon D. Levenson, *Sinai and Zion: An Entry into the Jewish Bible* (Minneapolis: Winston, 1985); see also Ronald E. Clements, *G-d and Temple: The Presence of G-d in Israel's Worship* (Philadelphia: Fortress Press, 1965).

[21] Jon D. Levenson, "The Temple and the World," *JR* 64 (1984): 275–98.

[22] Egyptian incantations indicate that proper pronunciation of a divine name gave the speaker control over the deity in question.

[23] See Campbell and O'Brien, *Sources of the Pentateuch*, 43, 144–46, 187–89.

[24] Campbell and O'Brien, *Sources of the Pentateuch*, 188–89.

[25] See Campbell and O'Brien, *Sources of the Pentateuch*, 199, who assign Exod 21–23 to the non-source materials of the Pentateuch.

[26] See my *The Twelve Prophets* (BO; Collegeville: Liturgical, 2000), 1:214–18.

[27] Levenson, *Sinai and Zion*, especially 187–217.

[28] Cf. my *King Josiah of Judah: The Lost Messiah of Israel* (Oxford: Oxford University Press, 2001), passim.

[29] Cf. Levenson, "The Temple and the World."

[30] See my discussion in *Reading the Hebrew Bible after the Shoah: Engaging Holocaust Theology* (Minneapolis: Fortress Press, 2008), 52–57.

[31] See my study, "The Wilderness Traditions of the Pentateuch: A Reassessment of their Function and Intent in Relation to Exodus 32–34," in *Society of Biblical Literature1989 Seminar Papers*, ed. D. J. Lull (Atlanta: Scholars Press, 1989), 291–99, which traces the intertexual relations of Exod 32–34.

[32] For discussion of these interrelationships, see Levenson, *Creation and the Persistence of Evil*, 85–86; Michael Fishbane, "Genesis 1:1–2:4a: The Creation," in *Text and Texture: Selected Readings of Biblical Texts* (New York: Schocken, 1979), 1–16, 143–44, especially 11–13, 144.

3) Revelation from the Tabernacle

With the completion of the Tabernacle and the manifestation of divine presence within, revelation may now proceed from the Tabernacle itself in Lev 1–27.[1] Insofar as the Tabernacle is constituted as the prototypical Temple, revelation from the Tabernacle sets the pattern for the function of the Temple as the source for divine revelation for Israel and the world at large at the holy center of creation.[2] Whereas the revelation from the mountain focused on the basic laws that would constitute Israel's social and religious life, as well as the laws concerning the construction of the Tabernacle at its center, revelation from the Tabernacle now focuses on the means by which Israel would sanctify itself and thereby enter into a relationship with YHWH that would enable Israel to serve as a priestly people that would undertake the task of initiating the sanctification and completion of creation at large.

The book of Leviticus asserts YHWH's holy character throughout and calls upon Israel to sanctify itself so that it will be able to relate to YHWH and thereby to carry out the divine will. Leviticus presumes YHWH's transcendent character, viz., YHWH is both wholly and holy other than the world of creation and stands above and beyond that world. As creator and sovereign of all creation, YHWH is in no way subservient to creation, but instead is able to direct all creation at will. As the eternal creator and sovereign of creation, YHWH brings life and fertility to the world, although YHWH is also capable of bringing death and devastation. As creator and sovereign, YHWH also brings wisdom, knowledge, and order to the world so that creation can flourish.

Human beings are created in the image of G-d (Gen 1:26-27). They possess knowledge of good and evil like that of YHWH and the capacity to create life as a result of Eve's actions in the Garden of Eden, but human beings still need to learn to employ that knowledge and capacity properly in order to carry out their task as partners with G-d in the completion and sanctification of creation. The completion and sanctification of creation facilitate the emergence of an ideal creation and ideal life within creation. In contrast to YHWH, however, human beings are not eternal and therefore are subject to death. Insofar as the improper use of knowledge is the antithesis of wisdom and death is the antithesis of life in Leviticus, human beings are antithetical to the divine presence, which therefore poses a danger to human beings insofar as they attempt to enter into the divine realm without proper preparation. The revelation from the Tabernacle in Lev 1–27 aims to prepare human beings to appear before YHWH in the holy realm of the Tabernacle or Temple and thereby to learn to fulfill their role as partners with G-d in the completion and sanctification of creation. The priesthood plays a key role in preparing Israel for its holy role, and Israel in turn will act as priests in instructing the rest of the world as well.

YHWH's revelation of divine instruction from the Tabernacle proceeds in three basic stages, viz., (1) instruction in Lev 1–7 concerning the presentation of offerings to YHWH at the Tabernacle or Temple that establish Israel's relationship with YHWH; (2) instruction in Lev 8–10 concerning the establishment of the priesthood that will represent Israel before YHWH and represent YHWH before Israel in order to facilitate their relationship; and (3) instruction in Lev 11–27 concerning the various dimensions of the purification or sanctification of the people so that their relationship with YHWH is possible.

Chapters 1–7 of Leviticus present the instructions concerning the offerings that the priesthood will make to YHWH on Israel's behalf at the holy Tabernacle or Temple in order to establish the holy relationship with YHWH. Five offerings are included in the instructions, viz., the *'ôlâ* or "whole burnt offering" in Lev 1; the *minḥâ*, "gift" or "grain offering," in Lev 2; the *zebaḥ šělāmîm* or "sacrifice of well-being" in Lev 3; the *ḥaṭṭa't*, "sin offering"; and the *'āšām*, "guilt offering," in Lev 4–5. Finally, the summation of the offerings appears in Lev 6–7. The first two offerings, the *'ôlâ* and the *minḥâ*, are voluntary offerings that are presented regularly in the Temple in order to establish a relationship with YHWH. The *šělāmîm* is also a voluntary offering that is presented on special occasions as a means to acknowledge or thank YHWH for some good or blessing that has occurred in the life of the party presenting the offering. The *ḥaṭṭa't* and the *'āšām* are expiatory offerings that are presented to atone for some wrong, whether done deliberately or in error, by the party presenting the offering. In all cases, the offerings are presented as a means to maintain the relationship between Israel—both collectively and individually—with YHWH and thereby to play a role in establishing the sanctity of the nation.

YHWH's first instruction speech to Moses in Lev 1–3 takes up the three voluntary offerings, the *'ôlâ*, the *minḥâ*, and the *zebaḥ šělāmîm*. YHWH's instructions for the first of these offerings, the *'ôlâ*, appears in Lev 1:2b-17.[3] The *'ôlâ* is a whole burnt offering that is presented by an individual or by the nation at large to honor YHWH. Insofar as the *'ôlâ* is entirely consumed upon the altar, it is a quintessential gift offering to YHWH that establishes and maintains the relationship of the presenter with YHWH. The instructions focus especially on the correct procedures to be followed by the priest in presenting the offering and thereby in ensuring its sanctity before YHWH. The *'ôlâ* may be chosen from the herd (cattle), the flock (sheep or goat), or birds (turtledoves or pigeons). In the case of herd or flock, it is to be a male without any blemish. The gender of the birds is not specified, although they are also presumed to be without blemish. The choice of animals for the offering is drawn from those that could be consumed as food by the people (see Lev 11). The choice of gender is not explained, although as regular offerings, the male animals would presumably correspond with the male priests who are obligated to present the offerings. The specification that the animals be without blemish ensures that the presenter does not undermine the sanctity of the honor given to YHWH by using the sacrifice as an occasion to dispose of defective livestock. Although YHWH has no need for food, the offering is presented as if it were a meal. In this manner, the procedure emphasizes that the presenter is honoring YHWH by giving to YHWH an animal that would otherwise be used for food. The offering thereby constitutes a sacrifice on behalf of the presenter. The blood is drained and dashed against the altar to signify the holiness of the life of the animal that is offered to YHWH, the animal is flayed and cut up, and its entrails are washed as if it were to be eaten, and finally the whole of the animal is placed upon the altar and burnt entirely as an offering to YHWH.

YHWH's instructions for the *minḥâ* appear in Lev 2:1-16. The *minḥâ* is an offering of fine flour, oil, and frankincense, which emphasizes its character as choice food that would otherwise have been consumed by the presenter. The *minḥâ* differs from the *'ôlâ*, however, in that the priests offer only a portion of the *minḥâ* on the altar but retain the rest for their own consumption. The *minḥâ* thereby functions not only as a means to honor YHWH, but as a means to support the priests as well. The instruction specifies the different types of *minḥâ* offerings, viz., unleavened cakes baked in an oven with oil baked in, wafers spread with oil and cooked on a griddle or pan. Leavened flour is not permitted since fermentation altars the state of the flour through a process of decomposition. Salt is to be included insofar as it impedes fermentation.[4] The offering of first fruits allows for the honoring of YHWH at the very outset of the harvest season.

The instructions for the *zebaḥ šĕlāmîm* appear in Lev 3:1-17. No occasion is listed for this sacrifice, but subsequent discussion in Lev 7:11-36 indicates that it is celebratory insofar as it is offered in thanks. Like the *'ôlâ*, the *zebaḥ šĕlāmîm* is a male animal without blemish, chosen from the herd or flock. No bird is specified, presumably because the *zebaḥ šĕlāmîm* is a celebratory offering and a bird is an offering made by someone who lacks the means to make a better offering. The *zebaḥ šĕlāmîm* is initially slaughtered and its blood drained and dashed against the altar like the *'ôlâ*, but it is not entirely consumed on the altar. All the kidneys and liver and the fat associated with them are offered on the altar and burned. The rest of the animal, however, is to be eaten by the presenter, although the right thigh and the breast are retained by the priest (see Lev 7:11-36).

YHWH's second instruction speech to Moses in Lev 4:1—5:13 takes up the *ḥaṭṭa't*, the "sin offering" or the "purification offering,"[5] which is made when a person—including the anointed priest of the sanctuary—or the community at large intentionally or unintentionally violates one of the prohibitions enjoined upon Israel in YHWH's Torah. Insofar as the majority of YHWH's commands in the priestly legislation are prohibitions, the *ḥaṭṭa't* covers a very wide range of acts. The instructions for presenting the *ḥaṭṭa't* presuppose that the violation of YHWH's Torah pollutes the Tabernacle/Temple altar or even the Tabernacle/Temple itself as well as the nation at large. Insofar as the Tabernacle and later the Temple serve as the holy center of creation, the violation of YHWH's Torah corrupts all of creation, requiring that the offenders and the sanctuary must be purified in order to restore the sacred order of creation as a whole.

Leviticus 4:1—5:13 provides instruction for a variety of circumstances in which the *ḥaṭṭa't* must be offered. The first appears in Lev 4:3-12, in which the anointed priest of the sanctuary—also known as the high priest (Lev 21:10; Num 35:25)—is the offending party. Such an offense would likely be some error committed in the course of his officiating on behalf of the people at the sanctuary, which would compromise both the sacred character of the nation as a whole and the order of all creation. In such an instance, the priest is required to bring a bull, the largest and presumably the most costly of the sacrificial animals, to the sanctuary as a *ḥaṭṭa't* offering. He sprinkles blood from the *ḥaṭṭa't* before the Holy of Holies of the sanctuary, upon the incense altar, and upon the sacrificial altar, to purify each from the corruption suffered as a result of the sin committed by the priest. He offers the *ḥaṭṭa't* much as the *zebaḥ šĕlāmîm* is offered, that is, the bull is flayed and the kidneys and liver are burned on the altar. Unlike the *zebaḥ šĕlāmîm*, however, the rest of the animal is not eaten. Instead, it is entirely burned at a clean place outside of the camp or city so that it does not provide the occasion for a festive meal, but instead functions as a sacrifice on behalf of the offending party.

Leviticus 4:13-21 specifies a similar procedure in case the transgression is committed by the entire nation. Although it is sometimes difficult to imagine how everyone in a nation might be guilty of transgression, Levitical law presupposes a sense of corporate responsibility in which the entire nation is collectively responsible for moral action in the world. The procedure for the community *ḥaṭṭa't* differs only in that the high priest offers the *ḥaṭṭa't* on behalf of the community, viz., the elders lay hands on the *ḥaṭṭa't* as representatives of the people and then the priest carries out the offering much as he would if he had been the offending party.

Leviticus 4:22-26 takes up the case in which the *nāśî'*, a tribal chieftain or leader of the people, transgresses YHWH's Torah. The transgression of the chieftain appears to be a less serious offense insofar as a presumably less expensive male goat rather than a bull is required for the *ḥaṭṭa't* and its blood is applied only to the sacrificial altar and not to the interior of the sanctuary. Leviticus 4:27-31 prescribes a similar procedure for a case in which an individual person from the nation inadvertently commits a transgression, except that it calls for a female goat to be offered as a *ḥaṭṭa't*. A female goat would be somewhat more precious than a male goat because its capacity to reproduce and to provide milk would also be sacrificed. Leviticus 4:32-35 presents an alternative case in which a female sheep, instead of a goat, is offered as a *ḥaṭṭa't*. In all cases, the offering of the *ḥaṭṭa't* symbolizes divine forgiveness for the transaction, although it must be recognized that divine forgiveness comes only from G-d, not from the offering per se.

Leviticus 5:1-13 concludes the *ḥaṭṭa't* instruction by envisioning a number of specifications to the general *ḥaṭṭa't* instructions. It specifies examples of the transgressions which a person might commit, that is, refusing to testify under oath when having knowledge of a matter; inadvertently coming in to contact with something unclean, such as an animal corpse; coming into contact with some human uncleanness; or failing to fulfill an oath. In addition, it specifies alternatives to the standard *ḥaṭṭa't* offerings in case a person cannot afford them. Alternatives include two turtledoves or two pigeons, one to be offered as a *ḥaṭṭa't* and the other as an *'ōlâ*, or a tenth ephah of fine flour. Again, the *ḥaṭṭa't* symbolizes divine forgiveness.

YHWH's third instruction speech in Lev 5:14-19 takes up the *'āšām* offering. The *'āšām* is often considered to be a "guilt offering," although the requirement to give restitution in the cases of transgression indicate that it must be considered as a "reparation offering."[6] The *'āšām* differs from the *ḥaṭṭa't* in that it calls for restitution, whereas the *ḥaṭṭa't* does not. It may apply to cases of the "sacred matters of YHWH" (Lev 5:15-16) as well as to the common matters in which the *ḥaṭṭa't* is required (Lev 5:17-19). Whereas the *ḥaṭṭa't* takes up offenses that cannot be repaid—because nothing tangible is lost—the *'āšām* presupposes that restitution is possible, either to YHWH (Lev 5:15-19) or to an individual (see on Lev 5:20-26, below). The *'āšām* offering in the case of the sacred things of YHWH is a ram without blemish from the flock or its equivalent in cash, and an additional 20 percent of its value, perhaps to be paid in cash, is given to the priest. In the case of common matters, the additional 20 percent is not required for the priest. Perhaps the offender was expected to make restitution to the party that sustained the loss. The *Lex Talionis* (Exod 21:23-24; Lev 24:17-21; Deut 19:21) makes it clear that an offending party is liable for death or injury and various laws specify liability for property loss or damage.[7] Although the offender must repay the party that sustained the loss, he also has an obligation to make reparation to YHWH for having disrupted the sacred order of creation.

YHWH's fourth instruction speech in Lev 5:20-26 makes this last principle clear by specifying restitution in relation to the *'āšām* offering. The instruction specifies cases of deliberate crimes against YHWH that are committed against individuals among the people, viz., deceit in deposits or pledges, robbery, fraud, lying about lost property that was found, or swearing falsely about a matter. The instruction requires reparation to the party suffering loss, including both the value of what was lost and an additional 20 percent. In addition, the *'āšām* offering must be presented at the sanctuary so that the offending party might seek forgiveness for the transgression.

The five instruction speeches by YHWH to Moses in Lev 6–7 both summarize the instructions concerning the offerings discussed in Lev 1–5 and add specifications to each of them. The first speech in Lev 6:1-11 takes up the *'ōlâ* and the *minhâ*. It specifies procedures for the removal of ash from the *'ôlâ*, while calling for the altar fires to burn continuously, and it adds instructions concerning the preparation and eating of the *minhâ*. The second speech in Lev 6:12-16 specifies the *minhâ* offering required of the priests. The third speech in Lev 6:17—7:21 specifies procedures for the handling and eating of the *hatta't*, the *'āšām*, and the *zebah šĕlāmîm*. The fourth speech in Lev 7:22-27 prohibits the eating of fat or blood (cf. Lev 17:10-16). The fifth speech in Lev 7:28-36 specifies the presentation of the *zebah šĕlāmîm*, and stipulates the portions that are due to the priest. Leviticus 7:37-38 concludes this section with a summary-appraisal form.[8]

Leviticus 8–10 turns to the consecration of the priesthood that will represent Israel before YHWH and YHWH before Israel. The ordination ceremony for the priests has already been prescribed in Exod 29, but it is carried out in Lev 8 to consecrate Aaron and his sons, Eleazer, Ithamar, Nadab, and Abihu, as priests. Consecration of the priests is necessary to establish relationship between the otherwise incompatible holy sphere of G-d and heaven and the profane sphere of creation and humanity. As representatives of Israel before the Holy G-d, the priests must also be made holy so that they may enter the holy precincts of the sanctuary without fear of death. Once ordained, the priests are expected to maintain their holy status by restricting contact with the profane world outside of the sanctuary.[9] The consecration comprises a series of acts that sanctify the priests for their holy service. First, they are washed with water to begin the process of purification. Second, they are dressed in the priestly garments, including the breast piece with the Urim and Thummim that mark them for their holy roles. Third, they are anointed with oil, a cleansing agent in the ancient world, to purify them for holy service, and the oil is also applied to the altar and its utensils. Fourth, they present a *hatta't* or sin offering as part of the process of purification, and blood from the *hatta't* is applied to the altar to purify it as well. Fifth, a ram is presented as an *'ôlâ* or whole burnt offering to establish relationship with YHWH. Sixth, a second ram is presented as a *millû'îm* (lit., "filling" their hands to undertake their task) or ordination offering and blood from the offering is applied to the ears, thumbs, and big toes of Aaron and his sons to consecrate them, much as the altar was consecrated with the blood of the *hatta't*. Together with the *minhâ*, Aaron and his sons offer the required portions of the *millû'îm* offering to begin their holy service. Blood from the *millû'îm* offering is mixed with oil and applied to the altar and to Aaron and his sons once again to purify them. At the conclusion of the ceremony, Aaron and his sons are given instructions for their preparation and eating of the *millû'îm* and *minhâ* offerings. They are instructed to remain in the sanctuary for seven days to complete the process of ordination, after which they are consecrated for holy service at the altar. Altogether, the ordination constitutes a holy rite of passage from the profane to the sacred sphere so that the priests can act as intermediaries between YHWH and the people.

With the instruction concerning the consecration of the priests complete, Lev 9–10 turn to the first episode in which the priests would officiate at the altar in order to reveal the presence of YHWH. In presenting this episode, these chapters illustrate both the proper role of the priests and the consequences of improper action when Aaron's sons, Nadab and Abihu, attempt to offer alien fire before YHWH. The passage underscores the importance of scrupulous adherence to holy ritual action before YHWH. Leviticus 9 narrates the first presentation of offerings before YHWH, in which Aaron and his sons first present the offerings of the people. Aaron and sons are instructed to offer a *ḥaṭṭa't* and an *'ôlâ* on their own behalf prior to offering the *ḥaṭṭa't*, *'ôlâ*, *zebaḥ šĕlāmîm*, and *minḥâ* offerings on behalf of the people. If all goes well according to holy procedure, Moses and Aaron enter the Tent of Meeting to appear before YHWH, and YHWH's presence is manifested when fire from YHWH consumes the offerings. Leviticus 10 then relates the consequence of the abrogation of holy procedure. Aaron's sons, Nadab and Abihu, put fire and incense into their fire pans and attempt to offer alien fire before YHWH. The problem emerges when Lev 10:1 stipulates that Nadab and Abihu were attempting to make an offering that was not stipulated by YHWH, that is, only the high priest makes incense offerings (Exod 30:7-8). On the one hand, Nadab and Abihu went beyond the holy actions enjoined upon the priests, perhaps in their zeal to serve YHWH, and on the other hand, perhaps they were taking upon themselves the role of high priest. By either interpretation, the consequences are disastrous; fire comes forth from YHWH—much like the fire that consumed the sacrifices—to consume Nadab and Abihu for their abrogation of holy ritual. YHWH's statement in Lev 10:3, "through those near to Me I show Myself holy, and gain glory before all the people," reiterates the principle of divine holiness and the strict requirement to adhere to holy action on the part of the priesthood. Leviticus 10:8-11 further stipulates that the priests are to drink no intoxicating beverages when serving in the sanctuary, and that their quintessential roles are to distinguish between the holy and the profane and the clean and the unclean, and to teach Israel all the statute commanded by YHWH to Israel through Moses.

Leviticus 11–27 then turns to instruction concerning the various dimensions of the sanctification of the people before YHWH. This section is organized as a series of instruction speeches by YHWH to Moses on the various topics, including human consumption of meat (Lev 11); impurity after childbirth (Lev 12); impurity resulting from skin diseases (Lev 13 and 14); impurities resulting from bodily discharges (Lev 15); the sanctification of the sanctuary (Lev 16); the proper slaughter of animals and treatment of blood (Lev 17); improper sexual relations (Lev 18); laws of holiness (Lev 19); the disposition of cases involving improper religious practice and sexual relations (Lev 20); proper conduct and status of the priests (Lev 21); priestly handling of offerings (Lev 22); observance of sacred times (Lev 23); burning of lamps and presentation of bread in the sanctuary (Lev 24:1-9); blasphemy (Lev 24:10-23); disposition of land (Lev 25–26); and Temple tax, vows, and tithes.

Leviticus 11 takes up the human consumption of meat. The killing of animals for food disrupts the stability and sanctity of creation by introducing death and the spilling of blood. The spilling of blood by human beings was one of the issues that led to the flood in Gen 6–9, but the issue was resolved by allowing humans to spill blood under a restricted set of conditions—that is, they may not consume the blood nor may they spill the blood of a human. Leviticus 11 aids in defining those conditions by stipulating that only a very few types of animal may be killed for food, which thereby limits the bloodshed that human beings may perpetrate. Animals designated for food include those that have cleft hooves and that chew the cud, fowl with the exceptions specified, fish with fins and scales, winged swarming things that have jointed legs and walk on all fours. All other animals, fowl, fish, and insects are prohibited for use as food in order to limit the disruption of creation by the shedding of blood by human for food. The chapter also includes instruction for purification in the case of contact with unclean animals.

Leviticus 12 takes up the issue of purification of woman following childbirth. Childbirth involves the discharge of blood and the continuing flow of fluid following the discharge of blood. Insofar as blood and the following birth discharges are living matter that dies when discharged from the body, purification following childbirth involves purification following contact with death (see on Lev 11:39-40, above). The birth of a male calls for a total of forty days for purification, seven for the flow of blood and an additional thirty-three days for subsequent discharge. The birth of a female calls for eighty days of purification, fourteen for the flow of blood and an additional sixty-six days for subsequent discharge. The basis for such a distinction is not entirely clear, although it may lie in the fact that an infant girl is presumed to be a potential source of childbirth herself.

Leviticus 13–14 includes three instruction speeches that together address impurities caused by skin diseases (see the summary statement in Lev 14:54-57). Although the Hebrew term ṣārāʿat is sometimes understood as a reference to leprosy, the symptoms described do not correspond to Hanson's disease and apparently refer to some other types of skin disease that involves inflammation, swelling, and the discharge of fluid, that is, blood, pus, or other fluids, from the body through the skin.[10] Again, the operative principle is that living fluids of the body are discharged and die, resulting in contact with death. The instruction speech in Lev 13:1-59 focuses on the diagnosis and basic treatment of the affliction, the instruction speech in Lev 14:1-32 focuses on the ritual for purification once the disease is cured, and the instruction speech in Lev 14:33-53 takes up the question of an analogous affliction, that is, mold or mildew, in the walls of a house.

The instruction speech in Lev 15 addresses impurity that results from bodily discharges, including the emission of semen in men and menstrual discharge in women. Again, both instances take up the discharge of living fluid that dies upon emission from the body. Procedures and rituals for purification are specified for each case.

Leviticus 16 takes up the purification of the sanctuary on Yom Kippur, the Day of Atonement, observed on the tenth day of the seventh month each year (see Lev 16:29-31; cf. Exod 30:10; Lev 23:26-32). The instruction speech makes reference to the deaths of Aaron's sons, Nadab and Abihu, while serving at the sanctuary (Lev 10), although the intervening chapters have all dealt with impurity that would defile the sanctity of the sanctuary. By stipulating an annual purification of the sanctuary, divine Torah insures that any lingering or accidental defilement of the sanctuary is purified. The instruction stipulates that only the high priest may enter the Holy of Holies behind the curtain where the ark resides to carry out the purification and that he may do so only once a year. The purpose of the priest's appearance is to present the *ḥaṭṭa't* and *ʿôlâ* offerings that are a necessary part of the purification ritual. Insofar as YHWH appears in the Holy of Holies, the act is considered to be a visionary event (cf. Isa 6; Ezek 1–3; 8–11). According to Rabbinic tradition, the priest invokes the name of YHWH as part of the ritual of purification (see *m. Yoma* 3:8). This is the only occasion when the holy name of YHWH may be pronounced. The priest offers a bull as a *ḥaṭṭa't* offering for himself and his household and a goat as a *ḥaṭṭa't* on behalf of the people to purify the sanctuary. An additional goat is then employed as a "scapegoat" that will symbolically carry the sins of the nation out to the wilderness. The priest lays his hands on the goat, confesses the sins of the people, and then sends the goat out to the wilderness for Azazel, a name perhaps once associated with a demon of the wilderness. The priest completes the purification ritual by washing himself, by making two *ʿôlâ* offerings, one for himself and his household and one for the people, and by burning the fat of the *ḥaṭṭa't* offerings.

Leviticus 17 takes up the proper treatment of blood. Although diachronic scholarship correctly treats Lev 17–26 as a distinct document known as the Holiness Code due to the repeated injunction that the people must be holy because YHWH is holy,[11] it follows Lev 16 naturally in a synchronic reading of the text because of its concern for the proper treatment of blood in relation to sacrifice. The instruction prohibits the slaughter of animals outside of the camp unless they are brought to the sanctuary as a *zebaḥ šĕlāmîm* offering. It prohibits the human consumption of blood under any circumstances, again because blood is holy due to its association with life. In cases when a wild animal is hunted and killed for food, its blood is to be drained and buried in the earth. Finally, contact with an animal corpse requires purification by bathing.

Leviticus 18 prohibits specific sexual acts attributed to the Egyptians and Canaanites, such as incestuous sexual relations, sexual relations with a woman during menstruation (due to the flow of blood), adultery, specific acts of male intercourse with another male,[12] and bestiality. Although some maintain that this passage is concerned with protecting sexual relations devoted to procreation, such a view does not fully explain the intent of this passage since incest and adultery may also result in procreation. Rather, the underlying concerns are the maintenance of the natural order of creation and the social order of the human world as perceived by the text.

Leviticus 19 turns to an instruction speech devoted to laws of holy conduct that include both ritual laws and social laws pertaining to interpersonal conduct, personal integrity, social justice, and the obligation to ensure the well-being of all in ancient Israelite or Judean society. By combining these spheres of life, Lev 19 demonstrates that all human conduct, both in the religious realm and the realm of human social life, has an impact on the holy order of creation and that people in general have an obligation to ensure that order.

Leviticus 20 returns to the issues of sexual conduct taken up in Lev 18. Whereas Lev 18 simply stated prohibitions of such conduct, Lev 20 prescribes the disposition of such cases so that the sanctity of the nation may be preserved or restored. Insofar as Lev 18 presupposes a statement of the ideals of human conduct as understood in the text, Lev 20 recognizes that such ideals are hardly to be presumed among human beings, and specifies action to be taken in the event that such ideals are abrogated.

Leviticus 21 focuses on instruction to the priests concerning the sanctity of the priests who would present offerings at the Temple. A basic principle of these instructions is a concern to preserve and maintain the integrity and sanctity of creation through those who would appear in the Temple, the holy center of creation in Judean thought, to offer sacrifice. A variety of instructions concern the priesthood at large. First is the instruction that the priests must avoid contact with the death—since death is the antithesis of sanctity and creation in Judean thought. Allowances are made, however, for close relatives related by blood, that is, his mother, father, son, and daughter. Brothers are not included, presumably because they have their own family lines, but sisters are included if they are unmarried virgins. Priests are forbidden to alter their bodies by shaving their heads and the side growth of their beards or by gashing their bodies in a manner common in mourning rituals. Instructions concerning the marriage of priests include prohibitions against marrying harlots or divorced women because the seed of other men has already entered their bodies. The priest is also responsible for the sanctity of his daughters, as any who commit harlotry—and therefore defile themselves and their family—are subject to death. The high priest is subject to additional requirements because of his extraordinary holy status as one who enters the Holy of Holies each Yom Kippur, viz., he may not come into the contact with the dead at all (including his parents), he may not leave the holy sanctuary and enter the profane world, and he may marry only a virgin from a priestly family. Finally, priests with physical defects or injuries are not permitted to offer sacrifices because such defects or injuries compromise their ability to represent the image of G-d in which humans are created (cf. Gen 1:26-27). Temple sanctity presupposes representation of an ideal creation.

Leviticus 22 focuses on the eligibility of those who would eat from the offerings presented in the sanctuary. Because the offerings are sacred and because they are assigned to the priests, their use is forbidden to those who are outside of the priestly circle of holiness. Those who are forbidden to eat from the sacred offerings include priests who have become defiled until such time as they are sanctified once again; lay persons, unless they are formally a part of the priest's household; daughters of priests who marry laymen, unless they are widowed and return to their father's house. Further instructions are given concerning the character of animals offered in the sanctuary—that is, like the priests, they cannot be defective or blemished because they, too, represent the sanctity and integrity of creation. Young animals are not to be offered within the first seven days of their lives and not on the same day as their mothers. Thanksgiving offerings are eaten on the same day in order to avoid decomposition and contamination of the holy precincts.

Leviticus 23 presents instruction concerning the sacred calendar. The calendar sanctifies time in keeping with the references to days and seasons in the creation account of Gen 2:1-3, and it also ties the sacred calendar to the natural cycles of creation in the agricultural year. The first observance is Shabbat, which marks the culmination of creation in Gen 2:1-3 with a day of rest following the six days of work. By stipulating observance of Shabbat, Lev 23 provides a means for human beings to give expression to their creation in the image of G-d. The first of the annual holidays then follows with the observance of Pesach (Passover) and seven days of Matzot (Unleavened Bread) beginning on the fourteenth day of the first month. Although Pesach commemorates the Exodus from Egypt, Lev 23 focuses on the ritual and agricultural aspects of the festival, that is, the offering of a lamb as the Pesach ʿôlâ together with the Matzot as the minḥâ offering. Because the month of Nisan (March–April) marks the beginning of the spring harvest season, the Pesach and Matzot offerings, required of all males in Israel (see Exod 23:14-15, 17; 34:18-20, 23; Deut 16:1-8, 16-17), represent the first-born of the flock and the first-fruits of the harvests in keeping with the agricultural cycle. Seven weeks, that is, fifty days, following the presentation of the first sheaf from the harvest at Pesach, the festival of Shavuot (Weeks, see v. 15) is observed. Although Shavuot, observed in the third month (May–June, Exod 19:1) commemorates the revelation of Torah at Sinai, Lev 23 focuses on its role as the conclusion of the grain harvest in keeping with the agricultural cycle of the natural world of creation (cf. Exod 23:16, 17; 34:22, 23: Deut 16:9-12, 16-17). The third set of festivals occurs in the seventh month (Tishri, September–October). The first day of the seventh month is a Shabbaton, or day of sacred rest, at the beginning of the fall festival season. The festival is otherwise known as Rosh ha-Shanah, the beginning of the year (see Ezek 40:1) in keeping with the Babylonian calendar adopted by Judaism at some time in the Exilic or Second Temple period. The tenth day of Nisan is Yom Kippur, a day of rest, fasting, and atonement that marks the occasion of the purification of the Temple and the nation (see Lev 16). The observances of the seventh month culminate in Sukkot (Tents, Tabernacles), observed for seven days beginning on the fifteenth day of the month. The eighth day is also observed as a day of special observance called Shemini Atzeret (Eighth Day Observance). Although Sukkot commemorates the period of wilderness wandering, Lev 23 emphasizes the conclusion of the fruit harvest immediately prior to the onset of the rainy season, again in keeping with the agricultural cycle of creation (cf. Exod 23:16, 17; 34:22, 23; Deut 16:13-15, 16-17).

Leviticus 24:1-9 follows with instructions concerning continuous observance of G-d in the sanctuary apart from the weekly Shabbat and the annual festivals. The instruction calls for the continuous burning of an olive oil lamp by the priest in the sanctuary (cf. Exod 27:20-21). The second command calls for the placement of twelve loaves of bread (Challah) in rows on the Table before the Holy of Holies as a continuous offering by the twelve tribes of Israel to be eaten by the priests.

Leviticus 24:10-23 takes up the problem of blasphemy, that is, the utterance of the holy name of YHWH, which is exclusively reserved for the high priest on Yom Kippur. The placement of this narrative here follows upon the fact that preservation of the sanctity of the sanctuary and people throughout Lev 17–27 also maintains the sanctity of G-d's holy name. The fact that the blasphemer is described as the son of an Egyptian father and an Israelite mother is immaterial; the prohibition against blasphemy applies equally to Israelites and to resident aliens (*gērîm*, later understood as converts to Judaism in Rabbinic Hebrew).[13] Compromise of YHWH's sanctity is a capital crime in ancient Israel and provides once again an opportunity for a statement of the *Lex Talionis* (cf. Exod 21:33-37; Deut 19:21) to indicate that punishment must be commensurate with the crime. Again, the instruction makes it clear that this standard applies to Israelites and resident aliens alike.

Leviticus 25–26 presents instructions concerning the sanctification of the land of Israel and its ramifications for the socio-economic life of the people once they take possession of the land. Just as the nation has an obligation to ensure the sanctity of the divine name by their observance of divine instruction, so they have the obligation to sanctify the land and their lives in it. Although his passage states that YHWH's instructions were given to Moses at Sinai, the present form of the narrative provides them only at the conclusion of the revelation from the wilderness Tabernacle. The instructions begin with the sabbatical laws as applied to the land. The land is to have a Shabbat every seventh year, based on analogy with the weekly Shabbat, so that the land will have rest and lie fallow. Such an instruction presupposes that the sanctity of the land—and indeed creation itself—must emulate divine rest on the Shabbat. Because the land will not be cultivated, the people are expected to subsist on what they have stored from the previous year and what grows naturally on the land during this time. Such an observance enables the land to renew itself by lying fallow, although this is never stated in the text, and it demonstrates to the people their own dependence on YHWH's bounty as author of creation. At the end of seven weeks of year, that is, the fiftieth year after every forty-nine year cycle of seven such Shabbats for the land, a Jubilee year is declared beginning on Yom Kippur to enable both the land and the people to return to their "natural" states. In the case of the land, the Jubilee again calls for the land to lie fallow. In the case of the people, the Jubilee calls for the people to return to their ancestral tribal land that is assigned to each of the tribes of Israel. Land assignments to the tribes in Israel are considered to be permanent, and the sale of land is not a permanent sale per se, but a form of debt relief in which the buyer leases the land from its owner with the intent that the owner or his heirs will one day repay the sale price and resume possession of the land. Ultimately, the Jubilee system presumes that the land belongs to YHWH (Lev 25:23-24), and that the people themselves live on the land and hold permanent assignments of land at YHWH's discretion. The instructions for the Jubilee year allow for a number of provisions to take care of the poor in ancient Israel. If a man or his heirs are unable to redeem their land during the Jubilee year, a kinsman must redeem the land for them in order to return it to the family or tribe. Houses in walled cities may be sold, but houses outside of walled cities are considered open land and are subject to redemption. The property of Levites is also subject to redemption on the same terms as the other tribes. Kinsmen in economic distress may be taken as slaves, but they must be treated as family members rather than resident aliens and not charged interest. Resident aliens in economic distress may be treated as slaves, although slavery in ancient Israel calls for release at the end of six years unless the slave decides to remain a slave permanently (see Exod 21:1-11). A resident alien may also be a creditor, but the kinsmen of the debtor may redeem slaves and land held by a resident alien. In all cases of redemption, the amount of the debt is adjusted to account for the number of years that have actually passed since the presumably seven-year arrangement commenced.

Overall, Lev 26:1-2 makes it clear that the people, by observing YHWH's instructions, avoid idolatry, keep YHWH's holy Shabbat, and revere YHWH's sanctuary. All of these concerns play a role in sanctifying YHWH, the nation, and creation at large.

The so-called blessings and curses section in Lev 26:3-46 makes it very clear that Israel's observance of YHWH's instruction has a major impact on the sanctity and stability of creation and their own place in the land of Israel. The blessings in vv. 3-13 tie Israel's observance of YHWH's instructions specifically to elements of creation, viz., the rains and the earth's ability to yield produce. It expands its purview by taking in peace from enemies in the land and the continuity of YHWH's covenant with the nation, culminating the continued presence of YHWH's holy sanctuary among the people. The curses in vv. 14-45 go into far greater detail, presumably to convey the reality of the threats as motivation for the people to observe YHWH's instructions. Again, the curses stress a combination of natural disasters, such as the withholding of rain and the loosing of wild beasts, that will result in inadequate harvests and an abundance of enemies that will destroy people, fields, crops, houses, and so on, and lead them into exile. Although YHWH promises to spurn the people, in the end YHWH makes it clear that memory of the covenant with Abraham, Isaac, Jacob, and the land will result in restoration once the people atone for their iniquity.

The final elements of instruction appear in Lev 27, which takes up the financial valuations of vows and other obligations made by the people to the sanctuary. Such considerations allow for the development of a diversified cash economy in the ancient world when the distance of travel to the sanctuary and the goods possessed by the people make it difficult to pay in quantities of animals or produce so frequently stipulated in the Torah. Each person is responsible for a Temple tax, and the instruction establishes valuations, for example, sixty shekels for an adult male aged twenty to sixty; thirty shekels for an adult female; twenty shekels for a young male aged five to twenty and ten shekels for a female; five shekels for male babies and toddlers to age five and three shekels for females; and fifteen shekels for old men sixty and above and ten shekels for women. The instruction makes it clear that a valuation will be set by the priests if a person is unable to afford these amounts. Instruction concerning the valuation and assessment of animals for offerings, houses, land, dedicated to the sanctuary then follow. The last instruction stipulates that any tithes of produce due to the sanctuary may be redeemed by adding one fifth of the value, but tithes of animals may not be substituted or redeemed.

Presupposing the Wellhausenian consensus of a late nineteenth- and early twentieth-century dating, interpreters have tended to view Leviticus as largely a P composition dating to the post-exilic period of Ezra and Nehemiah. The view that the priesthood and ritual concerns could be attributed only to the post-exilic period was hardly sustainable, however, due to the increasing recognition that it was based on Wellhausen's own anti-Semitic and anti-Catholic theological views and that Israel's religious establishment was based in temples, priesthood, and ritual from the earliest periods of its settlement in the land. The deep antipathy to the priesthood and ritual matters inherent in the Wellhausenian consensus has now begun to give way to greater critical study of the P material as scholars have distinguished the P ritual texts in Lev 1–16 from the so-called and purportedly later Holiness Code of Lev 17–26 (27). Nevertheless, dating of this material is now in flux as many scholars are now beginning to consider the possibility that the literature of Leviticus originates in the monarchic period or even earlier. The concern with cultic centralization in Lev 17–26 and the response to prophetic critique have prompted some to date the Holiness material to the reign of the eighth-century monarch Hezekiah, who mounted a Temple reform program as part of his efforts to extend Davidic rule over the north following the collapse of northern Israel in 722/1 BCE. Likewise, attempts are now being made to argue that the earliest forms of the P legislation may find their earliest setting in the Shiloh sanctuary of the pre-monarchic period.[14] The observations made above concerning the specification of more generalized instruction point to a process of continuous literary-historical growth in the instructions of Leviticus. The placement of the P and H materials in the monarchic or even the pre-monarchic period, however, does not change the Persian-period setting of the P redactional framework with its literary structure based in the *toledoth* formulas.

4) Census and Organization of the People around the Tabernacle

Numbers 1:1—2:34 presents an account of the census of the people and their organization by tribes around the Tabernacle as they prepare to depart from Mt. Sinai on their journey to the promised land of Israel. The census is dated to the first day of the second month in the second year following the Exodus from Egypt (Num 1:1), which indicates that the revelation from the Tabernacle took one month to complete insofar as the divine presence descended upon the Tabernacle on the first day of the first month of the second year (Exod 40:17). The narrative indicates that the census accounts for all males able to bear arms from the age of twenty upwards (Num 1:3). The military character of the march through the wilderness makes a certain degree of sense since Israel must defend itself from enemies in the wilderness and conquer the land of Israel from its Canaanite inhabitants, but it must also be noted that the definition of males able to bear arms also corresponds to males of the age of majority who will support the central sanctuary by means of the Temple tax (Lev 27).[15] Thus, the census and organization of the people is not simply a military matter; it is also a cultic matter insofar as it points to the responsibility for supporting and protecting the sanctuary. Indeed, the identification of tribal chieftains and the placement of the tribes in order around the Tabernacle for the march through the wilderness indicate a concern to portray the march as a cultic procession with Judah in the lead and Levi tending to the Tabernacle at the center of the nation.

NOTES

[1] For the distinction between revelation from the mountain (Sinai) and revelation from the tent (Tabernacle), see Rolf P. Knierim, "The Composition of the Pentateuch," in *The Task of Old Testament Theology: Substance, Method, and Cases* (Grand Rapids: Eerdmans, 1995), 351–79, especially 360–69.

[2] Jon D. Levenson, *Sinai and Zion: An Entry into the Jewish Bible* (Minneapolis: Winston, 1985); idem, "The Temple and the World."

[3] For a model of study for this material, see especially Rolf P. Knierim, *Text and Concept in Leviticus 1:1-9* (FAT 2; Tübingen: Mohr Siebeck, 1992).

[4] Cf. Jacob Milgrom, *Leviticus 1–16* (AB 3; New York: Doubleday, 1991), 191–92.

[5] For the terminology, "purification offering," see Milgrom, *Leviticus 1–16*, 253–54.

[6] For the characterization of the *'āšām* as "reparation offering," see Milgrom, *Leviticus 1–16*, 327–28.

[7] See Exod 21:37; 22:3; Lev 5:20–26; Num 5:6-8, all of which specify restitution for destroyed or damaged property or false oaths (Milgrom, *Leviticus 1–16*, 328–29).

[8] For discussion of the summary appraisal form, see my *Isaiah 1–39, with an Introduction to Prophetic Literature* (FOTL 16; Grand Rapids: Eerdmans, 1996), 539, and the literature cited there.

[9] This proves to be an important issue in Ezekiel's conceptualization of himself as a profaned priest who must define a new role as prophet in the profane land of Babylonia (see especially Ezek 4–7). For discussion of the distinction between the holy and the profane, see especially David P. Wright, "Holiness (OT)," *ABD* 3:237–49.

[10] For discussion of leprosy in the Bible, see especially David P. Wright and Richard N. Jones, "Leprosy," *ABD* 4:277–82.

[11] For discussion of the Holiness Code, see Milgrom, *Leviticus 17–22* (AB 3A; New York: Doubleday, 2000), 1319–1447.

[12] The text prohibits specific acts of male-on-male intercourse, most likely anal intercourse (although anal intercourse with a woman is not prohibited). It does not take into account the fact that homosexual orientation and resulting lifestyle is a product of creation itself, and it does not prohibit such orientation or lifestyle, only a specific sexual act.

[13] Although some interpreters regard the blasphemer as a foreigner or resident alien, based on the presumption of a principle of patrilineal descent in ancient Israel that was later reconceptualized as matrilineal descent in the rabbinic period, it is striking that the ancestral figures in Genesis are concerned to find wives for the male figures from among those related to Israel (see the cases of Abraham and Hagar in Gen 16 and 21; Isaac and Rebekah in Gen 24; Esau and his wives in Gen 27; and Joseph and Asenath in Gen 41).

[14] See especially Israel Knohl, *The Sanctuary of Silence: The Priestly Torah and the Holiness School* (Minneapolis: Fortress Press, 1995); cf. Milgrom, *Leviticus 17–22*, 1319–67; idem, "Priestly ('P') Source," *ABD* 5:454–61. See also Antony F. Campbell and Mark A. O'Brien, *Sources of the Pentateuch: Texts, Introductions, Annotations* (Minneapolis: Fortress Press, 1993), 61–67, 200.

[15] Cf. the discussion of genre in Numbers by Rolf P. Knierim and George W. Coats, *Numbers* (FOTL 4; Grand Rapids: Eerdmans, 2005), 17–23.

12. The Generations of Aaron and Moses: Israel under the Guidance of the Levites

Numbers 3:1—Deut 34:12 is a lengthy narrative that both concludes the Torah as a whole and that presents the early history of Israel from the time of the nation's departure from Mt. Sinai through the entire period of wilderness wandering until the eve of its entry into the promised land of Israel. The Sinai revelation narrative is now complete, but Num 3:1—Deut 34:12 continues to present divine Torah through the course of the wilderness wandering as Israel encounters new situations that require continued divine instruction. Although clearly of different origins than the preceding wilderness narratives in Numbers, the presentation of Moses' last speeches to Israel in Deuteronomy add to the body of divine instruction by purportedly recounting the Sinai revelation. A close reading of the laws in Deuteronomy indicates that its review includes major substantive refinement and specification of the earlier Sinai legal instruction and even new legislation that had not appeared in the Sinai narratives. But the wilderness narratives are not only—or even predominantly—concerned with the revelation of divine law. They are also concerned with examining the very difficult relationship between G-d and Israel, Israel and Moses, and Moses and G-d. Tensions between each of the major parties included in the narratives threaten to end the covenant relationship devised between YHWH and the ancestors from the time of creation, Noah, and Israel's ancestors. In order to facilitate this relationship and address the tensions inherent between the holy G-d of Israel and the very human people of Israel, the wilderness narratives focus on the designation of the tribe of Levi and the line of Aaron through his grandson Phineas ben Elazer as the priests of Israel. It will be the task of the priests to represent Israel before G-d as well as G-d before Israel in order to provide the means to allow the covenant relationship to realize its divine purpose, viz., the sanctification of Israel and all creation before YHWH.

As in the Exodus narratives, the wilderness itinerary formulas continue to provide the synchronic literary structural markers for the narrative as Israel moves from place to place during the period of wilderness wandering.[1] Thus, the major structural components of the narrative appear as follows, viz., a) sanctification of the people led by the Levites at Sinai (Num 3:1—10:10); b) from Sinai to the wilderness of Paran and Kibroth Hattaavah: rebellion in the wilderness (Num 10:11—11:35a); c) from Kibroth Hattaavah to Hazeroth: authority within Israel (Num 11:35a—12:15); d) from Hazeroth to the wilderness of Paran: the institution of the Levites as priests (Num 12:16—19:22); e) From Paran to the wilderness of Zin/Kadesh: Moses and Aaron condemned (Num 20:1-21); f) from Zin/Kadesh to Mount Hor: the death of Aaron (Num 20:22—21:3); g) from Mount Hor to Edom/Moab: defeat of Sihon and Og (Num 21:4-35); h) arrival at Moab: the blessing of Balaam and the census and organization of the people (Num 22:1—36:13); and i) Moses' final addresses to Israel: the repetition of the Torah (Deut 1:1—34:12).

The full structural diagram of Num 3:1—Deut 34:12 appears as follows:

Israel under the Guidance of the Levites

<table>
<tr><td>XII.</td><td colspan="2">History of Israel under the Guidance of the Levites</td><td>Num 3:1—Deut 34:12</td></tr>
<tr><td></td><td>A.</td><td colspan="2">Sanctification of the people led by the Levites</td><td>Num 3:1—10:10</td></tr>
<tr><td></td><td></td><td>1.</td><td>introduction: Identification of the Levites as those to be ordained to priesthood</td><td>3:1-4</td></tr>
<tr><td></td><td></td><td>2.</td><td>commission of the Levites to serve as priests in place of first-born</td><td>3:5—4:49</td></tr>
<tr><td></td><td></td><td>3.</td><td>instruction account concerning purification of the people Israel in preparation for journey through wilderness to promised land</td><td>5:1—6:27</td></tr>
<tr><td></td><td></td><td>4.</td><td>instruction account concerning purification of the Mishkan and Levites in preparation for journey through wilderness to promised land</td><td>7:1—10:10</td></tr>
<tr><td></td><td>B.</td><td colspan="2">From Sinai to Wilderness of Paran: rebellion in the wilderness</td><td>10:11—19:22</td></tr>
<tr><td></td><td></td><td>1.</td><td>departure from Sinai</td><td>10:11-27</td></tr>
<tr><td></td><td></td><td>a.</td><td>date of departure: second year, second month, twentieth day</td><td>10:11</td></tr>
<tr><td></td><td></td><td>b.</td><td>itinerary: from Sinai to Paran</td><td>10:12</td></tr>
<tr><td></td><td></td><td>c.</td><td>organization of the march: Tribes arrayed around the Mishkan with Judah in the lead</td><td>10:13-27</td></tr>
<tr><td></td><td></td><td>1)</td><td>at command of YHWH by agency of Moses</td><td>10:13</td></tr>
<tr><td></td><td></td><td>2)</td><td>first cohort: Judah, Issachar, Zebulun; the Mishkan borne by Gershom and Merari</td><td>10:14-17</td></tr>
<tr><td></td><td></td><td>3)</td><td>second cohort: Reuben, Shimon, Gad; the Mishkan set up by Kohathites</td><td>10:18-21</td></tr>
<tr><td></td><td></td><td>4)</td><td>third cohort: Ephraim, Manasseh, Benjamin</td><td>10:22-24</td></tr>
<tr><td></td><td></td><td>5)</td><td>fourth cohort: Dan, Asher, Naftali</td><td>10:25-27</td></tr>
<tr><td></td><td></td><td>2.</td><td>journey by stages</td><td>10:28—19:22</td></tr>
<tr><td></td><td></td><td>a.</td><td>introduction to journey by stages</td><td>10:28</td></tr>
<tr><td></td><td></td><td>b.</td><td>journey by stages proper</td><td>10:29—19:22</td></tr>
<tr><td></td><td></td><td>1)</td><td>preliminary issue: account of contract with Hobab to serve as guide</td><td>10:29-32</td></tr>
<tr><td></td><td></td><td>a)</td><td>Moses' request to Hobab: "guide us in the wilderness"</td><td>10:29</td></tr>
<tr><td></td><td></td><td>b)</td><td>Hobab's response: "I'm going home"</td><td>10:30</td></tr>
<tr><td></td><td></td><td>c)</td><td>Moses' counter offer</td><td>10:31-32</td></tr>
</table>

Although the synchronic literary form of Num 3:1—Deut 34:12 presents a purportedly coherent narrative sequence, modern critical scholarship has identified a complex diachronic process of literary formation that produced the present narrative.[2] Thus, Num 3–36 constitute a P redaction of an underlying EJ narrative. The P redaction, dating to the early Persian period, ties the narrative into the overall P literary framework of the Pentateuch and treats matters of priestly concern, such as the organization of the nation around the Tabernacle in Num 3:1—10:10; the definitions of the tribes of Israel and its leaders in Num 13–14; elements of the designation of Levi as the priests of Israel in Num 16–18; reflection on Moses' and Aaron's condemnation by YHWH in Num 20; and reflection on Moses' death and the designation of Joshua and the line of Phineas ben Elazar ben Aaron as his successors for leading the people in Num 27 and 31.[3] The underlying EJ narrative, dating to the period of the later Judean monarchy, is especially concerned with examining the tensions between Israel and YHWH in the wilderness.[4] These narratives also display a special concern for addressing the theological problem of the destruction of northern Israel by the Assyrians in 722–721 BCE insofar as they so frequently portray the source of tensions in relation to practices and institutional leadership identified with the northern kingdom of Israel. In this respect, the EJ narratives of Num 3–36 display a marked Judean perspective that views Judean practice and leadership as the means to resolve the tensions between Israel and YHWH. Although worked into the P literary frame-work by comments made in the account of the death of Moses in Deut 34, Deut-eronomy constitutes a discrete D source in the Pentateuch that also dates to the later period of the monarchy, particularly the reign of King Josiah of Judah in 640–609 BCE.[5] The D material constitutes the account of legal instruction that defined the theological perspectives and practices of King Josiah's program of religious reform and national restoration in the late seventh century BCE by which he hoped to reconstitute the former Davidic/Solomonic kingdom of a united Israel and Judah. Insofar as P serves as the final redactor of Num 3:1—34:12, P took up the EJ narratives of Num 3–36, the non-source materials of the same chapters, and the underlying D material to constitute the present form of the pentateuchal text.[6]

a. Sanctification of the People at Sinai Led by the Levites

Numbers 3:1—10:10 focuses on the sanctification of the people of Israel under the leadership of the Levites and their organization around the Tabernacle as they prepare to depart Sinai for their journey through the wilderness to the promised land of Israel. The goal of the journey is to place the holy Tabernacle at the center of the land of Israel where it will serve as the holy center of creation and thereby play its role in sanctifying and completing all of creation. Although the Levites are not yet designated as the priests of Israel, earlier elements of the Sinai narra-tive, for example, the golden calf episode in Exod 32–34 and the priestly instruc-tion of Leviticus, have made it clear that the Levites will serve in this capacity. By portraying Israel's organization around the Tabernacle and under Levitical leadership, Num 3:1—10:10 presents the journey through the wilderness as a ritual or liturgical procession that would later be represented ideally by Israel's organization around the Temple. The narrative comprises four major sub-units, including an introduction in Num 3:1-4 which identifies the Levites as those to be ordained to priesthood, the commission of the Levites to serve as priests in place of the first-born of Israel in Num 3:5—4:49, the instruction in Num 5:1—6:27 concerning the purification of the people in preparation for their journey to the

promised land of Israel, and instruction in Num 7:1—10:10 concerning the
purification of the Tabernacle and the Levites in preparation for their journey to
the promised land of Israel.

The introductory segment in Num 3:1-4 identifies the following narratives as
the account of the generations of Aaron and Moses within the larger structure of
the Torah narrative. It thereby focuses on the foundation of the priestly line of
Aaron and Moses as the culminating stage of the Torah's account of the history
of creation. Aaron is the primary figure in this presentation insofar as his son,
Eleazar, will through his own son Phineas (see Num 25:10-18) become the founder of the line of high priests that will ultimately serve in the Jerusalem Temple
(1 Chr 5:27-41). His brother Ithamar is generally identified as the ancestor of
Eli and Abiathar, the high priestly line that served in the Shiloh sanctuary and
later played a role in the Jerusalem Temple (see 1 Chr 24:3-19). The two older
sons of Aaron, Nadab and Abihu, perished when they attempted improperly to
offer incense before YHWH. Moses' sons, Gershom and Eliezer, are not listed.
Gershom's son Jonathan may be identified as the priest of Dan (Judg 18:30),
although his descendants and those of Eliezer later served in the Jerusalem
Temple (1 Chr 23:15-17).

Numbers 3:5—4:49 focuses on the commission of the Levites to serve as priests
in Israel and to carry the Tabernacle and its furnishings during the course of the
Wilderness journey. The narrative makes a special point of noting that the Levites
will replace the first-born of Israel who had previously served as priests before
YHWH. First-born (to the mother) sons were claimed by YHWH, but were to be
redeemed, presumably for service to YHWH (see Exod 13:2; 22:28-29; 34:19-20).
Such a practice is not explicitly stated in the Torah, but the figure of Samuel, the
first-born to his mother Hannah who was raised in the Shiloh sanctuary to serve
as a priest (see 1 Sam 1–3), exemplifies this practice. It is also likely that the
narrative concerning the binding of Isaac (Gen 22) has a background in such
practice.

The narrative also calls for a census of the Levites, and it assigns each of the
major Levitical ancestral houses, descended from the first generation of the four
sons of Levi, to their respective places and roles in the holy procession. The house
of Gershom is placed to the west of the Tabernacle and is assigned responsibility
for the Tabernacle, the tent, hangings, the entrance screen, the cords, and the
altar. The house of Kohath is placed to the south of the Tabernacle and is assigned
responsibility for the ark, the table, the lamp stand, the altars, the sacred utensils,
and the screen. The house of Merari is placed to the north of the Tabernacle and
is assigned responsibility for the planks of the Tabernacle, the bars, posts, sockets,
and the furnishings. Finally, Moses and Aaron and Aaron's sons are placed to the
east of the Tabernacle, at the entrance, where they will lead the Tabernacle on its
journey through the wilderness. Priestly service is reserved for those aged thirty
through fifty. Although Num 8:23-26 specifies service from the age of twenty-five

through fifty, rabbinic commentary speculates that the first five years of service were a period of training or apprenticeship before the priest could assume full duties in the sanctuary at the age of thirty.

Numbers 5:1—6:27 focuses on the purification of the people in preparation for their journey through the wilderness. The presence of the holy Tabernacle among the people requires their ritual and moral purification. Leviticus earlier focused on laws of purity pertaining to bodily afflictions, blood, incest and sexual relations, moral conduct, the priesthood, observance of festivals, blasphemy, and debt issues, but Num 5:1—6:27 includes a number of other considerations not fully addressed earlier.

The first case (Num 5:1-4) is eruption or discharge, which takes up skin afflictions, sexual emissions, menstruation, as well as corpse contamination (cf. Lev 13–15; 21–22). The lack of detail to be found in the Levitical texts indicates that Lev 5:1-4 is a statement of principle that such persons are to be removed from the camp, presumably until the issue is resolved.

The second case (Num 5:5-10) takes up the moral issue of some breach of trust among human beings and with G-d. The text appears to be a basic statement of the means to resolve such issues, including confession of the wrong, restitution of the value of the offence plus an additional 20 percent, and the offering of an 'āšām or "guilt/reparation offering" (cf. Lev 5:14-26; cf. 4:1—5:13).

The third (Num 5:11-31) is the case of a woman charged by her husband with adultery. Adultery is defined here as relations between a married woman and a man other than her husband. Whereas a woman could marry only one man at any given time, a man could marry multiple wives. The underlying issue is the question of paternity of the accused woman's children and the question of the inheritance of the father's possession. The procedure specifies the offering that is to be brought to the priest and the preparation of water mixed with dirt from the sanctuary floor to be ingested by the woman as she holds the offering and swears that she has not had relations with another man. The ritual presupposes that the ingestion of the bitter water would cause a physical reaction in her womb and genital area. In the absence of such reaction, she is to be considered innocent. In most cases, the procedure would not likely cause a reaction. Although the man is considered innocent in any case, the cost of such an accusation, both in terms of the offering and the humiliation—both for the woman and the man—would presumably ensure that such an accusation would be made infrequently. One can only imagine the state of the marriage following such an accusation that demonstrated the woman's fidelity.

The fourth case (Num 6:1-21) is the Nazirite vow, which is a ritual in which an Israelite man or woman consecrates him- or herself for holy service to YHWH somewhat analogous to priestly service. Such a vow entails abstention from alcohol, cutting of hair, and contact with the dead for the term of the Nazirite vow. Priests are prohibited from drinking alcohol when serving in the sanctuary (Lev 10:9-11), and they are forbidden from shaving their heads of the side-growth of the beard (Lev 21:5) and contact with the dead (Lev 21:1-3). Samson is an example of someone who undertook a Nazirite vow (Judg 13–16). The Nazirite vow calls for a substantial offering, so that the Nazir supports the sanctuary with the offering as well as with the service performed.

Finally, the priestly blessing concludes this sub-unit in Num 6:22-27 with a call for G-d's blessing, kindness, and favor for the people. The priestly blessing presupposes the essential role of the priests to ensure the sanctification of the people before YHWH so that such blessing will result.

Numbers 7:1—10:10 focuses on the purification of the Tabernacle and the Levites in preparation for their journey through the wilderness to the promised land of Israel. A series of sub-units presents the various elements of this purification.

The first element in Num 7:1-89 recounts the offerings made by each of the twelve tribes of Israel to consecrate or dedicate the Tabernacle so that it might serve as the central sanctuary of Israel as the nation journeys through the wilderness. The offerings include six carts and twelve oxen—one cart for two tribes and one oxen for each tribe—to carry the Tabernacle offerings through the wilderness. The offerings themselves, presented by the *nāśî'* or chieftain of each tribe, includes a combination of utensils, for example, silver bowls and basins to be used in the sanctuary, as well as the *'ôlâ*, "whole burnt offering," *minḥâ*, "grain," *ḥaṭṭa't*, "sin" or "purification offering," and the *šĕlāmîm*, "well-being offering," that accompany the utensils and play roles in the dedication of the sanctuary. At the conclusion of the dedication, Num 7:89 states that Moses would hear the voice of G-d addressing him when he would enter the Tent of Meeting to speak with YHWH.

The second element in Num 8:1-4 is a brief notice concerning the role of the Levites in mounting and lighting the lamp stands of the sanctuary. The placement of this notice indicates that once the sanctuary is dedicated, the lights of the sanctuary will burn to symbolize divine presence.

The third element in Num 8:5-26 takes up the purification of the Levites for service in the sanctuary. Although the Torah has already indicated that Aaron and his sons are to be designated for service in the sanctuary (see Exod 28–29; Lev 8), the present passage specifies that the Levites will assist Aaron and his sons in the sanctuary. Here, the Levites are characterized metaphorically as a *tĕnûpâ*, "wave" or "presentation offering," made to support the Aaronide priests. The distinction between Aaron and sons and the rest of the Levites provides the basis for the later distinction in Judaism between the *kōhānîm*, "the priests" of the Jerusalem Temple who serve at the altar, and the *lĕwîyim*, "the Levites" who perform secondary duties at the Temple. The passage reiterates YHWH's decision to employ the Levites as priests in place of the first-born sons of Israel.

The fourth element in Num 8:23-26 is a brief notice that the age of Levitical service is from twenty-five through fifty. Attempts have been made to argue that the discrepancy with the age of service mentioned in Numbers, viz., thirty to fifty, indicates a five-year period of apprenticeship.

The fifth element in Num 9:1-14 focuses on the observance of Passover. The placement of this passage here makes eminent sense, since the dedication of the sanctuary would call for the observance of the first festival of the year, viz., Passover, which was celebrated from beginning on the fourteenth day of the first month of the year. Instructions concerning the observance of Passover have already appeared in the pentateuchal narrative (for example, Exod 12), but the passage is far more concerned with the observance of a second Passover for those unable to observe the first. The festival is set in the second month rather than the first, and it is intended for those who could not observe Passover due to corpse contamination or who were on a long journey and therefore unable to offer the Passover offering. Such an instruction points to the importance of observing Passover in ancient Judean/Israelite society. Provision is also made for resident aliens (understood to be converts in Rabbinic Judaism) to offer the Passover offering.

The sixth element in Num 9:15—10:10 begins with an account of the cloud, symbolizing the divine presence, settling upon the Tabernacle and the Tent of Meeting in preparation for the departure from Sinai. The image recalls the descent of the pillar of fire and cloud on the completed Tabernacle in Exod 40 as well as the image of the column of fire and cloud that led Israel through the wilderness from Egypt to Sinai. The cloud will continue to represent the divine presence through the remaining years of the journey through the wilderness. The narrative introduces YHWH's commands to manufacture two silver trumpets, sounded by the priests, that will summon the people to travel when the Tabernacle-centered procession sets out on its journey. The instruction also sets the pattern for other functions for the trumpets, viz., to summon the people in times of war and at special liturgical occasions and new moons. Rabbinic tradition reads this narrative as a basis for sounding the shofar at Rosh ha-Shanah.

b. From Sinai to the Wilderness of Paran: Rebellion in the Wilderness

Numbers 10:11—19:22 relates the departure from Sinai and the rebellion of the people against Moses and YHWH during the course of their wilderness journey.[7] The rebellion motif is frequently read as an indication of Israel's unworthiness before YHWH, but interpreters must recognize that these narratives provide a tremendous opportunity to examine key theological issues or problems in ancient Judean thought, most notably the destruction of the northern kingdom of Israel by the Assyrians in 722/1 BCE, problems in the structure of the leadership of the nation of Israel, and the character of YHWH, who stands both as author of creation and deliverer of Israel and as the deity who brings judgment against the people. To serve these ends, Num 10:11—19:22 focuses especially on northern Israelite institutions and practices, for example, the council of seventy elders

(Num 11:4-34), the role of women in institutional authority (Num 11:35—12:15), the leadership of the tribes of Israel (Num 13:1—14:49), and priestly houses associated with the north (Num 16:1—17:15). Critical examination of northern Israelite institutions and practices is designed to point to problems that, in the eyes of the Judean writers of these narratives, led to northern Israel's destruction, but they also prepare the reader for the introduction of the Levites as the priestly tribe (Num 17:16—18:32) and, most importantly, Phineas ben Elazer ben Aaron as the founder of the priestly line that ultimately served in the Jerusalem Temple (Num 25:1-18).

The narrative begins with an account of the departure from Sinai in Num 10:11-27. The date of the departure is given as the twentieth day of the second month of the second year of the people's sojourn at Sinai. Insofar as Exod 19:1 states that they arrived on the first day of the third month, the duration of their sojourn was just ten days short of a year and one month. Insofar as the divine descended upon the completed Tabernacle on the first day of the first month of the second year (Exod 40:17), the lifting of the cloud from the Tabernacle to commence the journey indicates a fifty-day period, perhaps to be compared with the fifty-day period of the counting of the Omer that begins during Passover, beginning on the fourteenth day of the first month, and concludes with the festival of Shavuot in the third month (see Lev 23:15-21).

Numbers 10:12 states that the initial stage of the journey is from Sinai to the Wilderness of Paran, but the people do not arrive in Paran until Num 12:16. In the interim, stops at Taberah (Num 11:1-3), Qivroth ha-Taavah (Num 11:4-34), and Hatzerot (Num 11:35—12:15) will be made. Consequently, Num 10:11-27 limits itself to the organization of the tribes around the Tabernacle. The people move only by the command of YHWH through Moses. Judah takes the lead, accompanied by the tribes of Issachar and Zebulun, with the Levites, Gershom and Merari, bearing the Tabernacle. This arrangement points to the leading role of Judah among the tribes and it ensures that the Tabernacle, carried by Gershom and Merari also takes the lead. The second group to set out comprises the tribes of Reuben, Shimon, and Gad, with the Levitical Kohathites who bear the sacred vessels of the Tabernacle. This arrangement includes tribes in the Trans-Jordan and Shephelah adjacent to Philistia that ultimately disappear through the course of Israel's history, but it ensures the protection of the Kohathites who bear the most sacred vessels of the Tabernacle (cf. Num 4:15-20). The third group includes the tribes of Ephraim, Manasseh, and Benjamin, who proceed without Levites. These tribes are the key tribes of northern Israel, but, in keeping with Jeroboam's decision to admit non-Levites to the priesthood in the north (1 Kgs 12:31), they are bereft of Levites and trail the two preceding processions that include Levitical presence. Finally, the fourth group includes the tribes of Dan, Asher, and Naphtali, who travel without Levites and who comprise the rear guard of Israel. Each of these tribes is peripheral; Dan is forced to move from its tribal allotment (Judg 17–18), and portions of Asher are turned over the King Hiram of Tyre by

Solomon (1 Kgs 9:10-14).[8] Naphtali is located between Asher and Dan's later
location in the northernmost portions of Israel.

The account of the journey by stages appears in Num 10:28—19:22. Numbers
10:28 introduces the account with the superscription, "These are journeys of the
people of Israel according to their hosts, and they set out (journeyed)." The
account of the journeys per se then follows in Num 10:29—19:22.

Numbers 10:29-32 relates Moses' negotiations with Hobab ben Reuel, generally
recognized as an alternative name for his father-in-law Jethro, to serve as Israel's
guide in the wilderness.

Numbers 10:33—11:34 recounts the initial three-day stages of the journey to
Taverah and Qivrot ha-Taavah. Numbers 10:33-34 makes it clear that the people
are led through the wilderness by YHWH, portrayed metaphorically as the pillar
of fire and cloud associated with the Ark of the Covenant. Numbers 10:35-36
presents Moses' songs of the Ark, spoken when the Ark would set out and when it
would halt.[9] Both of these segments function as a means to convey the divine
leadership of the procession (through Moses), which will be challenged through
the course of the following narratives.

The initial accounts of the complaints of the people in the wilderness appear in
Num 11:1-34. The first account in Num 3:1-3 sets the basic pattern of conflict
between the people and G-d with basic statements of the people's complaints,
YHWH's angry reaction, and Moses' role as intercessor between the two parties.
The place is called Taberah, "Burning," after the fire from YHWH that threatened
the people. The second account in Num 11:4-34 is much more substantive, insofar
as it takes up questions of food for the people in the wilderness, the observance of
Shabbat, and the question of institutional authority or leadership in the nation.
The account begins in Num 11:4-9 with the complaints of the people concerning
the lack of meat. The portrayal of the people's complaints is a caricature, insofar
as they reminisce about the supposedly wonderful food they enjoyed in Egypt—as
slaves! But the narrative quickly shifts in Num 11:10-23 to the developing crisis in
the relationship between YHWH and Moses. Here, Moses complains to YHWH
about the burdens of his leadership over the people. Again, the narrative employs
caricature when Moses demands that YHWH kill him if he is to be subjected to
such abuse by YHWH. In a manner reminiscent of Exod 18, YHWH tells Moses
to gather seventy elders among the people to assist him in leading the people.
Again, caricature appears when YHWH snidely states that the people will eat
meat until it comes out of their noses. When Moses protests, YHWH rebukes him
for questioning divine power. Resolutions and further complications follow. The
seventy elders are endowed with divine spirit and begin to prophesy, which
presents a potential challenge to Moses' leadership of the people. Finally, the
people eat their fill of quail provided by YHWH, but YHWH then strikes the
people who craved meat with a plague, much like the plagues visited upon Egypt.
As a result, the place was named Qivroth ha-Taavah, "graves of craving." A key
element of this narrative is the authority granted to the seventy elders, the ruling

council of northern Israel both prior to the monarchy and during the monarchy itself.[10] Insofar as tensions between the nation, Moses, and YHWH increase in the following narratives, readers may question the effectiveness of the seventy elders as leaders. In this respect, the narrative both accounts for the origins of this northern Israelite institution and critiques its effectiveness.

Numbers 11:35—12:15 portrays the people's journey from Qivroth ha-Taavah to Hatzeroth where Aaron and Miriam question Moses' leadership. The basis for the challenge is his marriage to a Cushite woman. Cushite is generally understood to refer to an Ethiopian, but it may also refer to the Midianites as Hab 3:7 equates Cushan and Midian. Thus, the woman in question may be the Midianite Zipporah, or it could be another woman that Moses married after he sent Zipporah and her children away (Exod 18:2). In either case, the issue is Moses' marriage to a foreign woman, particularly since he is both a Levite and leader of the nation. Although relations with Midianite women are later condemned (see Num 25:6-18), the narrative makes it clear that YHWH supports Moses as leader. Miriam becomes the object of YHWH's punishment when she is stricken with leprosy for a period of seven days. Aaron is strikingly omitted from the punishment, perhaps because he is destined to sire the priestly line of Jerusalem. Once again, Judean polemic against the north emerges, insofar as women seem to play an important leading role in northern Israel. Miriam's leading the women in liturgical song at the Red Sea (Exod 15:20-21), Deborah's acting as judge over Israel (Judg 4–5), women taking part in the service and liturgy of the Shiloh temple (1 Sam 2; 21), and the inscriptional references from Kuntillet Ajrud to YHWH of Samaria and his Asherah, all indicate that women played liturgical roles in northern Israelite religious practice.[11] By contrast, women play no apparent institutional role in the Jerusalem Temple and their leadership functions were limited after King Asa of Judah deposed his mother, Maacah, as Gebirah or Queen Mother (1 Kgs 15:9-15).

Numbers 12:16—19:22 presents a series of episodes concerning Israel's rebellion against YHWH and Moses in the wilderness which culminate in the selection of the Levites, particularly Aaron and his sons, to serve as priests in Israel, that is, intermediaries in the relationship between YHWH and the nation. Insofar as the line of Aaron ultimately forms the basis of the Jerusalem priesthood, Judean polemics against the north continue to define the perspective of these narratives. The sequence begins with a brief notice in Num 12:16, which introduces the narrative block with a notice of Israel's journey from Hatzeroth to the Wilderness of Paran. The following sequence once again focuses on Judean polemics against northern Israelite figures and institutions.

The first narrative in the sequence is the spy narrative of Num 13:1—14:49. The narrative relates that twelve spies, one representing each of the twelve tribes of Israel, were sent to scout out the land of Canaan and report back to Moses. At the end of forty days, the spies return and complain that the people of Canaan are too powerful for Israel to overcome. Only Caleb, of the tribe of Judah, asserts that Israel can overcome the Canaanites. Much later in the narrative, he is joined in his assessment by Joshua ben Nun of the tribe of Ephraim. Because of the spies' report, the entire people rebel against Moses, Aaron, and YHWH, accusing YHWH of bringing the nation to the desert to die and demanding that they return to Egypt. YHWH responds by accusing the people of a lack of faith and by proposing to kill the entire nation and to make a new nation of Moses. Moses' response to YHWH lays out the theological problems of YHWH's response much as he did in the golden calf episode of Exod 32–34, viz., he argues that YHWH will appear powerless in the eyes of the Egyptians and the nations at large and that they will conclude that YHWH has broken the oath sworn to the people to bring them into the land of Canaan. The formulaic citation of YHWH's qualities of justice, drawn from the longer liturgical rehearsal of YHWH's mercy and justice in Exod 34:6-7, underlines the theological assessment of YHWH's character. By shortening the citation, Num 14:18 focuses only on YHWH's capacity for punishment, and it urges YHWH to refrain from doing so. As a result of Moses' arguments and appeal, YHWH retracts the original proposal but announces instead the decision to kill off the entire wilderness generation over forty years of wilderness wandering, with the exception of Caleb and Joshua, and to bring only the next generation into the promised land of Israel. The narrative thereby takes the opportunity to raise questions about YHWH's fidelity, that is, will YHWH hold to the covenant promises to the ancestors or not? Despite YHWH's initial decision to destroy Israel, YHWH does hold to the covenant but finds the means to carry out judgment as well. Once again, the Judean polemics against the north—including all of the other tribes—are clear, viz., the north is faithless but Judah, represented by Caleb, trusts in YHWH. Such a portrayal aids in explaining the fall of northern Israel, examining the character of YHWH following the debacle, and defining expectations for Judah in the aftermath of Israel's demise. Interestingly, Joshua ben Nun emerges as a faithful character as well, but only in Num 14:6 after the conflict between YHWH and the people had broken out. Interestingly, his name was mentioned in Num 13:8 as Hosea ben Nun, but Num 13:16 states that Moses called him Joshua ben Nun, a variation of the name based on the same verb root, *yš'*, "to deliver." Viewed diachronically, these observations suggest a Judean narrative critical of the northern tribes that has been edited to rescue the character of Hosea/Joshua ben Nun and to work the narrative into a larger literary framework that views Joshua as the successor of Moses who led Israel into the promised land.

Numbers 15:1-41 follows with an account of YHWH's instructions to Moses concerning purification offerings that would play a role in purifying the people and restoring their relationship with YHWH. Offerings include the standard offerings of the *'ōlâ*, "the whole burnt offering," the *minhâ*, "the grain offering," and the *zebah šĕlāmmîm*, "the offering of well-being," as well as the *hatta't*, "the sin/purification offering," known from Lev 1-7. But additional concerns with vows and freewill offerings, the deliberate violation of the Shabbat, and the instructions to wear *ṣîṣit*, "fringes," as a reminder of YHWH's instructions, suggest that Num 15 is designed in relation to the immediate literary context to treat the needs for purification when the people enter the land (Num 15:2). The absence of the *'āšām*, "the guilt/reparation offering," suggests that this chapter may be based on the work of an early or non-P law code. In any case, it further defines issues related to purification and sacrifice in the aftermath of the confrontation between YHWH and Israel during the spy episode.

Numbers 16–18 relates the rebellion of the Levite Korah ben Izhar, his Reubenite supporters, Dathan, Abiram, and On, and 250 chieftains of Israel together with the subsequent appointment of the Levites as the priests of Israel and Aaron and his sons as the chief priestly line. The issue is once again Moses' leadership of the nation. Because of the complexities of this narrative, many scholars argue that it is combination of accounts of rebellions by Korah, on the one hand, and Dathan, Abiram, and On, on the other hand. Although the possibility of a composite narrative is possible, a synchronic reading of the narrative notes how Levitical and Reubenite factions have joined forces with the support of the chieftains of Israel. In this respect, the socio-geographical identities of the parties at hand are important. The sons of Korah are known as a guild of Temple singers (2 Chr 20:19), gatekeepers (1 Chr 9:19; 26:1), and bakers (1 Chr 9:31), who are credited with writing Pss 42; 44–49; 84–85; and 87–88. Nevertheless, the Korahites are originally located as part of the non-Aaronide Kohathites in the Levitical cities of Ephraim, Dan, and Manasseh according to Josh 21:20-26, whereas the Aaronides, who are also descended from Kohath, are assigned to the Levitical cities of Judah, Shimon, and Benjamin according to Josh 21:9-19. In short, Korah is identified with Ephraim, Dan, and Manasseh in the north. The presence of the Korahites in the Jerusalem Temple can only be the result of some secondary association which is reflected in the present narrative, viz., because Korah, the ancestor of the house of Korah, was swallowed up by the earth when he tried to challenge Moses. His descendants are then relegated to secondary status as singers, gatekeepers, and bakers in the Temple, whereas the sons of Aaron officiate at the altar. As for Dathan, Abiram, and On, they are identified as Reubenites, which are known for their association with Manasseh and Gad in the Trans-Jordan. Joshua 22 allays any suspicion of revolt on the part of Reuben and its neighbors, and Gen 35:22 states that Reuben lay with his father's concubine, Bilhah, which constitutes a claim for leadership among the tribes. Jacob's reprimand of Reuben in Gen 49:3-4 might explain his loss of standing among the tribes in biblical narrative. The Moabite Stone points to Israel's loss of the Trans-Jordan, including the territories of Reuben and Gad, to Moab in the ninth century BCE when Aram invaded the region. With the Assyrian invasions of the mid-eighth century BCE, the Trans-Jordan, including Reuben, was stripped away from Israel. Any of these events may lay behind the punishment of Dathan, Abiram, and On as portrayed in Num 16. In such cases, the Torah narratives concerning Korah's revolt point to underlying events including the diminution of the status of the Korahites in relation to the Aaronides of the Jerusalem sanctuary and Israel's loss of Reuben in the Trans-Jordan.

The rise of the Aaronides must also be considered. During the course of the revolt against Moses and Aaron after the earth had swallowed Korah and his supporters, Aaron stood between the living and the dead to make expiation for the people until YHWH's plague against them had been checked (Num 17:8-15). This act points to an essential role of the priesthood in ancient Israel/Judah, that is, to serve as intermediary between the people and YHWH and to ensure the sanctity of the people before YHWH. Insofar as death represents the ultimate negation of sanctity in ancient Israel/Judah, Aaron's act to protect the people from death demonstrates his preparedness to undertake the priestly role. In the aftermath of this incident, YHWH instructs Moses to gather the staffs of the chieftains of each of the twelve tribes so that one might be chosen as the priestly tribe. The staff of Aaron, chieftain of the house of Levi, had sprouted almond leaves, indicating that Levi would serve as the priestly house in Israel. Indeed, the sprouting of almond leaves in the spring symbolizes the fecundity of creation, and it points to the priests' role in ensuring the sanctity and integrity of creation as well as of Israel. As a result of their selection, the Levites will bear the guilt of the sanctuary, that is, they are responsible for ensuring the sanctity of the sanctuary as the holy center of creation as well. In return, the Levites receive the gift offerings and tithes brought to the sanctuary by the people of Israel. Such offerings serve as a means of support for the priesthood since their holy duties in the sanctuary preclude their owning and working land to support themselves. Insofar as their offerings include the first fruits of the land, herd, and flock, their responsibility for the sanctity of Temple, creation, and people plays a direct role in their own support. Numbers 18:19 makes it clear that this arrangement is a *běrît melaḥ ʿôlām*, "an eternal covenant of salt." Not only does such a covenant ensure the sanctity and stability of creation, but the inclusion of salt, the well-known ancient preservative, reinforces the eternal nature of the covenant.

In the aftermath of the articulation of the Levites' role in ensuring the sanctity of creation, people, and Temple, Num 19 presents instruction concerning the ritual of the red heifer, which purifies persons, objects, and sites that have been compromised by contact with death. The ritual calls for the sacrifice of a heifer or cow which is completely red, an ideal portrayal of a cow that is rarely encountered but nevertheless represents the ideal, sacred nature of the act. The placement of Num 19 at this point takes up the role of the priesthood in ensuring the purity and sanctity of the nation, but it also sets the context for the condemnation of Moses and Aaron in the following narratives.

Numbers 20:1-21 relates Israel's arrival at the Wilderness of Zin after having sojourned at Paran. Numbers 20:14 makes it clear that they are located specifically at Kadesh in the Wilderness of Zin. Comparison with Num 33:36-38, which states that Aaron was 123 years old when he died (see Num 20:22-29), indicates that the arrival at Zin/Kadesh takes place in the fortieth year of wilderness wandering. Miriam's death and burial is noted in Num 20:1, immediately

after the statement of Israel's arrival at Zin. This statement is key to understanding the following narrative concerning water from the rock. Once again, the
people complain concerning the lack of water, and YHWH instructs Moses and
Aaron to assemble the people at the rock for a ritual that will produce the
necessary water. Interpreters have struggled for centuries to understand why
Moses and Aaron should be condemned and barred from entering the land of
Israel as a result of their actions at the rock.[12] YHWH claims that they did not
trust YHWH enough to affirm YHWH's sanctity in the sight of the people and
names the site, Meribah, to signify the rebellion of the people. Interpreters have
suggested a variety of reasons for YHWH's objection, viz., they showed lack of
trust by striking the rock twice; they acted cavalierly in questioning whether they
could bring water from the rock; they suggested that they and not YHWH would
bring water from the rock; they identified with the rebels, and so on. None of
these solutions has gained full acceptance, but interpreters have overlooked the
importance of the notice concerning the death and burial of Miriam. As her
brothers, Moses and Aaron would have been responsible for her burial, which
means that they had just come into contact with the dead. Although a priest may
bury a blood relative, such as a virgin sister (Lev 21:3), there is no notice that
Moses and Aaron had purified themselves before undertaking holy service for
YHWH at the rock. Such an omission is particularly striking following the
instructions for purification in Num 19. Having come into contact with the dead
body of Miriam, Moses and Aaron were defiled and could not undertake any holy
service until the process of purification was completed. By officiating in a state of
defilement due to corpse contamination, Moses and Aaron compromised the
sanctity of YHWH and the ritual act to produce water at the rock, resulting in
their condemnation as unfit priests.

Immediately following this episode, Edom refuses Israel passage through their
territory on the way to the promised land of Israel despite the fact that Esau, the
ancestor of Edom, was the brother of Jacob, ancestor of Israel.

Numbers 20:22—21:3 recounts Israel's journey from Kadesh to Mt. Hor on the
boundary of Edom, where Aaron dies. The reason for YHWH's decision that
Aaron should die is not given, although the incident at the rock of Meribah must
stand in the background of a synchronic reading of this text. Because Aaron is the
priest, he is stripped of his sacred garments before he dies so as not to compromise their sanctity, and his son Elazar is dressed in the holy garments to
signify his succession of his father as priest. Again, the local Canaanites resist, this
time from Arad in south Canaan. After the attacking forces from Arad are
defeated, the region is called Hormah, "proscribed."

Numbers 21:4-35 recounts Israel's journey from Mt. Hor to Edom and Moab.
This segment relates the people's rebellion once again as a continuing theme,
YHWH's introduction of sĕrāpîm, "fiery snakes," to punish the people, and the
production of a copper serpent as a standard that one day would be placed in the
Temple and removed as part of Hezekiah's reforms (see 2 Kgs 18:4). The key
element of the narrative, however, is the refusal of King Sihon of the Amorites in

Heshbon of Moab and King Og of Bashan to allow Israel to pass through its lands. Both kings are defeated and their land conquered by Israel to become the Trans-Jordanian regions of the land of Israel.

Diachronically speaking, these narratives (and those concerning Edom in Num 20:14-21 and Arad in Num 21:1-3 above) are important because they make claims to the Trans-Jordanian lands that were taken from Israel, first by Moab and Aram in the ninth century BCE, and later by Assyria in the eighth century BCE. From the standpoint of the EJ tradition, these narratives indicate the desire to restore these lands to Israel/Judah.

Numbers 22:1—36:13 comprises the balance of the book of Numbers, which relates a series of episodes concerned with Israel's arrival at Moab immediately prior to their entry into the promised land of Israel.

Following the notice of arrival in Num 22:1, Num 22:2—24:25 takes up the account of Balaam's blessing of Israel prior to their entry into the land. The narrative is well-known for its character development and use of satire in the portrayal of Balaam ben Beor as a major Aramean prophet, who was hired by Balak, King of Moab, to curse Israel. A key motif of the narrative is that the great seer can only see and speak what YHWH determines. When he is traveling to Moab, this point is made when the ass upon which he rides sees an angel of YHWH blocking the road, but Balaam does not. This incident is preparatory to the main concern with Balaam's oracles, in which he is unable to curse Israel as he is hired to do but can only bless Israel as that is what YHWH permits him to do. Thus, on the eve of Israel's entry into the promised land, a great seer from among the nations blesses Israel on behalf of YHWH, author of creation and sovereign of all the nations of the earth.

From a diachronic standpoint, the Balaam narrative is also a very important text. As the product of the EJ tradition, it represents an eighth-century BCE E composition that has been taken up and edited into the larger narrative framework by the J writer during the late eighth through the seventh century BCE. Balaam ben Beor is a known historical figure who is represented as a foreign prophet who speaks of Israel's defeat in the Deir Alla Inscription dating to the eighth century BCE. Deir Alla is located along the Wadi Jabbok just west of the Jordan River and may be identified with biblical Sukkoth. The inscription was mounted on a building as a display inscription for all to read. It was apparently written in the aftermath of the Aramean seizure of the Trans-Jordan during the late eighth and early eighth centuries as a propaganda measure. The underlying E Balaam narrative would have been composed as a response to the inscription, perhaps during the reigns of the later Jehu monarchs, Jehoash (801–786 BCE) and Jeroboam (786–746 BCE), when Israel allied with Assyria and contained Aram, enabling Israel to restore the Trans-Jordan to Israelite sovereignty. The Balaam narrative would have been taken up in the EJ tradition as a means to press Davidic claims over the Trans-Jordan as the successors to northern Israel who would re-establish the unity of northern Israel and southern Judah.

Numbers 25:1-18 relates the incident at Shittim, just east of the Jordan River near the Dead Sea in Jordan, in which Israelite men engaged in apostasy in worship of Baal Peor with Moabite and Midianite women. Key elements of the narrative include the identification of Midianite women as a source of apostasy with the men of Israel and the zealous action of Phineas ben Elazar ben Aaron to put a stop to the apostasy. In the first instance, the apostasy calls into question Moses' marriage to Zipporah, daughter of the priest of Midian, and it thereby also calls Moses' leadership into question. Whereas Moses only stands and watches in the narrative, Phineas takes action and kills an Israelite man and Midianite woman while they are engaged in illicit activity. The ensuing condemnation of Midian disrupts the relationship between Israel and Midian established through Moses' marriage to Zipporah, and it also signals the eternal covenant with Phineas to serve as priest forever, that is, *běrît kěhunnat 'ôlām*, "covenant of eternal priesthood." First Chronicles 6:34-45 identifies Phineas ben Elazar ben Aaron as the ancestor of Zadok, founder of the priestly line of the Jerusalem Temple. Insofar as Moses' son Gershom is believed to be founder of the priestly line at Dan (Judg 18:30), Num 25:1-18 narrates the means by which Mushite priestly leadership in the north was supplanted by Aaronide priestly leadership in Jerusalem. Of course, the present form of the narrative is the work of the EJ writers.

Numbers 26:1-65 presents an account of the census of Israel at Shittim. This is the second account of a census of all Israel, the first having been completed in Num 1. Numbers 26:64 makes it clear that this census was taken only after all of the earlier wilderness generation, with the exceptions of Caleb ben Jephunneh and Joshua ben Nun, had died in the desert as commanded by YHWH in Num 14:26-35. Numbers 26 therefore envisions a restored Israel following catastrophe. Synchronically speaking, the catastrophe is the wilderness debacle. Diachronically speaking, the EJ tradition would have in mind the restoration of a united Israel and Judah following the collapse of northern Israel. The P tradition would envision such restoration in the Second Temple period.

With questions of the apportionment of the land of Israel in mind, Num 27:1-11 considers what is to be done when a man dies without male heirs. The daughters of Zelophehad report that their father had died in the wilderness without sons and had only daughters to inherit his property. Such a consideration had to be a practical issue during all periods of Israel's and Judah's existence as landed nations. The decision to give the daughters a hereditary holding among their father's kinsmen partially resolves the problem insofar as the women will formally own the land, while male kinsmen would be responsible for any transactions involving the property. No mention is made of what would happen when the women marry. This concern is addressed later in Num 36:1-12.

Numbers 27:12-23 takes up the question of national leadership, insofar as Moses is old and not likely to live much longer, due in part to the incident at the rock of Meribah (Num 20:1-20). YHWH makes the decision that Joshua ben Nun should succeed Moses, a prophet and Levite, as national leader. Joshua is portrayed in prophetic terms as "an inspired man" (cf. Num 11:10-25) although other elements suggest a quasi-priestly role, for example, the laying on of hands in v. 18,[13] his exhortations to observe Torah in Josh 1, and his reading Torah to the people at Shechem in the land of Israel (Josh 8:30-35). Insofar as northern Israel was known for its non-Levitical priests (1 Kg 12:31), it is possible that Joshua was understood to have a priestly role in northern Israel. The succession is analogous to that of Elisha and Elijah (1 Kgs 19:19-21, both of whom also have priestly associations. The present P context, however, makes it clear that the line of Phineas ben Elazar ben Aaron will serve as priests in Israel (Num 25:1-18).

Numbers 28:1—30:1 presents a calendar of public festivals and the offerings to be presented at each. The festivals and offerings include the daily 'ôlâ, "whole burnt offering," with its minḥâ, "grain offering," and nesek, "libation offering"; the Shabbat offerings; the New Moon offerings; the Passover offerings; the Shavuot offerings; offerings for a sacred occasion on the first day of the seventh month elsewhere identified as Rosh ha-Shanah or New Year; the Yom Kippur offerings; and the Sukkot offerings. Whereas other calendars outline the festivals (see Exod 23:12-18; 34:18-26; Lev 23; Deut 16:1-17), the present text makes a point of specifying the offerings. When read in context, Num 28:1—30:1 presents instruction relevant to holy life once Israel takes possession of the land. Although Num 28:1—30:1 is sometimes judged to be unidentified source material,[14] it may well represent an originally northern Israelite calendar that is now placed in an EJ and later a P framework.

Numbers 30:2-17 takes up the question of vows made by women. Insofar as men alone enjoy full legal rights in ancient Israelite and Judean society, the instruction effectively places vows made by women under the authority of men, the father in the case of an unmarried woman and the husband in the case of a married woman. The instruction specifies that if the father of an unmarried woman or the husband of a married woman makes no objection to the vow, the vow will stand with full legal force. Should the father or husband object, the vow carries no legal force. At the synchronic level, Num 30:2-17 defines rights and responsibilities for vows made by women in general. Insofar as Num 30:2-17 is a non-source text,[15] it appears to have been taken up by the EJ tradition and applied also in P.

Numbers 31:1-54 recounts Israel's holy war against Midian. The causes for this war lie in the idolatry in Israel promoted by the Midianites in Num 25:1-18. Although Moses also plays a leading role, Phineas ben Elazar ben Aaron plays the key role as the priest who sanctifies the war. The war is conceived as a means to eradicate the threat of idolatry and apostasy in Israel against an enemy that has demonstrated its will and capacity to lead Israel into such actions in the past. But it must also be recognized as a blow to Moses' authority as well, since he was married to Zipporah, the daughter of Jethro, priest of Midian. Perhaps the narrative also represents the break with northern Israelite ritual establishment, insofar as Moses' son Gershom served as priest in the Israelite sanctuary at Dan (Judg 18:30) whereas the line of Phineas ben Elazar ben Aaron served as priests in the Jerusalem Temple. The instructions for holy war included dedication and purification of the spoils of war to the Temple, purification of the soldiers who had come into contact with death, distribution of shares of booty among the army and the rest of the people, and the tithe of all booty.

Numbers 32:1-41 addresses the question of land holdings for the tribes of Reuben and Gad. Both of these tribes would be assigned land holdings exclusively in the Trans-Jordanian region of Gilead. Although the tribe of Manasseh is noted in vv. 33-41, Manasseh would possess land in both the Trans-Jordan and the hill country of Israel. The instruction specifies that Reuben and Gad would be granted the right to land holdings in Gilead on condition that they join the other tribes in the conquest of the land of Canaan. Questions of the status of Reuben and Gad among the tribes of Israel would be raised in later times (for example, Josh 22) insofar as the Jordan River would form a natural boundary between the land of the hill country of Israel and Judah and the Trans-Jordan. The Trans-Jordan was stripped away from Israel, first by Aram and Moab in the late ninth through early eighth centuries and later by Assyria in the late eighth century. Because Num 32:1-41 is considered to be a combination of J and non-source elements,[16] it would appear to the product of the EJ edition of the Torah that was designed to lay claim to the Trans-Jordan during the period of the late Judean monarchy. The claim would have been reiterated by the P edition of the Torah as well.

Numbers 33:1-49 summarizes the journey of Israel from Egypt through the wilderness and on into Moab prior to entry into the promised land of Israel. The text is a non-source text that would have been taken up by both the EJ and P editions of the Torah.[17] The travel itinerary laid out here provides the basis for the P travel itinerary through the wilderness.

Numbers 30:50—36:13 contains the final instructions concerning the apportionment of the land of Canaan among the tribes of Israel. Numbers 33:50-55 begins with instruction to destroy the Canaanites so that they do not become a source of idolatry and apostasy for Israel. Numbers 34:1-29 defines the boundaries of the land and the process by which it shall be apportioned among the tribes. Numbers 35:1-8 takes up the responsibility of each tribe to apportion towns and land for Levitical use. Numbers 35:9-34 defines the cities of refuge to which persons who have committed unintentional manslaughter might flee to save their lives. Those guilty of intentional homicide, however, remain subject to the death penalty. Numbers 36:1-12 returns to the question of the daughters of Zelophehad (cf. Num 27:1-11). Women who inherit land because their fathers died without sons must marry within their own tribe. This is to be done to retain control of the land, which will pass to their sons. If such women marry outside of their own tribes, they lose the right to such land inherited from their father. The instruction is designed to maintain the integrity of tribal land holdings in Israel. Finally, Num 36:13 is a summary statement concerning the commands and regulations enjoined upon Israel by YHWH. Again, these texts are considered to be non-source texts which would have been taken up by the EJ and P writers.

NOTES

[1] See F. M. Cross, "The Priestly Work," in *Canaanite Myth and Hebrew Epic* (Cambridge, MA: Harvard University Press, 1973), 293–325.

[2] See especially Antony F. Campbell and Mark A. O'Brien, *Sources of the Pentateuch: Texts, Introductions, Annotations* (Minneapolis: Fortress Press, 1993), 70–89, 150–60, 190–93, 200–201. For commentaries on Numbers, see Rolf P. Knierim and George W. Coats, *Numbers* (FOTL 4; Grand Rapids: Eerdmans, 2005); Baruch Levine, *Numbers 1–20* (AB 4; New York: Doubleday, 1993); idem, *Numbers 21–36* (AB 4A; New York: Doubleday, 2000); Martin Noth, *Numbers: A Commentary* (OTL; Philadelphia: Westminster, 1968; Jacob Milgrom, *Numbers* (JPS Torah Commentary; Philadelphia: Jewish Publication Society, 1989); Horst Seebass, *Numeri 10,11–30,1* (BKAT 4/1–3.3; Neukirchen–Vluyn: Neukirchener, 1993–2006).

[3] For identification and discussion of the P materials in Num 3–36 and Deut 34, see Campbell and O'Brien, *Sources of the Pentateuch*, 70–90.

[4] For identification and discussion of the EJ materials in Num 3–36, see Campbell and O'Brien, *Sources of the Pentateuch*, 150–60, 190–93.

[5] For identification and discussion of the D material, see Antony F. Campbell and Mark A. O'Brien, *Unfolding the Deuteronomistic History: Origins, Upgrades, Present Text* (Minneapolis: Fortress Press, 2000), 39–99.

[6] For identification and discussion of the non-source material in Num 3–36, see Campbell and O'Brien, *Sources of the Pentateuch*, 200–201.

[7] For studies of the wilderness texts, see George W. Coats, *Rebellion in the Wilderness* (Nashville: Abingdon, 1968); Dennis T. Olson, *The Death of the Old and the Birth of the New: The Framework of the Book of Numbers and the Pentateuch* (BJS 71; Chico: Scholars Press, 1985); Won W. Lee, *Punishment and Forgiveness in Israel's Wilderness Campaign* (Grand Rapids: Eerdmans, 2003).

[8] See Marvin A. Sweeney, *1 and 2 Kings: A Commentary* (OTL; Louisville: Westminster John Knox, 2007), 143–44.

[9] This segment, considered to be a discrete book in Rabbinic traditions (*Siphre Num.* 84; see Jacob Milgrom, *Numbers* [JPS Torah Commentary; Philadelphia; Jewish Publication Society, 1990/5750], 375–76), appears as a key element in the service for the reading of the Torah.

[10] Note that the seventy elders are to be identified with the seventy sons of Gideon who were killed by Abimelech during his attempt to seize kingship in Israel (Judg 9), the elders who came to David to make him king following the death of Ishbosheth (2 Sam 5), and the seventy sons of Ahab killed by Jehu during his revolt against the house of Omri (2 Kgs 10; see also 1 Kgs 21).

[11] See Zeev Meshel, "Kuntillat Ajrud," *ABD* 4:103–9. Note that references to YHWH and his Asherah also appear in the Khirbet el Qom inscriptions from the region of Hebron in Judah (John S. Holiday, "Kom, Khirbet el-," *ABD* 4:97–99).

[12] For an overview of discussion of this issue from medieval times, see Milgrom, *Numbers*, 448–56.

[13] Note that the laying on of hands, Hebrew *sĕmîkâ*, later signifies ordination as a Rabbi.

[14] See Campbell and O'Brien, *Sources of the Pentateuch*, 201.

[15] See Campbell and O'Brien, *Sources of the Pentateuch*, 201.

[16] See Campbell and O'Brien, *Sources of the Pentateuch*, 147–49, 201.

[17] See Campbell and O'Brien, *Sources of the Pentateuch*, 201.

c. Moses' Final Addresses to Israel, Transfer of Leadership, and Death in Moab

Deuteronomy 1:1—34:12 constitutes the last book of the Torah and—within the synchronic literary structure of the Torah as a whole—the last major component of the account of Israel's history under the guidance of the Levites in Num 3:1— Deut 34:12. Deuteronomy 1:1—34:12 is formulated as an account of Moses' last addresses to Israel on the last day of his life. Insofar as Israel is located in Moab where it is about to cross the Jordan River in order to commence its life in the land of Israel, Moses' last speeches present a summation and review of divine Torah that will be incumbent upon Israel for its life in the land. A close reading of the divine instruction in Deuteronomy indicates, however, that it is not merely a repetition or summation of previously presented divine Torah. Instead, it constitutes a representation of earlier instruction in Genesis—Numbers that presupposes reflection upon the earlier materials and efforts to address questions left unanswered or to specify and apply earlier instruction so that it might achieve its aims of producing a holy, just, and viable society in Israel. From a synchronic standpoint, such reflection, specification, and application in Deuteronomy illustrates the principle that Mosaic Torah comprises both written and oral Torah, insofar as later generations of the Jewish people must reflect upon Torah from Sinai in order to discern all of the various nuances of divine Torah that are implicit in the written form of the text. From a diachronic standpoint, Deuteronomy illustrates the dynamic and evolving character of a legal system that adapts to meet the needs and circumstances of a changing and living society.[1]

The synchronic literary structure of Deuteronomy comprises two major components, viz., the account of Moses' last speeches to Israel in Deut 1:1—30:20 and the account of Moses' transfer of leadership to Joshua together with Moses' death and burial in Deut 31:1—34:12. The account of Moses' first speech to Israel in Deut 1:1—4:43 is an exhortational résumé of Israel's journey from Horeb/ Sinai, through the wilderness, and to the borders of the promised land that is designed to promote observance of YHWH's Torah. The second speech in Deut 4:44—26:19 is an example of Levitical Torah or a Levitical instruction sermon that is designed to teach divine expectations to the people.[2] It includes an introduction in Deut 4:44-49 that specifies the setting of the speech in Beth Peor across the Jordan in Moab and identifies it as divine Torah and an account of the speech itself in Deut 5:1—26:19. Following a brief speech formula in Deut 5:1aα$^{1-2}$, the Levitical sermon itself proceeds with an introductory exhortation to observe YHWH's Torah in Deut 5:1aα$^{3-6}$—11:32 and the Torah proper in Deut 12:1—26:19, which lays out in detail the statutes and cases that comprise the divine Torah. The account of Moses' third speech in Deut 27:1—28:69 recounts the blessings and curses that follow from Israel's observance of the covenant or its failure to observe the covenant with YHWH. The account of Moses' fourth speech in Deut 29:1—30:20 comprises Moses' final exhortation to observe the covenant with YHWH. The synchronic literary structure of Deuteronomy appears as follows:

Narrative Account of Moses' Final Address to Israel:
Repetition of the Torah   Deut 1–34
   I. Narrative Account of Moses' Last Speeches to Israel   1:1—30:20
      A. The account of Moses' first speech:
           exhortational résumé of Israel's journey   1:1—4:43
      B. The account of Moses' second speech:
           exhortational summary of YHWH's Torah   4:44—26:19
         1. introduction: setting of speech and identification
             as Torah   4:44-49
         2. report of speech proper: Levitical Torah   5:1—26:19
            a. speech formula   5:1aα$^{1-2}$
            b. speech proper: Levitical Torah   5:1aα$^{3-6}$—26:19
               1) introductory exhortation   5:1aα$^{3-6}$—11:32
               2) Torah proper: statutes and cases   12:1—26:19
                  a) superscription   12:1
                  b) statutes and ordinances proper   12:2—26:15
                     i. concerning cultic differentiation
                          from the nations   12:2—13:19
                         aa. instructions concerning exclusive
                             worship at YHWH's chosen altar   12:2-31
                       bb. cases concerning cultic/national
                             apostasy   13:1-19
                     ii. concerning holy conduct of treasured
                         people   14:1—26:15
                       aa. basic instruction:
                               holiness of people   14:1-2
                       bb. specific instruction   14:3—26:15
                           i) eating of meat   14:3-21
                           ii) tithes   14:22-29
                         iii) debt issues   15:1-18
                         iv) offering of first-born   15:19-23
                         v) observance of holidays   16:1-17
                         vi) judicial and political
                             authority   16:18—17:20
                       vii) religious authority   18:1—19:13
                       viii) territorial/boundary issues   19:14—21:23

Diachronic scholarship maintains that, with the exception of minor elements from the account of Moses' death and burial in Deut 34:1aα, 7-9,[3] Deuteronomy comprises the D source of the Pentateuch.[4] Interpreters argue that Deuteronomy or an earlier form of the book is to be identified with the Torah scroll found in the Temple during the reign of King Josiah ben Amon of Judah (r. 640–609 BCE), which in turn provided the basis for King Josiah's program of religious reform and national restoration.[5] Although many interpreters argue that Deuteronomy was originally written in northern Israel and brought south where it would form the basis for Josiah's reform efforts,[6] more recent scholarship maintains that Deuteronomy's emphasis on a single site for the worship of YHWH—in contrast to the north that recognized multiple sites in Beth El, Dan, and elsewhere—indicates that Deuteronomy was produced in Judean circles to support Josiah's reform.[7] It constituted an attempt to revise earlier law codes applied in Israel and Judah, such as the Covenant Code of Exod 20–24, in order to give greater rights to the poor (including women)—the very constituency that placed Josiah on the throne following the abortive coup that saw the assassination of his father, King Amon ben Manasseh of Judah (r. 642–640 BCE).[8] Deuteronomy functioned as the introduction to the Deuteronomistic History or Former Prophets in Joshua, Judges, Samuel, and Kings, insofar as it lays out the theological foundations of the covenant between YHWH and Israel and the basis on which YHWH granted the land of Israel to the nation of Israel. With the completion of the EJ and P editions of the Pentateuch, Deuteronomy concluded the Pentateuch, but it continued to provide a foundation for the Former Prophets.

1) The Account of Moses' Speeches to Israel in Moab

a) Moses' First Speech to Israel: Exhortational Summary
of Israel's Journey from Horeb/Sinai to Moab

The account of Moses' first speech to Israel in Deut 1:1—4:43 constitutes an exhortational summary of Israel's journey from Horeb (Sinai), through the wilderness and on into Moab where Israel would prepare to enter the promised land. Moses' lengthy summation of the journey is designed to remind the people of YHWH's role in leading Israel to the promised land and sustaining the nation in the wilderness. The speech thereby exhorts the people to observe YHWH's instructions in order that they might thrive as a nation in the promised land of Israel. The account of Moses' first speech begins with a narrative introduction to the speech in Deut 1:1-5, which states the location and date of Moses' speech together with the speech itself in Deut 1:6—4:40, which includes both the historical review in Deut 1:6—3:29 and the exhortation to observe YHWH's teaching in Deut 4:1-40. The narrative concludes with an account in Deut 4:41-43 of Moses' actions immediately following the speech in which he sets aside three cities of refuge in the Trans-Jordan and thereby formally incorporates the Trans-Jordan into the administrative and judicial structure of the land of Israel. The synchronic literary structure of the account appears as follows:

The Account of Moses' First Speech to Israel: Exhortational Summary	
of Israel's Journey from Horeb/Sinai to Moab	Deut 1:1—4:43
I. The Account of Moses' Speech	1:1—4:40
A. Narrative introduction: place and date of speech	1:1-5
B. Moses' speech proper	1:6—4:40
1. historical review of Israel's journey from Horeb	
to Moab	1:6—3:29
2. exhortation to observe YHWH's Torah	4:1-40
II. The Account of Moses' Actions Following the Speech:	
Establishment of Cities of Refuge in the Trans-Jordan	4:41-43

The introduction to Moses' first speech in Deut 1:1-5 specifies the location and date of Moses' speech. The location is first identified as "the other side of the Jordan," which prompted Ibn Ezra to recognize that the narrative framework could not have been written by Moses, insofar as this statement presupposes a perspective from a writer placed inside the land of Israel rather than Moses, who never entered the land of Israel. The exact location cannot be identified, although "in the Arabah near Suph" indicates a location in Moab close to the Jordan River. The date on the first day of the eleventh month in the fortieth year since the departure from Sinai/Horeb is deliberately contrasted with the eleven days that it normally takes to journey from Horeb/Sinai to the location in Moab. The contrast highlights the conflict between Israel and YHWH in the wilderness that called for a forty-year journey that would see the demise of the entire slave generation prior to entry into the promised land of Israel. The use of the term, *bē'ēr*, "to expound, to make plain," to describe Moses' presentation of the Torah to Israel emphasizes the role of the Levites in teaching divine Torah to Israel (cf. Lev 10:10-11). The term also points to the need to reflect on divine Torah in order to discern all of its dimensions when it is applied to the creation of a holy, just, and dynamic society.

The account of Moses' speech in Deut 1:6—4:40 begins with the historical review in Deut 1:6—3:29 in which Moses recounts Israel's forty-year journey from Horeb, through the wilderness, and on into Moab so that the people might enter the promised land of Israel. The historical review emphasizes a combination of YHWH's beneficent acts on behalf of Israel in the wilderness and Israel's complaints against YHWH and Moses that necessitated the decision to kill off the wilderness generation. The purpose of such a combination of themes is to instill within both the fictive audience of Israel and the reader an understanding of both YHWH's mercy and YHWH's capacity for judgment as a means to explain both YHWH's grant of the land of Israel and the realities of punishment at the hands of foreign invaders throughout the course of Israel's history. In such a manner, Deuteronomy is able to deal with the question of theodicy, that is, YHWH is powerful, righteous, and merciful, but Israel is rebellious, which in turn causes YHWH to inflict judgment upon Israel as a means to bring Israel in line with YHWH's expectations. In this respect, Deuteronomy posits that Israel's suffering in history is a result of its own rebelliousness against YHWH—it is not a result of YHWH's impotence, injustice, or absence as many might posit in the face of disaster. Deuteronomy is therefore formulated to explain YHWH's power and beneficence and to articulate Israel's responsibilities in relation to YHWH in order to ensure a secure life in the land. Deuteronomy therefore defends YHWH's righteousness, power, and mercy by positing that Israel is responsible for any misfortunes suffered as a result of its rebellion.

Indeed, the historical review begins with instances of tension or rebellion within Israel—for example, the need to appoint judges and chieftains to resolve tensions within Israel and Israel's refusal to enter Canaan despite YHWH's promises based on the reports brought back by the spies who searched out the land, which in turn prompted YHWH's decision to kill off the wilderness genera-tion before they could enter the land. Nevertheless, the review turns to YHWH's acts of beneficence and protection of Israel during the wilderness journey, such as the journey through Edom and Moab where YHWH protected Israel from attacks by the various kings of the region. The review concludes with Moses' pleas to YHWH to allow him to enter the promised land, but YHWH's refusal to do so prepares for the transition of leadership to Joshua and underscores YHWH's capacity for judgment when faced with rebellion.

The portrayal of YHWH's mercy and judgment prepares both the fictive audience of Israel and the reader of the narrative for the exhortational material in Deut 4:1-40. This portion of Moses' speech emphasizes the experience of divine revelation at Mt. Horeb/Sinai in which YHWH revealed the divine Torah to Israel which would provide the foundation for Israel's life in the land. The exhortational speech combines warnings of punishment for failure to comply with YHWH's Torah and promises of divine compassion in response to the observance of divine Torah. Only YHWH is G-d, and only YHWH is capable of the acts that brought Israel from Egypt to Sinai and the wilderness and on into the promised land of Israel. Moses reiterates YHWH's decision to refuse Moses entry into the land to underscore his own responsibility for the people as a prophet (or priest) whose task is to instruct the people in YHWH's expectations and to demonstrate that even Moses is subject to punishment due to wrongdoing. Such a demonstration underscores Deuteronomy's understanding of the importance of observance of the divine Torah that is to follow in Moses' second speech.

Finally, the narrative account in Deut 4:41-43 of Moses' establishment of three cities of refuge in the Trans-Jordan formally binds the Trans-Jordan into the administrative structure of Israel and emphasizes the importance of this tie insofar as Moses is the figure who instituted the cities.

Because Deut 1:1—4:43 both rehearses the wilderness journey already presented in Exodus—Numbers and anticipates the exhortational material tied to the presentation of divine Torah in Deut 4:44—26:19, many diachronically oriented scholars argue that Deut 1:1—4:43 is an editorial composition designed to bind Exodus—Numbers and Deuteronomy together within the larger literary framework of the Pentateuch.[9]

b) Moses' Second Speech: Exhortational Summary of Divine Torah

The account of Moses' second speech in Deut 4:44—26:19 constitutes the longest of Moses' four speeches to Israel, and it conveys the basic core of legal instruction to Israel in the book of Deuteronomy. It is formulated as a Levitical sermon or instruction speech that is designed to exhort the people to observe YHWH's Torah as well as to present that Torah in detail. We have already observed above that it does not simply repeat the earlier legal instruction of Exodus—Numbers, but reflects upon, develops, reformulates, and specifies the earlier material to provide a basis for both the relationship between YHWH and Israel and the foundations for a holy, just, and viable society in the land of Israel.

The account begins in Deut 4:44-49 with a brief introduction that identifies the following material as the Torah or instruction that Moses set before Israel, the location at Beth Peor in Moab where Moses delivered his speech, and the circumstances of the journey from Egypt and through the Trans-Jordan that brought Israel to that location. The emphasis given to the Trans-Jordan aids in claiming the region as part of the land of Israel.

The account of the speech per se follows in Deut 5:1—26:19. Following the brief speech formula in Deut 5:1aα$^{1-2}$, the speech follows in Deut 5:1aα$^{3-6}$—26:19. The speech comprises two major portions, viz., the introductory exhortation to observe YHWH's Torah in Deut 5:1aα$^{3-6}$—11:32 and the Torah or Instruction proper in Deut 12:1—26:19 which lays out the statutes and cases that comprise YHWH's Torah.

Moses' introductory exhortation in Deut 5:1aα$^{1-2}$—11:32 constitutes an elaborate sermon that is designed to persuade its audience to observe YHWH's Torah.
It is designed to identify YHWH as Israel's G-d, benefactor, and partner in a
covenant relationship; it lays out the basic ideal principles that are articulated
throughout the Deuteronomic Torah (Deut 5:1aα$^{3-6}$-30); it makes it clear that
loyalty to YHWH alone as G-d is an absolute requirement of the covenant relationship (Deut 6:1-25); it warns of the consequences to be suffered by the people
should they engage in actions that would compromise their loyalty to YHWH,
such as intermarriage with the pagan peoples of the land (Deut 7:1-11); it reminds
the people that the benefits of living in the land are provided by YHWH (Deut
7:12—8:20); it reminds the people that their choice by YHWH to live in the land
is not due to any special merit on their part, as amply illustrated by their rebellions in the wilderness (Deut 9:1—10:11); and it concludes with a renewed call to
observe YHWH's Torah with ample reminders of YHWH's actions on behalf of
Israel, YHWH's promises to the ancestors of Israel, the benefits to be reaped by
observing YHWH's Torah, and the curses to be suffered should Israel fail to
observe YHWH's Torah (Deut 10:12—11:32). The formal literary structure of
Moses' introductory exhortation appears as follows:

1)   Moses' introductory exhortation
   to observe YHWH's Torah   Deut 5:1aα$^{3-6}$—11:32
   a)   exposition of the ideal principles
        underlying YHWH's Torah   5:1aα$^{3-6}$-30
   b)   exhortation to observe YHWH's Torah   6:1—11:32
       i.   requirement of absolute loyalty
          to YHWH as sole G-d   6:1-25
       ii.   consequences of failure to show loyalty
          to YHWH   7:1-11
       iii.   benefits of living in the land provided
          by YHWH   7:12—8:20
       iv.   choice by YHWH not due to
          special merit   9:1—10:11
       v.   renewed call to observe YHWH's
          Torah   10:12—11:32

The exposition of the ideal principles underlying YHWH's Torah in Deut
5:1aα$^{3-6}$-30 presents once again the Ten Commandments from Exod 20, albeit in
modified form. The passage makes it clear that these principles constitute the
essential core of YHWH's expectations of Israel in its covenant relationship with
YHWH and that they were conveyed directly to Moses face to face at Mt. Horeb
(Sinai). The image of Moses standing before the fire that envelopes YHWH at
Sinai calls to mind the role of the priest who enters the holy of holies of the
Temple or who stands before the altar and thereby highlights YHWH's holy
character and the need for an intermediary, either in the form of the priest or the
prophet as represented by Moses. As noted in the discussion of Exod 20, the Ten

Commandments cannot be considered as law per se, insofar as they are not adjudicable in a court of law due to the absence of any means to resolve instances of violation. Rather, their instructive and imperative/prohibitive forms require that they be understood as statements of the basic principles that underlie the specific statutes and cases that comprise the totality of Deuteronomic Torah. The sequence is basically the same as in Exod 20, but individual instances differ due to the specific concerns of Deuteronomy over against Exodus. Deuteronomy 5:6 identifies YHWH as Israel's only G-d, who brought the nation out of Egyptian bondage. Deuteronomy 5:7-10 prohibits the worship of other gods and the making of any images of the gods. Deuteronomy 5:11 prohibits swearing false oaths in the name of YHWH. Deuteronomy 5:12-15 calls upon the people to observe the Shabbat. This command differs from Exod 20:8-11, which calls upon Israel to "remember" the Shabbat. The Deuteronomic version represents a stronger statement of action, but it also provides a different rationale. Whereas Exod 20:8-11 explains the basis of the command as YHWH's role as creator of the world in six days, Deut 5:8-11 explains it as a result of YHWH's role as deliverer of Israel from Egyptian slavery. Deuteronomy 5:8-11 also extends the command for Shabbat observance to the animals of the household as well as to the humans mentioned in Exod 20:8-11. Rabbinic tradition maintains that the two versions must be read together as a full statement of the command, but the Deuteronomic version appears to build upon and specify an earlier version in Exodus. Deuteronomy 5:16 commands that the people honor their parents, which plays a role in ensuring social stability through family structure. Deuteronomy 5:17 presents the prohibitions against murder, adultery, theft, and false witness against a neighbor. Deuteronomy 5:18 prohibits coveting a neighbor's house, wife, slaves, animals, and possessions. The following statements make it clear that the Ten Commandments were spoken publically to Israel at Horeb, but that Moses remained behind to receive the entire body of statutes and cases that comprise the totality of the divine Torah revealed at Horeb/Sinai.

Having laid out the basic principles of Deuteronomic Torah, the balance of Moses' introductory exhortation in Deut 6:1—11:32 turns to the task of exhortation per se.

The requirement of absolute loyalty to YHWH is a fundamental condition of the covenant relationship between YHWH and Israel. Indeed, Deut 6:4-5 constitutes the basic statement of the Shema, that is, "Hear (Hebrew, *šěmʻa*) O Israel, the L-rd is our G-d, the L-rd is One," the fundamental statement of Jewish adherence to YHWH as sole G-d, which is read as an essential element of every Jewish worship service. The following vv. 6-9 are also read as part of the Shema in the Jewish worship service, together with Deut 11:13-21 and Num 15:37-41. The practice of praying with Tefillin, small pouches containing miniature manuscripts of the Shema affixed to the head and arm is attested at Qumran in the second century BCE. Mezuzot manuscripts, meant for amulets to be affixed to the doorposts (Hebrew, *mězuzôt*) are also attested at Qumran. Such amulets may have once been understood in antiquity as a means to ward off evil, but they clearly function in Jewish tradition as a means to establish a context of sanctity for prayer and for home. Rabbinic tradition calls for the inclusion of Exod 13:1-10, 11-16; Deut 6:4-9; and 11:13-21 in the Tefillin and Deut 6:4-9 and 11:13-21 in the Mezuzah, although ancient examples include other texts.

Deuteronomy 7:1-11 turns to the consequences of the failure to show loyalty to YHWH by worshipping other gods. This concern is expressed through a prohibition against intermarriage with seven nations that might be encountered in the land of Canaan; indeed, the passage demands that these peoples be wiped out entirely in the land. The rationale for such a prohibition is the concern that these nations would lead Israel to abandon YHWH by engaging in the worship of foreign gods. Such a command is rooted in ancient practices of destroying an enemy, and the general presupposition that the inhabitants of a nation would worship the god or gods of that nation. Deuteronomy does envision that *gērîm*, "resident aliens," might also join Israel in the land. Insofar as *gērîm* are later understood to be converts to Judaism, Deuteronomy lays some of the foundations for the conversion of Gentiles to Judaism.

Deuteronomy 7:12—8:20 focuses on the benefits of living in the land provided by YHWH, and it therefore begins with statements of blessing that will follow from adherence to YHWH's expectations. Here, YHWH's role as creator comes forward as the blessings include agricultural abundance, fertility in herd and flock, the birth of children, and the absence of illness. YHWH's role as deliverer of Israel also comes into play as the text emphasizes that YHWH will protect Israel from enemies, much as YHWH delivered Israel from the Egyptians. A review of YHWH's acts of beneficence in the wilderness, viz., the use of hardships to strengthen Israel, the provision of manna, the granting of the land, the provision of crops and livestock, and so on, all point to YHWH's capacity for blessing if the people observe YHWH's expectations.

Deuteronomy 9:1—10:11 focuses on the question of Israel's status as the chosen people of YHWH. Moses' speech makes it very clear that YHWH did not choose Israel as a result of any special merit of the people. Indeed, his rehearsal of the bitter conflicts between YHWH and Israel in the wilderness is designed to demonstrate that Israel lacks any merit. Modern readers must again observe that such a portrayal of Israel is an expression of theodicy, that is, an attempt to protect the moral integrity and power of YHWH by charging that the people— and not YHWH—are at fault when they suffer reversal. Insofar as YHWH's commitment to the covenant with Israel' ancestors would come into question, Moses' speech stresses that YHWH's commitment to the oath sworn to Abraham, Isaac, and Jacob explains YHWH's decision to bring the peope into the promised land of Israel and not to destroy them in the wilderness.

Finally, Deut 10:12—11:32 concludes Moses' exhortation with a renewed call to observe YHWH's Torah. Having laid out the foundations, pitfalls, and benefits of the relationship throughout the speech, Moses may now come to the major point, viz., the attempt to persuade Israel (and the readers of the text) to observe YHWH's Torah and thereby to uphold the covenant that brings them into the promised land of Israel. The blessings and curses point once again to YHWH's role as the creator who provides food and fertility to the world and as the redeemer of Israel who protects Israel from enemies. Including the references to Mt. Gerizim and Mt. Ebal, the passage anticipates the blessings and curses texts that appear following the exposition of Deuteronomic Torah in Moses' third and fourth speeches in Deut 27:1—28:69 and 29:1—30:20.

When considered diachronically, Moses' exhortation speech shows striking affinities with the preambles of Assyrian vassal treaties from the eighth and seventh centuries BCE in which the Assyrian monarch lays out the expectations of his vassal, generally in the form of commands and prohibitions like those of the Ten Commandments, and attempts to persuade the vassal monarch to accept the terms of the treaty by pointing to the benefits of acceptance and the consequences of refusal.[10] Such treaties were well known to Judah and Israel in the eighth and seventh centuries BCE and played an influential role in Deuteronomy and other literary works which portray YHWH as a suzerain deity who enters into a relationship with the vassal people Israel. Such a rhetorical strategy enabled ancient Judah to think of YHWH as a monarch more powerful than the Assyrian—and later Babylonian and Persian—monarchs. Such a strategy enabled ancient Judah to explain its suffering as the result of YHWH's decision to impose covenant penalties on the nation by employing the Assyrians and other nations as agents of punishment, and it also enabled them to view YHWH as the ultimate authority behind acts of restoration, such as the identification of King Cyrus of Persia as YHWH's anointed monarch and Temple builder in Isa 44:28 and 45:1 who would see to the restoration of the exiles to the land of Israel.

The account of Moses' Torah or Instruction speech proper in Deut 12:1—26:19 present the statutes and cases that constitute YHWH's Torah in Deuteronomy. The account begins with a superscription in Deut 12:1 that identifies the following material in Deut 2:2—26:19 as the *haḥuqqîm*, "the statutes," and *hammiš-pāṭîm*, "the (legal) cases," that constitute YHWH's Torah in Deuteronomy. The distinction between "the statutes" and "the cases" is crucial for understanding the generic character and organization of Deut12:2—26:19 as legal instruction. "The statutes" refer to those legal paragraphs that include commands and prohibitions concerning specific actions that Israel might undertake. In modern critical scholars, such statutes are identified as apodictic law because they prescribe or proscribe certain types of conduct. Although such commands and prohibitions appear frequently in biblical law, more recent scholarship has begun to recognize that such statements do not constitute law at all because they are not adjudicable in a court of law insofar as they provide no legal means of redress should the particular instruction not be followed. Instead, the statutes or apodictic "laws" constitute statements of legal principle that underlie and inform the Israelite law codes which are in turn designed to implement those principles in actual court settings. "The cases," however, do constitute laws that are adjudicable in court insofar as they begin by positing a hypothetical set of circumstances, generally beginning with a circumstantial clause introduced by *'im*, "if," *kî*, "when/if," *'ăšer*, "when," and so on, that is followed by statement as to how the case is to be resolved. Such legal paragraphs have been identified in modern scholarship as "casuistic laws," insofar as they state a set of circumstances together with a statement of resolution. As interpreters have noted for over two millennia, the laws of the Bible hardly constitute a comprehensive catalog of every legal case that might arise in Israelite/Judean society. Yet, as the work of J. J. Finkelstein on the goring ox laws of the Bible and the Mesopotamian law codes demonstrates, the legal paragraphs in biblical law are to be taken as examples of the resolution of legal cases. Although each case law states a set of facts and a resolution for the case, the facts may vary in any given case that might come before a court, and the judge or judges would have to study the legal precedent stated in the case, take account of any variables in the circumstances of the court case at hand, and then come to a decision concerning the means to resolve the case. Such a model apparently explains the functions of both ancient Near Eastern and biblical law codes in general as well as the origins of the Rabbinic concept of oral Torah, in which a case had to be studied in order to apply it to different and newer sets of circumstances, thereby revealing the divine intent or oral Torah that is inherent in the specific case of written Torah.

Study of the interplay between the statutes and cases of Deuteronomic Torah indicates that the Deuteronomic Torah is organized according to a pattern of initial "statutes" that are concerned with a fundamental legal theme or concern followed by a series of "cases" that takes up the same legal theme or concern and demonstrates how that theme or concern comes to expression in selected legal cases. As noted in the analysis of the structure of Deut 12–26, these concerns include an initial section concerning Israel's and Judah's cultic differentiation from the nations in Deut 12:2—13:9, followed by a detailed discussion of specific legal instruction concerning Israel's or Judah's holy conduct in Deut 14:1—26:15. Following an introductory statement concerning the holiness of the people in Deut 14:1-2, the sixteen specific concerns addressed include: (1) the eating of meat (Deut 14:3-21); (2) tithes (Deut 14:22-29); (3) debt issues (Deut 15:1-18); (4) the offering of the first-born (Deut 15:19-23); (5) the observance of holidays (Deut 16:1-17); (6) judicial and political authority (Deut 16:18—17:20); (7) religious authority (Deut 18:1—19:13); (8) territorial and boundary issues (Deut 19:14—21:23); (9) treatment of what pertains to other (Deut 22:1-8); (10) mixing what does not belong together (Deut 22:9-29); (11) impurities (Deut 23:1-15); (12) improper transactions with human beings (Deut 23:16—24:5); (13) improper financial and lending transactions (Deut 24:6-13); (14) justice due to the poor (Deut 24:14—25:3); (15) rights to sustenance and continuation (Deut 25:4-12); and (16) the obligation to give what is due (Deut 25:13—26:15). A concluding exhortation to observe YHWH's Torah in Deut 26:16-19 closes out Moses' second speech.

A close reading of the Deuteronomic Torah indicates that many of the legal topics have been previously addressed in the law codes of Exodus—Numbers. In many instances, the Deuteronomic instruction revises legal cases from earlier law codes in order to address problems or gaps that would have arisen in the earlier instances. The Deuteronomic Torah demonstrates a heightened concern with the rights and welfare of the poor, particularly women, resident aliens, and Levites. At the synchronic level, such revision and concern represent an attempt to address expanding sets of circumstances in relation to the earlier law codes. At the diachronic level, such revision reflects the setting of the composition of Deuteronomic Torah in the court of King Josiah of Judah (640–609 BCE), who was placed on the throne by "the people of the land," the agricultural class of ancient Judah, who put down a revolt against the house of David from within the royal court that saw the assassination of Josiah's father, King Amon ben Manasseh (r. 642–640 BCE). The "people of the land" represented the poorer agricultural class that had to be rebuilt following the Assyrian invasions of Judah in the late eighth century BCE, and women, resident aliens, and Levites would have been important constituents of the lower economic echelons of ancient Judean society insofar as they were not able fully to own or control land which served as the economic basis for an agricultural society. The socio-economic aspects of Josiah's reforms were meant to address the needs of these groups and thereby secure their support of the throne.

The initial sub-section in Deut 12:2—13:19 focuses especially on Israel's/Judah's cultic differentiation and thereby establishes the foundations for the balance of the topics addressed in Deuteronomic Torah insofar as it portrays Israel/Judah as a distinctive people among the nations. The text begins with a series of statutes or apodictic commands in Deut 12:2-28 that take up a command to destroy foreign worship sites throughout the land (Deut 12:2-3); the prohibition against worshipping YHWH anywhere except for the one site where YHWH chooses to manifest the divine name or presence (Deut 12:4-7); the commands to bring all offerings to the one place where YHWH chooses to manifest the divine name or presence (Deut 12:8-16); the commands to eat all offerings in the one place where YHWH chooses to manifest the divine name or presence (Deut 12:17-27); and a concluding command to observe YHWH's commandments and not to follow in the practices of the foreign nations (Deut 12:28—13:1). The cases then follow in Deut 13:2-19, including instructions to adhere only to prophets of YHWH and to put foreign prophets to death (Deut 13:2-6); to put to death those who would lead the people into the worship of foreign gods (Deut 13:7-12); and to destroy any town in Israel that engages in the worship of foreign gods (Deut 13:13-19). Fundamentally, this sub-unit is concerned with the exclusive worship of YHWH in Israel/Judah, and it emphasizes that worship must be carried out only at the one (sanctuary) site where YHWH chooses to manifest the divine name or presence. This overriding concern with cultic centralization differs from Exod 20:19-23, which calls for worship of

YHWH, but allows for the building of altars in every place where YHWH's presence might be manifested. Synchronically, it allows for only one Temple site in Judaism, generally understood as a reference to the Jerusalem Temple. Diachronically, it points to Josiah's concern to centralize worship in Jerusalem and thereby to reunite the nation under Davidic rule in the aftermath of the collapse of the northern kingdom of Israel by undermining the former northern worship sites at Beth El and Dan.

Deuteronomy 14:1-2 introduces the paragraphs concerned with the holy conduct of the people by instructing them to refrain from the foreign practice of gashing oneself or shave the front of the head on behalf of the dead and instead to constitute themselves as a holy people dedicated to YHWH.

The first major legal paragraph in Deut 14:3-21 takes up the eating of meat. This section appears only in the form of statutes or apodictic instruction that prohibits the eating of anything abhorrent in Deut 14:3, and then goes on to define those animals, fish, birds, and insects that may be eaten over against those that are unfit for human consumption (Deut 14:4-21). These instructions expand upon Exod 22:30, which prohibits the consumption of meat from animals that have been killed by beasts in the wild, and it complements Lev 11, which also specifies animals fit for human consumption. Deuteronomy 14:3-21 thereby constitutes an example of the means by which Gen 9 proposed to limit human violence by allowing the slaughter of animals to be used as food, but limiting the animals that would be eligible for human consumption. At the diachronic level, Deut 14:3-21 predates Gen 9 and Lev 11, but it represents a stage in the development of Israelite/Judean sacrificial practice, particularly the treatment of animal life in creation.

Deuteronomy 14:22-29 focuses on the tithe in ancient Israel and Judah. It calls for one-tenth of each Israelite's income to be offered as a tithe at the sanctuary. The tithe is well-known in Israel from early times (see Gen 14:20; 28:22; 1 Sam 8:15, 17). Deuteronomy 14:22-29 specifies the earlier law in Exod 22:28-29 that requires Israelites to bring offerings to the sanctuary without specifying any quantity or percentage, and it states that such tithes are to support the poor, including the Levites, widows, and orphans (cf. Exod 23:10-11). Later texts, such as Lev 27:30-33 and Num 18, specify that all tithes belong to YHWH and that they will be used to support the priesthood.

Deuteronomy 15:1-18 takes up debt issues. Deuteronomy 15:1-8 begins with statutes that call for the remission of debt in every seventh year (Deut 15:1-3) and that prohibit poverty among the people (Deut 15:4-6). Specific cases then follow, including the requirement to lend to the poor even with the approach of the seventh year of remission (Deut 15:7-11) and specifications concerning the terms of service for debt slavery (Deut 15:12-18). The standard six-year term of service for debt slavery is already well known in Exod 21:1-11 (cf. the terms of Jacob's service to Laban to pay the bride price for Leah and Rachel in Gen 29–31), but Deut 15:12-18 modifies those terms by stipulating that the freed slave be granted a portion of the master's income to help ensure that he will not go back into debt so easily and that women slaves be freed on the same basis as male slaves, thereby providing greater incentive to a male slave who is married during the term of his service to choose to be freed as he will be able to leave with his wife.

Deuteronomy 15:19-23 takes up the offering of the first-born from herd and flock that are to be consecrated to YHWH. The basic statute appears in vv. 19-20, but the following case in vv. 21-23 stipulates that defective animals are not offered to YHWH but are slaughtered and eaten in the villages and towns. This law differs from earlier cases in Exod 13:1-2, 11-16; 22:28-29; and 34:19-20, which call for the offering of the first-born to YHWH. The Deuteronomic instruction allows the people living in the countryside to keep and eat a greater share of their herds and flocks. It nevertheless calls for the proper treatment of blood.

Deuteronomy 16:1-17 focuses on observance of the three major pilgrimage festivals in ancient Israel in which all males are to appear at the sanctuary to make the offerings required for each festival. The pilgrimage festivals include Pesach (Passover), Shavuot (Weeks), and Sukkot (Booths). This section includes statutes only, although it provides detailed instruction concerning the observance of each festival. This calendar elaborates upon the far more basic instructions in Exod 23:14-18; 34:18-26.

Deuteronomy 16:18—17:20 takes up the questions of judicial and political authority in ancient Israel, including the appointment of judges and tribal officials as well as the selection of a king. The statutes or apodictic instructions appear in Deut 16:18—17:2, which command the appointment of judges and tribal officials, call for the practice of justice in all judicial proceedings, forbid the installation of Asherot (sacred posts) or Matzevot (sacred pillars) that are identified with Canaanite practice, and prohibit the sacrifice of defective animals at the altar. The case laws appear in Deut 17:2-20, which define the judicial procedure for executing someone who commits religious apostasy, call for the submission of difficult cases to the Levites and judge who will act as chief judges, and define the procedure and qualifications for selecting a king in Israel. This section systematizes and clarifies procedures for the appointment of judges in Exod 18 and various judicial instructions in Exod 23:1-3, 6-9, 13.

Deuteronomy 18:1—19:13 deals with the questions of religious authority in ancient Israel and Judah, particularly the rights and responsibilities of the Levites as well as prophets. Apodictic instruction or statutes appear in Deut 18:1-5, and stipulate that the Levites will hold no territory in Israel, but will be supported by offerings from the people. The cases appear in Deut 18:6—19:13, which enables the Levites to live in the central sanctuary of the land, calls for the appointment of prophets to speak on behalf of YHWH rather than pagan soothsayers and augurs, and institutes cities of refuge where someone who commits manslaughter may flee for refuge from blood vengeance by the family of the victim. The instructions concerning YHWH's prophets indicate that the criterion for identifying a true prophet of YHWH is whether or not the prophet's words will come to pass, which provides apparently effective criteria when the prophet's words are fulfilled in a short period of time but poses problems when the prophet's words are not fulfilled for longer periods and even millennia. The role of the Levites presupposes the narratives of Num 17–18, which identify the Levites as the priestly tribe and defines their rites and responsibilities, and the question of the prophets presupposes Num 11, in which all of the elders of Israel prophesy. The prohibition of Canaanite practice presupposes Exod 23:24 and 34:11-16. Numbers 35:9-34 provides detailed discussion of cities of refuge and the treatment of those who commit manslaughter.

Deuteronomy 19:14—21:23 focuses on questions related to territorial boundaries and judicial oaths. The apodictic instructions or statutes appear in Deut 19:14-15, including the prohibition against moving territorial boundary markers and the requirement that two witnesses are necessary to convict an accused person in a court of law. The statutes include a statement of the *Lex Talionis* (cf. Exod 21:23-25; Lev 24:17-21). The cases then follow in Deut 19:16—21:23, and include the procedure for trying a case in court and a lengthy section that takes up procedures for engaging in war. Instruction concerning the procedure for war includes the role of the priests in blessing the army, the question of those who might be exempt from military service, instructions concerning the acceptance of surrender, instructions concerning the need to destroy a town that does not surrender, the treatment and use of trees in an enemy nation, procedures for making decisions concerning the discovery of a corpse in the land, instructions concerning the marriage of Israelite men to captive foreign women, the designation of a man's legal heirs, the treatment of a defiant son, and the disposal of the body of a man executed for a capital offense. In addition to the alternative versions of the *Lex Talionis* mentioned above, this section elaborates on laws concerned with warfare in Exod 23:23-33; 34:11-16; and Num 34:50-56, questions of murder and corpse contamination in Num 35:16-24, and questions not treated in the earlier law codes.

Deuteronomy 22:1-8 focuses on the treatment of property and social relationships or boundaries, that is, what pertains to others. The section begins with statutes in vv. 1-5, which present instruction concerning the return of a neighbor's ox, the return of a neighbor's ass, garment, or other property, and a prohibition against cross-dressing. These instructions develop earlier instruction concerning the return of property in Exod 23:4. The cases in vv. 6-8 prohibit the taking of a mother bird together her eggs, since the parent and offspring should not die together, and the requirement to build a parapet on the roof of a house to prevent fatal accidents. The case of the birds echoes the concern with boiling a kid in its mother's milk in Exod 23:19; 34:26 (cf. Lev 22:28). The concern with personal liability takes up analogous concerns in Exod 22:28-36.

Deuteronomy 29:9-29 focuses on the prohibition against mixing things that do not belong together, which pertains to issues of agriculture, clothing, social identity, and marital relations. The statutes in vv. 9-12 take up various concerns, including the mixing of seed in a field, plowing with an ox and an ass together, wearing clothing made of mixed fiber, and the instruction to affix tassels on a garment to identify oneself as a Jew. Such instructions are likely intended to protect against diluting agricultural produce with a cheaper seed and protecting animals with very different capabilities, and diluting clothing with cheaper fabric. The principle extends to social identity, insofar as v. 12 calls for distinctive clothing for Judeans. Tassels were known to be worn by monarchs and other members of higher social classes in the ancient Near Eastern world, and the fringe of a garment often functioned as an indication of legal signature. The following cases then extend the principle into cases of sexual relations, including the protection of a newly married woman against charges of promiscuity, the condemnation of adulterers, and the treatment of unmarried women who have relations with a man. These cases are designed to protect the woman in question if she does not consent to relations with the man. If she is raped by a man, the requirement that he marry her without the possibility of divorce is designed to ensure her economic support for life. The earlier law in Exod 22:15-16 required that the man marry her or at least pay the bride price, but it did not protect her from subsequent divorce.

Deuteronomy 23:1-15 develops the concern of the previous section by delving more deeply into the forbidden mixing of social relations of various types. The statutes in vv. 1-9 prohibit marriage to the wife of one's father and prohibit the entry of various classes of persons into the congregation of Israel who would worship in the sanctuary. Those prohibited include those with damaged reproductive organs rendering them unable to father children, persons born of prohibited marriages (for example, incest), and Ammonites and Moabites because of their past treatment of Israel in the wilderness period. Descendants of the Edomites and Egyptians are permitted, however, presumably due to Edom's status as descendants of Jacob's brother Esau and Egypt's status as a source for the mixed multitude that accompanied Israel through the wilderness. The case in vv. 10-15 takes up issues of purity in a military camp.

Deuteronomy 23:16—24:5 extends the concern for mixing what does not belong together by focusing on the questions of improper transactions between human beings. The statutes in vv. 16-21 include prohibitions against turning over an escaped slave who seeks refuge, prohibitions against cultic prostitution and the use of income derived from such activity, and prohibitions against charging interest to fellow Israelites/Judeans. The cases in Deut 23:22—24:5 call for the fulfillment of vows, eating of produce in a fellow Israelite/Judean's vineyard or field (but harvest is not allowed), and a ban on remarrying a former wife after she has married another man. Such laws protect the poor and women, that is, Israelites are given privileges that will carry them through times of need, and women are protected from abuse in potentially fraudulent marriage schemes concocted by their husbands.

Deuteronomy 24:6-13 takes up improper financial transactions, again building on the previous section. The statutes in v. 6 forbid taking hand mills and upper millstones in pawn because the implements necessary for grinding grain are essential for the preparation of food. The cases in vv. 7-13 call for a death penalty for kidnappers, special care in the treatment of skin disease, and the proper treatment of items given in pledge for a loan. All of these cases are concerned with the sustainability of life on behalf of the poor and develop principles stated in Exod 22:24-26.

Deuteronomy 24:14—25:3 then focuses on justice for the poor. The statutes in vv. 14-18 include prohibitions against abusing the poor, holding parents and children accountable for the deeds of the other, and subverting the rights of foreigners, orphans, and widows. The cases call for agricultural practice that will leave food for the poor at harvest time and they stipulate limits on punishment to be rendered in legal disputes. This section develops earlier laws in Exod 21:16; 22:20-26.

Deuteronomy 25:4-12 take up concerns with the sustainability of life. The statute in v. 4 prohibits muzzling a threshing ox, so that the ox can eat and sustain itself while working. The following cases develop this principle by calling for a Levirate marriage procedure by which the brother (or other male relative; cf. Ruth's marriage to Boaz) of a man who dies childless will father a child with the widow to ensure the continuity of the dead man's house and name. Likewise, a woman who tries to crush the genitals of a male opponent loses her hand because her act threatens the future descendants of the man so affected.

Deuteronomy 25:13—26:15 takes up obligations to give what is due. The statutes in vv. 13-19 call for the use of just weights for calculating measures in financial transactions and reminds the reader of Amalek's attempts to destroy Israel when it was defenseless. The case in Deut 26:1-15 calls for the presentation of tithes due to YHWH as obligatory offerings at the sanctuary given in return for YHWH's grant of land to Israel. The case develops the obligation to bring offerings previously discussed in Exod 23:14-19; 34:18-26; and Deut 16:1-17, and it specifically notes that the tithe will help to support Levites, foreigners, orphans, and widows in the land.

Finally, Deut 26:16-19 presents a concluding exhortation to observe YHWH's Torah in order to ensure Israel's status as a holy nation before YHWH.

c) Moses' Third Speech to Israel: Blessings and Curses

Deuteronomy 27:1—28:69 constitutes the account of Moses' third speech to Israel on the plains of Moab prior to the nation's entry into the promised land. Having completed the instruction speech that reiterates divine Torah, Moses now turns to the blessings and curses that will result depending upon Israel's observance of YHWH's instructions. Insofar as the interplay of blessings and curses is intended to persuade the audience, whether the audience is conceived as Israel as portrayed in the book of Deuteronomy or as the readers of the book, this section serves the

exhortational purposes of the framework of Deuteronomy. This section emphasizes the curses of agricultural failure, invasion by foreign enemies, exile, and even
the plagues visited on Egypt that will follow should Israel choose not to observe
divine Torah. It therefore represents an attempt to persuade by threat. But the
threats are designed to work together with the blessings that appear within this
section and the portrayal of possible repentance and return from exile in the
following account of Moses' fourth speech (Deut 29:1—30:20).

The result is a text that addresses the question of theodicy insofar as it attempts
to account for both the realities of Israel's suffering due to foreign invasion by
various enemies (for example, the Arameans, Assyrians, Babylonians) and the
possibilities of Israel's restoration in the aftermath of calamity. Thus YHWH
appears as a G-d who is capable of both justice or judgment and mercy (cf. Exod
34:6-7). In this respect, Deuteronomy—and indeed the Torah at large—holds that
YHWH is a moral deity whose morality calls for the punishment of YHWH's own
people when they purportedly do wrong and for the blessing of the people when
they purportedly do what is right. Insofar as YHWH's capabilities of justice and
mercy extend to Israel's experience of both the natural and human realms, that is,
the portrayals of agricultural blessings and curses together with the possibilities of
foreign invasion and return from exile, Deuteronomy makes an argument that
YHWH is sovereign of both the worlds of creation and human events.

But such a model of divine morality rooted in YHWH's roles as author of
creation and master of human events also raises problems. Insofar as the model
presupposes that the experience of evil is necessarily rooted in the presumption of
human wrongdoing and that the experience of blessing is likewise necessarily
rooted in the presumption of human righteousness, it ultimately produces a
model in which the victims of evil are charged with having committed some great
sin that prompted the judgment realized against them. The problems with such a
model of divine moral causation have become apparent in modern theological
discussion of the Shoah or Holocaust in which theologians have come to recognize that the Shoah cannot be explained adequately as the result of Jewish wrongdoing, but must be explained as the result of decisions made by the perpetrators
of such murders, that is, the Nazi government of Germany and its supporters in
Europe and beyond.[11] The Bible as a whole is also aware of this problem, for
example, Esther postulates a scenario of destruction in which YHWH is absent
and Job posits a scenario in which YHWH's morality comes into question.[12]
Deuteronomy emerges as one portrayal of divine power and morality—albeit a
foundational one since it is part of the Torah itself—among the various portrayals
offered throughout the books of the Bible. In this respect, Deuteronomy's well-
ordered portrayal of a moral and powerful G-d becomes both the foundation for
the Bible's understanding of YHWH and the basis for continued reflection and
debate on the question among the biblical books.

When considered diachronically, Deut 27–28 clearly presuppose covenant- or
treaty-making in the ancient Near Eastern world, particularly by the Neo-Assyrian

empire.[13] The Assyrian king appears as the suzerain monarch and the subject king as the vassal who must observe the suzerain's requirements in such treaties which call for blessings should the vassal obey and threaten punishment should the vassal refuse to observe the suzerain's terms. YHWH here plays the role of suzerain, and Israel plays the role of vassal subject to YHWH's requirements. Insofar as these chapters are frequently attributed to King Josiah's edition of Deuteronomy, the Josianic conceptualization of Israel's relationship with YHWH, sovereign deity of all creation and humankind, would reflect its experience as a vassal of the Assyrian empire during the late eighth and seventh centuries BCE.

A particular problem in diachronic scholarship appears in the portrayal of the covenant cursing ceremony at Mt. Ebal and Mt. Gerizim in Deut 27. The chapter portrays the site of Shechem in central Israel, and of course Moses never enters the land of Israel nor does he travel to Shechem. The text very carefully portrays Moses as calling upon the people to perform this ceremony once they have taken possession of the land. The significance of this act must be traced to the role that Shechem plays in Israel's early history. Shechem is the site where the major north–south and east–west routes come together in northern Israel. It also sits on the boundary of Ephraim and Manasseh, the two tribes that constitute the core of the northern kingdom of Israel, and it is portrayed in biblical texts as a site where Israel comes together to undertake major actions and make major decisions, such as the sealing of the covenant by Joshua in Josh 8:30-35; 24, the attempt to seize kingship in Israel by Abimelech in Judg 9, and the decision to reject the house of David and select Jeroboam ben Nebat as the first king of northern Israel in 1 Kgs 12. By placing the covenant-cursing ceremony in Shechem, Deuteronomy deliberately appeals to the former northern kingdom of Israel to accept that its destruction by Assyria in 722–721 BCE was the result of YHWH's judgment for Israel's failure to observe divine Torah (cf. 2 Kgs 17). But insofar as the means for repentance and return are spelled out in Deut 29–30, the covenant ceremony at Shechem also provides the foundation for a decision to accept YHWH's Torah as the basis for restoration under Davidic rule in the late monarchic period.

In later periods, Deut 27–28 would serve as a basis for explaining the Babylonian exile and other such setbacks in Jewish history as a consequence of a failure to observe divine Torah.

d) Moses' Fourth Speech to Israel: Final Exhortation to Observe the Covenant

Deuteronomy 29:1—30:20 constitutes Moses' final exhortation to Israel on the plains of Moab to observe YHWH's Torah as the basis for its relationship with YHWH and its life in the land of Israel. At this point, Moses takes the opportunity to rehearse Israel's history, including elements of its journey through the wilderness as well as YHWH's promises to the ancestors and the exodus from Egypt. It is somewhat of a piecemeal history that hits many of the high points of

YHWH's actions on behalf of Israel throughout the Pentateuch in an effort to remind Israel of the benefits of its relationship with YHWH.

Nevertheless, this speech presupposes the scenario of punishment laid out in the previous section and builds on that by presenting a scenario for a future after punishment and exile, viz., the possibility that Israel might repent from wrong-doing and return to the land of Israel from foreign exile. The speech does rehearse the possibility of curses, but it ultimately holds out the possibilities of repentance and restoration as a means to convince its audience—again both the fictive audience of Israel portrayed on the plains of Moab and the reading audience of the book of Deuteronomy—that they should choose to observe divine Torah even in the aftermath of exile.[14]

Once again, Deut 29–30 presumes that wrongdoing on the part of Israel explains national disaster, and observance of divine Torah explains blessing and restoration. Such contentions are clearly challenged by the experience of the Shoah in modern times, viz., such a murderous event does not take place because the victim Israel brought suffering on itself by refusing to observe Torah, but because a nation such as Germany chose to attack Jews to serve its own anti-Semitic understanding of the world.

These chapters share many of the same concerns of Deut 27–28. The emphasis on repentance and return from exile could serve the interests of the Josianic restoration, insofar as it would attempt to convince northern Israelites to return to YHWH and the Jerusalem Temple (and YHWH's Davidic monarch) in Josiah's Judah. Most interpreters prefer to read this text in relation to the realities of the Babylonian exile, so that Deut 29–30 provides a theological basis for YHWH's decision to restore Israel/Judah in the Persian period following the Babylonian exile.

2) The Account of Moses' Transfer of Leadership, Death, and Burial in Moab

Deuteronomy 31–34 closes both the book of Deuteronomy and the Pentateuch at large with an account of Moses' death and burial, together with provisions for the transfer of leadership to Joshua and the promulgation of divine Torah. The literary structure of this section appears as follows:

The Account of Moses' Transfer of Leadership to Joshua, Torah to the Levites,
and Death, and Burial in Moab   Deut 31:1—34:12
  I. Moses' Provisions for Transfer of Leadership to Joshua
     and Torah to the Levites   31:1-13
  II. YHWH's Provisions for Transfer of Leadership to Joshua
     and Torah to the Levites   31:14—32:47
  III. Moses' Preparations for Death: Blessing for Israel   32:48—33:29
  IV. Moses' Death and Burial   34:1-12

The account begins in Deut 31:1-13, in which Moses' announces to Israel that he is old, and that YHWH has appointed Joshua ben Nun to serve as his successor as leader of the nation. The narrative emphasizes that YHWH is the one who acts on Israel's behalf, which aids in legitimizing Joshua as Moses' successor. Moses' charge to Joshua likewise stresses that YHWH will go before Israel into the land based on the promises made to the ancestors. Moses' writing down of the Torah points to the traditional understanding that Torah is transmitted from YHWH to Israel through Moses, and his handing the Torah to the Levites ensures that the Levites will serve as the primary agents by which Torah is taught to Israel. Thus, Moses' leadership functions are divided insofar as Joshua takes on the administrative and military role, like that of the kings of Israel, and the Levites take on the religious role anticipating their function in the future Temple. The instruction to read Torah before the people every seventh year, that is, the year of Remission (Deut 15:1-11), at the festival of Sukkot, puts into place the liturgical structure by which this task is to be accomplished. A somewhat different chain of the transmission of Torah from Moses to Joshua to the elders to the prophets and to the men of the great assembly is presupposed by *m. Avot* 1:1. The Mishnah's chain of transmission bypasses the Levites, apparently because the Temple and priesthood had been eclipsed in the Rabbinic period.

Deuteronomy 31:14—32:47 shifts to YHWH's provisions for the transfer of leadership to Joshua and the responsibility for teaching Torah to the Levites. YHWH's speech to Moses confirms the selection of Joshua as Moses' successor, but it also provides a rationale for the teaching of Torah by anticipating Israel's apostasy against YHWH. Such a statement is remarkable insofar as it once again raises the question of theodicy, viz., despite YHWH's roles as author of creation and master of human events, it asserts that the people will suffer because they will fail to adhere to YHWH or to observe YHWH's Torah. Such an assertion is designed to explain suffering even though Israel's G-d is the ultimate power in the universe who has made absolute promises to Israel's ancestors. This concern then explains Moses' writing of the Song of Moses, which appears in Deut 32:1-43 to rehearse YHWH's relationship with the people of Israel. Many modern interpreters have asserted that the song is based on the covenant lawsuit genre employed by the prophets to portray YHWH's charges of apostasy against the people. The poem takes up the themes of divine justice and mercy together with YHWH's roles as author of creation and deliverer of Israel. It asserts divine fidelity at the outset and calls upon its audience to remember YHWH's acts on behalf of Israel, particularly granting Jacob the land of Israel, from the beginning. The poem explains Israel's setbacks by arguing that Israel/Jeshurun abandoned YHWH when it became fat and prosperous, which in turn provoked YHWH's anger and punishment. But after asserting that YHWH will hide the divine face from Israel, the poem turns to YHWH's decision to demonstrate fidelity to Israel and take vengeance against its/YHWH's enemies. The account concludes with statements of Joshua's/Hosea's recitation of the words to the people and Moses' exhortation to the people to observe YHWH's words. In a nutshell, the Song of Moses both summarizes the theology of Deuteronomy and accounts for the problem of evil by asserting that evil comes when the people abandon YHWH.

Although many diachronic scholars argue that the Song of Moses presupposes the Babylonian exile, the reference to Hosea ben Nun in Deut 32:44 suggests that the poem comes from a northern Israelite setting (cf. Num 13:8, 16, and the discussion of provenance there). The song just as easily addresses the problem of evil provoked by the collapse of the northern kingdom of Israel in the late monarchic period.

Deuteronomy 32:48—33:29 conveys Moses' preparations for death, including the blessing of Moses for the tribes of Israel. The account begins with YHWH's command to Moses to ascend Mt. Nebo in Moab overlooking the Jordan River and the Land of Israel, and it reiterates YHWH's decision that Moses would not enter the land due to his travesty at Meribath-Kadesh in the Wilderness of Zin (Num 20). The blessing of Moses then follows in Deut 33:1-29 in the form of a blessing of a father over his sons prior to death (cf. Isaac's blessings of Esau and Jacob in Gen 27 and Jacob's blessing of his sons in Gen 49). The blessing begins with references to YHWH's revelation at Sinai and Seir in Edom, and then turns to the individual tribes. It is noteworthy that Simon is not included in the list, but Joseph's blessing refers to both Ephraim and Manasseh. Key elements in the blessing include hopes for the restoration of (the royal tribe) Judah, Levi's role in teaching Torah to Israel, Joseph's bounty and power, and Jeshurun's/Israel's security. Diachronically speaking, the poem seems to presuppose a northern milieu given Joseph's power, but Judean concerns may appear in the hope that Judah will be restored.

Finally, Deut 34:1-12 recounts Moses' death and burial on the summit of Pisgah on Mt. Nebo in Moab. The narrative stresses Moses' view of the land of Israel and YHWH's promises to grant the land of Israel to the ancestors. It also makes sure that Moses' burial spot remains unknown, in part to ensure that it would not become a shrine. The narrative concludes with Joshua's assumption of power as the leader of Israel and an assessment of Moses' life identifying him as an incomparable prophet who spoke with YHWH face to face and who carried out the manifestations of YHWH's power in delivering Israel from Egypt. Already in Talmudic times, interpreters have recognized that this portion could not have been written by Moses (*b. Baba Batra* 14b-15a).

NOTES

[1] See especially Bernard M. Levinson, *Deuteronomy and the Hermeneutics of Legal Innovation* (New York: Oxford University Press, 1997).

[2] For discussion of the Levitical sermon form, see Gerhard von Rad, *Studies in Deuteronomy* (SBT 9; London: SCM, 1953), 11–24, and my *King Josiah of Judah: The Lost Messiah of Israel* (Oxford: Oxford University Press 2001), 142–43.

[3] See Antony F. Campbell and Mark A. O'Brien, *Sources of the Pentateuch: Texts, Introductions, Annotations* (Minneapolis: Fortress Press, 1993), 98–99.
[4] For overview discussion, see Antony F. Campbell and Mark A. O'Brien, *Unfolding the Deuteronomistic History: Origins, Upgrades, Present Text* (Minneapolis: Fortress Press, 2000), 1–99; Moshe Weinfeld, *Deuteronomy and the Deuteronomic School* (Oxford: Oxford University Press, 1972); idem, *Deuteronomy 1–11* (AB 5; Garden City: Doubleday, 991), 1–84.
[5] For an overview discussion, see Mark A. O'Brien, "The Book of Deuteronomy," *CR:BS* 3 (1995): 95–128; Ronald E. Clements, *Deuteronomy* (OTG; Sheffield: JSOT, 1989).
[6] For example, Albrecht Alt, "Die Heimat des Deuteronomiums," in *Kleine Schriften zur Geshichte des Volkes Israel II* (Munich: Beck, 1953), 250–75; E. W. Nicholson, *Deuteronomy and Tradition: Literary and Historical Traditions in the Book of Deuteronomy* (Philadelphia: Fortress Press, 1967).
[7] Ronald E. Clements, "Deuteronomy and the Jerusalem Cult Tradition," *VT* 15 (1965): 300–12, and my *King Josiah of Judah: The Lost Messiah of Israel* (Oxford: Oxford University Press, 2001), 137–69.
[8] See my *King Josiah*, 137–69, and Carolyn Pressler, *The View of Women Found in Deuteronomic Family Laws* (BZAW 216; Berlin: de Gruyter, 1993).
[9] See Campbell and O'Brien, *Unfolding the Deuteronomistic History*, 43–55.
[10] See, for example, D. J. Wiseman, *The Vassal Treaties of Esarhaddon* (London: British School of Archaeology in Iraq, 1958); S. Parpola and K. Watanabe, *Neo-Assyrian Treaties and Loyalty Oaths* (SAS 2; Helsinki: University of Helsinki, 1988).
[11] For discussion of the theological problem of the Shoah in modern Jewish thought, see especially Zachary Braiterman, *(G-d) After Auschwitz: Tradition and Change in Post-Holocaust Jewish Thought* (Princeton: Princeton University Press, 1998); Michael L. Morgan, *Beyond Auschwitz: Post-Holocaust Jewish Thought in America* (Oxford and New York: Oxford University Press, 2001); Steven T. Katz, *Post-Holocaust Dialogues: Critical Studies in Modern Jewish Thought* (New York and London: New York University Press, 1985).
[12] See my *Reading the Hebrew Bible after the Shoah: Engaging Holocaust Theology* (Minneapolis: Fortress Press, 2008).
[13] For the treaty background of Deut 28, see especially Hans Ulrich Steymans, *Deuteronomium 28 und die adê zur Thronfolgeregelung Asarhaddons: Segen und Fluch im Alten Orient und in Israel* (OBO 145; Freiburg: Éditions universitaires; Göttingen: Vandenhoeck & Ruprecht, 1995).
[14] See especially Jack Shechter, *The Land of Israel: The Theological Dimensions. A Study of a Promise and a Land's "Holiness"* (Lanham: University Press of America, 2010), who demonstrates that Deuteronomy does not hold to a strictly conditional understanding of Israel's covenant with YHWH, but envisions restoration following repentance in keeping with the unconditional nature of the covenant.

Part IIIA

נביאים ראשונים
The Former Prophets

A. OVERVIEW

The Former Prophets (Hebrew, *nĕbî'îm ri'šônîm*), which includes the books of Joshua, Judges, Samuel, and Kings, constitutes the first major portion of the Prophets in the Tanak.[1] Altogether, these books differ from the type of classical prophetic book found in the Latter Prophets. Instead of the standard mix of oracular and narrative material typical of the prophetic books, the books of the Former Prophets present a narrative history of the nation of Israel from the time of its entry into the promised land of Israel under the leadership of Joshua ben Nun until the aftermath of the Babylonian exile. Although these books are historical narratives, Jewish tradition maintains that they are composed by prophets (*b. Baba Batra* 15a), that is, Joshua is composed by Joshua ben Nun, who is viewed as a prophet; Judges and Samuel are composed by the prophet Samuel; and Kings is composed by the prophet and priest, Jeremiah ben Hilkiah. The designation Former Prophets is derived from Zech 1:4 where it is employed to describe the earlier prophets who had warned Israel to turn back from its evil ways and thereby avoid divine judgment in the form of the Babylonian exile.

The synchronic literary structure of the narrative is based on the sequence of books. The book of Joshua discusses Israel's entry into the land, the defeat of the Canaanites, and the apportionment of the land among the tribes of Israel. The book of Judges discusses the earliest history of Israel in the land under the rule of a series of Judges, who defended Israel against various enemies until it became apparent that central monarchic rule was necessary for Israel's future security and continuity. The book of Samuel, read as 1–2 Samuel in Christian tradition, discusses the origins of kingship in ancient Israel, beginning with the reign of King Saul ben Kish and culminating in the rule of King David ben Jesse and the foundation of the Davidic dynasty in Jerusalem. Finally, Kings, read as 1–2 Kings in Christian tradition, discusses the subsequent history of the Kings of Israel and Judah, beginning with King Solomon's reign over a united Israel, continuing through the histories of the separate monarchies of Israel and Judah, and culminating in the destruction of northern Israel by the Assyrian empire and later of Judah by the Babylonian empire. Kings concludes with a brief notice concerning the release of King Jehoiachin ben Jehoiakim from prison by King Evil Merodach of Babylon.

The Former Prophets employs a distinct theological perspective in its narrative presentation of Israel's history that interprets that history in relation to its own understanding of divine purpose. History is not written simply to provide an account of the past; it is written so that both its writers and readers can reflect on and learn from that past in order to build a better future. Whereas the Torah lays out an ideal understanding of Israel in the midst of creation, the Former Prophets takes up the disruption of that ideal. Indeed, the Former Prophets employs its own theological perspectives in the presentation of Israel's history so that it might address the major theological problems of ancient Israel's and Judah's history, the Babylonian exile of 587–586 BCE in which Jerusalem and the Temple of Solomon were destroyed, the ruling house of David was deposed, and large numbers of the surviving Jerusalemites and Judeans were forced into exile in Babylonia. Overall, the Former Prophets constitute an expression of theodicy, that is, they defend the righteousness and power of YHWH in the face of the realities of the destruction of Jerusalem and the Temple and the exile of the people to Babylonia. Rather than charging that YHWH is powerless, unreliable, unjust, or absent in times of crisis, the Former Prophets chooses to explain the Babylonian exile by charging that the people of Israel and Judah—and not YHWH—were responsible for their own fate, that is, the Former Prophets maintains that the people of Israel and Judah had failed to adhere to YHWH and YHWH's expectations of the people as expressed in divine Torah from the time of their entry into the land through the time of the Babylonian exile.

The narrative assigns primary responsibility for the Babylonian exile to one figure, King Manasseh ben Amon of Judah (r. 687–642 BCE), who is judged by YHWH to be so wicked that YHWH determined to destroy Jerusalem and send the people into exile. The charge that Manasseh was responsible for the Babylonian exile is analogous to the charge that Jeroboam ben Nebat, the first king of northern Israel, was responsible for the Assyrian destruction of northern Israel in 722/1 BCE by leading the entire nation into sin and thereby prompting YHWH to destroy the nation. In addition to the questions raised about Manasseh and Jeroboam, the Former Prophets display some ambiguity about the Jerusalem Temple and the royal house of David as well.[2] It is not always clear that YHWH wants or needs a temple in the Former Prophets (2 Sam 7), and King David ben Jesse, the founder of the house of David, is a flawed character who enjoys the favor of YHWH but nevertheless commits adultery and murder in his rise to power (2 Sam 10–12). Although the Former Prophets appears to be primarily interested in the questions of exile and punishment, readers must remember that the purpose of such reflection on history is to learn from the alleged mistakes and problems of the past in order to build a better future. Insofar as the Former Prophets charges that the Babylonian exile took place as an expression of YHWH's punishment against Israel and Judah for failing to observe divine Torah, it serves as a basis for exhorting the people to rebuild Jerusalem, Judah, and Israel on the foundations of divine Torah in order to ensure the achievement of the ideal as laid out in the Five Books of Moses.

Although the Former Prophets appears early in the canonical sequence of the Tanak immediately following the Torah, readers must recognize that the Former Prophets does not constitute the only narrative account of Israel's and Judah's history in the Bible. The books of Chronicles and Ezra–Nehemiah appear as an alternative account of Israel's history in the Writings. Chronicles shares much material from the Former Prophets, particularly from Samuel and Kings, but Chronicles and Ezra–Nehemiah are very different works from the Former Prophets insofar as they have their own distinct theological perspectives. Chronicles and Ezra–Nehemiah share a concern with the Former Prophets for the Babylonian exile, but Chronicles and Ezra–Nehemiah are far more concerned with questions of restoration once the exile is over. Chronicles recounts Israel's history from the time of creation, through the formation of Israel, the inauguration of the monarchy and the building of the Temple in Jerusalem, and culminates in the Babylonian exile and the decree of King Cyrus of Persia that Jews would be able to return to Jerusalem from their exile in Babylonian to rebuild the Temple, repopulate Jerusalem, and restore Jewish life to the land of Judah. Ezra–Nehemiah relates that the process of restoration from the time of Cyrus' decree through the restoration was carried out under Ezra and Nehemiah. Whereas the Former Prophets explains the exile as a result of a history of Israel's failure to observe divine Torah and points especially to Manasseh as the figure whose sins prompted YHWH's decision to destroy Jerusalem and the temple and to exile its people, Chronicles argues that the destruction was due only to the people of that generation who defiled the Temple and thereby brought about the destruction themselves. Although the Former Prophets was not written to challenge the reading of history in the Chronicles and Ezra–Nehemiah, the presence of two accounts of Israel's history in the Bible requires that they are in debate with each other, that is, readers of the Bible may reflect on two related but nevertheless different accounts of Israel's history, see the events of the past from two very different theological standpoints, and learn from both.

Diachronic scholarship adds much to modern perspectives concerning the Former Prophets. Archeological data and ancient Near Eastern textual sources confirm at least the broad outlines of ancient Israel's history, if not always the details presented in the Former Prophets. The fourteenth-century BCE Amarna tablets point to the presence of Habiru, semi-nomadic tribal groups that entered the land of Canaan from east of the Jordan and settled around major Canaanite cities.[3] Pharaoh Mernepthah's ca. 1220 BCE stele boasts of his victory over a Canaanite coalition that includes a semi-nomadic people called Israel, although most scholars recognize that his boasts were intended to mask the decline of Egyptian power in Canaan.[4] Destruction layers in sites along the boundaries of the hill country of Israel and the low-lying coastal plains and valleys point to conflict between the emerging Israelite nation in the hills and the Philistines of the coastal plain who were descended from the Sea Peoples that entered Canaan beginning in the twelfth century BCE.[5] Fortification of cities in Israel points to the emergence of a powerful kingdom at least by the ninth century BCE, and Assyrian and other textual sources refer to Israel, also known as the house of Omri, as well as a number of its monarchs, such as Ahab, Jehu, Joash, and others.[6] Countless archeological sites have been identified with locations mentioned in the Bible, and excavations illumine their historical life as cities and towns of ancient Israel and Judah. Inscriptional evidence, such as the Moabite stone and the Tel Dan inscription,[7] note elliptically the house of David, and later Assyrian and Babylonian records also name Judean kings, such as Hezekiah and Manasseh.[8] Extensive archeological evidence points to the Assyrian invasions of Israel and Judah in the late eighth century BCE and the Babylonian invasions of Judah in the early sixth century BCE.[9] Hebrew inscriptional material also documents the existence of Israel and Judah, including brief letters written on ostraca by Judean soldiers who defended Lachish against the Babylonian siege in the early sixth century BCE.[10] The destruction of Samaria in 722–721 BCE is noted in the records of King Sargon II of Assyria,[11] and the destruction of Jerusalem in 587–866 BCE by Nebuchadnezzar is well known, although the Babylonian Chronicle breaks off in 594 BCE.[12]

In addition to the issues of historical background, the literary accounts of the Former Prophets themselves have also been analyzed with the tools of historical-critical exegesis in an effort to reconstruct their compositional history.[13] The work of Martin Noth is especially important insofar as he identified the Former Prophets as a relatively unified historical account of Israel's history from the time of Joshua through the Babylonian exile.[14] Noth argued that several features of the books of Joshua, Judges, Samuel, and Kings, pointed to such an observation. A key observation was the role that major speeches by figures such as Joshua (Josh 1; 23), Samuel (1 Sam 12), Solomon (1 Kgs 8), and even the anonymous narrator (2 Kgs 17), played in unifying the work and giving it a relatively consistent literary, historical, and theological perspective that interpreted Israel's history from the standpoint of YHWH's covenant with Israel as expressed in the book of Deuteronomy. Noth called the work "the Deuteronomistic History" (DtrH), and argued that an author/editor had brought earlier traditions together to form an account of Israel's history under YHWH in the land of Israel from the time of Joshua through the Babylonian exile. He observed that the establishment of Israel in the land was grounded in the covenant as articulated in Deuteronomy that called upon Israel to acknowledge YHWH alone as its G-d and to observe YHWH's commandments as the condition for Israel's life in the land. Reversals in Israel's fortunes, that is, the attacks against Israel in the period of the Judges, the division of the kingdom following the reign of Solomon, the Aramean victories over Israel during the Omride period, the Assyrian destruction of Israel, and finally the Babylonian destruction of Jerusalem and Judah, were explained as the result of Israel's turning to other gods and failing to observe YHWH's laws. According to Noth, the DtrH was written following the Babylonian exile as a means to account for Israel's demise.

Later interpreters, while accepting Noth's overall thesis of a Deuteronomistic historical work, began to refine his work to account for problems in his understanding of the DtrH. Gerhard von Rad and Hans Walther Wolff noted that the DtrH was not entirely a history of Israel's decline as Noth had postulated, but that it displayed some rather positive and forward-looking elements. Von Rad argued that the DtrH is concerned with YHWH's promise to the house of David and the implications of that promise for future restoration.[15] Wolff noted the exhortational character of the DtrH that builds for the future by calling upon readers to adhere to YHWH and to observe YHWH's laws.[16] Hans-Detlef Hoffmann argued that patterns of Temple reform in the DtrH pointed to an agenda for Temple reform in the post-exilic period.[17]

Other scholars began to probe Noth's claims that the DtrH had collected older traditions and edited them into the larger DtrH historical framework. The American scholar Frank Cross noted that the foundational themes of the condemnation of Jeroboam ben Nebat and the northern kingdom of Israel and the eternal promise to the house of David culminated in the account of the reign of King Josiah of Judah (r. 640–609 BCE), whose attempts at religious reform and national restoration were based on the discovery of a Torah scroll in the Temple that appeared to be an early form of Deuteronomy.[18] Cross and his students, such as Richard Nelson, Richard Friedman, Steven McKenzie, Gary Knoppers, and others, therefore argue that an early edition of the DtrH was produced in the late seventh century BCE to portray King Josiah as the Davidic monarch who would reunite the twelve tribes of Israel under the rule of the house of David and restore the Jerusalem Temple as the central shrine of Israel where YHWH would be worshipped by the entire nation.[19] Different literary patterns concerning the reigns of the Judean monarchs in 2 Kgs 24–25 indicated that the DtrH was updated following the early death of Josiah at Megiddo at the hands of the Egyptians to account for the following years which led ultimately to destruction and exile.

European scholars, such as Rudolf Smend, Walter Dietrich, and Timo Veijola, examined references to divine Torah and prophecy throughout the history that pointed to three successive editions of the DtrH written from ca. 582–562 BCE, viz., the so-called *Grundschrift* or Foundational History; a Prophetic redaction that introduced prophetic narratives and interpretation of the history a short time later; and finally a Nomistic redaction that added material concerned with Israel's adherence to YHWH's "Law" only a few years later.[20]

Campbell and O'Brien account for the prevalence of prophetic material in the DtrH by positing a ninth-century BCE "Prophetic Record" that coalesces around narratives concerning the role of prophets in establishing and disestablishing monarchs, such as Samuel, Saul, and David; Ahijah, Solomon, and Jeroboam;

Elijah and Ahab; and Elisha and Jehu.[21] The Prophetic Record appears in texts from 1 Sam 1 through 2 Kgs 10 and provides an underlying narrative that was taken up and incorporated into the larger DtrH.

Baruch Halpern and David Vanderhooft examined patterns in the death and burial formulas for the kings of Judah and argued that they demonstrated a basis for a Hezekian edition of the DtrH written to support Hezekiah's reforms.[22] Iain Provan agreed that the Hezekiah narratives constituted an important point of historical culmination in the DtrH but postulated that the work was nevertheless designed to provide a paradigm for Josiah's reforms.[23]

It is difficult to navigate through the variety of models offered for the compositional history of the Former Prophets, but the Smend–Dietrich–Veijola model is especially problematic. Smend's identification of the Nomistic source is based on an outmoded Wellhausenian understanding of "law," that is, Torah (more properly "instruction"), that prompted him to identify references to Torah in texts from Joshua as later additions to an earlier text. Likewise, Dietrich's isolation of prophetic narratives is based on an overly strict form-critical exegetical basis that views genres such as prophecy as exclusionary Platonic ideals that can never mix with other genres, although more recent form-critical theory demonstrates that genres do indeed work together within texts.

The Cross model of a Josianic edition of the DtrH and an exilic update is far more promising. Helga Weippert had already demonstrated the shift in regnal formulas apparent in 2 Kgs 24–25 that made his hypothesis workable.[24] My own work on the DtrH points to the basis for reconstructing the redactional history of the Manasseh narrative in 2 Kgs 21:1-18 that provides the basis for postulating an exilic-period reworking of the Josianic DtrH.[25] The postulated Hezekian edition easily provides a foundation for the later Josianic edition, and the Campbell–O'Brien model of a Prophetic Record has already been adapted by the authors to the Cross model of the Josianic layer. My own work again modifies this model by extending it through 2 Kgs 14, which presents the reigns of the Jehu dynastic line when Israel was finally secure under King Jeroboam ben Joash.[26] The result is an underlying northern Jehu history that dates to the mid-eighth century BCE. An even earlier narrative that lauds King Solomon underlies 1 Kgs 3–10 and provides foundation for the ideals of the Jehu history.[27]

Although the discussion of scholarship concerning the compositional history of the DtrH may seem overly complicated, it serves an essential theological point, viz., Israel and Judah were constantly engaged in reflecting upon their own understandings of their relationships with YHWH and their experiences in the larger ancient Near Eastern world. The result was the continued writing and rewriting of history to account for their understandings of YHWH's actions in the world and their own fortunes—or lack thereof—within it. The results appear in the Former Prophets, which constantly posit divine involvement in the world and promise of the land to Israel (and Judah) and which constantly argue that human failings—not YHWH's failings—account for the reversals that each nation experienced. In all cases, the reflection on history evident in the Former Prophets, in all of its postulated stages, represents the effort to learn from that history in order to learn from the experience of the past and to build a better future.

NOTES

[1] For introductory discussions and overviews of the Former Prophets, see Antony F. Campbell, *Joshua to Chronicles: An Introduction* (Louisville: Westminster John Knox, 2004); Antony F. Campbell and Mark A. O'Brien, *Unfolding the Deuteronomistic History: Origins, Upgrades, Present Text* (Minneapolis: Fortress Press, 2000); Richard D. Nelson, *The Historical Books* (IBT; Nashville: Abingdon, 1998); Thomas Römer, *The So-Called Deuteronomistic History: A Sociological, Historical, and Literary Introduction* (London: Continuum, 2007).

[2] See, for example, Serge Frolov, *The Turn of the Cycle: 1 Samuel 1–8 in Synchronic and Diachronic Perspectives* (BZAW 342; Berlin: de Gruyter, 2004), who points to ambiguities in 1 Sam 1–8 concerning the Temple.

[3] Nadav Na'aman, "Amarna Letters," *ABD* 1:174–81.

[4] Donald B. Redford, "Merenptah (Person)," *ABD* 4:700–701.

[5] Albrecht Alt, "The Settlement of the Israelites in Palestine," in *Essays on Old Testament History and Religion* (Garden City: Doubleday, 1967), 173–221; Amihai Mazar, *Archaeology of the Land of the Bible, 10,000–586 B.C.E.* (New York: Doubleday, 1990), 295–367.

[6] Mazar, *Archaeology*, 368–530.

[7] For the Moabite Stone, see J. Andrew Dearman and Gerald L. Mattingly, "Mesha Stele," *ABD* 4:708–709; Andrew Dearman, ed., *Studies in the Mesha Inscription and Moab* (SBLABS 2; Atlanta: Scholars Press, 1989). For the Tel Dan Inscription, see Avraham Biran and Joseph Naveh, "An Aramaic Stele Fragment from Tel Dan," *IEJ* 43 (1993): 81–98; idem, "The Tel Dan Inscription: A New Fragment," *IEJ* 45 (1995): 1–18.

[8] See Sennacherib's account of the 701 BCE siege of Jerusalem, which refers specifically to Hezekiah (*ANET* 287–88) and Esarhaddon's references to Manasseh as one of his vassals (*ANET*, 291, 294).

[9] Mazar, *Archaeology*, 544–49; Ephraim Stern, *Archaeology of the Land of the Bible*. Vol. 2, *The Assyrian, Babylonian, and Persian Periods (732–332 B.C.E.)* (New York: Doubleday, 2001), 1–350.

[10] Robert A. Di Vito, "Lachish Letters," *ABD* 4:126–28; *ANET*, 321–22.

[11] *ANET*, 284–85.

[12] For the Babylonian Chronicle, see *ANET*, 303–5; for a reference to Nebuchadnezzar's first siege of Jerusalem in 598 BCE, see *ANET*, 563–64.

[13] For detailed discussion of research on the Deuteronomistic History, see in addition to the introductory works cited above, Thomas Römer and Albert de Pury, "L'historiographie deueronomiste (HD): Histoire de la recherché et enjeux du débat," in *Israël construit son histoire*, ed. A. de Pury et al. (Geneva: Labor et Fides, 1996), 9–120.

[14] Martin Noth, *Überlieferungsgeschichtliche Studien I* (Tübingen: Max Niemeyer, 1957), 1–110; ET, *The Deuteronomistic History* (JSOTSup 15; Sheffield: JSOT, 1981).

[15] Gerhard von Rad, *Studies in Deuteronomy* (SBT 9; London: SCM, 1953), 74–91.

[16] Hans Walter Wolff, "The Kerygma of the Deuteronomic Historical Work," in *The Vitality of the Old Testament Traditions*, ed. Walter Brueggemann and Hans Walter Wolff (Atlanta: John Knox, 1975), 83–100.

[17] Hans-Detleff Hoffmann, *Reform und Reformen. Untersuchungen zu einem Grundthema der deuteornomistischen Geschichtschreibung* (AThANT 66; Zürich: Theologischer Verlag, 1980).
[18] Frank Moore Cross, Jr., "The Themes of the Books of Kings and the Structure of the Deuteronomistic History," in *Canaanite Myth and Hebrew Epic* (Cambridge, MA: Harvard University Press, 1973), 274–89.
[19] Richard D. Nelson, *The Double Redaction of the Deuteronomistic History* (JSOTSup 18; Sheffield: JSOT, 1981); Richard Friedman, *The Exile and Biblical Narrative: The Formation of the Deuteronomistic and Priestly Works* (HSM 22; Chico: Scholars Press, 1981); Steven L. McKenzie, *The Trouble with Kings: The Composition of the Books in the Deuteronomistic History* (VTSup 42; Leiden: Brill, 1991); Gary N. Knoppers, *Two Nations under G-d: The Deuteronomistic History of Solomon and the Dual Monarchies* (HSM 52–53; Atlanta: Scholars Press, 1993–94).
[20] Rudolf Smend, "Die Gesetz und Völker: Ein Beitrag zur deuteronomistischen Redaktions-geschichte," *Probleme Biblischer Theologie*, ed., H. W. Wolff (Fs. G. von Rad; Munich: Chr. Kaiser, 1971), 494–509; Walter Dietrich, *Prophetie und Geschichte. Eine redaktionsgeschichtliche Untersuchung zum deuteronomistischen Geschichtswerk* (FRLANT 108; Göttingen: Vandenhoeck & Ruprecht, 1972); Timo Veijola, *Die ewige Dyastie: David und die Enstehung seiner Dynastie nach der deuteronomistischen Darstellung* (Helsinki: Suomalainen Tiede-akatemia, 1975); idem, *Das Königtum in der Beurteilung der deuteronomistischen Historio-graphie* (Helsinki: Suomalainen Tiedeakatemia, 1977).
[21] Antony F. Campbell, *Of Prophets and Kings: A Late Ninth-Century Document* (CBQMS 17; Washington: Catholic Biblical Association, 1986); Mark A. O'Brien, *The Deuteronomistic History Hypothesis: A Reassessment* (OBO 92; Freiberg: Universitätsverlag, 1989).
[22] Baruch Halpern and David Vanderhooft, "The Editions of Kings in the 7th–6th Centuries," *HUCA* 62 (1991): 179–244.
[23] Iain W. Provan, *Hezekiah and the Books of Kings* (BZAW 172; Berlin: de Gruyter, 1988).
[24] Helga Weippert, "Die 'deuteronomistischen' Beurteilungen der Könige von Israel und Juda und das Problem der Redaktion der Königsbücher," *Bib* 53 (1972): 301–39.
[25] Marvin A. Sweeney, *King Josiah of Judah: The Lost Messiah of Israel* (Oxford: Oxford University Press, 2001), 33–136, especially 52–64.
[26] Marvin A. Sweeney, *1 and 2 Kings: A Commentary* (OTL; Louisville: Westminster John Knox, 2007), 4–32, especially 26–30.
[27] Sweeney, *1 and 2 Kings*, 31–32.

B. THE BOOK OF JOSHUA

The book of Joshua introduces the Former Prophets with an account of Israel's conquest of the promised land of Israel under the leadership of Moses' successor, Joshua ben Nun.[1] The account is a highly idealized narrative in which divine intervention in the form of miraculous events ensures Israel's success in taking possession of the entire land. Indeed, only thirty-six Israelites die in the campaign for the land of Israel, and those deaths occur only during the campaign against Ai when the integrity of the nation is compromised by one man, Achan ben Carmi, who had stolen from the booty dedicated to YHWH gained from earlier victories (see Josh 7). Only when Achan is identified as the culprit—and he and his family are punished for his transgression against the nation—does Israel successfully defeat Ai without loss of Israelite life. Otherwise, Israel crosses the Jordan River with divine assistance as the waters of the Jordan part to allow the people to pass (Josh 1–5), and the land falls to Israelite control with three very swift campaigns against the central regions of Israel, including Jericho and Ai (Josh 6–8); the southern regions once allied with Gibeon (Josh 9–10); and the north represented by Hazor (Josh 11). With the land conquered in its entirety (Josh 12), it is apportioned among the twelve tribes (Josh 13–23), who then gather at Shechem to ratify their covenant with YHWH that grants them possession of the land.

The synchronic literary form of the book constitutes an account of YHWH's granting the land to Israel, including the sacred conquest of the land, its apportionment to Israel, and the concluding covenant at Shechem. The account displays the following literary structure:[2]

Account of YHWH's Granting the Land to Israel		
I.	Account of the Sacred Conquest of the Land	1–12
	A. YHWH's instructions to Joshua	1:1-9
	B. Joshua's compliance with YHWH's instructions	1:10—12:24
	1. Joshua's instructions to Israel concerning the campaign	1:10-18
	2. the spy narrative: Rahab as righteous Canaanite	2:1-23
	3. the crossing of the Jordan River: waters divide	3:1—4:24

The account of the sacred conquest and apportionment of the land of Israel among the tribes is designed to demonstrate that YHWH has fulfilled the divine promise to grant the land to the people of Israel. It is idealistic in that it portrays the complete conquest of the land by Israel and YHWH's use of miracles and other elements of divine intervention to ensure the success of Israel's campaign. Examples of such miracles include the division of the waters of the Jordan River to allow Israel to cross into the land much as the waters of the Red/Reed Sea parted to allow Israel to escape from Egypt (Josh 3–4); the appearance of the angelic commander of YHWH's army to Joshua (Josh 5); the collapse of the city walls of Jericho which enabled Israel to conquer the city (Josh 6); the failure of the attack on Ai as a result of Achan's theft (Josh 7); the role played by the sun standing still to enable Israel to destroy the southern Canaanite coalition (Josh 10); and YHWH's divine promise that Hazor would fall to Israel (Josh 11). In addition to the miraculous nature of YHWH's intervention to ensure the success of the conquest, Israel engages in ritual or liturgical action throughout to ensure that the campaign for the land is sacred. Examples of such action include Joshua's exhortations to adhere to YHWH and divine Torah (Josh 1); the leading role of the Levites who bear the ark of the covenant in the crossing of the Jordan and the campaigns of conquest (Josh 3–4; 6); the circumcision and celebration of Passover at Gilgal (Josh 5); the liturgical circumvention of the city of Jericho that facilitates its conquest (Josh 6); the ritual purification of the nation as a result of Achan's theft (Josh 7); Joshua's ratification of the covenant at Shechem (Josh 8:30-35; 24); and Israel's determination to observe its oath to Gibeon as an aspect of its fidelity with YHWH (Josh 9–10).

Both sets of factors, viz., the miraculous and the liturgical, point to the conceptualization of Israel's conquest of Canaan as a result of its relationship with YHWH in which each side must meet expectations. YHWH's role is to grant the land to Israel, which the book of Joshua portrays. Israel's role is to adhere to YHWH and to observe YHWH's requirement, which the book of Joshua makes clear. It will be left to the books of Judges, Samuel, and Kings to demonstrate that Israel's failure to meet these expectations prompted divine punishment in the form of foreign invasion and the eventual exile from the land of both Israel (2 Kgs 17) and Judah (2 Kgs 25). For the time being, Joshua portrays YHWH's fidelity to the covenant with Israel, that is, YHWH fulfills the promises made to the ancestors in the Torah. The narratives concerning the apportionment of the land in Josh 13–23 underscore YHWH's fulfillment of the promise of the land to the ancestors as a fundamental element of the covenant struck with the ancestors of Israel. Joshua 24 likewise underscores the covenant itself; now that YHWH has granted Israel the land, Israel is obliged to adhere to YHWH and to YHWH's expectations.

And yet a very important twist appears in the conquests narratives insofar as the Canaanites are not completely destroyed, and some are allowed to remain in Israel. Rahab, the innkeeper or prostitute from Jericho, plays a special role in the spy narrative of Josh 2 by taking in the Israelite spies and hiding them from the king of Jericho when they come to spy on the city prior to Israel's attack. Because Rahab takes on the role of righteous gentile, she and her family are spared when the inhabitants of Jericho are put to the sword. Indeed, Rabbinic tradition maintains that she later married Joshua and became the ancestor to a line of prophets in Israel, including the prophet and priest Jeremiah and the prophetess Huldah (*b. Megillah* 14b).[3] Likewise, the Gibeonites, who enact a ruse to trick Israel into signing a treaty with them, survive the conquest of the land as a result of their treaty with Israel and are allowed to remain, albeit in a subservient status. The role of the Gibeonites in later Israelite history proves to be crucial.[4] According to 1 Sam 6 and 2 Sam 6, the ark of the covenant resided for some twenty years at Kirath Jearim, a city that was federated with Gibeon's own coalition, before David brought it up to Jerusalem. Likewise, David's rise to the throne of all Israel was made possible by his victory over Ish-Boshet's/Abner's forces at Gibeon (2 Sam 2). Although the exact terms of David's relationship with Gibeon are unclear, the expectation that he will turn Saul's sons over to Gibeon for execution (2 Sam 21) makes it clear that David is indebted to the Gibeonites. Furthermore, Solomon's vision of YHWH in 1 Kgs 3 in which YHWH grants him wisdom takes place while Solomon is worshipping YHWH at Gibeon—albeit in a dream— which indicates once again a tie between the early house of David and Gibeon. Both cases show that Canaanites do remain in the land, and that they do so for legitimate reasons. And yet as Judges, Samuel, and Kings argue, the continued presence of Canaanites in the land plays a key role in prompting Israel to turn to other gods and thereby in bringing about divine punishment culminating in the Babylonian exile. Such a feature points to some tension in defining Israel's relationship with the Canaanites in the Former Prophets, viz., to what extent should Canaanites be recognized and allowed to become part of Israel? And to what extent does the presence of Canaanites present a threat to Israel's national and religious integrity? Indeed, the book of Joshua appears designed in part to examine these questions.

Such questions are bound up with diachronic factors in the interpretation of the book of Joshua as well, particularly since it is quite clear that the nation of Israel is derived to a large degree from a Canaanite ethnic, cultural, and even religious base. Such an observation indicates that Israel's struggle to define the role of Canaanites in Israelite society is in fact a struggle with its own religious and national identity.[5] A number of factors contribute to this conclusion.

The first is the observation that the historical portrayal of the complete conquest of the land of Israel and the destruction of the Canaanite population is simply not true. Archeological surveys of the land of Israel during the transition from the Late Bronze to the Early Iron Age point to conflict in the land, but the conflict does not indicate an outside conquest of a settled Canaanite land as the book of Joshua suggests.[6] Rather, it is a conflict that is motivated by the movement of two different population groups into the land that settle into two different geographic regions and blend with the resident Canaanite population. The first is the Sea Peoples, who migrated from the Greek Islands through the eastern Mediterranean, came into conflict with various cultures, such as the Hittites of Asia Minor and the Egyptians, and ultimately settled along the Eastern Mediterranean coast in the regions of Gaza, Ashkelon, Ashdod, Ekron, and Gath to form the Philistine coalition in the coastal plain. The other is the Habiru, semi-nomadic tribal groups who crossed into the land of Israel from the Trans-Jordanian region to settle among the Canaanites of the hill country ultimately to form the basis of Israel. The patterns of conflict in the land during this period are found along the boundaries of the coastal plain and the hill country, which points to conflict between the Philistine/Canaanite and Israelite/Canaanite populations that dominated these respective areas. Such a pattern of conflict is better represented in the narratives of Judges, for example, Judg 13–16; 17–18, and Samuel, for example, 1 Sam 4–6; 28–31; 2 Sam 5–6—which point to a long struggle between the Philistines and Israelites—than in the idealistic portrayal of the book of Joshua. Although Israel was hardly able to conquer the entire land of Israel so easily in its early history, the book of Joshua chooses to portray the conquest of Canaan as a very easy victory that was won for Israel by YHWH, who fulfilled divine promises to the ancestors by doing so. Such a contention must be considered as a fundamental theological concern of the book of Joshua.

A second factor takes up questions concerning the historical portrayal of the book of Joshua involving the four major Canaanite cities that play important narrative roles in the book, namely, Jericho, Ai, Gibeon, and Hazor. Archeological investigation of each site raises problems regarding their historical representation in the book of Joshua. Three of the cities, Jericho, Ai, and Gibeon, are only ruined sites at the outset of the Iron Ages, ca. 1200 BCE, which marks the beginning of Israel's emergence in the land. Jericho is well known as one of the world's largest and oldest cities, dating back to ca. 9000 BCE, but in 1200 BCE, Jericho had been a ruin for about a millennium.[7] Although the city appears to have been destroyed by an earthquake in the late third millennium BCE, it was not resettled and rebuilt until the Iron Age, after Israel emerged in the land. To be sure, there are problems with erosion on the site, so it is possible that evidence of Late Bronze or Early Iron Age settlement might be lost, but interpreters must recognize that Jericho was a very large and visible ruined tel or archeological mound during much of ancient Israel's history. Likewise, Ai was a ruined site from the end of the Middle Bronze Age, ca. 1550 BCE, through the Iron Age.[8] Indeed, the name of the city in Hebrew, hāʿay, means, "the ruin." Like Jericho, Ai was a very visible ruin in ancient Israel and its name indicates that it was remembered as such. Gibeon was also a ruin from the end of the Middle Bronze Age and it was only resettled and rebuilt at the beginning of the Iron Age when Israel emerged in the land.[9] Furthermore, Gibeon is identified as a Canaanite city in biblical narrative, and it heads a coalition that includes Chephirah, Beeroth, and Kirath-Jearim (see Josh 9:17), which were under Philistine control early in

Israel's history (see 1 Sam 6). Biblical narrative in 2 Sam 3–6; 21; and 1 Kgs 3 indicates that Gibeon was very important to the rise of the house of David, insofar as Gibeon's support was key to David' defeat of northern Israel under Ish-Boshet and the Philistines, and that the city was incorporated into David's kingdom. The narrative in Josh 9–10 highlights Gibeon's foreign origins, its covenant with Israel, and its incorporation into Israel.

Hazor is the only city whose existence in 1200 BCE is confirmed by archeo-logical excavation.[10] Nevertheless, although Hazor was a huge city during the Bronze Age, it was much reduced in the Iron Age, and even a large portion of the city was left as a ruined tel during the Iron Age. But the major problems with Hazor relate to its representation elsewhere in biblical narrative. Although Hazor and its King Jabin are defeated and destroyed in Josh 11, they re-emerge in Judg 4–5 as the leading element of the forces arrayed against Israel in the time of Deborah. Jabin's commander, Sisera, takes center stage in this narrative, but interpreters note the historical improbability of Hazor's destruction in the time of Joshua and its continuing role in Israel's early history. Hazor appears in Joshua, which otherwise focuses on cities located in or near Benjaminite tribal territory, to fill out the ideal portrayal of the complete conquest of the land in Joshua. Indeed, the ideal portrayal of complete conquest is compromised in Judg 1:1—2:5, which notes the continued presence of the Canaanites in the land despite the claims of the book of Joshua. Indeed, Judg 1:8 notes the Judean conquest of Jerusalem, despite the claim in Josh 10 that Jerusalem was one of the five cities defeated and conquered by Joshua. Likewise, 2 Sam 5 relates Jerusalem's conquest (once again) by David.

It is striking that each of these cities was either completely or partially unin-habited in the time postulated for Joshua, but the ruined tels of Jericho, Ai, Gibeon, and Hazor would have been clearly visible throughout the monarchic period, and Jericho, Gibeon, and Hazor were inhabited or reinhabited during the monarchic period as well. One could easily go to each of the sites during the Iron Age and see in the continuing existence of their ruined tels and their resettlement in the monarchic period evidence that would have confirmed the truth of the Joshua narrative in the minds of its Judean readers.

A third factor takes up the portrayal of Shechem as the assembly site for all Israel, both in Josh 8:30-35 where Joshua enacts a covenant ceremony during the conquest of the land and in Josh 24 where Joshua reiterates the covenant with all Israel before he passes away. The first narrative focuses on a covenant that calls upon all Israel, indigenous and resident alien alike, to observe YHWH's Torah as the foundation of the covenant that grants Israel possession of the land. The second rehearses Israel's history from the time of the ancestors and calls upon the people to renounce the worship of other gods, including those worshiped by the ancestors long ago and those of the Amorites that might be found in the land itself. In both cases, the question of continued Canaanite or foreign identity comes to the forefront in the form of the resident aliens included among Israel and the gods of the land that might be worshipped by Israel. But another factor also comes into consideration, viz., Shechem is known in the Amarna letters as a city with which the Habiru are closely associated.[11] Letters by the kings of Megiddo and Jerusalem complain to the Pharaoh that King Labayu of Shechem has allied with the Habiru to harass them and encroach upon their territory. Furthermore, archeological investigation indicates that Shechem was not destroyed in the conflicts evident in the land in the early Iron Age. Subsequent tradition indicates that Shechem continued to function as an assembly point for northern Israel since Shechem was the site where Abimelech ben Gideon attempted to claim kingship over Israel (Judg 9) and where the northern Israelite kingdom initially ruled by Jeroboam ben Nebat was formed. Clearly, Shechem is important to Joshua and the historical presentation in the Former Prophets/Deuteronomistic History, and historically speaking it does serve as a focal point in Israel's early history.

The reason for the interest of the Former Prophets/Deuteronomistic History in Shechem is because of the central role it plays in Israel's—and particularly northern Israel's—national identity. Shechem lies at the intersection of the major north–south and east–west routes that tie the hill country of northern Israel together.[12] The city also lies on the boundary between Ephraim and Manasseh, the two major tribal units that form the foundation for northern Israel. Indeed, Shechem is the focal point for the federation of tribes that constitute northern Israel from the early Iron Age at least through the foundation of the northern Israelite monarchy.

Cross points to the fundamental interest in the northern kingdom of Israel by the Josianic edition of the Deuteronomistic History which explained the fall of the northern kingdom to Assyria by asserting that Jeroboam ben Nebat, northern Israel's first king, led the nation into sin by worshipping golden calves at the sanctuaries at Beth El and Dan.[13] All of the kings of northern Israel are said to have followed Jeroboam by leading the nation into sin in this manner. Shechem was the site where Jeroboam was chosen as king, but in the eyes of the Josianic DtrH writer, Shechem was also the site where Israel swore fidelity to YHWH, YHWH's Torah, and its covenant with YHWH. By contrast, Jeroboam and all of the northern kings are portrayed in the DtrH as leading Israel into Canaanite-style worship and rejection of YHWH as Israel's G-d. Such a portrayal serves the Josianic DtrH agenda that calls for all Israel to repent in the aftermath of punishment and to return to the land (see Deut 30), to YHWH, to YHWH's sanctuary at Jerusalem, and to YHWH's Davidic monarch in Jerusalem. The emphasis on Shechem serves as a reminder of Israel's obligations to YHWH, obligations which enable Israel to live in the land, but it also serves as a reminder of the DtrH contention that Israel, beginning with the reign of its first king, Jeroboam, failed to live up to that ideal and suffered defeat at the hands of Assyria and exile as a result. In the eyes of the Josianic DtrH, the time for northern Israel's repentance is at hand.

There are, however, some problems with the portrayal of northern Israel's apostasy against YHWH that must be considered. Although biblical narrative charges Jeroboam ben Nebat with apostasy on the basis of his institution of the golden calves as objects of worship for Israel, there is no indication that the golden calves actually functioned as gods that could be worshipped.[14] Ancient Near Eastern iconography is replete with examples of gods and goddesses portrayed mounted on the backs of bulls, calves, lions, and so on, that is, the golden calves mentioned in the Jeroboam narratives of 1 Kgs 12 would have functioned as mounts upon which YHWH would have been conceived to be invisibly mounted. Such an understanding is actually consistent with the understanding of the ark of the covenant in southern Judah, which is conceived as YHWH's throne or footstool (see Isa 66:1). Indeed, the phrase identifying YHWH as "YHWH Seba'oth who is enthroned/seated upon the Cherubim," refers to the ark as YHWH's throne insofar as figures of cherubim are affixed to the top of the ark and appear around it, as well in the holy of holies of the Jerusalem Temple. The golden calves served the same function in northern Israel as the ark of the covenant in southern Judah. The difference between them on this point is simply a matter of different iconographical portrayals of YHWH's throne, not a case of apostasy in which Jeroboam encouraged Israel to abandon YHWH for the worship of the golden calves.

Other religious crimes of which Jeroboam is accused also appear to be empty. The charge that Jeroboam allowed anyone to serve as priest rather than the Levites is apparently a characteristic of ancient northern Israelite practice. Numbers 3–4 and 8 indicate that prior to choosing the Levites to serve as the priestly tribe, YHWH had designated the first-born sons of Israel to serve in this capacity. Such a role explains the statement that first-born sons belong to YHWH but that they are to be redeemed, and examples in which first-born sons are delivered from sacrifice or death at the hands of the deity (see Exod 34:19-20; cf. Gen 21; Exod 4:24-26). It also explains how a figure like Samuel, the son of the Ephraimite Elkanah and first-born son to his wife Hannah, is placed in the Shiloh sanctuary to be raised as a priest (1 Sam 1–3). It likewise explains how such figures as Elijah and Elisha, who are never identified as priests, function as such. Elijah engages in sacrifice at Mt. Carmel (1 Kgs 18), has a vision of YHWH in a setting that deliberately recalls the holy of holies of an Israelite temple (1 Kgs 19), and designates his successor (1 Kgs 19; 2 Kgs 2). Elisha delivers oracles accompanied by liturgical music that would be characteristic of temple worship (2 Kgs 3) and presides over an association of prophets who represent YHWH (2 Kgs 3–8). Northern Israel simply had a different conceptualization of priesthood, and southern Judah's understanding of the Levitical priesthood may actually have grown out of a similar background. Likewise, Jeroboam's setting the festival, presumably Sukkot, on the fifteenth day of the eighth month rather than in the seventh month as observed in Judah simply represents a different liturgical calendar, not rejection of YHWH. Jeroboam and northern Israel continued to adhere to YHWH, but northern Israel employed different means from those employed in Judah to express their adherence to YHWH. The narratives that condemn Jeroboam and northern Israel are polemical, in that they charge both with apostasy, but such a charge is explained by Judah's own attempts to explain the theological problem of Israel's destruction, viz., because YHWH must be viewed as righteous, all-powerful, and present, whereas Jeroboam and northern Israel must have committed sins that explain their demise as a punishment from the all-righteous, all-powerful, and ever-present YHWH. Nevertheless, the polemics against the north also point to an interest in reclaiming northern Israel or persuading it to return to YHWH in keeping with the early covenant ceremonies enacted by Joshua at Shechem.

Recognition of the book of Joshua's polemical interest in the northern kingdom of Israel points to a fourth element that must be considered, namely, the Judean perspective of the book of Joshua. Although the book of Joshua portrays the conquest of the entire land, three primary cities that are involved in the conquest, Jericho, Ai, and Gibeon, are located in Benjaminite territory in the case of Jericho and Gibeon, or close to the Benjaminite border in the case of Ai, which is located just to the east of Beth El, which in turn forms the Ephraimite border with Benjamin in Josh 16:2.[15] Furthermore, the cities of the anti-Gibeonite coalition defeated by Israel, viz., Jerusalem, Hebron, Jarmuth, Lachish, and Eglon, were all later to become Judean cities. By contrast, only Hazor stands outside the orbit of Benjamin and Judah, insofar as the city is situated on the northern Galilee region far beyond the hill country of Ephraim and Manasseh. Its allies in battle against Israel, Madon, Shimron, and Achshaph are of uncertain location, although most interpreters maintain that they would have been in the vicinity of Hazor. To be sure, Josh 11:1-5 indicates that Hazor's coalition also included all the other cities of the north in the hill country, the Arabah, the lowlands, and in the region of Dor along the Mediterranean coast, but the narrative does not bother to name these cities. Such a perspective shows a special interest in Benjamin, which later becomes the first royal tribe of Israel, but Benjamin is closely aligned with Judah from the time of David on, due in large measure to the fact that David came to the throne of Israel as the son-in-law of King Saul of Benjamin, having married Saul's daughter Michal and demanded her return to him as a condition for his assuming the throne of Israel (2 Sam 3:12-16). As the first royal tribe that stood between Judah to the south and the northern Israelite tribes to the north, Benjamin was key to unifying the twelve tribes of Israel under the rule of a single king. David came to the throne of all Israel as a member of the royal house of Saul, and even following the rupture between Judah and the northern tribes after the death of Solomon, Benjamin continued to be closely associated with Judah.

Judean interests in geographical perspective also appear in the narratives concerning the apportionment of the land in Josh 13–22. Following an initial concern in Josh 13:8-33 with the Trans-Jordanian tribes in which the allotments of the tribes of half-Manasseh, Gad, and Reuben were treated in detail, Judah is the first major tribe to be allocated land and its territory is defined in great detail in specifying Judean cities in Josh 14:6-63. The narrative in Josh 16:1—17:18 shows far less interest in specifying the cites of Ephraim and Manasseh, the two major tribes of the northern kingdom of Israel, and focuses instead on the inability of these tribes to expel the Canaanites completely as well as their complaints that their allotted land was insufficient. The narrative in Josh 18:11-28 treats Benjamin's allotment in detail. Likewise, the narratives in Josh 19:1-51 specify the cities and territories of the remaining tribes, Simeon, Zebulun, Issachar, Asher, Naphtali, and Dan, in detail. The relative lack of attention to the Joseph tribes, Ephraim and Manasseh, is striking. Such a perspective suggests Judean interests that also took into account the tribes of the Galilee, coastal plain, and Trans-Jordan that surrounded Ephraim and Manasseh, but not in Ephraim and Manasseh themselves. Interpreters have pointed to P elements in Josh 13–23[16] or Josianic interests,[17] both of which would presuppose Judean interests either in the post-exilic or late monarchic periods respectively. Given the concern with the status of the Trans-Jordanian tribes, which appears at the beginning and near the end of the apportionment narratives, these narratives would have to be placed broadly in the Hezekian and Josianic periods when concern for the recovery of these territories would have been paramount after they had been stripped away from Israelite control, first in the ninth century by the Arameans and later in the mid-eighth century by the Assyrians.[18] In any case, the focus on land indicates a Judean interest in surrounding and containing the central northern tribes of Ephraim and Manasseh, which is how David arranged his marriages with women from powerful families in these regions so that he might surround and contain the northern tribes, thereby preparing for his own rise to power.[19]

Joshua 15:63 notes that the Judeans were unable to conquer Jerusalem or to dispossess the Jebusites who lived there, which would suggest Jerusalem's status prior to David's capture of the city without loss of life (see 2 Sam 5:6-12). Although such a suggestion might indicate a pre-Davidic date, interpreters have noted the degree to which the figure of Joshua himself in the book of Joshua is modeled on the Judean King Josiah ben Amon (r. 640–609 BCE), who is credited in much of biblical scholarship with the composition of a major edition of the Deuteronomistic History.[20] Indeed, Nelson observes that statements concerning Joshua's integrity in Josh 1:7 and 23:6 are parallel to those concerning Josiah in 2 Kgs 22:2; statements concerning Joshua's royal sponsorship of Passover in Josh 5:10-12 are parallel to those concerning Josiah in 2 Kgs 23:21-23; and statements concerning royal loyalty to YHWH in pledging adherence to divine

Torah in Josh 8:30-35 are parallel to those concerning Josiah in 2 Kgs 23:2-3. Statements in Josh 1:6-9 concerning Joshua's royal standard of courage and obedience to YHWH are parallel to those concerning Solomon (1 Kgs 2:1-4) and the ideal king (Deut 17:18-20). Altogether, such parallels point to an effort in the book of Joshua to present Joshua as the model for the ideal monarch that is ultimately fulfilled in Josiah. Such a concern points to Josianic interests in the composition of Joshua, including Joshua as the model of the ideal king Josiah, Joshua's role in swearing the tribes to loyalty to YHWH and YHWH's Torah at the central northern site of Shechem, and a perspective on the distribution of land among the tribes that would serve Josianic interests in reuniting the land on the example of David.

When viewed from the perspective of these four factors, the portrayal of Israel's conquest of the land of Canaan and the efforts to wipe out the Canaanite inhabitants in the land appear in a very different light.[21] Israel did not attack and destroy an indigenous Canaanite culture in order to displace the Canaanites and take control of their land; rather, Israel/Judah grew out of that very same Canaanite culture to develop a very distinctive understanding of themselves as a nation and of YHWH as creator of the land/world and G-d of Israel/Judah. Underlying the formulation of the Joshua narrative are very clear interests in portraying an ideal Israelite identity and unity in the land of Israel that is based on adherence to YHWH and YHWH's Torah; pointing to present-day (at least from the perspective of the monarchic period) ruins and resettled sites such as Jericho, Ai, Gibeon, and Hazor as evidence that the historical claims of the book of Joshua are true; interest in presenting Shechem, a central meeting site for northern Israel in its early history, as the site where all Israel, including the north, affirms its covenant with YHWH; and Joshua is presented as the model of the ideal king which is later fulfilled in the form of King Josiah of Judah, whose reform program was based on an attempt to reunify the twelve tribes of Israel throughout the entire land on the basis of adherence to YHWH and YHWH's Torah. When read in this light, Joshua is not a call to go out and destroy the Canaanite peoples of the land—indeed, Israel itself appears to have been descended from those very Canaanites—instead, the book of Joshua is addressed to Israelite readers to convince them to assert their Israelite identities, to adhere to YHWH and YHWH's Torah as the basis for their life in the land, and to reunify the nation as it was purportedly unified in the days of Joshua. To such an end, the book of Joshua portrays YHWH as having kept the promises given to the ancestors in the Torah narratives by granting Israel the promised land in a very swift campaign that resulted in the complete conquest of the land and the disappearance of all the Canaanites, with the exception of those who showed loyalty to Israel and to YHWH. Having portrayed YHWH's covenant fidelity to Israel in the book of Joshua, the Former Prophets/Deuteronomistic History can then turn to Israel's response to YHWH's actions beginning in the book of Judges.

NOTES

[1] For current discussion of the book of Joshua, see especially Richard D. Nelson, *Joshua: A Commentary* (OTL; Louisville: Westminster John Knox, 1997); Volkmar Fritz, *Das Buch Josua* (HAT 1/7; Tübingen: Mohr Siebeck, 1994); Robert Boling and G. Ernest Wright, *Joshua* (AB 6; Garden City: Doubleday, 1982); and my *King Josiah of Judah: The Lost Messiah of Israel* (Oxford: Oxford University Press, 2001), 125–36.

[2] Cf. my *King Josiah of Judah*, 131, for the details of argumentation and a slightly different assessment of the structure of the book of Joshua. For alternative structure analyses of the book of Joshua, see Brian Peckham, "The Significance of the Book of Joshua in Martin Noth's Theory of the Deuteronomistic History," in *The History of Israel's Traditions*, ed. S. McKenzie and M. P. Graham (JSOTSup 182; Sheffield: Sheffield Academic, 1994), 213–34.

[3] See "Rahab," *EncJud* 13:1513–15.

[4] For discussion of the historical background of the Gibeonites and their role in the rise of the house of David, see especially Joseph Blenkinsopp, *Gibeon and Israel: The Role of Gibeon and the Gibeonites in the Political and Religious History of Israel* (SOTSMS 2; Cambridge: Cambridge University Press, 1972).

[5] See also Lori Rowlett, *Joshua and the Rhetoric of Violence: A New Historicist Analysis* (JSOTSup 226; Sheffield: Sheffield Academic, 1996).

[6] For historical and archeological discussion, see Albrecht Alt, "The Settlement of the Israelites in Palestine," in *Essays on Old Testament History and Religion* (Garden City: Doubleday, 1967), 173–221; J. Maxwell Miller and John H. Hayes, *A History of Ancient Israel and Judah* (Philadelphia: Westminster, 1986), 25–85; Gösta W. Ahlström, *The History of Ancient Palestine* (Minneapolis: Fortress Press, 1993), 282–370; Amihai Mazar, *Archaeology of the Land of the Bible, 10,000–586 B.C.E.* (New York: Doubleday, 1990), 295–367; Israel Finkelstein, *The Archaeology of the Israelite Settlement* (Jerusalem: Israel Exploration Society, 1988).

[7] For discussion of Jericho, see Kathleen M. Kenyon, "Jericho: Tell Es-Sultan," *NEAEHL* 2:674–81.

[8] For discussion of Ai, see Joseph A. Calloway, "Ai," *NEAEHL* 1:39–45.

[9] For discussion of Gibeon, see James B. Pritchard, "Gibeon," *NEAEHL* 2:511–14; Blenkinsopp, *Gibeon and Israel*.

[10] For discussion of Hazor, see Amnon Ben-Tor, "Hazor," *NEAEHL* 2:594–606.

[11] For discussion of the Amarna letters and the role of Shechem, see especially Nadav Na'aman, "Amarna Letters," *ABD* 1:174–81. For translations of selected Amarna letters, see *ANET*, 482–90.

[12] For discussion of the historical geography of Shechem, see Edward F. Campbell, "Shechem," *NEAEHL* 4:1345–54.

[13] Cross, "The Themes of the Books of Kings and the Structure of the Deuteronomistic History," in *Canaanite Myth and Hebrew Epic* (Cambridge, MA: Harvard University Press, 1973), 274–89.

[14] For detailed discussion of this point, see Sweeney, *1 and 2 Kings: A Commentary* (OTL; Louisville: Westminster John Knox, 2007), 172–82; idem, *Reading the Bible after the Shoah: Engaging Holocaust Theology* (Minneapolis: Fortress Press, 2008), 67–72.

[15] See also Zecharia Kallai, *Historical Geography of the Bible* (Jerusalem: Magnes, 1986), 398–415.

[16] For example, Enzo Cortese, *Josua 13–21: Ein priesterschriftlicher Abschnitt im deuteronomistischen Geshichtswerk* (OBO 94; Freiburg: Universitätsverlag, 1990).

[17] Albrecht Alt, "Judas Gaue under Josia," in *Kleine Schriften zur Geschichte des Volkes Israel II* (Munich: Beck, 1953), 276–88.

[18] For discussion of the Aramean and Assyrian conquests of the Trans-Jordan, see Ahlström, *The History of Ancient Palestine*, 639–64.

[19] Jon D. Levenson and Baruch Halpern, "The Political Import of David's Marriages," *JBL* 99 (1980): 11–28.

[20] Nelson, *Joshua*, 21–22; idem, "Josiah in the Book of Joshua," *JBL* 100 (1981): 531–40.

[21] For expressions of concern with violence in the book of Joshua, see John J. Collins, *An Introduction to the Hebrew Bible* (Minneapolis: Fortress Press, 2004), 193–95; see also Collins, *Does the Bible Justify Violence?* (Minneapolis: Fortress Press, 2004); but cf. Rowlett, *Joshua and the Rhetoric of Violence*.

C. THE BOOK OF JUDGES

The book of Judges presents an account of Israel's earliest history as a nation in the land of Israel from the time immediately following Israel's entry into the land under Joshua until the time of Samuel immediately prior to the rise of kingship.[1] The book presupposes the unity of the twelve tribes of Israel, but it does not presuppose an institutionalized central monarchy. A monarchy would strive to ensure national stability and unity by instituting a system of dynastic succession in which a ruling monarch would be succeeded upon his death by one of his sons. Such monarchies would emerge in Israel and Judah only with the emergence of the dynastic houses of Saul, David, and the various northern dynasties. In the interim, Israel would be ruled by local leaders known as "judges," Hebrew, šôpēṭ, which is best translated as "rulers," rather than as the judicially oriented term, "judges." The term, šôpēṭ, frequently presupposes judicial connotations, but it refers more broadly to one who combines political, military, and judicial authority. Indeed, the governors of the city-states of Canaan prior to the emergence of Israel were identified by the cognate Akkadian term, *shappatum*, "ruler." Although the judges of Israel are generally portrayed as leaders of all Israel in the literary framework of the book of Judges, the individual narratives generally associate the judges with individual tribes or smaller coalitions of tribe, that is, Othniel is from Judah; Ehud is from Benjamin; Deborah is from Ephraim, although her coalition includes Naftali in Judg 4 and Naftali, Zebulun, Benjamin, Manasseh, and Issachar in Judg 5; Gideon is from Manasseh; Jepthah is from Gad; and Samson is from Dan. Such a portrayal suggests that the Judges narratives may originally have focused on local tribal heroes from the pre-monarchic period who were later understood to be leaders of all Israel.[2]

The judges are known primarily as military heroes who deliver Israel from its various enemies. Within the theological framework of the book of Judges, YHWH brings enemies to afflict Israel when Israel follows the practices of the Canaanite nations to worship foreign gods. As a consequence of Israel's abandonment of YHWH, Judg 2:6-23 indicates that YHWH brings foreign enemies to punish Israel for its apostasy, which prompts Israel to return to YHWH and ask for deliverance from the enemy, which in turn prompts YHWH to raise up a judge who will deliver Israel from the threat. Thus, Othniel defeats a Mesopotamian coalition led by King Cushan Rishathaim of Aram Naharaim in Judg 3:7-11; Ehud kills the Moabite King Eglon in Jericho and leads the people against the Moabites in Judg 3:12-30; Deborah and her companion Barak assemble a coalition to defeat King Jabin of Hazor and his commander Sisera in Judg 4–5; Gideon defeats the Midianites in Judg 6–8/9; Jepthah defeats the Ammonites in Judg 10–12; and Samson humiliates the Philistines repeatedly in Judg 13–16.

And yet the narrative concerning the last judge, Samson, raises questions concerning the purpose of the book of Judges insofar as Samson fails to defend his people against a foreign enemy. Samson was compromised in the view of the Judges narrative as a result of his relationship with Philistine women, and he ultimately commits suicide in the course of exacting vengeance against his Philistine captors. Readers might think that such an act settles the score, but suicide is the ultimate betrayal of G-d's gift of life to human beings in Judaism, and suicides are therefore viewed with a combination of pity and contempt. But more to the point from a narrative standpoint, Samson fails to deliver his people from the Philistines even though he succeeds in killing a large number of them when his strength returns and enables him to bring the Philistine temple crashing down on himself and his enemies.

Although many readers presuppose that the Samson narrative ends with Samson's "triumph" over his captors, the following narrative in Judg 17–18, viewed by Noth and many scholars who followed him as an appendix to the book of Judges,[3] must also be considered. Judges 17–18 relates what happens to Samson's own tribe of Dan in the aftermath of their hero's failed exploits, viz., the tribe of Dan is forced to abandon its allotted territory in the land of Israel due to continuing Philistine pressure and to resettle in the northernmost regions of the land around the city of Laish, which is conquered by the men of Dan and renamed Dan after their own eponymous ancestor. The specter of one of Israel's tribes being forced to leave its tribal territory is a very troubling episode following the Joshua narrative in which YHWH had granted the entire land to Israel and apportioned the land among the tribes. Such an event hardly fits with an understanding of the judges as the deliverers of Israel.

But the narrative also has a larger significance within the Former Prophets or Deuteronomistic History, for Dan becomes the site of one of the illicit golden calves established by King Jeroboam ben Nebat of Israel for the people to worship as an idol together with the other golden calf at Beth El (1 Kgs 12).[4] Such a notorious reputation is even foreshadowed in the Judg 17–18 narrative insofar as Dan becomes the site of an idolatrous sanctuary founded by an Ephraimite named Micah, who embezzles money from his mother and uses it to form a molten image for illicit worship. In addition to this act of apostasy, Micah hires a Levite from the city of Beth Lehem in Judah to officiate as priest over the worship of this idol, thereby compromising the sanctity of the Levite. When the men of Dan conquer Laish and establish it as their own city, they bring Micah's idol and the now-corrupted Levite with them and establish both the idols and the Levite in a sanctuary at Dan for the worship of the people. Thus, Judg 17–18 explains the origins of the sanctuary at Dan as a site of illicit worship in Israel, later to be established by Jeroboam as a site for the worship of the golden calf. Such a portrayal suggests that things have gone awry in Israel, particularly in the aftermath of Samson's failed career. Samson's relationship with a Philistine woman, viewed as a travesty in Deut 7:1-6 and in the book of Judges, costs Samson his own life and his home tribe of Dan its tribal territory, ultimately resulting in Dan's idolatry at the sanctuary of Dan.

The problems do not end with the origins of the sanctuary at Dan in Judg 17–18. Apostasy at Dan and its sister sanctuary at Beth El ultimately costs Israel dearly as Jeroboam's golden calves at Dan and Beth El are cited as key considerations in YHWH's decision to destroy the northern kingdom of Israel in 2 Kgs 17. The more immediate context has more to say as well, for Judg 19–21 relates a horrific narrative which sees the rape and murder of a Levite's concubine—she is also from Beth Lehem in Judah like Micah's Levite—in the city of Gibeah of Benjamin as well as the outbreak of civil war in Israel when the tribes of Israel attempt to destroy Benjamin when the tribe of Benjamin refuses to bring the city of Gibeah to justice for the rape and murder of the Levite's concubine. Although Judg 19–21 is also frequently considered as an appendix to the book of Judges like the narratives concerning the establishment of the city of Dan in Judg 17–18,[5] a closer reading of this narrative indicates that—like Judg 17–18—it plays a far more important role both in the context of the book of Judges and in the larger narrative framework of the Former Prophets or Deuteronomistic History.[6]

Judges 19–21 relates the account of the rape and murder of the Levite's concubine in the city of Gibeah and the consequences of that act when the tribes of Israel nearly destroy the tribe of Benjamin for its role in refusing to bring the perpetrators of this crime to justice. The pro-Judean and anti-Saulide perspectives of the narratives are clear. The Levite's concubine is from the city of Beth Lehem in Judah, and she and her partner travel to Gibeah in the tribal territory of Benjamin, later known as the capital city of the first king of Israel, Saul ben Kish. When the men of the city of Gibeah demand that they be allowed to rape the visiting Levite, they are refused, but seize the Levite's concubine and rape her all night, leaving her for dead.[7] Upon finding his concubine dead the next morning, the Levite cut her body into twelve pieces and sent them to the tribes of Israel to alert them of the crime committed in Gibeah. When Benjamin refuses Israel's demands that the perpetrators of this crime be brought to justice, the tribes of Israel went to war with Benjamin. After initial defeats, the tribes of Israel gather at Beth El—the future site of Jeroboam's golden calves—and were promised victory over Benjamin by YHWH. All but six hundred Benjaminites were killed in the battle. Following the battle, the tribes of Israel gathered again at Beth El to consider what to do about a tribe in Israel that was now threatened with extinction. Having vowed not to marry their daughters to the men of Benjamin, the tribes of

Israel concocted two plans to find wives for the Benjaminite survivors. The first was to destroy Jabesh Gilead, a city that had not joined the battle against Benjamin, and give the four hundred surviving maidens from the city as brides to Benjamin. The second plan was to allow the remaining two hundred Benjaminites to hide in the vineyards near the sanctuary at Shiloh and seize the maidens who came out to dance in the vineyards at the annual festival.

Both the pro-Judean and anti-Saulide elements play key roles in defining the function of this narrative as a conclusion to Judges and as an introduction to the following material concerning the rise of kingship in Israel—particularly the rise of King Saul ben Kish. Gibeah's identity as the capital of Saul is already known, but other elements of the narrative also point to Saul, such as the cutting up of the concubine's body into twelve pieces to summon the tribes of Israel and the role of Jabesh Gilead as a source for Benjaminite brides. First Samuel 11 relates an adulatory narrative about Saul's deliverance of the city of Jabesh Gilead when it is attacked by Nahash the Ammonite and his army. When Saul hears of the crisis, he cuts up his own oxen into twelve pieces, and sends the pieces throughout the land to summon Israel to war on behalf of Jabesh Gilead. Jabesh Gilead remains closely associated with Saul; when Saul's body is affixed to the wall of Beth Shean following his death in battle against the Philistines in 1 Sam 31, the men of Jabesh Gilead take it down and give him a proper burial. By incorporating Saulide-associated elements into the story of the rape of the Levite's concubine and the subsequent war against Benjamin, Judg 19–21 prepares the reader for the introduction of Saul in 1 Sam 8–31, and ensures that the reader will view Saul as a figure unfit for royal leadership due to his associations with Gibeah and its murderous reputation.

But the pro-Judean elements of Judg 19–21 and 17–18 must also be considered in relation to the preceding material from the book of Judges insofar as both narratives highlight the mistreatment of natives of the city of Beth Lehem in Judah, David's own home city.[8] Both narratives emphasize that the problems articulated in each take place at a time when there was no king in Israel and everyone did what was right in their own eyes (Judg 18:1; 19:1; 21:25). Such statements frame the concluding narratives in Judg 17–18 and 19–21 with repeated signals of the need for a king, but the contents of Judg 19–21 signal that Saul will not be adequate to the task and the references to Dan and Beth El in the two narratives provide a more distant signal that the later northern Israelite monarchy founded by Jeroboam ben Nebat will not be adequate either. The victimization of the anonymous citizens from Beth Lehem, the Levite who served in Micah's sanctuary, and the Levite's concubine in turn signals the need for a Judean king from Beth Lehem, who would of course be David ben Jesse and his successors.

Although the concern with Beth Lehem and Judah might seem a minor element at first sight, a survey of the judges in Judg 3–16 suggests that concern with ideal leadership from the tribe of Judah and corrupt or inept leadership from Benjamin and the other northern tribes of Israel plays an important role in the presentation of the judges. But the problems may be traced back to even earlier concerns in the book of Judges insofar as the continued presence of Canaanites in the land provides the basis for Judges' portrayal of the progressive corruption and disintegration of Israel throughout the period of the judges and through the concluding episodes of the sordid foundation of the sanctuary at Dan, the shocking behavior of the people of Gibeah and Benjamin, and the civil war in which Benjamin is pitted against the other tribes of Israel.

Judges 1:1—2:5 begins the presentation of judges with a very problematic narrative that relates the failure of the Israelite tribes to expel the Canaanites in the land.[9] Despite the claims of the book of Joshua that Israel had conquered the entire land of Canaan (see Josh 11:23), Judg 1:1—2:5 discusses in detail the many Canaanite enclaves that the tribes of Israel were not able to root out. Judah is unable to conquer the coastal plain; Benjamin is unable to conquer the Jebusite inhabitants of Jerusalem; Manasseh did not conquer Beth Shean, Taanach, Dor, Ibleam, and Megiddo; Zebulun did not conquer Nahalol: Asher did not conquer Acco, Sidon, and other cities; Naftali did not conquer Beth Shemesh and Beth Anath; the Danites were forced out of their own tribal territory by the Amorites. Judges 2:1-5 makes it clear that Israel's failure to dispossess the Canaanites constitutes an affront against YHWH. YHWH reiterates how YHWH kept covenant with the Israelites, harking back to the theological claims of Joshua by noting how YHWH granted Israel the entire land, but charges that Israel has failed to keep that covenant by failing to destroy the Canaanites in the land. As a result YHWH declares that the Canaanites will become Israel's oppressors.

Such a declaration raises some troubling theological problems in the portrayal of YHWH. In Joshua, YHWH defeated Israel's enemies; in Judges, Israel is unable to do so on its own and gets no support from YHWH. Such a scenario points to at least some degree of failure on YHWH's part; rather than act decisively on behalf of Israel as in the book of Joshua, YHWH chooses instead to place the blame on Israel for its own weakness and vulnerability while YHWH does nothing to help.

Judges 2:6-23 points to the consequences of allowing the Canaanites to remain in the land. The problem with continued Canaanite presence in the viewpoint of Deut 7:1-6 and Judg 2:1-5 is that the Canaanites would influence Israel to worship foreign gods. Indeed, this is precisely what happens in Judg 2:6-23. Judges 2:6-10 presents a reprise of the death and burial of Joshua and his entire generation which takes the reader back to the point of the conclusion of the book of Joshua to portray Israel from a very different angle, not as a people who have just heard Joshua's exhortations to observe divine Torah, but as the next generation that grew up after the time of Joshua to adopt the religious practices of the Canaanites who remained in the land. The resulting pattern of action then forms the basis or the four-part motific pattern in the presentation of each of the judges, viz., (1) Israel worships foreign gods; (2) YHWH becomes angry at Israel and brings a foreign oppressor to punish the people; (3) the people suffer under the oppressor and return to YHWH to ask forgiveness; and (4) YHWH sends a deliverer to save the people from the oppressor allowing the land to have peace until the cycle resumes once again.[10]

Judges 3:1-6 introduces the judges cycle with the claim that YHWH would allow the Canaanites to remain in the land so that they might test Israel's loyalty to YHWH. Read uncritically, such a statement lays the foundations for the conclusion that Israel would continue to sin against YHWH by following other gods, but a more critical reading of these statements indicates that YHWH is a duplicitous figure who sets up Israel to fall by failing to drive out the Canaanites as in the book of Joshua. One might consider YHWH a failed G-d who chose to blame Israel for YHWH's own failures. In either case, Judg 3:1-6 indicates that the action of the people in worshipping other gods is the immediate cause for Israel's oppression by foreign nations in the judges cycle.

The first instance of the cycle relates a very basic example of Judges' narrative pattern in which the people turn to other gods, suffer foreign invasion, return to YHWH, and see the rise of a judge to deliver them from the oppressor. Thus Judg 3:7-11 states that the people did evil in the eyes of YHWH; YHWH became angry at Israel and sent King Cushan Rishathaim of Aram Naharaim to oppress them; Israel cried out to YHWH; and YHWH sent Othniel the Kenizzite and youngest kinsman of Caleb to deliver them so that the land would have peace for forty years. Othniel is a Judean judge, who sets the ideal pattern of the book of Judges with little elaboration.

The narratives concerning subsequent judges, however, display two important features, viz., (1) they come from the northern tribes of Israel; and (2) their narratives indicate problems in their leadership and actions that grow progressively worse in each instance.[11] Although those problems are initially minor, they grow to become cases of apostasy that result from the continued presence of the Canaanites in the land and ultimately result in one tribe, Dan, losing its tribal inheritance, and civil war as the tribes attempt to destroy one of their own, that is, the tribe of Benjamin.

The narrative concerning Ehud ben Gera in Judg 3:12-30 follows the usual pattern of apostasy by Israel, oppression of Israel by foreigners, repentance by Israel, and the appearance of deliverer for Israel. It relates that the Moabite Eglon was able to take control of Jericho for eighteen years until he was killed by the left-handed judge, Ehud, of the tribe of Benjamin. It is noteworthy first of all that Benjamin lost control of a part of its tribal allotment for a period of time, but it is striking that the city taken by Eglon was Jericho, the first city to be granted by YHWH to the people of Israel at the outset of Joshua's campaign. The problems associated with Ehud are somewhat minor, viz., he is able to kill Eglon and deliver his people but he must practice deception to do so by hiding his weapon on his right thigh where no one would think to look since most right-handers would carry weapons on the left thigh. Nevertheless, the episode underscores Benjamin's and Ehud's weaknesses in controlling and recovering territory allotted by YHWH.

The next narrative in Judg 4–5 takes up the judge, Deborah, a woman from the tribe of Ephraim who is identified as a prophet and who exercises judicial authority in Israel. Other roles include that of liturgical singer, insofar as the song of Deborah is attributed to her, and military commander in some form or other together with Barak ben Abinoam. When faced with a Canaanite coalition led by King Jabin of Hazor, who was supposedly defeated and destroyed by Joshua in Josh 11, and his military commander Sisera, Deborah and Barak lead an Israelite army that defeats the Canaanite coalition. When Sisera attempts to flee following the disaster, he is killed by a Kenite woman named Yael. The Song of Deborah gives due credit to YHWH for the victory, insofar as the stars from heaven and the Wadi Kishon appear to have played roles in the victory, apparently through a flash flood that somehow disabled the Canaanite army.[12] But problems emerge as well in that Deborah is unable to rally all Israel to the battle. The Song of Deborah chastises several tribal groups from Israel that do not join their fellow tribes, that is, Reuben, Gilead (Gad?), Dan, and Asher. All of these tribes are outlying tribes that might be distant from the center of Israel where the battle took place, but their absence from the battle and the complaints expressed in the Song of Deborah about their absence raise questions about Deborah's—and perhaps Ephraim's— ability to unite all Israel and serve as its leader. It also raises questions about whether all Israel is able to unite even in self-defense.

Judges 6–9 relates the narratives about the judge Gideon ben Joash of the tribe of Manasseh. When Israel is attacked by the Midianites and their allies, Gideon takes action to raise an army to defeat them. His choice of three hundred soldiers is well-considered insofar as he observes how they drink water and chooses only those who keep watch for enemies even while refreshing themselves. His defeat of the Midianites is complete, and the nation has rest for forty years. But a number of problems emerge in this narrative. The first is Gideon's Canaanite associations. The first is his father's altar dedicated to Baal, which Gideon destroys at YHWH's behest. The second is Gideon's Canaanite name, Jerubbaal, a theophoric name which means "let Baal contend," which would have been given to him by his Baal-worshipping father. Although Gideon could hardly be held responsible for these lapses, his actions following his victory also speak to his Canaanite association insofar as he constructs an ephod of gold for Israel to worship as an idol. There are other problems as well that emerge in the narrative. One is the threat made against Gideon and his army by the Ephraimites, who demand to know why they were not called out to battle and who are placated only when he acknowledges that their deeds in the war were greater than his own. Of course, such a threat points to Ephraim's willingness to threaten other tribes of Israel and raises questions once again about Ephraim's capacity for leadership. The last problem is Gideon's son, Abimelech, identified ironically by his father's Canaanite name as ben Jerubbaal rather than as ben Gideon. Although Gideon turns down a request that he serve as king of all Israel, his son Abimelech actively seeks kingship and plunges Israel into civil war as he kills the seventy sons of Gideon, apparently a reference to the ruling council of Israel at this time, to press his claims. Abimelech is only stopped when he is killed by a woman who drops a millstone on his head while he is besieging her city. The Canaanite associations of Gideon and the disintegration of Israel into civil war prepare the reader for greater calamity to follow.

The narratives in Judg 10:6—12:7 concerning Jepthah ben Gilead, apparently from the region of Gilead where the tribes of Manasseh and Gad resided, begin inauspiciously by identifying him as the son of a prostitute who is forced to flee from his father's holdings by his brothers, who would not tolerate such a family member in their midst. Despite any questions that might be raised about him, Jepthah emerges as the hero of the Trans-Jordan who fights off the Ammonites who attempt to seize Israel's territory. But problems emerge once again during his rule. The first is once again the threat of the tribe of Ephraim, which, as in the time of Gideon, questions why they were not called to battle in a time of crisis. Of course such a demand is an assertion of leadership. This time, however, Ephraim is not placated and goes to war against Jepthah, plunging the nation into civil war once again, but Jepthah and his followers were able to defeat them. The other problem is Jepthah's oath to YHWH that he would sacrifice whatever came out of his house to meet him if YHWH would grant him victory over the Ammonites. No doubt expecting cattle or sheep, Jepthah is shocked to find that his own daughter emerged from the house to greet him when he returned from his victory. Jepthah's daughter spent two months lamenting before she was sacrificed in a manner that recalls the Bible's claims that the earlier Canaanite and Moabite inhabitants of the land had practiced child sacrifice, which of course prompted YHWH to expel them from the land.

The narratives concerning Samson ben Manoah in Judg 13–16 focus on a local hero from the tribe of Dan whose birth is announced by an angel of YHWH.[13] The boy is raised as a Nazirite, which would indicate a special vow of holy service to YHWH (see Num 6), but Samson's behavior is hardly holy. His long, untrimmed hair, in keeping with the Nazirite vow (as well as the avoidance of alcohol and contact with the dead), give him great strength, and he spends much of his time harassing the Philistines who live near the Danite tribal territory along the coastal Mediterranean plain. In contrast to the instruction of Deut 7:1-6, which forbids Israel to intermarry with the Canaanite nations, and the understanding of this instruction in Judg 3:1-4, which places the Philistines at the top of the list even before the Canaanites, Samson marries Philistine women. His first marriage to a Philistine woman from Timnah provides the occasion for conflict and competition with the Philistines in which his new bride plays a role in undermining Samson. When Samson proposes a contest with the Philistines in which they would give him thirty sets of expensive clothing if they were unable to guess the answer to a riddle, his wife nagged him to such an extent that he finally told her the answer. She promptly turned the information over to the Philistines who correctly guessed the answer and required Samson to give them thirty sets of clothing as agreed in their wager. Samson paid off the wager by killing thirty Philistines, taking their clothing, and turning these garments over to the Philistines with whom he had made the wager. When his bride's father married her off to another man, this provoked continued conflict between Samson and the Philistines, which Samson would invariably win with his great strength. When Samson later took up a relationship with another Philistine woman named Delilah, the Philistine lords conspired with her to learn the secret of Samson's strength. After much nagging Samson told Delilah that his long hair was the secret to his strength. She then called the Philistines, who cut Samson's hair while he slept, thereby depriving him of his great strength and enabling the Philistines to overcome and imprison him. When the now-blinded Samson was brought to a Philistine temple for entertainment and mockery, Samson prayed to YHWH for his strength to return. Having been placed between two supporting pillars for the temple structure, YHWH granted Samson's request. This enabled him to push the pillars apart and bring down the entire structure, killing himself and all the Philistines inside.

Although this narrative might be perceived to have ended in triumph for Samson, readers must remember that suicide is strictly forbidden in Jewish tradition. Samson's action represents a betrayal of YHWH's gift of life and marks him as a failure. The fact that he is done in by means of his relationships with Philistine women underscores his failure to observe divine Torah. But the narrative cannot be read only in isolation. It functions in relation to the larger literary context of Judges where it stands as the culmination of the narratives concerning the major judges of Israel and as the introduction to the above-discussed narratives concerning the forced migration of the Danites and the establishment of the idolatrous temple at Dan in Judg 17–18 and the rape of the Levite's concubine and near-destruction of Benjamin in Judg 19–21. Samson emerges as the most problematic of the judges insofar as his failures are not insignificant, as in the case of Ehud, or accidental, as in the case of Jepthah. Rather, Samson's failures are the result of his willful disregard of divine Torah, which ultimately costs the tribe of Dan their original tribal inheritance in the Israelite coastal plain. The Samson narratives mark the beginning of the full disintegration of Israel in the judges narratives as the tribes at first successfully fend off their enemies, but show increasingly Canaanite traits as they decline throughout the narrative under the leadership of northern judges. Such decline begins with the need for deception by Ehud to defeat Eglon of Moab, the failure of Deborah to rally all of the tribes to the defense of the nation against Jabin and Sisera, the threat of civil war by Ephraim against Gideon of Manasseh, the realization of civil war by Ephraim against Jepthah of Gilead, and the loss of the tribal territory of Dan under Samson. The displacement of Dan, the construction of an idolatrous sanctuary, the outrage of the rape and murder of a Levitical woman in Gibeah, the nearly successful attempt to destroy the tribe of Benjamin, and the questionable means by which the men of Benjamin seize their wives points to a complete breakdown in the moral, social, and political order of the tribes of Israel, prompting the narrator to state repeatedly how there was no king in Israel and everyone did whatever they pleased (Judg 21:25; cf. 18:1; 19:1).

The narratives in Judg 17–18 and 19–21 are hardly appendices to the narratives of the judges; rather, Judg 17–18 and 19–21 demonstrate the horrific consequences of the decline among the tribes of Israel that is attributed to the Canaanization of the tribe under the leadership of the northern judges. Indeed, the ramifications of these narratives reach far beyond the boundaries of only the book of Judges. The portrayal of the actions of the men of Gibeon and Benjamin at large has implications for the reader's assessment of the first king of Israel, Saul ben Kish, who proves to be an inadequate leader who must finally give way to David ben Jesse of the city of Beth Lehem in the tribe of Judah. Likewise, the repeated statements that Israel did evil in the eyes of YHWH at the outset of each narrative concerning a judge anticipate the formulaic statement of the evil behavior of each of the northern Israelite kings—and many of the Judean kings as well—in the book of Kings in which each northern monarch is said to have done evil in the eyes of YHWH like that done by Jeroboam ben Nebat, the first northern Israelite king. Judges attempts to make the case that the northern Israelite tribes are incapable of ruling themselves in large measure by charging that their moral perspectives and political integrity have been compromised by their inability to separate themselves from the Canaanites and to adhere only to YHWH.

The synchronic literary form of the book of Judges displays literary coherence that posits decline in Israel due to the failure of Israel to separate itself from the Canaanites.[14] The literary structure of Judges may be represented as an account of Israel's Canaanization and degeneration during the premonarchic period:

Account of Israel's Canaanization and Degeneration during the Premonarchic Period

When read within the synchronic literary framework of the Former Prophets, the book of Judges stands in stark contrast to the preceding book of Joshua. Joshua portrays YHWH's commitment to the covenant with Israel insofar as YHWH grants the land of Canaan to Israel and calls upon Israel to fulfill its obligation to observe YHWH's expectations within the framework of that covenant. Judges then turns to the question as to whether or not Israel will meet its obligations to YHWH and answers that question with a resounding no. Judges maintains that Israel failed to observe YHWH's requirement to drive out the Canaanites from the land, and it further maintains that YHWH resolved therefore to turn the Canaanites into a test and snare for Israel. As Canaanite influence progressively permeated Israel in the book of Judges, the people progressively engaged in the pursuit of idolatry and other gods and progressively saw their moral base and political unity disintegrate through the progression of the judges, each with their progressively worsening faults, and culminating in the loss of the tribal territory of Dan, the establishment of the idolatrous sanctuary at Dan's new home once they had been displaced, the moral outrage committed by Benjamin, one of the tribes of Israel, and the resulting civil war that nearly saw the destruction of the tribe of Benjamin by the other tribes.

By portraying Israel in this fashion, the Judges narrative maintains that Israel did not live up to its obligations to YHWH, and thereby laid the foundations for punishment and exile in keeping with the terms of the covenant articulated in Deut 28–30 and in Joshua's public speeches to Israel in Josh 1; 23; 24. But the narrative goes further than that insofar as it also looks forward to the following books of Samuel and Kings in the Former Prophets. Samuel and Kings provide a critical examination of the institution of kingship in Israel—maintaining that it is an institution that makes Israel resemble the nations around it (1 Sam 8)—together with a critical examination of the first kings of Israel—Saul ben Kish, David ben Jesse, and Solomon ben David—followed by all of the later kings of Israel and Judah. These examinations demonstrate the inadequacies of these kings as leaders of Israel, insofar as they bear primary responsibility for the exiles of both Israel and Judah. In the end, all of the major royal families of Israel and

Judah, including the house of Saul, all of the northern kings, and even the house of David, are portrayed as inadequate, incompetent, idolatrous, and even criminal to a degree, in leading Israel and Judah into judgment from YHWH. There are certain exceptions in the house of David—for example, Asa, Jehoshaphat, Hezekiah, and Josiah—but the righteousness of these figures is overwhelmed by the inadequacies of the other members of the line, beginning with David and Solomon, so that by the end of the history, King Jehoiachin ben Jehoiakim, the last legitimate monarch of the Davidic line, is reduced to eating at the table of his captor, the king of Babylon, much like Mephibosheth ben Jonathan ben Saul, was reduced to eating at the table of his own overlord, King David.

Judges points to the need for righteous kingship at the conclusion of the narrative and therefore prepares the way for the introduction and exercise of kingship throughout the balance of Israel's history in the land through the Babylonian exile, but in doing so, Judges prepares the reader for a history of kingship that leads to Israel's and Judah's exile from the land in contradistinction to the expectations laid out in Deuteronomy and Joshua. This does not mean that Israel has no future in the land—Deut 30 makes sure to state that Israel will return to the land when it returns to YHWH—but it does mean that the kings of Israel and Judah are the primary culprits responsible for their respective exiles. It also does not mean that kingship itself or its corollary, political independence, are forbidden or somehow antithetical to YHWH's will. The so-called Torah of the King in Deut 17:14-20 makes the expectations of kingship clear insofar as it portrays the righteous king as one who keeps a copy of YHWH's Torah with him, studies it daily under the tutelage of the Levitical priests, and implements its teachings in the exercise of the royal office. Readers of the narrative are expected to draw the proper conclusions, that is, remove the influence of Canaanite idolatry and immorality and establish proper observance of YHWH and YHWH's Torah as the foundation for Israel's life in the land, including the exercise of kingship as laid out in Deut 17:14-20 and exemplified by the righteous monarchs, Asa, Jehoshaphat, Hezekiah, and especially Josiah.

The diachronic dimensions of this narrative must also be considered. In the current form of the text, the Judges narratives lay a foundation for understanding the downfall of Judah in the exilic period as well as the downfall of northern Israel to the Assyrians by pointing to patterns of idolatry for the entire twelve-tribe nation of Israel as early as the premonarchic period. As part of the exilic edition of the DtrH, Judges would therefore call upon its readers to observe YHWH's Torah as the fundamental basis for any efforts to restore Jewish life in the land of Israel following the end of the Babylonian exile. The return to the land in the late sixth century and the rebuilding of the Jerusalem Temple under Zerubbabel and Joshua ben Jehozadak, as well as the late fifth-century efforts at restoration and reform by Nehemiah and Ezra, would presuppose the general DtrH portrayal of Israel's past sins as models from which to learn as they pursued their own efforts at reconstituting Jewish life in the land of Israel.

The Josianic edition of the DtrH would also have made great use of the Judges narrative in its entirety. The portrayal of the shortcomings of the northern Israelite judges, the establishment of an idolatrous sanctuary at Dan, the Benjaminite outrage committed against the Levite's concubine, and the efforts of the tribes to destroy Benjamin from their base at Beth El would have provided the basis for the charge that northern Israel was incapable of ruling itself and was destroyed by Assyria as a result of its own apostasy against YHWH. The more ideal portrayal of the Judean judge, Othniel, would have supported Josian efforts to restore Judean/Davidic rule over the former northern kingdom of Israel.

The Judges narrative would have played a similar role in the Hezekian edition of the DtrH, which also promoted the efforts of the house of David to re-establish its rule over the former northern tribes. When read in relation to the Jehu history of Israel, the Judges narrative would have employed the critique of Israel's premonarchic rulers as a foil for the development of righteous rule of Israel by the Jehu dynasty. King Jeroboam ben Joash, the fourth monarch of the line, who ruled a kingdom much like that of Solomon, extending from Lebo Hamath in the north to the Arabah in the south (2 Kgs 14:23-29), is said to have "delivered" (Hebrew, *wayyôšî'ēm*, "and he delivered them") Israel much as the judges delivered Israel during the premonarchic period.

Finally, the Judges narrative also plays a role in the Solomonic history of Israel insofar as the concluding narratives concerning Dan and the rape of the Levite's concubine makes the case for a righteous king to rule over Israel. Both narratives posit victims from Beth Lehem, viz., the Levites in the case of Judg 17–18 and the Levite's concubine in the case of Judg 19–21, as victims of northern apostasy and immorality. The Judges narratives concerning the incompetence of the northern judges points to Judean monarchs, that is, David and Solomon, as the righteous kings necessary to overcome the problems of the tribes of Israel. The concluding narrative concerning the rape of the Levite's concubine very clearly undermines the house of Saul, which ceases to be a threat to the house of David once Solomon comes to the throne and eliminates Shimei, the last member of the house of Saul to pose any threat, real or perceived, to the house of David (1 Kgs 2:36-46; cf., respectively, 2 Kgs 2:8-9; 2 Sam 16:5-8; 19:22-24).

NOTES

[1] For commentaries on the book of Judges, see Robert Boling, *Judges* (AB 6A; Garden City: Doubleday, 1975); J. Alberto Soggin, *Judges: A Commentary* (OTL; Philadelphia: Westminster, 1981); Yairah Amit, *Judges* (Miqra leYisrael; Jerusalem: Magnes, 1999 [Hebrew]); Tammi J. Schneider, *Judges* (BO; Collegeville: Liturgical, 2000); Mark Brettler, *The Book of Judges* (London: Routledge, 2002); Susan Niditch, *Judges: A Commentary* (OTL; Louisville: Westminster John Knox, 2008). See also Yairah Amit, *The Book of Judges: The Art of Editing* (BibInt 38; Leiden: Brill 1999); Robert H. O'Connell, *The Rhetoric of the Book of Judges* (VTSup 63; Leiden: Brill, 1996).

[2] For the distinction between the literary framework of Judges and the narratives concerning the individual Judges, see especially Wolfgang Richter, *Traditionsgeschichtliche Untersuchungen zum Richterbuch* (BBB 18; Bonn: P. Hanstein, 1963); idem, *Die Bearbeitungen des "Retterbuches" in der deuteronomischen Epoche* (BBB 21; Bonn: P. Hanstein, 1964).

[3] Martin Noth, "The Background of Judges 17–18," in *Israel's Prophetic Heritage*, ed. B. W. Anderson and W. Harrelson (Fs. J. Muilenburg; London: SCM, 1962), 68–85; idem, *The Deuteronomistic History* (JSOTSup 15; Sheffield: JSOT, 1981), 121 n. 29.

[4] See M. A. Sweeney, *King Josiah of Judah: The Lost Messiah of Israel* (Oxford: Oxford University Press, 2001), 110–24; Yairah Amit, "Hidden Polemics in the Conquest of Dan: Judges xvii–xviii," *VT* 40 (1990): 4–20.

[5] Noth, *Deuteronomistic History*, 121 n. 29.

[6] Sweeney, *King Josiah*, 110–24; Yairah Amit, "Literature in the Service of Politics: Studies in Judges 19–21," in *Politics and Theopolitics in the Bible and Postbiblical Literature*, ed. H. Graf Reventlow and B. Uffenheimer (JSOTSup 171; Sheffield: Sheffield Academic, 1994).

[7] The narrative also draws on the account of the men of Sodom in Gen 19 who demand to rape the two angels who visited Lot (see also Gale Yee, "Ideological Criticism: Judges 17–21 and the Dismembered Body," in *Judges and Method: New Approaches in Biblical Studies* [Minneapolis: Fortress Press, 1995], 146–70).

[8] For a full assessment of the literary structure of the book of Judges, see my "Davidic Polemics in the Book of Judges," *VT* 47 (1997): 517–29, and *King Josiah*, 110–24.

[9] See Moshe Weinfeld, "Judges 1.1–2.5: The Conquest under the Leadership of the House of Judah," in *Understanding Poets and Prophets*, ed. A. G. Auld (Fs. G. W. Anderson; JSOTSup 152; Sheffield: JSOT, 1993), 388–400.

[10] Noth, *Deuteronomistic History*, 46–47.

[11] See my "Davidic Polemics," passim.

[12] Schneider, *Judges*, 91.

[13] See also James A. Crenshaw, *Samson: A Secret Betrayed. A Vow Ignored* (Atlanta: John Knox, 1978).

[14] See my "Davidic Polemics," 529, and *King Josiah*, 120.

D. THE BOOK OF SAMUEL

The books of Samuel were originally considered as one book in Jewish tradition. They only came to be viewed as two books in Judaism when printed Rabbinic Bibles, which followed the Christian tradition of dividing Samuel into 1 and 2 Samuel/Kingdoms, began to appear in the fifteenth century. Traditional Jewish scholarship considers Samuel to be the author of the books (*b. Baba Batra* 14b–15a; see 1 Sam 10:25; 1 Chr 29:29), although R. Abraham Ibn Ezra notes in his commentary on Isa 40:1 that it would have been impossible for Samuel to write the portions of the book that followed his death (see 1 Sam 25:1; 28:3). Modern scholarship attributes authorship of the books to the circles that produced the Deuteronomistic History in the exilic, Josianic, or perhaps the Hezekian periods, and some push the composition of some of Samuel's major components back into the circles that produced the Jehu history of the eighth century BCE or even into the early Davidic dynasty of the tenth and ninth centuries BCE.[1]

The books of Samuel examine the origins of kingship in ancient Israel from the time of Samuel, the prophet and priest who acts as Judge of Israel, through the reigns of King Saul ben Kish of the tribe of Benjamin and King David ben Jesse of the tribe of Judah.[2] The narrative begins in 1 Sam 1–7 with an account of Samuel's leadership of Israel, who rules Israel when the priestly house of Eli at the Shiloh sanctuary proves to be inadequate and who will subsequently prepare for the transition to a formal monarchy near the end of his life. The narrative then turns in 1 Sam 8–12 to the inauguration of the monarchy and the selection of Saul as the first King of Israel, although the narrative makes it clear throughout that Saul will prove to be an inadequate king for Israel. First Samuel 13–31 presents an account of the reign of King Saul from his earliest battles against the Philistines and the Amalekites until his death by his own hand in battle against the Philistines at Mt. Gilboa near Beth Shean. The narrative portrays Saul's decline as Israel's leader, in contrast to David's rise to power, first as a member of Saul's own household and later as an enemy of Saul allied with the Philistines. Second Samuel 1–8 portrays David's own rise to kingship, first over Judah, later over all Israel, and ultimately over the nations that surrounded Israel and Judah. Finally,

2 Sam 9–24 examine David's exercise of kingship, with particular attention to David's own inadequacies, including his adulterous affair with Bath Sheba, his role in murdering her husband, Uriah the Hittite, when she became pregnant, and the tensions within his own household as his sons engaged in rape, murder, and revolt against even David himself.

Although 1–2 Samuel present an account of the public events that led to the institution of the house of David as the ruling dynasty of Israel, the Samuel narratives focus on the characterization of the major figures of that history, including their personal and private interactions as well as their very clear moral and personal failings together with their strengths. It appears that the books of Samuel are concerned with much more than with a simple account of the public history of the origins of Israel's monarchy. To be sure, G-d also plays a role in the narrative, but frequently serves as more of a background figure for the more engaged and engaging human characters of the text. Samuel's focus on the unflattering personal and often private dimensions of Israel's founding figures suggests an interest in presenting these figures, their motivations, their strengths, and their weaknesses, as subjects of study in their own right in the larger context of history. Such a focus on the private or personal human dimensions of history would perhaps provide the means for Samuel's readers, perhaps future kings, officers, priests, and other potential leading figures of Israel, to learn from the examples of human conduct offered in the Samuel narratives as they prepared for their own roles and responsibilities in guiding the nation. Samuel therefore emerges as a type of didactic history that presents both the major public events of the origins of Israel's monarchy and character studies that illustrate how individual personalities, for good or for ill, function in relation to the major events of the narrative.

The literary structure of Samuel is based in the successive presentation of the central figures involved in the inauguration of kingship in Israel. The synchronic literary structure of the work may be presented as follows:

Didactic History of the Origins of Israel's Monarchy

I.	The Rule of Samuel ben Elkanah: Priest, Prophet, and Judge	1 Sam 1–7
	A. Samuel's introduction to Shiloh and the house of Eli	1–3
	B. The Philistine defeat of Israel and capture of the Ark	4–6
	C. Samuel's exercise of leadership over Israel	7
II.	Samuel's Institution of Kingship in Israel under Saul	8–12
	A. The people's demand for kingship	8
	B. The selection of Saul as king	9–11
	C. Samuel's farewell	12
III.	The Reign of King Saul ben Kish	13–31
	A. Samuel's condemnations of Saul	13:1—15:34
	B. David's selection as the next king	15:35—17:58
	C. David's rivalry with Saul	18–27
	D. The death of Saul	28–31

The first major component of the books of Samuel is the presentation of Samuel's rule over Israel as priest, prophet, and judge in 1 Sam 1–7.[3] Although the account of Samuel's rule does not appear among the Judges of Israel, it is clear that he is a transitional figure whose pattern of rule closely resembles that of the Judges but who also plays the key role in inaugurating dynastic kingship in Israel. Samuel comes to prominence to deliver Israel at a time of crisis when the Philistines threaten Israel's freedom and perhaps even its existence, and it is equally clear that his sons are inadequate successors for their father (1 Sam 8:1-3). The boundaries of this component of the narrative are defined by Samuel's lifetime, from the account of Samuel's birth and his early years that appears in 1 Sam 1–3 through his exercise of leadership over Israel in 1 Sam 7. Although the account of the Philistine capture of the Ark of the Covenant in 1 Sam 4–6 does not explicitly feature Samuel, the introductory statement in 1 Sam 4:1 concerning Samuel's words in Israel and the transition from the ark narrative back to Samuel in 1 Sam 7:1-2 makes it clear that the ark narrative appears as a sub-unit of the larger account of Samuel's life and rule over Israel. The following account of the inauguration of kingship in Israel in 1 Sam 8–12 begins with a notice of Samuel's old age and the inadequacy of his sons for rule in 1 Sam 8:1-3 as a means to provide a transition into the concern with the establishment of dynastic kingship in Israel.

Concern with the major personalities featured in the account of Samuel's birth and early years in 1 Sam 1–3 is paramount insofar as the portrayal of the major characters establishes both the need for major change in Israel's leadership and the role of YHWH behind the scenes in bringing the necessary change about.[4] The account begins in 1 Sam 1:1—2:11 with Samuel's birth to Ephraimite parents and his placement in the Shiloh sanctuary where he will be raised under the tutelage of the high priest Eli to serve as a priest in Israel. Samuel's father is identified as an Ephraimite from Ramathaim of the Zuphites, Elkanah ben Jeroham, although the genealogy in 1 Chr 6:13 identifies Samuel as a Levite. First Chronicles 6:10-12 curiously does not identify Samuel as one of the sons of Elkanah, who is tied into the genealogy of the Levites. Traditional scholarship attempts to resolve this problem by arguing that Elkanah is a Levite who resides in Ephraim. The reference to Elkanah's two wives, Hannah and Peninah, provides the opportunity to introduce typical Israelite motifs concerning the rival wives of the same husband and the barrenness of the wife who is loved (cf. Sarah and Hagar in Gen 12–24 and Rachel and Leah in Gen 29–35). Such a motif signals that the loved wife will ultimately overcome her rival by giving birth to a son who will emerge as a leading figure in Israel, viz., the birth of Isaac to Sarah and the births of Joseph and Benjamin to Rachel.

The purpose here is not simply to signal the birth of Samuel, but to point to the inadequacies of the priestly house of Eli at Shiloh. When Hannah comes with her husband to celebrate the festival at Shiloh each year, she is given a lesser portion of the festival meal than her rival Peninah, who has already born children and who torments Hannah for her inability to conceive. Hannah's weeping and fervent prayer to YHWH to give her a son provides the opportunity for her to vow that her son would be raised as a Nazirite (Num 6) so that he might serve in the Temple at Shiloh, but it also provides the first opportunity for Eli to demonstrate his incompetence as high priest. When Eli sees Hannah praying, he does not recognize that she is at prayer, but assumes instead that she is drunk—which in turn might suggest that this, rather than prayer, is something that Eli knows from his own experience—and upbraids her for her conduct. He is forced to back down, however, when Hannah insists that she is not drunk, but is merely praying to YHWH. Of course, Hannah bears her son, Samuel, in the aftermath of this incident and brings him to Shiloh to serve as a Nazirite, in keeping with her vow, once he is weaned. Her song of praise to YHWH in 1 Sam 2:1-10 highlights YHWH's role in bringing about such a wonderful outcome.

A second opportunity to demonstrate Eli's incompetence as high priest appears in 1 Sam 2:11-36, in which an anonymous prophet of YHWH comes to condemn the house of Eli for its reprehensible conduct in supervising the holy shrine at Shiloh. The condemnation focuses on the behavior of Eli's two sons, Hophni and Phineas, who abuse the sacrifices offered at Shiloh as well as the women who served at the entrance to the sanctuary. Although Eli reprimands his sons, he is ineffective in this most elemental human responsibility, which in turn raises questions about his ability to serve as the key figure tasked with instructing Israel in its holy obligations to YHWH. As a result, YHWH sends an anonymous man of G-d who condemns Hophni and Phineas and thereby seals the fate of the house of Eli which will ultimately be replaced by another priestly line in the Jerusalem Temple. As it happens, Solomon later replaces Abiathar, the high priest of the line of Ithamar ben Aaron through Eli, with Zadok, the high priest of the line of Phineas ben Eleazar ben Aharon (1 Kgs 2). Questions may be raised about

YHWH in this narrative insofar as the refusal of Hophni and Phineas to listen to their father is attributed to YHWH, who intends for them to die whereas Samuel grows in favor with YHWH (v. 25). Although YHWH insures the continuity of the line of Eli, YHWH also insures that Hophni and Phineas do not take the opportunity to correct their actions.

A third opportunity to demonstrate Eli's incompetence appears in 1 Sam 3, which relates Samuel's call to serve as a prophet of YHWH. Young Samuel sleeps in the sanctuary by the Ark of the Covenant and one night hears a voice calling to him. Of course the voice is YHWH's, but when Samuel awakens Eli thinking that the priest has called him, Eli the High Priest does not recognize that YHWH has been calling to Samuel. Eli only realizes what is taking place after the third time he is awakened by young Samuel. When Samuel finally hears from YHWH, YHWH reiterates the condemnation of the house of Eli and sets young Samuel on his career as a seer or prophet of YHWH.

The narrative takes a temporary departure from its focus on Samuel to relate the capture of the Ark of the Covenant by the Philistines and the deaths of Hophni, Phineas, and Eli in 1 Sam 4–6.[5] This narrative serves several functions within the larger contexts of the Samuel narrative. First, it demonstrates YHWH's initial fulfillment of the condemnation of the house of Eli insofar as Hophni, Phineas, and Eli all die when the ark is seized by the Philistines in their defeat of Israel at Aphek. Second, it demonstrates both the Philistines' recognition of YHWH's power and the reality of YHWH's power over the Philistines and their gods when plagues break out against the Philistines in the cities where the captured ark is taken as a war trophy and when the image of the Philistine god Dagon topples over each night when the ark is placed before it. Third, the narrative highlights the absence of the Ark of the Covenant from Israel for the next twenty years when the Philistines send it off to Kiriath Jearim for safe-keeping after it becomes apparent that it cannot remain in Philistia itself. The absence of the ark is a key element in the subsequent account of the rise of Saul to kingship and the exercise of his rule as king. Insofar as the Ark of the Covenant symbolizes YHWH's presence in the world, its absence from Israel indicates YHWH's absence throughout the entire period in which Saul is selected as king and serves as such. The ark only returns to Israel when David's kingship is secure in Jerusalem (see 2 Sam 6–7).

First Samuel 7 then concludes the account of Samuel's leadership of Israel rule with an overview of Samuel's roles as priest, judge, and military leader. Samuel is very much a figure like Moses in these roles, and his key accomplishment is to defeat the Philistines and keep them at bay for the duration of his time as Israel's leader.

The second major component of the Samuel narratives is the account of Samuel's institution of kingship in Israel under Saul in 1 Sam 8–12.[6] This sub-unit is demarcated initially by the reference to Samuel's old age and the inadequacy of his sons in 1 Sam 8:1-3, which signals the need for change in Israel's leadership.

The sub-unit focuses throughout on the process by which Saul ben Kish is selected to serve as Israel's first king. The initial reference to Saul's age and the duration of his reign in 1 Sam 13:1 marks the beginning of a new sub-unit concerned with the reign of King Saul.

First Samuel 8–12 is designed to prompt critical reflection on the institution of kingship in Israel in general and the selection of Saul ben Kish as Israel's first king in particular. Although the narrative can hardly be considered anti-monarchic, it takes care to raise concerns about the character of kingship and its costs to the nation at large and it demands that proper kingship in Israel must be exercised in accordance with the divine will. Although Saul is portrayed very positively in 1 Sam 9:1—10:16 as a handsome and capable young man who stumbles unknowingly into kingship and in 1 Sam 11 as a hero in Israel who delivers the town of Jabesh Gilead from Ammonite oppressors, the positive stories about Saul are framed with narratives that are critical of kingship in general (1 Sam 8), that are critical of Saul himself (1 Sam 10:17-27), and that stress the importance of adhering to divine expectations in the exercise of kingship (1 Sam 11). This last element is particularly important since the following narratives in 1 Sam 13–15 immediately portray Saul's failure to abide by divine expectations in his exercise of kingship as the cause for YHWH's rejection of him as king. Overall, the negative framework for the Saul narratives prompts the reader to rethink the positive portrayals of Saul, and view him as a flawed character and a questionable choice for king.

The initial episode in 1 Sam 8 begins the sub-unit with a critical examination of the institution of kingship in Israel. Following the reference to Samuel's old age and the corrupt character of his sons in the exercise of justice in Israel, 1 Sam 8:4 turns to the people's demand for a king. The people are represented by "the elders of Israel," who serve as the governing body of Israel that is typically involved in the selection of a king (see 2 Sam 5:3; cf. 1 Kgs 12:1, 20). Their demand for a king indicates that they wish to be ruled "like all the nations" (v. 5) raises questions about Israel's self-understanding insofar as Israel is not to be like the nations that YHWH had expelled from the land, although the Torah of the King in Deut 17:14-20 envisions such a possibility and stipulates that the king should be well-versed in divine Torah in order to avoid such a problem. The stance of the narrative continues to be critical insofar as it portrays Samuel's conversation with YHWH about the matter, that is, Samuel is upset because he believes that the people have rejected him as leader, but YHWH makes it clear to Samuel that the people have rejected YHWH to follow other gods. Although YHWH (and Samuel) accedes to the people's demands, Samuel makes sure to warn the people of the costs of kingship, viz., kingship will result in a draft of the people's sons for military service and their daughters for service in the royal court, appropriation of agricultural land to supply the needs of the military and the royal court, a one-tenth tax of all agricultural produce and animals, and so on. From Samuel's (and

YHWH's) perspective, the people will cry out much as they did during the period
of Egyptian slavery and during the period of the Judges when they were oppressed
by foreign nations.

First Samuel 9:1—10:16 then turns to a very positive portrayal of Saul and his
selection by YHWH (and Samuel) as Israel's first king. Saul ben Kish of Benjamin, the son of a wealthy family, is described as handsome and tall. He is sent out
on a task to find his father's lost asses, but in fairy-tale style he ultimately finds
himself a kingdom. The choice is made when Saul and his servant travel to
Ramah to consult the seer of the city, Samuel, who displays none of the doubts
about kingship expressed in the preceding chapter. After inviting Saul to sit at the
place of honor in a festival celebration in the city, Samuel invites Saul to spend the
night and anoints him as king of Israel the next morning. YHWH's role in the
matter is clear throughout, insofar as YHWH tells Samuel that the new king is
about to visit and points Saul out to Samuel when he arrives the next day.
YHWH's view of Saul at this point will raise some questions later on when Saul
proves to be inadequate as king.

First Samuel 10:17-27 then turns to a very critical portrayal of Saul during the
process in which the tribes selected the king, which of course demonstrates at the
outset that Saul is unfit to rule Israel. The process for the selection of the king calls
for a series of lots, first among the tribes of Israel, then among the clans of the tribe
of Benjamin, and finally among the men of the Matrite clan. When Saul's lot is
chosen, he is nowhere to be seen, but is found hiding among the baggage after
inquiry is made to YHWH. Such an act is hardly fitting for the man who has just
been selected as the new king of Israel. To reinforce the point, the narrative
concludes with the statement of two scoundrels (lit., sons of Belial) who question
Saul's ability to deliver the nation (from the Philistine threat) and refuse to bring
any gift. For his own part, Saul ignores this sleight, indicating his inability to quell
dissent in Israel, not unlike the problems that Deborah had in uniting the nation
(Judg 4–5). The notice that Saul returned home to Gibeah signals to the reader
that Saul is from the same town responsible for the rape of the Levite's concubine
and the near destruction of his own tribe of Benjamin (Judg 19–21).

First Samuel 11 then turns to another favorable portrayal of Saul, who saves the
city of Jabesh Gilead from Nahash, King of the Ammonites. Saul is clearly a hero
in this narrative, and he earns the undying gratitude of the people of Jabesh
Gilead, who will ultimately see to his proper burial in 1 Sam 31. But various elements of this narrative have already been incorporated into the narrative concerning the rape of the Levite's concubine in Judg 19–21, clearly to undermine
Saul. When Saul hears of Jabesh Gilead's plight, he cuts up his oxen and sends the
pieces throughout all Israel to call the people to war, just as the body of the
Levite's concubine was used for the same purpose in Judg 19–21. The role of
Jabesh Gilead in the narrative also recalls Judg 19–21. Brides for the surviving
men of Benjamin were found by slaughtering the people of Jabesh Gilead and

giving the surviving four hundred maidens of the city to the men of Benjamin after all Israel swore never to give their daughters to Benjamin. Although Saul is a hero for saving Jabesh Gilead, the larger literary context makes it clear that Saul is an inadequate king with potentially murderous tendencies.

Having portrayed Saul in three episodes, 1 Sam 12 then returns to Samuel and his address to Israel after having installed Saul as king. The old prophet takes his leave of the nation as he is about to retire from public service. Before he goes, he delivers a public speech in which he rehearses YHWH's actions on behalf of Israel from the times of Jacob, Moses and Aaron, and the Judges, and exhorts the people to adhere to YHWH and to observe YHWH's expectations now that they have a king. Samuel's exhortation speech—and indeed the entire block of material in 1 Sam 8–12—of course signals Saul's failure to do so in the narratives that follow.

The third major component of the books of Samuel is the lengthy account of the reign of King Saul in 1 Sam 13–31.[7] The unit begins with an introductory regnal formula in 1 Sam 13:1 like those of the books of Kings, stating Saul's age at his accession to the throne and the duration of his reign.[8] There are clearly textual problems with this statement, in that it indicates that Saul was a one-year-old when he began his reign,[9] and the Hebrew word employed for the duration of his reign, šĕtê, "two," is a construct that must be joined with another element that does not appear in this text. The narrative concludes in 1 Sam 31:13 with a notice of Saul's burial in Jabesh following his death by his own hand in battle against the Philistines at Mt. Gilboa.

The account of Saul's reign in 1 Sam 13–31 is clearly designed to portray him as an inadequate monarch whose reign must be considered an absolute failure. His basic task is to protect Israel from foreign enemies, most notably the Philistines who are his primary nemesis throughout his reign, but he is never able to defeat the Philistines fully and dies in battle against them near Beth Shean by his own hand at the end of his reign. Saul's suicide is the culmination in the portrayal of an ultimately tragic life that never achieved the potential greatness signaled in the accounts of his anointing as king in 1 Sam 9:1—10:16 and his deliverance of Jabesh Gilead in 1 Sam 13. But Saul's tragic end follows naturally upon his own failure to rally Israel against the Philistines, in part because he spent so much of his efforts in trying to track down David, who emerged as a rival when it became evident to the Israelite public—particularly the women of Israel—that David was far more capable of protecting Israel and defeating the Philistines than Saul. Readers, of course, must learn to read through the propagandistic elements of the Saul–David narratives, which are clearly written to serve David's interests by portraying the rise of David over against the downfall of Saul. David does after all go over to the Philistine side during Saul's reign, indicating that Saul likely had ample reason to be concerned about a man of questionable allegiance. Nevertheless, the outcome speaks for itself, viz., Saul was never able to overcome the Philistines and died in his failed attempts to do so, whereas David subdued the Philistines very quickly at the outset of a long reign that saw Israelite dominance

over most of its immediate neighbors and good relations with many of the more
distant nations. The house of David survived to write the history; the house of
Saul lost its position to the Davidides and its voice and perspectives are therefore
left unheard.

The Saul narratives raise another important dimension, viz., the role of YHWH
in setting up Saul as king and YHWH's very active role in Saul's failure. On the
one hand, readers might observe that YHWH somehow failed in selecting Saul as
Israel's first king despite the signs very early on (for example, 1 Sam 10:17-27;
contra 1 Sam 9:1—10:16; 11) that he was inadequate for the role. On the other
hand, readers must observe that Saul had ample opportunity to fulfill his task in
accordance with YHWH's expectations, but he fails to do so as the initial narratives in 1 Sam 13:1—15:34 concerning Saul's battles against the Philistines and the
Amalekites demonstrate. Saul grows tired of waiting for Samuel prior to the battle
against the Philistines and makes the pre-battle sacrifices himself in 1 Sam 13–14,
seriously compromising the sanctity of the priesthood by taking on the holy task
himself, despite his lack of qualification to do so. When Saul wins a victory
against the Amalekites in 1 Sam 15:1-34, he deliberately ignores Samuel's instructions to destroy completely the Amalekites and their cattle. In both cases, Samuel
declares Saul's transgressions and the punishments for them. In 1 Sam 13:13-14,
Samuel declares that Saul's dynasty will not endure, but will be replaced by
another royal house—clearly a reference to the house of David. A further dimension of Saul's tragic side is his oath in 1 Sam 14:24 that none of his soldiers will
taste food until the Philistines are entirely defeated. Of course, Jonathan, Saul's
first-born son and presumed heir to the throne, does not hear Saul's oath and
unwittingly eats honey in 1 Sam 14:25-30, thereby sealing his own fate to die in
battle with his father at Mt. Gilboa. In 1 Sam 15:26 Samuel declares that YHWH
has rejected Saul as king because Saul had rejected YHWH's commands.

The question of YHWH's righteousness and power appears in 1 Sam 15:29
when Samuel states that the Glory of Israel, that is, YHWH, does not deceive or
change the divine mind since YHWH is not human. Yet, Samuel's statement
must be read as an attempt to defend YHWH's character in the Saul narratives.
YHWH after all did select Saul as king and the subsequent narratives will indicate
that YHWH deliberately set an evil spirit on Saul in 1 Sam 16:14 that would afflict
him for the rest of his life. Although the pro-Davidic stance of the narrative is
clear, viz., Saul is condemned to prepare the way for David, the narrative must
also be recognized for its adherence to the notion of human free will. YHWH may
have chosen Saul, and YHWH may even know how Saul will ultimately fair as
king, but Saul is responsible for his own decisions—at least in 1 Sam 13:1—15:34
prior to affliction by the evil spirit from YHWH—and he must be held responsible for his own loss of kingship. Such a portrayal stands in contrast to YHWH's
hardening of Pharaoh's heart in the Exodus narrative or YHWH's commission to
Isaiah in Isa 6 to close the eyes, ears, and minds of the people of Israel so that they
would not repent. But the portrayal of Saul here conforms to the portrayal of Eve

in Gen 3, viz., she exercises her own free will, and pays the consequences when she proves to be wrong. With the portrayal of Saul's choices in 1 Sam 13:1—15:34, the book of Samuel joins in a debate concerning divine righteousness and power and human responsibility that runs throughout the Bible.

With the condemnation of Saul, the narrative turns to the introduction of David and the beginnings of his rivalry with Saul in 1 Sam 15:35—17:58. The pro-Davidic stance of the three narratives that comprise these chapters and the role of YHWH in supporting David and acting against Saul is clear throughout. The narrative block begins in 1 Sam 15:35 with statements of Samuel's grief and YHWH's regret concerning Saul, which must be read in relation to the preceding statements in 1 Sam 15:29 that YHWH does not deceive or change the divine mind. Such a statement demonstrates a degree of divine (and prophetic) vulnerability in the face of human free will, that is, YHWH is affected by human choice.

The first narrative in 1 Sam 16:1-13 builds on the portrayal of Saul insofar as it depicts Samuel's secret journey to the house of Jesse in Beth Lehem at YHWH's behest to anoint David as Saul's replacement. Both Samuel and YHWH conspire to deceive Saul. When Samuel expresses fear that Saul might learn of the purpose of his journey, YHWH instructs him to masquerade his actions as an effort to make an offering to YHWH. YHWH remains involved. When the sons of Jesse are brought before Samuel, YHWH informs Samuel that the boys are inadequate. Only when Jesse's youngest son, David, is brought before Samuel does YHWH indicate that David is the divine choice. The reason for David's earlier absence, that he was tending the sheep, indicates his royal role. Mesopotamian kings typically portrayed themselves as shepherds to depict metaphorically their leadership of their peoples.[10]

The second narrative in 1 Sam 16:14-23 has little to do with the first, but the narrative context draws a connection between them as David is introduced to Saul. The narrative makes YHWH's involvement clear when it begins with a statement that YHWH's spirit had departed from Saul only to be replaced by an evil spirit from YHWH. Readers may observe symptoms of depression in Saul, which comes as no surprise given Saul's chronic failure to defeat the Philistines and his resulting failure to gain popular support. David appears as a means to soothe the troubled Saul because of David's abilities in music, military skills, speech, and so on. Only David is able to soothe Saul, and the emphatic statement that YHWH is with David in 1 Sam 16:18 suggest that YHWH may have had a hand in David's ability to soothe his king.

The third narrative in 1 Sam 17:1-58 returns to the Philistine wars with an account of David's slaying of the Philistine giant, Goliath. Under Saul's leadership, Israel is at a stalemate with the Philistines, who daily send out their champion to challenge any of the Israelites to fight him one-on-one. Of course, no Israelite accepts the challenge until young David, who only comes to bring his older brothers food after he has fulfilled his duties in tending his father's flocks, arrives on the scene and determines that he will accept Goliath's challenge.

David's capacity to place himself in the right place at the right time emerges in the narrative when he is forced to defend himself against his brother Eliab's charges that he has just come to watch the fighting. The pro-David perspective of the narrative continues when David is offered Saul's armor—a pointed reference to the fact that Saul himself would not accept the Philistine challenge but would allow a young boy like David to do so—but the armor is far too big for him to wear. Readers are then treated to a heroic tale in which the young David, armed only with his sling, kills Goliath with a well-placed stone to the head. An ancient sling is a lethal weapon used in combat by Mesopotamian armies,[11] but the point is made, viz., David kills Goliath but Saul is unable to do so. Saul's inadequacies are highlighted at the end of the narrative when Saul does not even recognize the boy who soothes his soul with music.

The after-effects of David's victory over Goliath—and its consequences for Saul—are clear throughout the following block of material in 1 Sam 18–27, which portrays the rivalry between David and Saul. Saul spends much of his time in attempts to kill David, and David ultimately goes over to the Philistines to escape from Saul, but the narrative makes it clear throughout that David has the support of the Israelite population and of YHWH. Again, the propagandistic aspect of the narrative must be considered, because the house of Saul is unable to give its own account. The interests of the house of David, however, are well represented throughout.

The first sub-unit appears in 1 Sam 18–20, which recounts David's initial flight from Saul. The narrative begins with notices of David's rising popularity. Jonathan, Saul's oldest son and presumed heir to the throne, becomes David's greatest friend, despite the fact that he has the most to lose should David rise to power. Some have argued that Jonathan's love for David is homosexual, but such a view overlooks the use of the language of love to define political relationships in the ancient Near East and the clearly political interests on the part of David that would be served by such a portrayal of Jonathan's devotion to David.[12] Those interests stand behind the songs of the women of Israel, who sing in 1 Sam 18:7 that "Saul has slain his thousands, and David his ten thousands," signaling that David's star is rising while Saul's is falling. The results are predictable, viz., Saul is gripped once again by the evil spirit from YHWH as his jealousy of David grows. Following Saul's two attempts to kill him, David is made a military commander in the hope that he will be killed in battle. But in contrast to Saul, David is a stunning success.

David's popularity extends to Saul's daughters as well. Saul offers his oldest daughter Merab to David in marriage, but marries her to another man before David can claim her. When Saul offers his younger daughter Michal, he stipulates that the bride price is one hundred Philistine foreskins, thinking that David will be killed when he attempts to procure them. David of course brings two hundred Philistine foreskins and marries Michal. For her part, Michal loves her husband.

Saul's attempts to kill David continue, even when David plays the lyre for Saul in his house. Both Jonathan and Michal, again the two people who have the most to lose if their father's house is overthrown, act on David's behalf in aiding David to escape from Saul. Michal places a dummy in her bed to fool Saul's soldiers while David escapes. Jonathan secretly signals David that the time to flee has come after he has nearly been killed himself by his rapidly deteriorating father.

The sequence of episodes in 1 Sam 21–27 depicts David's flight from Saul and Saul's attempts to track David down. Each of these episodes continues the pro-Davidic and anti-Saul stance of the previous narratives by demonstrating David's righteousness, divine favor, and magnanimity in contrast to Saul's paranoia, utter incompetence, and murderous intent. They further demonstrate the rising support for David among the people and David's own efforts to build a constituency that would support him.

First Samuel 21 depicts David's arrival at Nob, where the priest Ahimelech, a descendant of the house of Eli, aids David by giving him bread consecrated in the sanctuary and the sword of Goliath. From Nob, David flees to the Philistine King Achish of Gath, who remarks that he has no lack of madmen when David appears at his gate foaming at the mouth. Although the narrative portrays David's flight from Saul's attempts to kill him, David eventually does become a vassal of King Achish of Gath in 1 Sam 27.

First Samuel 22 portrays David's continued flight from Saul and Saul's attempts to pursue him. A particularly despicable episode appears in this chapter when Saul orders the execution of the priests at Nob for their role in aiding David. Although Saul's own soldiers refuse the order, Doeg the Edomite carries out the atrocity. Only the priest Abiathar ben Ahitub escapes to join David's forces. First Samuel 23 continues the portrayal of David's flight from Saul and Saul's intention to destroy the Israelite town, Keilah, until he learns that David is no longer in the town. First Samuel 24 makes a special effort to demonstrate David's continuing fidelity to Saul despite Saul's efforts to kill him. When Saul enters a cave at En-gedi to relieve himself, David and his six hundred men are inside. Saul of course does not notice how David refuses to consider the proposals of his men to kill YHWH's anointed, and follows Saul out of the cave loudly proclaiming his loyalty and innocence. For his own part, Saul accepts David's claims and acknowledges that David will one day become king.

First Samuel 25 is a key episode which begins with a notice of Samuel's death. David marries Abigail, the widow of a Calebite man named Nabal who lives in Carmel. The narrative emphasizes Nabal's churlishness—his name means "fool" in Hebrew—and depicts his death following his refusal to aid David and his men. Nabal's refusal is important to consider because he charges that David is nothing more than a servant who has fled from his master—which describes David precisely. Nabal's wife, Abigail, however, recognizes that David will become ruler of Israel and provides him with food and support to prevent him from killing her husband. After Nabal dies, perhaps by heart attack or stroke, Abigail marries David. This is a key marriage for David. As the widow of a Calebite man of wealth, she brings to David social and political standing in the tribe of Judah, standing which David will employ to build his own constituency in Judah.[13]

First Samuel 26 returns to the depiction of David's flight from Saul with a narrative similar in motif to 1 Sam 24. This time, David finds Saul and his men asleep, and enters the camp to take Saul's spear and water bottle. Of course, David spurns suggestions to kill YHWH's anointed. David again loudly proclaims his innocence to Saul and his refusal to harm YHWH's anointed. Saul in turn accepts David's claims, blesses him, and declares that David will prevail. In 1 Sam 27, however, David concludes that it is time to go over to the Philistine side, and he submits to King Achish of Gath. When Achish grants David the town of Ziklag, expecting that David would use it as a base to harass Judah on his behalf, David and his men use Ziklag as a base to protect Judah from attackers, thereby further building his constituency in Judah. Achish is none the wiser since David sends his overlord regular shares of booty that he claims were taken from Judah. At all times, David is a loyal servant of Saul, Judah, and YHWH, even though he is now in the service of the Philistines against his own tribe of Judah.

David's association with the Philistines and residence in Ziklag will be key factors in the fourth sub-unit of the account of Saul's reign, 1 Sam 28–31, which depicts the death of Saul in battle against the Philistines. Because David is at Ziklag during the battle at Mt. Gilboa when Saul dies, he can clearly have no hand in Saul's death. To underscore this point, 1 Sam 29 emphasizes Philistine objections to David's presence with their army, viz., because David is an Israelite servant of Saul, he must remain behind lest he turn against the Philistines when they fight Saul's forces. As for Saul, the polemic against him continues in 1 Sam 28 with a portrayal of his secret consultation of the now dead Samuel through the witch at Endor. Despite his own decree against such mediums, Saul consults her anyway and learns from the ghost of Samuel that he and his sons will die in battle against the Philistines. Samuel's ghost reiterates that this punishment is a result of Saul's failure to kill the Amalekites as instructed in 1 Sam 15. First Samuel 28 concludes with a portrayal of Saul's terror at the news of his impending death so that he must be consoled by the witch of Endor whose profession Saul had condemned by his own decree. Once again, Saul's incompetence as king is clear.

While the Philistines attack Saul at Mt. Gilboa in the Jezreel Valley, David remains in the south where he tracks down the Amalekite raiders who had despoiled Ziklag and other towns in southern Judean. Such a notice further undermines Saul; whereas Saul failed to destroy the Amalekites, David goes out to attack and destroy them. In the course of doing so, he further builds his Judean constituency and wins support among his own men when he declares that those of his soldiers who protect the baggage are entitled to a share of the spoils along with those who actually do the fighting.

The portrayal of Saul's death in 1 Sam 31 concludes the account of the reign of Saul with a tragic portrayal of his own suicide when the battle turns against him. Saul's sons, Jonathan the first-born and presumed heir to the throne, Abinadab, and Malchishua, are all killed by the Philistines as Saul's forces are routed. Wounded by Philistine archers, Saul demands that his armor bearer kill him lest he become a Philistine captive. But even the armor bearer will not strike down YHWH's anointed, leaving Saul to kill himself with his own sword. Saul's suicide is a final testimony to his failed monarchy and ultimately tragic life, but it will also leave the way open for David to become King of Israel.

The fourth major component of the books of Samuel, 2 Sam 1–8, portrays David's rise to kingship over all Israel. The block begins with the temporal notice in 2 Sam 1:1, "And it came to pass after the death of Saul that David returned from striking the Amalekites and remained two days in Ziklag," which introduces the sequence of events that leads David to kingship over all Israel. The block concludes in 2 Sam 8 with a portrayal of David's rule over an empire that includes all the territory around Israel. Most notable in the concluding sequence is the statement in 2 Sam 8:15-18 that "David ruled over all Israel, and David acted justly and righteously for all his people," followed by a listing of the major figures in his administration. A new plot sequence concerned with David's exercise of kingship begins in 2 Sam 9.

Once again, the narrative portrays David as YHWH's favored choice to rule over all Israel. At all points, David is portrayed as free of wrongdoing, even though it is clear throughout the narrative that David begins as a Philistine vassal who must serve his overlords by fighting against the remnants of Israel's forces under the leadership of Saul's son, Ishboshet. During the course of David's rise, the key figures associated with the house of Saul either die or are otherwise removed as obstacles to clear the way for David's assumption of kingship over all Israel. In each case, David is portrayed as acting righteously. Nevertheless, David benefits from each death or setback in the house of Saul, and he is consistently favored by YHWH throughout the narrative.

The narrative begins with its first sub-unit in 2 Sam 1, which portrays David's receipt of the news that Saul and Jonathan are dead. From the standpoint of David's ambitions to rule over all Israel, the deaths of the king and first-born son and heir apparent present David with an opportunity. On the other hand, David is the son-in-law of the king, although Michal has been married to another man since David fled from Saul and abandoned his wife, and he must present himself as a loyal servant of Saul to ensure his reputation and popular support. When a runner from Saul's camp appears with his clothing torn as a sign of mourning, David bows low in anticipation of bad news, thereby demonstrating very publically his loyalty to the king. The runner is identified in the narrative as one of the Amalekites, who are well known as the sworn enemies of Israel whom David had just been fighting. When the runner claims to have killed Saul—even at Saul's own request—David very publically mourns for the deaths of Saul and Jonathan and has the Amalekite runner put to death for having killed YHWH's anointed king. These actions and David's dirge over Saul and Jonathan would dispel any doubts in the minds of the fictive audience of the narrative or on the part of the readers of the narrative that David had a hand in the deaths of Saul and Jonathan or that he would have viewed it as opportunity to serve his own interests.

The second sub-unit of the narrative in 2 Sam 2–5 presents David's rise to kingship, first over the tribe of Judah alone and then over all Israel. The favor of YHWH is indicated from the outset when David consults YHWH, presumably through the Ephod or Urim and Thummin carried by the priests, as to whether he should go up to Hebron. Such a move is strategically important because Hebron is the center or capital of the tribe of Judah, and David's move there amounts to a claim of leadership over his own home tribe. His marriage to Abigail, the widow of the Calebite Nabal, would support his claims to the throne, and his status as a Philistine vassal would ensure that the Philistines would see his move as an extension of their own authority over Judah. David's first move as king is to establish a relationship with Jabesh Gilead, a city very closely associated with Saul whose men gave Saul a proper burial following his death at Mt. Gilboa. For David's part, this is a wise political rule that demonstrates loyalty to Saul and stakes out an ally in the northern trans-Jordan that would enable him to contain northern Israel. But it must also be viewed as a move against Ish-Boshet, the surviving son of Saul, who was made king over the Gilead in place of his father, and Saul's general, Abner, who clearly is the power behind Ish-Boshet's throne.

The resulting conflict between David and Ish-Boshet—as well as between David's general Joab and Ish-Boshet's general Abner—would ultimately decide the leadership of all Israel. When the Judean and Israelite armies meet in battle at Gibeon, David's forces defeat the Israelites, but Abner manages to kill Asahel, the brother of David's general Joab.[14] In the aftermath of the battle, David's power begins to rise as Ish-Boshet's power begins to wane, which in turn creates tensions in the leadership of northern Israel. The tension comes to expression when Abner demands Ritzpah, a concubine of Saul, for himself. A marriage to a former wife or concubine of the previous king amounts to a claim to kingship itself from the perspective of the Samuel narratives, and Ish-Boshet interprets Abner's demand as a claim to the throne. For his own part, David demands the return of his wife, Michal bat Saul, which demonstrates that David is also a member of the house of Saul and therefore has his own claim on the Israelite throne. Having been rebuffed by Ish-Boshet, Abner opens negotiations with David for a settlement that would see an end to hostilities as all Israel would be united under David's rule, and of course Abner would then emerge as a likely candidate for David's top general. But when Joab returns and hears the news of Abner's negotiations with David, he sends forces to overtake the departing Abner and kills him in the gate of Hebron to avenge the death of his brother Asahel. The narrative informs the reader that David knew nothing about Joab's actions, although David clearly benefits from the death of Israel's military commander. For his part, David mourns loudly and publically for Abner just as he did for Saul and Jonathan.

The death of Abner is quickly followed by the assassination of Ish-Bosheth. The assassins are two of his own army officers, Baanah and Rechab, the two sons of Rimmon of the town of Beeroth, which was part of a federation led by Gibeon (see Josh 19:17). Because David had just defeated Ish-Bosheth's forces at Gibeon, the actions of Baanah and Rechab suggest part of a larger scenario in which Gibeon had defected from an alliance with the house of Saul to ally instead with David. Obviously, David benefits from the assassination of Ish-Boshet, but once again the narrative goes to great lengths to demonstrate that David has nothing to do with Ish-Boshet's death. When Baanah and Rechab report their actions to David, apparently expecting to be handsomely rewarded, David very loudly condemns them for having killed YHWH's anointed and has them executed for their actions.

With both Ish-Boshet and Abner dead and David cleared of any wrongdoing, 2 Sam 5:1-3 states that all the tribes of Israel came to Israel at Hebron to make him king over all Israel and thereby end the fighting between Judah and Israel. Second Samuel 5:4-5 presents an introductory regnal formula for David, noting that he was thirty years old when he began to reign, and that he reigned for forty years, including seven years and six month over Judah in Hebron and thirty-three years over both Israel and Judah.

Several more events must transpire for David to consolidate his rule over Israel. First is the selection of a capital, for if David remains in Hebron, he will be far too distant from the more powerful and numerous northern Israelite confederation that has just named him king. But if David leaves Hebron for a northern location, he will lose the support of Judah. The solution is Jerusalem, a Benjaminite town inhabited by Jebusites that sits on the border between Judah and the north. When David captures it with his own mercenaries and without any deaths among the Jebusites, he has a capital that cannot be claimed by either Judah or northern Israel and can thereby consolidate his rule on ground neutral to the two major components of his own federation. With David's capture of Jerusalem, the City of David, 2 Sam 5:10 reiterates that YHWH of Hosts is with him. Recognition of David's kingship by Hiram of Tyre quickly follows, which suggests that David made overtures that would demonstrate his autonomy as king. It is only at this point that David's Philistine overlords recognize what David has done, but when they attack to force him to submit, David now has the power to defeat the Philistines easily and turn them into his own vassals. At this point, David has accomplished what Saul never could, viz., defeat of the Philistines and security for his own people.

Three more sub-units, each concerned with demonstrating David's consolidation of power, then follow. Second Samuel 6 narrates David's return of the Ark from Kiriath Jearim where it had resided since the time of its capture by the Philistines, to Jerusalem. The move signifies David's overthrow of the Philistines, his own assumption of power in Jerusalem, and the recognition of David by YHWH insofar as YHWH's shrine is now moved to Jerusalem under David's patronage. In short, David's kingship is now supported by YHWH's presence and favor, and YHWH is supported as G-d of Israel by David. But a further important dimension also appears in this narrative. When Michal upbraids her husband for dancing before the Ark and exposing himself in his ecstasy, David retorts that he will never have relations with her again. Although such an event might be dismissed as a marital spat, it ensures that David has no sons by Michal, who would then be blood descendants of Saul—unlike David—and thereby have a greater claim to the throne. David's spurning of Michal ensures that he is able to found his own dynasty and not sit on the throne merely as a member of the house of Saul.

The next sub-unit in 2 Sam 7 then portrays unequivocally YHWH's support for David and the foundation of his own dynasty.[15] When David inquires through the prophet Nathan concerning the possibility for building a "house," that is, a temple, for YHWH, YHWH responds that there is no need for a Temple since YHWH has always moved about the world freely, but that YHWH would build a "house," that is, a dynasty, for David. The narrative plays an important role in defining the conceptualization of temples in the history, that is, YHWH's presence could be manifested at Gilgal, Shiloh, Jerusalem, and anywhere else YHWH might choose, which very interestingly lays the foundations for a theological understanding of divine presence in the Babylonian exile when the Temple of Jerusalem was destroyed and yet prophets such as Ezekiel and Second Isaiah articulated YHWH's divine presence throughout the world of creation and human events at large. As for David, YHWH promises him an eternal dynasty so that even his sons will rule after him in Israel forever. From the standpoint of the larger history articulated in the Former Prophets, this understanding of the house of David will be qualified by the stipulation that the house of David will rule forever if the Davidic kings observe YHWH's commands (see 1 Kgs 2:1-4; 8:25-26; 9:1-9). Such qualification clearly results from reflection on an early tradition of David's eternal dynasty grounded in the creation of the world itself, but of course historical events, most notably the Babylonian exile, would see to the end of the house of David, necessitating the explanation that David's descendants would need to observe YHWH's Torah (see Deut 17:14-20) to ensure their continued rule.

The last major component of the narrative concerning David's rise to kingship appears in 2 Sam 8, which outlines all of David's conquests throughout his reign to establish an empire that would include Philistia, Moab, Aram, Edom, Ammon, and the Amalekites as well as all Israel and Judah.

Second Samuel 9–24 constitutes the fifth and concluding major component of the books of Samuel with an account of David's exercise of kingship. Having secured the throne following the lengthy account of his rise to power over against Saul, David now faces a very new situation in which he must be held accountable for the security of the nation and his relationships with his subjects and his own family. David appears to be a very different character in these narratives. Whereas he was favored by YHWH from 1 Sam 16 through 2 Sam 8, his unsavory conduct, including his adultery with Bath Sheba, the murder of her husband Uriah the Hittite, and his failure to act when his own sons engage in similar acts of rape, murder, and rebellion, results in a situation in which David no longer appears to enjoy the full support of YHWH as in the earlier narratives. Indeed, YHWH appears to play a relatively limited background role in these narratives as the human characters stand in the forefront, offering readers the opportunity to study and learn from their many character flaws and questionable actions as the narratives proceed. Nevertheless, David's own character flaws and weaknesses emerge in the actions of his sons, which might suggest a principle of moral retribution at work in these narratives.

Most interpreters follow Leonhard Rost and later followers of his work who identify these narratives diachronically as the Succession Narrative or the Court History of David and argue that their major concern is the question of which of David's sons will succeed him on the throne.[16] The grounds for identifying this narrative sequence as a discrete diachronically defined narrative are well founded even if the details of its demarcation, intention, and setting remain disputed. But the view that these chapters are primarily concerned with the question of David's succession by one of his sons is only partially correct. To be sure, Solomon emerges as the heir to the Davidic throne in 1 Kgs 1–2 when David's sons, Amnon, Abshalom, and Adonijah, are eliminated one by one, primarily due to their own weaknesses and flaws of character, yet readers must remember that David comes to the throne as a member of the house of Saul, even if 2 Sam 7 relates YHWH's promise of a dynasty for David himself. David is the son-in-law of Saul, having married Saul's daughter Michal. Even though she may never have children, David's status as a member of the house of Saul plays a role in his acceptance as king, especially by the northern tribes of Israel. He is no usurper, technically speaking, even though he so often acted to undermine his father-in-law while loudly proclaiming his innocence and loyalty to the king.

The prior narratives emphasize David's loyalty to Saul, but they mask the fact that David was a very poor son-in-law who frequently acted to undermine Saul. He abandoned his wife, Michal, leaving her to be married to another; he went over to the Philistine side when Philistia was at war with Saul; he went to war as a Philistine vassal against Saul's son Ish-Bosheth; he accepted the kingship of Israel when a number of Saul's sons and grandsons remained alive, and indeed, 2 Sam 9 and 20 relate how David kept control of Mephibosheth ben Jonathan ben Saul and handed Saul's other descendants over to the Gibeonites for execution; and he refused to have relations with Michal, ensuring that she would never produce a grandson for Saul. David's actions clear the way for the foundation of his own family as the ruling dynasty of Israel in place of the family of his father-in-law Saul

Nevertheless, the narratives in 2 Sam 9–24 offer an ironic twist insofar as they present David's sons as figures very much like their father, though without his finesse or savvy. Whereas the earlier narratives mask David's actions against Saul with a cloak of loyalty, 2 Sam 9–24 show the reader how David's own sons fundamentally defy parental authority and moral principle in relation to their father, viz., Amnon rapes his half-sister Tamar; Abshalom murders his half-brother Amnon for the rape of his sister; Abshalom revolts against his father and even takes his own father's concubines; and Adonijah—about whom 1 Kgs 1 very pointedly states that David had never taught him anything regarding proper conduct—demands David's concubine (and therefore the throne), even when it is clear that Solomon is the designated successor to his father. Of course, their father provides no moral example, having committed adultery with Bath Sheba and murdered her husband to cover up the affair. As a result of these actions and the overall neglect of parental responsibility in relation to his own sons, the entire house of David from his days in Hebron and before is destroyed as Solomon, the son of Bath Sheba, comes to the throne with a new cohort of supporters who push David's earlier supporters from his Hebron days to the side. Just as Saul's family is pushed aside by David with many killed, so David's Hebron-based family and supporters are pushed aside by the latest branch of his family formed in adultery and murder. Such a portrayal of the house of David raises questions about its continuity in the larger framework of the Former Prophets or the Deuteronomistic History, viz., the history ends in 2 Kgs 25 with a notice that King Jehoiachin ben Jehoiakim, the last legitimate king of the house of David, ate at the table of the Babylonian King Evil Merodach while in Babylonian exile, which is parallel to the experience of Mephibosheth ben Jonathan ben Saul, the last member of the house of Saul who gives up his claims to his father's heritage in 2 Sam 19 when David returns to Jerusalem following his defeat of Abshalom's revolt. In the end, the house of David suffers the same fate as the house of Saul, albeit that David's actions are the ultimate cause in both cases.[17]

The first sub-unit of the account of David's exercise of kingship appears in 2 Sam 9, which relates David's magnanimity to Mephibosheth, the surviving son of Jonathan and grandson of Saul. David's motives are presented as pure, that is, he wishes to show favor to the son of his late friend, Jonathan, and sees to the well-being and support of the crippled young man and his family (see 2 Sam 4:4). The narrative stance toward Mephibosheth is clear, insofar as the name means, "from the mouth of Shame," apparently a deliberate corruption of MepiBaal (*mippîba'al*). But David's motives are not so transparent, particularly when one recognizes that eating at the king's table means that David is able to keep watch over Mephibosheth to ensure that he never becomes a threat to David's rule. The attention given to Ziba, the servant of Mephibosheth, is also indicative of David's intentions, insofar as Ziba will later denounce Mephibosheth to David and, despite a veneer of fairness in the matter, receive Mephibosheth's inheritance in 2 Sam 19. Indeed, the interest in Mephibosheth at the outset of the narrative marks the interest of 2 Sam 9–24 in the house of Saul, particularly since 2 Samuel relates how David gave up the other surviving members of the house of Saul for execution by the Gibeonites. With the removal of the house of Saul, the way will be clear for Solomon ben David to succeed his father on the throne and found the house of David.

The second narrative block in 2 Sam 10–12, which relates David's affair with Bath Sheba and the murder of her husband Uriah, shows David at his worst.[18] Having been left behind while the army went out to war against Ammon, perhaps because David was perceived to be too old to fight, the now idle king immediately gets himself into trouble by having an affair with Bath Sheba, wife of Uriah the Hittite, who is serving in David's army during the campaign against Ammon. When Bath Sheba informs David that she is pregnant, David attempts to cover the affair by summoning Uriah home on some pretext so that he will have relations with his wife and no one will be the wiser concerning the cause of her pregnancy. Of course, the altruistic Uriah refuses to return home to enjoy his wife while his comrades are fighting and dying in the field, and David sees no other recourse than to ensure Uriah's murder by ordering Joab to place Uriah in the front lines and then abruptly withdrawing, abandoning the unsuspecting Uriah (who bore the written orders to Joab himself!) to his fate. The narrative portrays YHWH's actions against David through the agency of the prophet Nathan, the same prophet who conveyed YHWH's promise of an eternal dynasty in 2 Sam 7. Nathan cleverly employs a ruse to prompt David to condemn himself and seek forgiveness from YHWH. As a result, the son conceived by Bath Sheba dies, but she conceives another, Solomon, who will ultimately become the next king of Israel. But YHWH is not done with David yet.

The third sub-unit of the narrative appears in 2 Sam 13, which relates Amnon's rape of his half-sister Tamar. Amnon is the son of David's wife Ahinoam of Jezreel, whom some identify as the former wife of Saul, although this identification is not secure.[19] Amnon is the first-born son of David and presumptive heir to the throne (see 2 Sam 3:2-5). Even if he is not the son of Saul's former wife, his behavior displays the Benjaminite association with rape so evident in the account of the rape of the Levite's concubine in Judg 19–21. Following his father's callous behavior with Bath Sheba and Uriah in the previous chapters, Amnon emerges very much as his father's own son. Using deception to overpower and rape Tamar, Amnon then spurns her, leaving her to a life of solitude in her brother's house since no one would marry her after such an incident. But Abshalom, Tamar's brother, born to David's second wife, Maacah bat Telmai, King of Geshur, is incensed at his sister's treatment. When David does nothing to punish Amnon for his crime, Abshalom takes matters into his own hands and murders Amnon through deception of his own. Following the murder of Amnon, Abshalom fled to his grandfather in Geshur. David did nothing to Abshalom, but mourned for his self-exiled son.

The fourth sub-unit in 2 Sam 14–19 relates Abshalom's revolt against his father David. The sub-unit begins with an account of Abshalom's return to Jerusalem engineered by Joab, who acted in order to get David to focus on his role as king rather than pine away for his exiled son. Here, readers see David as a failed father and king, viz., he is unable to discipline his sons and, as a result, David neglects his responsibilities as king. Joab brings the wise woman of Tekoa to convince David to send for Absalom and bring him home. As it happens, the wisdom of this decision is very questionable because it brings back an Absalom whose anger has festered so much that he carries out his own revolt against his father.[20]

The account of the revolt per se in 2 Sam 15–19 is a study in the effective rule of a nation, the causes of revolt, the means to undermine a revolt, military tactics, public relations, and even the relationship between a king and his own son. YHWH plays very little role in this narrative as the human characters carry the action and provide the grist for careful reflection on the part of the readers of this narrative. Such readers might include kings, government officers, priests, military figures, and anyone else who might aspire to the exercise of authority in ancient Israelite and Judean society. The lessons of this narrative are many.

The first lesson pertains to the causes of Absalom's revolt. The accounts of Amnon's rape of Tamar and Absalom's subsequent exile to Geshur following his murder of Amnon provide ample basis to understand the bitterness that grows within Absalom against his father David, who did nothing to train his sons in proper conduct or to do justice concerning Amnon's rape of Tamar or even Absalom's murder of Amnon. A key element in Absalom's thinking therefore is the issue of justice, and he prepares his revolt by seeking support among the people in return for his pledge to do justice in the kingdom as expected of the monarch. Several additional factors must be considered. First, the narrative presupposes that people in the kingdom are in fact dissatisfied with the dispensation of justice by the king—otherwise, Absalom would never have a hearing. Second, Absalom's public conduct, calling for justice in the gates of Jerusalem and moving about the city with a chariot and runners like that of a king, could not have been unknown to David, who nevertheless fails to recognize the significance of Absalom's actions to call him to account. Third, is the federated nature of David's kingdom, including Judah and northern Israel, which he rules from his own city in Jerusalem. The narrative presupposes that both major components of David's empire are disaffected by their king's distance from them. All of these factors enable Absalom to prepare carefully for his revolt by garnering support among the people outside Jerusalem by playing on their dissatisfaction with the king.

The second lesson pertains to David's actions in abandoning the city and yet leaving his own agents to undermine Absalom and prepare him for defeat. David may be a negligent father and monarch, but he is a wily, experienced, and tough warrior. David's retention of his own mercenary force proves its worth and loyalty in this challenge in that it ensures him of military support in a time of crisis when he is rejected by his own people led by his own son. David makes several key moves. He leaves the ark in Jerusalem, loudly proclaiming that YHWH will ultimately decide the matter, which of course gives David a public relations advantage in that he demonstrates his own fidelity to and trust in YHWH. But he also makes sure that the two priests who bear the ark, Zadok and Abiathar, and their respective sons, Ahimaaz and Jonathan, remain in the city to act as spies and to inform David of Abshalom's actions and plans. A telling comment is his statement that he will remain in the wilderness when in fact David will fortify himself in Mahanaim, viz., David is already preparing an ambush for Abshalom. In addition to the priests, David sends Hushai the Archite back to the city with orders to serve as a counter-agent to frustrate the advice of Ahitophel, a well-regarded councilor, who remained in Jerusalem to support Abshalom. Finally, David's departure from the city, barefoot and weeping, functions as an effective ploy to feign weakness when in fact David is already planning his ambush of Abshalom's forces.

The third lesson pertains to the portrayal of the reactions to David's flight from Jerusalem among key people in the kingdom. Ziba, the servant of Mephibosheth takes the opportunity to curry favor from David by bringing supplies and denouncing Mephibosheth as disloyal to David, a charge that later proves to be a lie. By granting Ziba Mephibosheth's property, David buys Ziba's support and undermines Mephibosheth. Shimei ben Gera, a member of Saul's clan, curses David as his procession proceeds through the tribal territory of Benjamin. Although Shimei will later reconcile with David, David will remember and will see to it that Solomon will find the grounds to kill him (1 King 2). By letting Shimei live for now in a show of royal weakness, David adds further bait to the trap he is setting for Abshalom.

The fourth lesson pertains to the means by which the council of Ahithophel is frustrated. Ahithophel's advice is in fact well-considered. His advice to Abshalom to lie with David's concubines on entering the city constitutes Abshalom's pub-lic declaration that he is now king, which would receive wide support in a city whose loyalty to the king was already in question, especially after the king had fled. Ahithophel's advice to strike at David immediately is also well-considered. As a fugitive, David would need time to consolidate his forces and position in the Trans-Jordan. A rapid strike would hit him when he was most vulnerable and ensure success for Abshalom. But Hushai's counter-advice to wait and gather all of the forces of Israel and Judah before taking on David ensures that David will have sufficient time to prepare and to spring the trap against Abshalom. When David hears from Ahimaaz and Jonathan that Hushai's advice had prevailed, he fortifies himself at Mahanaim, gathers his Trans-Jordanian allies, and prepares to confront Abshalom in the open and away from Jerusalem where casualties would cost him Judean, Israelite, and Jerusalemite support. As for Ahithophel, the frustration of his counsel leaves him little recourse but suicide, because he understands that Abshalom now has no hope of winning. As a traitor to David, Ahithophel's life is now over.

The fifth lesson pertains to the brilliant military plan employed David to defeat Abshalom's much larger army. He lures the army into the Trans-Jordan where

David can choose his own ground to fight just as he did against the Philistines in Emek Rephaim (2 Sam 5). The crushing defeat of Israel and Judah will demonstrate once again David's power, but it will do so at a distance from Jerusalem, Israel, and Judah, so that the people of Israel, Judah, and Jerusalem will not suffer the repercussions of military destruction themselves. The isolation of Absalom also plays a role. Acting against David's orders not to harm his son, Joab makes sure to kill Absalom when he finds him caught by his hair in a tree—a metaphorical portrayal as to how his own vanity results in his death. By killing Absalom, Joab does David a favor by eliminating the primary instigator of the revolt—even though Absalom is David's son.

The sixth lesson pertains to the public relations repair that must be undertaken in the aftermath of David's victory. When David mourns loudly and publicly for the death of his son, Joab must remind him to mind the attitudes of the men who fought and died for David as a result of Absalom's revolt. David shuts up, but he never forgets that Joab killed his son and again has Solomon settle issues with Joab later in life (1 Kgs 2). Shimei ben Gera hurriedly runs to David to submit to him again as overlord. Although David forgives him, which ensures Shimei's support, he will later advise Solomon to find the grounds to kill Shimei and thereby eliminate one more potential challenger from the house of Saul (1 Kgs 2). Mephibosheth also submits to David and in the course of David's interrogation of Mephibosheth, it becomes clear that Mephibosheth is loyal to David and that Ziba had lied to David about Mephibosheth's loyalty. David resolves the matter by splitting Saul's inheritance between them, thereby ensuring the loyalty of both. But Mephibosheth gives up any claim to his grandfather's inheritance, thereby signaling the end of any potential challenges to David and likely saving his own life. Barzillai the Gileadite, one of those who supported David in the Trans-Jordan (2 Sam 17:27), finalizes an alliance with David that sees his servant Chimham moving to Jerusalem under the king's protection much like Mephibosheth. Finally, both Israel and Judah reconcile with David, although the rivalries and tensions between them remain evident.

The fifth sub-unit of 2 Sam 9–24 appears in 2 Sam 20, which relates Sheba ben Bichri's attempted revolt against David. The significance of this narrative is frequently overlooked in relation to the preceding and larger narrative concerning Absalom's revolt. The source of the revolt in Benjamin suggests continuing dissatisfaction with David, who continues to rule Israel as a member of the house of Saul. The role played by northern Israel in the revolt also suggests dissatisfaction in the north that anticipates the later revolt against Rehoboam in 1 Kgs 12 and the ties between Israel and the house of Saul from earlier days. A side issue is the conflict between Amasa and Joab. Amasa had been appointed commander by Absalom in place of Joab (2 Sam 17:25) and apparently part of the deal that led to Israel's return to David involved Amasa's retention of his new post. Joab's assassination of Amasa—notably in Gibeon, which had supported David in his conflict with Saul (2 Sam 3–4)—resolves this particular problem, and Joab goes on to resolve the revolt by negotiating the surrender of Sheba on the condition that the city of Abel of Beth Maacah where Sheba and his followers had fortified themselves hand Sheba over to him. The people of Abel were only too glad to comply with Joab's demand. When Sheba's head was tossed over the wall, Joab called off the siege of Abel.

The sixth sub-unit appears in 2 Sam 21, often considered by interpreters as part of an appendix to the David narratives in 2 Sam 21–24. Yet, 2 Sam 21 is key to the overall narrative insofar as it resolves the questions of the house of Saul and David's place in it, as well as lingering threats by the Philistines. Second Samuel 21 relates that David hands over seven sons and grandsons of Saul, two sons born to Saul by his concubine Ritzpah and five grandsons born to him by his daughter Merab. The basis for the request is Saul's attempt to wipe out the Gibeonites, perhaps associated with David's defense of the city against the forces of Ish-Bosheth (2 Sam 3–4). By acceding to the Gibeonite demand, David both solidifies his relationship with a key coalition that housed the ark during the reign of Saul and eliminates potential challengers to the throne from the house of Saul itself. Such an act would also signal that he may no longer be considered a member of the house of Saul, but clears the way for the recognition of his own house as the ruling dynasty of Israel. The actions against the Philistines function much like the actions against revolts by Abshalom and Sheba. David suppresses dissent in his empire. When David's warriors are named for their exploits, Elhanan ben Jaare-Oregim of Beth Lehem is named as the man who killed Goliath, which has triggered endless speculation as to whether Elhanan was David's personal name before he ascended to the throne of Israel or if David took credit for one of his own warrior's actions.

The seventh sub-unit appears in 2 Sam 22 as the song of David. This song is a thanksgiving song that appears in a slightly different form as Ps 18. As a thanksgiving psalm that would have been employed in the Temple liturgy, it expresses praise and thanks to YHWH for YHWH's role in rescuing David from enemies, it conveys David's reliance on YHWH in times of danger, and it conveys David's pledge to observe YHWH's laws and statutes.[21] Diachronic interpreters have observed that it appears to be a very ancient psalm, although no one can be sure if it was actually written by David. From a synchronic standpoint, the psalm's placement following the narratives that are concerned with David's containment of the house of Saul and his defeat of the revolts of Abshalom and Sheba makes a great deal of sense. The initial notice that David addressed this song to YHWH after YHWH had delivered him from his enemies and from Saul, which also appears in Ps 18, makes this psalm a fitting culmination for the books of Samuel.

The eighth sub-unit is 2 Sam 23:1-7, which is labeled as the last words of David. This poetic composition is formulated as an oracular speech that functions much like the last words or testaments of Jacob (Gen 49) or Moses (Deut 33). Here, David acknowledges YHWH's role in making him king with an eternal covenant (cf. 2 Sam 7) and instructions to rule justly in order to sweep aside all evil.

The ninth sub-unit in 2 Sam 23:8-39 is a listing of David's warriors who served him throughout his lifetime and brief accounts of the respective exploits for those listed in vv. 8-23. Verses 24-39 only list the names and essential elements of identity of a group of "thirty" (actually thirty-six, although v. 39 indicates thirty-seven; perhaps Joab should be included).

The tenth and final sub-unit in 2 Sam 24 presents an account of how David acquired the threshing floor of Araunah as the site for the future Temple of Solomon. The choice of a threshing floor makes eminent sense since it would facilitate the processing of grain brought as offerings to YHWH. The narrative is quite troubling theologically because it indicates YHWH's anger against Israel—although it does not identify the reason for YHWH's anger—and YHWH therefore incites David against the people by demanding that he take a census of the nation. On the one hand, a census would demonstrate the power of David's kingdom with some 800,000 men of Israel and 500,000 men of Judah, but it would also provide the basis for David to tax the people as forewarned by Samuel in 1 Sam 8. When David reproaches himself for having undertaken the census, YHWH offers him three afflictions for the nation to atone for what has been done. David chooses a plague to afflict the people, which results in some 70,000 deaths. The plague only subsides when David, on the advice of the prophet Gad, sets up an altar to YHWH on the threshing floor of Araunah and purchases the site to serve as the site of the future Temple of Solomon. The narrative points to the dangerous nature of YHWH's holy presence among the people, which recalls YHWH's outbreaks of punishment against Israel in the wilderness (Num 11–25) and against Uzzah when the ark was brought to Jerusalem (2 Sam 6). The altar and Temple then emerge as necessary institutions that are designed to address YHWH as the holy author of creation, thereby ensuring the stability of creation. The placement of the narrative at this point is crucial insofar as it points forward to the reign of David's son, Solomon, who will build the Temple to YHWH in Jerusalem in 1 Kgs 3–11.

NOTES

[1] For discussion of recent research on 1–2 Samuel, see Richard D. Nelson, *The Historical Books* (IBT; Nashville: Abingdon, 1998), 109–28; Campbell, *Joshua to Chronicles*, 111–86; Thomas Römer, *The So-Called Deuteronomistic History: A Sociological, Historical, and Literary Introduction* (London: Continuum, 2007), especially 91–97; Antony F. Campbell and Mark O'Brien, *Unfolding the Deuteronomistic History: Origins, Upgrades, Present Text* (Minneapolis: Fortress Press, 2000), 215–321.

[2] For commentaries on 1–2 Samuel, see S. R. Driver, *Notes on the Hebrew Text and Topography of the Books of Samuel* (Oxford: Clarendon, 1913/1960); Hans Joachim Stoebe, *Das erste Buch Samuelis* (KAT 8/1; Gütersloh: Gerd Mohn, 1973); idem, *Das zweite Buch Samuelis* (KAT 8/2; Gütersloh: Gerd Mohn, 1994); P. Kyle McCarter, *1 Samuel* (AB 8; Garden City: Doubleday, 1980); idem, *II Samuel* (AB 9; Garden City: Doubleday, 1984); Antony F. Campbell, *1 Samuel* (FOTL 7; Grand Rapids: Eerdmans, 2003); idem, *2 Samuel* (FOTL 8; Grand Rapids: Eerdmans, 2005.

[3] Interpreters generally maintain that 1 Sam 1–15 is an edited text in which underlying traditions concerning the origins of Saul's monarchy and the Ark narrative have been reworked and placed into a larger literary framework that recounts David's rise to kingship in 1 Sam 16—2 Sam 8. Accordingly, the earlier Saul tradition portrayed Israel's first monarch very positively, but the pro-Davidic redaction presented Saul in a far more critical light. The David narratives were later reworked again when they were incorporated into the DtrH. In addition to the commentaries, see Ivar Hylander, *Der literarische Samuel-Saul-Komplex (1. Sam. 1–15). Traditionsgeschichtlich Untersucht* (Uppsala: Almqvist & Wiksell, 1932); Antony F. Campbell, *Of Prophets and Kings: A Late Ninth-Century Document (1 Samuel 1—2 Kings 10)* (CBQMS 17; Washington: Catholic Biblical Association, 1986); and especially Serge Frolov, *The Turn of the Cycle: 1 Samuel 1–8 in Synchronic and Diachronic Perspective* (BZAW 342; Berlin: de Gruyter, 2004). For treatment of the historical issues in the formation of the Israelite/Judean monarchy, see especially Albrecht Alt, "The Formation of the Israelite State in Palestine," in *Essays in Old Testament History and Religion* (Garden City: Doubleday, 1967), 223–309; idem, "The Monarchy in the Kingdoms of Israel and Judah," in *Essays in Old Testament History and Religion*, 311–35; Giorgio Buccellati, *Cities and Nations of Ancient Israel: An Essay on Political Institutions with Special Reference to the Israelite Kingdoms* (Rome: Istituto di Studi del Vicino Oriente, Università di Roma, 1967); Tomoo Ishida, *The Royal Dynasties in Ancient Israel* (BZAW 142; Berlin: de Gruyter, 1977).

[4] For the role of characterization in biblical narrative, see especially Meir Sternberg, *The Poetics of Biblical Narrative: Ideological Literature and the Drama of Reading* (Bloomington: Indiana University Press, 1987).

[5] For study of the Ark Narrative in 1 Sam 4–6; 2 Sam 6, see Antony Campbell, *The Ark Narrative (1 Sam 4–6; 2 Sam 6): A Form-Critical and Traditio-Historical Study* (SBLDS 16; Missoula: Scholars Press, 1975).

[6] For study of the DtrH redaction of 1 Sam 8–12, see Martin Noth, *The Deuteronomistic History* (JSOTSup 15; Sheffield: JSOT, 1981), 47–53; Hans Jochen Boecker, *Die Beurteilung der Anfänge des Königtums in den deuteronomistischen Abschnitten des 1. Samuelbuches* (WMANT 31; Neukirchen–Vluyn: Neukirchener, 1969).

[7] Of this material, 1 Sam 16—2 Sam 8 is generally considered as discrete text known as the history of the rise of David, a pro-Davidic account that played a role in the editing of the Samuel-Saul traditions of 1 Sam 1–15 to serve its pro-Davidic agenda. See especially Jakob H. Grønbæk, *Die Geschichte vom Aufstieg Davids (1. Sam. 15–2. Sam. 5). Tradition und Komposition* (Copenhagn: Prostant apud Munksgaard, 1971). For discussion of the historical dimensions of David's rise to power and his reign, see Baruch Halpern's interesting but often speculative study, *David's Secret Demons: Messiah, Murderer, Traitor, King* (Grand Rapids: Eerdmans, 2001); Steven L. McKenzie, *King David: A Biography* (Oxford: Oxford University Press, 2000).

[8] For discussion of the regnal résumé form, see Burke Long, *1 Kings, with an Introduction to Historical Literature* (FOTL 9; Grand Rapids: Eerdmans, 1984), 259.

[9] See Driver, *Notes*, 96–97; McCarter, *1 Samuel*, 222.

[10] See, for example, *ANEP*, 182, 184.

[11] See *ANEP*, 372–73, which portray Assyrian slingers among Sennacherib's forces that attacked Lachish in 701 BCE.

[12] Thomas Marland Horner, *Jonathan Loved David: Homosexuality in Biblical Times* (Louisville: Westminster John Knox, 1978). For discussion of the language of love in the ancient Near Eastern world in relation to treaty relationships, see William L. Moran, "The Ancient Near Eastern Background of the Love of G-d in Deuteronomy," *CBQ* 25 (1963): 77–87.

[13] For discussion of the political importance of David's marriages, see Jon D. Levenson and Baruch Halpern, "The Political Import of David's Marriages," *JBL* 99 (1980): 507–18.

[14] For discussion of Gibeon's importance to David, see Joseph Blenkinsopp, *Gibeon and Israel: The Role of Gibeon and the Gibeonites in the Political and Religious History of Early Israel* (SOTSMS 2; Cambridge; Cambridge University Press, 1972).

[15] See Philip J. Calderone, *Dynastic Oracle and Suzerainty Treaty. 2 Samuel 7, 8-16* (Manila: Manila University, 1966); Donald F. Murray, *Prerogative and Royal Pretension: Pragmatics, Poetics and Polemics in a Narrative Sequence about David (2 Samuel 5.17–7.29)* (JSOTSup 264; Sheffield: Sheffield Academic, 1998).

[16] Leonhard Rost, *The Succession to the Throne of David* (Sheffield: Almond, 1982). For discussion of the Succession Narrative hypothesis, see especially R. N. Whybray, *The Succession Narrative: A Study of II Sam. 9–20 and I Kings 1 and 2* (SBT 2/9; Naperville: Allenson, 1968); Gillian Keys, *The Wages of Sin: A Reappraisal of the 'Succession Narrative'* (JSOTSup 221; Sheffield: Sheffield Academic, 1996).

[17] See my *1 and 2 Kings: A Commentary* (OTL; Louisville: Westminster John Knox, 2007), 464–65.

[18] Interpreters generally view this block as a later insertion meant to discredit David. See especially Steven L McKenzie, "The So-Called Succession Narrative in the Deuteronomistic History," in *Die sogenennte Thronfolgegeschichte Davids. Neue Einsichten und Anfragen* (OBO 176; Freiburg: Universitätsverlag, 2000), 123–35.

[19] See Diana Edelman, "Ahinoam," *ABD* 1:117–18.

[20] See Larry L. Lyke, *King David with the Wise Woman of Tekoa: The Resonance of Tradition in Parabolic Narrative* (JSOTSup 255; Sheffield: Sheffield Academic, 1997).

[21] Cf. Campbell, *2 Samuel*, 194–98.

E. The Book of Kings

The book of Kings were originally considered as one book in the Jewish Bible.
The first printed editions of the Rabbinic Bible in the fifteenth century began to
change this convention by following the Christian practice of dividing Kings into
two books. The Rabbinic sages maintain that the prophet Jeremiah is the author
of Kings (*b. Baba Batra* 15a), which makes some sense due to similarities in literary style and theological outlook, but no one can be certain as to the individual
identity of the author or authors of Kings.[1] Modern scholarship generally maintains that the present form of the books of Kings was written by a writer or circle
of writers whose viewpoints are heavily influenced by the theological perspectives
of Deuteronomy.[2] Although the present form of Kings comprises a portion of the
Exilic edition of the Deuteronomistic History, American scholars in particular
maintain that an earlier edition of the work was produced during the reign of
King Josiah of Judah (r. 640–609 BCE) to support his program of national restoration and religious reform. Other editions may also be identified, such as a
Hezekian edition of the history produced to support Hezekiah's efforts to restore
Davidic rule over the former northern kingdom of Israel; a Jehu history designed
to explain and support the rule of the Jehu dynasty of northern Israel; and a
Solomonic history that is designed to laud King Solomon's rule as the divinely
sanctioned successor of King David. European scholars tend to posit a three-stage
exilic edition of the work, but this model is hardly viable due to its rigid reliance
on outdated Wellhausenian principles.

The books of Kings provide an account of the reigns of the kings of Israel and
Judah from the end of the lifetime of King David ben Jesse of Israel and Judah
through the reign of his son Solomon, the division of the kingdom into northern
Israel and southern Judah following Solomon's death, the overthrow of the house
of Omri in northern Israel during the late ninth and early eighth centuries BCE,
the destruction of northern Israel by the Assyrians in 722/1 BCE, King Josiah's
program of religious reform and national restoration in the mid- to late seventh
century BCE, the destruction of Jerusalem, Solomon's Temple, and the kingdom
of Judah in 587/6 BCE, and finally the release of King Jehoiachin ben Jehoiakim,
the last legitimate monarch of the Davidic line, from prison in Babylonia.[3] The

books of Kings provide an explicitly theological account of the history of Israel
and Judah. In most cases, the account of each king's reign is framed by introductory and concluding regnal accounts that state essential information, that is,
the year in which he began his rule, the duration of his reign, the theological
evaluation of his reign, major events in the reign, the death and burial of the king,
and the identity of his successor.[4] Some of these accounts are quite elaborate,
whereas others present only a minimum of information. The synchronic literary
structure of Kings may be represented as follows:[5]

Account of the History of the Kings of Israel and Judah

I.	The Death of David and Designation of Solomon	1 Kgs 1:1—2:11
II.	Regnal Account of Solomon ben David	2:12—14:20
	A. Solomon secures his throne	2:12-46a
	B. Solomon's subsequent rule	2:46b—4:19
	C. Solomon's reign and its consequences;	
	Jeroboam ben Nebat	4:20—14:20
	1. Solomon's wealth and power	4:20—5:32
	2. Solomon's construction of the Temple complex	
	and royal palace	6:1—9:9
	a. palace and Temple complex	6:1—7:12
	b. the construction of the Temple implements	7:13-51
	c. Solomon's dedication of the Temple	8:1-66
	d. Solomon's second encounter with YHWH	9:1-9
	3. the rise of Solomon's adversaries	9:10—11:40
	a. introduction	9:10
	b. Solomon's association with Hiram of Tyre	9:11-28
	c. Solomon's association with the Queen of Sheba	10:1-29
	d. Solomon's apostasy	11:1-25
	e. the rise of Jeroboam ben Nebat	11:26-40
	4. Solomon's death and the consequences of his reign;	
	the establishment of the Northern Kingdom	
	of Israel	11:41—14:20
	a. Solomon's death; regnal résumé	11:41-43
	b. The establishment of the Northern Kingdom	
	of Israel; Israel's revolt against Rehoboam	12:1-24
	c. Jeroboam's apostasy	12:25—13:34
	d. Ahijah's oracle against the house of Jeroboam	14:1-18
	e. Regnal summary for the reign of Jeroboam	
	ben Nebat of Israel	14:19-20
III.	Regnal Account of Rehoboam ben Solomon of Judah	14:21-31
IV.	Regnal Account of Abijam ben Rehoboam of Judah	15:1-8
V.	Regnal Account of Asa ben Abijam of Judah	15:9-24
VI.	Regnal Account of Nadab ben Jeroboam of Israel	15:25-32
VII.	Regnal Account of Baasha ben Ahijah of Israel	15:33—16:7
VIII.	Regnal Account of Elah ben Baasha	16:8-14
IX.	Regnal Account of Zimri of Israel	16:15-22
X.	Regnal Account of Omri of Israel	16:23-28

Each king of Israel and Judah is judged to have been wicked or righteous in the eyes of YHWH according to whether or not he observed divine Torah in the eyes of the narrator. In the case of the northern Israelite monarchs, every king of the north is judged as wicked. Most of the Judean monarchs are also judged to have been wicked, although a select few, that is, Asa, Jehoshaphat, Hezekiah, and Josiah, are judged as righteous.

The book of Kings is therefore a theological history whose purpose is to assess the theological character of the kings of Israel and Judah in an effort to explain the two major disasters of the monarchic period in ancient Israel and Judah, viz., the destruction of the northern kingdom of Israel in 722/1 BCE and the destruction of the southern kingdom of Judah in 587/6 BCE. Because as the history targets the kings of Israel and Judah as the primary parties responsible for leading the people astray from YHWH's expectations, the history emerges as a form of theodicy insofar as it portrays YHWH as righteous, powerful, and faithful to the covenant with the people and the people, led by their kings, as idolatrous, rebellious, and ultimately unfaithful to the covenant with YHWH. In the case of the northern kingdom of Israel, the founding monarch of the northern kingdom, King Jeroboam ben Nebat, sets the patterns of idolatry followed by every one of the northern kings, that is, worship of the golden calves at Dan and Beth El, which ultimately explains the downfall of the northern kingdom as a judgment brought by YHWH against the nation. In the case of Judah, some of the monarchs are considered righteous, but the sins of King Manasseh ben Hezekiah of Judah are so great that YHWH ultimately decides to destroy Jerusalem, the Temple, and the kingdom of Judah, and not even the righteousness of King Josiah ben Amon can avert the judgment. Clearly, the theological viewpoint of Kings is teleological insofar as the actions of a monarch such as Manasseh bear consequences for the people of Judah some six decades after his death.

Such contentions raise tremendous theological problems. Diachronic scholarship demonstrates that northern Israelite religious practice differed in some details from that of the south; for example, the golden calves at Dan and Beth El functioned as mounts upon which YHWH was seated or enthroned much like the ark of the covenant in the Jerusalem Temple.[6] The charges of idolatry, therefore, cannot be taken at face value. Rather, they are intended to demonstrate that YHWH remains the powerful protector of Israel even in the aftermath of Israel's destruction. Such a contention therefore functions as a means to call upon the people to adhere to YHWH's expectations as expressed in divine Torah, worship at YHWH's sanctuary in Jerusalem, and recognize YHWH's divinely selected monarch from the house of David in Jerusalem. But when Jerusalem is destroyed, the writers of Kings choose not to blame all of the monarchs for the disaster, but focus instead only on Manasseh, whose purported sinful deeds prompt the destruction of Jerusalem some fifty-five years after his death. In such a view, the suffering of the inhabitants of Jerusalem and Judah at the time of the Babylonian exile is prompted by the actions of one man who lived at a time prior to the birth of most of the people who inhabited Jerusalem and Judah at the time of the catastrophe. Such a view is inherently unfair to those who suffer for the sins of their monarchs, but it nevertheless highlights the responsibility of the monarchs as commonly viewed in Israel/Judah and throughout the larger ancient Near Eastern world for ensuring the welfare of their people. The Chronicler's history in 1–2 Chronicles recognizes these problems and presents a very different scenario, that is, neither Jeroboam nor Manasseh nor any of the other kings of Israel or Judah are to blame for the disasters. Instead, Chronicles assigns blame to the generation that actually suffered the disaster. Such a view of corporate human responsibility likewise must be recognized as an attempt to defend the power, sanctity, and righteousness of YHWH, but it also presents its own set of theological problems that will be examined in discussion of the historical worldview of 1–2 Chronicles.[7]

The initial accounts of the death of David and the designation of Solomon as his successor in 1 Kgs 1:1—2:11 and the regnal account of Solomon ben David in 1 Kgs 2:12—14:20 illustrate the theological perspective of Kings. Whereas the core account of Solomon's reign in 1 Kgs 3–10 is quite laudatory, the framing narratives for his reign in 1 Kgs 1–2 and 11 are quite critical of the process by which Solomon was chosen as king and the consequences of his conduct and rule. Although Solomon is a wise, prosperous, and pious monarch who works to ensure the welfare of his people, the critical literary framework raises questions concerning his integrity and wisdom. Ultimately, this framework judges him to have been an inadequate monarch whose lust for women—not unlike that of his father—led to his apostasy against YHWH and the dissolution of a united kingdom of Israel into the competing northern kingdom of Israel and southern kingdom of Judah.[8]

First Kings 1:1—2:11 serves as a literary or narrative bridge between the Samuel and Kings narratives insofar as it portrays the process by which Solomon is selected to be king of Israel in David's old age. David appears as an old man who is unable to consummate a relationship with a beautiful young Shunamite woman, Abishag, who is brought to tend to him and serve as a concubine. At this point, two major facets of David's past life come into play. First, his son Adonijah, who, like his brothers Amnon and Absalom, is very pointedly described as a son who was never disciplined by his father, presumes that he is David's successor and immediately acts to have himself declared as king. Second, his wife Bath Sheba, supported by the prophet Nathan, convinces David that he had declared that Solomon would be his heir. The reader will never know if this claim is true, but it becomes true when, prodded by Bath Sheba and Nathan, David states that it is so. Although David is portrayed as old and malleable at the outset of the narrative, by its conclusion he has his wits about him as he instructs Solomon in the need to assert his power as king and thereby to ensure the continuity of the dynasty. David instructs Solomon to deal with several problematic figures, viz., Joab is to be killed; Barzillai is to be shown favor; and Shimei is to be killed. David's reign comes to a close, but the account sets up a settling of scores at the outset of Solomon's reign. Solomon is the youngest son of the house of David born in Jerusalem who supplants his older brother Adonijah, born to David in Hebron. Furthermore, Solomon was born as a result of an adulterous relationship between David and Bath Sheba and the murder of Bath Sheba's first husband, Uriah the Hittite. This account is deliberately designed to raise questions about Solomon, who is never divinely designated as king, but is designated only by David and the acclamation of the people. When David's adultery with Bath Sheba and his role in the murder of Uriah the Hittite are considered, Solomon's prospects for establishing a secure dynasty as promised unconditionally in 2 Sam 7 are actually quite debatable. Such questions aid in explaining why—from a narrative standpoint—David's statements concerning the future of the dynasty in 1 Kgs 2:2-4 must be conditioned on the observance of YHWH's Torah.

The narrative strategy of raising questions about Solomon continues with the account of his reign in 1 Kgs 2:12—14:20. The initial sub-unit concerning the securing of Solomon's throne in 1 Kgs 2:12-46a builds on David's instructions to Solomon concerning the settling of old scores. The sub-unit begins with Adonijah's ill-considered request for David's concubine Abishag. Prior experience with claims for the king's harem by Abner (2 Sam 3:6-11) and Abshalom (2 Sam 16:20-23) make it quite clear that Adonijah's demand would be understood to be a claim for the throne. The fact that his request was delivered to Bath Sheba, the mother of the king who would be displaced, raises many questions as to whether Adonijah had fully understood the import of his demand and indeed if he had in fact made such a claim—after all, Adonijah does not survive to give his side of the story. Adonijah is executed by order of the king as a result of his ill-considered demand, and Solomon also notes that Adonijah's supporters include Joab the general and Abiathar the priest. Joab is also executed in keeping with David's instructions, and Abiathar is expelled to Anathoth, leaving Zadok alone as high priest in Jerusalem. Finally, Shimei, the kinsman of Saul who had cursed David during Abshalom's revolt (2 Sam 16:5-14) is executed, again in keeping with David's instructions, based on charges—perhaps contrived—that he had violated Solomon's orders to remain in Jerusalem. With the measures taken against these figures, Solomon's throne is secured. It is striking to note that with Solomon's succession to the throne, the Hebron branch of the house of David represented by his sons, Amnon, Abshalom, Adonijah, their mothers, Ahinoam, Maacah, Haggit, and their supporters, Joab and Abiathar, have been replaced by a Jerusalemite branch of the family centered on Solomon and Bath Sheba and their supporters, Nathan, Zadok, and Benaiah. Solomon's accession to the throne constitutes a coup within the house of David.[9]

The account of Solomon's subsequent rule in 1 Kgs 2:46b—4:19 begins with a notice that his throne is secured and focuses especially on the laudatory elements of his reign. But even these laudatory elements come into question when read in relation to the larger contexts of the Torah and the Former Prophets. The initial notice in 1 Kgs 3:1 of Solomon's marriage to the daughter of Pharaoh is an indication of Solomon's high status in the world, insofar as he is allied by marriage to one of the great superpowers of the day. Yet, the Pharaoh of Egypt is the very same figure that once represented the enslavement of Israel in the Torah. Solomon's vision of YHWH in a dream recounted in 1 Kgs 3:4-15 lauds him for his choice of wisdom as a gift from YHWH by which he will rule his people, but the setting at Gibeon reminds the reader that Solomon worships YHWH—even if only in a dream—at a site that remains inhabited by Canaanites (Josh 9–10). Solomon's decision in settling the case of two women who claim the same baby in 1 Kgs 3:16-28 lauds him for his wisdom, but it also reminds the reader that Solomon acts as chief magistrate of the nation when this role is supposed to be reserved for the priests (Deut 16:18—17:13). The account of his administration in 1 Kgs 4:1-19 lauds Solomon for his wisdom in ruling the people, but the fact that it identifies Adoniram as the officer in charge of forced labor and notes that the twelve administrative districts—all constituted among the northern tribes but not in Judah—are responsible for the support of the royal court lays the foundations for the charge that Solomon acted like the Pharaoh of Egypt by imposing state slavery on his own people (1 Kgs 5:1-8, 27-32).[10]

Indeed, the major sub-unit concerning Solomon's reign and its consequences in 1 Kgs 4:20—14:20 is also designed to contextualize and question Solomon's greatness. Although 1 Kgs 4:20—14:20 continues to laud Solomon for his wealth, his building of the royal palace and the Temple, and his building projects throughout Israel, it ultimately points to the dissolution of his kingdom with the revolt of the northern tribes against his son Rehoboam and the rise to kingship over the north of Jeroboam ben Nebat who had once served Solomon as the officer in charge of the forced labor imposed on the house of Joseph.

The account of Solomon's wealth and power in 1 Kgs 4:20—5:32 begins with a notice that Judah and Israel were as numerous as the sands of the sea, in keeping with YHWH's promises to the ancestors (Gen 22:17; 32:12), and the observation that they were happy. But the notices of Solomon's power, wealth, and wisdom appear with notices that he was allied with King Hiram of Tyre and that he imposed forced labor on Israel to carry out his building projects. Although Hiram is a key ally, he is a Canaanite king, which raises questions about Solomon's alliances with Canaanites, contrary to the prohibition of marriage with the Canaanite nations in Deut 7:1-6 which in turn warns that Israel would follow Canaanite gods if they intermarried with the Canaanites. This becomes a key issue later in the narrative when Solomon cannot pay his bill to Hiram and cedes twenty Israelite cities to the Canaanite king in order to settle his debt (1 Kgs 9:10-14). Again, the imposition of forced labor on Israel to carry out the work likens Solomon to Pharaoh. Although 1 Kgs 9:15-22 very carefully states that only Canaanites were so enslaved, the association of these notices with the statement in 1 Kgs 9:24 that the daughter of Pharaoh moved into the royal palace built in front of the Temple reinforces the identification of Solomon as a ruler like Pharaoh.

The account of Solomon's construction of the Temple complex and the royal palace in 1 Kgs 6:1—9:9 again presents some of the most laudatory material concerning Solomon and yet places it once again in a context that raises questions about the future of the house of David and even the Jerusalem Temple itself in the eyes of YHWH. The basic account of Temple and palace construction in 1 Kgs 6:1—7:12 describes the details of the two buildings, including their general lay-outs, measurements, materials for construction, decoration, and so on, indicating that Solomon spared no effort and expense to create an edifice that would symbolize both the glory and presence of YHWH as the sovereign of creation and the Davidic monarch as YHWH's duly designated regent over Israel at the center of creation.[11] The three-room pattern of the Temple itself is structured after the pattern of royal palaces, which include an entrance hall or porch (Hebrew, ʾûlām), a great hall or palace (Hebrew, hêkāl), and the Holy of Holies or Shrine (Hebrew, dĕbîr) which functions as the divine throne room where the Ark of the Covenant will reside. The interior decoration of the Temple symbolizes its role as the holy center of creation; indeed, the engraved and gold inlaid palm trees, lions, pome-granates, cherubim, and so on, symbolize the Garden of Eden from which Adam and Eve were first expelled (Gen 3) and to which human beings aspire to return in order to repair their relationship with YHWH and thereby complete the process of creation initiated in Gen 1.[12] Insofar as the high priest of the Temple is the only figure allowed to enter the Holy of Holies guarded by the Cherubim surrounding the Ark, he represents Adam as Ben Adam (son of Adam) attempting to re-enter the Garden of Eden. As the holy center of creation, the Temple is the place where heaven and earth meet and from which YHWH is revealed to humankind. With its orientation to the east, meaning that the open gate of the Temple will allow the rising sun to illuminate its interior, once again creating light in the midst of darkness, the Temple and its daily liturgy symbolize the creation of the world each and every day.

The construction of the Temple implements in 1 Kgs 7:13-51 reinforces the imagery of the Temple as the holy center of creation. The two pillars, Jachin and Boaz, placed at the entrance of the Temple symbolize the pillars or foundations that support all of creation (Pss 18:16; 75:4; 82:5; Job 9:5; 26:11; Prov 8:29; 2 Sam

22:16; Isa 24:18; Jer 31:37, respectively). The large molten sea or water tank is the place where the priests purify themselves by immersion in the water to serve at the altar, but the tank also represents the sea from which the earth emerged at creation as well as the sea through which Israel passed at the Exodus from Egypt. The incense burners (not laver stands) add the dimensions of smoke, cloud, and sweet aroma that symbolize YHWH's presence in deep darkness, and the lamp stands with their flickering lights represent the lightening and flame that so frequently accompany divine theophanies.

Solomon's dedication of the Temple in 1 Kgs 8:1-66 provides the occasion for the narrative to display Solomon's power, wisdom, and piety before YHWH, but it also enables Solomon to serve as a mouthpiece for the theology represented by the Temple as the locus for YHWH's divine presence in the world. The dedication ceremony begins with the placement of the Ark of the Covenant in the Holy of Holies of the Temple to symbolize its role as YHWH's divine residence and throne room. Solomon's opening statements concerning YHWH's residence in the thick clouds of the Temple reinforce the theophanic imagery associated with the incense burners and lamp stands describe above. His reference to YHWH's promise to the house of David once again expresses the promise in conditional terms (cf. 1 Kgs 2:2-4) unlike the unconditional formulation of 2 Sam 7. Such a formulation anticipates the reality of the end of the books of Kings when the future of the house of David is in doubt and the reason for such doubt is the alleged failure of the dynasty—or at least Manasseh—to observe YHWH's will. Likewise, although the presence of the Ark represents the purportedly permanent presence of YHWH in creation, Solomon's conditional reference to the Temple anticipates its destruction by the end of Kings. The function of the Temple is also addressed. It is the place where humans worship and pray to YHWH in an effort to maintain the stability and sanctity of creation, so that enemies do not come to threaten the land, the rains will come to ensure the stability and bounty of creation, disease and pestilence will be held back, and all the foreigners and nations of the world will recognize YHWH as the sovereign G-d of creation.

The final segment of the construction account in 1 Kgs 9:1-9 reinforces the specter of potential destruction and exile. YHWH appears once again to Solomon to reaffirm the relationship between YHWH and Israel, but YHWH reiterates the conditional nature of the royal covenant with the house of David and even calls into question the continued existence of the Temple itself. According to Kings, if Israel and its monarchs do not adhere to YHWH and to the divine will, the promise of land and the continuity of the monarchy and Temple are not assured. In this respect, Kings ensures that the onus for maintaining the relationship with YHWH is placed squarely on Israel's and the king's shoulders.

The account of the rise of Solomon's adversaries in 1 Kgs 9:10—11:40 builds upon the questions raised about the relationship between YHWH and Israel and the house of David in the previous sections to depict the process by which the house of David and its rule over all twelve tribes of Israel would begin to disintegrate in the aftermath of Solomon's death. After the introductory notice in 1 Kgs 9:10 of Solomon's completion of the palace and the Temple after some twenty years of work, the following sub-units outline a series of problems inherent in Solomon's reign.

The first sub-unit in 1 Kgs 9:11-28 focuses on Solomon's relationship with King Hiram of Tyre. Although Hiram was the key ally of Solomon who supplied him with the raw materials and architectural expertise necessary to build the Temple and palace, he is a Canaanite monarch, which raises questions about Solomon's association with him. Tensions quickly emerge when Solomon is unable to pay Hiram and cedes twenty Israelite cities to Hiram to settle his debt, which explicitly undermines YHWH's promise to grant the land of Canaan to Israel. Instead, Solomon returns land to Canaan. Solomon's imposition of forced labor on the people also emerges as a problem. Although the narrative is careful to state that only Canaanites were enslaved and that Israelites supervised them, Solomon clearly emerges as a figure like Pharaoh of Egypt and Israel becomes a nation of taskmasters like Egypt at the time of the Exodus.[13] With the move of Solomon's first wife, the daughter of Pharaoh, to the royal palace before the Temple, the equation of Solomon with Pharaoh is secured. Even so, Solomon's construction of a sailing fleet with the aid of Hiram constitutes another problem insofar as his acquisition of gold would stand in contradiction to the guidance offered to the king in Deut 17:14-20, which expressly prohibits the king from amassing gold for himself. Furthermore, Solomon's fleet on the Red Sea meant that he sent Israelites back across the Red Sea to Egypt for trade, an act that ran counter both to the instructions of Deut 17:14-20 and to the Exodus from Egypt itself.

The second sub-unit in 1 Kgs 10:1-29 recounts the celebrated visit of the Queen of Sheba to Solomon. The queen's visit marks Solomon's reputation for wisdom, wealth, and power to the very ends of the earth, at least as understood in the world of ancient Israel. The opening of trade relations with Sheba, a kingdom situated along the Red Sea coast of Africa according to some scholars or the Arabian peninsula according to others, would aid in bringing wealth, power, and influence to Solomon's court, all of which is sumptuously described in the narrative.[14] Although this narrative was clearly composed to laud Solomon, an element of critique is imbedded within and brought out when read in the larger context of the Torah and the Former Prophets, viz., Solomon engaged in the trading of horses and chariots, again contrary to the Torah of the King in Deut 17:14-20.

The third sub-unit in 1 Kgs 11:1-25 takes up the matter of Solomon's apostasy against YHWH. The text emphasizes Solomon's love for foreign women, noting that he had seven hundred wives and three hundred concubines. Such an assemblage of wives would be ample testimony to Solomon's standing in the world of international relations, that is, a treaty with each nation would be sealed by a royal marriage. In the eyes of the Kings narrator, Solomon's love for foreign women runs counter to the divine instruction of Deut 7:1-6, which holds that Israel must not intermarry with the Canaanite nations because they would lead Israel to follow other gods. First Kings 11:1-25 clearly envisions more than just the seven Canaanite nations of Deut 7:1-6, viz., the daughter of Pharaoh heads a list of foreign women who come from the various nations that surrounded ancient Israel. The text holds to Deut 7:1-6 insofar as it points out that Solomon began to abandon YHWH by building shrines for the gods of his various wives in Jerusalem and worshipping at those shrines himself. As a result, the narrative recounts that YHWH raised enemies against Solomon, for example, Hadad of Edom and Rezon ben Eliada of Damascus. Although revolts against a powerful king like Solomon are to be expected, the narrator makes the point that this is a theological issue in which YHWH chose to punish Solomon for apostasy.

The fourth sub-unit in 1 Kgs 11:26-40 relates the rise of Jeroboam ben Nebat, who would go on to become the first king of northern Israel following its revolt against Solomon's son Rehoboam in 1 Kgs 12. The narrative makes it clear that YHWH is motivated by Solomon's intermarriages and his apostasy in choosing to raise up Jeroboam as the next king of the ten northern tribes of Israel. Never-theless, other factors are also evident, namely, Jeroboam is identified as Solomon's officer in charge of the forced labor of the house of Joseph, the core of northern Israel. Such a role for Jeroboam highlights the association of Solomon's reign with the policies of Pharaoh as articulated in the Exodus tradition and surely served as a motivating force in northern Israel's revolt (see below on 1 Kgs 12). There is a question of YHWH's theological integrity as well. YHWH had promised David that his sons would rule after him (2 Sam 7). The narrative goes to pains to show that YHWH will keep the promise to David by allowing his descendants to rule over Judah (and Benjamin) while nevertheless handing ten tribes over to Jero-boam to rule as northern Israel's next king. But this will raise another theological question, viz., why did YHWH designate Jeroboam as king when it becomes so clear later that Jeroboam is portrayed as an apostate worse than Solomon, parti-cularly when Jeroboam becomes the figure whose sins are emulated by all other northern Israelite monarchs, resulting ultimately in the destruction of northern Israel according to Kings (2 Kgs 17)? The choice must allow for YHWH's recognition of human free will, but later interpreters would struggle with this question.

The account of Solomon's death and the consequent establishment of the northern kingdom of Israel in 1 Kgs 11:41—14:20 serves an important theological agenda in the books of Kings, viz., explaining why the northern kingdom of Israel would ultimately be destroyed by the Assyrian empire in 722/1 BCE.

The first sub-unit is the regnal résumé in 1 Kgs 11:40-43, which ends Solomon's reign with standard notices of his death, reputation, the duration of his reign, burial, and the succession of his son Rehoboam to the throne. But it also signals the initiation of the chain of events that would lead to the revolt of the northern tribes against Solomon's son, Rehoboam ben Solomon, the establishment of the northern kingdom of Israel under the leadership of Jeroboam ben Nebat, and the condemnation of Jeroboam and the northern kingdom at large.

The second sub-unit in 1 Kgs 12:1-12 takes up northern Israel's revolt against Rehoboam and the establishment of the northern kingdom of Israel under Jeroboam. Although the narrative presumes the accounts of Solomon's apostasy and YHWH's designation of Jeroboam as king in 1 Kgs 11:1-25, 26-40, the present account presupposes a very different set of reasons for northern Israel's revolt from the house of David, that is, the tremendous burdens imposed on the people by Solomon's heavy spending and extravagant building policies. Although these factors were noted in the account of Solomon's reign, the earlier narrative chose to explain dissatisfaction with Solomon on the basis of religious apostasy. First Kings 12:1-24 therefore draws out the underlying causes for dissatisfaction in the north on a synchronic level—and indeed, this represents a very plausible historical cause for the revolt, but on the diachronic level the narrative suggests that an older account of northern Israel's revolt has been taken up by the DtrH which chose to frame the issues with its own theological perspective. The narrative very carefully stipulates that Jeroboam was in Egypt at the time of the revolt so that he cannot be charged with conspiracy; rather, the issue is framed as a popular revolt against the king. As for Rehoboam, his behavior and response to the people's questions concerning his rule indicate that he is an immature, self-interested, and overindulged prince of the house of David, much like his uncles Amnon, Absalom, and Adonijah. Indeed, his younger advisors with whom he grew up are called "children" (Hebrew, yĕlādîm), a striking label for the lifelong companions of a 41 year-old man (1 Kgs 14:21).

The following sub-unit concerned with Jeroboam's apostasy in 1 Kgs 12:25—13:34 returns to the theological perspectives of 1 Kgs 11:1-40, but it now shifts to an accusation of apostasy against Jeroboam ben Nebat that will ultimately determine the theological evaluation of the northern kingdom of Israel throughout the books of Kings.[15] Once he is designated as king, Jeroboam acts quickly to establish sanctuaries at Dan in the north and Beth El in the south to serve as centers for the worship of YHWH in the newly formed kingdom, to collect the tithes and other offerings of the people for the support of the state, and to prevent the people from continuing to go south to the Jerusalem sanctuary. Key factors in Jeroboam's alleged apostasy are his establishment of the golden calves for the people to worship at Dan and Beth El, the charge that Jeroboam allowed anyone to serve as a priest rather than only the Levites, and a change in the festival calendar so that the major festival of the seventh month, that is, Sukkot, would be observed in the eighth month instead. The narrative concerning the condemnation of Jeroboam at Beth El by the man of G-d from Judah reinforces the portrayal of Jeroboam and the Beth El sanctuary. Jeroboam officiates at the Beth El altar as if he were a priest, thereby reprising a role for which Saul was condemned (1 Sam 3–14). The Judean man of G-d states that some day King Josiah of Judah will destroy the Beth El altar, which signals the account of Josiah's reforms in

2 Kgs 22–23. The prophet from Beth El lies to the Judean man of G-d, which prompts the death of the Judean prophet for violating divine instructions against eating and drinking in Beth El. The account therefore associates Beth El with mendacity, and it once again signals the account of Josiah's reforms insofar as Josiah takes the bones of the men from the Beth El prophet's tomb to desecrate the Beth El altar.

Although at the synchronic level the accounts of Jeroboam's sins provide the foundations for the condemnation of northern Israel and all of its kings culminating in 2 Kgs 17 in the Former Prophets, diachronic perspectives must also be considered. The narrative is clearly written or edited to serve the interests of the Josian edition of the DtrH by portraying northern Israel as sinful and misguided and in need of proper Davidic leadership. But the charges against Jeroboam must also be critically evaluated. Beth El is a revered sanctuary in the north whose origins are traced back to the patriarch Jacob, insofar as it was the site of a revelation from YHWH promising him a covenant that his descendants would become a great nation (Gen 28). As for the claim that the golden calves were gods for the people to worship, in fact they function as mounts upon which YHWH is invisibly seated or enthroned, much like the Ark of the Covenant in the Jerusalem sanctuary. Jeroboam's action was not a deliberate act of idolatry, but simply the use of a different type of iconography to depict and honor YHWH. The choice of priests represents the older pattern in Israel in which first-born sons would have served as priests from an early period until the institution of the Levitical priests replaced them (see Num 3; cf. 1 Sam 1–3, where Samuel, first-born son of Hannah, is raised to serve as a priest in the Shiloh sanctuary). The difference in the timing of the celebration of Sukkot is nothing more than the use of an alternative calendar. Jeroboam was hardly an apostate; rather, he understood adherence to YHWH differently than it was understood in the south. The condemnation of Jeroboam and northern Israel must be recognized as a means to serve Judean interests, particularly in relation to the Josian reform that was designed to reinstitute Davidic rule over the former northern kingdom. The charge that Jeroboam and northern Israel had sinned aids in supporting that program. It also aids in defending the power, righteousness, and fidelity of YHWH, insofar as the destruction of northern Israel is not charged to YHWH's inadequacies but to Israel's instead. In this respect, the portrayal of the sins of Jeroboam and northern Israel is a means to defend YHWH's integrity against charges that YHWH was somehow inadequate in protecting northern Israel and showing fidelity to the covenant. In the view of Kings, YHWH did not fail Israel; rather, Israel failed YHWH.

The account of Ahijah's condemnation of the house of Jeroboam in 1 Kgs 14:1-18 makes this point clear. When the wife of Jeroboam comes to the prophet Ahijah to ask for a cure for her ill son, Ahijah, although blind, recognizes her and emphatically states that the boy will die and that the house of Jeroboam will come to an end as a result of his sins. Ahijah's condemnation of Jeroboam sets the pattern for the condemnation of the house of Omri as well. Just as every male, bond and free, will be cut off to Jeroboam and the dogs and birds will devour anyone of the house of Jeroboam, so the same will happen to the house of Omri (1 Kgs 21:20-24; 2 Kgs 9:34-37). The condemnation of Jeroboam becomes the paradigm for the condemnation of the northern dynasties and all of the northern kings. As discussion of the reigns of Kings Manasseh and Josiah of Judah will demonstrate, it also plays a role in the condemnation of Judean monarchs and in YHWH's decision to destroy Jerusalem.

The regnal summary of Jeroboam's reign in 1 Kgs 14:19-20 closes the account of his reign with typical notices of the events and duration of his reign, his death, and the succession of his son Nadab.

The following seven regnal accounts provide relatively brief treatment of the kings of Judah and Israel, including Rehoboam ben Solomon of Judah (1 Kgs 14:21-31); Abijam ben Rehoboam of Judah (1 Kgs 15:1-8); Asa ben Abijam of Judah (1 Kgs 15:9-24); Nadab ben Jeroboam of Israel (1 Kgs 15:25-32); Baasha ben Ahijah of Israel (1 Kgs 15:33—16:7); Elah ben Baasha of Israel (1 Kgs 16:8-14); and Zimri of Israel (1 Kgs 15–22). Although treated perfunctorily, these accounts note the righteousness of Asa, who undertook religious reform in Judah, the continuing conflicts between northern Israel and southern Judah, and the instability of the northern throne, which saw the overthrow of Nadab ben Jeroboam, Elah ben Baasha, and Zimri. Apart from Asa, every one of these kings, whether Judean or Israelite, is condemned in the narrative.

The reigns of the northern monarchs from the house of Omri, including Omri (1 Kgs 16:23-28), Ahab ben Omri (1 Kgs 16:29—22:40), Ahaziah ben Ahab (1 Kgs 22:52—2 Kgs 2:25), and Jehoram ben Ahab (2 Kgs 3:1—8:15), together with their Judean allies or vassals, Jehoshaphat ben Asa (1 Kgs 22:41-51) and Jehoram ben Jehoshaphat (2 Kgs 8:16-24), come under special scrutiny in the Former Prophets. This is because of the role that the house of Omri plays in demonstrating northern Israel's apostasy against YHWH and because of the continuing influence it has on the house of David by virtue of the marriage of Athaliah bat Ahab or Omri to Jehoram ben Jehoshaphat of Judah, viz., from the time of Jehoram on, every member of the house of David is also a descendant of the house of Omri and shares in Elijah's condemnation of the dynasty (1 Kgs 21:20-29).

The regnal account of Omri's reign in 1 Kgs 16:23-28 conceals more than it reveals insofar as Assyrian sources portray Omri as the founder of a powerful kingdom that was known in Assyrian records for years as the land of Omri, even after the house of Omri had been overthrown. From a synchronic standpoint, however, the narrative is only interested in Omri's role in doing evil in the eyes of YHWH, following the pattern of Jeroboam ben Nebat, and in founding Samaria as the new capital of Israel.

The regnal account Ahab ben Omri in 1 Kgs 16:29—22:40, however, is far more substantive insofar as its focuses on the prophet Elijah the Tishbite and his conflict with Ahab and his Phoenician wife Jezebel over the dynasty's alleged adherence to the Canaanite/Phoenician deity Baal as opposed to YHWH. The initial notice of Ahab's reign takes note of these issues in 1 Kgs 16:31-33. The marriage to Jezebel is a particularly contentious issue in the narrative. Jezebel is a Canaanite, and Ahab's marriage to her illustrates the consequences of inter-marriage, that is, apostasy against YHWH as Israel turns to foreign gods. Ahab's erection of an Asherah or sacred post dedicated to the Canaanite goddess Asherah will also appear again when King Manasseh of Judah erects such a post in Jerusalem (2 Kgs 21:3). The reference in 1 Kgs 16:34 to Hiel's fortification of Jericho by laying the foundations of the city at the cost of his son should also be noted. The notice fulfills Joshua's curse against anyone who re-establishes Jericho in Josh 6:26, but it also anticipates the demise the house of David in 2 Kgs 25:5 when King Zedekiah ben Josiah is captured at Jericho while attempting to escape the Babylonians and ultimately exiled to Babylon.[16] Insofar as Zedekiah was the last sitting monarch of the house of David, and his nephew Jehoiachin never returned to Jerusalem to reclaim the throne, Jericho emerges as an important indicator of the fate of Israel's and Judah's monarchs in the Former Prophets, especially when it is considered that the house of David is descended from the house of Omri through Ahab's sister or daughter, Athaliah (see 2 Kgs 8:18, 26; 11:1-20). Such a relationship becomes especially important in the history when Elijah curses the entire house of Omri and all of its descendants in 1 Kgs 21:20-29 as a result of Ahab's role in the murder of Naboth of Jezreel.

The narrative concerning Ahab's reign in 1 Kgs 17:1—22:40 focuses especially on Ahab's conflict with prophets of YHWH, particularly Elijah the Tishbite. The initial block of Elijah narratives in 1 Kgs 17–19 emphasizes the conflict between the deities of both parties, YHWH of Israel as represented by Elijah and Baal of Phoenicia as represented by Jezebel and her apparently compliant husband Ahab. Diachronically speaking, Ahab's marriage to the Phoenician princess undoubt-edly sealed a very important alliance between the two nations that would give them control over the sea and land trade routes of the Eastern Mediterranean. It also explains the hostility of Aram, which would want to break that relationship in order to enlist Israel as an ally in its own conflicts with Assyria. At the syn-chronic level, however, the conflict only represents a theological struggle for control of Israel by YHWH or Baal.[17]

The narrative proceeds with a pronounced anti-Baal polemic throughout. Baal is the Canaanite/Phoenician god of fertility who brings the rains so that creation will produce an abundance of food and life. Elijah first appears in the Wadi Cherith of the Trans-Jordan, the very area that is contested by Aram, where he is supported by the forces of nature, that is, the Wadi provides water and the ravens provide food. The polemic is clear, viz., YHWH controls creation, not Baal. The point is made even clearer in the subsequent narratives. When Elijah moves to Zarephat, a Phoenician city under the control of Baal, he finds a widow and her son starving to death because Baal does not provide. Not only does YHWH provide for the widow through Elijah, the prophet also saves the boy's life by purportedly bringing him back from the dead, an important motif in the Baal mythology insofar as Baal is a dying and rising god whose return from the dead in the autumn inaugurates the yearly rainy season that ensures the growth of new crops. The contest on Mt. Carmel between Elijah, the prophet of YHWH, and the 450 prophets of Baal (and four hundred prophets of Asherah) further accentuates the polemic. Whereas the prophets of Baal are unable to prompt their deity to respond to their liturgical pleas for rain, Elijah immediately elicits a response from YHWH that brings an end to the drought and inundates the land in rain. The culminating sub-unit of these narratives is Elijah's encounter with YHWH on Mt. Horeb. Fleeing for his life following the Carmel incident, Elijah seeks refuge at Horeb, the alternate name for Mt. Sinai, where he has an experience of YHWH's presence analogous to that of Moses in Exod 34. Elijah hides in a cave like Moses, but he sees several visions of a mighty wind, an earthquake, and a great fire, all of which are major natural phenomena, but the narrative takes care to point out that YHWH is not to be identified with any of these as Baal might be conceived; rather, YHWH as sovereign of creation controls nature. YHWH's presence is revealed through "the still small voice" (Hebrew, qôl děmāmâ daqqâ), literally, "the sound of crushed/sheer silence," in which the deliberate use of antonyms is intended to express YHWH's incorporeality and intangible nature when compared to Baal or other pagan gods. Indeed, the visionary appearance of YHWH to Elijah while the latter resides in the cave is analogous to the role of the priest at Yom Kippur when he enters the Holy of Holies to experience the presence of YHWH.[18] The episode ends with YHWH's instructions to Elijah to anoint Hazael as king of Aram and Jehu ben Nimshi as king of Israel and to designate Elisha ben Shaphat as his own successor as prophet. These instructions prepare the reader for the continuation of the conflict through the revolt against the house of Omri led by Jehu ben Nimshi at the instigation of Elisha long after Elijah is gone. They indicate that the Elijah narratives in 1 Kgs 17–19 function as an introduction to the narratives concerning Elisha in 2 Kgs 3–14 insofar as Elisha is actually credited with instigating the overthrow of the house of Omri.

Subsequent narratives then portray divine judgment against Ahab and his death. First Kings 20 portrays Ahab's condemnation by an anonymous prophet in the context of the war with Aram. First Kings 21 portrays Ahab's role in the murder of Naboth of Jezreel—at the instigation of his wife Jezebel—in order to gain control of Naboth's property in Jezreel. When Elijah condemns Ahab for his actions, he emphasizes the destruction of the entire house of Omri, but when Ahab repents, Elijah states that Ahab will die before seeing the demise of his entire house. This form of mercy will also come into play in the Josiah narratives in 2 Kgs 22–23, when Josiah is granted an early death as an act of mercy for his own repentance despite the fact that YHWH had already decided to destroy Jerusalem on account of the sins of Josiah's grandfather, Manasseh. First Kings 22:1-40 portrays Ahab's death in battle against the Arameans at Ramoth Gilead. An important dimension of this narrative is the motif of concealment. YHWH conceals plans to kill Ahab by calling for a lying spirit to entice Ahab to his death, but the plan is revealed by the prophet Micaiah ben Imlah who is the only prophet to announce that Ahab will die when he goes to battle against Aram. Although the narrative is designed to follow upon Elijah's grant of a merciful death to Ahab, it raises the theological question of divine deceit in relation to human beings.[19] The motif of hiddenness also comes to expression in Ahab's attempts to conceal his identity so that he will not be targeted on the battlefield, but the narrative goes to great lengths to demonstrate how an entirely random arrow shot by an Aramean archer found its mark despite Ahab's attempts to protect himself, thereby fulfilling Elijah's prophecy of Ahab's death. Nevertheless, Elijah's prophecy is not entirely fulfilled since Ahab's sons are still alive.

The account of the reign of Jehoshaphat ben Asa in 1 Kgs 22:41-51 emphasizes his righteousness, but notes that he was forced to submit to the king of Israel as a vassal. Such a notice then explains the later marriage of his son, Ahaziah, to Athaliah, the daughter or sister of Ahab.

The account of the reign of Ahaziah ben Ahab of Israel in 1 Kgs 22:52—2 Kgs 1:18/2:1-25 plays an important role in the narrative insofar as it explains the demise of one of Ahab's sons and accounts for the miraculous disappearance of Elijah from the scene and the succession to his prophetic role by Elisha ben Shaphat. The importance of these narratives lies in its attempts to portray the power of the prophet Elijah as the representative of YHWH and the transference of that power to his successor Elisha. The demonstration of Elijah's power begins with the account of Ahaziah's accident and the attempts to secure aid for the injured monarch from Baal Zebub, a manifestation of Baal associated with the Philistine city of Ekron. Although Ahaziah's fall is an accident, its occurrence following the condemnation of the house of Omri and the divinely directed death of Ahab in battle suggests that it was no accident at all, but an act of YHWH to carry out the curse against the house of Ahab. The attempt to secure aid from Baal Zebub only highlights the contention of the history that the house of Omri is completely corrupt insofar as it has abandoned YHWH for Phoenician and now Philistine gods. The motif of YHWH's power comes to expression when an angel of YHWH informs Elijah about the developments with Ahaziah in order to prompt the prophet to demand adherence to YHWH and to proclaim Ahaziah's death because of his failure to do so. When the royal palace sends successively three units of soldiers to summon the man of G-d, the first two units are completely destroyed because of their failure to approach Elijah with the respect due to a prophetic representative of YHWH. The third unit succeeds, but only because its commander knelt before Elijah to ask for aid from YHWH and the prophet, much as a priest would do when officiating before YHWH in the Temple. Although the military unit survives its encounter with the prophet, Ahaziah does not survive due to his own adherence to Baal Zebub. An appended narrative in 2 Kgs 2 further demonstrates Elijah's divine power together with its transference to Elisha. When Elijah is carried to heaven in a fiery chariot, he leaves behind his hairy mantle for Elisha to retrieve. Following Elijah's departure, Elisha now emerges as the major power figure and representative of YHWH. Elisha purifies the bad water of Jericho, but he also demonstrates the dangers of approaching him without proper respect when he unleashes wild bears to kill forty-two boys who taunted him for his baldness. Such a portrayal is once again analogous to approaching YHWH in the Temple without attending to the proper ritual requirements that YHWH's holy presence demands. Underlying these portrayals is a diachronic reality that must be explained, viz., Elijah disappears from the scene and Elisha takes his place. Perhaps Elijah was killed by the Israelite monarchy, but his departure is portrayed in terms that point to divine reality beyond the empirical world of creation, thereby laying a foundation for the development of the later Heikhalot tradition in Rabbinic times.

The regnal account of Jehoram ben Ahab of Israel in 2 Kgs 3:1-3 (see also 2 Kgs 8:23-24) reiterates the standard condemnation of the fall of the kings of northern Israel, viz., he is condemned for acting wrongfully in the eyes of YHWH for following in the sins of Jeroboam ben Nebat, despite removing a shrine for Baal built by his father. The major purpose of his regnal account is to relate the narratives concerning the prophet Elisha. As signaled in the accounts of Elijah and Elisha in 2 Kgs 1–2, the Elisha narratives also focus on the holy power of the prophet as representative of YHWH, the G-d of Israel and sovereign of creation. Elisha's and YHWH's power are applied both to the realm of human events and to the realm of creation, although the worldview of these narratives appears to be focused on Israel and its immediate neighbors, that is, Moab, Edom, Philistia, Aram, and so on. Elisha has a priestly dimension as well, insofar as his prophecies are accompanied by music (2 Kgs 3:15), a feature of Temple worship, and he presides over a guild of prophets, who appear to function much like a cadre of temple priests. The purpose of these demonstrations is to prepare the reader for the contention that YHWH, working through Elisha, is ultimately responsible for the overthrow of the house of Omri by Jehu in 2 Kgs 8–10. Throughout the Elisha narratives, YHWH's power remains hidden to the human protagonists, whether Israelite or Aramean, unless revealed by the prophet. The motif of YHWH's hiddenness aids in preparing the reader for the contention that YHWH remains the hidden factor in Jehu's revolt.

The account of Jehoram's attack against Moab in 2 Kgs 3:4-27 emphasizes Elisha's role in securing military victory for Jehoram ben Ahab and his allies over King Mesha of Moab. Despite YHWH's support, however, the narrative makes it clear that the soldiers of Israel did not trust in YHWH's support insofar as they fled upon observing King Mesha sacrificing his own son to deliver his city from the Israelite attack. The account of Elisha's efforts to save the sons of the widow and the Shunammite woman in 2 Kgs 4:1-37 builds upon the motif of Elijah's actions to save the son of the woman of Zarephath in 1 Kgs 17. Elisha provides abundant food for the first woman and her sons. As for the Shunammite woman, Elisha first declares that she will bear a son soon after he moves in with her and her husband, and then he saves the boy's life after he collapses while working in the fields. All of these acts are intended as polemic against Baal by demonstrating YHWH's power to provide food, life, and even to bring the dead back to life, all of which are acts that Baal is known for in the ancient world. Elisha's purification of a pan of food in 2 Kgs 4:38-41 and his feeding of one hundred men in 2 Kgs 4:42-44 serve similar functions, which are accentuated by the motif of famine in a land whose people worship Baal. Elisha's powers of restoration are illustrated in 2 Kgs 5:1—6:7 when he heals the Aramean army commander, Naaman, from leprosy, and retrieves an ax head from a river by making it float. Elisha's power over the king of Aram is aptly demonstrated in 2 Kgs 6:8—7:20 when he plays the key role in capturing Aramean forces, with the aid of the unseen heavenly army of YHWH, and prompting them to flee when they think reinforcements have arrived to support the besieged men of Samaria. Despite the actions of Elisha and YHWH, the narrative takes care to portray the people's disbelief in YHWH despite the famine that afflicts the land due to its devotion to Baal under the Omride kings. The final narrative concerning Elisha's power in 2 Kgs 8:1-15 emphasizes his power in the human realm once again when he plays key roles in restoring the property of the Shunammite woman and in anointing Hazael as the next king of Aram in keeping with YHWH's instructions to Elijah in 1 Kgs 19:15-18.

The regnal account of Jehoram/Joram ben Jehoshaphat of Judah in 2 Kgs 8:16-24 emphasizes his alliance with the house of Omri by marrying a daughter of Ahab (Athaliah) and his adherence to their evil practices. YHWH's decision not to destroy Judah for his actions is explained by YHWH's promise to the house of David (2 Sam 7). Nevertheless, the successful revolt against Judah by Edom signals YHWH's displeasure in the narrative insofar as Edom had been subject to David (2 Sam 8:13-14).

The regnal account of Ahaziah ben Jehoram of Judah in 2 Kgs 8:25—11:20 is a key narrative in the books of Kings because of its account of Jehu ben Nimshi's overthrow of the house of Omri in 2 Kgs 9:1—10:36 and the reign of Athaliah bat Ahab/Omri over Judah in 2 Kgs 12:1-22. The introductory regnal account for Ahaziah ben Jehoram in 2 Kgs 8:25-29 signals Ahaziah's ties to the house of Omri. It identifies his mother as Athaliah bat Omri, which means that he is born to the house of Omri even though he is also a member of the house of David. The regnal account emphasizes that Ahaziah joined his northern Israelite ally, Joram ben Ahab, in battle against the Arameans under King Hazael. When Joram was wounded at Ramoth Gilead, he retired to Jezreel to recover, and Ahaziah went to visit him there. Ahab's murder of Naboth and his seizure of Naboth's property in Jezreel of course prompted Elijah to announce the downfall of the house of Omri in 2 Kgs 21. Ahaziah's regnal notice therefore signals that the judgment against the house of Omri will apply to Ahaziah and also the entire house of David within the larger framework of the books of Kings.

The account of Jehu's overthrow of the house of Omri is a highly theologized narrative that emphasizes the ties of Jehoram ben Ahab of Israel and Ahaziah ben Jehoram of Judah with Baal worship, as well as the ties of Jehu ben Nimshi with YHWH, the prophet Elisha, and Jehonadab ben Rechab, the leader of a group known for its devotion to YHWH.[20] Although the revolt is portrayed at the synchronic level as YHWH's victory over the forces aligned with Baal, the narrative shows clear signs of redaction that point to its origins in the Jehu Dynastic History as well as its reading and interpretation in relation to the Hezekian, Josianic, and exilic editions of the DtrH. The narrative presupposes the earlier Elisha narratives, insofar as it portrays Elisha as the figure who instigated the revolt by sending a messenger to name Jehu as YHWH's chosen king over Israel, but Elisha and Jehu never meet. Instead, Jehonadab appears to be the representative of YHWH who supports Jehu's revolt. As part of the Jehu Dynastic History and the later DtrH editions, the narrative emphasizes that Jehu's killing of Jehoram of Israel, Ahaziah of Judah, and Jezebel, the Phoenician widow of Ahab, at Jezreel fulfills Elijah's earlier proclamation of judgment against the house of Omri for Ahab's and Jezebel's roles in the murder of Naboth and the seizure of his property at Jezreel. Yet, the narrative also goes on to demonstrate how Jehu destroyed all of the supporters of the house of Omri in Jezreel and Samaria, here portrayed as Baal worshipers, by declaring a gathering at the temple of Baal in Samaria, barricading everyone inside the building, and then burning it down on top of them to ensure that all of the supporters of Baal (and the house of Omri) would perish in keeping with Elijah's announcement of judgment.

Although Jehu's revolt must be viewed as a victory for YHWH, at least at the level of the Jehu Dynastic History, the overall framework of Kings in its various DtrH editions will nevertheless condemn Jehu in 2 Kgs 10:30-35 for following in the path of Jeroboam ben Nebat. The reason for this at the diachronic level would be the reverses suffered by Israel at the hands of the Arameans as a result of Jehu's coup. Israel was severely weakened and left vulnerable to the Arameans until the reign of Jehu's grandson, Jehoash ben Jehoahaz, who finally defeated the Arameans. Ancient Near Eastern sources indicate that Jehoash's victories were aided by the alliance between the house of Jehu and the Assyrian empire, which contained the Arameans between the two allies and forced their capitulation. At the synchronic level, the condemnation of Jehu is explained by the need to condemn all of the kings of northern Israel in order to portray the fall of northern Israel as an act of divine punishment due to the nation's apostasy under the leadership of its kings.

The account of Athaliah's reign over Judah in 2 Kgs 11:1-20 also serves the theological agenda of the Jehu Dynastic History, as well as the Hezekian, Josianic, and Exilic editions of the DtrH. The account portrays Athaliah's coup against the house of David after hearing of the death of her son, Ahaziah ben Jehoram, and the overthrow of the house of Omri. As a descendant of the house of Omri herself, she illustrates the dangers posed by this ruling house in the eyes of the ancient historians by immediately acting to destroy the entire royal family of the house of David. She fails to kill her own infant grandson, Jehoash ben Ahaziah, however, when the baby is hidden away in the Temple by his aunt, Jehosheba bat Jehoram and the high priest Jehoiada. When Jehoash turned seven, Jehoiada engineered a successful coup against Athaliah. Although she was killed in the coup, she is nevertheless the grandmother of Jehoash, which means that the entire house of David is descended also from the house of Omri, and will ultimately come under the judgment announced to Ahab by the prophet Elijah.[21]

The next five regnal notices concerning Jehoash ben Ahaziah of Judah (2 Kgs 12:1-22), Jehoahaz ben Jehu of Israel (2 Kgs 13:1-9), Jehoash ben Jehoahaz of Israel (2 Kgs 13:10-25), Amaziah ben Joash of Judah (2 Kgs 14:1-22), and Jeroboam ben Joash of Israel (2 Kgs 14:23-29) emphasize the struggle of the house of Jehu to free itself from the threat of Aram and to assert its rule over southern Judah as its vassal. These efforts culminate in the regnal account of Jeroboam ben Joash, who ruled in peace over a kingdom extending from Lebo-Hamath in the north to the sea of the Aravah in the south, which means that his kingdom was comparable to that of Solomon. The account of Jeroboam's reign signals the conclusion of the Jehu Dynastic History, although the narrative was later employed in the Hezekian, Josianic, and Exilic DtrH editions to illustrate the sins of northern Israel. Although the biblical accounts are silent on the matter, the success of the house of Jehu was due to its alliance with Assyria, which had a common interest with Israel in keeping the Arameans under control.[22]

A second set of eight regnal accounts illustrates the rise of Assyria as a threat to both Israel and Judah, including the reigns of Azariah/Uzziah ben Amaziah of Judah (2 Kgs 15:1-7), Zechariah ben Jeroboam of Israel (2 Kgs 15:8-12), Shallum ben Jabesh of Israel (2 Kgs 15:13-16), Menahem ben Gadi of Israel (2 Kgs 15:17-22), Pekahiah ben Menahem of Israel (2 Kgs 15:23-26), Pekah ben Remaliah of Israel (2 Kgs 15:27-31), Jotham ben Uzziah/Azariah of Judah (2 Kgs 15:32-38), and Ahaz ben Jotham of Judah (2 Kgs 16:1-20). The rise of Assyria is instigated by Aramean attempts to assassinate the pro-Assyrian ruling monarchs of Israel, that is, Zechariah ben Jeroboam and Pekahiah ben Menahem, in order to replace them with kings who would shift Israel's alliance to Aram, that is, Shallum ben Jabesh and Pekah ben Remaliah, so that the resulting Syro-Ephraimitic alliance might confront Assyria. Judean kings, including Jotham ben Uzziah/Azariah and Ahaz ben Jotham, were threatened by the Syro-Ephraimitic coalition when they refused to join, apparently to ensure a united front when confronting Assyria. When Ahaz ben Jotham of Judah appealed to his suzerain monarch, Tiglath Pileser III of Assyrian, Tiglath Pileser invaded Syria-Israel, destroyed Damascus, subjugated Israel and stripped it of its outlying territories, and imposed greater tribute on Judah for having saved it and its king from destruction. Ahaz's orders to copy an Assyrian altar for placement in the Jerusalem Temple earn him the condemnation of the narrator. The northern kings are uniformly condemned for following in Jeroboam's paths.[23]

The regnal account of Hoshea ben Elah of Israel in 2 Kgs 17:1-41 is a key narrative in the larger framework of the books of Kings as well as in the Hezekian, Josianic, and Exilic editions of the DtrH because it explains the fall of northern Israel to Assyria in 722/1 BCE as an act of YHWH intended to punish northern Israel for its sins in following the apostasy of Jeroboam ben Nebat throughout the entire history of the northern kingdom as presented in Kings.[24] The narrative commentary on the fall of Israel must be recognized theologically as a form of theodicy, insofar as its defends the fidelity, moral character, power, and presence of YHWH by contending that northern Israel's collapse was not the result of YHWH's failures to keep the covenant with Israel and to protect the nation. Rather, 2 Kgs 17 charges that the fault lies with the kings of Israel from Jeroboam ben Nebat on, who prompted the people to abandon YHWH in favor of foreign gods. The historical causes of Israel's destruction, however, lie in Assyrian interests in expanding westward to control the eastern Mediterranean trade routes to Egypt and to subjugate their vassal Israel, which had revolted against them. Within the synchronic context of Kings, this narrative presents the fall of northern Israel as a model or paradigm for the subsequent fall of southern Judah and the Babylonian exile. When considered diachronically in relation to the Hezekian and Josianic editions of the DtrH, the fall of northern Israel provides an example that is designed to motivate readers to adhere to the reform programs instigated by both monarchs to adhere to YHWH through the Jerusalem Temple and to support efforts to restore the original unity of the twelve tribes of Israel under Davidic rule. The accounts of both Hezekiah and Josiah will offer them as faithful contrasts to the models of apostasy exemplified in the history by the northern monarchs.

The regnal account of Hezekiah ben Ahaz in 2 Kgs 18:1—20:21 is a key narrative in the Former Prophets insofar as it deliberately contrasts the repentance of King Hezekiah with the alleged apostasy of all of the kings of northern Israel as portrayed in 2 Kgs 17.[25] The point of the narrative is to encourage readers to turn to YHWH by contrasting the fate of the northern kingdom of Israel, all of whose kings were charged with apostasy against YHWH, with that of Hezekiah, who turned to YHWH when the Assyrian army invaded Judah and thereby saved Judah and Jerusalem from destruction. The narrative includes five major components, viz., the regnal introduction in 2 Kgs 18:1-7, which states that Hezekiah did what was right in the eyes of YHWH and provides an overview of his various reform measures that indicate his righteousness; the account of YHWH's deliverance of Jerusalem in 2 Kgs 18:8—19:37, which relates how YHWH saved Jerusalem in terms analogous to the deliverance of Israel from Pharaoh at the time of the Exodus when Hezekiah turned to YHWH in repentance following the failure of his attempted revolt against Assyria; the account of YHWH's healing of Hezekiah from sickness in 2 Kgs 20:1-11 prior to the revolt, again when Hezekiah turned to YHWH; the account of Isaiah's condemnation of Hezekiah for receiving an embassy from Babylonia in 2 Kgs 20:12-19 while preparing for his revolt against Assyria, which anticipates the Babylonian exile in the larger framework of the Former Prophets; and the concluding regnal resume in 2 Kgs 20:20-21. The narrative emphasizes the role of the prophet Isaiah throughout. The narrative also appears in Isaiah 36–39, although the Isaian version of the narrative removes any explicit or implicit criticism of Hezekiah in order to present the king in as exemplary a manner as possible.

A number of diachronic features of the narrative must also be considered.[26] First is the contrasting viewpoints of the results of Hezekiah's revolt as portrayed in the present narrative and in the records of the Assyrian King Sennacherib who invaded Judah in 701 BCE when Hezekiah revolted against him. Second Kings 18–20 maintain that YHWH delivered Jerusalem from siege, killing 185,000 Assyrian troops, and that Sennacherib was assassinated by his own sons, whereas Sennacherib claims a victory over Hezekiah and provides details concerning the numbers of Judeans that he exiled and the amount of booty that he gained as a result of his invasions. Historians generally maintain that the conflict resulted in a draw in which Hezekiah was allowed to maintain his throne due to Sennacherib's need to put down the revolt in the eastern Assyrian empire by Hezekiah's ally, Merodach Baladan of Babylonia. An underlying version of the narrative appears to have originated as part of a Hezekian edition of the DtrH which was designed to demonstrate YHWH's fidelity to the house of David and to support Hezekiah's claims to rule over the former northern kingdom. The edited present form of the narrative would also have functioned as a means to support Josiah's reform program insofar as it posited Hezekiah as a model of piety and adherence to YHWH—in contrast with the northern monarchs—in keeping with the religious ideals and political goals of Josiah's reforms. When read in relation to the Exilic edition of the DtrH, the Hezekiah account presents Hezekiah as a pious model for readers, although it also points to his alliance with Babylon as a misstep that ultimately anticipates the Babylonian exile.

The regnal account of King Manasseh ben Hezekiah in 2 Kgs 21:1-18 is also a key narrative in the Former Prophets insofar as it is designed to explain YHWH's decision to destroy Jerusalem and Judah and to bring about the Babylonian exile as a result of Manasseh's sins against YHWH. Manasseh is portrayed as the worst monarch of the Davidic line due to his apostasy against YHWH—described in terms reminiscent of his ancestor, King Ahab ben Omri of Israel—and his killing of so many innocent people during his reign. This account raises tremendous theological problems,[27] the most significant of which is why should later generations of Judeans suffer for the sins of one man? The problem becomes especially acute when the account of Manasseh's reign in 2 Chr 33:1-20 is considered. Although the Chronicler's account begins much like Kings, Manasseh is dragged in chains to Babylon to appear before the Assyrian king, apparently to intimidate him during the Babylonian revolt against Assyria in 652–648 BCE. As a result of this experience, the Chronicler's account maintains that he repented and became a righteous monarch for the rest of his reign. The contrasting portraits of Manasseh illustrate two important principles in biblical literature, viz., the capacity to interpret events according to theological worldview and the capacity to engage in dialog with earlier texts that present problematic viewpoints and to address problems in the earlier narratives by providing a very different viewpoint of the event or issue in question. The willingness to engage in such inner-biblical exegesis points to the origins of midrashic interpretation of the Bible even within the Bible itself.

Following the brief account in 2 Kgs 21:19-26 of the reign of Amon ben Manasseh, who was assassinated in a failed coup d'état, 2 Kgs 22:1—23:30 presents a lengthy account of the reign of Josiah ben Amon, who ascended the throne of Judah at the age of eight following the assassination of his father.[28] The account of Josiah's reign is especially important in the Former Prophets because he is judged as righteous and emerges in the Kings narrative as the most exemplary king of the entire house of David. Josiah is well known for his program of religious reform and national restoration in which he reinvigorated the covenant with YHWH and attempted to extend Davidic rule over the former northern kingdom of Israel. Indeed, his reform program is based on a book of Torah, discovered during Temple renovations, which appears to be some form of the book of Deuteronomy. Although he is initially compared to his ancestor David for exemplary righteousness in 2 Kgs 22:2, the text adds that he did not deviate to the right or to the left. Additionally, the concluding regnal account in 2 Kgs 23:25 maintains that there was no king like him who turned back to YHWH with all his heart and soul and might in full accord with the Torah of Moses. Such descriptions fit well with the portrayal of the ideal king in Deut 17:20 and in Joshua's exhortation speeches to the people in Josh 1:7; 23:6. In his efforts to conform to YHWH's expectations, the Kings narrative indicates that he corrected many of the cultic abuses of his predecessors; for example, he destroyed the altar at Beth El erected by Jeroboam ben Nebat as well as the various foreign cultic installations of Solomon, Ahaz, Manasseh and the other kings of Israel and Judah, and he reinstituted the observance of Passover which had not been observed since the days of the Judges.

Yet, the narrative presents a major theological problem.[29] Despite Josiah's exemplary righteousness as resented in the Kings narrative, the reality of his early death at the age of thirty-nine in Megiddo at the hands of Pharaoh Necho of Egypt and the subsequent destruction of Jerusalem and the Temple by the Babylonians only twenty-two years after Josiah's death must be explained. As noted above, the account of Manasseh's reign in 2 Kgs 21:1-18 emphasizes that YHWH had decided to destroy Jerusalem and the Temple due to Manasseh's excessive sinfulness, and the present narrative maintains that even Josiah's repentance and exemplary behavior was insufficient to avert the divine decree. The prophetess Huldah informs Josiah that YHWH will show him mercy for his repentance and allow him to die an early death in peace so that he will not have to witness the destruction in terms much like those offered to Ahab in 1 Kgs 21 after he had repented for his role in the murder of Naboth and the seizure of his property in Jezreel. As a descendant of the house of Omri through Athaliah as well as the house of David, Josiah can hardly avoid the judgment decreed against the house of Omri by Elijah. Later tradition, particularly the account of Josiah's reign in 2 Chr 34–35, attempts to address the theological problems posed by these narratives by portraying Manasseh as repentant, Josiah as responsible for his own death, and assigning responsibility for the destruction of the Temple to the people of the time who are charged with having corrupted the Temple. Again, the differing portrayals of Manasseh, Josiah, and the destruction of the Temple in Kings and Chronicles point to the Bible's own capacity for disagreement, debate, and reinterpretation.

The diachronic elements must also be considered. The present account of Josiah's reign fits well within theological purview of the exilic edition of the DtrH, but the exemplary presentation of Josiah's reign indicates that these narratives were intended to form the culmination of the Josianic edition of the DtrH.

The final regnal accounts of Jehoahaz ben Josiah in 2 Kgs 23:31-35, Jehoiakim ben Josiah in 2 Kgs 23:36—24:7, Jehoiachin ben Jehoiakim in 2 Kgs 24:8-17, and Zedekiah (Mattaniah) ben Josiah in 2 Kgs 24:18—25:30 trace the final years of the kingdom of Judah through the destruction of Jerusalem and the Temple by the Babylonians in 587/6 BCE and the Babylonian exile. Again, the narrative stresses YHWH's decision to destroy Jerusalem due to the sins of Manasseh (2 Kgs 24:1-4). When Zedekiah, who was installed as a puppet king by the Babylonians following their deportation to Babylon of Jehoiachin ben Jehoiakim, is unable to prevent revolt, the Babylonians invade Judah, crush all resistance, and capture Zedekiah near Jericho when he tries to escape. Zedekiah's capture by Jericho, after which he is forced to watch the execution of his own sons before he is blinded and sent into exile himself, brings the narrative of the Former Prophets full circle insofar as Israel's life in the land begins with conquest of Jericho under Joshua. Afterwards, the Babylonians destroyed the Temple on the seventh day of the fifth month (Av), although Jer 52:12 places the event on the tenth of Av. This discrepancy is reconciled by b. Taanith 29a, which argues that the Babylonian commander Nebuzaradan entered the Temple on the seventh of Av, ordered it burned on the ninth of Av, and the fire burned until the tenth of Av. The ninth of Av is afterwards observed as the anniversary of the destruction of both the first and the second Temples—as well as other calamities—in Jewish tradition.

The final episode of the history in 2 Kgs 25:27-30 concludes the narrative with an account of Jehoiachin's release from prison by the Babylonian monarch Evil Merodach (Amel Merodach), the son of Nebuchadnezzar who reigned from 562 to 560 BCE. Some interpreters view this act as an indication of hope in the restoration of the house of David,[30] but the fact that Jehoiachin remains in Babylon to eat at the king's table establishes an analogy with Mephibosheth ben Jonathan ben Saul who ate at King David's table (2 Sam 9) and ultimately gave up his right to

reclaim the throne of his father (2 Sam 19).[31] Given the critical stance taken by the
Former Prophets towards the kings of Israel and Judah, such a portrayal raises
questions as to whether the history envisions the reinstitution of Davidic kingship. The narrative consistently calls for the observance of divine Torah, but
kingship is granted only as a concession to the demands of the people (1 Sam 8)
and the Temple is granted only as a concession to David (2 Sam 7).

NOTES

[1] For traditional Jewish commentary on Kings, see A. R. Rosenberg, *The Book of Kings* (2 vols.;
Judaica Books of the Bible; New York: Judaica, 1998, 1993).

[2] For overviews of modern scholarship on Kings, see Sweeney, *King Josiah of Judah: The Lost
Messiah of Israel* (Oxford: Oxford University Press, 2001), 33–109; idem, *1 and 2 Kings: A
Commentary* (OTL; Louisville: Westminster John Knox, 2007) 1–47; Antony F. Campbell and
Mark O'Brien, *Unfolding the Deuteronomistic History: Origins, Upgrades, Present Text*
(Minneapolis: Fortress Press, 2000), 329–470.

[3] For modern commentaries on Kings, see especially my *1 and 2 Kings*; Mordechai Cogan,
1 Kings (AB 10; New York: Doubleday, 2001); Mordechai Cogan and Haim Tadmor, *2 Kings*
(AB 11; New York: Doubleday, 1988); Robert L. Cohn, *2 Kings* (BO; Collegeville: Liturgical,
2000); Simon J. DeVries, *1 Kings* (WBC 12; Waco: Word: 1985); Volkmar Fritz, *1 and 2 Kings*
(ContCom; Minneapolis: Fortress Press, 2003); John Gray, *I and II Kings: A Commentary*
(OTL; Philadelphia: Westminster, 1970); T. R. Hobbs, *2 Kings* (WBC 13; Waco: Word, 1985);
G. H. Jones, *1 and 2 Kings* (NCenB; Grand Rapids: Eerdmans, 1984); Burke O. Long, *1 Kings,
with an Introduction to Historical Literature* (FOTL 9; Grand Rapids: Eerdmans, 1984); idem,
2 Kings (FOTL 10; Grand Rapids: Eerdmans, 1989); James A. Montgomery and Henry Snyder
Gehman, *The Books of Kings* (ICC; Edinburgh: T. & T. Clark, 1951); Jerome T. Walsh, *1 Kings*
(BO; Collegeville: Liturgical, 1996).

[4] For discussion of the regnal account form, see Long, *1 Kings*, 158–65, 259.

[5] For critical discussion of this structure analysis, see Sweeney, *1 and 2 Kings*, 4–15.

[6] In addition to the discussion of individual texts in my *1 and 2 Kings*, see my "The Religions
of Israel and Judah," in *The Cambridge History of Ancient Mediterranean Religions*, ed.
M Salzman et al. (Cambridge: Cambridge University Press, forthcoming).

[7] For critical theological discussion of the presentations of the reign of Manasseh in Kings and
Chronicles, see my "King Manasseh of Judah and the Problem of Theodicy in the Deutero-
nomistic History," in *Good Kings, Bad Kings*, ed. L. L. Grabbe (LHBOTS 393; London: T&T
Clark International, 2005), 264–78.

[8] See my "The Critique of Solomon in the Josianic Edition of the Deuteronomistic History,"
JBL 114 (1995): 607–22, and "Synchronic and Diachronic Considerations in the Portrayal of
the Demise of Solomon's Kingdom," in *Birkat Shalom: Studies in the Bible, Ancient Near
Eastern Literature, and Post-Biblical Judaism Presented to Shalom Paul on the Occasion of his
Seventieth Birthday*, ed. Ch. Cohen et al. (Winona Lake, IN: Eisenbrauns, 2008), 1:175–89.

[9] See especially Gwillym H. Jones, *The Nathan Narratives* (JSOTSup 80; Sheffield: JSOT, 1990).

[10] For discussion of the portrayal of Solomon as a monarch like the Pharaoh of Egypt, see
especially Pekka Särkiö, *Die Weisheit und Macht Salomos in der Israelitischen Historiographie*
(Schriften der Finnischen Exegetischen Gesellschaft; Helsinki; Finnish Exegetical Society;
Göttingen Vandenhoeck & Ruprecht, 1994).

[11] For discussion of the construction of Solomon's Temple on the pattern of royal palaces in ancient Syria and Canaan, see especially Baruch Halpern, *The First Historians: The Hebrew Bible and History* (San Francisco: Harper & Row, 1988), 46–54.

[12] For discussion of the association of Solomon's Temple and the Garden of Eden, see Jon D. Levenson, "The Temple and the World," *JR* 64 (1984): 275–98; idem, *Sinai and Zion: An Entry into the Jewish Bible* (Minneapolis: Crossroad, 1985), 89–184, especially 142–45; Moshe Weinfeld, "Sabbath, Temple, and the Enthronement of the L-rd—The Problem of the Sitz im Leben of Genesis 1:1–2:3," in *Mélanges bibliques et orientaux en l'honneur M. Henri Cazelles*, ed. A. Caquot and M. Delcor (AOAT 212; Kevelaer: Butzon & Bercker, 1981), 501–12.

[13] See especially Särkiö, *Die Weisheit und Macht Salomos*, 103–81.

[14] For discussion and bibliography, see my *1 and 2 Kings*, 149–51.

[15] For discussion of the portrayal of Jeroboam in Kings, see especially my *Reading the Hebrew Bible after the Shoah: Engaging Holocaust Theology* (Minneapolis: Fortress Press, 2008), 67–72, and *1 and 2 Kings*, 162–86.

[16] For discussion, see especially my "On the Literary Function of the Notice concerning Hiel's Reestablishment of Jericho in 1 Kings 16.34," in *Seeing Signals, Reading Signs: The Art of Exegesis*, ed. M. A. O'Brien and H. N. Wallace (JSOTSup 415; Sheffield: Sheffield Academic, 2004), 104–15.

[17] For discussion of the Canaanite mythological background of the Elijah and Elisha narratives, see especially Leah Bronner, *The Stories of Elijah and Elisha as Polemics against Baal Worship* (POS 6; Leiden: Brill, 1968); Alan J. Hauser, "YHWH versus Death—The Real Struggle in 1 Kings 17–19," in Alan J. Hauser and Russell Gregory, *From Carmel to Horeb: Elijah in Crisis* (JSOTSup 85; Sheffield: Almond, 1990), 9–89.

[18] See my *1 and 2 Kings*, 232.

[19] See especially James L. Crenshaw, *Prophetic Conflict* (BZAW 124; Berlin: de Gruyter, 1971); Simon J. DeVries, *Prophet against Prophet* (Grand Rapids: Eerdmans, 1978).

[20] See especially Susan Otto, *Jehu, Elia und Elisa* (BWANT 152; Stuttgart: Kohlhammer, 2001), 29–117; Marsha C. White, *The Elijah Legends and Jehu's Coup* (BJS 311; Atlanta: Scholars Press, 1997).

[21] See my *1 and 2 Kings*, 340–47, and *King Josiah*, 9–50.

[22] For discussion of the political background for these regnal accounts, see especially my *1 and 2 Kings*, 347–69.

[23] For discussion of the political background for these regnal accounts, see especially my *1 and 2 Kings*, 369–86.

[24] Martin Noth, *The Deuteronomistic History* (JSOTSup 15; Sheffield: JSOT, 1981), 73; Frank Moore Cross, "The Themes of the Books of Kings and the Structure of the Deuteronomistic History," in *Canaanite Myth and Hebrew Epic* (Cambridge, MA: Harvard University Press, 1973), 281; see also my *1 and 2 Kings*, 386–96.

[25] See my *1 and 2 Kings*, 397–424, and *Isaiah 1–39*, 454–511.

[26] For discussion of the historical aspects of this narrative, see especially *The Cambridge Ancient History* 3/2, 109–11; G. W. Ahlström, *The History of Ancient Palestine* (Minneapolis: Fortress Press, 1993), 707–16.

[27] See my *1 and 2 Kings*, 424–32, and "King Manasseh of Judah and the Problem of Theodicy."

[28] See my *1 and 2 Kings*, 434–50, and *King Josiah of Judah*.

[29] See my *Reading the Hebrew Bible after the Shoah*, 77–81.

[30] For example, Gerhard von Rad, *Old Testament Theology* (2 vols.; New York: Harper & Row, 1962–65), 1:334–47.

[31] See my *1 and 2 Kings*, 464–65.

Part IIIB

נביאים אחרונים

The Latter Prophets

A. OVERVIEW

The collection of books known as the Latter Prophets (Hebrew, *nĕbî'îm 'aḥrônîm*) of the Bible includes the prophetic books of Isaiah, Jeremiah, Ezekiel, and the Twelve Prophets (Hosea, Joel, Amos, Obadiah, Jonah, Micah, Nahum, Habakkuk, Zephaniah, Haggai, Zechariah, Malachi). Each book presents a combination of oracular and narrative material that portrays the words, activities, socio-historical setting, and concerns of the prophet in question. The prophets are especially well known for their attempts to interpret the major historical, economic, and religious events of their day, to identify the divine will in relation to those events, and to call upon the people of their times to follow the prophet's understanding of the divine will. Although prophets are frequently understood as figures who predict the future, their basic function is to persuade people to follow the divine will. Their efforts to envision the future were a means to indicate to people what the possible consequences or outcomes their actions might hold, either for judgment or for blessing, and to convince them to adopt a course of action that was in keeping with the will of YHWH.

Although each of the prophets is placed in relation to a particular historical setting, Talmudic tradition does not arrange the books of the Latter Prophets in chronological order. The Rabbis considered a chronological order for the presentation of the Latter Prophets, but rejected it in favor of a thematic or theological basis for the presentation of the prophetic books (*b. Baba Batra* 14b). The Former Prophets conclude with the book of Kings, which is concerned throughout with destruction, that is, of northern Israel and later of southern Judah, Jerusalem, and the Jerusalem Temple. The Rabbis conclude, therefore, that the book of Jeremiah must appear first among the Latter Prophets, because it, too, is concerned with destruction throughout. Ezekiel then follows because it begins with destruction, but concludes with consolation, and Isaiah follows Ezekiel because Isaiah is concerned with consolation throughout. The book of the Twelve Prophets concludes the sequence without discussion as to the reasons why, although the presentation of prophets beginning with those who are concerned with destruction and concluding with those who are concerned with consolation suggests that the Twelve

Prophets presents an overarching set of concerns that coincides with those of the first three books. The prophets are set in periods ranging from the eighth century, which saw the Assyrian invasions of Israel and Judah, through the seventh and sixth centuries, which saw the Babylonian destruction of Jerusalem and the exile, and finally through the sixth and fifth centuries, which saw the Persian-period restoration of Jerusalem and the Temple. Nevertheless, the Rabbinic concern with destruction and consolation represents their underlying preoccupation with the interrelated issues of the destruction of Jerusalem and the Temple and the exile of the people from the land of Israel together with the restoration of the Jerusalem Temple and the return of the exiled people to the land. Insofar as the Talmudic Rabbis lived and worked in the aftermath of the Roman destruction of Jerusalem in 70 CE and the destruction of the population of Judah in 132–135 CE, they looked to the Babylonian exile as a model for considering the future restoration of Israel when the period of Roman-instigated oppression would come to an end.

Each of the books of the Latter Prophets is identified with a particular prophet, but it is not entirely clear that the prophets composed their own books. Each book begins with a superscription or narrative introduction that identifies the prophet in question and generally situates him in relation to a particular socio-historical context and set of concerns. Many of the prophetic books also include extensive narrative sections that present third-person accounts of the prophet's activities. Although the prophets may (or may not) have composed much of the oracular material found within their respective books, these narrative features indicate to modern interpreters that the present forms of the prophetic books were composed, arranged, and edited by parties other than the prophets themselves. Indeed, the books of Isaiah, Zechariah, and perhaps others appear to include the works of anonymous prophets who lived and worked long after the prophet in question. Talmudic tradition recognizes this reality as well (*b. Baba Batra* 15a) insofar as it argues that the book of Isaiah was composed by Hezekiah and his colleagues and that both Ezekiel and the Book of the Twelve Prophets were composed by the men of the great assembly. Only Jeremiah is ascribed to the prophet himself, which is ironic insofar as Jeremiah includes more third-person narrative than any other prophetic book. But then the Rabbis maintain that Jeremiah wrote Kings and Lamentations as well, indicating their belief in his capacity for narrative and poetic composition. Such observations underscore the fact that interpreters must recognize that the individual prophetic books present the prophets as they are understood by the composers and editors of their respective books, and sometimes the presentation of the prophet may differ to some degree from the self-understanding of the prophet himself, such as Isaiah, who envisions a righteous Davidic monarch (Isa 9:1-6; 11:1-16), but whose book envisions the Persian monarch Cyrus as YHWH's divinely appointed ruler and Temple builder (Isa 44:28; 45:1).

Each book has a distinctive outlook based in part on the social identity of the prophet portrayed therein.[1] Isaiah's royalist viewpoint relates to his role as royal advisor; Jeremiah's concern with the application of Torah stems from his role as a priest of the line of Eli or Ithamar; and Ezekiel's concern with the re-establishment of the Holy Temple stems from his identity as a priest of the line of Zadok that served as the high priests of the Jerusalem Temple. Although the Book of the Twelve includes twelve originally discrete prophetic compositions, they are now arranged so that they function as a single composition with a pervasive concern for the city of Jerusalem. Indeed, the differences between the prophets are such that the books of Jeremiah, Ezekiel, and the Twelve frequently cite or allude to Isaiah and express their differences with Isaiah's views. Altogether, the four books of the Latter Prophets each present their respective understandings concerning the significance of the fall of Jerusalem and the projected restoration of Jerusalem, the Temple for both Judah/Israel and the world at large.

Each book of the Latter Prophets therefore addresses the problems of exile and restoration in its own distinctive way.[2] The royalist book of Isaiah envisions a restored Jerusalem/Israel that will serve as a source for divine Torah and be ruled by a foreign monarch in the context of the recognition of YHWH's divine sovereignty throughout the world. The priestly book of Jeremiah envisions the restoration of Israel to Jerusalem following the punishment of the nation according to divine Torah. The Zadokite priestly book of Ezekiel envisions the purification of Jerusalem and the world at large as the process by which a new Temple will be built at the center of Israel and all creation. The multifaceted Book of the Twelve anticipates a period of world conflict in which the nations will recognize YHWH at the Jerusalem Temple after their defeat by YHWH's Davidic monarch. Indeed, each takes up the problem of Israel's exile as articulated in the Former Prophets by envisioning a restoration of Jerusalem/Israel at the center of a new creation. Each engages in debate, both with the tradition and with the prophetic colleagues, concerning the character of the future restoration.

The Latter Prophets therefore play a key role within the three-part structure of the Tanak. The Torah presents Israel arrayed around the Wilderness Tabernacle or Temple as the ideal culmination of creation, and the Ketuvim present the restoration of that ideal in the aftermath of the Babylonian Exile.[3] Insofar as the Tabernacle/Temple serves as the ideal, holy center of creation in the Tanak,[4] its destruction by the Babylonians and the question of its restoration stands as a central concern in both the Former and the Latter Prophets.[5] The Former Prophets (Joshua, Judges, Samuel, and Kings) present a narrative history of Israel's/Judah's existence in the land of Israel, from the time of the conquest under Joshua through the time of the Babylonian exile, that reflects theologically upon this history by attempting to demonstrate that the destruction of the Temple resulted from Israel's failure to abide by G-d's Torah. The Latter Prophets (Isaiah, Jeremiah, Ezekiel, and the Twelve Prophets) likewise attempt to explain the destruction of the Temple as the result of Israel's/Judah's failure to abide by

YHWH's expectations, but it also outlines divine plans to re-establish both the Temple and Israel/Judah at the center of creation once the period of punishment is over. In this regard, the Prophets play the central role in the Tanak, insofar as they provide the link between the ideal portrayal in the Torah of creation with Israel and the Temple at the center and the re-establishment of that ideal in the Writings following its disruption.[6]

NOTES

[1] For introductions to each of the prophetic books that comprise the Latter Prophets, see, in addition to my *The Prophetic Literature* (IBT; Nashville: Abingdon, 2005), Joseph Blenkinsopp, *A History of Prophecy in Israel* (Louisville: Westminster John Knox, 1996); David L. Petersen, *The Prophetic Literature: An Introduction* (Louisville: Westminster John Knox, 2002).

[2] See especially Abraham Joshua Heschel, *The Prophets* (New York: Harper & Row, 1962), who discusses the role of divine pathos in selected prophets as a means to illustrate how they grappled with the problems of evil and potential judgment or exile in their own experience. See also my *Reading the Bible after the Shoah: Engaging Holocaust Theology* (Minneapolis: Fortress Press, 2008).

[3] For discussion of the literary and theological structure of the Tanak and the Christian Old Testament, see my "Tanak versus Old Testament: Concerning the Foundation for a Jewish Theology of the Bible," in *Problems in Biblical Theology: Essays in Honor of Rolf Knierim*, ed. H. T. C. Sun and K. L. Eades (Grand Rapids: Eerdmans, 1997), 353–72.

[4] For discussion of the role of the Temple in creation, see Jon D. Levenson, "The Temple and the World," *JR* 64 (1984): 275–98, and *Sinai and Zion: An Entry into the Jewish Bible* (Minneapolis: Winston, 1985). See also the discussion of world order in Rolf P. Knierim, "Cosmos and History in Israel's Theology," in *The Task of Old Testament Theology: Substance, Method, and Cases* (Grand Rapids: Eerdmans, 1995), 171–224, especially 175–98, who points to the significance of sacred, cosmic space at the center of creation.

[5] For discussion of the significance of the destruction of the Jerusalem Temple in 587 BCE and 70 CE and its relation to contemporary theological discussion of the *Shoah* or Holocaust, see Emil L. Fackenheim, *G-d's Presence in History: Jewish Affirmations and Philosophical Reflections* (New York: Harper Torchbacks, 1972); cf. idem, *The Jewish Bible after the Holocaust: A Rereading* (Bloomington: Indiana University Press, 1990), for general discussion of the question of a post-Shoah reading of the Bible.

[6] Cf. Gerhard von Rad's treatment of the prophets in his acclaimed *Old Testament Theology*, trans. D. M. G. Stalker (2 vols.; New York: Harper & Row, 1962–65). By devoting the entire second volume to the prophets, von Rad pointed to their central theological importance as the culmination of the Old Testament tradition, where they constitute the conclusion of the Old Testament and thus point to the New Testament in the Christian form of the Bible.

B. The Book of Isaiah*

The book of Isaiah is the best known of all the prophetic books of the Tanak. Isaiah generally appears as the first of the Latter Prophets, but there are exceptions insofar as one Talmudic tradition places it as the third book of the Latter Prophets following Jeremiah and Ezekiel (*b. Baba Batra* 14b). Judaism looks to Isaiah as the primary prophet who announced the famous vision of world peace, in which all nations would journey to Mt. Zion to learn YHWH's Torah and to hear YHWH's word, to turn their swords into plowshares and their spears into pruning hooks, and to learn war no more (Isa 2:2-4; cf. Mic 4:1-5). Although Isaiah anticipates punishment, Judaism views Isaiah as a book of comfort (*b. Baba Batra* 14b) because it looks forward to the time when Jews will bring divine Torah to the world at large and exiled Jews will return home to Jerusalem.

Isaiah presents a combination of prophetic oracles and narrative materials concerning the prophet's vision of divine plans for Judah and Jerusalem. The superscription in Isa 1:1 identifies the entire book as the vision of the eighth century prophet, Isaiah ben Amoz, who lived during the reigns of the Judean Kings Uzziah (783–742 BCE), Jotham (742–735 BCE), Ahaz (735–715 BCE), and Hezekiah (717–687/6 BCE). Major historical events during his lifetime included the Syro-Ephraimitic War (735–734 BCE) in which Aram and Israel formed an anti-Assyrian coalition that attacked Judah in an effort to force it into their alliance; the first Assyrian invasions of Aram and Israel (734–732 BCE) by King Tiglath Pileser III, which resulted in the destruction of Damascus, Assyria's annexation of Israel's territory in the Trans-Jordan, the Galilee, and the coastal plain, and Judah's subjugation to Assyria; Israel's revolt against Assyria (724–722/1 BCE), including the destruction of Samaria and the deportation of large numbers of its surviving population by the Assyrian monarchs Shalmaneser V and Sargon II; and finally Sennacherib's invasion of Judah (701 BCE) following Hezekiah's revolt. The book also addresses events beyond the lifetime of the prophet, including the assassination of Sennacherib in 681 BCE; the downfall of the Assyrian empire in the latter half of the seventh century BCE; the Babylonian exile of Jerusalem and Judah in the sixth century BCE; the fall of Babylon to King

Cyrus of Persia in 539 BCE; and the restoration of Jerusalem from the late sixth through the fifth centuries BCE.

Although Isaiah appears to present the work of Isaiah ben Amoz alone, interpreters from the Rabbinic period on contend that the book is the product of other editors and authors as well. The apparent Babylonian-period setting of Isa 40–66 and the explicit references to the sixth-century monarch, Cyrus of Persia, who conquered Babylon in 539 BCE, indicate that these chapters may have been composed near the end of the Babylonian exile or even in the early post-exilic period. Thus *b. Baba Batra* 15a attributes the composition of the book to Hezekiah and his colleagues; Abraham ibn Ezra (d. 1167 CE) raises questions concerning the Babylonian-period setting of the material beginning in Isa 40–66; R. David Kimḥi raises questions concerning the date and character of Isaiah's commissioning narrative in Isa 6 because of its placement within the book and not at the beginning; and Samuel David Luzzato argues that Isa 40–66 were addressed by Isaiah to the Judean exiles but these chapters were not published until after the exile had begun.

Modern scholars generally agree that the book of Isaiah is the product of a long compositional history. The composition of Isaiah began in the time of the Assyrian invasions of Israel and Judah during the latter half of the eighth century BCE. It continued through the period of Josiah's restoration, the end of the Babylonian exile, and the projected restoration of Jerusalem and Judah in the early Persian period during the latter half of the sixth century BCE, and it came to a conclusion in the late fifth century BCE during the times of Nehemiah and Ezra.[1]

The book of Isaiah presents the prophet as a royal counselor who advises the kings and people of Jerusalem and Judah during the crises of the latter half of the eighth century BCE. Isaiah's oracles and actions are based consistently in the royal Davidic or Zion covenant tradition, which maintains that YHWH had chosen Jerusalem/Zion and the house of David as the eternal representative institutions of YHWH's role as sovereign of all creation and that YHWH alone would defend Zion and David from all threats.[2]

The synchronic literary structure of the book of Isaiah is organized to emphasize the royal Davidic/Zion covenant tradition in an effort to present the prophet's oracles in relation to the major events of Jerusalem's and Judah's experience from the late eighth-century Assyrian invasions through the Persian-period restoration of the late sixth through the fifth centuries BCE.[3] Many interpreters argue that the structure of the book includes three basic parts, including Isa 1–39, which presents the eighth-century prophet Isaiah ben Amos, Isa 40–55, which presents the work of the anonymous exilic prophet Second Isaiah, and Isa 56–66, which presents the work of anonymous writers generally designated as Third Isaiah. But such a model is based on a diachronic reconstruction of the book's compositional history, not on its synchronic literary features.[4]

The synchronic literary structure of the book includes two basic parts, Isa 1–33, which projects a scenario of judgment and restoration on the Day of YHWH for

Jerusalem, Israel/Judah, and the nations that will reveal YHWH's sovereignty to the entire world of creation, and Isa 34–66, which presupposes that the judgment of the Day of YHWH against Babylon, Assyria, and the other nations has now taken place and that the time of Jerusalem's restoration is at hand. Isaiah 1–33 begins in Isa 1 with an address to the heavens and earth to witness YHWH's punishment of Israel, Judah, and Jerusalem, and Isa 34–66 begins in Isa 34–35 with an address to the nations to witness YHWH's punishment of the nations and restoration of the exiles to Jerusalem. The narrative concerning the Syro-Ephraimitic War in Isa 7:1—9:6 portrays King Ahaz's lack of trust in YHWH at a time when his nation faces invasion, and Isa 36–39 portrays King Hezekiah's appeal to YHWH at the time of the Assyrian invasion.[5] Isaiah 1–33 looks forward to the reign of a righteous Davidic monarch who will preside over a period of peace and restoration, and Isa 34–66 argues that the reign of Cyrus of Persia points to the realization of YHWH's plans for righteous rule.[6]

This two-part structure for the book is designed to address the problem of evil, that is, it presents its oracles and narratives in order to argue that the tragedies of the Assyrian invasions and the Babylonian exile were not the result of YHWH's failure to protect Jerusalem and the house of David from threats. Rather, these events were the result of YHWH's deliberate plans to reveal divine sovereignty to the entire world. YHWH brought the Assyrians to demonstrate to the people of Israel, Judah, and Jerusalem that YHWH was not simply the deity of a single nation, but the deity of all the nations of the world. When the Assyrians arrogantly claimed that they and not YHWH held power over Jerusalem, they were likewise condemned by YHWH together with the nations of the world. Following the Babylonian exile, the book of Isaiah maintains that YHWH decreed that the time had come for Jews to return to their homeland in Jerusalem, Judah, and Israel, and that the nations of the world would acknowledge YHWH's world-wide sovereignty in bringing the exiled Jews home.

The structure and contents of the book of Isaiah are far more complex. Isaiah 1–33 begins with a prologue in Isa 1 that lays out the basic themes of punishment and restoration for Jerusalem for the entire book. Isaiah 2–33 then lays out Isaiah's instruction concerning YHWH's projected plans for the Day of YHWH that will transform the entire earth. Within these chapters, Isa 2–4 focuses on the judgment and restoration of Jerusalem for its role as the center for YHWH's sovereignty in the world; Isa 5–12 focuses on YHWH's judgment against Israel and the restoration of righteous Davidic rule; Isa 13–27 focuses on YHWH's judgment against the nations and the subsequent gathering of Israel and the nations to Jerusalem in the aftermath of that punishment; and Isa 28–33 focuses specifically on YHWH's plans for Jerusalem and the emergence of the royal figure who will represent YHWH's sovereignty. Isaiah 34–66 begins in Isa 34–35 with the prophet's announcement concerning YHWH's punishment of the nations and the imminent restoration of Jerusalem; Isa 36–39 demonstrates these principles with a narrative that relates Assyria's defeat and Jerusalem's deliverance in the time of Hezekiah; Isa 40–54 draws upon earlier traditions concerning the covenants with Noah, Abraham, David, Jacob's exile and return, Sarah's barrenness and subsequent childbirth, the exodus through the wilderness, the portrayal of Zion as YHWH's bride, and so on, to argue that YHWH is now restoring Jerusalem; and Isa 56–66 presents a series of oracles that calls upon the audience of the book to adhere to YHWH's covenant as Jerusalem is restored. The following outline provides an overview of the synchronic literary organization and message of the book:

The Vision of Isaiah Ben Amoz: Prophetic Exhortation to Jerusalem/Judah to Adhere to YHWH

I. Concerning YHWH's Plans to Reveal Worldwide Sovereignty at Zion — 1:1—33:24
  A. Prologue to the book of Isaiah: Introductory parenesis concerning YHWH's intentions to purify Jerusalem — 1:1-31
  B. Prophetic instruction concerning YHWH's projected plans to reveal worldwide sovereignty at Zion: announcement of the Day of YHWH — 2:1—33:24
    1. prophetic announcement concerning the preparation of Zion for its role as the center for YHWH's worldwide sovereignty — 2:1—4:6
    2. prophetic instruction concerning the significance of Assyrian Judgment against Jacob/Israel: restoration of Davidic rule — 5:1—12:6
    3. prophetic announcement concerning the preparation of the nations for YHWH's worldwide sovereignty — 13:1—27:13
      a. announcements concerning the nations — 13:1—23:18
      b. restoration for Zion/Israel at the center of the nations — 24:1—27:13
    4. prophetic instruction concerning YHWH's plans for Jerusalem: announcement of a royal savior — 28:1—33:24
II. Concerning the Realization of YHWH's Plans for Revealing Worldwide Sovereignty at Zion — 34:1—66:24
  A. Prophetic instruction concerning the realization of YHWH's sovereignty at Zion — 34:1—54:17
    1. prophetic instruction concerning YHWH's power to return redeemed exiles to Zion — 34:1—35:10
    2. royal narratives concerning YHWH's deliverance of Jerusalem and Hezekiah — 36:1—39:8
    3. prophetic instruction that YHWH is maintaining covenant and restoring Zion — 40:1—54:17
      a. renewed prophetic commission to announce YHWH's restoration of Zion — 40:1-11
      b. contention: YHWH is master of creation — 40:12-31
      c. contention: YHWH is master of human events — 41:1—42:13
      d. contention: YHWH is redeemer of Israel — 42:14—44:23
      e. contention: YHWH will use Cyrus for the restoration of Zion — 44:24—48:22
      f. contention: YHWH is restoring Zion — 49:1—54:17

The book of Isaiah has diachronic dimensions as well. In pointing to a period of restoration for the city of Jerusalem and its population, the book presupposes the period of Persian rule in the late sixth and fifth centuries BCE. It posits that a member of the royal house of David no longer sits on the throne in Jerusalem, but that King Cyrus of Persia will first be designated as YHWH's messiah and Temple builder (Isa 44:28; 45:1) and that later YHWH will be recognized as the divine sovereign in Jerusalem (Isa 66:1). Even the oracles concerning the nations in Isa 13–23 presuppose the period of Persian rule, since no oracle against Persia appears in these chapters and all of the nations listed, viz., Babylon, Assyria, Philistia, Moab, Aram, Israel, Ethiopia, Egypt, Babylon again, Dumah, Arabia, Jerusalem, and Tyre, were incorporated into the Persian empire. Indeed, the oracle against Babylon in Isa 21 mentions Elam and Media, elements of the Persian empire, as nations that would bring down Babylon. Insofar as Isaiah points to the restoration of Jerusalem under Persian rule and the restoration of divine Torah in the city and throughout the world, the present form of the book presupposes the fifth- century restoration efforts of Nehemiah and Ezra. Much of the material in Isa 56–66, and perhaps in other sections of the book, would have been composed during the Persian-period restoration of the late sixth through the fifth centuries BCE.

Other stages in the composition of the book are evident. The work of the so-called Second Isaiah, the anonymous prophet of the Babylonian exile, presupposes the events of the latter stages of the Babylonian exile during the years 545–538 BCE when King Cyrus of Persia was advancing against Babylon. The material in Isa 40–55, and perhaps in other sections of the book, such as Isa 2–4; 13–14; 24–27; 34–35; 36–39; and 60–62, also appears to have been composed during this period. Thus, a sixth-century edition of the book, including much of Isa 2–55; 60–62, appeared at the end of the Babylonian exile in an effort to announce that the rise of Cyrus, the collapse of Babylon, and the potential return of Jews to Jerusalem were the fulfillment of the oracles of Isaiah ben Amoz. There are also indications of a late seventh-century edition of the book that supported the program of national restoration and religious reform sponsored by King Josiah ben Amon of Judah (r. 640–609 BCE).[7] Such an edition would look to the collapse of the Assyrian empire and the anticipated restoration of Davidic rule over all Israel during this period as the fulfillment of the oracles of Isaiah ben

Amoz. Isaiah 7; 11–12; 32, and other texts presuppose this period, and would contribute to an edition of the book that comprised Isa 5–12; 14–23; 28–32; 33; and 36–37. Finally, a great deal of material derives from the prophet Isaiah ben Amoz himself, which suggests that an eighth-century form of the book, including materials from Isa 1; 2–3; 5; 6; 8–10; 14–23; and 28–31, appeared during the prophet's lifetime or shortly thereafter. Such an edition would argue that the threat of the Assyrian empire came directly from YHWH, but that Judah would survive the onslaught under the rule of a righteous Davidic monarch.

The full form of the book of Isaiah constitutes a sustained theological reflection on Jerusalem's and Judah's experience from the time of the Assyrian invasions of the eighth century BCE through the Persian-period restoration of the late sixth and fifth centuries. It is not a historical work in the same sense as Kings or Chronicles, but it nevertheless reads and constructs history in keeping with its own theological worldview in a manner analogous to works such as Kings and Chronicles. It attempts to interpret the significance of the disasters suffered by Israel in the Assyrian and Babylonian periods as well as the restoration carried out during the Persian period, and it projects an ideal period of world-wide recognition of YHWH's sovereignty beyond the restoration. The theological worldview of Isaiah is based consistently in the theological traditions of the royal house of David and the Zion tradition that posited an eternal relationship between YHWH and Jerusalem based on the Davidic monarchy and the presence of the Jerusalem Temple. The book therefore employs a royalist model of YHWH as sovereign author of creation as well as the ultimate authority in the human realm. Insofar as Isaiah is rooted in the Davidic Zion tradition, YHWH appears as an idealized Davidic monarch with the full authority to decree the fate—for good or for evil—of all persons and nations in the realm. As an ideal monarch, YHWH also demands loyalty on the part of the divine subjects, here understood first as Israel and Judah, who are tied to YHWH by a special covenant, but YHWH's expectations also extend to the nations at large who are also a part of creation and therefore obligated to recognize YHWH's sovereignty. Not only may Jerusalem, Judah, and the Davidic king be punished for alleged failures to place their trust in YHWH, so also the nations brought to punish Israel and Judah on YHWH's behalf also suffer judgment when they fail to recognize YHWH's sovereignty. The book of Isaiah puts forward a model of human submission to YHWH, on the parts of Israel and Judah as well as the nations of the world, as its ideal model for the divine–human relationship.

The book of Isaiah grapples with the theological problem of evil—expressed through the historical realities of Assyrian invasion and Babylonian exile—by positing that such an experience was necessary for the revelation of YHWH's sovereignty to the entire world. It defends YHWH from charges of powerlessness and absence by claiming that YHWH was not defeated by foreign gods and nations, but that YHWH brought punishment on Israel and Judah as part of the process of divine revelation to Israel, Judah, and the world at large. In this respect, the book of Isaiah takes on a teleological view of theology and ethics, insofar as it is willing to justify the sacrifice of generations of Israelites and Judeans during the Assyrian and Babylonian periods in its efforts ultimately to reveal YHWH's world-wide sovereignty by the end of the book. This is evident especially in Isa 6, in which the prophet is commissioned to ensure that the people are blind, deaf, and lacking in understanding so that they will not repent and be saved from the disaster that YHWH has in mind for them. Isaiah's theological viewpoint is therefore akin to the book of Exodus, which is willing to sacrifice Pharaoh and Egypt for the same purpose by hardening Pharaoh's heart so that the punishment of Egypt and revelation of YHWH to Israel and the nations of the world may take place. Such a contention raises tremendous theological problems, particularly in the aftermath of the Shoah, insofar as it justifies the sacrifice of generations for the greater glory of G-d. Of course modern readers must also understand that Isaiah's model represents one attempt to make sense out of Israel's and Judah's suffering in the world. When placed in dialog with other biblical books, such as Jeremiah, the Twelve Prophets, Lamentations, or Job, such a theological world-view is shown to have its defects. Nevertheless, it represents an early attempt by Judean thinkers to grapple with the problem of evil and to maintain their adherence to G-d even in the aftermath of the overwhelming disasters of the fall of northern Israel, the destruction of Jerusalem and the Temple, the fall of the house of David, and the exile of major portions of the populations of Israel and Judah out of the land of Israel.

One of the major theological issues addressed in the book of Isaiah is the question of the continuity of the house of David through the Babylonian and Persian periods. Although the book is clearly based in the Davidic Zion tradition that posits an eternal covenant with the house of David, it must grapple with the fact that King Jehoiachin ben Jehoiakim was the last legitimate monarch of the house of David to sit on the throne in Jerusalem. His uncle, Zedekiah ben Josiah, was chosen by the Babylonians to serve as monarch following the deportation of Jehoiachin in 597 BCE, and therefore functioned as a Babylonian puppet who was unable to control his population on their behalf. Although Jehoiachin was released from confinement during the reign of Evil Merodach/Amel Merodach, Nebuchadrezzar's successor, he never returned to Jerusalem. Although his grandson, Zerubbabel did return to Jerusalem to play a key role in rebuilding the Temple, he disappears from the scene for unknown reasons. No Davidic monarch has ascended the throne since that time.

When considered diachronically, oracles in Isa 9; 11; and 32 affirm Isaiah ben Amoz's support for righteous Davidic monarchs, but when the book is read synchronically, a different model emerges. Isaiah's affirmation of Hezekiah at the time of the Assyrian siege of Jerusalem in Isa 36–37/38 is followed by Isaiah's condemnation of Hezekiah for his alliance with the Babylonians in Isa 39. The projection of the Babylonian exile of Hezekiah's sons in that passage prepares the reader for the work of Deutero- and Trito-Isaiah in Isa 40–55 and 56–66, which presuppose the Babylonian exile and Persian-period restoration when no Davidic monarch ever returns to the throne in Jerusalem. Second Isaiah's assertion in Isa 44:28; 45:1 that King Cyrus of Persia is YHWH's chosen monarch and Temple builder overturns the Davidic tradition by positing that a foreign monarch, not a Davidic monarch, is YHWH's chosen king. The problem is addressed in Isa 55, which posits that YHWH's eternal covenant with David is applied to the people of Israel at large. It is further addressed in Isa 56–66, which posits that YHWH is the true monarch, which of course is in keeping with traditional Davidic ideology that portrayed YHWH as the true monarch behind the Davidic throne. By splicing the tradition in this fashion, the book of Isaiah upholds the continuity of the Davidic tradition in principle while accounting for the realities of history in which no Davidic monarch was ever restored to the throne. Throughout the book, YHWH identifies with the nations that come to punish or restore Israel and Judah, most particularly the Persian Empire which subdued every one of the nations, beginning with Babylon, included in Isaiah's oracles concerning the nations in Isa 13–23. But Isaiah ultimately argues that all of the nations, including Persia, will recognize YHWH's sovereignty in Jerusalem and submit to YHWH's authority.

The book of Isaiah is especially concerned throughout with the fate of Jerusalem in the midst of creation. Like David, YHWH had also chosen Jerusalem as the site for the Temple, which functions as the holy center of creation in Judean thought. One of the major theological problems of the book is the destruction of Jerusalem and the Temple of Solomon insofar as both shared in YHWH's promise of eternal protection. The ideals of Jerusalem are clear at the outset of the book in Isa 2:2-4, viz., Jerusalem is the site where all the nations of the world will come to recognize YHWH and to learn YHWH's Torah as part of the larger effort to bring peace and stability to the world under YHWH's sovereignty. Indeed, the portrayal of Jerusalem as the locus for YHWH's world-wide sovereignty and the source of YHWH's Torah to the world draws upon the role of the Jerusalem Temple, analogous to that of Mt. Sinai in Exod 19—Num 10, as the source for YHWH's revelation to Israel/Judah and the word at large.[8] Likewise, Jerusalem or Bat Zion, Daughter Zion, is the bride of YHWH abandoned by her husband who is now to be restored to her former status as her husband and children return to her in Isa 54. The theme of the return to Jerusalem permeates the book in Isa 8:23—9:6; 11:11-16; 24–27; 35; 40:1-11; 49–54; 60–62; and culminating in Isa 66 makes this point clear by portraying the nations of the world returning exiled Jews to Jerusalem. It is striking, however, that the book of Isaiah never actually portrays a ruined or destroyed Jerusalem. From the book's standpoint, Jerusalem is always the holy city bound to YHWH and will serve not only as the holy center of creation, but as the locus from which YHWH exercises world-wide sovereignty as well.

Each of these theological concerns appears throughout the major components of the book of Isaiah.[9]

Isaiah 1

The prologue for the book in Isa 1 functions both as an introduction to the first part of the book in Isa 1–33 and to the book as a whole.[10] It begins with the superscription in Isa 1:1, which identifies the contents of the book as the vision of Isaiah ben Amoz. The superscription also identifies Judah and Jerusalem as the subjects of the vision and the purported historical setting of the prophet's visions during the reigns of the Judean kings, Uzziah (783–742 BCE), Jotham (742–735 BCE), Ahaz (735–715 BCE), and Hezekiah (715–687/6 BCE). The address in Isa 1:2-31 lays out the basic themes that appear throughout the rest of the book, that is, Jerusalem's punishment and restoration, in the form of a trial speech that includes elements of accusation (vv. 2-20) and an announcement of Jerusalem's restoration once the punishment is complete (vv. 21-31). The passage appeals to the audience to do justice by observing YHWH's Torah and to abandon past practices of wrongdoing and idolatry.

Isaiah 2–4

Isaiah 2–4 announces YHWH's plans to reveal worldwide sovereignty. Isaiah 2–4 is concerned specifically with the preparation of Jerusalem for this role.[11] As the site of YHWH's holy Temple, Jerusalem/Zion naturally stands at the center of all creation where YHWH will reveal divine Torah to the world at large.

Isaiah 2–4 begins with its own superscription in Isa 2:1, which again identifies the following material according to its genre or literary type as a prophetic word attributed to Isaiah ben Amoz and its concern with Judah and Jerusalem.

The initial oracle depicts the pilgrimage of the nations to Zion so that they might learn YHWH's Torah, which will in turn lead to the abandonment of war.[12] This oracle serves as the basic premise for the three prophetic addresses that follow in Isa 2:5—4:6, addresses which explain the process of Jerusalem's cleansing on the Day of YHWH by which this idyllic scenario will be achieved.

The first address in Isa 2:5-9 takes up the need for Jerusalem's cleansing so that it might serve in this role. The passage begins with an address to Jacob or Israel in v. 5, inviting Jacob to join the procession of the nations to walk in the light of YHWH. Verses 6-9, however, explain that Jacob is unfit for such a role, insofar as the house of Jacob has forsaken YHWH by aligning itself with foreign powers bent on war and idolatry.

Isaiah 2:10-21 takes up the process of cleansing by announcing the Day of YHWH. The Day of YHWH is rooted in the liturgy of the Jerusalem Temple where it expresses YHWH's efforts to defeat enemies and to manifest divine glory. Although it is frequently employed against foreign enemies who threaten Jerusalem, it may also be employed against the people of Israel or Jerusalem when

YHWH's holiness is compromised. Here it is directed against those who purportedly exalt themselves by relying on their power rather than upon YHWH.
This is a classic expression of the Zion tradition which maintains that YHWH
alone will protect Jerusalem.

Isaiah 2:22—4:6 provides an extended discussion of the process by which
Jerusalem and Judah will be cleansed in preparation for its role as the center for
YHWH's worldwide sovereignty. Following the prophet's plea in Isa 2:22 to
desist from self-reliance, a prophetic judgment speech in Isa 3:1—4:1 respectively
threatens both the men and the women of Jerusalem with punishments for
wrongdoing. The passage concludes in Isa 4:2-6 with a portrayal of the purified
Jerusalem in which the surviving remnant of the people will once again be
gathered around the Temple.

Isaiah 5–12

Isaiah 5–12 takes up YHWH's plans to reveal worldwide sovereignty in Isa 2–33.[13]
This sub-unit is specifically concerned with the significance of Assyrian judgment
against Jacob/Israel and the threat posed by Assyria to Judah and Jerusalem
during the Syro-Ephraimitic War. Although Israel will suffer punishment in the
scenario laid out in these chapters, it projects that Israel will ultimately return to
righteous Davidic rule after the Assyrian king is brought down for his arrogance.

Isaiah 5–12 lacks its own superscription, but the shift in concern from
Jerusalem and Judah to northern Israel and Judah is clear from the first oracle in
Isa 5:1-7, and it continues through the portrayal of the righteous Davidic monarch in Isa 11:1-16 who will reunite Israel and Judah. The block includes a
mixture of prophetic oracles, autobiographical and third person narrative, and
liturgical poetry. It is organized to proclaim a prophetic announcement of
judgment against Israel and Judah in Isa 5 and to explain the significance and
results of that judgment in the establishment of righteous Davidic rule as a result
of that judgment in Isa 6–12.

The initial sub-unit in Isa 5:1-30 employs a combination of oracle types to
announce YHWH's intentions to bring a foreign nation in judgment against
Israel and Judah. The chapter begins in Isa 5:1-7 with an allegorical song that
portrays the care given by a friend of the prophet to a vineyard in the hopes that it
would produce good grapes. But when the time came to harvest the fruit of the
vineyard, it had only produced sour grapes. It is only when the prophet asks his
audience what the friend should do about his failed vineyard that the meaning
of the allegory becomes clear, that is, the friend is YHWH, the vineyard is Israel,
and the vines are Judah.

A series of woe oracles in Isa 5:8-24 illustrates the basis for the prophet's
condemnation of Israel. He charges the leadership of Israel with abuse, insofar

as they take people's homes and land, drink and feast all day on the proceeds of extortion, and deny that YHWH would bother to do anything about it. Ultimately, the prophet contends that the people have rejected YHWH's Torah. The passage concludes in Isa 5:25-30 with the prophet's depiction of YHWH raising a hand to call for a nation from far away to bring punishment against Israel.

The following in Isa 6–12 elaborates upon the expected judgment against Israel and Judah. The narratives in Isa 6:1—8:15 recount the prophet's understanding of the reasons for the punishment, whereas Isa 8:16—12:6 presents the prophet's announcements concerning the impending fall of the Assyrian king and the rise of a new righteous Davidic king.

Isaiah 6:1—8:15 provides an explanation for YHWH's decision to bring punishment on Israel and Judah. These narratives contrast Ahaz's refusal to place trust in Isaiah's promises of YHWH's protection at a time of threat with Hezekiah's appeal to YHWH for protection in a very similar situation of threat in Isa 36–39. The pointed contrast between the two kings is an important link that binds together the two major halves of the book of Isaiah.

Isaiah 6:1—8:15 contains two narrative sub-units that explain the reasons for YHWH's judgment. Isaiah's autobiographical vision in Isa 6:1-13 raises issues of tremendous theological importance.[14] The vision of YHWH enthroned and surrounded by a court of winged, fiery angelic creatures (*sĕrāp*, derived from a Hebrew verb that means, "to burn") presents YHWH as a holy, divine monarch. Such a vision presupposes the imagery of the Holy of Holies in the Jerusalem Temple and the Ark of the Covenant that symbolizes YHWH's throne on earth (1 Sam 4:4; 6:2; Isa 37:16; 66:1; Pss 80:2; 99:1). Indeed, Solomon's three-room Temple employs the same basic structure as a royal palace with its throne room in the Holy of Holies.[15] The fiery Seraphs and the smoke that fills the Temple recall the imagery of the Temple *mĕnōrôt* (lamp stands) and incense altars employed during festival worship. The call, "Holy, holy, holy is the L-rd of Hosts; the whole earth is full of his glory," is an expression of YHWH's holy nature as divine monarch that appears as the Kedushah in Jewish liturgy. Isaiah's lips are purified in a manner similar to the mouth purification rituals of ancient Near Eastern oracle diviners,[16] which enables Isaiah to respond to YHWH's call.

The prophet's commission, however, is very disturbing.[17] His task is to make sure that the people do not understand the judgment that will overtake them lest they repent and be saved from that judgment. As the narrative concludes, the imagery of the burning stump makes it clear that YHWH intends to destroy some 90 percent of the people until only a remnant remains. By maintaining that the disaster was part of a divine plan, the prophet contends that YHWH is indeed sovereign over the world.

The narratives in Isa 7:1—8:15 present an account of Isaiah's actions in the Syro-Ephraimitic War when Aram and Israel attacked Judah in an effort to force it into the anti-Assyrian alliance.[18] The narrative portrays King Ahaz's refusal to trust in YHWH's promises of protection. It portrays Isaiah's encounter with Ahaz while the king was inspecting Jerusalem's water system, a crucial element in the defenses of an ancient city expecting a siege, at the end of the conduit of the upper pool on the highway to the fullers' (that is, washers') field. Isaiah's symbolically named son, Shear Yashuv, "a remnant will return," expresses Isaiah's belief that many Judeans would die in the attack, but that YHWH would protect the city. When Ahaz balked at accepting Isaiah's assurances, Isaiah announced a sign in the birth of Immanuel, "G-d is with us," whose name indicates that YHWH would be with Judah to punish it for Ahaz's refusal to accept Isaiah's assurances. It is striking that while Ahaz's refusal to test YHWH is actually a very pious act, his failure to do so nevertheless results in an Assyrian invasion of the region that subjugates Judah as well as Israel.

The command by Isaiah in Isa 8:16 to bind up the testimony and seal the teaching among his disciples marks the beginning of his announcements concerning the downfall of Assyria and the rise of a righteous Davidic king in Isa 8:16—12:6. The first portion of the prophet's announcements in Isa 8:16—9:6 envision a long period of darkness and distress prior to the emergence of a righteous Davidic king who would preside over a period of peace, justice, and righteousness. Interpreters generally maintain that the prophet's oracle points to the birth of King Hezekiah, but the anonymity of the oracle has enabled it to be read in later times as a reference to royal or messianic figures, such as Josiah, Cyrus, Zerubbabel, Jesus, Simon Bar Kochba, and so on. The prophet's statements are very important for understanding the formation of the book, particularly since his decision to wait for YHWH, "who is hiding his face from the house of Jacob," points to the portrayal of future action by YHWH in the book that ultimately would be revealed in the Babylonian exile and the Persian-period restoration of Jerusalem.

The second portion of the prophet's announcements in Isa 9:7—12:6 presents a far more detailed scenario of judgment and restoration. Isaiah 9:7—10:4 begins with a series of oracles that expresses YHWH's judgment against the northern kingdom of Israel. It continues in Isa 10:5—12:6 with a portrayal of the arrogance of the Assyrian king, who maintained that his own power enabled him to threaten Jerusalem. Isaiah's oracles maintain that YHWH would bring down the Assyrian king just as one would chop down the branches of an olive tree at harvest time. This in turn would allow for a new shoot to grow from the stump of Jesse to produce a new Davidic monarch who would reunite Israel and Judah, defeat the nations that oppress them, and return the exiles from Assyria just as YHWH had returned the slaves from Egypt in an earlier time. Indeed, the concluding hymn in Isa 12:1-6 even cites statements from the Song of the Sea in Exod 15 (cf. Isa 12:2b, 5a with Exod 15:1b; see also Pss 105:1; 118:14).

Isaiah 13–27

Isaiah 13–27 announces YHWH's plans to reveal worldwide sovereignty. The sub-unit builds upon the earlier concerns with Jerusalem and Judah in Isa 2–4 and Israel and Judah in Isa 5–12 by focusing specifically on the role of the nations in YHWH's plans. Isaiah 13:1 is the first in a series of superscriptions throughout chs. 13–23 that are formulated similarly as "the oracle (Hebrew, *māśśā'*) concerning . . ." to introduce each of the oracles concerning the nations that appear in this sub-unit. Isaiah 24–27 are linked to chapters 13–23 by their common concern with the role of the nations in the world following the period of judgment when YHWH reveals divine sovereignty at Zion.

The literary structure for this text is relatively simple. The oracles concerning the nations in chapters 13–23 constitute the first portion of this text. Each oracle begins with the characteristic superscription, "the oracle (*māśśā'*) of . . ." identified above, and it continues with a prophetic oracle that discusses YHWH's judgment against the nation in question. Chapters 13–23 therefore present a succession of nations, including Babylon (with comments concerning Assyria and Philistia as well) in Isa 13:1—14:32; Moab in Isa 15:1—16:13; Damascus (with comments concerning northern Israel, since both Aram and Israel formed the Syro-Ephraimitic coalition, and the recognition of YHWH by all the nations of the earth beyond even Ethiopia) in Isa 17:1—18:7; Egypt in Isa 19:1—20:6; Babylon (identified as the wilderness of the sea, a designation for the southern part of Babylonia ruled by Merodach-baladan in the late eighth century) in Isa 21:1-10; Dumah, an oasis located in the Arabian desert between Babylonia and Aram, in Isa 21:11-12; the desert plain, a designation for the Arabian desert, in Isa 21:13-17; the valley of vision, a designation for Jerusalem, in Isa 22:1-25; and Tyre in Isa 23:1-18.

A cursory scan of the nations named herein indicates that it is a very selective list. Major nations, such as Persia, are missing, and even more familiar smaller countries, such as Edom and Ammon, are also absent. All of the nations found within these chapters once formed part of the Persian Empire in the fifth century BCE, and the oracle concerning Babylon in Isa 21:1-10 names Elam and Media, two regions of the Persian Empire, as nations that led the assault against the Babylonians.

Isaiah 24–27 is sometimes identified as "the Apocalypse of Isaiah" because it purportedly takes up the eschatological judgment and restoration of the world. Nevertheless, the passage does not portray the end of time. Prophetic literature is filled with mythological language concerning cosmic disruption that signals YHWH's judgment against Israel, Judah, or the nations within the framework of historical events (for example, Hos 4; Zeph 1; Jer 4–6, respectively). Isaiah 24–27 looks forward to the nations' recognition of YHWH at Jerusalem, which in fact took place under Persian rule when the Persian Achaemenid dynasty enabled figures such as Nehemiah and Ezra to govern Judah under Jewish law.

Isaiah 28–33

Isaiah 28–33 builds upon the previous material by returning to a concern with Jerusalem culminating in the announcement of a just and righteous royal monarch. Isaiah 28–33 is identified as a discrete textual block by its sequence of introductory "woe" oracles (Hebrew, *hôy*, "woe!") which appear at the head of each sub-unit in Isa 28:1; 29:1; 30:1; and 31:1. The concluding unit differs, however, insofar as an introductory *hēn* ("behold!") appears in place of the expected *hôy* to signal the announcement of the righteous king. The *hôy* in Isa 33:1 marks the prophet's announcement of the downfall of "the destroyer," that is, Assyria or later Babylon, as the righteous king assumes his rule. Such a concern indicates that chapters 32 and 33 together form the concluding sub-unit of Isa 28–33. The result is a logical sequence of texts that outlines YHWH's plans for the announcement of a royal savior in Jerusalem.

Isaiah 28 begins the sequence with a presentation of the prophet's instruction concerning YHWH's purpose in bringing Assyrian hegemony over Israel and Judah. The prophet announces that YHWH will assume leadership of the people (vv. 1-4) when the leaders of both Israel (vv. 7-13) and Judah (vv. 14-22) are removed. The passage concludes in vv. 23-29 with the prophet's allegory of the farmer, which illustrates that just as a farmer must plow land and crush grain to produce food, so YHWH must bring punishment to produce the desired result.

Isaiah 29 follows with the prophet's instruction concerning YHWH's purposes in bringing about an assault against Ariel or Mt. Zion. Two "woe" oracles identify YHWH as the cause of the assault against Ariel together with YHWH's plans to overthrow Jerusalem's oppressors once the punishment is complete. The statements that the deaf and the blind will hear and understand the words of the prophet's scroll take up motifs from other parts of the book, such as the prophet's commission to ensure that the people remain blind and deaf in Isa 6, his decision to bind up the scroll during a time of darkness in Isa 8:16—9:6, and the announcements of the second part of the book, for example, Isa 35:5; 42:18; 43:8, that the blind and deaf will understand YHWH's purposes.[19]

Isaiah 30 explains YHWH's delay in delivering the people from Assyria by expressing YHWH's dissatisfaction with plans to send embassies to Egypt rather than to rely solely on YHWH's protection (cf. Isa 7). The delay in deliverance has tremendous importance for understanding why the book projects deliverance following the Babylonian exile rather than after the downfall of Assyria. The concluding theophanic announcement concerning the fall of Assyria is associated with the fall of Babylon elsewhere in the book (see Isa 13:1—14:23 and 14:24-27; see also Isa 52:3-6).

Isaiah 31 compares YHWH to a lion, the symbol of Judah, who stands watch over prey. The metaphor conveys once again the prophet's view that YHWH will first punish the people before restoring them.

The climactic passage of this textual unit—and indeed of the first half of the book—appears in Isa 32–33, which presents the prophet's instruction concerning the rise of a royal savior together with the downfall of the oppressor of the people. The oppressor is never identified, but the book as a whole makes it clear that it is first Assyria and then Babylon.

Isaiah 34–66

Isaiah 34–66 constitutes the second half of the book of Isaiah. These chapters are fundamentally concerned with the revelation of YHWH's plans for worldwide sovereignty at Zion. They presuppose that YHWH's punishment of Israel and the nations, particularly Babylon, is complete, and that the time for Jerusalem's restoration at the center of the nations is at hand.[20]

Isaiah 34–35

Isaiah 34–35 functions as the introduction to the second half of the book. These chapters display some important parallels with Isa 1 that point to their introductory role in relation to Isa 34–66. Parallels include the calls to attention in Isa 34:1 and 1:2; the focus on YHWH's vengeance in Isa 34:8 and 1:24; the unquenchable burning of Edom in Isa 34:10 and of YHWH's enemies in 1:31; the mouth of YHWH that speaks in Isa 34:16 and 1:20; YHWH's sword of punishment in Isa 34:5, 6 and 1:20; the sacrificial blood and fat of cattle in Isa 34:6-7 and 1:11-15; the references to Sodom and Gomorrah in Isa 34:9-10 and 1:7-9, 10; and the references to wilting leaves in Isa 34:4 and 1:30. Whereas Isa 1 focuses on the punishment of Israel and the removal of the wicked as the prelude for restoration, Isa 34–35 focuses on the punishment of the nations, especially Edom, as the prelude for the restoration of Zion. Isaiah 34–35 employs the Day of YHWH motif to portray Edom's downfall, much as it portrayed the downfall of the arrogant in Isa 2 and Babylon in Isa 13, as well as the rejoicing of the people as they return to Zion in a new Exodus.

Isaiah 36–39

Isaiah 36–39 constitutes the second element of the prophetic instruction concerning the realization of YHWH's sovereignty in Zion in Isa 34–54. Many interpreters consider these chapters as the conclusion to the First Isaiah tradition in Isa 1–39 because they present narrative accounts of Isaiah's interactions with King Hezekiah in relation to the Assyrian invasion of Judah in 701 BCE. Nevertheless, more recent interpretation points to the contrast in the portrayal of

Hezekiah with that of King Ahaz (see Isa 7:1—9:6) in similar times of crisis.[21] Whereas Ahaz refused Isaiah's advice to rely solely on YHWH for the protection of Jerusalem at the time of the Syro-Ephraimitic invasion, Hezekiah turned to YHWH at the time of Sennacherib's invasion. Whereas Judah suffered subjugation to Assyria as a result of Ahaz's actions, the Assyrian army was defeated and driven from the land as a result of Hezekiah's piety. The parallels and contrasts in these narratives point to their roles in relation to the two halves of the book of Isaiah, that is, whereas the Ahaz narratives illustrate the basis for YHWH's punishment of Jerusalem and Judah, the Hezekiah narratives illustrate the basis for YHWH's restoration of Jerusalem at the center of creation.

A second narrative in Isa 38 portrays Isaiah's healing of Hezekiah following the king's prayer to YHWH. A third narrative in Isa 39 points to the Babylonian exile by portraying Isaiah's condemnation of Hezekiah for receiving a Babylonian delegation as he prepared for revolt against Assyria. Although Isaiah claims that some of Hezekiah's sons would be taken to Babylon, the Babylonian exile is the precursor for the return to Zion in the book of Isaiah.

Isaiah 40–55

Most modern interpreters treat Isa 40–55 (or 40–66) as an entirely separate unit from the preceding material in Isa 1–39 based upon the identification of an anonymous prophetic writer from the sixth century as the author of the work.[22] Although such a diachronic conclusion is undoubtedly correct, it has unduly influenced the synchronic literary reading of this material. Isaiah 40–54/66 is designed to be read as a larger literary unit within the book of Isaiah. It is presented to the reader as part of the vision of Isaiah ben Amoz concerning the realization in the early Persian period of earlier prophecies of restoration from the Assyrian period. It is designed to convince its readers that YHWH is acting to restore Zion. These chapters are organized to make a progressive series of arguments—that YHWH is creator, that YHWH is master of human events, that YHWH is redeemer of Israel, and that YHWH has appointed Cyrus as king—in order to demonstrate the primary contention that YHWH is acting to restore Zion. Each sub-unit within this text is identified by a combination of formal and thematic factors, and each has a place in the argumentative structure of the whole.

Isaiah 40:1-11

Isaiah 40:1-11 introduces Isa 40–54 by reiterating the prophetic commission to announce YHWH's restoration of Zion. The prophet begins by announcing YHWH's message of comfort to Jerusalem that her term of punishment is over and that the time for restoration is at hand. A variety of voices speak, perhaps from YHWH's heavenly council (cf. Isa 6; 1 Kgs 22:19-23; Ps 82, respectively), to call for the preparation of a new highway in the wilderness to lead the people home. An important element of this section is the assertion that "the word of our G-d will stand forever" (v. 8), which in the context of Isaiah indicates that the prophet's earlier prophecies of restoration are now coming to fruition. The passage concludes in vv. 9-11 with a commission to *mebaṣṣeret Ṣion*, "the herald of good tidings to Zion," to proclaim YHWH's act of restoration.

Isaiah 40:12-31

Isaiah 40:12-31 asserts that YHWH is the master of all creation and therefore is quite capable of redeeming Jacob/Israel. The text begins with a series of rhetorical questions in vv. 12-20 that asserts that only YHWH could have set the world in order and established justice in it. A second set of rhetorical questions in vv. 21-26 carries the argument further by asserting that the audience for this text, that is, the people of Israel, should know that this is the case from tradition. Indeed, this assertion is key to understanding the argument, particularly since the prophet draws on past traditions, Noah's and Abraham's covenant, the birth of a son to the barren Sarah and Rachel, Jacob's exile and return, the exodus, the wilderness, and so on, to make the point that YHWH is acting once again. The concluding section in vv. 27-31 employs rhetorical questions once again to assert that YHWH is the everlasting creator of the earth who does not grow weary and whose understanding is unsearchable.

Isaiah 41:1—42:13

Isaiah 41:1—42:13 presents the next stage in the sequence of argumentation with an assertion that YHWH is the master of human events who is therefore able to redeem Jacob. This particular sub-unit employs the rhetorical devices of speech before a court of law to make its case. The passage begins in Isa 41:1-4 with YHWH's court speech, which again employs rhetorical questions to make its points, that is, YHWH has brought a victor from the east to subdue nations (Cyrus), and YHWH is the first and the last. YHWH then addresses Israel/Jacob in vv. 5-20 to assert that Israel is YHWH's servant and that YHWH will continue to be Israel's G-d. These contentions draw upon the traditions of YHWH's covenant with Abraham (v. 8) and YHWH's provision of water in the wilderness (vv. 17-20). YHWH addresses the court once again in Isa 41:21—42:4 with appeals to past traditions and demands that the other gods of the nations prove their power by demonstrating their ability to tell the former things and the things to come. In the context of the book of Isaiah, such traditions include the oracles of Isaiah ben Amoz. When the gods are unable to provide proof, YHWH addresses the servant in Isa 42:5-9 to assert that the servant (Israel) will serve as a covenant people and light to the nations, and thereby open their eyes to YHWH's role in planning and carrying out the restoration of Jacob. A hymn of praise for YHWH concludes the segment in Isa 42:10-13.

Isaiah 42:14—43:7

Isaiah 42:14—44:23 contends that YHWH is the redeemer of Israel. The first part of this sub-unit in Isa 42:14—43:7 employs a combination of motifs from the wilderness traditions and Isaiah's characterization of Israel as blind and deaf to provide an overview of YHWH's actions, that is, YHWH brought punishment on Israel for failing to observe YHWH's Torah, and YHWH will restore Israel now that the punishment is complete. Isaiah 43:8—44:22 then shifts back to the language of the courtroom to assert YHWH's role as redeemer of Israel. Again, the speech draws upon the traditions of the exodus and wilderness to assert that YHWH will lead a new Exodus from Babylon through the sea and the wilderness. An important component of this section is the contention that the idols are powerless to answer YHWH and the call to look to tradition to see that YHWH acts on behalf of Israel. Once again, the sub-unit concludes in Isa 44:23 with a hymn that extols YHWH's redemption of Jacob/Israel.

Isaiah 44:24—48:22

Isaiah 44:24—48:22 makes the extraordinary assertion that YHWH will employ King Cyrus of Persia for the restoration of Israel. Such an assertion is particularly innovative insofar as it posits that YHWH's agent will be a foreign monarch rather than the expected Davidic king. The assertions in Isa 44:24—45:8 draw upon the imagery of the Babylonian *akitu* or New Year festival in which Cyrus was proclaimed king of Babylon in 539 BCE. A series of trial speeches follows in Isa 45:9—48:19. Isaiah 45:9-25 contends that no one can challenge YHWH's role as creator and redeemer of Israel. Isaiah 46–47 present evidence for this contention by portraying the bowing and stooping of the Babylonian gods, Bel and Nebo, and the humiliation of Babylon now sitting in the dirt. Isaiah 48:1-19 rehearses the earlier arguments of YHWH's knowledge and power to assert that the time of Jacob's redemption has come. The concluding hymn in Isa 48:20-21(22) calls upon Jacob to flee from Babylonian captivity into the wilderness where YHWH will again provide water, as in the exodus from Egypt (cf. Exod 17:1-7; Num 20).

Isaiah 49–54

The climactic sub-unit of the sequence of argumentation in Isa 40–54 appears in Isa 49:1—54:17, in which the prophet contends that YHWH is restoring Zion. It draws extensively on past tradition in its efforts to reformulate the classical Zion tradition. It focuses especially on the enigmatic servant figure, and it calls for the restoration of Bat Zion, "Daughter Zion," at the center of creation without a simultaneous restoration of the Davidic monarchy.[23]

Isaiah 49:1-13 announces the role of the servant, here identified as Israel. The servant speaks in vv. 1-6 and employs imagery from Jeremiah's call narrative (Jer 1) to announce his own call by YHWH while still in the womb. YHWH's speech in vv. 7-12 reaffirms the choice of the servant and the servant's role as "a covenant people" (Hebrew, bĕrît 'ām). A concluding hymn in v. 13 calls for creation to rejoice at YHWH's comforting of the people.

Although the hymn in Isa 49:13 would normally mark the conclusion of a unit, Isa 49:14—52:12 is clearly joined to Isa 49:1-13 by its introductory conjunctive statement, "But/and Zion said, 'YHWH has forsaken me. . . .'" Such a bond indicates that Isa 49:14—52:12 is designed to elaborate on the significance of the preceding text. In this case, Isa 49:14—52:12 elaborates upon the significance of the servant's role by pointing specifically to YHWH's restoration of Zion. The three components of this text make a series of points to demonstrate this contention. Isaiah 49:14-26 employs the metaphors of mother–child and marriage relationships to argue that YHWH has not forsaken Zion. Isaiah 50:1-11 returns again to the language and rhetorical questions of the court room to assert that YHWH has not divorced Zion. Isaiah 51:1—52:12 calls upon the people to look to the traditions of Abraham and Sarah, the Garden of Eden, the slaying of the dragon Rahab, the crossing of the Red Sea, and so on, to assert YHWH's capacity to restore Zion and her children. Again, YHWH personifies Zion as a bride, and calls upon her to awaken and to see the messenger who proclaims "peace" to Zion and announces to her that "Your G-d reigns." This segment concludes with a renewed call to depart from captivity and to begin the journey to return to Jerusalem.

Isaiah 52:13—53:12 portrays the suffering servant. Although interpreters continue to debate the identity of the servant,[24] the appearance of this section immediately following the announcement of YHWH's restoration of Zion in Isa 49:14—52:12 suggests that the servant should be identified as Israel (cf. Isa 49:4, 6). The portrayal of the servant draws on the image of sacrifice, particularly in Isa 53:10-12, insofar as sacrifice is made in part to play a role in the expiation of sin. In the context of Isaiah, the portrayal of the suffering servant functions as one means to address the problem of evil or exile by asserting that it was divinely ordained. The dangers of such a theology become apparent when it is used to justify the killing of Jews (or other groups) as an act of divine will.

The hymnic portrayal of Zion's restoration in Isa 54 concludes Isa 49–54. The unit draws upon traditional portrayals of Zion or Israel as the bride of YHWH (see Zeph 3:14-20; cf. Jer 2; Hos 1–3; Ezek 16) and the traditions of the barren ancestral wife (for example, Sarah, Rachel) to portray Zion's restoration.[25] The passage draws upon the tradition of YHWH's hidden face in Isa 8:16—9:6 in which Isaiah ben Amoz announces that YHWH will hide the divine face from Israel and that Isaiah's children will serve as signs and portents until YHWH acts to restore Israel with righteous (Davidic) kingship. YHWH's assertions of everlasting love and covenant for Zion also draw upon the tradition of YHWH's eternal covenant with Noah (Gen 9:1-17).

Isaiah 55–66

The last major sub-unit of Isa 34–66—and indeed of the book as a whole—appears in Isa 55–66, which constitutes the prophet's exhortation to adhere to YHWH's covenant. Although most modern scholars correctly maintain that Isa 55 was composed to function as the conclusion to the work of the anonymous sixth-century prophet, Second Isaiah, synchronic literary analysis of the book indicates that this chapter functions as an introduction to Isa 56–66. Isaiah 55 is set off from the preceding material by an introductory *hôy* ("woe!" or "Ho!") that calls the reader's attention to the following material. Isaiah 55 asks the reader to come, listen, and seek YHWH, who is making an eternal covenant with them. Insofar as Isa 56–66 is designed to define YHWH's expectations of the people within the context of such a covenant in the restored Jerusalem, Isa 55 signals a new concern with adherence to YHWH's covenant.

Isaiah 55

Isaiah 55 functions as the basic exhortation to adhere to YHWH's covenant in Isa 56–66. It does not spell out what such adherence entails—that is left to Isa 56–66—but it employs a combination of imperative addresses and rhetorical questions to invite the audience to accept YHWH's covenant. Once again there is a reformulation of the Davidic or Zion tradition in this passage insofar as it refers to YHWH's eternal covenant with the people with Davidic language even though no Davidic monarch is envisioned.[26] Essentially, the eternal covenant applied by earlier tradition to the house of David (see 2 Sam 7; Pss 89; 110; 132) is now applied to the people of Israel at large. The passage reiterates the continuity of YHWH's word, which will accomplish what YHWH purposes (v. 11).

Isaiah 56–66

The major component of this unit then follows in Isa 56–66. The chapters have generally been identified as the work of Trito-Isaiah from the late sixth or fifth centuries BCE.[27] When read synchronically, Isa 56–66 emerges as a literary unit that is fundamentally concerned with defining the expectations of the restored people in Jerusalem. These chapters presuppose that a restoration of the people to Jerusalem is imminent, but that it has not yet been fully accomplished. They presuppose that opponents of YHWH's will remain among the people, and that the restoration will take place as those opponents are removed from the people or convinced to join in observing YHWH's will. The presentation of consequences for the wicked together with restoration for the righteous constitutes a very powerful theme within these chapters, one which plays an important role in attempting to persuade the readers of Isaiah to count themselves among the righteous by observing YHWH's expectations. A combination of formal and thematic criteria indicates that Isa 56–66 comprises three major components: Isa 56–59; 60–62; and 63–66.

Isaiah 56–59

Isaiah 56–59 is fundamentally concerned with the proper observance of YHWH's covenant and YHWH's willingness to forgive those who repent. An oracle in Isa 56:1-8 calls upon the people to observe justice and righteousness, the Shabbat, and Temple worship, including both sacrifices and prayer, as the basic elements of YHWH's covenant. The oracle also calls for the acceptance of eunuchs and foreigners who observe YHWH's covenant. Many Jews who were compelled to serve as officers in the Babylonian government were made into eunuchs as an expression of their subservient status and many were also born of intermarriages between Jews and foreigners. Although such persons might not have been accepted in the Temple in the past (cf. Deut 23:1-8), the realities of life in the Babylonian exile called for change. The reference to "a monument and a name" (Hebrew, *yād vāšēm*) indicates that the eunuchs would have a future as part of the people. The expression is today employed as the name of modern Israel's museum for the Shoah/Holocaust. Interpreters often overlook the fact that this passage speaks of foreigners who have in essence converted to Judaism, in keeping with Exod 12:48-49; Lev 16:29; 19:33-34; 24:22; Num 9:14; 11:14-16; Deut 24:17-18; 16:11, 14; 26:11. The second element of this text in Isa 56:9—57:21 emphasizes YHWH's willingness to forgive those who repent. The following text in Isa 58:1-14 calls specifically for such repentance, and indicates that YHWH expects both ritual observance and just behavior (cf. Lev 19). The lamentation in

Isa 59:1-21 draws upon earlier Isaian themes of YHWH's hidden face and blindness to express the people's expectation that YHWH will restore Zion and enable justice to be realized.

Isaiah 60–62

Isaiah 60–62 proclaims YHWH's restoration to Zion. The passage presents alternating statements by the prophet and YHWH concerning what the people might expect. Isaiah 60:1-9 begins with an announcement of restoration directed to Zion concerning the return of YHWH's glory and the approach of the nations, who will return Zion's sons and daughters and bring gifts and sacrifices to YHWH's altar. YHWH reiterates in Isa 60:10-22 the scenario of punishment and restoration articulated throughout the book. YHWH's characterization of Zion's people as "the shoot of my planting" recalls both the vineyard allegory of Isa 5:1-7, in which YHWH metaphorically planted Israel and Judah as a vineyard (Isa 5:2), and the oracle concerning the righteous monarch in Isa 11:1-16, which called for the growth of a righteous Davidic shoot (Isa 11:1) who would ultimately see to the restoration of Israel and Judah from exile among the nations (Isa 11:10-16). The prophet speaks in Isa 61:1-7 to proclaim liberty to captives and to declare that they will serve as priests for YHWH among the nations (cf. Exod 19:6). YHWH announces in Isa 61:8-9 an everlasting covenant with the people. The prophet speaks once again in Isa 61:10—62:12 to rejoice in YHWH's restoration of Jerusalem.

Isaiah 63–66

Isaiah 63–66 anticipates the period of violence and struggle that will take place as the remaining wicked are punished prior to the full realization of restoration. The unit begins in Isa 63:1-6 with a depiction of YHWH's punishment of Edom on the day of YHWH's vengeance, which will fulfill the earlier call for Edom's punishment on the Day of YHWH in Isa 34. Isaiah 63:7—64:11 presents the people's lament in which they appeal to YHWH for mercy at a time when adversaries have trampled the sanctuary. The culmination of the book appears in Isa 65–66, where YHWH answers the lament by declaring death for the wicked and restoration for the righteous as YHWH's kingship is finally realized. This passage refers repeatedly to earlier Isaian texts. For example, Isa 65:2 recalls the portrayal of the peaceful existence of the wolf and the lamb in Isa 11:6-9. Similarly, the role of the nations in restoring the exiles of Israel and Judah in Isa 66:18-24 refers back to Isa 11:10-16; 60:1-7.[28] Although some understand Isa 66:21 to indicate that YHWH will take some of the nations for priests and Levites, the syntax of the Hebrew requires that it refer to YHWH's taking priests and Levites from among the restored Israelite exiles mentioned in v. 20. The result will be a new creation in which all the world will recognize YHWH. This is in keeping with the ideal expressed in Isa 2:2-4.

NOTES

* This chapter is a heavily revised and condensed version of my chapter concerning Isaiah in *The Prophetic Literature* (IBT; Nashville: Abingdon, 2005), 45–84. Readers wishing a much fuller and earlier version of this discussion should turn there.

[1] See my *Isaiah 1–39, with an Introduction to Prophetic Literature* (FOTL 16; Grand Rapids: Eerdmans, 1996), 31–62.

[2] See especially Moshe Weinfeld, "Covenant, Davidic," *IDBSup* 188–92, and "Zion and Jerusalem as Religious and Political Capital: Ideology and Utopia," in *The Poet and the Historian: Essays in Literary and Historical Biblical Criticism*, ed. R. E. Friedman (HSS 26; Chico: Scholars Press, 1983), 75–115.

[3] For discussion of the literary structure of Isaiah, see my *Isaiah 1–39*, 31–62, and H. G. M. Williamson, *The Book Called Isaiah: Deutero-Isaiah's Role in Composition and Redaction* (Oxford: Clarendon, 1994).

[4] The classic model for the modern interpretation of a First, Second, and Third Isaiah was developed by Bernhard Duhm, *Das Buch Jesaia* (HKAT 3/1; Göttingen: Vandenhoeck & Ruprecht, 1892), especially v–xxi.

[5] See Peter R. Ackroyd, "Isaiah 36–39: Structure and Function," in *Studies in the Religious Tradition of the Old Testament* (London: SCM, 1987), 105–20, 274–78.

[6] See also Craig A. Evans, "On the Unity and Parallel Structure of Isaiah," *VT* 38 (1988): 129–47.

[7] See also my *King Josiah of Judah: The Lost Messiah of Israel* (Oxford: Oxford University Press, 2001).

[8] Cf. Jon D. Levenson, *Sinai and Zion: An Entry into the Jewish Bible* (Minneapolis: Winston, 1985); idem, "The Temple and the World," *JR* 64 (1984): 275–98; and my "The Book of Isaiah as Prophetic Torah," in *Form and Intertextuality in Prophetic and Apocalyptic Literature* (FAT 45; Tübingen: Mohr Siebeck, 2005), 13–27.

[9] For much of the interpretation of Isaiah presented here see my *Isaiah 1–39*, ad loc.

[10] See Roy F. Melugin, "Figurative Speech and the Reading of Isaiah 1 as Scripture," in *New Visions of Isaiah*, ed. R. F. Melugin and M. A. Sweeney (JSOTSup 214; Sheffield: Sheffield Academic, 1996), 282–305.

[11] Cf. Ronald E. Clements, "The Prophecies of Isaiah and the Fall of Jerusalem in 587 B.C.," *VT* 30 (1980): 421–36.

[12] See Hans Wildberger, *Isaiah 1–12: A Commentary* (ContCom; Minneapolis: Fortress Press, 1991), 81–96.

[13] See Bernhard W. Anderson, "'G-d with Us'—in Judgment and in Mercy: The Editorial Structure of Isaiah 5–10(11)," in *Canon, Theology, and Old Testament Interpretation*, ed. Gene M. Tucker et al. (Philadelphia: Fortress Press, 1988), 230–45.

[14] See especially Wildberger, *Isaiah 1–12*, 246–78.

[15] For discussion of the parallels between the structures of temples and royal palaces, see Baruch Halpern, *The First Historians: The Hebrew Bible and History* (San Francisco: Harper & Row, 1988), 46–54.

[16] Victor Hurowitz, "Isaiah's Impure Lips and their Purification in Light of Akkadian Sources," *HUCA* 60 (1989): 39–89.

[17] See my "Isaiah and Theodicy after the Shoah," in *Strange Fire: Reading the Bible after the Holocaust*, ed. T. Linafelt (Sheffield: Sheffield Academic, 2000), 208–19.

[18] See Stuart Irvine, *Isaiah, Ahaz, and the Syro-Ephraimitic Crisis* (SBLDS 123; Atlanta: Scholars Press, 1990).

[19] For discussion of the role of blindness and deafness within the whole of the book of Isaiah, see especially Ronald E. Clements, "The Unity of the Book of Isaiah," *Int* 36 (1982): 117–29; idem, "Beyond Tradition-History: Deutero-Isaiah's Development of First Isaiah's Themes," *JSOT* 31 (1985): 95–113.

[20] For analysis of the literary structure of Isa 34–66, including Isa 40–54; 55–66, see my *Isaiah 1–39*, 31–62. For discussion of Isa 40–55 in general, see especially Roy F. Melugin, *The Formation of Isaiah 40–55* (BZAW 141; Berlin: de Gruyter, 1976).

[21] For example, Ackroyd, "Isaiah 36–39."

[22] See the standard introductions and commentaries, for example, John J. Collins, *An Introduction to the Hebrew Bible* (Minneapolis: Fortress Press, 2004), 379–400, especially 380–89.

[23] See now Patricia Tull Willey, "The Servant of YHWH and Daughter Zion: Alternating Visions of YHWH's Community," in *Society of Biblical Literature 1995 Seminar Papers*, ed. Eugene H. Lovering, Jr. (Atlanta: Society of Biblical Literature, 1995), 267–303.

[24] See T. N. D. Mettinger, *A Farewell to the Servant Songs: A Critical Examination of an Exegetical Axiom* (Lund: Gleerup, 1983).

[25] See Patricia Tull Willey, *Remember the Former Things: The Recollection of Previous Texts in Second Isaiah* (SBLDS 161; Atlanta: Scholars Press, 1997), 229–61. For further discussion concerning intertextuality in Isa 40–66, see now Benjamin D. Sommer, *A Prophet Reads Scripture: Allusion in Isaiah 40–66* (Stanford: Stanford University Press, 1998).

[26] See my "The Reconceptualization of the Davidic Covenant in the Book of Isaiah," in *Studies in the Book of Isaiah: Festschrift Willem A. M. Beuken*, ed. J. van Ruiten and M. Vervenne (BETL 132; Leuven: Leuven University Press and Peeters, 1997), 41–61.

[27] See Joseph Blenkinsopp, *Isaiah 56–66* (AB 19B; New York: Doubleday, 2003), 25–66.

[28] See my "Prophetic Exegesis in Isaiah 65–66," in *Form and Intertextuality*, 46–62.

C. THE BOOK OF JEREMIAH*

Jeremiah lived in Jerusalem during one of the most important and challenging periods in biblical history, that is, the final years of the kingdom of Judah, from the time when the nation lost its independence following the unexpected death of King Josiah in 609 BCE through the Babylonian destruction of Jerusalem and the exile of much of its surviving population in 587 BCE. The book of Jeremiah portrays his attempts to grapple with the tragedy that overtook the entire nation. On the one hand, the prophet argues that the destruction of Jerusalem and the suffering of its people are consequences of their own failure to abide by YHWH's Torah. On the other hand, he looks forward to the restoration of Israel and Jerusalem following a period of seventy years of punishment in which YHWH's Torah will be written upon the hearts of the people. Jeremiah represents the necessity of life guided by Torah as the means to overcome evil in the world.

The book of Jeremiah generally appears as the second book of the Latter Prophets in the Tanak, although some Rabbinic authorities maintain that it should be the first book because, like Kings, it is concerned with destruction throughout (*b. Baba Batra* 14b). The superscription in Jer 1:1-3 identifies the book as "the words of Jeremiah ben Hilkiah, of the priests who were in Anathoth in the land of Benjamin. . . ." Talmudic tradition maintains that Jeremiah wrote the book (*b. Baba Batra* 15a).

But the book of Jeremiah contains much more than simply the words of Jeremiah. There is a great deal of narrative material about the prophet, major events in his lifetime, and his oracles. Jeremiah therefore presents the prophet, his actions, and his words, but the superscription does not indicate that Jeremiah actually wrote the whole book. Other writers are responsible at least for the superscription and the narratives. Many interpreters point to the scribe Baruch ben Neriah, who wrote down Jeremiah's words after the prophet was banned from speaking in the Temple (see Jer 36; 45), as the composer of the book,[1] but interpreters cannot be certain that he was in fact the author of the book.[2] The prose portions of Jeremiah, however, have much in common with the books of the DtrH (Joshua; Judges; Samuel; Kings).[3]

Jeremiah's identification as a priest from Anathoth is crucial for understanding the prophet as a representative of the Elide priestly line. According to 1 Kgs 2:26-27, Solomon expelled the high priest Abiathar from Jerusalem to Anathoth, leaving only Zadok to found the Zadokite priestly line. First Samuel 22:2-23 states that Abiathar ben Ahimelech, the great grandson of Eli (1 Sam 14:3) escaped the slaughter of the priests at Nob, and later served as David's priest (1 Sam 23:6-11; 2 Sam 20:25). Jeremiah later refers to the destruction of his ancestral sanctuary at Shiloh (Jer 7:12-14) and to Samuel, who served at Shiloh (Jer 15:1) in an effort to challenge the view that the presence of the Jerusalem Temple would ensure the security of the city. Jeremiah's identity as a priest explains his role as a teacher of YHWH's Torah like Moses (see, for example, Jer 7:1—8:3, in which Jeremiah quotes from the Ten Commandments; cf. Lev 10:11, which states that the Levites are to teach Israel all YHWH's statutes). It also explains in part the presence of the so-called confessions or laments of Jeremiah (Jer 11:18-23; 12:1-6; 15:10-21; 17:14-18; 18:18-23; 20:7-13, 14-18), in which the prophet expresses his frustration concerning his prophetic task, his relationship with YHWH, and the persecution that he suffers from his opponents. Jeremiah's "confessions" are formulated after the pattern of liturgical psalms.[4] The Levites formed the Temple choirs responsible for the singing of psalms in worship (1 Chr 16:4-37; cf. the Psalms of Asaph in Pss 50; 70–83 and the Psalms of Korah in Pss 42–49). Indeed, the Mosaic covenant tradition bases Israel's relationship with YHWH on the observance of divine Torah, and defines the basic theological outlook of the book of Jeremiah.

Jeremiah 1:1-3 claims that Jeremiah spoke for forty years from the thirteenth year of Josiah (627 BCE) through the captivity of Jerusalem in the eleventh year of Zedekiah (587 BCE). The superscription notes the reigns of Josiah (640–609 BCE), Jehoiakim (609—598 BCE), and Zedekiah (597—587 BCE). It omits the brief reigns of Jehoahaz (609 BCE), who was exiled by the Egyptians, and Jehoiachin (597 BCE), who was exiled by the Babylonians. This was a crucial period in Judah's history. Judah's Assyrian overlord, Assurbanipal, had died by 627, which enabled Josiah to begin a program of religious and national restoration in his twelfth year (see 2 Chr 34:3). Following Josiah's tragic death at the hands of the Egyptians in 609 BCE, Judah was subjugated first to Egypt and then to Babylon in 605 BCE. Following Jehoiakim's unsuccessful revolt against Babylon in 598, the Babylonians deported his son Jehoiachin and other leading Judeans to Babylon. When Jehoiakim's brother, Zedekiah, whom the Babylonians had placed on the throne, failed to prevent a second revolt, the Babylonian king Nebuchadnezzar destroyed Jerusalem and the Temple in 587 BCE, and deported thousands more to Babylon. In 582 BCE, a third revolt, in which Gedaliah ben Ahikam ben Shaphan, the Babylonian-appointed governor of Judah was assassinated, was put down before the Babylonian army arrived. The book shows little evidence of oracles spoken during the reign of Josiah (Jer 3:6; cf. Jer 22:11-19), but it demonstrates that Jeremiah continued to speak in Egypt after the assassination of Gedaliah in 582 BCE (Jer 41–45). This suggests that the superscription idealizes the span of

Jeremiah's career in an effort to make a theological point by comparing Jeremiah to Moses, that is, whereas Moses spent forty years leading Israel from Egypt to the promised land, Jeremiah's forty years saw Israel/Judah exiled from the land and Jeremiah ultimately in Egypt (cf. *Pesik. Rab.* xiii 112a).[5]

Study of the book of Jeremiah is complicated by the existence of two distinct but interrelated versions of the book in the Masoretic Hebrew form that appears in the Tanak and Septuagint Greek form that was originally written by Jews in Egypt but later served as sacred scripture in Christianity. Many scholars maintain that the Masoretic text appears to be an expanded version of the Hebrew text underlying the Greek Septuagint, although some evidence suggests that both texts have undergone extensive editing since the times of their respective origins.[6] Interpreters maintain that the Masoretic version of the book was produced in Babylonia during the Second Temple period. Because the Masoretic text serves as sacred scripture in Judaism, discussion will focus on the Masoretic form of the book.

Past attempts to explain the structure of the book of Jeremiah have been largely unsuccessful because they employ diachronic criteria, which are better suited to explaining the literary growth of the text than its final literary structure. Because both the Septuagint and Masoretic text versions begin with a very similar structure in chapters 1–25, most interpreters presuppose that they represent the first major unit within the literary structure of the book. But such a view overlooks the role of the superscriptions as the most fundamental markers of literary structure within both versions of the book. Superscriptions appear throughout the book to introduce and characterize the individual blocks of material that comprise both versions of the book of Jeremiah.[7] The book begins with the superscription in Jer 1:1-3, which identifies the contents of the book as "the words of Jeremiah ben Hilkiah. . . ." It is noteworthy that variations of the standard formula, "the word that came to Jeremiah from YHWH," appear at the beginning of textual sub-units in Jer 7:1; 11:1; 14:1; 18:1; 21:1; 25:1; 30:1; 32:1; 34:1; 34:8; 35:1;.40:1; 44:1; 45:1; 46:1; 46:13; 47:1; 50:1; and 51:59. A number of examples of this formula begin with the conjunction, "and," which indicates that they introduce sections that are subsumed structurally into the preceding material. The result is a general statement of the superscription of the book as "the words of Jeremiah" in Jer 1:1-3 followed by a succession of individual words given by YHWH to the prophet throughout the book. The narrative concerning the fall of Jerusalem in Jer 52 stands outside of this structure as a concluding appendix.

The sequence of superscriptions cuts through the major blocks of material, including the oracles concerning Judah and Israel in Jer 1–25, the narratives in Jer 26–45, and the oracles concerning the nations in Jer 46–51. The placement of the individual oracles concerning the nations points to a concern to demonstrate the realization of YHWH's plans to bring about the downfall of the nations, culminating in Babylon. Such a structure indicates a prospective, hopeful interest in the book, insofar as it is designed to point to the rise of the Persian Empire as the agent of YHWH's restoration for Jerusalem and punishment against Babylon and the nations that oppressed Judah. The structure of Jeremiah appears as follows:

The Words of Jeremiah Ben Hilkiah Concerning the Restoration of Jerusalem and the Downfall of Babylon

I.	Oracles Concerning Israel and Judah	1–6
	A. Superscription	1:1-3
	B. Commissioning of the prophet	1:4-10
	C. Signs concerning YHWH's purpose	1:11-19
	D. Oracles calling for Israel and Judah to return to YHWH	2–6
II.	Account Concerning Jeremiah's Temple Sermon	7–10
III.	Oracles Concerning the Rejection of YHWH's Covenant	11–13
IV.	Oracles Concerning Drought and Marriage	14–17
	A. Drought	14–15
	B. Marriage	16–17
V.	Oracles Concerning the Shattered Pot/Judgment against Judah	18–20
VI.	Oracles Concerning Davidic Kingship	21–24
VII.	Narratives Concerning Jeremiah's Warnings to Submit to Babylon	25–29
VIII.	Oracles Concerning the Restoration of Israel and Judah	30–31
IX.	Narrative Concerning the Field at Anathoth	32–33
X.	Narrative Concerning YHWH's Decision to Give Jerusalem to Nebuchadnezzar	34:1-7
XI.	Narrative Concerning Reneging on the Year of Release	34:8-22
XII.	Narrative Concerning the Fall of Jerusalem	35–39
XIII.	Narrative Concerning Jeremiah's Removal to Egypt	40–43
XIV.	Narrative Concerning Jeremiah's Oracles in Egypt	44
XV.	Narrative Concerning Word to Baruch	45
XVI.	Oracle Concerning Egypt	46:1-12
XVII.	Oracle Concerning the Babylonian Conquest of Egypt	46:13-28
XVIII.	Oracle Concerning Small Nations	47–49
XIX.	Oracle Concerning Babylon	50:1—51:58
XX.	Narrative Concerning Jeremiah's Instructions about Babylon	51:59-64
XXI.	Appendix Concerning the Fall of Jerusalem	52

The book of Jeremiah portrays the struggle of the prophet Jeremiah to discern divine will in relation to the decline and ultimately the collapse of Judah in the late seventh and early sixth centuries BCE. During this period, the kingdom of Judah shifted from a time of optimism in keeping with King Josiah's attempts at religious reform and national restoration following the collapse of the Assyrian empire, to a time of downfall and destruction. The nation witnessed King Josiah's unexpected death at the hands of Pharaoh Necho of Egypt in 609 BCE, the subsequent subjugation of Judah first to Egypt and then to Babylon, the invasions of Judah by the Babylonians in 597, 588, and 582 BCE, and ultimately the destruction of Jerusalem and the Temple in 587–586 BCE and the exile of much of the surviving population. Throughout the book, Jeremiah appears as a prophet and priest who attempts to interpret the events of his day in relation to earlier traditions extant in his time, including early forms of Mosaic Torah and Isaian prophecy. In the end, the book of Jeremiah portrays a reversal of the Exodus tradition, as Israel returns to Egypt and Babylon at the conclusion of Jeremiah's forty-year career. Nevertheless, Jeremiah anticipates restoration of the nation following its period of judgment (cf. Deut 28–30).

Synchronic analysis of the book indicates its theological concern with the issue of theodicy insofar as it argues that the destruction of Jerusalem was caused, not by YHWH's lack of power or commitment to the kingdom of Judah, but by the failure of the people to observe YHWH's Torah. Much like Isaiah, Jeremiah is designed to protect YHWH against such charges by claiming that the people are at fault instead. Indeed, the concern with observance of divine Torah is rooted in Jeremiah's identity as a priest of the line of Ithamar. One of the primary duties of the priesthood is to teach the people YHWH's Torah or instruction concerning the distinction "between the sacred and the profane, and between the unclean and the clean, and you must teach the Israelites all the laws which YHWH has imparted to them through Moses" (Lev 10:10-11). Jeremiah proceeds on this premise throughout the book. His initial Temple sermon in Jer 7, for example, is a classic example of priestly instruction to the people in which he is commanded to stand in the gates of the Temple and to speak to the people concerning YHWH's will. In the course of this speech, Jeremiah is to quote from the Ten Commandments as part of his efforts to teach the people that reliance on the Temple alone will not ensure their safety. Rather, they must observe YHWH's will as articulated through divine Torah, such as the Ten Commandments. He continues to make his point by citing the fate of the Shiloh sanctuary, his own ancestral sanctuary from the time of the high priest Eli, which was apparently destroyed as a result of YHWH's dissatisfaction in the early days of Israel's life in the land of Israel. Jeremiah's argument is meant to make an essential point: the Davidic Zion theology that posits YHWH's eternal protection of the city of Jerusalem and the house of David does not work. In Jeremiah's view, only observance of YHWH's Torah will see the people safely through.

Ironically, Jeremiah's adherence to divine Torah includes a political dimension as well, viz., Egypt was the enemy of YHWH and Israel in the Torah tradition of Israel's origins. Consequently, Jeremiah opposes efforts to ally with Egypt and instead calls for alliance with—or more properly submission to—Babylon as a key element in Judah's survival during the late seventh and early sixth centuries BCE. Throughout the prophet's lifetime, sentiment ran high in Judah concerning an alliance with Egypt to oppose the Babylonians. Such sentiment was rooted in the failure of Josiah's reforms. Josiah's program was based upon the centralization of Judean religious life around adherence to YHWH alone, worship only at the Jerusalem Temple, and observance of YHWH's Torah. But there were other dimensions as well, such as the reunification of northern Israel and southern Judah in the aftermath of Assyria's collapse and alliance with Babylonia based on Judah's and Babylon's common interest in seeing to the downfall of Assyria as a means to set both nations free from Assyrian control. Because Egypt was a close ally of Assyria, Josiah's program was inherently anti-Egyptian as well, a statement which would only be reinforced by the role that Egypt had played as Israel's enemy in the Torah traditions concerning Israel's early history in the Exodus. But when Josiah was killed by the Egyptians in 609 BCE, Egypt became the overlord of Judah and replaced Josiah's son and successor, Jehoahaz, with his older brother, Jehoiakim, who consistently pursued a pro-Egyptian and anti-Babylonian policy throughout his reign. Jeremiah, an early adherent to Josiah's reform program, opposed Jehoiakim's pro-Egyptian and anti-Babylonian policy, arguing that it was contrary to the will of YHWH. Egypt's defeat by the Babylonians in 605 BCE had proved that Egypt was unable to stand up to Babylon. Plans by Jehoiakim and his followers to revolt against Babylon following Babylon's subjugation of Judah in 605 BCE could only result in disaster for Judah.

One of the dimensions of the theological viewpoint of the book of Jeremiah is the rethinking of the significance of Josiah's reform and its failure. There are few references to Josiah in the book of Jeremiah, but texts such as Jer 2–6, 30–31, and even Jer 7 and 22–24 indicate Jeremiah's support of Josiah's reform even though these had to be reworked after the great king's death. Despite his efforts at religious reform and political restoration, Josiah's early death at the hands of Pharaoh Necho of Egypt in 609 BCE would have demonstrated that the process of judgment that YHWH had unleashed against Israel and Judah beginning in the late eighth century BCE had not yet run its course. Although Judah, unlike Israel, had survived the Assyrian invasions and weathered the long years of Assyrian hegemony, Judah could still be subject to punishment by Babylon even though they had earlier been allies against Assyria under Hezekiah and later under Josiah. Jeremiah understood all too well Babylon's strength, and an attempt to challenge that strength, particularly by relying on Assyria's old ally, Egypt, was certain to fail with disastrous consequences for Judah. As events transpired, Jeremiah proved to be right on this point.

Jeremiah's adherence to the principles of Josiah's reform, and his recognition that the process of judgment had not yet run its course, also influenced the way in which he read past tradition. Jeremiah shows engagement with an early form of the Isaian traditions as well as with the tradition of Mosaic Torah. Isaiah had argued that adherence to YHWH would ensure the security of Jerusalem and the house of David. Jeremiah's reading of events in his time apparently convinced him that this was not quite the truth. As noted above, only adherence to YHWH's Torah could ensure the security of Jerusalem, the house of David, and the people at large. Consequently, the book of Jeremiah is filled with continuous interaction with the Isaian tradition. We have already noted the prophet's challenge of the Davidic Zion tradition in his famous Temple sermon in Jer 7, but we must also note other instances. Jeremiah 2–6 begins with an indictment of northern Israel and call for Israel to return to YHWH and Jerusalem in keeping with Josiah's reform and Isaiah's own teachings, but it then shifts to a similar call for Judah and Jerusalem to repent and return to YHWH. Interestingly, the depiction of the approaching army "from a far off nation" (from the north, that is, Babylon) that would threaten Jerusalem in Jer 5:15-17 echoes Isaiah's depiction of the approaching army "from a nation afar" (Assyria) bent on the same ends in Isa 5:25-29. Much the same might be said of Jer 30–31, which calls for Israel's return to Jerusalem, but these chapters appear to have been reworked to account for Jerusalem's restoration after judgment as well. Jeremiah's rejection of Hananiah as a false prophet for proclaiming that YHWH would protect Jerusalem from Babylon in Jer 27–28 entails rejection of Isaiah's claims a century earlier, claims on which Hananiah's message was based (cf. Isa 10; 13–14). And Jeremiah's vision of a righteous Davidic monarch in Jer 24:1-7 echoes Isaiah's depiction of the righteous Davidic monarch in Isa 11:1-10, although Jeremiah's recasting of the Davidic promise to pertain to Jerusalem and the Levites in Jer 33:14-26 echoes the book of Isaiah's recasting of the tradition in Isa 55. Jeremiah was apparently an avid reader or hearer of the Isaian tradition, but he had to disagree, viz., Isaiah's promises of an ideal period of peace and protection by YHWH were not to be achieved anytime soon given Judah's penchant for challenging YHWH and Babylonia. Judgment against Jerusalem and Judah would come first if the nation continued its course of action.

Jeremiah is in constant conflict with YHWH, unlike Isaiah, who consistently submits to YHWH's will. Indeed, Jeremiah's conflicts with YHWH are analogous to his conflicts with human authorities as well, such as the priests from his home town of Anathoth, the kings Jehoiakim and Zedekiah, the priest Pashhur, and the people of Jerusalem and Judah in general. Unlike Isaiah, who is known for his children through his wife the prophetess, Jeremiah never marries (Jer 16). Indeed, his conflicts with human beings appear to feed his conflict with YHWH. At the outset of his career, Jeremiah attempts to resist YHWH's demand in Jer 1 that he serve as a prophet, and YHWH finally has to tell him that he is going to do it whether he like it or not. Jeremiah is arrested and tried for treason and sedition when he speaks his famous Temple sermon in Jer 7; 26, and he is only saved from execution by Ahikam ben Shaphan, formerly an officer in Josiah's court and apparently a powerful ally for the prophet. He is again sought by King Jehoiakim in Jer 36 for publishing a written form of his Temple sermon. He is arrested by the priest Pashhur for his symbolic depiction of the judgment of Jerusalem in Jer 18–20, and he is again arrested during the siege of Jerusalem and thrown into a pit (Jer 37; 38). Jeremiah's conflict with YHWH comes to full culmination in his laments in which he charges YHWH with raping and impregnating him with the divine word that he does not want to speak to his people, but he nevertheless must (Jer 20:7-18). He ends up cursing the day of his birth because he must preside as a prophet over his people at a time when Jerusalem, the Temple, the nation, and the house of David will all be destroyed. Even at the end of his life, he is dragged against his will to Egypt, the very enemy of Israel as portrayed in the Torah tradition, where he will become a figure who reverses Moses' exodus, viz.,

Moses left Egypt to lead the people to the promised land; Jeremiah leaves the promised land to return to Egypt. Indeed, Jeremiah's conflicts with YHWH and with people prompted Heschel to speak of YHWH's divine pathos and pain at seeing what had become of the people of Judah. Jeremiah, with his bitter relationship with YHWH and people, was the focal point of that pathos.

For all his bitterness and sense of impending judgment, Jeremiah also holds to a vision of restoration once the punishment is over. Jeremiah 30–31; 32–33 lays out a process of restoration in which the northern kingdom of Israel will return to Jerusalem, Jerusalem itself will be re-established, a new covenant will be established in which YHWH's Torah will be imbedded in the people's hearts, and the eternal Davidic promise will be applied to the city of Jerusalem and the Levites who serve in its Temple. Such restoration in the aftermath of punishment is consistent with Deut 28–30, which calls for curses in case of Israel's failure to observe divine Torah, but envisions restoration following the punishment once the people repent. Jeremiah's understanding of restoration appears to be rooted in the ideals of Josiah's reform, which looked to the restoration of Israel to Jerusalem once the long period of Assyrian subjugation had come to an end. We observed above that Jeremiah had been compelled to conclude as a result of Josiah's death that the judgment had not yet run its course. But he still held to the ideals of Josiah's reform once the period of punishment had finally come to an end. In Jer 25 and 29, the prophet envisions a seventy-year period of punishment, which happens to correspond to the time between the destruction of Solomon's Temple in 587/6 BCE and the construction of the Second Temple in 520–515 BCE. As part of the process, the nations that had played a role in Jerusalem's punishment, culminating in Babylon, would also be punished in turn by YHWH (Jer 46–51). As far as Jeremiah was concerned, Josiah's reform was still on, despite the king's death, but a long period of punishment would have to be endured before the full restoration could take place.[8]

Examination of the various components of the book of Jeremiah indicates that these theological concerns are addressed throughout the book.

Jeremiah 1–6

Jeremiah 1–6 serves as an introduction to the basic concerns of the book by pointing to the impending punishment of both Israel/Judah and the nations, as well as the restoration of both. The block is defined by the superscription in Jer 1:1-3, which introduces both Jer 1–6 and the book as a whole. Examples of the formula, "and/now the word of YHWH came to me, saying . . . ,'" in Jer 1:4, 11; and 2:1 are joined together by their introductory conjunctions, "and/now," to introduce each of the following three sub-units of chapters 1–6. Although the third-person formulation of the superscription indicates that it is the work of the book's final editor, the first-person formulation of the following sub-units indicates that they are autobiographical. They include an account of the prophet's commission to serve as a prophet in Jer 1:4-10, an account of the signs given by YHWH to Jeremiah to indicate YHWH's purpose in Jer 1:11-19, and oracles in Jer 2–6 formulated as the prophet's call for Israel and Judah to return to YHWH.

Jeremiah 1:4-10 presents Jeremiah's account of his commissioning as a prophet. YHWH's claims to have formed Jeremiah in the womb and to have consecrated him as a prophet to the nations before birth frequently prompt interpreters to posit that Jeremiah must have considered his birth to be the beginning of his prophetic career. This would suggest that the prophet was born in 627 BCE, and that he would have been eighteen years old in 609, the year in which Josiah was killed by the Egyptians.[9] The reference to Jeremiah's birth is important because of his priestly identity. Like Moses (cf. Exod 3–4), Jeremiah attempts to persuade YHWH that he is inadequate for his role by claiming that he is only a boy. But YHWH places the words in his mouth and reassures him with the statement, "Do not fear them, for I am with you to deliver you" (cf. Exod 3:12; Isa 6:6-7; Ezek 3:1-3). As a priest, he is born to this role and cannot escape it (cf. Jer 20:7-18). Because the Jerusalem Temple was considered to be the focal point of creation,[10] Jeremiah's role as both priest and prophet would have an impact on the nations as well. YHWH's commission of the prophet employs six verbs, four of destruction ("to pluck up and to pull down, to destroy and to overthrow") and two of restoration ("to build and to plant") to express the basic themes of judgment and restoration that appear throughout the book (see also Jer 12:14-17; 18:5-9; 24:5-7; 31:27-30, 38-40; 42:7-12; 45:2-4).

The account of the two signs from YHWH in Jer 1:11-19 again indicates YHWH's intentions to bring judgment and to stand by the prophet, and they presuppose Jeremiah's identity as a priest. Symbolic visions frequently presuppose visions of common phenomena (cf. Amos 7:1-3; Zech 2:1-4). The first appears in vv. 11-12, and follows a standard form for the presentation of a symbolic vision (cf. Amos 7:7-9; 8:1-14; Zech 4:1-13; 5:1-4). The sign depends upon a pun, that is, Jeremiah's vision of an almond branch (Hebrew, *maqqēl šāqēd*) indicates that YHWH is watching (*šōqēd*) over the divine word to carry it out. The almond branch symbolizes the Levitical staff that indicates the Levites' roles as priests (Num 17). The second appears in vv. 13-19 in the form of a boiling pot tilted away from the north. This symbolizes the gathering of tribes and nations from the north that will attack Jerusalem. Although Babylon is situated to the east of Jerusalem, the presence of the Arabian Desert requires that Mesopotamian armies march through the Fertile Crescent in Syria to approach Jerusalem from the north. Jeremiah's oracles concerning the enemy from the north appear in Jer 4:5—6:30 and 8:4—10:25. As a priest, Jeremiah would have been responsible for food preparation, including the boiling of sacrificial meat in pots (cf. 1 Sam 2:12-17; Ezek 24:1-14).

Jeremiah 2–6 presents the prophet's account of YHWH's call for Israel and Judah to repent.[11] This material is organized by three prose statements in 2:1; 3:6; and 3:11 in which the prophet relates YHWH's instructions to proclaim the following oracles.

Jeremiah 2:1—3:5 employs the metaphor of marriage between YHWH and Israel to recount YHWH's dissatisfaction with the people. The use of the marriage metaphor to express the relationship between YHWH and Israel appears frequently in the prophets (see Isa 54; Ezek 6; Hos 1–3; Zeph 3:14-20). In contrast to the Pentateuch's presentation of continuous tension between Israel and YHWH in the wilderness (for example, Exod 32–34; Num 14), YHWH alludes to the wilderness period in vv. 2-3 as an ideal time when Israel first became YHWH's bride. But YHWH's tone changes markedly in Jer 2:4—3:5 with calls for a divorce, claiming that Israel has other lovers.

Jeremiah 3:6-10 employs the metaphor of sisters to compare Judah's abandonment of YHWH to that of Israel. The passage is formulated as a retrospective look to the days of Josiah. In the synchronic form of the text, such a claim merely entails that the prophet is concerned with judgment against Judah. But this is also very important from a diachronic perspective because it indicates that the prophet ultimately reconsidered his early support for Josiah's program to conclude that Judah would suffer YHWH's judgment just as northern Israel had suffered during the Assyrian period.

Jeremiah 3:11—6:30 gets to the main point of these chapters by portraying YHWH's call for Israel's and Judah's repentance. Jeremiah 2–6 is formulated rhetorically as an attempt to persuade the prophet's audience to change their course of action. It thereby builds upon the previous accusations of faithlessness to make the case that YHWH is justified in bringing punishment, and then it portrays the punishment as a threat of attack by the enemy from the north to be realized if the people do not heed YHWH's call for return. YHWH's formal call for repentance appears in Jer 3:11-17, which emphasizes Israel's return to Zion in keeping with Josiah's program of restoring northern Israel to Judean/Davidic rule. The following material in Jer 3:18—6:30 emphasizes an idyllic future in which Israel and Judah are joined together again (Jer 3:18-25), the benefits of repentance and the costs of a failure to repent are outlined in true parenetic fashion (Jer 4:1-4), and the scenario of judgment by an enemy from the north is laid out in great detail should the people not respond to YHWH's and Jeremiah's call (Jer 4:5—6:30). Jeremiah 5:15-17 and 6:19, 22-23 draw heavily on Isaiah's portrayal of the advancing enemy army in Isa 5:25-30; Jer 6:12 recalls Isaiah's repeated statement of YHWH's "outstretched hand" in Isa 5:25-30 and 9:7—10:5, and Jer 5:20-21 and 6:10 reiterate Isaiah's depiction of the people as blind and deaf in Isa 6. Such citations suggest that Jeremiah was very aware of the Isaian tradition. In keeping with Isaiah, Jerusalem would ultimately be restored, but a period of judgment would be realized first if Judah did not submit to Babylon.[12]

Jeremiah 7–10

Jeremiah 7–10 presents YHWH's instructions to the prophet to deliver his famous Temple sermon. An account of Jeremiah's subsequent trial for sedition appears in Jer 26. By presenting the sermon in the context of YHWH's instructions, the narrative aids in answering charges (see Jer 26) that Jeremiah misrepresented the will of YHWH.

YHWH's instructions call upon Jeremiah to deliver a typical Levitical sermon like that spoken by Moses to the people of Israel in Deuteronomy as they stood on the banks of the Jordan River prior to entering the Promised Land.[13] One of Jeremiah's primary tasks as a priest is to teach YHWH's Torah to the people (see Lev 10:11). By standing in the gate of the Temple, he stands at the position of the Levitical gatekeepers who ensure the sanctity of the Temple by admitting those who had sanctified themselves for divine service (1 Chr 9:17-27; cf. the entrance liturgies in Pss 15; 24).[14] Jeremiah's sermon focuses specifically on calling the people to amend their ways by observing YHWH's Torah. This is a particularly crucial issue because of the prevailing view, represented in the Zion/Davidic tradition of Isaiah and many of the Psalms, that the presence of YHWH's Temple would ensure the security of Jerusalem, the Davidic monarchy, and the people at large. Jeremiah, however, represents the Mosaic understanding of the covenant that security also depends upon the people's observance of YHWH's Torah. He cites elements of the Ten Commandments and refers to the fate of his ancestral sanctuary at Shiloh to make his point, viz., if YHWH's sanctuary at Shiloh could be destroyed, YHWH's sanctuary at Jerusalem could suffer the same fate.

The purpose of this narrative is not simply to record Jeremiah's speech; rather, it reflects upon the significance of the speech and the subsequent destruction of Jerusalem. Because it argues that the people did not observe YHWH's instruction and emphasizes YHWH's own struggle with Jerusalem's destruction, the narrative serves as a form of theodicy that attempts to demonstrate YHWH's righteousness while placing the responsibility for Jerusalem's destruction on the people themselves.

Jeremiah 11–13

Jeremiah 11–13 builds upon the concern of the preceding section with proper observance of YHWH's Torah by emphasizing that the people broke their covenant with YHWH (Jer 11:10). The passage therefore plays a key role in the prophet's debate with the Zion/Davidic tradition by calling into question the notion of an eternal covenant with Jerusalem and the house of David (see 2 Sam 7; Pss 89; 110; 132; cf. Gen 15).

The initial charge in Jer 11:1-17 introduces a series of additional passages that prompts the reader to reflect on the significance of the prophet's contention. The first are two examples of Jeremiah's so-called complaints or laments in Jer 11:18-23 and 12:1-6. Both are formulated after the model of liturgical complaint psalms in which the prophet raises questions concerning suffering in an attempt to request intervention and redress by YHWH.[15] The first refers to threats against Jeremiah made by the people of his hometown in Anathoth who apparently sought to silence the prophet. Jeremiah appears to be one of the few priests outside of Jerusalem who responded to Josiah's call to serve in the Jerusalem Temple (2 Kgs 23:8-9). Such a move on his part would likely be opposed by family members and colleagues in Anathoth. The second lament demands to know why YHWH allows the wicked to prosper in the expectation that YHWH's righteousness will ultimately prompt action against them.

YHWH in turn expresses sorrow in a lament in Jer 12:7-13 much like the prophet.[16] The lament expresses the struggles that both YHWH and Judean society undergo in the aftermath of the death of Josiah and the subsequent failure of his reforms. The prophet's own struggle with the Isaian tradition emerges with references to Isaiah's vineyard parable (Isa 5:1-7) and the birds of prey that threaten Jerusalem (Isa 31). A series of oracles then addresses the fate of the nations around Israel and Judah (Jer 12:14-17); a symbolic act involving Jeremiah's loin cloth (Jer 13:1-11); a symbolic act involving a jar filled with wine (Jer 13:12-14); and a concluding oracle that draws upon Isaiah's oracle of gloom and darkness (Isa 8:23—9:6) to anticipate YHWH's punishment (Jer 13:15-27).

Jeremiah 14-17

Jeremiah 14-17 takes up the themes of drought and marriage to symbolize YHWH's decision to bring punishment against Jerusalem. The introductory statement in Jer 16:1, "and the word of YHWH came to me," simultaneously marks the transition between the two concerns while joining them with its initial conjunction. Both themes draw upon traditional metaphors to express YHWH's relationship with Israel. As author of creation, YHWH brings rain to the land to ensure fertility and the life of the people in the land (see especially Deut 28-30), and the relationship between YHWH and Israel is frequently expressed through the metaphor of marriage between YHWH and Israel (see Isa 54; Jer 2; Ezek 16; Hos 1-3; Zeph 3:14-20).

Jeremiah 14:1—15:21 emphasizes the mourning that engulfs the land when the rains fail and the land withers for lack of water. Such a lament is particularly pertinent at the autumn festival of Sukkot (Booths), which commemorates the onset of the rainy season and the wilderness wandering tradition when YHWH and Israel were "married." The lack of rain points to YHWH's decision to punish the people for wandering after other gods. Jeremiah's third lament in Jer 15:10-21 expresses regret over his birth and prophetic vocation, but it prompts YHWH's reassurance that Jeremiah's return to YHWH will be accepted and that his words to the people will result in their return as well.

Jeremiah's own marital situation becomes a symbol for the upcoming punishment of the people in Jer 16:1—17:27. Although the first commandment in Judaism is to "be fruitful and multiply" (Gen 1:28), YHWH commands Jeremiah not to marry in order to symbolize the death and mourning that will overtake the land. The passage does not presuppose a full end, however, but looks to restoration when the punishment is over in order to teach the world about YHWH's power to punish and to restore. Jeremiah's fourth lament in Jer 17:14-18 calls upon YHWH for healing and defense. A concluding oracle calls for the observance of Shabbat as a basis for Jerusalem's restoration.

Jeremiah 18–20

Jeremiah 18–20 presents the prophet's condemnation of Jerusalem and Judah based upon his symbolic actions concerning the potter and the shattered pot. The segment includes the final two laments by the prophet as he calls for the punishment of those who persecute him and expresses his frustration over the role that YHWH has assigned to him.

The first sub-unit is the account in Jer 18:1-17 of Jeremiah's oracles against Judah and Jerusalem based upon his observation of a potter at work. The making of pottery serves as a particularly instructive representation for the prophet's oracles, particularly since the word employed for "potter" (Hebrew, *yōṣēr*, "one who forms, fashions") is used frequently both for the making of pottery (Isa 29:16; 41:25; Lam 4:2) and for YHWH's fashioning of human beings (Gen 2:7, 8), animals and birds (Gen 2:19), the nation Israel (Isa 27:11; 43:1; 44:21; 45:9), and even Jeremiah himself (Jer 1:5). As Jeremiah observes the potter fashioning and then refashioning pots as he makes mistakes and corrects them, the prophet concludes that this represents YHWH's relationship with the people of Jerusalem and Judah, that is, YHWH had fashioned the people, but the work had gone wrong and needed to be redone. This provides the opportunity to repeat a basic theme of the book, viz., YHWH calls for repentance, but will bring judgment if the people do not change their ways.

Jeremiah's fifth lament in Jer 18:18-23 relates the words of his enemies and reiterates his strong support for submission to Babylon (see Jer 27–29; 32).

Jeremiah 19–20

Jeremiah 19–20 illustrates Jeremiah's persecution. Jeremiah purchases an earthenware jug and gathers some of the priests and elders for a symbolic action that will illustrate YHWH's condemnation of the people. The prophet takes them to the Valley of Hinnom (Tophet) by the Potsherd Gate, located along the south-western edges of the eighth- through seventh-century site of Jerusalem. The site was used for the burning of waste, and it apparently was also used for pagan rites of human sacrifice (cf. Jer 7:30-34; 2 Kgs 23:10, respectively).[17] Because of its reputation, the Valley of Hinnom provides a suitable location for Jeremiah's symbolic action in which he shatters the earthenware jug to symbolize YHWH's decision to shatter Jerusalem and Judah. Jeremiah's action prompts his arrest by the priest Passhur ben Immer. Jeremiah's final laments then follow in Jer 20:7-13 and 20:14-18, in which he denounces YHWH for having forced him to condemn his own people. He employs the language of rape, "you enticed me . . . , you have overpowered me, and you have prevailed," to describe how YHWH forced him to speak. Jeremiah's final lament bitterly curses the day of his birth, because of the grim task of condemnation that YHWH requires of the prophet.

Jeremiah 21–24

Jeremiah 21–24 presents the prophet's oracles against Jerusalem and the house of David, which directly challenges the Davidic/Zion tradition of YHWH's protection of Jerusalem and the house of David.

The initial episode takes the reader forward to the reign of Zedekiah (597–587 BCE) and the imminent Babylonian siege of Jerusalem in 588–587 BCE in an effort to present the siege of Jerusalem as the outcome of the prophet's condemnations of the Davidic monarchy. Jeremiah states unequivocally in Jer 21:1-14 that YHWH will fight against Zedekiah and Jerusalem and support the Babylonians in their efforts to take the city. Only those who submit to Babylon will survive.

Jeremiah 22:1-30 then presents a series of oracles in which Jeremiah condemns Kings Jehoiakim and Jehoiachin for their alleged lack of justice. The oracle shows signs of having been delivered originally at the death of Josiah and the Egyptian deportation of his son Jehoahaz, nicknamed Shallum, when Pharaoh Necho placed Jehoiakim on the throne (2 Kgs 23:28-35). The prophet accuses Jehoiakim of looking to his own needs by building a large palace while ignoring the needs of his people—Jehoiakim, after all, was a loyal supporter of Egypt throughout his reign, and was responsible for Judah's policy of confrontation against the Babylonians. When Jehoiakim died during Judah's first revolt against Babylon in 598–597 BCE, the Babylonians deported his son, Jehoiachin (Coniah), and placed his brother Zedekiah on the throne to rule as a Babylonian puppet (2 Kgs 24:1-19). Jeremiah looks forward to the rule of a righteous Davidic monarch, whom he calls the "branch," apparently presupposing the imagery employed in Isa 11:1-16 to describe the righteous "shoot" of Jesse or David who will preside over a restored Israel and Judah. The placement of Jeremiah's oracle against the false prophets in Jer 23:9-40 immediately after his oracle concerning the house of David is particularly striking. Many maintain that the prophet was opposed to the monarchy altogether, but his comments concerning Josiah's righteousness (see Jer 22:15-16) indicate that this is not the case.

The concluding oracle in Jer 24:1-10 metaphorically depicts two baskets of figs to argue that those who go into captivity, for example, Jehoiachin, will form the basis for restoration, whereas those who remain, for example, Zedekiah, are condemned.

Jeremiah 25–29

Jeremiah 25–29 presents Jeremiah's warnings to submit to Babylon. This unit anticipates a seventy-year period of exile, which corresponds to the period from the destruction of Jerusalem in 587 BCE until 520–515 BCE when the Temple was rebuilt. The retrospective narrative viewpoint of this section suggests that it has been edited and organized to point to just such a period as the fulfillment of the prophet's words.

Jeremiah 25 begins with a retrospective view of the prophet's words to the people of Jerusalem and Judah from the thirteenth year of Josiah (627 BCE) until the fourth year of Jehoiakim (605 BCE) when the Babylonians took control of Jerusalem. The prophet contends that the people did not listen to his warnings, and that the time of judgment has now begun. Once the seventy years are complete, YHWH will bring punishment against Babylon and its supporting nations (cf. Isa 40–66).

Jeremiah 26 then turns to a retrospective look at Jeremiah's trial for sedition at the beginning of Jehoiakim's reign. The prophet was charged as a result of his statements in his Temple sermon (Jer 7–10) that Jerusalem would be destroyed. Insofar as the unit is set in the fourth year of Jehoiakim when Babylon took control of Jerusalem, the placement of the text here aids in vindicating the prophet's message that Jerusalem and Judah would suffer punishment. The prophet Micah, who also announced Jerusalem's destruction (Mic 3:12), is cited in Jeremiah's defense, particularly since his words are said to have prompted Hezekiah to turn to YHWH so that the city was saved from the Assyrians (but see Isa 36–37; 2 Kgs 18–19, respectively). Jeremiah's accusers cite the case of an otherwise unknown prophet named Uriah, who was hunted down and executed by King Jehoiakim for his statements that Jerusalem would be destroyed. Jeremiah is saved only when Ahikam ben Shaphan intervenes. Although we may be prone to think of Jeremiah as a lonely figure, he had considerable support from the Shaphan family.[18]

The chronology of Jeremiah's confrontation with the prophet Hananiah in Jer 27–28 is uncertain because Jer 27:1 places it at the beginning of Jehoiakim's reign while Jer 28:1 places it at the beginning of Zedekiah's reign. It should likely be placed at the beginning of Zedekiah's reign (see especially Jer 27:12) since the text of Jer 27:1 may have been influenced by the retrospective presentations of the previous chapters. Jeremiah engages in a symbolic action, appearing in the city wearing a yoke that is designed to illustrate his contention that Jerusalem and Judah must submit to Babylon.[19] He is challenged by the prophet Hananiah, who breaks Jeremiah's yoke to proclaim that the exiles taken to Babylon with Jehoiachin would be returned within two years. But Jeremiah returns with an iron yoke that could not be broken to reinforce his call for submission to Babylon and his contention that Hananiah was a false prophet (cf. Jer 23:9-40) who would soon die. Notably, Hananiah's message of deliverance for Jerusalem echoes Isaiah's similar message to Ahaz a century before (Isa 7).

The final episode in Jer 29 concerning Jeremiah's letter to the exiles reiterates the prophet's call for submission to Babylon for seventy years.

Jeremiah 30–31

Jeremiah 30–31 presents the prophet's oracles of restoration for Israel and Judah. This section has frequently been viewed as a later addition to the book because of its focus on restoration rather than judgment. A significant number of scholars have noted, however, that Jeremiah's focus on the restoration of both Israel and Judah signals the concerns of the pre-monarchic period when King Josiah of Judah attempted to reunite the former northern kingdom of Israel with Judah. This suggests that the unit represents an early cycle of oracles by the prophet that supported Josiah's efforts to restore northern Israel to Davidic rule, but that the passage was updated after Josiah's death to account for the restoration of both Israel and Judah.[20]

The theme of punishment followed by restoration is correlated with Jeremiah's call narrative in Jer 31:27-28 by the appearance of the key words used to describe YHWH's punishment, that is, "to pluck up, break down, overthrow, destroy, bring evil," and those used for restoration, "to build, plant" (cf. Jer 1:10; see also 1:11, which mentions YHWH's "watching"). Concern with restoration is inherent in the Levitical worldview, which calls for humans to restore their relationships with YHWH and with their own people after having committed some wrong (cf. Lev 4:1—5:13).

Jeremiah 32–33

Jeremiah 32–33 relates Jeremiah's oracles based upon his attempt to redeem family property during a lull in the Babylonian siege of Jerusalem in 588 BCE. Jeremiah 37:11-21 states that the prophet was arrested as a traitor when he tried to leave the city at the time of the Babylonian withdrawal. Jeremiah 32–33 explains Jeremiah's act in relation to the interplay between punishment and restoration in YHWH's plans.

The narrative is set at the time of Jeremiah's arrest, when King Zedekiah demanded to know why the prophet had stated that Nebuchadnezzar would capture Jerusalem and take Zedekiah to Babylon. The prophet explains his statements in relation to his attempt to redeem family property in his home town of Anathoth. In cases when a family member used land as collateral for a debt, priestly law requires that the land be redeemed by a family member (Lev 25:25-28). The prophet describes the transaction in detail, and states that he redeemed the land at YHWH's instruction. The purpose of the transaction was to symbolize YHWH's intentions to redeem Jerusalem after punishment.

Jeremiah 33 continues the motif of YHWH's intentions to restore Jerusalem following its punishment, but it focuses specifically on YHWH's intentions to restore a righteous Davidic monarch, here designated as the "branch" (cf. Jer 23:1-7; Isa 11:1-16, respectively). Just as Jerusalem's restoration is tied to creation in Jer 30–31, so is the house of David (cf. Pss 89; 110). It is noteworthy that the covenant shifts the Davidic covenant of Jer 23:1-8 to the city of Jerusalem and the Levitical priests.[21]

Jeremiah 34:1-7

Jeremiah 34:1-7 presents Jeremiah's condemnation of King Zedekiah. The prophet states that Zedekiah will not be killed, but will be taken to Babylon where he will die in peace.

Jeremiah 34:8-22

Jeremiah 34:8-22 presents the prophet's condemnation of Zedekiah for reneging on his promise to release the slaves in the city of Jerusalem. Biblical law indicates that people may become slaves to pay a debt, but they are to be released after six years of service (Exod 21:1-11; Deut 15:1-18; Lev 25:39-55).

Jeremiah 35–39

Jeremiah 35–39 relates Jeremiah's experiences at the fall of Jerusalem. The narrative provides an overview of the prophet's actions and message from the time of Jehoiakim's reign through the fall of the city during the reign of Zedekiah. These narratives attempt to demonstrate that Kings Jehoiakim and Zedekiah do not meet the standards for righteous Davidic kingship as portrayed in Jer 23:1-7 and 33:14-26 (cf. Jer 22:15-16).

The narrative begins with an account of Jeremiah's use of the Rechabites to illustrate loyalty to YHWH. The narrative is set in the reign of Jehoiakim in order to demonstrate that the reasons for the destruction of the city are rooted in the earlier monarch's reign (contra 2 Kgs 21, which attributes the city's destruction to Manasseh's actions). The Rechabites were a group founded by Jonadab ben Rechab, who is described as zealous for YHWH and who supported Jehu's revolt against the house of Omri (2 Kgs 9–10). Biblical tradition identifies the Rechabites as Kenites (1 Chr 2:55), who were descended from Moses' father-in-law, Jethro (Judg 1:16; Exod 3:1; 18:1), and ultimately from Cain after whom the Kenites are named (Gen 4:1-16). The prophet offers them wine, which the Rechabites refuse because of their vows to avoid wine and to live in tents in keeping with their understanding of YHWH's expectations (cf. the Nazirite vow in Num 6:1-21). He then contrasts the loyal Rechabites with the people of Judah and Jerusalem, whom he maintains have not shown such loyalty to YHWH.

Jeremiah 36 points to Jehoiakim's contempt for YHWH and Jeremiah following Jeremiah's Temple sermon (see Jer 7–10; 26). The narrative is set in the fourth year of Jehoiakim (605 BCE) when the Babylonians took control of Jerusalem. The prophet apparently had been banned from speaking in the Temple, but he simply had the scribe, Baruch ben Neriah, write a scroll with his words so that Baruch could read them in the Temple in Jeremiah's place. After Baruch read the scroll, it was taken to the home of Gemariah ben Shaphan, a highly placed member of the Shaphan family that supported the prophet,[22] for discussion among the scribes as to how to proceed. When it was taken to the king, he burned each column after it was read to show his contempt for Jeremiah.

The final segment of this unit appears in Jer 37–39, which focuses on Jeremiah's imprisonment by Zedekiah during the Babylonian siege of Jerusalem (see Jer 32–33). Zedekiah ben Josiah was the brother of Jehoiakim, who was placed on the throne by the Babylonians as a puppet to control the population following the death of his brother and the exile of his nephew Jehoiachin. The narrative portrays him as a very weak figure who was unable to control the pro-Egyptian forces loyal to Jehoiakim.

Zedekiah had Jeremiah imprisoned, although he continued to consult the prophet. When the prophet continued to speak out for submission to Babylon, several officials called for Jeremiah to be cast into a cistern where he would be left to die without food. Zedekiah complied, but an Ethiopian slave, identified only as Ebed-Melech, "servant of the king," pulled Jeremiah out of the pit and placed him back in the court of the guard. This was done at Zedekiah's command, as the king continued to consult the prophet, who repeated his claims that YHWH would give Jerusalem and the king to the Babylonians.

Finally, Jer 39 describes the Babylonian conquest of Jerusalem, the killing of Zedekiah's sons before his eyes, and the blinding and deportation of the king. The Babylonians' treatment of Jeremiah is noteworthy, apparently because they were aware of his calls for submission to Babylon. He is released from prison and placed in the care of Gedaliah ben Ahikam ben Shaphan, a member of the pro-Babylonian Shaphan family, who was appointed by the Babylonians as governor of Judah.

Jeremiah 40–43

Jeremiah 40–43 presents Jeremiah's decision to remain in Judah following the Babylonian destruction of Jerusalem and his subsequent move to Egypt following the assassination of Gedaliah ben Ahikam. This section is particularly important because it points to Jeremiah's removal to Egypt—against his will—at the end of his forty-year prophetic career, and thereby plays a crucial role in presenting him as an antithetical character to Moses, whose forty-year period of leadership led to Israel's journey from Egyptian bondage to the land of Israel.[23]

The narrative relates the circumstances of Jeremiah's removal to Egypt by focusing on the assassination of Gedaliah ben Ahikam, whom the Babylonians appointed as governor of Judah following the destruction of Jerusalem and the deportation of a large number of its surviving population. It begins with a portrayal of Jeremiah's decision to remain in the land of Judah. Although he was initially among those whom the Babylonians planned to exile, Nebuzaradan, the captain of the guard, decided to release him. Perhaps Nebuzaradan saw Jeremiah as a Babylonian loyalist—certainly many in Judah viewed him as a traitor—and he offered to make sure that the prophet was well cared for in Babylon. Jeremiah declined the offer, and remained with Gedaliah.

Gedaliah was a member of the Shaphan family that had served the royal court as officers under King Josiah and later continued to advocate Josiah's policy of alliance with Babylon after the pro-Egyptian Jehoiakim was placed on the throne. Gedaliah would have been associated with the royal house of David, but he was not of the Davidic line. The narrative portrays Gedaliah as a capable administrator who is able to convince many Judeans who had fled the country to return and to begin the process of rebuilding. Johanan ben Kareah, described as leader of the military forces left in the field, provides support for Gedaliah, and warns him of assassination plots.

The assassination plot by Ishmael ben Nethaniah ben Elishama succeeded. Ishmael is described as a member of the royal house of David who had fled to Ammon. In the absence of the sons of Zedekiah or Jehoiachin, he would then be in a position to claim the Judean throne. His assassination of Gedaliah is portrayed as an act of treachery, and his murder of the mourners who came from Shechem also raises questions about his character. Such acts contradict Jeremiah's image of the righteous Davidic monarch (Jer 23:1-7; 33:14-26).

The assassination of Gedaliah and the defeat of Ishmael set up the circumstances in which Jeremiah is taken to Egypt against his will. Johanan ben Kareah is justifiably concerned about what might happen if the Babylonian army were to return. After two invasions of Judah in 598–597 and 588–587 BCE, the assassination of Gedaliah would provoke a return of the army with potentially brutal consequences. Jeremiah consults YHWH in order to determine what to do, and YHWH's reply reiterates Jeremiah's initial call to build and to plant now that the punishment is over (cf. Jer 1:10). Johanan's rejection of the prophet's position is consistent with the portrayal of Judah's rejection of YHWH.

The final episode in Jer 43:8-13 begins with its own introduction, which is tied to the preceding material with a conjunction, "and the word of YHWH came to Jeremiah in Tahpanhes." It portrays the prophet in the city of Tahpanhes, identified with the site of Tel Hisn, about seven miles northeast of modern Cairo,[24] where he engages in symbolic actions and delivers oracles to demonstrate that Babylon would conquer Egypt as well. Babylon never conquered Egypt, but the Persians took Egypt in 525 BCE.

Jeremiah 44

Jeremiah 44 presents Jeremiah's oracles against the Judeans who had fled to Egypt to escape the Babylonians. The experience of invasion and exile would hardly promote confidence in YHWH among the exiles, but Jeremiah charges that abandonment of YHWH prompts the punishment.

Jeremiah 45

Jeremiah 45 presents Jeremiah's oracle to his scribe, Baruch ben Neriah, who had so loyally supported him and went with him to exile in Egypt. In response to Baruch's own laments, Jeremiah promises that YHWH will spare his life despite the destruction.[25]

Jeremiah 46:1-12

Jeremiah 46:1-12 presents Jeremiah's first oracle against Egypt. The superscription in Jer 46:1 functions as an introduction to all of the oracles concerning the nations, but the appearance of superscriptions in Jer 46:14; 47:1; and 50:1 indicates separate groupings of the oracles within the present form of the oracles concerning the nations in Jeremiah.

The oracle in Jer 46:2-12 is addressed specifically to Pharaoh Necho of Egypt. Necho II took control of Egypt in 609 BCE following the death of his father Psamtek (664–609 BCE).[26] Necho was an ally of the Assyrians, and killed King Josiah of Judah at Megiddo in 609. Following the Babylonian defeat of Assyria in 609, Necho took control of Judah, deposed Jehoahaz ben Josiah, apparently because he would follow his father's pro-Babylonian policy, and replaced him with his older and pro-Egyptian brother Jehoiakim ben Josiah. Following the Babylonian defeat of Egypt at Carchemesh in 605 BCE (the fourth year of Jehoiakim), the Egyptians were forced to relinquish Judah to Babylonian control, which set in motion a chain of events that ultimately led to the unsuccessful Judean revolts against Babylon.

Jeremiah's oracle clearly reflects his own pro-Babylonian views. He draws on the Day of YHWH tradition, which is well known in Isaiah (Isa 2; 13; 34) and other prophets (Amos 5:18-20; Obadiah; Joel; Zephaniah) as a day when YHWH would punish enemies. He also draws upon the imagery of the rising Nile River to depict Egypt's arrogance, but his portrayal of the Babylonian defeat of Egypt recalls elements of the Song of the Sea (Exod 15), in which the Egyptian horses and chariots are destroyed with the rising waters of the Nile by the River Euphrates in Mesopotamia. The placement of this oracle at the head of the oracles concerning the nations in Jeremiah makes eminent sense in the book of a prophet who is also a priest insofar as Egypt is the quintessential enemy of YHWH in the Pentateuchal tradition.

Jeremiah 46:13-28

Jeremiah 46:13-28 presents Jeremiah's second oracle against Egypt. This oracle differs from the first insofar as it anticipates Nebuchadnezzar's conquest of Egypt. Although Nebuchadnezzar invaded Egypt in 601–600 BCE, he did not succeed in conquering the nation. The prophet employs the motif of the enemy from the north that he had previously employed against Judah (see Jer 1:14-19; 4–6). He concludes the oracle with assurances to Jacob that Jacob/Israel would suffer punishment, but Jacob would ultimately be delivered from captivity.

Jeremiah 47–49

Jeremiah 47–49 presents the prophet's oracles against the Philistines, Moab, the Ammonites, Edom, Damascus, Kedar, and Elam. This section takes up the smaller nations that, with the exception of Elam, stood in close proximity to Israel and Judah.

The first oracle against the Philistines appears in Jer 47:1-7. The passage again employs the image of rising waters to depict the threat posed to Philistia by Egypt, but the reference to the north suggests that the oracle may have been modified to account for the threat from Babylon. The Babylonians ultimately took control of the region following their defeat of Egypt in 605.

The oracle against Moab appears in Jer 48:1-47. The initial depiction of threat in vv. 1-10 draws heavily on the language and imagery from the oracle against Moab in Isa 15–16. This would suggest once again that Jeremiah was familiar with the Isaian traditions, and drew upon them in his work.[27] Isaiah depicts a threat posed by Assyria and then applies it to Babylon, and Jeremiah apparently sees the Babylonian threat as a fulfillment of Isaiah's oracles. Later statements also draw on other prophets, such as the references to Moab's arrogance in vv. 29-30, 42, which recall Zeph 2:8-11, and vv. 45-46, which draw upon Num 21:28-29.

The oracle against the Ammonites appears in Jer 49:1-6. Ammon served as refuge for Judeans who fled the Babylonian assault, including Ishmael ben Nethaniah, the Davidic figure who assassinated Gedaliah ben Ahikam (see Jer 40–43). The Babylonians later destroyed the Ammonites along with Moab in the sixth century.

The oracle against the Edomites appears in Jer 49:7-22. Various texts in the Bible indicate that the Edomites assisted the Babylonians in the destruction of the Temple and the city of Jerusalem (see Ps 137:7; Lam 4:21-22; Obad 10–16). The Edomites, later known as Idumeans, survived the Babylonian period, although they were eventually displaced by the Nabateans.

The oracle against Damascus appears in Jer 49:23-27. The city had been destroyed by the Assyrians in 734–732 BCE, and later functioned as an administrative center. Verse 27 quotes Amos 1:4 to indicate judgment that is now fulfilled.

The oracle against Kedar in Jer 49:28-33 is directed against the Arab tribes that inhabited the north Arabian Desert. The ancient Arabs gave extensive support to the Babylonians in their campaigns against Assyria and later against southwestern Asia.

Finally, the oracle against Elam in Jer 49:34-39 focuses on a nation that was subdued by Assyria, Babylon, and finally Persia.

Jeremiah 50:1—51:58

Jeremiah 50:1—51:58 presents the lengthy oracle against Babylon. This oracle forms the climactic conclusion to the oracles concerning the nations in Jeremiah, which indicates the book's fundamental concern with the downfall of Babylon following the exile.

The oracle portrays Babylon's fall as the opportunity for exiled Jews to depart from Babylon and return to their homeland. The oracle ironically employs the same motif of an enemy from the north (Jer 50:3) that will carry out the punishment, much as earlier material in Jer 4–6 made the same claims for the punishment of Judah. Like Isaiah, the oracle envisions the nations' recognition of YHWH and their efforts to join with Judah to return to Jerusalem under the auspices of an eternal covenant (cf. Isa 2:2-4; 11:1-16; 56:1-8; 60–62; 66:18-24). The portrayal of Israel as lost sheep (Jer 50:6-7) echoes Ezek 34 and Mic 2:12-13, and the command to flee from Babylon (Jer 50:8-10) echoes Isa 48:20-21. The descriptions of the army that threatens Babylon may well presuppose the Persian King Cyrus' advance against Babylon in 545–539 BCE and perhaps even his defeat of the Babylonian army in the field, but the lurid descriptions of Babylon's destruction never came to pass, since the priests of Marduk submitted to Cyrus, declared him to be Marduk's chosen monarch, and opened the gates of the city to allow him and his army to enter peacefully.

The oracle makes an effort to establish an analogy between the punishment of Assyria and the punishment of Babylon, much like Isaiah (see Isa 10:5—11:16; 13:1—14:27). The passage makes a special effort to point to the Medes, one of the primary nations incorporated into the Persian Empire, as the agents of YHWH's judgment (Jer 51:11, 28). Indeed, the following statements concerning a raised standard against Babylon recalls motifs from Isa 11:10-16, and the depiction of YHWH's power as creator recalls Isa 41:12-31. The depiction of the rising waters that inundate Babylon (Jer 51:42) reverses the motif of the Babylonian creation epic in which Marduk, the city god of Babylon, establishes order in creation by defeating the sea goddess, Tiamat. The motif also recalls the defeat of the Egyptians at the Red Sea (Exod 15). The final call for the exiles to go out from Babylon (Jer 51:45) and to remember YHWH and Jerusalem (Jer 51:50) likewise recalls motifs that appear throughout Isa 40–66.

Jeremiah 51:59-64

Jeremiah 51:59-64 presents Jeremiah's instructions to Seraiah ben Neriah ben Mahseiah to engage in a symbolic act concerning the punishment of Babylon. Seraiah is the brother of Baruch ben Neriah, Jeremiah's scribe. Seraiah is to accompany Zedekiah to Babylon in Zedekiah's fourth year (ca. 593 BCE), apparently to present tribute to the Babylonian king. Jeremiah instructs him to take a scroll with his oracles concerning Babylon, read them in the city (cf. Jer 36) and to sink the scroll in the Euphrates River. Such an act would symbolize the fact that Babylon would sink, fulfilling the oracle of judgment against the city. The concluding statement, "thus far are the words of Jeremiah," signals the conclusion of the prophet's oracles prior to the following historical appendix.

Jeremiah 52

Jeremiah 52 portrays the Babylonian destruction of Jerusalem, the exile of much of its surviving population, and the release of Jehoiachin from prison by King Evil Merodach of Babylon. This material is drawn from 2 Kgs 25. Evil Merodach is identified with Amel Marduk, the son of Nebuchadnezzar, who ruled for only two years (562–560 BCE) before he died. Although this material is clearly appended to Jeremiah's oracles (note Jer 51:64), it is apparently placed here to confirm Jeremiah's oracles of judgment against Judah and Jerusalem. The concluding notice concerning Jehoiachin's release also suggests that Jeremiah's oracles of restoration would come to pass.

NOTES

* This chapter is a heavily revised and condensed version of my chapter concerning Jeremiah in *The Prophetic Literature* (IBT; Nashville: Abingdon, 2005), 85–125. Readers wishing a much fuller and earlier version of this discussion should turn there.

[1] For discussion concerning the composition of the book of Jeremiah, see especially Jack R. Lundbom, *Jeremiah 1–20* (AB 21A; New York: Doubleday, 1999), 92–101; Douglas R. Jones, *Jeremiah* (NCenB; London: Marshall Pickering, 1992), 17–37.

[2] See Nahman Avigad, *Hebrew Bullae from the Time of Jeremiah: Remnants of a Burnt Archive* (Jerusalem: Israel Exploration Society, 1986) 28–29, which presents a clay bulla or seal with the name Baruch ben Neriah from the time of the Babylonian destruction of Jerusalem.

[3] See, for example, E. W. Nicholson, *Preaching to the Exiles: A Study of the Prose Traditions in the Book of Jeremiah* (New York: Schocken, 1971).

[4] For discussion of the confessions of Jeremiah, see A. R. Diamond, *The Confessions of Jeremiah in Context: Scenes of a Prophetic Drama* (JSOTSup 45; JSOT, 1987); Kathleen M. O'Connor, *The Confessions of Jeremiah: Their Interpretation and Role in Chapters 1–25* (SBLDS 94; Atlanta: Scholars Press, 1988); Mark S. Smith, *The Laments of Jeremiah and their Contexts* (SBLMS 42; Atlanta: Scholars Press, 1990).

[5] Christopher R. Seitz, "The Prophet Moses and the Canonical Shape of Jeremiah," *ZAW* 101 (1989): 3–27; cf. idem, *Theology in Conflict: Reactions to the Exile in the Book of Jeremiah* (BZAW 176; Berlin: de Gruyter, 1989), especially 222–35.

[6] Emmanuel Tov, "Some Aspects of the Textual and Literary History of the Book of Jeremiah," *Le livre d'Jérémie. Le prophète et son milieu. Les oracles et leur transmission* (BETL 54; Leuven: Leuven University Press and Peeters, 1981), 145–67; cf. J. Gerald Janzen, *Studies in the Text of Jeremiah* (HSM 6; Cambridge, MA: Harvard University Press, 1973); Andrew G. Shead, *The Open and the Sealed Book: Jeremiah 32 in its Hebrew and Greek Recensions* (JSOTSup 347; London: Sheffield Academic, 2002).

[7] For discussion of superscriptions, see Gene M. Tucker, "Prophetic Superscriptions and the growth of the Canon," in *Canon and Authority*, ed. G. W. Coats and B. O. Long (Philadelphia: Fortress Press, 1977, 56–70.

[8] See my *King Josiah of Judah: The Lost Messiah of Israel* (Oxford: Oxford University Press, 2001), 208–33.

[9] See J. Philip Hyatt, "The Beginning of Jeremiah's Prophecy," in *A Prophet to the Nations: Essays in Jeremiah Studies*, ed. L. G. Perdue and B. W. Kovacs (Winona Lake, IN: Eisenbrauns, 1984), 63–72.

[10] Jon D. Levenson, "The Temple and the World," *JR* 64 (1984): 275–98; cf. idem, *Sinai and Zion: An Entry into the Jewish Bible* (Minneapolis: Winston, 1985).

[11] For discussion of the literary structure, theological outlook, and compositional history of Jer 2–6, see my "Structure and Redaction in Jeremiah 2–6," in *Form and Intertextuality in Prophetic and Apocalyptic Literature* (FAT 45; Tübingen: Mohr Siebeck, 2005), 94–108.

[12] See my study, "The Truth in True and False Prophecy," in *Form and Intertextuality*, 78–93.

[13] For discussion of Levitical sermons, see especially Rex Mason, *Preaching the Tradition: Homily and Hermeneutics after the Exile* (Cambridge: Cambridge University Press, 1990), although he fails to see that the sermonic form has antecedents prior to the exile.

[14] For discussion of the entrance liturgies, see my *Isaiah 1–39, with an Introduction to Prophetic Literature* (FOTL 16; Grand Rapids: Eerdmans, 1996), 520.

[15] For discussion of the complaint psalms that influence Jeremiah's confessions, see Erhard S. Gerstenberger, *Psalms, Part 1, with an Introduction to Cultic Poetry* (FOTL 14; Grand Rapids: Eerdmans, 1988), 11–14.

[16] Cf. Abraham Joshua Heschel, *The Prophets* (New York: Harper & Row, 1969), 103–39, who emphasizes G-d's divine pathos concerning Judah's wrongdoing and suffering in Jeremiah.

[17] See Duane F. Watson, "Hinnom Valley," *ABD* 3:202–3; Philip C. Schmitz, "Topheth," *ABD* 6:600–601.

[18] For discussion of the political background of the last years of the kingdom of Judah and Jeremiah's own political viewpoints and alliances, see Jay Wilcoxen, "The Political Background of Jeremiah's Temple Sermon," in *Scripture in History and Theology: Essays in Honor of J. Coert Rylaarsdam*, ed. A. Merrill and T. Overholt (Pittsburgh: Pickwick, 1977), 151–66.

[19] See David Stacey, *Prophetic Drama in the Old Testament* (London: Epworth, 1990), 151–57, and my "The Truth." See also James A. Sanders, "Hermeneutics in True and False Prophecy," in Coats and Long, eds., *Canon and Authority*, 21–41.

[20] See my "Jeremiah 30–31 and King Josiah's Program of National Restoration and Religious Reform," in *Form and Intertextuality*, 109–22, and *King Josiah*, 225–33.

[21] See especially Yohanan Goldman, *Prophétie et royauté au retour de l'exil* (OBO 118; Freiburg: Universitätsverlag, 1992), 9–64.

[22] Wilcoxen, "The Political Background."

[23] Seitz, "The Prophet Moses."

[24] Richard N. Jones and Zbigniew T. Fiema, "Tahpanhes," *ABD* 6:308–9.

[25] For a study of Baruch ben Neriah in Jeremiah and the development of his image in later tradition, see now J. Edward Wright, *Baruch Ben Neriah: From Biblical Scribe to Apocalyptic Seer* (Columbia: University of South Carolina Press, 2003).

[26] See Amélie Kuhrt, *The Ancient Near East, c. 3000–330 BC* (London: Routledge, 1998) 2:636–44; Donald B. Redford, *Egypt, Canaan, and Israel in Ancient Times* (Princeton: Princeton University Press, 1992), 430–69.

[27] See my "The Truth."

D. THE BOOK OF EZEKIEL*

The book of Ezekiel presents some of the most profound and challenging theological literature in the entire Bible.[1] Ezekiel was a Zadokite priest who would have served in the Jerusalem Temple had he not been among the exiles taken by Nebuchadnezzar with King Jehoiachin of Judah to Babylonia in 597 BCE. As a priest in exile, Ezekiel was compelled to apply his highly mythologized worldview of the holiness of YHWH and creation in his attempts to grapple with the meaning and significance of the exile, the destruction of Jerusalem and the Temple, and his expectations of a return to the holy center of creation in Jerusalem. Ezekiel represents an important figure in the foundation of the Jewish mystical tradition, with its emphasis on the manifestation and recognition of the holy divine presence within the world, and a key proponent for the restoration of Israel around the Temple in Jerusalem.

The book of Ezekiel generally appears immediately after Jeremiah as the third book of the Latter Prophets in the Tanak, although some authorities consider it to be the second book (*b. Baba Batra* 14b). Rabbinic tradition raises questions about the canonical status of Ezekiel, however, since the book frequently conflicts with halakhic statements found in the Torah. Talmudic tradition states that Rabbi Hanina ben Hezekiah burned three hundred barrels of oil working at night to reconcile the differences so that Ezekiel might be accepted as sacred scripture (*b. Shabbat* 13b; *b. Haggigah* 13a; *b. Menahot* 45a).[2]

The superscription for the book in Ezek 1:1-3 presents a mixed introduction which combines a first-person autobiographical statement, purportedly by the prophet, with third-person descriptive statements apparently made by an editor of the book. Verse 1 places the prophet among the exiles by the River Chebar, in the thirtieth year, on the fourth day of the fifth month, when he began to see visions of G-d. The third-person statements in vv. 2-3 specify that it was the fifth year of King Jehoiachin's reign when the word of YHWH came to Ezekiel ben Buzi by the River Chebar in the land of the Chaldeans. The term Chaldeans refers to the Neo-Babylonian Empire established in 627 BCE by Nabopolassar, the father of Nebuchadnezzar. The fifth year of Jehoiachin's exile would be 593–592 BCE, and the fifth day of the fourth month would be 5 Tammuz in the ancient Jewish and Babylonian calendars, approximately late June or early July. The River Chebar is a canal that ran by the ancient city of Nippur.³ Ezekiel's later reference to a city called Tel Aviv (Ezek 3:15), after which the modern Israeli city was named in 1909 to signify the restoration of modern Israel, corresponds to the site of a town called *til abūbi*, located along the Chebar canal.⁴

The significance of Ezekiel's initial reference to the thirtieth year has prompted considerable speculation. Some posit that it refers to the thirtieth year since King Josiah's reform began in 627 BCE; others posit that it refers to Ezekiel's initial call.⁵ It most likely refers, however, to the prophet's age at the time of his initial visions, which would coincide with the initiation of Josiah's reform.⁶ As a Zadokite priest, Ezekiel would have assumed his priestly duties at the age of thirty, and he would have continued service until the age of fifty (see Num 4:3, 23, 30, which specify that the lines of Kohath, the ancestor of the high priest Aaron, Gershom, and Merari would begin their specialized service in relation to the tent of meeting at the age of thirty; cf. Num 8:23-25, which specifies twenty-five, Ezekiel's age at the time of his exile, as the initial year of service for Levites in general). As the chronology of the book indicates, all but one of the prophet's oracles are placed from Ezekiel's initial vision in the fifth year of Jehoiachin's exile through the twenty-fifth year when Ezekiel saw the vision of the restored Temple (see Ezek 40:1). The result is a twenty-year chronological framework for Ezekiel's oracles that would take him from the age of thirty through the age of fifty, the years of active service normally expected of a Zadokite priest. Only the reference to the twenty-seventh year in Ezek 29:17, which introduces an oracle that refers to Nebuchadnezzar's campaign against Tyre, stands outside of this framework. Interpreters note, however, that this oracle was updated and its date likely changed to account for the actual timing of Nebuchadnezzar's conquest of Tyre following a thirteen-year siege that finally concluded in 572 BCE.⁷

The literary structure of the book of Ezekiel is evident in the sequence of chronological statements that introduce the major components of the book. These appear in Ezek 1:1-3 (cf. Ezek 3:6), which introduces the initial account of Ezekiel's visions in the fifth year of Jehoiachin's exile; Ezek 8:1, which describes YHWH's departure from the Temple in the sixth year, sixth month, fifth day; Ezek 20:1, which introduces a sequence of oracles concerned with the punishment of Israel in the seventh year, fifth month, tenth day; Ezek 24:1, which introduces oracles concerned with the fall of Jerusalem and the nations in ninth year, tenth month, tenth day; Ezek 26:1, which introduces the initial oracle against Tyre in the eleventh year on the first day of an unspecified month; Ezek 29:1, which introduces the first oracle against Egypt in the tenth year, tenth month, twelfth day; Ezek 29:17, which introduces the second block of oracles concerned with Egypt in the twenty-seventh year, first month, first day; Ezek 30:20, which introduces the first oracle against Pharaoh in the eleventh year, first month, seventh day; Ezek 31:1, which introduces the second oracle concerning Pharaoh in the eleventh year, first month, seventh day; Ezek 32:1, which introduces an oracle concerning Pharaoh and Egypt in the twelfth year, twelfth month, first day; Ezek

32:17, which introduces an oracle sequence concerning the nations and Ezekiel's role as watchman in the twelfth year and the first day of an unspecified month; Ezek 33:21, which introduces oracles concerned with the restoration of Israel in twelfth year, tenth month, fifth day; and Ezek 40:1, which introduces Ezekiel's vision of the restored Temple in the twenty-fifth year, on the tenth day of the beginning of the year (Rosh Ha-Shanah in the seventh month).

Insofar as the sequence envisions a process of punishment, restoration, and purging that extends from the destruction of Jerusalem to its re-establishment, the book may be characterized as Ezekiel's visions concerning the purge of Jerusalem.

Much of Ezekiel appears to represent the work of the prophet himself, although it has been lightly edited.[8] Ezekiel's vision of the restored Temple was never achieved—representations of the Second Temple built in 520–515 BCE differ markedly from Ezekiel's portrayal. The book is dated to the period of the Babylonian exile prior to the early Persian restoration.

The book of Ezekiel presents a programmatic Zadokite priestly rationale for the restoration of the land and people of Israel centered at the Temple in Jerusalem. Ezekiel is a Zadokite priest who was raised and educated to serve in the Jerusalem Temple, but his exile to Babylonia together with King Jehoiachin in 597 BCE removed him from the holy precincts of the Temple and brought him instead to a foreign land. Beginning with his thirtieth birthday, which would have initiated his twenty-year service as an active priest, Ezekiel sought to interpret the significance of the divine will in relation to YHWH's efforts to resanctify the Temple at the center of all creation. The result is a scenario in which Ezekiel maintains that divine presence and sanctity are evident and active throughout all creation, and that YHWH will restore both Israel and the Temple at the center of a renewed creation.

Ezekiel functions simultaneously as both prophet and Zadokite priest. Ezekiel's language, use of visual imagery, and theological concepts indicate an attempt to combine the traditional perspectives and worldview of a Zadokite priest with the very new circumstances of life in Babylonian exile.[9] Ezekiel was raised in the holy precincts of the Jerusalem Temple for a life of service within the sanctuary, whereas Babylonia was an impure foreign land that stood outside of the Temple compound. Thus Ezekiel's visions, oracles, and symbolic actions indicate an effort to recognize the manifestation of YHWH in creation at large and to adapt the usual practices and perspectives of life in the holy Temple to account for YHWH's presence throughout all of creation and to explain the significance of YHWH's destruction of Jerusalem and the Temple itself.

Fundamental to Ezekiel's attempts to portray the manifestation of the holy divine presence is his use of the expression, "the glory of YHWH" (Hebrew, *kĕbôd yhwh*), which is employed throughout the biblical tradition to describe YHWH's presence among the people (Exod 16:7, 10-12), in the Tabernacle (Exod 40:34-38), and in the Temple (1 Kgs 8:10-11; 2 Chr 7:1-3; cf. 1 Sam 4:21-22). The expression appears throughout Ezekiel's visions to describe YHWH's presence in relation to the destruction of Jerusalem and the Temple in Ezek 1–11 and the re-establishment of the Temple at the center of creation in Ezek 40–48. Ezekiel's portrayal of the glory of YHWH in Ezek 1:4-28 presupposes the imagery of the ark of the covenant located in the Holy of Holies of the Jerusalem Temple.[10] As a priest, Ezekiel would be familiar with such imagery as part of his preparation for divine service in the sanctuary. His description of YHWH's glory as a cloud from the north takes up a combination of elements from priestly tradition and from the general ancient Near Eastern cultural environment. On the one hand, the ten incense stands would fill the great hall of the Temple with clouds of smoke to symbolize the divine presence at times of worship. Likewise, both biblical and ancient Near Eastern traditions portrayed YHWH, the Ugaritic/Canaanite god Baal, and the Assyrian god Assur as divine figures who rode through the clouds on a chariot or other suitable vehicle to symbolize their power and mastery in the world of creation (see 2 Sam 22:7-20; Pss 18:6-19; 68:17-20, 32-35; Hab 3). The four living creatures or cherubim that bear the glory of YHWH through the heavens correspond to the two cherubim that are constructed on top of the ark of the covenant and the two cherubim that are constructed in the Holy of Holies of the Temple (Exod 25:1-22; 37:1-9; 1 Kgs 6:23-28; 2 Chr 3:10-14). Such figures typically appear beside the thrones of kings in the ancient Near East. Because Judaism prohibits the tangible portrayal of G-d, Ezekiel employs the language of simile to describe YHWH's holy presence; for example, "above the expanse over their heads was the semblance of a throne, in appearance like sapphire; and on top, upon this semblance of a throne, there was the semblance of a human form" (Ezek 1:26). The four faces of each of the living creatures or cherubim represent divine characteristics, that is, the bull represents divine power; the lion, symbol of the royal tribe of Judah, represents divine sovereignty; the eagle represents divine freedom to be everywhere and anywhere; and the human face represents divine intelligence. Because the living creatures represent the holy other nature of the divine, they are said to move in the direction of each of their four faces at once, that is, in all four directions at once, a movement impossible for humans to conceptualize.

The vision also reflects Temple imagery. The gleaming bronze recalls the description of the ark as overlaid with gold, and perhaps reflects the realities of the ark after the gold was stripped from the Temple by foreign invaders and replaced with bronze (1 Kgs 14:25-28; cf. 2 Kgs 18:14-16). The burning coals of fire presuppose the burning incense altars within the great hall of the Temple or perhaps even the sacrificial altars themselves. The wheel within the wheel pre-supposes the four rings used with poles to convey the ark through the wilderness (Exod 25:12-15) or perhaps the wheels of the cart later used to carry the ark from Kiriath Jearim to Jerusalem (2 Sam 6:3; 1 Chr 13:7). The firmament that shines like crystal above the heads of the creatures that bear the glory of YHWH sym-bolizes the mercy seat of the ark (Exod 25:17) or the clear pavement underneath the throne of YHWH at the time when Moses, Aaron, Nadab, Abihu, and the seventy elders of Israel ascend Mt. Sinai to engage in a banquet with YHWH (Exod 24:9-11). Such a banquet represents the sacrificial meals eaten at the Temple on holy festivals. The image of the bow in the clouds (Ezek 1:28) repre-sents the bow that appeared in relation to YHWH's covenant with Noah (Gen 9:8-17).

Other images from the vision reflect Ezekiel's priestly role and practice. YHWH's designation of Ezekiel as "Mortal," literally, "Son of Man/Adam," reflects the belief that the high priest in the Temple was the descendant of Adam, the first human being, who represented all humanity before YHWH. The por-trayal of his eating the scroll presented to him by YHWH (Ezek 2:8—3:3) reflects the priestly role for learning Torah and teaching it to the people, most notably in public readings of the Torah at the Temple (Lev 10:11; Deut 31:9-13; cf. Hag 2:10-19). Ezekiel's role as watchman or sentinel who warns the people of YHWH's words so that they might avoid wrongdoing (Ezek 3:16-21; 33:1-20) presupposes the role of the Levitical Temple gatekeepers, who would ensure the sanctity of the Temple by permitting only those who were properly prepared for Temple worship to enter the Temple grounds (see 1 Chr 9:17-27; 26:1-19; cf. Pss 15; 24; 2 Chr 23).

Further elements and images in the book point to Ezekiel's priestly identity. Ezekiel's sitting in silence for seven days (Ezek 3:15) reflects the seven-day period of seclusion when priests are first ordained for service at the altar (Lev 8:33). Ezekiel bears the guilt of his people (Ezek 4:4-8) in keeping with the priestly task to bear the guilt of the people (Lev 9:1-21; Num 18:1). His portrayal of the destruction of Jerusalem as a sort of purging sacrifice reflects the presentation of sin offerings at the Temple (Lev 4:1—5:19) and the scapegoat sacrifice for Yom Kippur (Lev 16). His discussion of moral responsibility (Ezek 18) draws heavily on the teachings of the Holiness Code in Lev 17–26, which define holy, righteous life in ancient Israel. His concern with the profanation of YHWH's holy name

(Ezek 20; 33) reflects the priestly concern with YHWH's holiness in general. The portrayal of besieged Jerusalem as a sacrificial cauldron that must be cleansed (Ezek 24:1-14) draws upon the fundamental priestly duty to prepare sacrifices for consumption in the Temple. His portrayal of YHWH's lack of mourning at the fall of Jerusalem in relation to the death of his own wife (Ezek 24:15-27) draws upon the extensive tradition of Israel as the bride of YHWH (Jer 2; Hos 1–3; Zeph 3:14-20; Ezek 16; Isa 54) and the prohibition of mourning for priests except for blood relatives (Lev 21). The portrayal of the cleansing of the land through the resurrection of the dead (Ezek 37) and the burning of enemy corpses (Ezek 38–39) presupposes the priestly concern with death as the ultimate form of impurity (Lev 21). Even the vision of the restored Temple embodies the fundamental image for a pure and stable creation (Ezek 40–48).

As a Zadokite priest, Ezekiel would view the Jerusalem Temple as the holy center of creation. Given this role, the sanctity of the Temple plays a key role in maintaining the sanctity and stability of creation at large. Thus, when the sanctity of the Temple is compromised or the Temple is destroyed, all creation suffers or even perishes as a result. Such a view is evident in the final vision of the restored Temple in Ezek 40–48, which culminates in a vision of the restored creation with a restored twelve tribes of Israel gathered around the new Temple at the center. In this vision, water wells up from under the Temple mount, flows down into the Dead Sea, and turns this dead zone into a living lake filled with fish and lined with verdant vegetation and fruit as evidence that the restoration of the Temple has resulted in the restoration of creation as well, indeed, on terms not seen before. But the purging of the Temple in the book of Ezekiel also has its impact on the nations of the world that inhabit creation. A sequence of nations, including Ammon, Moab, Edom, Tyre, and Egypt, will suffer punishment in Ezek 25–32 as part of the process by which YHWH will be revealed to Israel and the world at large. These nations hardly constitute all the nations of the world; rather, they are nations that Ezekiel projects will fall to the Babylonian Empire, thereby identifying YHWH with Babylon in much the same way that Isaiah identifies YHWH with Assyria, and later Babylonia and Persia. In contrast to the models in Isaiah, Babylon is never brought down in the book of Ezekiel nor does it factor in to YHWH's role as the One who carries out the purge of the Temple. Throughout the book, Ezekiel makes clear that YHWH and YHWH alone is the key actor on the scene who brings about punishment and restoration, so that "they will know that I am YHWH."

Indeed, the so-called recognition formula, "so that they will know that I am YHWH," appears to be the key factor in YHWH's actions as presented in the book of Ezekiel.[11] Throughout the book, Ezekiel contends that the world has gone awry in idolatry and apostasy, and that YHWH's actions are taken to manifest a process of revelation in which YHWH will be recognized throughout Israel, the nations, and creation at large as the one holy G-d of all creation.

Clearly, the destruction and restoration of the Temple are the key events around which the book of Ezekiel turns, but the role of the monarchy is also noteworthy. The books of Isaiah and Jeremiah both recognize that the Davidic monarchy is finished, and both thereby reconceive the Davidic covenant to apply to the people of Israel at large in the book of Isaiah (Isa 55) and the city of Jerusalem and the Levites in the book of Jeremiah (Jer 33). Ezekiel makes no such move. He generally views the Davidic monarch as a "prince" (*nāśî'*), analogous to the tribal leaders of Israel in the wilderness period, and portrays the Davidic monarch as subservient to YHWH and the Temple establishment. But in a strik-ing oracle in Ezek 37:15-28, he refers to the Davidic monarch as "king" (*melek*) in the context of an oracle that calls for the reunification of Joseph, that is, northern Israel, and Judah. Such reunification of northern Israel and southern Judah under the rule of a Davidic monarch and the purging of the Temple were central to King Josiah's program of religious reform and national restoration in the late seventh century BCE. Given Ezekiel's age of thirty in 592 BCE at the time of his inaugural vision, Ezekiel would have been born in 622 BCE, the eighteenth year of King Josiah, which was the year that Josiah began the Temple restoration that launched his reform program (2 Kgs 22:3; 2 Chr 34:8). Given Ezekiel's birth at the outset of Josiah's reform, he would have been raised and educated to serve as a priest in the Jerusalem Temple throughout the course of Josiah's reform program. But of course, with the death of Josiah at the hands of Pharaoh Necho of Egypt in 609 BCE the entire program came apart. Nevertheless, Ezekiel appears to have been heavily influenced by the reform, insofar as his visions of a restored Temple and a reunited Israel with a Davidic monarch gathered around that Temple appear to embody the ideals of Josiah's reform as the centerpiece of a new creation.[12]

The following examines the major components of the book of Ezekiel in an effort to delineate the theological concerns of the book.

Ezekiel 1–7

Ezekiel 1–7 begins with Ezekiel's initial vision of YHWH by the banks of the River Chebar in Babylonia. Following the account of Ezekiel's vision in Ezek 1:4—3:15, the appearance of the formula, "the word of YHWH came to me," in Ezek 3:16; 6:1; and 7:1 marks the other sub-units of this section. Overall, Ezek 1–7 presents YHWH's commission of Ezekiel to act as a prophet.

Ezekiel's initial vision of YHWH is based largely on the imagery of the ark of the covenant in the Holy of Holies of the Jerusalem Temple, and it appears to function as Ezekiel's response to the earlier vision of Isaiah ben Amoz in Isa 6.[13] The image has been modified, however, to account for YHWH's mobility and manifestation in the world of creation. Such an image may well depend in part on representations of YHWH flying through the heavens in a divine chariot or pagan representations of deities such as Baal, who is portrayed in Ugaritic texts as the rider of clouds,[14] or Assur, who is depicted in Assyrian art in relation to a winged solar disc who appears at the head of the Assyrian armies as well as in other contexts.[15] Although Ezekiel is a priest, raised to serve in the Jerusalem Temple, his unexpected presence as an exile in a foreign land obviously influences his view of the world, and his visions and actions reflect his adaptation to the circumstances and culture in which he finds himself. Ezekiel never gives up his identity as a Zadokite priest, but instead finds the means to serve as a priest outside of the sanctuary in which he would normally have spent his life.

In his thirtieth year, the time when he would normally begin his service in the Temple, Ezekiel's initial vision of YHWH reflects an adaptation of the priestly ordination in which young priests would commence their holy service. According to Lev 8 (see also Exod 28), the priestly ordination ceremony calls for a seven-day period of incubation in which the priest remains in the sanctuary (tent of meeting) as daily sacrifices are made in order to consecrate him for holy service (see especially Lev 8:31-36; Exod 28:35-37).[16] Insofar as the priest remains in the sanctuary, he is located before the Holy of Holies and the ark of the covenant, which represents the divine presence in the Temple. The presence of the cherubim and the ark contribute markedly to the image. Presumably, the incense altars and *mĕnōrôt* (candelabra) add smoke and light to the imagery of divine presence. Moses' experience in the tent of meeting (Exod 33:7; 34:29-35; Num 7:89), Samuel's experience before the ark in Shiloh (1 Sam 3), and Zechariah's experience at the ordination of the high priest Joshua ben Jehozadak (Zech 3) suggest that visions of the divine presence could well be a part of the ordination process. Ezekiel receives his commission to act from YHWH in the form of specific instructions to speak YHWH's words to the people of Israel and a scroll which he is to eat in order to internalize the divine message (Ezek 2:1—3:11). Such a commission, of course, recalls the priestly task to teach YHWH's Torah to the people (Lev 10:10-11). He sits stunned among the exiles at Tel Aviv for a period of seven days (Ezek 3:15), and it is only at the end of his seven days of silence among his fellow exiles that he begins to carry out the divine commission (Ezek 3:16), much as a newly ordained priest begins his service at the altar on the eighth day immediately following his ordination (Lev 9, especially v. 1).

Ezekiel 3:16—5:17 presents a series of divine commands to the prophet/priest that defines his role and message in relation to the exiled people. YHWH begins by informing him that he will serve as a sentinel for the people to warn them of their wickedness. This role represents an adaptation of the priestly gatekeepers who were to ensure that only those who were properly prepared could enter the holy precincts of the Temple. Ezekiel's task is to inform the people of wrongdoing so that they might correct themselves and not die or otherwise suffer punishment. Should Ezekiel fail in his task, he is held accountable just as the priest is expected to bear the sins of Israel or the Temple (Num 18:1). It is noteworthy that Ezek 3:22-27 specifies that Ezekiel is to remain silent in his house and to speak only when YHWH commands him to deliver an oracle to the people. Such a role conforms to that of Moses as oracle diviner in the Tent of Meeting (see Exod 33:7-11; 34:29-35; Num 11). It also reflects priestly service at the altar, insofar as the priests carry out the sacrifice without speaking.[17] Speech is left to the Levitical choirs, whose singing constitutes a form of prophetic speech that corresponds to the singing of the angelic choirs of the heavenly Temple (see 1 Chr 15–16). Ezekiel cannot serve at the Jerusalem Temple, so his service in Babylonia reflects an adaptation of his expected Temple role.

YHWH's instructions include several symbolic acts that represent the profanation or punishment of Israel. In the first instance, YHWH commands Ezekiel to construct a model of the city of Jerusalem under siege and to lie on his side to symbolize the time of the punishment of Israel and Judah. He is to lie on his left side for 390 days to symbolize the years of the punishment of Israel and on his right side for forty days to symbolize the years of the punishment of Judah. The significance of these periods of time is uncertain. They are noteworthy, however, because forty years corresponds to the time from Josiah's reform in 627 BCE until the destruction of the Temple in 587 BCE. The 390 years would then correspond roughly to the time from Saul's kingship (ca. 1020 BCE; see 1 Sam 13:1) or David's establishment of Jerusalem as the site for the Temple ca. 1000 BCE to the beginning of Josiah's reform. Such a chronology accepts biblical claims that the northern kingdom of Israel was punished for idolatry (2 Kgs 17) and that Josiah attempted to atone for past wrongdoing through his reform (2 Kgs 22–23). His early death, however, signaled the end of his reform and led ultimately to Jerusalem's destruction by the Babylonians.

This action is to be accompanied by the preparation of impure food, which Ezekiel is to eat while lying on his side for the specified periods of time. The food is impure because it is cooked over a fire fueled by human dung. As a priest, Ezekiel was enjoined to eat only food that had been sanctified for presentation at the altar and prepared for consumption in the holy Temple (Lev 7; 10–11; Num 18; Deut 14). When Ezekiel protests to YHWH, he is allowed to use cow dung instead. Such an act symbolizes Ezekiel's own profanation as a priest.

The second symbolic action calls for Ezekiel to cut his hair and divide it into thirds so that each third will represent the fate of a segment of Jerusalem's population; one third will be burned, one third will be stricken with the sword, and one third will be scattered to the wind. Such an act likewise symbolizes Ezekiel's loss of sanctity as a priest. Although the priests were to cut their hair, they were not to shave it off entirely as Canaanite or Egyptian priests apparently did (Lev 21:5; 19:27). This action is followed by Ezekiel's announcement of judgment against Jerusalem in Ezek 5:5-17, viz., because Jerusalem rebelled against YHWH's expectations and defiled YHWH's Temple, YHWH will execute judgment against the city.

Ezekiel 6 presents YHWH's instruction role for Ezekiel to prophesy against the hills of Israel. The oracle continues the themes of the symbolic acts in Ezek 4–5, but it adds references to the profanation of the land of Israel by the presence of unauthorized cultic high places and altars. As the holy center of creation and the land of Israel,[18] the Jerusalem Temple was to serve as the only sanctuary in the land. With the profanation of Jerusalem and the Temple, the land becomes unclean and subject to punishment.

The concluding sub-unit in Ezek 7 presents a prophecy of judgment against the entire nation. The oracle draws upon the Day of YHWH traditions in the Hebrew Bible (for example, Amos 5:18-20; 8:1-14; Isa 2:6-13; 13; 34; Zeph 1:7-18, respectively), which frequently announce YHWH's judgment against either the nations or Israel and Judah.

Ezekiel 8–19

Ezekiel 8–19 presents Ezekiel's vision of the departure of the glory of YHWH from Jerusalem in Ezek 8:1—11:13 together with a series of oracles that takes up the significance of this event. Each of the following oracles is introduced with the phrase, "and the word of YHWH came to me, saying. . . ." The first appears in Ezek 11:14, which introduces an oracle in vv. 14-24 concerning YHWH's intentions to restore Israel with a new heart following the conclusion of the exile. Successive prophetic word formulas, each of which introduces a new oracle in the sequence, appear in Ezek 12:1, 17, 21; 13:1; 14:1-2; 15:1; 16:1; 17:1, 11; and 18:1. Although these oracles take up the coming punishment of the people, Ezek 11:14-24 defines Israel's restoration as the ultimate goal of the punishment articulated throughout this section.

Ezekiel's portrayal of YHWH's departure from the Temple draws heavily on priestly notions of purification in an effort to interpret the anticipated destruction of the Temple as an attempt to purge the Temple and Jerusalem of impurity.[19] Various biblical and apocryphal narratives portray attempts at Temple purification during the reigns of Hezekiah (2 Kgs 18:1-8; 2 Chr 29–31), Josiah (2 Kgs 23:1-25), and Judah the Maccabee (1 Macc 4:36-51). Portrayals of attempts to purge the people of Israel appear in the golden calf episode (Exod 32), the narrative concerning the deaths of Korah, Dathan, and Abiram for conducting improper worship (Num 16), and the narrative concerning Achan's theft of booty during the conquest of Canaan (Josh 7). The expiatory ḥaṭṭa't, "sin offering," and 'āšām, "guilt offering" (Lev 4:1—5:26; 6:17—7:10), accompany attempts to purge the Temple or the people.[20]

Ezekiel begins with a description of a heavenly figure who transports him to the Temple. He portrays the Temple as a sanctuary that has been corrupted by foreign worship, where he describes the presence of "an infuriating image." The precise meaning of this term is uncertain, but it clearly suggests something improper, as do the references to abominations, creeping things, loathsome animals, idols, and so on, that appear within the Temple. The reference to the elders of Israel and Jaazniah ben Shaphan deserve attention, since the elders were an important authoritative body in Israel, and Jaazniah is a member of the Shaphan family that supported Jeremiah. Interpreters frequently take Ezekiel's description as an account of true idolatry in the Temple, but his perspective as an exiled Zadokite priest must be considered. If the Babylonians had taken Zadokite priests like Ezekiel from the Temple, those who were left behind might have been viewed as inadequate to maintain Temple sanctity. Ezekiel's vision need not depict people who deliberately committed sins, but only reflect his understanding of the compromised sanctity of the Temple following the removal of Zadokite priests. Late summer mourning rituals that call for rain are cast as worship of the Babylonian fertility god, Tammuz, and morning prayer directed to the east is cast as worship of the sun.

The portrayal of the executioners is particularly important for its use of priestly imagery. Ezekiel describes six men with weapons in hand supervised by a man dressed in white linen with a writing case at his side. White linen is the characteristic dress of the priests (Exod 28:29) and of the angels who are the heavenly counterparts of priests (Dan 10:5). Rabbinic literature notes that a priestly officer typically supervised other priests during times of sacrifice (*m. Tamid* 1.2; 3.1-9). Although interpreters often claim that the executioners are to destroy the guilty,[21] there is little indication that "those who sigh or groan over all the abominations that are committed in it" are guilty of sighing or groaning in support of the abomination or in disgust at them. The following command to show no pity in cutting down old men, women, and children likewise suggests little interest in determining individual guilt or innocence. In Ezekiel's estimation, guilt or impurity are corporate insofar as they affect the entire nation, and the people suffer accordingly. We may recall the scapegoat ritual of Yom Kippur (Day of Atonement) in which two goats are employed as sin offerings for the people (Lev 16). One is sacrificed at the altar, and the other is sent out to the wilderness to carry away the sins of the people. Insofar as Ezekiel later claims that those who survive are to be sent into exile to be judged, whereas those who died are likened to meat in a sacrificial pot (Ezek 11:5-12), it appears that Ezekiel's understanding of the destruction of Jerusalem is heavily influenced by the scapegoat ritual in which the people are purged in part by the sacrifice of the one goat and the expulsion of the other.

The destruction of the city represents a form of sacrifice. YHWH commands the man in white linen to take coals from among the cherubim and scatter them over the city to ignite it. Such an image represents the procedure of sacrifice, and the portrayal of smoke and brightness represents the incense altars and sacrificial altar in operation during worship. The rise of the cherubim who bear YHWH represents the departure of the glory of YHWH from the Temple in contrast to the descent of the glory of YHWH into the wilderness tabernacle (Exod 40:33-38; 1 Kgs 8:1-13).

The following oracles attempt to explain the significance of the destruction of Jerusalem. The initial oracle, Ezek 11:14-24, portrays the destruction as an act of purification and states YHWH's intentions to restore Jerusalem and the people once the process of purification is complete. YHWH pledges to serve as a "little sanctuary" for the people and to give them a new heart and spirit to observe divine expectations. Many see in this statement the beginnings of diaspora Jewish organization and worship that led ultimately to the emergence of the synagogue, as exiled Jews attempted to establish community religious life outside of the land of Israel.[22]

The remaining oracles, each introduced by the formula, "and the word of YHWH came to me, saying . . . ," reflect on the message of judgment and restoration laid out in Ezekiel's vision. Ezekiel 12:1-16 presents YHWH's call for Ezekiel to carry out a symbolic act to represent the exile of the people. He is to carry his baggage, dig through the wall, cover his face, and then explain to the people that this act symbolizes YHWH's intentions to exile the people among the nations. Such a portrayal draws upon the observance of Pesaḥ (Passover) in the Temple, in which the people are dressed for travel as they eat the sacrificial offering in the Temple (see Exod 12–13, especially 12:11). Ezekiel 12:17-20 likewise draws upon the Passover tradition by calling on the people to drink water and eat bread in fear, much like the slaves of the Exodus tradition, as they go out into the wilderness away from the land of Israel. Ezekiel 12:21-25 emphasizes that the realization of Ezekiel's vision is near, which would dispel any notions that judgment is far off. Ezekiel's language draws upon the Day of YHWH tradition, which frequently states that YHWH's day of judgment is near (see Isa 13:6; Obad 15; Joel 1:15; 2:1; Zeph 1:7, 14; cf. Ezek 30:3). Ezekiel 12:26-28 envisions a long period of fulfillment before the entire process of exile and restoration is complete.

Ezekiel 13 takes up the issue of false prophecy (see Deut 18:9-22; 1 Kgs 13; 22; Jer 23:9-40; 27–29). One of the major hermeneutical questions of biblical prophecy is whether it is true or false, which entails that a prophecy cannot be considered true until it is fulfilled (see Deut 18:9-22).[23] Ezekiel agrees with Jeremiah (Jer 27–28) in claiming that those prophets who announce peace must be false. From Ezekiel's perspective, judgment followed by restoration is inevitable.

Ezekiel 14:1-11 takes up the question of repentance, insofar as YHWH calls for the people to change, but justifies judgment by charging that the people defiled themselves by turning to idols. Ezekiel 14:12-23 argues that even the presence of righteous figures, such as Noah, Daniel, and Job, could not save the lives of those who acted against YHWH (cf. Jer 15:1, which cites Moses and Samuel for similar reasons).

Ezekiel 15 presents an allegory in which the prophet compares the wood of the vine to the people of Israel. Just as the twisted wood of the vine is useless for anything but burning, so YHWH will give up Israel to burning (cf. Judg 9:7-21). Such an analogy is typical of the wisdom tradition (see Prov 30), although prophets frequently make use of wisdom perspectives (see Isa 5:1-7; 28:23-29; Amos 2:13; 3:3-8).

Ezekiel 16:1-63 represents another example of the use of the marriage metaphor to portray the relationship between YHWH and Jerusalem as husband and bride (cf. Hos 1–3; Jer 2; Isa 54; Zeph 3:14-20, respectively).[24] Ezekiel's portrayal is particularly harsh, insofar as he presents Jerusalem as an abandoned baby girl, whom YHWH takes in, clothes, raises to maturity, and then marries, only to be abandoned when the grown up girl goes off with other lovers. The metaphor is not to be understood strictly in religious terms. The designation of Egypt, the Assyrians, and the Chaldeans/Babylonians, indicates that the prophet has in mind Jerusalem's history of alliances with foreign nations that frequently resulted in defeat or conquest. The charge that Jerusalem's mother was a Hittite and her father an Amorite calls to mind Jerusalem's background as a Jebusite city, whose population was never destroyed when David took control (2 Sam 5). The portrayal of the fate of the sisters, Samaria and Sodom, is intended to demonstrate that Jerusalem had ample warning in the fate of the northern kingdom of Israel (2 Kgs 17) and in the portrayal of Sodom's destruction (Gen 18–19). The concluding portrayal of Jerusalem's restoration, like that of Samaria and Sodom, draws upon the Zadokite concept of an eternal covenant with creation in which the Temple and its practices (Gen 9:8-17; Exod 31:12-17), the priesthood (Num 18:23; 25:10-13), and the house of David (2 Sam 7; 23:1-7; Pss 89; 110) are rooted. It is not a new covenant as in Jeremiah (Jer 31:31-34), but an eternal covenant which YHWH remembers.

Ezekiel 17:1-10 presents an allegory about two great eagles. The first came to Lebanon to break off the top shoot of a cedar. It placed the shoot in a land of merchants where it sprouted and flourished. When a second eagle came, the vine reached out again, but YHWH raised questions whether it will thrive after it is pulled up. Ezekiel 17:11-24 then explains the allegory, which draws upon earlier prophetic tradition that portrays the Davidic monarchy as a shoot or vine (Isa 11:1-9; Jer 23:1-8). The first eagle refers to Nebuchadnezzar, the king of Babylon, who took the Judean king Jehoiachin into exile and placed his uncle Zedekiah on the throne. The second refers to the Egyptian Pharaoh, Psamtek II, with whom Judah allied in a futile attempt to revolt against Babylon. The oracle concludes by stating that only YHWH will raise a righteous Davidic monarch.

Ezekiel 18:1—19:14 calls for the repentance of the current generation as it laments the downfall of the Davidic monarchy. The two sub-units of this section, Ezek 18:1-32 and 19:1-14, are linked together by their concern with the deterioration of Judah's position following the deportation of Jehoiachin. In view of the growing sentiment for renewed revolt against Babylon, the prophet apparently hopes to convince people to change their course before it is too late. The first part of this sub-unit in Ezek 18:1-32 focuses on the question of moral responsibility.[25] Although many see this text as a statement of Ezekiel's view of the moral responsibility of the individual human being, the examples indicate that it focuses on the individual generation. In this respect, it is designed to answer a popular proverb that contends that the current reverses suffered by Jerusalem and Judah are punishments for the sins of past generations (cf. Jer 31:29-30). Ezekiel responds with a disputation speech that is designed to demonstrate that only the current generation must be held accountable for its own suffering and that, by repentance and change, it has the capacity to change its fate.[26] Ezekiel's contention conflicts with the Decalogue (Exod 20:5; Deut 5:9; cf. Exod 34:7), which states that YHWH holds sinners accountable to the third and fourth generation. The prophet presents four cases of moral action that draw upon the commandments of the Pentateuch, particularly the Holiness Code of Lev 16–26. Ezekiel concludes his illustration with a call for his generation to repent and live.

The second sub-unit of this section appears in Ezek 19:1-14, where the prophet illustrates the preceding principles by lamenting the downfall of the princes of Israel, viz., the royal house of David. The laments employ the typical Qinah (lament) 3/2 metrical pattern. The first lament employs the metaphor of the lion, the symbol of Judah and the house of David (Gen 49:8-12), and her cubs. The first cub is caught and taken to Egypt to symbolize the Egyptians' removal of King Jehoahaz ben Josiah from the throne in 609 BCE (2 Kgs 23:31-34; 2 Chr 36:1-4). The second cub is caught and taken to Babylon to symbolize Nebuchadnezzar's deportation of Jehoiachin (2 Kgs 24:8-17; 2 Chr 36:9-10). The second lament employs the imagery of the vine (see Isa 11:1-9; Jer 23:1-8; Ezek 17:1-24) to depict the demise of a vine that is transplanted to the desert. It likely refers to Zedekiah, the son of Josiah and uncle of Jehoiachin, who was placed on the throne by the Babylonians following Jehoiachin's exile. By employing laments for lost monarchs in this manner, Ezekiel warns the people that a weak monarch like Zedekiah offers little chance for successful resistance against the Babylonians.

Ezekiel 20–23

Ezekiel 20–23 presents Ezekiel's oracles concerning the punishment of all Israel. The unit employs elements of past tradition to reiterate the sins of the people that will lead to judgment and YHWH's intention to restore them after the punishment is complete.

Ezekiel 20:1-44 draws upon the wilderness traditions to provide an assessment of Israel's past and future (see especially Exod 32–34; Num 14). The discourse draws a deliberate analogy between Israel's rebellion in the wilderness and the charge that Israel has rebelled against YHWH in the land to justify YHWH's decision to punish the nation once again. YHWH's statement, "I acted for the sake of my name," and the focus on Shabbat emphasize the priestly concern with the holiness of YHWH. The oracle concludes with a portrayal of Israel's redemption from foreign lands and service of YHWH on YHWH's holy mountain. Such claims indicate a renewed Exodus and restoration of the Temple that will call for the recognition of YHWH.

The oracle in Ezek 21:1-5 against the Negeb employs the imagery of seasonal fires in the late summer to indicate that this region will suffer punishment as well.

Ezekiel 21:6-12 is the first of three oracles concerning YHWH's drawn sword against Jerusalem. The statement that the sword will cut off both righteous and wicked supports the claims in Ezek 9–11 that YHWH will act against all the inhabitants of Jerusalem. The second oracle in Ezek 21:13-22 employs the image of a polished and sharpened sword that strikes its victims. The third oracle in Ezek 21:23-37 makes it clear that the sword will be used by the king of Babylon against Israel and the Ammonites.

Ezekiel 22:1-16 is the first of three oracles that draw upon the imagery of Isa 1:2-31 to express YHWH's judgment against Jerusalem. The focus on bloodshed both emphasizes the concerns with bleeding wounds, sacrifice, and hands stained with blood from Isa 1:6, 10-17, 18-20, and the priestly concern with the proper treatment of blood (Lev 17). The crimes of incest, bribery, extortion, and contempt for parents appear throughout Lev 18–20 in the Holiness Code. The second oracle in Ezek 22:17-22 draws upon the smelting imagery of Isa 1:21-26 to portray YHWH's purification of Jerusalem much as one smelts metal to remove its dross or impurities. The third oracle in Ezek 22:23-31 draws upon Isa 1:10, 23, and 26 to charge Jerusalem's leadership, including the prophets, priests, officials, and people of the land with failure to exercise proper leadership as they attempt to serve their own interests. Altogether, Ezekiel's use of the oracle from Isa 1 indicates his priestly responsibility to teach (Lev 10:10-11).

Ezekiel 23:1-49 concludes this segment with a metaphorical portrayal of Samaria and Jerusalem as the sisters Oholah and Oholibah.[27] The word Oholah employed for Samaria means "her tent," and refers to YHWH's presence in the northern kingdom of Israel since YHWH is portrayed as dwelling in a tent or wilderness tabernacle. The term Oholibah employed for Jerusalem means "my tent is in her," which alludes to the presence of YHWH's Temple in Jerusalem. The passage presupposes the traditional relationship between Israel and Judah, and uses the marriage metaphor as a basis to portray each nation's abandonment of YHWH (cf. Hos 1–3; Jer 2; Ezek 16, respectively). The passage focuses on Israel's and Judah's relationships in the international sphere with Egypt, Assyria, and Babylonia from the period of the Jehu dynasty (ninth and eighth centuries) through the death of Judah's submission to Babylon in the late seventh century. From Ezekiel's perspective, such alliances defile YHWH's sanctuary insofar as YHWH protects Judah. The prophet apparently intends to condemn current attempts at alliance with Egypt that might lead to a second revolt against Babylon.

Ezekiel 24–25

Ezekiel 24–25 presents the prophet's symbolic actions and oracles concerning the impending fall of Jerusalem, Ammon, Moab, Edom, and Philistia. Although Ezek 25 presents the first of Ezekiel's oracles concerning the nations in Ezek 25–32, these oracles are grouped together with his oracles concerning the onset of the Babylonian siege of Jerusalem because these nations are charged with various past acts against Israel and Judah and supporting the Babylonians in their efforts to take the city. Each sub-unit is introduced by the formula, "and the word of YHWH came to me, saying. . . ."

The first sub-unit, Ezek 24:1-14, presents Ezekiel's allegory of the pot. As a Zadokite priest in the Jerusalem Temple, Ezekiel's duties would have included carrying out the sacrifices at the altar and preparing the sacrificial meat for consumption by the priests and other worshipers. References to the thigh and shoulder indicate the choice offerings that are presented to the priests for their service in the Temple (see Num 18:12; Exod 29:26-28; Lev 7:28-36; 10:12-18; Num 18:18; Gen 32:32, respectively). Ezekiel focuses on the images of blood and sludge at the bottom of the pot to characterize Jerusalem as the "bloody city" that must be purified. In priestly thought, blood is holy and must be covered when shed (Lev 17:13-16; Gen 9:1-7, respectively). Ezekiel proposes to clean the pot by burning it with fire until the sludge at the bottom is burned away. Such an image calls to mind the burning of Jerusalem by the Babylonians.

The second symbolic action appears in Ezek 24:15-27, in which YHWH commands Ezekiel to refrain from mourning for his dead wife to symbolize YHWH's attitude at the destruction of Jerusalem and the Temple. As a Zadokite priest, Ezekiel is forbidden to come into contact with the dead, with the exception of his own blood relatives, and the high priest is forbidden even to mourn (Lev 21:1-12; cf. Lev 10:1-7). Leviticus 21:4 specifically prohibits a priest from mourning for his wife. The reason for these commands is because death represents the ultimate impurity in priestly thought. Because of the priests' holy status before YHWH, they are forbidden to come into contact with death except as indicated above. Ezekiel draws upon his own experience and expectations as a Zadokite priest to illustrate YHWH's lack of remorse at the fall of Jerusalem and the Temple, symbolically portrayed once again as YHWH's bride (cf. Isa 54; Hos 1–3; Jer 2; Zeph 3:14-20; Ezek 16, respectively).

The oracles against Judah's immediate neighbors in Ezek 25:1-17 include YHWH's instructions for Ezekiel to speak out against Ammon, Moab, Edom, and Philistia. The passage presupposes that each of these nations somehow assisted or supported Babylonia in its attack against Jerusalem.

Ezekiel 26–28

Ezekiel 26–28 presents Ezekiel's oracles concerning Tyre and its rulers. Tyre joined Jerusalem in revolt against the Babylonians (see Jer 27:3). Shortly after the conquest of Jerusalem, Nebuchadnezzar laid siege to Tyre. Although he was never able to conquer the city, he did force its capitulation. The lament concerning Tyre in Ezek 27 employs the 3/2 Qinah ("Lamentation") meter, and portrays Tyre's importance as a maritime trading power. The oracles against the king of Tyre in Ezek 28:1-19 draw on Canaanite mythology, particularly the legend of Aqhat, which portrays the descent of Aqhat, son of the wise man Dan El, to the underworld, and the Garden of Eden tradition. The oracle concerning Sidon targets Tyre's primary ally, which also joined the revolt against Babylon (Jer 27:3). The final verses envision the restoration of Israel.

Ezekiel 29:1-16

Ezekiel 29:1-16 portrays Egypt as a great dragon that will be hooked and drawn from the Nile. The oracle draws upon the images of fishermen who populated its banks and earlier mythological portrayals of Egypt as a sea monster that would be defeated by YHWH (Isa 11:11-16; cf. Exod 15).

Ezekiel 29:17—30:19

Ezekiel 29:17—30:19 again focuses on Egypt. Following the conclusion of his siege against Tyre in 573 BCE, Nebuchadnezzar launched an invasion of Egypt in 668 BCE, but failed to conquer the country. Because Tyre controlled the Mediterranean coast leading to Egypt, it was an important step in his campaign against Egypt. The oracle employs the Day of YHWH tradition in Ezek 30:3 (cf. Isa 2; 13; 34; Zeph 1; Obadiah; Joel) to describe the projected fall of Egypt to Nebuchadnezzar.

Ezekiel 30:20-26

Ezekiel 30:20-26 focuses specifically on Pharaoh. The oracle refers to Nebuchadnezzar's defeat of Pharaoh Hophra, who sent an army against Nebuchadnezzar in an unsuccessful attempt to relieve the siege of Jerusalem (Jer 37).

Ezekiel 31

Ezekiel 31 presents a second oracle concerning Pharaoh, which draws heavily on Isaiah's depiction of the downfall of the king of Assyria in Isa 10:5-34 and the downfall of the king of Babylon in Isa 14:3-23.

Ezekiel 32:1-16

Ezekiel 32:1-16 presents another oracle concerning Egypt and Pharaoh. The lament employs the 3/2 Qinah meter and depicts Egypt mythologically as the slain dragon Leviathan (see Isa 11:15; 27:1; Pss 74:12-17; 104:7-9; Job 38:8-11; cf. Exod 15).

Ezekiel 32:17—33:20

Ezekiel 32:17—33:20 takes up the prophet's final oracles concerning the nations and an oracle concerning Ezekiel's role as "sentry" or "watchman" for Israel. The oracle in Ezek 32:17-32 concerning Egypt and the other nations lists a succession of nations that have fallen to the Babylonians. Although Egypt was not conquered by Babylon, the fall of Jerusalem would have signaled to Ezekiel that Egypt, too, would succumb. The following oracle in Ezek 33:1-20 returns to the theme of Ezekiel's role as watchman for the people (cf. Ezek 3:16-21). This role is based upon the roles of the Levitical gatekeepers whose task is to ensure the sanctity of all who enter the holy Temple precincts (see 1 Chr 9:17-27; 26:1-19; cf. Pss 15; 24; 2 Chr 23). The oracle also draws upon the discussion of moral culpability and repentance in Ezek 18, in which the prophet argues that only those who actually commit evil are liable for punishment and that those who repent may be spared punishment. Such a concern would anticipate the following units in Ezek 33:21—39:29 and 40:1—48:35, which are explicitly concerned with restoration.

Ezekiel 33:21-29

Ezekiel 33:21—39:29 presents the prophet's oracles concerning the restoration of Israel.[28] The introductory prophetic word formulas in Ezek 33:23; 34:1; 35:1; 36:15; 37:15; and 38:1 mark the beginning of each sub-unit in this text. The first sub-unit in Ezek 33:23-29 sets the theme for the prophet's contentions through-out the rest of the unit, that is, that YHWH is legitimately punishing the people for defiling themselves and that Ezekiel is YHWH's prophet.

Ezekiel 34:1-31 presents Ezekiel's oracle against the leaders of the nation. He employs the metaphor of shepherd, which appears throughout biblical and ancient Near Eastern tradition to portray kings and other leading figures (see, for example, David in 1 Sam 16:11; 17). His basic charge is that the nation's leaders have failed in their responsibility to care for the people as they served their own interests. In keeping with Davidic ideology, which maintains that YHWH is the true king and the Davidic monarch is YHWH's son or agent (see Ps 2), Ezekiel argues that YHWH will function as the true shepherd for the people. Ezekiel's oracle draws upon Isa 11:1-16 in arguing that YHWH will establish a righteous Davidic monarch (cf. Jer 23:1-8; 33:14-26).

Ezekiel 35:1—36:15 presents the prophet's contrasting oracles concerning Edom and Israel. Ezekiel condemns Edom because of its support for Babylon in the destruction of Jerusalem and the Temple (cf. Obad 11-14; Ps 137:7-9). The reference to an ancient enmity (v. 5) refers to the traditions of conflict between Esau, the ancestor of Edom, and Jacob, the ancestor of Israel (see Gen 25–25). In contrast to Edom, which was displaced by Arab Nabatean people in the Second Temple period, Israel will be restored.

Ezekiel 36:16—37:14 focuses on the purification and restoration of Israel. Although Ezek 36:16-38 and 37:1-14 appear to be entirely different oracles, both appear here because they take up the question of purification. Ezekiel 36:16-38 employs the imagery of menstrual purification to portray the restoration of Israel, which has been defiled by the blood shed upon the land. In priestly tradition, blood was a defiling agent and a woman needed to purify herself from the effects of blood following her menstrual period (see Lev 15:19-30; note also that men are defiled by an emission of semen, Lev 15:1-18). The imagery of blood also conveys the presence of idolatry (see Ps 104:38). The impurity of the land defiles the holy name of YHWH, and thereby compromises YHWH's holy standing among the nations and throughout creation. The menstrual imagery continues with the metaphorical portrayal of the cleansing of the land through pure water. Both women and men immerse themselves in pure water to purify themselves (Lev 11:36), and a priest must purify himself before he serves in the Temple (Lev 8). Ezekiel understands that such purification will include a new heart for the people that will enable them to observe YHWH's requirements (see Ezek 11:19; 18:31; Jer 31:31-34). The second element in Ezek 37:1-14 takes up the famous vision of dry bones, in which the prophet sees the bones of Israel's dead return to life. Death is the epitome of defilement in priestly thought, and the Babylonian conquest of Jerusalem and the Temple left many dead, with the corpses defiling the city and the site of the Temple. Ezekiel's vision therefore conveys a very powerful image of YHWH's intent to restore Israel and to purify it from the defilement of death.

Ezekiel 37:15-28 presents Ezekiel's symbolic action concerning the two sticks. Ezekiel's visions of restoration invariably involve the ideal of all Israel, that is, both the northern kingdom of Israel and the southern kingdom of Judah arrayed around the Jerusalem Temple as in the days of Solomon (1 Kgs 6–8). The prophet writes the names of Judah and Joseph (father of the tribe of Ephraim, the key tribe of Israel) on two sticks and then joins them together to symbolize the reunification of all the people of Israel. To complete the restoration, Ezekiel also includes the restored Davidic monarch (2 Sam 7; Pss 89; 132) in the eternal "covenant of peace" granted to the priest Phineas ben Eliezer, the grandson of Aaron (Num 25:10-13; cf. Ezek 34:25).

Finally, Ezek 38:1—39:29 concludes with the prophet's oracles concerning Gog of Magog. Many consider this text to be an apocalyptic addition,[29] but it functions as an integral part of the book of Ezekiel in that it portrays the purification of the land from the defilement of corpses in preparation for the restoration of the holy Temple in chapters 40–48. Although the identity of Gog is uncertain, he functions as an evil threat against Israel. Such a threat is key to the Zion tradition, which presents YHWH as the protector of Zion from threats by the nations (Pss 2; 46–48). His defeat is portrayed as the fulfillment of prophetic tradition with cosmic consequences for all of creation. Most importantly, it demonstrates the holy name of YHWH. In the aftermath of Gog's defeat, the land is filled with corpses that leave it defiled. The land must be purified by the fires that burn for seven years and the burial of the corpses of Gog and his army. The sacrificial feast by the birds and wild animals removes the meat and the blood of the dead that mimics the sacrificial feast of the Temple. The result is the worldwide recognition of YHWH and the purposes of the exile of Israel.

Ezekiel 40–48

The concluding segment of the book of Ezekiel is the prophet's vision of the restored Temple in Ezek 40–48. Many modern scholars argue that this section is a late addition to the book of Ezekiel, but such a contention is based largely on the view that prophets and priests are diametrically opposed to each other.[30] Insofar as Ezekiel combines both identities, a vision of the restored Temple makes a great deal of sense as the culmination of his book, in which the prophet contends that the destruction of Jerusalem must be viewed as part of a process of purification and restoration of holiness at the site of the Temple. The portrayal of the structure and dimensions of the Temple and its courts in these chapters does not correspond to the Wilderness Tabernacle (Exod 25–30; 35–40), Solomon's Temple (1 Kgs 6–7; 2 Chr 3–4), or the Second Temple that was built shortly following the exile (m. Middot 5; cf. Ezra 3–6; Zech 1–8, respectively). Medieval commentators on Ezekiel, such as Rashi and David Kimhi, came to regard Ezekiel's vision as a description of the third Temple that would be built in the days of the Messiah.

The vision is dated to the tenth day of the month at the beginning of the year (Rosh ha-Shanah) of the twenty-fifth year of exile. This would place the vision on 10 Tishri (late September or early October), 573 BCE. The tenth of Tishri is Yom Kippur, the Day of Atonement, when the high priest would enter the Holy of Holies of the Temple to experience the presence of YHWH as part of the observance of the day (Lev 16; m. Yoma 3:8; see also Lev 23:26-32; Num 29:7-11). Yom Kippur marks the day when the people would ask forgiveness from YHWH for wrongdoing throughout the prior year. In Ezekiel's case, the twenty-fifth year of exile would mark the twentieth year from the time of his initial vision of YHWH as presented in Ezek 1–7. If he was indeed thirty years old at the time of his initial vision (see Ezek 1:1), he would be fifty years old in the twenty-fifth year, when he would have retired from active service as a priest (see Num 4:3; 8:23-25) had he remained in the Jerusalem Temple. Because he is in exile, the vision expresses his expectation that YHWH would act to restore the Temple and the people of Israel, and thereby restore the holy center of all creation.

Ezekiel's vision includes three major sub-units, each of which focuses on a different aspect of the envisioned Temple: Ezek 40:1—43:12 provides instruction for the building of the Temple and the return of YHWH's glory; Ezek 43:13—47:12 provides instruction for building the associated structures and activities of the larger Temple complex; and Ezek 47:13—48:35 provides instruction for the re-establishment of the land and people of Israel around the Temple together with the renewal of creation. Because the prophet's vision is formulated as instruction, it represents an attempt to fulfill one of the basic tasks of the priest-hood, that is, to instruct the people in holiness (Lev 10:10-11).

Ezekiel 40:1—43:12 claims that the prophet is transported supernaturally to Israel to receive instructions for the building of the Temple. The site is apparently Mt. Zion where the Temple was situated, since the biblical city of Jerusalem lay immediately to the south of the Temple Mount. His guide is described as a man whose appearance shone like bronze, much like the four living creatures or cherubim who bore the presence of YHWH through the heavens in Ezekiel's earlier visions (Ezek 1–3; 8–11).

The guide begins in Ezek 40:5-47 by instructing Ezekiel in the dimensions of the Temple walls, gates, and courtyards. He provides full dimensions for the gates and buildings of both the outer court, identified as the women's court in later tradition (m. Middot 2:5), and the inner court, identified as the Israelites' court (m. Middot 2:6).

Ezekiel 40:48—41:26 presents instruction concerning the building of the Temple itself. The Temple is constructed according to the three-room pattern of Solomon's Temple, with a vestibule or porch (Hebrew, 'ûlām), a nave or main hall (Hebrew, hêkāl), and the Holy of Holies (Hebrew, dĕbîr). Indeed, this three-room pattern is typical of Temple construction in ancient Israel, Canaan, and Syria. The vestibule is an entry hall or reception room. The nave or main hall is where the Temple furnishings are placed, such as the lamp stands, incense burners, and table for the bread of the presence. The Holy of Holies is where the ark of the covenant had been kept in Solomon's Temple. Because the ark seems to have disappeared either during or prior to the Babylonian exile—it may have been taken by the Babylonians or hidden by the Temple priests—no mention of the ark is made here. Ezekiel does not enter the Holy of Holies since only the high priest may enter, and only on Yom Kippur (Lev 15; m. Yoma 5:1). Ezekiel's Temple is decorated with cherubim and palm trees to symbolize the Garden of Eden and the role of the Temple as the holy center of creation.

The vision then depicts the return of YHWH's glory in Ezek 43:1-12 (cf. Ezek 1–3; 8–11). The divine presence returns through the east gate from which it had earlier departed (see Ezek 10:19). YHWH informs Ezekiel that the Temple will be the place of the divine throne, and that Israel will sanctify the divine name. Ezekiel's task is to inform the people of YHWH's requirements, including the plan and laws for the Temple.

Ezekiel 43:13—47:12 presents instructions concerning the Temple complex and its activities. It begins with a description of the altar, which is a four-stepped structure that resembles a Mesopotamian ziggurat (contra Exod 20:21-23). Both altar and priests are sprinkled with blood as part of the process of their sancti-fication for holy service (cf. Lev 16:18-19; Exod 29:16), although the use of goat as a sin offering for the dedication of the Temple is otherwise unknown.

Ezekiel's guide brings him back to the eastern gate, which will remain closed to all except YHWH. Once again, Ezekiel sees the glory of YHWH, who informs him that those who engage in idolatry and abomination are not to be admitted to the Temple. Foreigners who are uncircumcised of heart and flesh are not to enter, but the Levites may serve in secondary functions. This instruction presupposes the distinction between the Levitical priests who served outside of Jerusalem and the Zadokite priests who served in the Jerusalem Temple. Because the Levites were considered to have compromised their holiness (cf. the portrayal of Eli and his sons in 1 Sam 2), they are not permitted to serve at the altar. By contrast, the Zadokites will serve at the altar and abide by the regulations for holy life in the Temple.

A series of instructions then defines the holy precincts of the Temple, the prince, and the people, proper weights and measures, Temple offerings to be made by the people, and observance of the Temple festivals. Once the Temple is established, water wells up from below the threshold of the Temple to water the entire land. This points to the role of the Temple as the center of creation, insofar as the Temple becomes the source of rain, fertility, and life for the created world. The water flows down into the Jordan Valley and the Dead Sea to restore life in the formerly desolate region.

The final sub-unit, Ezek 47:13—48:35, portrays the re-establishment of the land and the people of Israel. The boundaries of the land are an idealized portrayal of the greatest extent of the kingdoms of David or Jeroboam ben Joash (2 Sam 8:5-12; 2 Kgs 14:25; cf. Num 34). The tribes of Israel are assigned equal portions of land that are aligned along its entire length from north to south. The priestly and Levitical allotment is placed in the center of the tribes together with that of Judah and surrounded by the portion allotted to the prince. The concluding statement that the name of the city shall be "YHWH is there" signifies the return of YHWH's presence to Jerusalem, closing the circle that began at the outset of the book with YHWH's departure from Jerusalem.

NOTES

* This chapter is a heavily revised and condensed version of my chapter concerning Ezekiel in *The Prophetic Literature* (IBT; Nashville: Abingdon, 2005), 127–64. Readers wishing a much fuller and earlier version of this discussion should turn there.
[1] For surveys of discussion on the book of Ezekiel, see Katheryn Pfisterer Darr, "Ezekiel Among the Critics," *CR:BS* 2 (1994): 9–24.
[2] For discussion of the differences between Ezekiel and the Torah in Rabbinic literature, see my "The Problem of Ezekiel in Rabbinic Literature," in P. M. Joyce and A. Mein, eds., *After Ezekiel: Essays on the Reception of a Difficult Prophet* (LHBOTS 535; New York: T&T Clark International, 2011), 11–23.
[3] Henry O. Thompson, "Chebar," *ABD* 1:893.
[4] See Yoshitaka Kobayashi, "Tel-Abib," *ABD* 6:344.

[5] For discussion of the thirtieth year, see Moshe Greenberg, *Ezekiel 1-20* (AB 22; Garden City: Doubleday, 1983), 39–40; Katheryn Pfisterer Darr, "Ezekiel," in *The New Interpreters' Bible*, ed. L. Keck et al. (Nashville: Abingdon, 2001), 6:1110.

[6] See Sweeney, "Ezekiel: Zadokite Priest and Visionary Prophet of the Exile," in *Form and Intertextuality in Prophetic and Apocalyptic Literature* (FAT 45; Tübingen: Mohr Siebeck, 2005), 125–43.

[7] For discussion of Ezek 29:17, see Moshe Greenberg, *Ezekiel 21-37* (AB 22A; New York: Doubleday, 1997), 616–17; Walter Zimmerli, *Ezekiel 2: A Commentary on the Book of the Prophet Ezekiel Chapters 25-48*, trans. J. D. Martin (Hermeneia; Philadelphia: Fortress Press, 1983), 210–11.

[8] Cf. Greenberg, *Ezekiel 1-20*, 3–27. Others, for example, Walter Zimmerli, *Ezekiel 1: A Commentary on the Book of the Prophet Ezekiel 1-24*, trans. R. E. Clements (Hermeneia; Philadelphia: Fortress Press, 1979), 68–77; Ronald M. Hals, *Ezekiel* (FOTL 19; Grand Rapids: Eerdmans, 1989), 2–7, suggest a longer process of composition and redaction.

[9] For an introduction to the worldview and perspectives of the Zadokite priesthood, see Jon D. Levenson, *Sinai and Zion: An Entry into the Jewish Bible* (Minneapolis: Winston, 1985).

[10] See my "Ezekiel's Debate with Isaiah," in *Congress Volume: Ljubljana, 2007*, ed. A. Lemaire (VTSup 133; Leiden: Brill, 2010), 555–74.

[11] For discussion of the recognition formula, see Walther Zimmerli, "I am YHWH," in *I am YHWH* (Atlanta: John Knox, 1982), 1–28.

[12] See my "The Royal Oracle in Ezekiel 37:15-28: Ezekiel's Reflections on Josiah's Reform," in *Israel's Prophets and Israel's Past: Essays on the Relationship of Prophetic Texts and Israelite History in Honor of John H. Hayes*, ed. B. E. Kelle and M. B. Moore (LHBOTS 446; New York: T & T Clark, 2006), 239–53.

[13] See my "Ezekiel's Debate with Isaiah," 555–74.

[14] See the Ugaritic Baal Cycle, which refers frequently to the storm god Baal "the Rider of the Clouds" (for example, Baal Cycle IIAB 3:11 [*ANET*, 132]; I*AB 2:7, [*ANET*, 138]).

[15] See, for example, *ANEP*, 534, 535, 536.

[16] See Margaret S. Odell, "You Are What You Eat: Ezekiel and the Scroll," *JBL* 117 (1998): 229–48.

[17] Israel Knohl, *The Sanctuary of Silence: The Priestly Torah and the Holiness School* (Minneapolis: Fortress Press, 1994).

[18] Jon D. Levenson, "The Temple and the World," *JR* 64 (1984): 275–98.

[19] See my "The Destruction of Jerusalem as Purification in Ezekiel 8-11," in *Form and Intertextuality*, 144–55.

[20] For discussion of these offerings, see Jacob Milgrom, "Sacrifices and Offerings, OT," *IDBSup* 763–71, especially 766–69.

[21] See Greenberg, *Ezekiel 1-20*, 177.

[22] L. I. Rabinowitz, "Synagogue," *EncJud* 15:579–84, especially 580.

[23] Cf. James A. Sanders, "Hermeneutics in True and False Prophecy," in *Canon and Authority*, ed. G. W. Coats and B. O. Long (Philadelphia: Fortress Press, 1977), 21–41.

[24] See especially Julie Galambush, *Jerusalem in the Book of Ezekiel: The City as YHWH's Wife* (SBLDS 130; Atlanta: Scholars Press, 1992); for a survey of the marriage metaphor in the Hebrew Bible, see Gerlinde Baumann, *Love and Violence: Marriage as Metaphor for the Relationship between YHWH and Israel in the Prophetic Books*, trans. L. Maloney (Collegeville: Liturgical, 2003).

[25] Knohl, *Sanctuary*; Gordon H. Matties, *Ezekiel 18 and the Rhetoric of Moral Discourse* (SBLDS 126; Atlanta: Scholars Press, 1990).

[26] Adrian Graffy, *A Prophet Confronts his People* (AnBib 104; Rome: Pontifical Biblical Institute, 1984), 58–64.

[27] See Galambush, *Jerusalem as YHWH's Wife.*

[28] See my "The Assertion of Divine Power in Ezekiel 33:21–39:29," in *Form and Intertextuality,* 156–72.

[29] These chapters draw heavily on earlier pentateuchal and prophetic tradition; see my "The Priesthood and the Proto-apocalyptic Reading of Prophetic and Pentateuchal Texts," in *Form and Intertextuality,* 239–47.

[30] See Jon D. Levenson, *Theology of the Program of Restoration of Ezekiel 40–48* (HSM 10; Missoula: Scholars Press, 1976); Steven Shawn Tuell, *The Law of the Temple in Ezekiel 40–48* (HSM 49; Atlanta: Scholars Press, 1992).

E. The Book of the Twelve Prophets*

The Book of the Twelve Prophets functions simultaneously as a collection of twelve individual prophetic works and as a single prophetic book. The twelve individual prophets include Hosea, Joel, Amos, Obadiah, Jonah, Micah, Nahum, Habakkuk, Zephaniah, Haggai, Zechariah, and Malachi.[1] Each work within the Book of the Twelve begins with its own superscription or narrative introduction that identifies the prophet and provides information concerning the historical background of the work, its literary characteristics, and its overall concerns. No common material binds the twelve together. The book is called *těrê ʿāśār* in Jewish tradition, which is Aramaic for "the twelve." The Twelve Prophets appear as the fourth book of the "Latter Prophets" in the Tanak (*b. Baba Batra* 14b), but the Talmud also stipulates that only three lines separate the individual books of the Twelve Prophets whereas four lines normally separate biblical books (*b. Baba Batra* 13b).

The Book of the Twelve presents a sequence of books that emphasizes divine purpose in relation to the fate of Jerusalem. The book begins with Hosea and ends with Malachi, so that it employs the metaphorical portrayal of marriage to depict the tension in the relationship between YHWH and Israel and the concern to call upon the people to maintain the relationship despite the suffering of conquest and exile that the people have endured. Although Hosea addresses the fate of northern Israel, its frequent references to Judah (Hos 1:7; 5:5, 10, 14; 6:4, 11; 8:14; 10:11; and 12:3) and its concern for reunification of Israel and Judah under a Davidic monarch (Hos 3:5) facilitate a reading of the book in relation to a larger concern with Jerusalem. The placement of Joel in the second position ensures that the questions of Jerusalem and the threat posed by the nations will set the agenda for the rest of the sequence. Insofar as Joel depicts YHWH's intention to defend Jerusalem on the Day of YHWH from the threats posed by the nations, it demonstrates how the reunification signaled in Hosea will take place and establishes the concern from which the remaining books will be read. In filling such an agenda, the ahistorical portrayal of the nations allows the scenario presented in Joel to serve as a typological model for the historically based models that appear throughout the rest of the sequence, that is, YHWH will bring the nations to punish Jerusalem for wrongdoing, but YHWH will deliver the city once the punishment is complete, when YHWH's sovereignty is revealed to the entire world. Amos then calls for judgment against the northern kingdom of Israel and its reunification with Judah under the rule of a restored Davidic monarchy. Obadiah calls for the punishment of Edom and its submission to Israel at Zion on the Day of YHWH. Jonah tempers Obadiah's message with a contention that YHWH will show mercy to Nineveh when it repents, but later books also indicate YHWH's judgment against Nineveh when it oversteps its bounds in acting against Israel. Micah presupposes that Assyria and later Babylon will be YHWH's agents of punishment against Israel and Judah prior to their restoration around Jerusalem under the rule of a righteous Davidic monarch. Nahum celebrates the downfall of the oppressive Nineveh as an example of YHWH's justice. Habakkuk reassures readers of YHWH's justice by pointing to YHWH's plans to punish the Chaldeans or Neo-Babylonians for their oppression even though YHWH authorized them to enter Judah in the first place. Zephaniah calls for a purge of Jerusalem on the Day of YHWH which would represent the Babylonian destruction of the city. Haggai calls for the restoration of the Temple and the house of David under Zerubbabel. Zechariah outlines the significance of the restoration of the Temple as Israel, Judah, and the nations will ultimately recognize YHWH at the Jerusalem Temple. Finally, Malachi calls for its audience to maintain the covenant while waiting for YHWH's manifestation on the Day of YHWH.

With its emphasis on YHWH's purposes with regard to the fate of Jerusalem, the Book of the Twelve reflects the concerns of Judean elements during the Persian period from the time of the rebuilding of the Temple through the reforms of Ezra and Nehemiah, who focused on the restoration of Jerusalem as the holy center of Persian-period Judah and perhaps the world at large.

The Book of the Twelve shares an intertextual relationship with the book of Isaiah in particular that points to a very different understanding of the significance of world events for understanding divine purpose.[2] Like the Book of the Twelve, Isaiah contends that YHWH brought the nations to punish Israel and Judah for wrongdoing and to reveal YHWH's sovereignty throughout the world. But Isaiah identifies the manifestation of YHWH's sovereignty with the rise of the Persian empire, particularly the rise of the Persian monarch Cyrus who is identified as YHWH's Messiah and Temple builder (Isa 44:28; 45:1). It thereby calls upon its audience to submit to the Persian empire as the will of YHWH. The Book of the Twelve is very different. Although it, too, presupposes that YHWH brought the nations to punish Israel and Judah, it calls upon its audience to fight against the nations that oppress Israel/Judah/Jerusalem under the rule of YHWH and the Davidic monarch in order to realize the promised restoration of Jerusalem. Such a scenario is particularly evident when one considers the role of the very famous swords into plowshares passage in Isaiah and the Twelve. Isaiah 2:2-4 envisions a scenario of world peace in which Israel will join the nations in a pilgrimage to Zion to learn YHWH's Torah and to end war. Israel and the nations alike will suffer YHWH's judgment on the Day of YHWH before this idyllic scenario is realized. The Book of the Twelve cites this passage at three points, and presents a very different scenario of YHWH's or Israel's warfare against the nations in order to realize this goal. It first appears in Joel 4:10, which calls for the people to beat their plowshares into swords and their pruning hooks into spears to carry out YHWH's judgment against the nations on the Day of YHWH. Micah 4:1-5 cites the passage as a whole, but states categorically that Israel and the nations will serve their own deities prior to the rise of the Davidic monarch who will lead Israel and Judah in battle to subdue the nations that oppressed them. Zechariah 8:20-23 likewise cites the nations' call to make a pilgrimage to Zion as an introduction to its apocalyptic scenario of YHWH's battle against the nations in Zech 9–14 that will result in their recognition of YHWH at the Jerusalem Temple at the festival of Sukkot. Whereas Isaiah calls for submission to Persia, the Book of the Twelve calls for warfare against the oppressive nations—including Persia—to realize the recognition of YHWH's sovereignty at Zion. Such differences point to debate within the Second Temple-period Jewish community, expressed through the writing and redaction of prophetic (and other) biblical literature, concerning its relationship with Persia.

Each of the individual prophetic books that comprise the Book of the Twelve contributes distinctive elements to the theological concerns of the whole.

1. Hosea

The book of Hosea begins with a portrayal of Hosea's strained relationship with his wife Gomer bat Diblaim and the birth of their three children as a metaphor for the strained relationship between YHWH and Israel.

The superscription in Hos 1:1 places the prophet in the reigns of the Israelite monarch Jeroboam ben Joash (786–746 BCE) and the Judean monarchs Uzziah (783–742 BCE), Jotham (742–735 BCE), Ahaz (735–715 BCE), and Hezekiah (715–687 BCE). The period given for Hosea's career was particularly bloody as four of Israel's last six monarchs were assassinated as Israel veered between a policy of alliance with Assyria and alliance with Aram before finally suffering invasion by the Assyrians. The Jehu (842–815 BCE) dynasty began in revolt against the house of Omri, and shifted Israel's political position from a very troubled alliance with Aram to a far more stable alliance with Assyria that ensured Israel's power and prosperity for the balance of the Jehu dynasty's reign. In the aftermath of Jeroboam's reign, his son Zechariah (746 BCE) was assassinated by Shallum (746 BCE), who sought to break Israel's alliance with Assyria so that it might ally with Aram instead. Shallum in turn was assassinated by Menahem (745–738 BCE), who returned the nation to its alliance with Assyria. Menahem's son Pekahiah (738–737 BCE) was assassinated by Pekah (738–732 BCE), who broke relations with Assyria once again to ally with Aram. Pekah was killed during the course of the

Syro-Ephraimic War, when Assyria invaded Aram and Israel following their attack on Judah in 734–732 BCE. Although Assyria subdued Israel, the country revolted in 724 BCE under the leadership of King Hoshea. The result was the complete destruction of Israel by 722/1 BCE and the deportation of many surviving Israelites.

The book of Hosea addresses the problem of evil by positing that Israel suffered punishment because it had abandoned YHWH. Hosea draws upon the traditional portrayal of Israel as the bride of YHWH to charge that Gomer/Israel had engaged in harlotry by pursuing other lovers, prompting Hosea/YHWH to punish the wayward bride with divorce.[3] Such a portrayal presupposes Israelite conceptions of Canaanite fertility rites and Israel's political relations with Assyria and Egypt. The book does not consider judgment to be the final word, but it calls upon its audience to repent and return to YHWH. For Hosea, such a return called for both religious and political action, including a rejection of Canaanite religion and a return to YHWH, together with a rejection of Assyria and a return to alliance with Aram, the homeland of Israel's ancestors.

Close attention to the Hebrew syntax and narrative perspective of Hosea and the role of repentance in its presentation indicates a literary structure that is designed to convince its audience to reject alliance with Assyria and to return to YHWH and alliance with Aram.[4] An anonymous narrative provides the superscription for the book in Hos 1:1, introduces the main body of the book in Hos 1:2—14:9, and provides the concluding exhortation in Hos 14:10:

Hosea's Call for Israel's Return to YHWH
I.	Superscription	1:1
II.	Main Body of the Book: Appeal for Israel's Return	1:2—14:9
	A. narrative account of YHWH's instructions to Hosea to marry a harlot and give their children symbolic names	1:2—2:2
	B. Hosea's speeches to Israel	2:3—14:9
	1. Hosea's appeal to his children for their mother's return	2:3—3:5
	2. YHWH's basic charges against Israel: abandonment of YHWH	4:1-19
	3. specification of YHWH's charges against Israel	5:1—14:1
	4. appeal for Israel's return to YHWH	14:2-9
III.	Concluding Exhortation Concerning YHWH's Righteousness	14:10

The body of the book appears in Hos 1:2—14:9. The anonymous narrative introduces this section with a portrayal of YHWH's instructions to Hosea to marry a harlot and to have children with her in Hos 1:2—2:2. This narrative establishes the metaphorical portrayal of YHWH as the husband of the wayward wife Israel in order to illustrate Hosea's understanding of the tension in Israel's relationship with YHWH as a cause for the dangers that Israel faces in its relationship with Assyria. By arguing that Gomer/Israel is acting as a harlot, the prophet contends that the threats posed to Israel are punishment for abandoning YHWH and that Israel must return to YHWH (and an alliance with Aram) in order to ensure its well being. The names given to each of the children symbolize the tension. The name of Jezreel, the first son, recalls the site where Jehu overthrew the house of Omri and established his own dynasty (2 Kgs 9–10). Although Israel was allied with the Arameans at this time, tension with Aram prompted Jehu and his successors to turn to the Assyrians for support, which provided the basis for Israel's power and prosperity during the Jehu dynasty's reign (see 2 Kgs 13–14). The name of the daughter, Lo Ruhamah, means, "No mercy," to signify YHWH's lack of mercy for the purportedly recalcitrant bride. The name the second son, Lo Ammi, "Not my people," signifies YHWH's willingness to break the relationship.

The book turns to Hosea's own prophetic speeches in Hos 2:3—14:9. Each sub-unit of this section begins with an imperative in which the prophet addresses his Israelite audience. Hosea 2:3—3:5 begins with the prophet's appeal to his children for their mother's return. Given the metaphorical character of the speech,[5] the appeal is directed to the people of Israel so that the nation as a whole might return to YHWH. By employing the names Ammi, "my people," and Ruhamah, "mercy," for the children, Hosea signals his interest in restoration. He begins with descriptions of punishment for Gomer's marital infidelity, but references to parched land, thorns, grain, wine, festivals, Baals, and so on, make it clear that he is ultimately concerned with Israel's life in the land, its agricultural produce, its festivals, and its gods. Ultimately, the prophet/YHWH envisions a restoration of the relationship when Israel returns to the wilderness to renew the marriage/covenant as in the days of the exodus from Egypt and the wilderness period when Israel was formed as a nation. The passage concludes with YHWH's instructions to Hosea to marry the adulterous woman. The Judean setting for the final composition of the book is evident in Hos 3:5, which holds that return to YHWH entails northern Israel's return to the house of David.

Hosea 4:1-19 lays out YHWH's basic charges against Israel. The metaphor of marriage is dropped as the prophet presents YHWH's charges that Israel has abandoned its covenant. Hosea's statements employ a verb, *yāda'*, "to know," that has sexual connotations to indicate that the people lack knowledge of YHWH, but the passage also emphasizes a combination of natural images and the forensic language of the courtroom to charge that Israel has violated YHWH's commandments. Such an approach presupposes the blessings and curses of legal codes that promise rain, crops, and security in the land if the people observe YHWH's commands, and drought, famine, and exile from the land if they do not (see Deut 28–30; Lev 26). Indeed, v. 3 cites specific provisions of the Ten Commandments (see Deut 5; Exod 20) in charging that Israel's priests and prophets have not done their job in instructing the people in YHWH's expectations.

Hosea 5:1—14:1 takes up specific discussion of the general charges made in Hos 4. Throughout this passage, Hosea and YHWH alternate as speakers. Readers must pay close attention to the use of pronouns and other indicators to determine the identity of each. Hosea begins in Hos 5:1-7 with an address to the priests, the nation, and the king to charge Israel with harlotry or abandonment of YHWH.

He cites the locations of major events in Israel's history—Mizpah, where Saul was made king (1 Sam 10:17-27); Tabor, where Deborah defeated Jabin and Sisera (Judg 4–5); and Shittim, where Israel committed apostasy with the Moabites at Baal Peor (Num 25:1-5)—to illustrate Israel's abandonment of YHWH. A lengthy speech by YHWH in Hos 5:8—7:16 emphasizes YHWH's reluctance to accept the people because of their alliances with Egypt and Assyria (Hos 5:13-14; 7:11-12). Hosea 8:1-14 focuses on the establishment of illegitimate kings and the golden calves in the capital city of Samaria as symbols of Israel's rebellion and return to Egypt. Northern Israel was formed by revolt against the house of David and Jeroboam ben Nebat's establishment of calf images at Beth El and Dan (1 Kgs 12); Hosea contends that the house of Jehu stands in the same tradition.

Hosea 9:1—14:1 presents an overview of YHWH's relationship with Israel throughout history. Again, the words of the prophet alternate with those of YHWH. YHWH's voice frequently cites episodes of Israel's apostasy to provide background and justification for the current threat. YHWH envisions no end to the relationship, but the deity anticipates Israel's repentance. The other motif that holds this section together is the fertility and natural growth of creation, which asserts that YHWH and not Baal is the creator deity. Hosea 9:1-9 emphasizes the celebration of the festival of Sukkot, "Booths," or "Tabernacles," which marks the conclusion of the fruit and olive harvest—and indeed the entire harvest season—shortly after the New Year celebration in the fall. It anticipates the onset of the winter rains, which will provide the water that will ensure fertility and bountiful crop for the coming year. Despite the celebration, the prophet argues that Sukkot will be a time of punishment because of Israel's relationship with Assyria and Egypt. The reference to Gibeah recalls the capital of Saul (1 Sam 10:26), the first king of Israel, as a basis for the roots of YHWH's dissatisfaction. YHWH chimes in with a recollection of Israel's apostasy with the Moabite women at Baal Peor in Hos 9:10-13 (Num 25). YHWH recalls Gilgal, where Joshua made his first alliance with the Canaanites (Josh 9–10) and Israel renewed Saul's kingship (1 Sam 11). The prophet continues his criticism in Hos 9:17—10:8 with charges that YHWH will reject Israel because they continue idolatry at Beth Aven ("house of iniquity," a term used to describe Beth El and its golden calf) and see to it that the calf is carried off to Assyria. YHWH's recollection of Gibeah once again recalls Saul's capital and the rape of the Levite's concubine (Judg 19–21).

YHWH waxes nostalgic in Hos 11:1-9 with a metaphorical recollection of Israel as a child in the wilderness, first learning to walk. After bitterly condemning them to return to Egypt under Assyrian rule, YHWH vacillates by declaring that Israel cannot be given up like Admah and Zeboiim, two cities that were destroyed with Sodom and Gomorrah (Gen 14:2; 19:24-28). A series of statements by Hosea and YHWH culminates with the charge that Israel has made a treaty with Assyria to carry oil to Egypt (Hos 12:2), apparently a nod to Assyria's commercial ambitions in the ancient world. The prophet once again turns to Israel's early history in Hos 12:3-9, with recollections of Jacob's wrestling with the angel at

Jabbok (Gen 32:22-32) and his encounter with YHWH at Beth El (Gen 28), in order to charge that Israel engages in dishonest trade and claims to have become rich without YHWH. This serves as an introduction to YHWH's assertion in Hos 12:10-12, "I am YHWH, your G-d," which echoes the Ten Commandments. YHWH refers to the prophets sent to Israel. The passage has suffered poor translation because of its enigmatic language, that is, v. 11 should read, "through the prophets I speak in metaphors/oracles," and v. 12 should read, "if Gilead is iniquity, they (the prophets) were nothing." Gilead recalls Jacob's treaty with Laban, that is, Israel's alliance with Aram, in Gen 31:44-46, which serves as a reminder that Israel's natural allies are the Arameans, since their ancestors came from Aram. Jacob found his beloved wife Rachel (and Leah; Gen 29–31) in Aram, whereas the prophet (Moses) had to lead Israel out of Egyptian bondage. From Hosea's perspective, the choice between alliance with Aram and Egypt/Assyria should be obvious when one considers the past. YHWH recalls the Exodus in Hos 13:4-14, but Hosea concludes in Hos 13:15—14:1 that the east wind, which once split the Red/Reed Sea (Exod 14–15) must now come to punish Israel for rebellion against YHWH if the people do not return.

Hosea 14:2-9 concludes the lengthy segment of the prophet's speech to Israel in Hos 2:3—14:9 with an appeal for Israel's return. This constitutes the rhetorical goal of the book, and demonstrates that the prophet's images of judgment are intended to persuade the audience to return rather than to announce irrevocable judgment. He notes the political aspect of his efforts by stressing that Assyria cannot save Israel, and provides a religious dimension by claiming that reliance on Assyria is equivalent to idolatry. YHWH speaks as creator to emphasize the healing of Israel like dew, so the nation will blossom as a lily, olive tree, vine, and so on—a final appeal for Israel to recognize its G-d.

The concluding verse of the book, Hos 14:10, calls upon readers to recognize YHWH's righteousness in the midst of the evil that threatens the nation.

2. Joel

Joel emphasizes the central importance of threats to Jerusalem and its deliverance from the nations on the Day of YHWH. Its typological portrayal of Jerusalem serves as a Leitmotif for the theological concerns of the Book of the Twelve. Joel is notoriously difficult to interpret historically since the superscription in Joel 1:1 simply notes the otherwise unknown Joel ben Pethuel without reference to historical setting. The references to other biblical literature—for example, Exod 10:1-20, 21-29 (Joel 1–2); Isa 13:6 (Joel 1:15); Ezek 30:2-3 (Joel 1:15); Amos 1:2; 9:13 (Joel 4:16, 18); Obadiah; Mic 4:1-4/Isa 2:2-4 (Joel 4:10); Zeph 1:14-15 (Joel 2:1-2); and 2 Chr 20:20-26 (Joel 3–4)—indicate that the book dates to the fifth or fourth century BCE.[6]

Because Joel lacks specific historical referents and emphasizes elements of nature, it is frequently perceived to be a proto-apocalyptic book. Its portrayal of the portents in heaven and earth on the Day of YHWH—that is, the darkened sun and stars, the moon turned to blood, the pouring out of the divine "spirit" (literally, "wind") on all flesh prior to judgment against the nations—suggests an apocalyptic scenario of cosmic disruption. Familiarity with the climate of the land of Israel indicates that this is no cosmic upheaval, but a description of the very real effects of the so-called "east wind" or sirocco (Hebrew, Sharav; Arabic, Ḥamsin), a phenomenon similar to the Santa Ana winds of the American southwest, which typically appears in Israel at the transitions between the dry and wet seasons.[7] The Sharav blows so much dust and dirt that it obscures the sun during the day and gives the moon a reddish cast at night. It threatens crops and people, and therefore frequently serves as a natural agent of divine action in the Bible (for example, at the Red Sea in Exod 14–15). Overall, Joel portrays the threat posed by hostile nations to Jerusalem as a locust plague that is defeated by the east wind. Joel serves as an enduring assurance of YHWH's pledge of protection for Jerusalem.

The book displays a coherent literary pattern of YHWH's response to national lamentation at a time of threat. Joel's use of liturgical forms marks him as a figure who stands within priestly circles, perhaps as a prophetic Temple singer.[8] The structure of the book may be portrayed as follows:[9]

YHWH's Response to Judah's Appeals for Relief from Threat
- I.   Superscription   1:1
- II. Body of the Book: YHWH's response to Judah's appeal   1:2—4:21
  - A.   prophet's call to communal complaint concerning the threat of the locust plague   1:2-20
  - B.   prophet's call to communal complaint concerning the threat of invasion   2:1-14
  - C.   prophet's announcement of YHWH's response to protect people from the threat   2:15—4:21

The superscription identifies the following material as "the word of YHWH which came to Joel ben Pethuel" without further elaboration. Joel presents YHWH's response and reassurance of protection to Judah's complaint concerning the threat posed by the nations, here portrayed as locusts that threaten both crop and city. The initial call for communal complaint by the prophet in Joel 1:2-20 presupposes the typical form and setting of the psalms of complaint or lamentation (for example, Ps 7), which appeal to YHWH for deliverance at a time of threat. Because of the conception of YHWH as creator and Jerusalem as the holy center of creation, the initial complaint draws heavily on the Exodus locust plague tradition (Exod 10:1-20) to portray the threat against Jerusalem. Such portrayals are typical of the Day of YHWH tradition, in which YHWH's judgment is frequently expressed in natural or cosmic terms (see, for example, Isa 2; 13; 34; Obadiah; Zeph 1).

The prophet's discourse shifts to the imagery of military invasion with a second call for communal complaint in Joel 2:1-14. Such a shift effectively demonstrates the correlation between the natural and human worlds that is so frequently articulated in biblical tradition (for example, the Exodus and Wilderness traditions, which draw upon the natural world to depict YHWH's deliverance of the people from Egyptian bondage). The second call continues the Day of YHWH imagery, but the enemy clearly appears to be hostile nations. The prophet announces YHWH's deliverance in Joel 2:15—4:21. The call to spare the people is about to be realized, and the question "where is their G-d?" is about to be answered. YHWH's response culminates in warfare in the Valley of Jehoshaphat against the nations that threaten Jerusalem. The tradition reverses Micah's and Isaiah's calls to turn swords into plowshares and recalls (Mic 4:1-5; Isa 2:2-4) Jehoshaphat's victory over the Ammonites and Moabites who threatened Jerusalem in the Valley of Barakah/Blessing (2 Chr 20:20-26). The passage also draws heavily on Obadiah's portrayal of YHWH's judgment against Edom on the Day of YHWH. Altogether, Joel upholds the tradition of YHWH's role as creator and protector.

3. Amos

Amos focuses on the northern kingdom of Israel. The book is set against the background of the rise of the Israelite state under the rule of Jeroboam ben Joash (786–746 BCE) and his Judean vassal, Uzziah ben Amaziah (783–742 BCE). This was a period of wealth and power for the northern kingdom that was brought about by the Jehu dynasty's policy of alliance with the Assyrian empire. Jeroboam's kingdom extended from Lebo Hamath in Aram to the sea of the Arabah (Gulf of Aqabah) in the south (2 Kgs 14:25). This would make the kingdom about as large as that of Solomon.

Although northern Israel was powerful during this period, Amos points to problems in the kingdom that in his estimation will bring about disaster for the state. Amos does not mention the rising power of the Assyrian empire, although his oracles are set in the period immediately prior to the time of Assyria's westward expansion beginning in 745 BCE. The reasons for his condemnation of Israel lie in his Judean identity. Amos was a sheep herder and tender of sycamore trees who lived in the town of Tekoa, located south of Jerusalem in the Judean wilderness overlooking the Dead Sea. Following the Judean King Amaziah's failed attempt to revolt against the more powerful northern Israel (2 Kgs 14:8-14), Judah remained a vassal of Israel, and apparently was compelled to pay a heavy tribute. Such a tribute fell upon the Judean population at large, and Amos traveled to Beth El, the royal sanctuary of the northern kingdom of Israel, in order to pay a portion of Judah's tribute. The major festivals, Pesach (Passover), Shavuot (Weeks), and Sukkot (Booths), marked the times of harvest in the agricultural season, and people were required to bring a portion of their flocks and harvest to the Temple at that time as a form of taxation that would support Temple and state.[10] Judah had a subsistence-level agricultural economy, and the imposition of such a tax had grave implications for the people, particularly when natural catastrophes took their toll from the annual harvest. Amos points repeatedly to the poverty of his people who have suffered these disasters and yet still have to pay tribute to the north. But Amos does not tell us the reason for Israel's exploitation of Judah. As a vassal of Assyria, Israel would have been forced to pay tribute to Assyria or suffer the consequences.

The book is organized rhetorically to present an argument for the overthrow of the sanctuary at Beth El and an exhortation to seek YHWH. Following the superscription in Amos 1:1 and the associated motto in 1:2, the book begins broadly with a focus on judgment against the nations that surround Israel, following which it narrows its focus to Israel at large and finally to Beth El, before concluding with a call for the restoration of Davidic rule over all Israel. Although the prophet's oracles emphasize judgment against the northern kingdom, they include calls to seek YHWH (Amos 5:4, 6) to indicate the prophet's ultimate intentions. The structure of the book may be outlined as follows:[11]

Amos' Exhortation to Seek YHWH

I.	Introduction	1:1-2
	A. Superscription	1:1
	B. Motto: YHWH roars from Zion	1:2
II.	Exhortation Proper	1:3—9:15
	A. Oracles against the nations (culminating in northern Israel)	1:3—2:16
	1. Damascus/Aram	1:3-5
	2. Gaza/Philistia	1:6-8
	3. Tyre/Phoenicia	1:9-10
	4. Edom	1:11-12
	5. Ammon	1:13-15
	6. Moab	2:1-3
	7. Judah	2:4-5
	8. Israel	2:6-16
	B. Indictment of northern Israel	3:1—4:13
	C. Call for repentance of northern Israel	5:1—6:14
	D. Amos' vision reports: call for destruction of Beth El and rise of the house of David	7:1—9:15

The introduction for the book appears in Amos 1:1-2 as a combination of the superscription and the following motto. The motto indicates the prophet's Judean identity by stating that YHWH roars from Zion/Jerusalem, so that the top of Carmel (a very fertile northern Israelite chain of hills along the Mediterranean coast) withers. Insofar as Judah was subjugated to Israel during the eighth century, Amos' Judean identity becomes a foundational issue throughout the book.

The initial set of oracles against the nations begins the prophet's discourse with a very broad perspective. The nations listed here are all Israel's neighbors and the events noted all stem from their interrelationships with Israel during the ninth century BCE. During that period, Aram successfully attacked its ally, Israel, and the various nations listed actively supported the move or failed to come to Israel's aid as expected. The rhetorical strategy of the prophet in his indictment of each nation is clear, viz., he condemns each one for its past transgressions against Israel and YHWH, and thereby wins over his Israelite audience. It is only after Amos has won over his audience that he begins to focus on his true target, and concludes the sequence with a diatribe against Israel that highlights its abuses against the poor, that is, the people of Judah.

Amos 3:1—4:13 focuses on the prophet's charges against the northern kingdom of Israel. He points to signs of coming judgment, and claims that YHWH is bringing judgment against the nation as in the past (for example, Sodom and Gomorrah).

Amos 5:1—6:14 continues to emphasize his charges against Israel, but he couples them with calls for the people to seek YHWH and to reject Beth El and the other northern Temples. Amos envisions the Day of YHWH, a day that signals YHWH's defense of the nation (see Joel), as a day of YHWH's judgment against Israel (Amos 5:18-20).

Amos's vision reports in Amos 7:1—9:15 relate the experiences that prompted him to speak his message at the Beth El sanctuary. It is striking that in each case Amos cites an image or an event that would represent a common experience of the ancient Israelite/Judean farmer, but he sees in each an expression of the will of YHWH. Throughout the book, he observes divine purpose in common images, such as a cart laden with sheaves (Amos 2:13) or lions roaring in the wild when they catch prey (Amos 3:4). His observation that horses cannot run on rocks (Amos 6:12) shows the reader how Amos observes the world around him, much like the wisdom tradition (Prov 30), to determine the will of YHWH.[12] He notes the plague of locusts (Amos 7:1-3), a common and recurring threat to ancient (and modern) farmers, that eat the crop and leave little behind after the king's portion of the harvest has been taken. He notes the fires that dry up the deep (Amos 7:4-6), a common occurrence at the end of Israel's dry summer season. In both cases, he sees them as communications from YHWH, and successfully appeals to YHWH to show mercy. The third vision, YHWH holding a plumb line (7:7-9), again employs a common image of a weighted line used to measure the straightness of a wall—an essential tool in a society in which house walls were built by hand from stone foundations and mud brick—an error would quickly result in the collapse of the typical Israelite two-story house. Here it serves as a metaphor for measuring Israel's moral straightness. A brief editorial narrative in Amos 7:10-17 informs the reader of the circumstances of Amos' speech at the Beth El Temple, and how he is expelled from Israel for his charges against Temple and monarch. The fourth vision employs a pun on Amos' presentation of a basket of summer fruit (qāyiṣ), which YHWH states represents the end (qēṣ) of Israel. Such a presentation explains why Amos, a dresser of fig trees, appears at the Beth El altar in the first place, that is, to present the fruit harvest at the sanctuary. The final image of YHWH calling for the destruction of the Beth El capitals draws upon the imagery of a Temple altar in operation, with the carcasses of sacrificial animals, the knives, the blood, the fire, and the smoke, that all evoke images of destruction. For Amos, such images call for the destruction of the sanctuary itself.

Amos concludes his vision sequence with a call for the fallen booth of David, which expresses the prophet's Judean viewpoint and hopes for the ideal of a restoration of Davidic/Judean rule over the north, as it was in the days of Solomon.[13]

4. Obadiah

Obadiah focuses on Edom as the object of punishment on the Day of YHWH.

The superscription simply identifies the book as "the vision of Obadiah." Although some traditional authorities identify Obadiah with the ninth-century Israelite official who assisted Elijah and hid the prophets from persecution by Ahab and Jezebel (1 Kgs 18), there is no conclusive evidence that the present work is to be identified with the ninth-century figure. The dependence of Obad 1-7 on Jer 49:7-22 and the explicit references to the exiles of Israel and Jerusalem in Obad 19-21 indicate a late exilic or early post-exilic dating for the book.[14] In this case, it is read in relation to other texts that indicate Edom's assistance in the capture and destruction of Jerusalem by the Babylonians (see Ps 137:7; Isa 34:5-17; 63:1-6; Jer 49:7-22; Lam 4:21-22, respectively; and so on).

The rest of the book in Obad 1b-21 presents an oracular condemnation of Edom for its treachery against Jerusalem. The oracle begins with a prophetic messenger formula in Obad 1bα^{1-5}, which introduces the prophet's call to punish Edom in Obad 1bα^{6-12}-7 and the prophet's announcement of punishment against Edom in Obad 8-21. The structure of the book appears as follows:[15]

Prophetic Announcement of Judgment against Edom
- I. Superscription — 1a
- II. Oracle Concerning the Condemnation of Edom — 1b-21
  - A. Prophetic messenger formula — 1bα^{1-5}
  - B. Oracle proper — 1bα^{6-12}-21
    1. call to punish Edom — 1bα^{6-12}-7
    2. announcement of punishment against Edom — 8-21

5. Jonah

Jonah tempers the portrayal of YHWH's judgment against Edom in Obadiah with a portrayal of YHWH's mercy for a repentant Nineveh. The portrayal of the prophet draws on 2 Kgs 14:25, which presents Jonah ben Amittai as an eighth-century prophet who foresees the greatness of Jeroboam ben Joash's

(786–746 BCE) restored kingdom of Israel. The narrative makes extensive use of irony, parody, and exaggeration: for example, a prophet of YHWH attempts to flee from YHWH; the pagan characters of the narrative do not hesitate to acknowledge YHWH; a great fish swallows Jonah for three days; YHWH saves Nineveh, which ultimately destroys the northern kingdom of Israel; and so on. The book is not designed to present a historical account of the prophet. It is designed to examine the question of YHWH's justice and mercy.[16]

Many interpreters maintain that the book poses a conflict between the universalism of YHWH and the particularism of the Jewish community, but such constructions depend largely on a misreading of the book informed by anti-Jewish stereotypes. Jonah is not a selfish and petulant figure who questions why YHWH's mercy should be shown to Gentiles. He is a prophet who has foreseen the greatness of Jeroboam II, and presumably he also has foreseen that Nineveh, the capital of the Assyrian Empire, will see to the destruction of his own nation in 722–721 BCE only a few years after Jeroboam's reign. Even if one argues what Jonah may or may not know, the reader of the Bible knows what Nineveh will ultimately do, and it is to the readers of biblical tradition that the book is addressed. Why should YHWH show mercy to a nation that will ultimately serve such a destructive purpose? Such a question fundamentally entails the question of YHWH's righteousness and fidelity to the covenant with Israel. Ultimately, the book argues that YHWH responds to repentance with mercy, which has important implications for the post-exilic Judean audience of the book.

Jonah differs from most prophetic literature in that it is fundamentally a narrative and not a presentation of prophetic oracles. It appears in two distinct and yet parallel parts to emphasize the contrast between Jonah's attempt to flee his initial commission to condemn Nineveh in Jonah 1–2 and his frustration over YHWH's mercy when Nineveh repented in Jonah 3–4. The structure of the narrative appears as follows:[17]

Narrative Concerning YHWH's Mercy toward a Repentant Nineveh
I.   Jonah's Attempt to Flee from YHWH   1:1—2:1
    A.   Jonah's attempt to flee from YHWH's initial commission   1:1-3
    B.   Jonah's encounter with the sailors during the storm   1:4-16
    C.   Jonah's prayer to YHWH from the belly of the fish   2:1-11
II. Encounter between YHWH and Jonah Concerning
    YHWH's Mercy toward a Repentant Nineveh   3:1—4:11
    A.   YHWH's renewed commission to Jonah and its outcome   3:1-10
    B.   YHWH's assertion of the right to mercy in the encounter
        with Jonah   4:1-11

The narrative includes two parallel episodes that are designed to highlight the contrast (and comparisons) between YHWH's two commissions to Jonah. In each half, YHWH commissions Jonah to condemn Nineveh, but something entirely unexpected happens, namely, Jonah, the prophet of YHWH, attempts to flee from the sovereign of the universe in chapters 1–2, and YHWH reverses judgment and grants mercy to Nineveh in chapters 3–4.

Jonah 1–2 prepares the reader for the primary examination of issues in Jonah 3–4. It includes three basic episodes, each of which begins with action by YHWH that serves as the basis for action by the other major protagonists of the narrative. Jonah 1:1-3 presents YHWH's initial commission to Jonah and his unexpected attempt to flee. The reader knows that Jonah is a prophet and that YHWH is sovereign of the universe, so that such an attempt is patently absurd. The absurdity of the situation is highlighted by the portrayal of Jonah's experiences on board ship in Jonah 1:4-16. YHWH brings a storm that threatens to sink the ship. While Jonah, the prophet of YHWH, sleeps soundly in the hold while attempting to escape his G-d, the pagan sailors call upon Jonah to pray to YHWH and offer sacrifice themselves in a futile attempt to stop the storm. They finally and reluctantly accede to Jonah's advice that they throw him into the sea. In Jonah 2:1-11, Jonah finally acknowledges YHWH and prays for mercy until YHWH prompts the fish to vomit him out onto dry land.

Jonah 3–4 then focuses on the primary questions of YHWH's righteousness and fidelity in relation to the questions of judgment and mercy. YHWH commissions Jonah once again to announce judgment against Nineveh in chapter 3. The prophet obeys, and the unexpected happens when Nineveh actually listens to the prophet and repents. The hyperbole of the narrative is such that even the animals of the city repent. Jonah 4 presents Jonah's indignation at YHWH's mercy toward Nineveh and the key examination of the issues posed in the book. Jonah cites the merciful aspects of the formulaic characterization of YHWH from Exod 34:6-7, and demands that YHWH take his life in his exasperation at having his message of judgment reversed. But such a reversal highlights the purposes of the prophetic judgment speech, viz., it is designed to convince people to change, not serve as irreversible judgment as some contend. To illustrate the principle of pity or mercy, YHWH provides a caster bean plant to give Jonah shade and comfort, and then sends a worm to destroy it. Despite his sorrow at the loss of the plant, Jonah still contends that he would rather die than give up his anger at YHWH. At this point, YHWH concludes the book by asking Jonah (and the audience of the book) if YHWH should not pity Nineveh with its 120,000 people and many animals, just as Jonah had pitied the plant. The answer to YHWH's rhetorical question of course is "yes." Such an answer is of particular importance to the post-exilic Jewish community, which viewed the Babylonian exile as an expression of divine judgment, and the restoration as an expression of divine mercy that resulted from community repentance. Such a portrayal is designed to call for the people to repent and rebuild as exilic and post-exilic Judah sought restoration.

6. Micah

The book of Micah emphasizes the restoration of Jerusalem and Judah at the center of the nations following the experience of the Babylonian exile.

The superscription attributes the book to Micah the Morashtite, who lived in the days of the Judean kings Jotham (742–735 BCE), Ahaz (735–715 BCE), and Hezekiah (715–687 BCE). It states that his words concern Samaria and Jerusalem, which indicates the correlation between the experiences of the northern and southern kingdoms. Micah's home town is identified with Moresheth-Gath, a town on the southwestern border of Judah and Philistia, near the Philistine city of Gath.[18] This location is significant because it is precisely where the Assyrian king Sennacherib concentrated his attack against Judah at the time of Hezekiah's revolt in 701 BCE.[19] It enables readers to understand that Micah was a war refugee, who had to flee his home for Jerusalem as the Assyrians advanced. Such a portrayal informs his images of suffering on the part of the people and his anger at the monarchies of Israel and Judah for bringing such disaster on the heads of the Judean population. Unlike his better-known colleague Isaiah, Micah calls for the destruction of Jerusalem (Mic 3:12).

Micah has a very different perspective from the urbane Isaiah. Both books include nearly identical versions of the famous oracle in Isa 2:2-4 and Mic 4:1-5 that calls for nations to come to Zion to learn YHWH's Torah and turn their swords into plowshares to bring about world peace, but each book has a very different perspective as to how such an idyllic scenario is to be brought about.[20] Isaiah maintains that YHWH will judge all the world (Isa 2:6-21), and invites Jacob/Israel to join the pilgrimage of the nations to Zion to submit to YHWH (Isa 2:5). Ultimately, the book of Isaiah calls for Israel/Judah to submit to punishment by Assyria and Babylon, and finally to the rule of Persian monarch Cyrus, who is identified as YHWH's Messiah (Isa 44:28; 45:1). Micah, however, notes that Israel/Judah and the nations all follow their respective gods (Mic 4:5). The prophet's scenario of punishment by the nations in the form of the Babylonian exile (Mic 4:10) and the rise of a new Davidic king who will punish the oppressive nations then follows as the means to achieve the ideal scenario of Mic 4:1-5. Whereas Isaiah calls for submission to the rule of the nations, most notably Persia, as the will of YHWH, Micah calls for the overthrow of the oppressive nations and restoration of a righteous Davidic monarch. The reference to the Babylonian exile in Mic 4:10 and the intertextual references to Isa 2:2-4; 14:24-27; and 2:6-21 in Mic 4:1-5 and 5:4, 9-14, respectively, indicate that the book was edited during the early Second Temple period, when the question of Judah's relationship with the Persian Empire was in question.

The literary structure of Micah raises the question of Jerusalem's (or Israel's) future in the aftermath of the Babylonian exile. It begins in typical fashion with the superscription in Mic 1:1, and the balance of the book in Mic 1:2—7:20 is formulated as a prophetic announcement concerning YHWH's future exaltation of Jerusalem at the center of the nations. Micah 1:2-16 begins with a portrayal of YHWH's punishment of Samaria as a paradigm for that of Jerusalem. Micah 2:1—5:14 provides a detailed overview of the process of punishment and restoration for Jerusalem. Micah 6:1-16 appeals to the people of Israel/Judah to return to YHWH as a prelude for this process, and Mic 7:1-20 expresses the prophet's trust that YHWH will act to bring the restoration about once the punishment is complete. The structure may be portrayed as follows:[21]

Micah's Announcement concerning YHWH's Future Exaltation of Jerusalem at the Center of the Nations

I.	Superscription	1:1
II.	Announcement of YHWH's Exaltation of Jerusalem Proper	1:2—7:20
	A. YHWH's punishment of Samaria as paradigm for Jerusalem	1:2-16
	B. Process of punishment and restoration for Jerusalem: Babylonian exile, new Davidic monarch to punish oppressive nations	2:1—5:14
	1. concerning the process of punishment	2:1-13
	2. concerning YHWH's plans to punish and exalt Jerusalem	3:1—5:14
	C. Appeal to Israel/Judah for return to YHWH	6:1-16
	D. Liturgical psalm of confidence in YHWH	7:1-20

The body of the book takes its audience through a literary progression of sub-units that are organized to convince the reader that YHWH will act to exalt Jerusalem at the center of the nations after having brought punishment upon it for the erroneous decisions of the kings of Israel and Judah. Micah 1:2-16 begins with a trial scenario in which the prophet accuses Samaria and Jerusalem of transgression that brought conquerors against both Israel and Judah. The passage does not specify the transgression, but one may surmise that the transgression was Israel's and Judah's individual decisions to go to war against Assyria in the latter half of the eighth century BCE. The result was disaster for both as the Assyrians invaded Israel and subjugated Judah in the Syro-Ephraimitic War of 734–732 BCE, destroyed Israel when it revolted in 724–722/1 BCE, and devastated Judah when it revolted in 701 BCE.

The second major component of the book appears in Mic 2:1—5:14, which is held together by syntactical connectors at 3:1, "and I said," 4:1, "and it shall come to pass," and 5:1, "but you, O Bethlehem Ephrata." It presents the exile of the northern kingdom as the model and impetus for that of the south in the later Babylonian period. The initial sub-unit of this section is a woe speech in Mic 2:1-13 that accuses the leadership of Israel with lack of concern for the people. The prophet accuses the leaders of rising against the people as an enemy (v. 8), and the portrayals of suffering among the people represent the experience of people fleeing for their lives while the leaders act as if they were drunk. The chapter ends with a portrayal of the king leading the people like sheep out of their fold and into exile. The prophet then turns to the future of Jerusalem in Mic 3:1—5:14. He begins in Mic 3:1-8 with accusations of injustice and disregard for the welfare of the people in general, and then turns specifically to Jerusalem in Mic 3:9—5:14. The claim in Mic 3:9-12 that Jerusalem and Zion will be destroyed introduces his concern with Jerusalem and indicates that, unlike his Jerusalemite colleague, Isaiah, the rural Micah had no stake in the claims of Davidic or Zion theology that YHWH would protect Jerusalem forever. Micah 4–5 begins with the above-mentioned portrayal of world peace as the nations stream to Zion to give up war. It shifts to the process by which that ideal is achieved when it focuses on the nations that oppressed Israel (4:10), together with the rise of the Davidic monarch who would defeat the nations and restore the remnant of Jacob in the midst of the nations.

Micah 6:1-16 appeals to the people for righteous action or observance of YHWH's justice, and demands that they not act like the notorious King Ahab ben Omri of Israel (cf. 1 Kgs 17–22).

Micah 7:1-20 concludes the book with a liturgical expression of confidence that YHWH will act to realize the plans laid out in the book.

7. Nahum

The book of Nahum points to the ultimate downfall of Assyria following the restoration of the righteous Davidic monarch who will defeat the nations that oppress Israel/Judah.

The superscription identifies Nahum as "the oracle concerning Nineveh" and "the vision of Nahum the Elqoshite," but it provides no further information concerning the historical setting of the book or the prophet. Nineveh fell to a combined force of Babylonians and Medes in 612 BCE, two years after the fall of Assur in 614 BCE and three years prior to the final defeat of the Assyrian army at Haran in 609 BCE. The book refers to the fall of Thebes (No-Amon; Nah 3:8-10) to the Assyrians in 663 BCE.

The portrayal of Nineveh's conquest is a key factor in the rhetorical strategy of the book, which is designed to convince its audience that YHWH is indeed the powerful and just sovereign of all creation who punishes Nineveh for its abusive treatment of other nations. The body of the book appears as a prophetic *māśśā'*, "oracle," in which the prophet attempts to convince his audience to abandon their doubts about YHWH's justice and power to recognize YHWH as the cause of Nineveh's destruction. The prophet employs a form of the disputation speech to challenge the contention of a Judean audience that Assyria's domination of the world showed that YHWH lacks power or righteousness. The prophet attempts to refute the notion that YHWH is powerless by pointing to the fall of Nineveh as an act of YHWH.[22] The argument proceeds with an initial masculine plural address to Judah and Assyria in Nah 1:2-10 that challenges their low estimation of

YHWH's power with a partial acrostic poem in vv. 2-8 and a rhetorical question, "how do you reckon/consider YHWH?," that is, "what do you think about YHWH?" Nahum 1:11—2:1 follows with a second person feminine singular address to Judah asserting that the fall of Nineveh and the end of its oppression is an act of YHWH. A key statement is v. 11, which reads correctly, "from you has gone forth wrong thinking about YHWH, worthless council." Nahum 2:2—3:19 then concludes the book with a second person masculine singular address to Nineveh and the Assyrian king that again asserts YHWH as the true cause of Nineveh's destruction. The structure of the book appears as follows:

Nahum's Argument that YHWH is the True Power of the World
I. Superscription   1:1
II. *Māśśā'* Proper: Refutation of Contention that YHWH
    is Powerless   1:2—3:19
    A. Address to Judah and Assyria challenging their
        low estimation of YHWH   1:2-10
    B. Address to Judah asserting that the end of Assyrian
        oppression is an act of YHWH   1:11—2:1
    C. Address to Nineveh and the Assyrian king asserting
        that the fall of Nineveh is an act of YHWH   2:2—3:19

8. Habakkuk

The book of Habakkuk raises questions concerning YHWH's role in bringing the Neo-Babylonian empire as a threat against Jerusalem and Judah. The two superscriptions for the book in Hab 1:1 and 3:1 simply identify each portion of the book with Habakkuk the prophet. Nevertheless, the portrayal in Hab 1:6 of the rise of the Chaldeans, that is, the Neo-Babylonian dynasty founded in 625 BCE by Nabopolassar, provides an indication of the historical context. When Nabopolassar's son Nebuchadnezzar defeated Egypt in 605 BCE and took control of Judah, many in Judah saw the Babylonians as foreign oppressors rather than former allies from the days of King Josiah.[23] Habakkuk raises the question as to why YHWH would bring an oppressor against Judah. Although many interpreters have argued that Habakkuk's portrayal of the wicked must initially refer to Judeans who rejected YHWH's Torah (Hab 1:2-4), the usage of the term throughout the rest of the book indicates that it refers to the Babylonians as "the wicked who swallow the righteous" (Hab 1:13; cf. 1:12-17). The portrayal of the Babylonian king as the wicked oppressor who will be destroyed by YHWH (Hab 2:5-20) is opposed to the depiction in Hab 2:4 of "the righteous who shall live by their faith" (in YHWH).

    The two-part structure of the book is indicated by the superscriptions in Hab 1:1 and 3:1.[24] Habakkuk 1:1—2:20 is a prophetic *māśśā'*, "oracle," that presents a dialogue between Habakkuk and YHWH concerning YHWH's righteousness.

Habakkuk laments to YHWH over the oppression of the righteous by the wicked in Hab 1:2-4; YHWH claims to have brought the Chaldeans in Hab 1:5-11; Habakkuk demands to know how YHWH can tolerate such wickedness in Hab 1:12-17; and Hab 2:1-20 portrays YHWH's assurances that the wicked oppressor will ultimately fall. The Prayer of Habakkuk in Hab 3:1-19 draws on the imagery of theophany to assert that YHWH will respond to Habakkuk's complaint by destroying the oppressor. The structure of the book appears as follows:

Habakkuk's Oracle and Prayer Concerning YHWH's Righteousness
   I. Habakkuk's Oracle: Dialogue Concerning YHWH's
      Righteousness   1:1—2:20
      A. Superscription   1:1
      B. *Māśśā'* proper   1:2—2:20
         1. Habakkuk's initial complaint to YHWH concerning
            oppression of righteous by wicked   1:2-4
         2. YHWH's response: I brought the Chaldeans   1:5-11
         3. Habakkuk's second complaint: why tolerate evil?   1:12-17
         4. Report of YHWH's response: oppressor will fall   2:1-20
  II. Prayer of Habakkuk: Petition for YHWH to Act   2:1-19
      A. Superscription   3:1
      B. Prayer proper: YHWH will act   3:2-19a
      C. Instructions for the choirmaster   3:19b

9. Zephaniah

Although the superscription for the book in Zeph 1:1 places it in the reign of King Josiah of Judah (640–609 BCE), its position following Habakkuk, which relates Habakkuk's concerns over the rise of the Neo-Babylonian empire, and Haggai, which calls for the restoration of the Temple, indicates that its scenario of judgment and restoration for Jerusalem is read in relation to the Babylonian destruction of the city and the exile of much of its surviving population.

The body of the book exhibits a two-part structure that reflects the rhetorical effort to convince the people to support Josiah's reform. Zephaniah 1:2-18 announces the coming Day of YHWH (cf. Isa 2; 13; 34) as a day of punishment and sacrifice for those who would adhere to foreign gods. Zephaniah 2:1—3:20 presents an exhortation to seek YHWH, that is, to support Josiah's reform. It is based upon the exhortation in Zeph 2:1-3 and the prophet's explanatory address in Zeph 2:4—3:20. Zephaniah 2:4 points to the destruction of the Philistine cities as the basic evidence of YHWH's actions, and Zeph 2:5-15 and 3:1-20 respectively point to YHWH's actions against selected nations and the projected restoration of Jerusalem as further reason to support the reform. The structure appears as follows:

10. Haggai

Haggai is sct in the second year of the reign of King Darius of Persia (520 BCE), and appears as the prophet's call for the people of Jerusalem to support efforts to rebuild the Jerusalem Temple (cf. Ezra 3; 6). He is mentioned together with Zechariah in Ezra 5:1 and 6:14 as a prophet who called for the building of the Temple at the time that Zerubbabel ben Shealtiel, the grandson of King Jehoiachin of Judah, and Joshua ben Jehozadak, the high priest, returned to Jerusalem to commence the reconstruction efforts. During this period, the Persian empire was wracked by internal conflict as several major figures fought to gain control of the empire following the death of Cambyses, the son of Cyrus, in 522 BCE. Darius, the son in law of Cyrus, ultimately won control of the empire.

The book of Haggai appears in narrative form, and it presents a series of oracles dated to the year 520 BCE, in which the prophet lays out his calls for the rebuilding of the Temple and the designation of Zerubbabel as YHWH's designated regent.[25] Haggai 1:1-15a begins with a narrative concerning the people's compliance with the prophet's first oracle that calls upon the people to rebuild the Temple so that YHWH will provide rain and good harvest. Haggai 1:15b—2:9 presents the prophet's second oracle concerning the future glory of the new Temple to which the nations will bring gifts to acknowledge YHWH's sovereignty. Haggai 2:10-23 presents two oracles that respectively call upon the people to complete the Temple to ensure community purity and announce Zerubbabel as YHWH's signet ring, a metaphor for regent, who will ensure the overthrow of the nations that subjugate Judah. The structure of the book appears as follows:

11. Zechariah

Zechariah presents an account of the visions and the oracles of the prophet Zechariah concerning the significance of the Temple's restoration. The book appears in narrative form, and it is set in the second and fourth years of the reign of the Persian monarch Darius, that is, in 520 and 518 BCE (see Zech 1:1, 7; 7:1). Darius, the son–in-law of Cyrus, came to the throne following the unexpected death of his brother-in-law Cambyses. The empire was plunged into civil war as several figures attempted to seize control of the throne. Darius was able to quell opposition and begin his campaign against the Greek colonies in Asia Minor and the Greek mainland in 520–517 BCE. He authorized Zerubbabel ben Shealtiel, the grandson of King Jehoiachin of Judah, and the priest Joshua ben Jehozadak to return to Jerusalem in 522 BCE to begin construction of the Second Temple. The narrative setting of the book would therefore also coincide roughly with the years of the building of the Temple in 520–515 BCE.

Modern interpreters argue that Zechariah is a composite book like Isaiah insofar as Zech 1–8 appears to represent the visions of the prophet Zechariah, whereas Zech 9–14 represents a later apocalyptic scenario. Many also argue that Zech 9–11 and 12–14 are separate compositions that should be designated as Second and Third Zechariah. Although past interpreters have placed this material in the Hellenistic period, contemporary interpreters are beginning to recognize that Zech 9–14 may well date to the Persian period.

A synchronic literary reading of Zechariah notes the literary coherence of the book, particularly when the structural role of the date formulas in Zech 1:1, 7; and 7:1 is taken into consideration. The date formulae indicate a two-part structure for the book in which the narrator guides the reader into a presentation of the prophet's eight visions and two major oracles.[26] Zechariah 1:1-6 presents the introduction to the book with YHWH's initial word to the prophet, and Zech 1:7—14:21 presents YHWH's later words to the prophet concerning the visions in Zech 1:7—6:15 and the oracles in Zech 7:1—14:21. The present synchronic literary structure for the book appears as follows:

Account of Zechariah's Visions and Oracles concerning the Significance of the Restoration of Jerusalem

The introduction to the book in Zech 1:1-6 signals the concern with earlier prophetic tradition by constructing Zechariah's identity in relation to the figure of Zechariah ben Yeberechiah in Isa 8:1-4 (cf. the references to Zechariah bar Iddo in Ezra 5:1; 6:14) and by its references to the "former prophets" (v. 4). By referring to the calls for repentance made to the ancestors by the former prophets, the introduction emphasizes YHWH's ability to act in the world as announced by the prophets. Such an argument prepares the reading audience to anticipate the realization of the claims made in the following material concerning Zechariah's visions and oracles.

The narrative account of Zechariah's visions in Zech 1:7—6:15 lays out a sequence of the prophet's visions, each of which is based upon his observations of activities connected with the building of the new Temple and its preparation to serve as the holy center of creation. The first vision in Zech 1:7/8-17 draws upon the typical use of horse-mounted messengers by the Persian empire to portray the four horsemen who announce YHWH's plans to rebuild the Temple. The second vision in Zech 2:1-4 draws upon the imagery of workmen constructing the four-horned altar for the Temple (cf. Exod 27:2) to symbolize the scattering or exile of Israel in all directions and the punishment of all nations that carried out the exile. The third vision in Zech 2:5-17 draws upon the imagery of workmen laying out the plans for the reconstruction of the Temple and the city to depict Jerusalem as an unwalled, holy city, ringed by fire, much like the Persian holy city of Pasargadae, as a representation of YHWH's presence in the center of the nations. The fourth vision in Zech 3:1-10 portrays the ordination of Joshua ben Jehozadak as high priest for service in the new Temple (cf. Exod 28–29; Lev 8–9). The fifth vision in Zech 4:1-14 describes the Temple menorah, "candelabrum," flanked by two olive branches to symbolize YHWH's presence and the role of the two anointed figures, the royal Zerubbabel and the priestly Joshua, at the foundation of the new Temple. The sixth vision in Zech 5:1-4 employs the image of the flying scroll to symbolize the reading of Torah from the *'ûlām* or "porch" of the Temple as the basis for the holy life of the people. The seventh vision in Zech 5:5-11 portrays the removal of a woman in an ephah basket to Shinar, the site of Babylon, to symbolize the purity of the priests and the offerings made at their ordination. The eighth and final vision in Zech 6:1-15 presents the images of four chariots and the priest, Joshua ben Jehozadak, seated on the throne to symbolize the re-establishment of the Temple.

The narrative account of the transmission of YHWH's word to Zechariah in Zech 7:1—14:21 poses a question concerning mourning for the lost Temple in Zech 7:1-7 and answers the question with a lengthy depiction of rejoicing and righteous action at the restoration of the Temple in Zech 7:8—14:21. Within this second section, three sub-units, each introduced by the prophetic word-transmission formula, lay out YHWH's concerns. Zechariah 7:8-14 begins with an initial oracle concerning YHWH's call for righteous action that reiterates concerns from the introduction of the book to emphasize the reasons for the exile. Zechariah 8:1-17 recalls the earlier words of the prophets to emphasize that restoration will follow the period of punishment. Zechariah 8:18—14:21 calls for joy at the restoration of the Temple by portraying how the nations will come to seek YHWH (see Zech 8:18-23). The two major prophetic *māśśā'ôt*, "oracles," in Zech 9–11 and 12–14 respectively present YHWH's judgment against the shepherds, that is, the three Persian kings, Cyrus, Cambyses, and Darius, that failed to bring about YHWH's purposes as articulated in Isa 40–54 (see especially Isa 44:24—45:1), and YHWH's judgment against the nations. The scenario depends upon the rise of a new shepherd or Davidic monarch (Zech 11:16; cf. Jer 23:1-8) who would lead the combat that would eventually result in the nations' acknowledgment of YHWH at the Temple during the festival of Sukkot. Such a proposal runs counter to Isaiah, which envisions submission to the Persians as recognition of YHWH's world-wide sovereignty.

12. Malachi

Finally, Malachi calls for the return of the people to YHWH and rejects the notion of divorce, which had been employed metaphorically to represent the rupture of the relationship between YHWH and Israel in Hosea.

Nothing is known of the prophet Malachi, and many suspect that he does not even exist since the name in Hebrew means simply, "my messenger, angel." The term does not appear elsewhere in the Bible as a proper name. The book's concern with the neglect of the Temple and the marriage of Jewish men to pagan women suggests that it is to be set some time prior to the arrival of Ezra in Jerusalem. This suggests that Malachi should be dated to the fifth century, and perhaps played a role in building the case for Ezra's placement in Jerusalem. Indeed, Ezra's reforms address the issues raised in Malachi.

   The literary form of Malachi supports such a contention.[27] The structure of the
book may be represented as follows:

Parenetic Address to Priests and People Calling for Proper
Reverence for YHWH

I.	Superscription	1:1
II.	Body of the Book: Parenetic Address Proper	1:2—3:24
	A. First disputation: YHWH loves the people	1:2-5
	B. Second disputation: people and priests have mishandled cultic matters	1:6—2:16
	C. Third disputation: justice will be done on the Day of YHWH	2:17—3:5
	D. Fourth disputation: call for proper treatment of YHWH's tithes	3:6-12
	E. Fifth disputation: YHWH's justice will be realized on Day of YHWH	3:13-21
	F. Concluding summation: observe YHWH's Torah	3:22-24

The superscription in Mal 1:1 identifies the book simply as "An oracle. The word
of YHWH to Israel by Malachi." The body of the book in Mal 1:2—3:24 appears
as a parenetic address to priests and people designed to convince them to provide
proper reverence and support for YHWH and the Temple. This section includes
six disputation speeches that challenge popular perceptions, arguing for adherence to YHWH. Malachi 1:2-5 contends that YHWH loves the people. Malachi
1:6—2:16 argues that both people and priests have mishandled cultic matters.
Malachi 2:17—3:5 answers concerns about YHWH's justice to contend that the
Day of YHWH's justice is about to arrive. Malachi 3:6-12 calls for the proper
treatment of YHWH's tithes. Malachi 3:13-21 again asserts that YHWH's justice
will be realized on the Day of YHWH. The concluding statements in Mal 3:22-24
sum up the argument by calling for observance of YHWH's Torah and announcing the return of the prophet Elijah prior to the Day of YHWH (cf. 2 Kgs 2, which
contends that Elijah did not die, but ascended to heaven in a fiery chariot).

NOTES

* This chapter is a heavily revised and condensed version of my chapter concerning the Twelve
Prophets in *The Prophetic Literature* (IBT; Nashville: Abingdon, 2005), 165–214. Readers
wishing a much fuller and earlier version of this discussion should turn there.
[1] For discussion of the different versions of the Book of the Twelve extant in the ancient world,
see Ehud Ben Zvi, "Twelve Prophetic Books or 'The Twelve': A Few Preliminary Considerations," in *Forming Prophetic Literature: Essays on Isaiah and the Twelve in Honor of J. D. W.
Watts*, ed. J. W. Watts and P. R. House (JSOTSup 235; Sheffield: Sheffield Academic, 1996),
125–56; Barry Alan Jones, *The Formation of the Book of the Twelve: Study in Text and Canon*
(SBLDS 149; Atlanta: Scholars Press, 1995). For discussion of the sequence of the books in the
Masoretic text and Septuagint versions of the Book of the Twelve Prophets, see my "Sequence
and Interpretation in the Book of the Twelve," in *Reading and Hearing the Book of the Twelve*,

ed. J. D. Nogalski and M. A. Sweeney (SBLSymS 15; Atlanta: Society of Biblical Literature, 2000), 49–64; idem, *The Twelve Prophets* (BO; Collegeville: Liturgical, 2000), 1:xv–xxix.

[2] Cf. Odil Hannes Steck, *The Prophetic Books and their Theological Witness*, trans. J. D. Nogalski (St. Louis: Chalice, 2000).

[3] See Gerlinde Bauman, *Love and Violence: Marriage as Metaphor for the Relationship between YHWH and Israel in the Prophetic Books*, trans. L. Maloney (Collegeville: Liturgical, 2003), 85–104; for discussion of this theme in Hosea, cf. Francis Landy, *Hosea* (Readings; Sheffield: Sheffield Academic, 1995), 21–52.

[4] See my *The Twelve Prophets*, 3–7, and *King Josiah of Judah: The Lost Messiah of Israel* (Oxford: Oxford University Press, 2001), 256–72.

[5] For discussion of metaphor in Hosea, see, for example, Göran Eidevall, *Grapes in the Desert: Metaphors, Models, and Themes in Hosea 4–14* (ConBibOT 43; Stockholm: Almqvist & Wiksell, 1996).

[6] For discussion of the intertextual references in Joel, see Siegfried Bergler, *Joel als Schriftinterpret* (BEATAJ 16; Frankfurt: Lang, 1988); for discussion in English, see, in addition to my own, the commentaries by Wolff and Crenshaw.

[7] For discussion of the Hamsin/Sharav, see "Israel, Land of (Geographical Survey)," *EncJud* 9:189–90.

[8] Gösta W. Ahlström, *Joel and the Temple Cult of Jerusalem* (VTSup 21; Leiden: Brill, 1971).

[9] For discussion of the structure of Joel, see my *Twelve Prophets*, 1:147–52.

[10] See Moshe Weinfeld, "Tithe," *EncJud* 15:1156–62.

[11] For discussion of the structure of Amos, see Sweeney, *Twelve Prophets*, 1:191–95; idem, *King Josiah*, 273–86.

[12] For discussion of Amos's relation to the wisdom tradition, see especially Hans Walter Wolff, *Amos the Prophet: The Man and his Background*, trans. F. McCurley (Philadelphia: Fortress Press, 1973).

[13] See the treatment of this passage in the commentaries by Paul and Sweeney; cf. Max Polley, *Amos and the Davidic Empire* (New York: Oxford University Press, 1989).

[14] See especially Ehud Ben Zvi, *A Historical-Critical Study of the Book of Obadiah* (BZAW 242; Berlin: de Gruyter, 1996), 99–109; Hans Walter Wolff, *Obadiah and Jonah*, trans. M. Kohl (ContCom; Minneapolis: Fortress Press, 1986), 37–42.

[15] See my *Twelve Prophets*, 1:279–85.

[16] See now the treatment of Jonah in J. William Whedbee, *The Bible and the Comic Vision* (Cambridge: Cambridge University Press, 1998); Ehud Ben Zvi, *Signs of Jonah: Reading and Rereading Jonah in Ancient Yehud* (JSOTSup 367; London: Sheffield Academic, 2003).

[17] Sweeney, *Twelve Prophets*, 1:303–7.

[18] Lamontte M. Luker, "Moresheth," *ABD* 4:904–5.

[19] See Sennacherib's account of his invasion of Judah in 701 BCE in *ANET*, 287–88; cf. Isa 36–37/2 Kgs 18–19.

[20] See my "Micah's Debate with Isaiah," in *Form and Intertextuality in Prophetic and Apocalyptic Literature* (FAT 45; Tübingen: Mohr Siebeck, 2005), 210–21.

[21] See my *Twelve Prophets*, 2:339–43, and *King Josiah*, 287–300.

[22] For discussion of the formal features and rhetorical strategy of Nahum, see my *The Twelve Prophets*, 2:419–47.

[23] For discussion of the political situation presupposed in Habakkuk, see Jay Wilcoxen, "The Political Background of Jeremiah's Temple Sermon," in *Scripture in History and Theology: Essays in Honor of J. Coert Rylaarsdam*, ed. A. Merrill and T. Overholt (Pittsburgh: Pickwick, 1977), 151–66; cf. Robert D. Haak, *Habakkuk* (VTSup 44; Leiden: Brill, 1992), 107–49.

[24] See my *The Twelve Prophets*, 2:453–58; idem, *King Josiah*, 301–10.

[25] For discussion of the literary form of Haggai, see the commentaries by Petersen, Meyers, and Sweeney.

[26] Sweeney, *The Twelve Prophets*, 2:561–67; cf. Edgar W. Conrad, *Zechariah* (Readings; Sheffield: Sheffield Academic, 1999).

[27] For discussion of the literary form of Malachi, see, in addition to my own, the commentary by Petersen.

Part IV

The Ketuvim/Writings

A. Overview

The Writings (Hebrew, *kĕtûbîm*) of the Bible include the books of Psalms, Proverbs, Job, the Five Megillot (Song of Songs, Ruth, Lamentations, Qoheleth, Esther), Daniel, Ezra–Nehemiah, and Chronicles.[1] Unlike the Torah, Former Prophets, and Latter Prophets, the Writings is a variegated collection of material including hymnic, wisdom, apocalyptic, and historical narrative, which appears to have no common theme, generic characteristics, or purpose. The Writings is the last major segment of the Bible to be canonized, a fact which has led interpreters to speculate that the segment is an ill-defined, "catch all" section that provides a place for books that are considered canonical and yet have little or no common characteristics with other, better known, biblical works. These books are not read regularly in the synagogue service, as are the Torah or the Haftarah readings of the Prophets. Some of them appear on various occasions, viz., many of the Psalms are read individually within the services or as part of the Hallel, and the Five Megillot are read in relation to major festival observances, that is, Song of Songs on Passover, Ruth on Shavuot, Lamentations on Tisha b'Av, Qoheleth on Sukkot, and Esther on Purim.

Rabbinic tradition sets the order of Ketuvim as Ruth, Psalms, Job, Proverbs, Qoheleth, Song of Songs, Lamentations, Daniel, Esther, Ezra–Nehemiah, and Chronicles (*b. Baba Batra* 14b). This order is understood to be roughly chronological insofar as Ruth is written by Samuel, Psalms by David, Job by Job, Proverbs, Qoheleth, and Song of Songs by Solomon, Lamentations by Jeremiah, Daniel by Daniel in the Babylonian Exile, and both Ezra–Nehemiah and Chronicles by Ezra and Nehemiah. Job is an exception to this rule, however, insofar as Job is considered to be a contemporary with Moses. But the Baraita continues by noting that Job has been displaced because the Ketuvim should not begin with a record of suffering. Although Ruth also suffers, the Rabbis point out that her suffering leads to happiness because she is the ancestor of David who replenished G-d with hymns and praises. Because Job is wisdom literature, Job is therefore placed within the wisdom material ascribed to Solomon. Some manuscript traditions place Chronicles at the head of the Ketuvim insofar as Chronicles begins its history with Adam, leaving Ezra–Nehemiah to conclude the segment with the reconstruction of the Temple and the restoration of Jerusalem.[2] The current order of books cited above is based on the orders of books as presented in printed editions of the Mikra'ot Gedolot beginning in the sixteenth century CE.

Because no common thread appears to tie these books together, scholars have developed no compelling diachronic model for the composition of the Ketuvim as a distinct and coherent segment of the Bible. Instead, they have had to focus on the compositional history of the individual books of the Ketuvim. Many presume that the Ketuvim was a gradually growing collection of distinct books that began with the Psalms and was finalized only at the yeshivah or council of Yavneh (Jamnia) founded by Rabbi Yohanan ben Zakkai in the years between the destruction of the Second Temple in 70 CE and the outbreak of the Bar Kochba Revolt in 132 CE.[3] Ben Sira 39:1 refers to wisdom literature together with Torah and Prophets; 2 Macc 2:13-14 refers to Ezra–Nehemiah; and Luke 24:44 refers to the Psalms, although it is never clear in any of these sources that a coherent unit such as the Ketuvim is intended. Nevertheless, close study of the Rabbinic traditions concerning the compilation of the biblical books demonstrates that the final status of the individual books of the Writings was not decided until well into the period of the composition of the Talmuds, ca. 300–600 CE. Indeed, the book of Ben Sira is frequently cited as sacred scripture in Rabbinic literature even though it was never included in the Jewish Bible and appears only in the Deutero-Canonical or Apocryphal literature of Christian Bibles.[4]

Despite the lack of clarity on the diachronic models of composition and function, it is possible to posit a synchronic model for the form and function of the Ketuvim within the Jewish Bible.[5] Overall, the Ketuvim provides a model for the restoration of the ideals of Jewish life in the land of Israel and the world at large laid out in the Torah and disrupted in Prophets. Psalms presents the hymn book (perhaps) of the Second Temple, and thereby provides a liturgical basis for Jewish worship of G-d in the yet-to-be-restored Third Temple of the future. It also provides alternative viewpoints on biblical history, insofar as many of the Psalms provide overviews of biblical events as well as reflection on the role of G-d in various aspects of Jewish life and the world at large. Proverbs is a wisdom book that instructs its readers on how to live in the world. Insofar as it posits a stable world of creation and ideal means of human conduct based on G-d's consultation with wisdom as the first of the creation (see Prov 8), it provides an alternative means to learn divine Torah by observing the world of creation and learning to live according to its norms. Job questions the stable world of creation and moral order by arguing that human beings really do not understand the divine principles by which our world works, insofar as divine wisdom is so difficult to understand (for example, Job 28). The Megillot are each tied to a holiday and thereby provide a means to reflect on the lessons and observance of the festival. Song of Songs reflects on the intimate nature of the relationship between YHWH and Israel established at the time of the Exodus from Egypt celebrated at Passover. Ruth reflects on the revelation of Torah in the world celebrated at Shavuot by focusing on the life of Ruth, a Moabitess who converts to Judaism. Lamentations mourns the destruction of the Temple at Tisha b'Av and thereby gives voice to the suffering of the Jewish people throughout their history. Qoheleth probes the futility and transitory nature of human life in the world at the time of Sukkot, which celebrates Israel's transitory life in the wilderness. And Esther celebrates the deliverance of Jews from the Persian decree of death at the time of Purim while reflecting on the questions of divine absence and human responsibility in the world. Daniel posits a future restoration of the world in which Jews will ultimately overcome the threats posed against them in the world with the aid of G-d. It is perhaps no accident that Daniel appears before Ezra–Nehemiah, which portrays the restoration of the Second Temple and the city of Jerusalem during the early Persian period. Such a portrayal obviously anticipates another restoration of the Temple and Jewish life in the land of Israel. And finally, Chronicles presents a history of Israel, focused on the Jerusalem Temple planned by David and built by Solomon, from the time of Adam to the time of King Cyrus of Persia. Chronicles provides an alternative interpretation of history to that of the Former Prophets by positing that those who suffer do so on account of their own actions rather than because of the actions of ancestors as posited in the Former Prophets. But it also points forward to the restoration of the Temple, this time under the authority of the Persians rather than under the authority of the house of David. In this respect, Chronicles points to new possibilities for the realization of ideal Jewish life in the land of Israel and the world at large.

NOTES

[1] See especially Sid Z. Leiman, *The Canonization of Hebrew Scripture: The Talmudic and Midrashic Evidence* (New Haven: Connecticut Academy of Arts and Sciences, 1976); Roger T. Beckwith, "Formation of the Hebrew Bible," in *Mikra: Text, Translation, Reading, and Interpretation of the Hebrew Bible in Ancient Judaism and early Christianity*, ed. M. J. Mulder et al. (CRIANT 2; Philadelphia: Fortress Press, 1988), 39–86; idem, *The Old Testament Canon of the New Testament Church* (Grand Rapids: Eerdmans, 1986); James A. Sanders, "Canon," *ABD* 1:837–52; Donn F. Morgan, *Between Tex and Community: The "Writings" in Canonical Interpretation* (Minneapolis: Fortress Press, 1990).
[2] See the Leningrad/St. Petersburg Codex, which gives the order as Chronicles, Psalms, Job, Proverbs, Ruth, Song of Songs, Qoheleth, Lamentations, Esther, Daniel, and Ezra–Nehemiah.
[3] Jack P. Lewis, "What do we Mean by Jabneh?," *JBL* 32 (1964): 125–32.
[4] See Leiman, *Canonization*, 92–102.
[5] Cf. Morgan, *Between Text and Community*, passim.

B. The Book of Psalms

The book of Psalms is known as *těhillîm*, "praises," which indicates its character as a book of praises for G-d, even when it raises questions concerning G-d's power, presence, and will to act on behalf of justice and righteousness. Indeed, Psalms constitutes a marked change in the presentation of the literature that appears within the Tanak. Currently standing at the head of the *Ketuvim*,[1] Psalms is the first book of the Bible to address G-d directly on behalf of the people of Judah and Israel, rather than to present the customary history and prophecy concerning G-d's interrelationship with Israel and Judah that the reader has come to expect. Psalms therefore constitutes the first instance of a book in which human beings are able to talk directly to G-d, rather than be addressed by G-d as in the Torah and Prophets.

Such a change points to the dialogical character of the Bible in which human beings not only speak to G-d, but frequently challenge the theological constructs of divine righteousness and human wrongdoing that stand at the basis for the understanding of divine involvement in the history and experience of Israel and Judah throughout the Torah and Prophets.[2] Insofar as the Torah and Prophets presuppose a righteous and powerful YHWH, who creates the universe, enters into a covenant with the people of Israel, grants of the land of Israel to the people, and brings punishment against them when they allegedly do wrong, the book of Psalms offers the opportunity to praise YHWH for the many blessings experienced by the people and to question YHWH in times of threat. Because the Prophets, both Former and Latter, focus so pointedly on the problems of destruction and exile, most notably the destruction of the northern kingdom of Israel by the Assyrians in 722/1 BCE and the destruction of Jerusalem and the Temple in 587/6 BCE, the book of Psalms provides the opportunity to "talk back" to YHWH, often challenging the notions of a righteous, powerful, moral, and present deity who so often remains hidden in human experience.[3]

As the opening book of the *Ketuvim*, Psalms asks the critical questions of G-d and it offers the praise of YHWH. In this manner, Psalms opens the way for the process of critical reflection on G-d and the world and the restoration of Jerusalem and Israel/Judah within the world that proceeds throughout the third major component of the Bible. The critical questions of Psalms anticipate those of the wisdom literature, Job and Proverbs (as well as those of Qoheleth, Lamentations, and Esther). The liturgical qualities of Psalms anticipate the Megillot, which are each identified with a liturgical celebration in Judaism. The concern for future divine action anticipates the book of Daniel in the *Ketuvim*. Finally, the realization of divine action appears in Ezra–Nehemiah, which sees the restoration of the Temple, and in Chronicles, which surveys the history of Jerusalem from the time of creation to anticipate the restoration of the city with the Temple and king at its center.

The book of Psalms likely constituted the hymnbook of the Jerusalem Temple in Second Temple times and perhaps to some extent also in First Temple times. A wide variety of psalmic types appears within the book in which Jews address YHWH with a variety of concerns and needs, such as the praise of YHWH, critical questioning of YHWII in times of threat or need, thanksgiving to YHWH, reflection on the monarch, reflection on divine teaching, and other concerns.[4] The Temple would have been the place where most of the ancient Jewish population would have encountered YHWH and divine service and instruction in ancient times, and it therefore would have been the primary setting in which people interacted with the divine.[5]

Most interpreters recognize the hymns of praise as the fundamental genre of psalms.[6] Hymns praise and extol YHWH at festivals or other joyous occasions for YHWH's various acts as creator, deliverer and protector of Israel, the source of justice and righteousness in the world, and so on. The hymns appear in Pss 8; 19; 29; 33; 47; 65; 66; 78; 93; 95–100; 103–106; 111; 113; 114; 117; 134; 135; 136; and 145–150. They comprise a very simple two-part structure that includes (1) the call to praise in which the people are called to assemble in the sacred sanctuary to sing praise of YHWH, and (2) the basis for praise of YHWH, which would include YHWH's power, sovereignty, righteousness, mercy, presence, acts of deliverance on behalf of the people, and so on.

The most numerous type of psalm in the book of Psalms is the communal and individual lament or complaint that presents difficult problems and questions to G-d, such as the threat of impending enemies, famine, illness, and so on, as well as the problem of divine absence or failure to respond in the face of such threats.[7] Insofar as the lament constitutes nearly half of the Psalter, the laments point to the fundamental role that need for YHWH plays in the relation between deity and people.[8] Perhaps the lament should actually be recognized as the most fundamental psalm type. Communal laments appear in Pss 12; 44; 60; 74; 79; 80; 83; 85; 90; 94; 108; 123; 129; and 137. Individual laments appear in Pss 3–7; 9–10; 13; 14; 17; 22; 25; 26; 28; 31; 35; 36; 38; 39; 40; 41; 42–43; 51; 52; 53; 54–59; 61; 64; 69; 70; 71; 77; 86; 88; 102; 109; 120; 130; and 140–143. Typical elements of both versions of the lament include (1) the address to YHWH in which the psalmist calls upon the deity; (2) the complaint or lament proper in which the psalmist lays out the problem or threat that has prompted an appeal to YHWH for assistance or intervention; (3) the request for help from YHWH to resolve or alleviate the problem or crisis at hand; (4) an expression of trust in YHWH that confirms the psalmist's and the nation's confidence in YHWH's ability and willingness to resolve the issue; and (5) a vow to praise YHWH once the crisis has passed.

The thanksgiving psalms give thanks to YHWH for various acts of beneficence.[9] They appear in Pss 18; 30; 32; 34; 40; 66; 92; 116; 118; and 138. They may have been sung during liturgical processions to the Temple or the presentation of thanksgiving offerings at the Temple altar. The standard elements of the thanksgiving songs include (1) an invitation to give thanks to YHWH, generally employing a version of the formula, *hôdû lyhwh*, "give thanks to YHWH"; (2) an account of the problem or crisis that YHWH has resolved on the people's behalf; (3) praises for YHWH for having taken such action; (4) offertory formulae to accompany the presentation of thanksgiving offerings at the altar; (5) a statement of blessings for the participants in the ceremony; and (6) an exhortation to trust in YHWH.

The royal psalms focus on the divinely anointed king of Israel in Jerusalem.[10] They appear in Pss 2; 18; 20; 21; 45; 72; 89; 101; 110; 132; and 144. The setting for the royal psalms was likely some event in the life of the king, such as a coronation, wedding, victory in battle, deliverance from enemies, or other major events that would celebrate the role of the king in the life of the nation. They have no typical structural elements, and are identified solely by their focus on the monarch. They may include various forms of hymns, thanksgiving, complaints, and other elements found elsewhere in the psalms, which raises questions as to whether the royal psalms actually constitute a distinct genre rather than an expression of interest in messianism on the part of modern scholars.

The Zion psalms focus on the well-being and central role of Zion or Jerusalem in the world at large.[11] They appear in Pss 46; 48; 76; 84; 87; and 122. Again, the Zion songs display no typical structure or structural elements. Rather, they are identified thematically by their celebration of YHWH's choice of Zion as the site for the Temple as the holy center of creation and divine presence in the world. Insofar as the Zion psalms appear to presuppose a ritual procession, they appear to function in the context of a celebration of YHWH's creation of the world or establishment of the Temple at the center of creation.

The wisdom and Torah psalms celebrate the wisdom with which YHWH endows human beings and creation at large.[12] They appear in Pss 1; 19; 37; 49; 73; 112; 119; 127; 128; and 133. They appear to be designed for reflection and meditation on issues pertaining to G-d, worship, study of Torah, and life in the world. They have no typical structure or elements, but are defined thematically, again raising questions as to whether they represent a distinct genre or simply the interests and perspectives of modern interpreters.

A variety of liturgical psalms appears in Pss 15; 24; 50; 68; 81; 82; 95; 115; and 132.[13] They include the entrance liturgies of Pss 15 and 24, which define the qualities of moral and ritual purity that should characterize one who would enter the Temple precincts.[14] Covenant renewal is the subject of Ps 50. Liturgical processions appear in Pss 68; 91; 118; and 132. Psalm 81 focuses on repentance by

the people, and Ps 82 calls for judgment against foreign gods for their failure to
do justice in the world.

Finally, a number of psalms, including Pss 11; 16; 23; 27; 62; 63; 67; 75; 91; 107;
121; 124; 125; 126; 131; and 139 are unique or mixed types that are difficult to
classify adequately.[15]

The book of Psalms therefore constitutes an anthology or a repository for the
many hymnic compositions that might be employed in the liturgy of the
Jerusalem Temple and perhaps elsewhere. Unfortunately, our knowledge as to
how individual psalms would have been selected for use in the Temple liturgy or
how they would have functioned within it is limited. First Chronicles 16 provides
us with a window as to how the Psalms might have functioned within the context
of liturgical worship. When David had the Ark of the Covenant moved from
Kiriath Jearim to Jerusalem, the liturgy for the occasion, sung by Asaph and his
sons, included portions of Pss 105:1-15; 96:1-13a; and 106:47-48. Second Chronicles 6:41-42 notes that Ps 132:8-10 was sung as part of the liturgy accompanying
Solomon's dedication speech for the Jerusalem Temple. Second Chronicles 35:15
indicates that the sons of Asaph were present to sing the Temple liturgy during
Josiah's celebration of Passover, although the text provides no clue as to which
psalms were sung. Furthermore, Ezra 2:70 and 3:10-11 indicate that the sons of
Asaph were present to sing at the ceremony for the foundation of the Second
Temple, where they sang "for [YHWH] is good; [YHWH's] fidelity for Israel is
eternal" (see Pss 106:1; 107:1; 118:1, 29; 136:1). Although the choice of psalms is
clearly appropriate for the occasion celebrated, the psalms employed in the liturgy
appear throughout the present form of the book of Psalms with no indication that
the Psalms are arranged according to the occasion on which they might be sung.

Although the book of Psalms comprises 150 individual psalmic compositions,
it is organized into five major components or books, each of which concludes
with a distinctive formulaic refrain or doxology, bārûk yhwh, "blessed is YHWH,"
in Pss 41:14; 72:18-20; 89:53; 106:48, and hallĕlû-yah, "praise YHWH," in Ps
150:1-6.[16] Thus, the five books that comprise Psalms are Pss 1–41; 42–72; 73–89;
90–106; and 107–150. Midrash Shoher Tov on Pss 1:2 maintains that the five
books of Psalms correspond to the five books of the Torah, viz., "Moses gave the
five books of the Torah to Israel, and David gave the five books of the Psalms to
Israel." It further maintains that the book of Psalms actually contains only 147
psalms to correspond to the number of sĕdārîm, "orders," or Torah portions that
would have been read in the triennial cycle of Shabbat Torah readings read in
antiquity and the Middle Ages (b. Berakot 9b–10a). The number 147 results from
the rabbinic position that Pss 1 and 2; 114 and 115; and 117 and 118 each constitute one psalm. But ancient versions of the Psalms indicate that there were more
psalms in antiquity than those that appear within the present Masoretic form of
the book. Additional psalms appear throughout the Bible, for example, Exod 15;
Deut 32; Judg 5; 1 Sam 2:1-10; 2 Sam 23:1-7; Isa 12; Jonah 2; Hab 3. Some psalmic
compositions in the Bible correspond to known psalms, such as 2 Sam 22 and

Ps 18. Otherwise unknown psalms appear in other versions of the Bible. The Septuagint, for example, includes Ps 151, and the Syriac Peshitta includes Pss 151–155. The Qumran Psalms scroll (11QPsalms) includes all or parts of 41 psalms that appear in Books IV and V of the Psalms, albeit in a different order from that of the Masoretic text, as well 2 Sam 23:1-7, the apocryphal Pss 151; 154; 155; and Sir 51:13-19, 30, and four non-biblical works that appear throughout the scroll.[17] Some argue that such psalms might have filled a need for additional psalms to correspond to the Torah readings of the triennial cycle. Although it is possible that the five-fold structure of the book of Psalms is intended to correspond to the five books of the Torah, no clear proof for such a hypothesis has yet been achieved. It is possible that the five-book arrangement presupposes the periods between the five holiday observances of Judaism, viz., Passover in the first month during the early spring, Shavuot in the third month during the late spring, Tisha b'Av in the fifth month during the late summer, Sukkot in the seventh month during the early autumn, and Purim in the twelfth month during the late winter—but again, no convincing proof is forthcoming.

A close examination of each of the five books suggests a different basis for the organization of the Psalms. Book I (Pss 1–41) includes 41 psalms, of which 37 are attributed to David. Some 21 of these psalms are classified as psalms of lament, whereas the representation of other types is limited, that is, four hymns, four thanksgiving psalms, three royal psalms, no Zion psalms, two liturgical psalms, three wisdom psalms, and four of mixed or unique type. Book II (Pss 42–72) include 31 psalms of which 18 are attributed to David, one to Solomon, one to Asaph, and seven to the sons of Korah. Again, laments predominate, with 18. Other types are less well represented, with three hymns, one thanksgiving psalm, two royal psalms, two Zion psalms, two liturgical psalms, one wisdom psalm, and three of mixed or unique type. In addition, Book II concludes with the statement, "end of the prayers of David ben Jesse" in Ps 72:20. Book III (Pss 73–89) includes 17 psalms, with eleven attributed to Asaph, four to the sons of Korah, one to David, and one to Ethan the Ezrahite. Among them are eight laments, one hymn, no thanksgiving psalms, one royal psalm, three Zion psalms, two liturgical psalms, one wisdom psalm, and one of mixed or unique type. Book IV (Pss 90–106) includes 17 psalms, of which two are attributed to David and one to Moses. Among them are ten hymns, three laments, one thanksgiving psalm, one royal psalm, no Zion psalms, one liturgical psalm, one wisdom psalm, and one of mixed or unique type. Book V (Pss 107–150) includes 44 psalms, of which 15 are attributed to David, one to Solomon, and 15 are identified as "songs of ascent (Hebrew, *maʿălôt*), which were presumably sung as worshippers made their ascent to the Temple courtyard. Of the songs of ascent, four are among those attributed to David and one is the previously identified psalm attributed to Solomon. Among these psalms are thirteen hymns, eleven laments, three thanksgiving psalms, three royal psalms, one Zion psalm, two liturgical psalms, five wisdom psalms, and seven of mixed or unique type.

Modern scholars have suggested that the statement, "end of the prayers of David ben Jesse" in Ps 72:20 marks the end of an early collection of Psalms to which the materials in Books III, IV, and V have been later added.[18] But the predominance of psalms attributed to David in Books I–II and V, the predominance of psalms attributed to Asaph in Book III, and the predominance of unattributed psalms in Book IV suggests that perhaps the original collection is based in Books I–II and V, and that Books III and IV, with their Asaphite and unattributed collections, are the supplementary material. Such contention would presuppose that the psalms attributed to David would have been sponsored or commissioned under the patronage of the royal house of David.[19] The Asaphite Psalms would have been commissioned by the royal house of David at some later time (see 1 Chr 6:16-33; 25:1-31, which notes David's commission of the Levitical singers, including Asaph, among others).[20] The Korahite Psalms, which are included together with Davidic Psalms in Book II, would have been incorporated into Book II after the initial Davidic collection.[21] They would have been the product of a priestly line that was somehow discredited in relation to the line of Aaron, perhaps because of some power struggle among the priestly families or because of some foreign association (see Num 16, which narrates Korah's rebellion), together with the Reubenites, Dathan, and Abiram, against Moses and Aaron (see 1 Chr 26, which identifies the Korahites as the line of priestly gatekeepers, although they are also linked to the Asaphites). The Songs of Ascent in Book V, some of which are attributed to David, may well be original to the book.[22] Of course, this model is speculative, but it might help to explain the formation of the book from so many disparate elements.

Apart from questions of the diachronic formation of the book, the synchronic literary form of Psalms points to a predominance of laments in Books I, II, and III, and a predominance of hymns in Books IV and V (see also 11QPsalms, noted above, which draws all of its biblical psalms from Books IV and V although it employs a different order and includes both apocryphal and non-canonical psalms). Other psalm types appear in every one of the books, but the fundamental distinction between laments and hymns, the two most numerous types of the psalms, may well explain at least some basis for the current form of the book. In such a case, Books I–IIII would serve as a repository for lament psalms to be drawn upon as the occasion requires, and Books IV–V would serve as a repository for hymns, again to be drawn upon as the occasion requires.

Book I

Book I of the Psalms focuses especially on the problems or fears that are addressed to G-d, insofar as over half of the psalms included in this section, 22 of 41, may be classified as laments. In addition, 37 of the psalms in Book I are ascribed to David, suggesting that some form of this book could derive from monarchic patronage.

The book begins with Pss 1–2, which are considered as one psalm in rabbinic tradition because Ps 2 lacks its own introduction and because of the formulaic statements, "happy is the man who . . . ," that introduce Ps 1 and close Ps 2 (*b. Berakot* 9b–10a).[23] Psalm 1 is a wisdom psalm that extols the path of righteousness and knowledge of divine Torah over that of wickedness and sin. Psalm 2 then illustrates G-d's commitment to come to the aid of the Davidic monarch in Jerusalem when threatened by the nations of the earth, and advises foreign monarchs to accept the sovereignty of YHWH. When read as one, Pss 1–2 begins with a reassurance to those who would look to YHWH for security in the world and thereby provides a fitting introduction for a book that so emphasizes the laments of Israel.

A series of lamentation psalms then follows in Pss 3–7 in which each psalm builds dramatically on the threat posed to the psalmist and the need for divine action. Psalm 3, ascribed to David when he fled from his son Absalom (2 Sam 15–16), states David's confidence in YHWH's protection even as his enemies attack and deny divine protection. Psalm 4, ascribed to David but without specific occasion, is an appeal for divine protection on behalf of those who are devoted (*ḥāsîd*) to YHWH. Psalm 5, ascribed to David, again appeals for divine protection, but it elaborates on the issue by stating that G-d does not desire wickedness and emphasizes that G-d will surely bless the righteous. Psalm 6, ascribed to David, displays great distress insofar as its appeals for divine deliverance indicate that the psalmist is already suffering punishment from G-d and begs G-d to know "how long?" (Hebrew, *'ad mātāy*) the punishment will continue until G-d hears this plea. Psalm 7, ascribed to David when he sang concerning Cush the Benjaminite, takes the appeal to G-d a step further by allowing that the psalmist should be punished if he is indeed guilty. The psalm nevertheless presumes the innocence of the psalmist, and it emphasizes that when one who is evil is unchecked, he will continue to do more mischief until checked by divine intervention.[24] The Benjaminite Cush mentioned is unknown, and so the Targum to Psalms reads the reference in relation to Saul ben Kish.

Psalm 8, ascribed to David, is a hymn that extols G-d's role as creator and meditates on G-d's choice to take up such extraordinary concern with human beings as divine agents who have responsibility for tending to creation. Within the context of the laments, Ps 8 stands as a reminder that G-d will act on behalf of human beings.

Psalms 9–14 return to the concern with lamentations, but unlike the first sequence in Pss 3–7, presents a greater sense of distress and threat. Psalm 9, ascribed to David, begins with calls to praise YHWH, but clearly presupposes a situation a threat insofar as it elaborates on the divine role as righteous judge against oppressors. Psalm 10, which many maintain is a continuation of Ps 9 due to its lack of title or ascription,[25] sounds a note of alarm in that it opens with direct address to YHWH, asking why G-d stands aloof as the wicked rampage freely. The extended descriptions of the words of the wicked are designed to goad YHWH insofar as the wicked state that G-d does not care, that G-d hides the divine face, and that G-d never looks, which then provide the basis for the psalm-ist's appeal for divine intervention. Psalm 11, ascribed to David, is a unique type insofar as it engages in debate with those who would hear the psalmist, although the situation of need clearly presupposes lamentation. The debate focuses on the advice of those who counsel flight to the hills as the enemies approach, whereas the psalmist states the case that G-d will act to protect the righteous. Psalm 12, ascribed to David, is a communal lament that expresses confidence that G-d will act against the wicked who speak lies and oppress the needy. Psalm 13, ascribed to David, pointedly addresses G-d with the question, "how long" will G-d ignore the plight of the psalmist and hide the divine face? The psalmist demands an answer from G-d, indicated by the crisis of divine neglect in a time of threat, and yet it concludes with statements of confidence that G-d will answer the plea. Psalm 14, ascribed to David, focuses especially on the wicked who maintain that G-d does not care and that the actions of humans are always corrupt, but it concludes with the hope—but not the absolute certainty—of divine deliverance for Israel. The psalm is nearly identical to Ps 53. It is exceptional in that it is not addressed to YHWH, but instead represents reflection on YHWH. In this respect, Ps 14 presents the reader with the opportunity for reflection at the end of a sequence of lamentations.

Psalm 15, ascribed to David, interrupts the sequence of lamentation psalms with an example of an entrance liturgy. The entrance liturgies define the moral qualities of one who would enter the sacred Temple precincts, and rejects the entry of one who lacks such moral perspective.[26] Psalm 15 therefore serves as a reminder to humans to maintain their purity and righteousness, and it affirms the principal that G-d will grant refuge to the righteous. Psalm 16, ascribed to David, is a unique type that expresses the psalmist's confidence in G-d at a time when the psalmist seeks refuge. It appeals to G-d for protection, and grants divine sovereignty, morality, guidance, and fidelity.

Psalm 17, ascribed to David, returns to the lament form and presents a lengthy appeal for G-d to respond to the psalmist's prayer for deliverance in the face of the wicked. The intensity of this psalm prepares the reader for the final appeal for YHWH to rise up against the enemies and to save the psalmist and companions so that their children may have a future.

Psalm 18, ascribed to David at the time that YHWH delivered him from Saul (see 1 Sam 18–27), corresponds quite closely to 2 Sam 22. It is a lengthy song of thanksgiving that affirms the power and presence of YHWH, but does so by extensive appeal to the role of YHWH as creator who is manifested from the heavenly realm in the world of creation.[27] Thus YHWH responds to the psalmist by riding from the divine palace on a cherub (cf. Ezek 1) to defeat the forces of chaos that threaten the psalmist. The psalm must have been a major liturgy in its time insofar as it extols the righteousness of the psalmist, YHWH's fidelity and power, and YHWH's commitment to act on behalf of the Davidic king. Psalm 19, ascribed to David, is hymn of praise intermixed with wisdom elements that extols YHWH as creator and as the author of divine teaching (Torah). The psalmist makes it clear that such divine Torah enables life to proceed in the world of creation. The concluding verse of the psalm (v. 15), "may the words of my mouth and the meditations of my heart be acceptable to you, O YHWH, my rock and my redeemer," appears as part of the conclusion of the Amidah, the main prayer segment of the Jewish worship service. Psalm 20, ascribed to David, is a royal psalm which expresses the hope that YHWH will protect the king in battle against enemies. It is not a direct address to G-d, but a third-person expression of hope that may have been adopted from Egyptian or Canaanite prayers for the king addressed to Horus or Baal. Psalm 21, ascribed to David, is another royal psalm that expresses gratitude for YHWH's blessings to the king and thereby expresses the hope that YHWH will continue to grant the king blessings by defeating enemies that would stand against him.

Psalm 22, ascribed to David, is a lamentation that begins with an appeal to G-d, "My G-d, my G-d, whey have you abandoned me?," that is well known to Christian readers of the New Testament as the basis for Jesus's appeal to G-d at the time of the crucifixion (Matt 27:46; Mark 15:34). The depth of crisis in such an appeal will be well known to those Jews throughout history who faced the pogroms of Christians and Muslims who viewed Jews as infidels. The psalmist expresses confidence that G-d will act, just as Israel's ancestors had such confidence in G-d that was not betrayed. Nevertheless, the psalm presents a heart-wrenching description of the psalmist's plight as enemies surround him and mock him for his adherence to G-d.

Psalm 23, ascribed to David, is a well-known hymn that expresses the psalmist's confidence in G-d, the shepherd who guides him while walking "through the valley of the shadow of death." Psalm 24, ascribed to David, is another example of an entrance liturgy that speaks of the qualities one must possess when ascending the holy mountain to appear in the sanctuary of YHWH.[28] Unlike Ps 15, it speaks more generally of moral purity, citing avoidance of false oaths in YHWH's name as a primary expression of such moral action.

Psalms 25–28 then return to the sequence of lamentations in Book I. Psalm 25, ascribed to David, is lamentation written in acrostic literary style, viz., each verse begins with a successive letter of the Hebrew alphabet from 'aleph in v. 1 through taw in v. 21. Following upon the entrance liturgy in Ps 24, Ps 25 appeals to YHWH to teach the psalmists YHWH's ways, affirming YHWH's righteousness and mercy, while taking due note of the psalmist's wickedness (and therefore need for instruction) as well as the psalmist need for protection from enemies. Psalm 26, ascribed to David, is a lament in which the psalmist asserts moral righteousness, but asks for G-d to probe or test him in order to verify his righteous status. The purpose of such an assertion is not arrogance, but the references to the holy Temple suggest that the psalmist intends to approach the Temple for divine service and appeals for divine mercy as he does so. Such a psalm might apply to a priest who approaches the altar to present offerings, or even to the high priest who enters the Holy of Holies on Yom Kippur to atone for the people. Psalm 27, ascribed to David, has confused interpreters who identify it as a lamentation or as a psalm of trust or confidence in YHWH. The psalm clearly expresses confidence in YHWH, but it appeals to YHWH to show mercy to the psalmist and answer him as he seeks the divine face.[29] Again, this psalm may have given expression to the anxieties of priest as he approaches the Temple altar or even the high priest as he approached the Holy of Holies. Psalm 28, ascribed to David, is a lament that appeals to YHWH for mercy as the psalmist approaches the Holy of Holies of the Temple, which suggests that the psalmist is the high priest about to enter the Holy of Holies to atone for Israel on Yom Kippur.

Psalm 29, ascribed to David, is a hymn that celebrates YHWH's power over creation. The command to divine beings to celebrate as well as the reference to YHWH's enthronement in the Temple suggest that this hymn might be employed as part of the overall New Year period, when Rosh ha-Shanah, Yom Kippur, and Sukkot would be celebrated. Psalm 30, ascribed to David, is a thanksgiving psalm that is to be sung at the dedication of the Temple, although the contents suggest that the psalmist has recovered from death. The Temple is dedicated at Sukkot (2 Chr 7:8; Ezra 3), which celebrates the end of the dry summer season and the onset of rains often associated in the ancient Near Eastern world with motifs of life triumphing over death.

Psalm 31, ascribed to David, is an anthological lament that draws on other Psalms and Jeremiah (vv. 1-3, cf. Ps 71:1-3; v. 9, cf. Ps 25:15, v. 14, cf. Jer 20:10; v. 21, cf. Ps 76:3) in an appeal to YHWH for deliverance from enemies.

Psalm 32, ascribed to David, is a thanksgiving song with wisdom affinities in which the psalmist thanks YHWH for deliverance after repenting from sins. Psalm 33 is an unattributed hymn that celebrates YHWH's righteousness, fidelity, and protection from enemies. Psalm 34, ascribed to David when he feigned madness before Abimelek (see 1 Sam 21:12-15, which identifies the Philistine king as Achish), is an acrostic thanksgiving song for divine deliverance from unspecified threats.

Psalm 35, ascribed to David, is a lament that appeals to YHWH for assistance against attacking enemies that threaten the psalmist. Psalm 36, ascribed to David, is a lament, in which the psalmist asks for divine protection on behalf of those who are devoted to G-d.

Psalm 37, ascribed to David, is an acrostic wisdom psalm that calls upon the righteous to trust in divine support and protection.

Psalm 38, ascribed to David, is a lament in which the psalmist appeals to YHWH for relief from illness and enemies. Psalm 39, ascribed to David, is a lament that meditates on human frailty and mortality as a basis to appeal for divine deliverance from transgression and plague. Psalm 40, ascribed to David, is a lament that appeals for divine compassion while recalling past acts of deliverance.

Finally, Book I closes with Ps 41, a lament ascribed to David, that appeals for healing. As noted above, the blessing formula in Ps 41:14 concludes the first book.

Book II

Book II of the Psalms comprises Pss 42–72. The preponderance of lamentation psalms in Book II, that is, 18 of 31 psalms, indicates that Book II also gives expressions to the problems and fears of the people when they address G-d as in Book I. But this book differs from Book I in two major respects. First, although the attribution of the psalms in this book is primarily to David, with 18 of 31 psalms, another seven are attributed to the sons of Korah, one is attributed to Asaph, and one is attributed to Solomon. Korah, as noted above, was the ancestor of the Levitical Korahite line who perished in the wilderness following a failed attempt to challenge the Aaronide line (see Num 16). Second, Ps 42 marks the beginning of the so-called Elohistic psalter in Pss 42–83, in which YHWH is identified by the term, "G-d" (*'ĕlōqîm*), rather than by the personal name YHWH. These factors suggest that Book II (or perhaps Pss 42–83) was a discrete collection of psalms, perhaps from another sanctuary, such as Shiloh, Beer Sheva, or elsewhere, which entered the book of Psalms at some point following the initial selection in Book I and perhaps Book V.[30] Such a combination of psalms may be rooted in scenarios of early expansion and unification of Israel under Solomon or perhaps reform and consolidation programs carried out by figures such as King Hezekiah or King Josiah, in which outlying sanctuaries were closed as worship was centralized in Jerusalem.

The book begins with Pss 42 and 43. As with Pss 1 and 2 at the beginning of Book I, interpreters maintain that Pss 42 and 43 together constitute one psalm, as indicated by their common refrain in Pss 42:6, 12 and 43:5, their common interest in the desire to appear before G-d in the Temple, and the attribution of Ps 42 to the sons of Korah whereas Ps 43 is unattributed.[31] Both psalms are laments. Together they cry out to G-d to ask for divine remembrance in the face of challenge by foes, and both express the will to have hope in G-d in the midst of such challenge. Psalm 44, a community lament attributed to the sons of Korah, follows with a trenchant appeal to G-d for assistance in the face of danger. Here, G-d is charged with abandoning the psalmists despite their fidelity to G-d and the covenant.[32]

Psalms 45–50 then break the pattern of lamentation with a combination of royal, Zion, wisdom, and liturgical psalms. Psalm 45 is a love or friendship (Hebrew, *yĕdîdōt*, "intimate female friends") song attributed to the sons of Korah which portrays the relationship between a woman and the king, perhaps at their wedding. The identity of the Tyrian princess (vv. 13, 14) has suggested to some that King Ahab of Israel is the subject of the psalm, just as Solomon is the subject of Song of Songs. Psalm 46, ascribed to the sons of Korah, is a song of Zion that celebrates G-d's power over creation and nations from the holy abode, although notably Zion is never mentioned in the psalm. Psalm 47, ascribed to the sons of Korah, is hymn that celebrates the enthronement of G-d, identified as YHWH

Elyon at one point in v. 3, over all the earth. Psalm 48, ascribed to the sons of Korah, is a Zion song that celebrates G-d's (identified as YHWH in v. 2) enthronement in the Temple at Zion/Zaphon to the dismay of the nations who would threaten the city. Psalm 49, ascribed to the sons of Korah, is a wisdom psalm that extols wisdom and adherence to G-d over wealth in view of the reality of human mortality. Psalm 50, ascribed to Asaph, is a liturgical psalm in which G-d is revealed from Zion to summon the people to be mindful of G-d. The other Asaphite psalms appear in Pss 73–83, which conclude the so-called Elohistic collection of Book III.

The balance of the psalms in Book II is attributed primarily to David, so that they are generally viewed as a discrete collection.[33] Psalm 51, attributed to David when Nathan came to him concerning his affair with Bath Sheba (2 Sam 12), is a lament in which the psalmist appeals to G-d for mercy as he is purged of his sins. Psalm 52, ascribed to David at the time that Doeg informed Saul of David's presence at Nob (1 Sam 22), is a lament addressed to an evil man that informs him of G-d's efforts to punish him for his sins. Psalm 53, ascribed to David, is a lament. It is the Elohistic version of Ps 14 that meditates on G-d's attention to human beings.[34] Psalm 54, attributed to David at the time that the Ziphites informed Saul of David's presence among them (1 Sam 23), is a lament in which the psalmist asks for divine deliverance from foes. Psalm 55, attributed to David, is a lament in which the psalmist appeals for divine aid against enemies, but it also contends that the enemy is a former friend who has now turned against him. Psalm 56, attributed to David at the time that the Philistines seized him in Gath (perhaps 1 Sam 21, but the event is unknown), is a lament in which the psalmist appeals for divine mercy at a time when he is threatened by enemies. Psalm 57, attributed to David when he hid from Saul in a cave (1 Sam 24), is a lament that appeals for divine mercy at a time when the psalmist metaphorically lies among man-eating lions. Psalm 58, attributed to David, is a lament that challenges the justice of other divine beings whom the psalmist maintains will be destroyed by G-d. Psalm 59, attributed to David when Saul sent men to kill him (1 Sam 19), is a lament in which the psalmist calls upon G-d to trap—but not kill—enemies who are metaphorically portrayed as growling dogs. Psalm 60, attributed to David at the time of his campaigns against Aram Naharaim and Aram Zobah (2 Sam 8:3-8; 10:6-18), is a community lament that charges G-d with having rejected the people before appealing to G-d for support in conquering enemies and uniting Israel. Psalm 61, attributed to David, is a lament that appeals to G-d for refuge, apparently on behalf of the king.

Psalm 62, attributed to David, breaks the sequence of lament psalms. This psalm has a unique form with hymnic elements that extols G-d as the psalmist's hope for protection against enemies. Psalm 63, ascribed to David while he was in the wilderness of Judah (for example, 1 Sam 24–27), has a unique form with thanksgiving elements that expresses the psalmist's efforts and desire to search for G-d and behold G-d in the sanctuary as he eludes enemies.

Psalm 64, ascribed to David, is a lament that pleads for G-d to hide the psalmist from enemies.

Psalm 65, ascribed to David, is a hymn that celebrates G-d's role as creator in Temple at Zion, who forgives iniquity while bestowing the earth with bounty. Psalm 66, unascribed, is a combination of hymn and thanksgiving song that employs creation imagery to honor G-d for defeating enemies, thereby saving the people from threat. Psalm 67, likewise unascribed, is a unique form with thanksgiving elements that asks for divine blessing. Psalm 68, ascribed to David, is a lengthy liturgical psalm that recounts divine theophany against enemies, that is, actions against enemies, revelation at Sinai, revelation at Bashan in the Trans-Jordan, and others, while calling upon the people to sing praises to G-d.[35]

Psalm 69, ascribed to David, is a lament that appeals for divine deliverance while recounting the fidelity and suffering of the psalmist, emphasizing the appeal to cease hiding the divine face. Psalm 70, ascribed to David, is a lament that appeals for divine assistance against enemies on behalf of a poor and needy psalmist. Psalm 71, unascribed, is a lament that appeals for divine assistance on behalf of a psalmist who recounts life-long fidelity to G-d.

Finally, Ps 72 concludes Book II. This is a royal psalm, ascribed to Solomon, that appeals for G-d to endow the king with wisdom, the capacity to rule, to care for the needy, to receive blessings of wealth and bounty, and so on.

As noted above, Ps 72 concludes with the blessing formula in vv. 18-19 and the statement that the prayers of David ben Jesse have come to a close in v. 20.

Book III

The third book of the Psalms comprises Pss 73–89, including Pss 73–83, which conclude the so-called Elohistic Psalter in Pss 42—83. Psalms 73–83 are all ascribed to Asaph. Of the remaining psalms in the book, four are ascribed to the sons of Korah, one to David, one to Ethan the Ezrahite, and one to Heman the Ezrahite (although this psalm is also ascribed to the sons of Korah). As in Books I and II, the lament psalms predominate, with eight examples. Other types include one hymn, one royal psalm, three Zion songs, two liturgical compositions, one wisdom psalm, and one unique type that is often labeled an exhortation. Given its affinities with the Elohistic Psalter and the ascriptions to Asaph, Book III appears to be a later expansion of Books I and II that fills out the predominantly lamentation portion of the Psalter.

Psalm 73, ascribed to Asaph, is a wisdom psalm that begins the book with a meditation on the question of divine righteousness and power. This psalm is especially noteworthy insofar as it depicts a psalmist who questioned divine power and righteousness based on observations of the success of the wicked, but who, through study, reflection, commitment to the tradition, and divine support, ultimately affirms divine power and righteousness. Thus Ps 73 forms a fitting introduction to Book III, in which such questions posed to G-d continue to predominate.[36]

Psalm 74, ascribed to Asaph, is a community lament that demands to know why G-d has rejected the people and how long the enemies will continue to threaten. Such questions prepare for the further demands that G-d remember the covenant and defend the people as in times past.

Psalm 75, ascribed to Asaph, is a unique psalm that is sometimes labeled as an exhortation, although it displays elements of the hymn. The psalm affirms G-d's decision to act on behalf of the people against their enemies at the time that G-d will choose. Psalm 76, ascribed to Asaph, is a Zion song that celebrates G-d's manifestation in Judah and Zion, from where G-d will be recognized throughout the earth.

Psalm 77, ascribed to Asaph, is a lament in which the psalmist cries aloud to G-d and questions whether G-d will abandon the divine promises and compassion. Ultimately, it reiterates G-d's past actions in an expression of hope that G-d will yet act.

Psalm 78, ascribed to Asaph, is a lengthy hymn that recounts G-d's acts on behalf of Israel from the time of the Exodus from Egypt, the wilderness murmuring, the period of the Shiloh sanctuary, and ultimately the sanctuary at Mt. Zion in Jerusalem where G-d chooses the tribe of Judah over Ephraim. Overall, the historical review is designed to demonstrate Jerusalem's and Judah's preeminence among the tribes of Israel, while pointing to G-d's power and volition to act on Israel's behalf.[37]

Psalm 79, ascribed to Asaph, is a community lament that mourns the defilement of the Temple by foreign invaders, prompting many to argue that this is an exilic psalm. The psalm pleads for G-d to cease divine anger against the people and to act against their enemies. Psalm 80, ascribed to Asaph, is a community lament that asks again for G-d to appear and to act against the enemies of the people, and it recounts past actions, such as the redemption of Israel from Egypt and its transplantation in the promised land. Although it makes mention of northern tribes, viz., Ephraim, Benjamin, and Manasseh, the portrayal of G-d enthroned upon the cherubim presupposes the imagery of the Ark of the Covenant, which was moved from Benjamin to Jerusalem at the outset of David's reign (2 Sam 6; 1 Chr 16).

Psalm 81, ascribed to Asaph, is a liturgical psalm in which the psalmist calls upon the people to sing praises to G-d. G-d speaks within the psalm to recall divine acts on behalf of the people, but recalls the people's refusal to listen to G-d before calling upon them to return so that their enemies might be subdued. Psalm 82, ascribed to Asaph, is a liturgy, which recounts G-d's condemnation of all of the foreign deities because of their failure to judge the peoples of the world with justice.

Psalm 83, the final Elohistic psalm ascribed to Asaph, is a community lament that appeals to G-d no longer to remain silent in the face of enemies that rage against the people, threatening to wipe them out. The psalmist recalls G-d's actions on Israel's behalf from the time of the Judges as a basis for demanding divine action.

Psalm 84, ascribed to the sons of Korah, is a Zion song that extols the beauty and serenity of G-d's sanctuary in Zion.

Psalm 85, ascribed to the sons of Korah, is a community lament that calls upon G-d to withdraw divine anger and to forgive the people in order to restore justice and well-being in the world. Psalm 86, ascribed to David, is a lament in which a psalmist recounts his own piety and asks for divine guidance as part of an appeal for divine support against arrogant oppressors.

Psalm 87, ascribed to the sons of Korah, is a Zion song that celebrates G-d's love for Zion in the midst of the nations.

Psalm 88, ascribed to both the sons of Korah and to Heman the Ezrahite, is a lament in which the psalmist desperately pleads with G-d to answer his prayer and to end his suffering.

Finally, Ps 89, ascribed to Ethan the Ezrahite (see 1 Kgs 5:11), is a royal psalm that celebrates G-d's role as creator and ruler of the earth together with the eternal covenant with the house of David. The psalm is careful to state the conditions for the Davidic covenant, that is, that the king observe G-d's Torah and expectations, and it concludes with charges that G-d has repudiated the covenant and appeals that G-d act to restore the fortunes of the Davidic king. Because of the questions raised concerning the continuity of the house of David, interpreters maintain that Ps 89 is an exilic psalm. By placing this royal psalm at the end of the book, it becomes clear that Book III takes up the suffering of the entire nation culminating in the king.[38]

Book III concludes with the blessing formula in Ps 89:53.

Book IV

Book IV of the Psalms marks a major shift insofar as the predominance of the lament form in Books I–III comes to an end and the predominance of the hymn now begins. Of the seventeen psalms in this book, which comprises Pss 90–106, ten are hymns, whereas only three are laments, one is a thanksgiving psalm, one is a royal psalm, one is a unique type sometimes classified as a sermon, and one of the hymns is sometimes identified as a liturgy. Most of these psalms are not ascribed to any particular author, although one is attributed to Moses and two to David. Overall, the shift to emphasis on praise of YHWH provides a means to respond to the many laments laid out in Books I–III with statements of confidence in YHWH's righteousness, power, compassion, fidelity, and willingness to act on behalf of the people. As noted above, three psalms from this book (Pss 96; 105; 106) were employed in 1 Chr 16 to depict the liturgy celebrating the arrival of the Ark in Jerusalem in the time of David.

The book begins with Ps 90, attributed to Moses, the man of G-d. This psalm is a community lament that recounts the frailty of human mortality in relation to the eternity of G-d as a basis for asking that G-d turn aside from divine anger. Such a lament facilitates the transition in the book of Psalms from the laments of Books I–III to the hymns of Books IV–V.

Psalm 91 has been difficult to classify, although interpreters observe that it displays sermonic elements. The psalmist recounts his confidence in YHWH, here identified as Elyon and Shaddai, as protector and deliverer. The psalmist's confidence in YHWH is intended to inspire others to similar trust in YHWH, especially following the lengthy emphasis on laments in Books I–III. Psalm 92 is a thanksgiving psalm for the Shabbat that celebrates G-d's fidelity, works in the world, and defeat of enemies on behalf of the people. Psalm 93 is a hymn that celebrates YHWH's role as the king who secures the foundations of creation.

Psalm 94 is a community lament that once again appeals for divine assistance and justice in a time of threat, but this psalm is unique in that it celebrates divine discipline as a means to prepare human beings for times of trial. In this respect, the psalm continues to show confidence in YHWH as protector of the people.

Psalm 95 is a hymn that is sometimes defined as a liturgy. It begins a lengthy section of hymns with classic calls to give praise to YHWH combined with admonitions to observe divine instruction. The psalm cites past rebellion on the part of Israel to drive home the consequences in contrast to the blessings of adherence. Psalm 96 is a hymn that celebrates YHWH's righteous rule over all the nations, their gods, and creation. Verses 1-13a appear in 1 Chr 16:23-33 as part of the liturgy for bringing the Ark into Jerusalem. Psalm 97 is a hymn that employs theophany imagery, ultimately derived from the imagery of incense smoke and the lights of the *menorot* or lamp stands of the Temple, to celebrate YHWH's role as king over all the earth. Psalm 98 is a hymn that celebrates YHWH's victories over enemies in the sight of the nations as it calls upon all creation to rejoice. Psalm 99 is a hymn that celebrates YHWH's enthronement upon the cherubim in Zion as it claims Moses, Aaron, and Samuel as YHWH's priests who conveyed the divine will to the people even as they suffered for their misdeeds. Psalm 100 is a brief hymn that calls upon all the earth to worship YHWH at the Temple as it celebrates divine goodness and fidelity. Psalm 101, ascribed to David, is a royal psalm in which the psalmist, presumably representing the king, pledging to live according to YHWH's justice and righteousness and to destroy all the wicked from the land and the city.

Psalm 102 is a lament sung on behalf of a lowly man as he prays to YHWH. The psalm calls upon YHWH to hear the man's prayer, and it points to YHWH's enthronement in Zion as a basis for an appeal to look upon and to relieve the suffering of the man and of Zion.

Psalm 103, ascribed to David, is a hymn that praises YHWH for forgiving sins, delivering humans from death, acting righteously by revealing the divine will to Israel through Moses, and keeping covenant. Psalm 104 is hymn that celebrates

YHWH's role as creator of the universe. Its affinities with the Egyptian Hymn to Aten have convinced many interpreters that it was adapted from an Egyptian model.[39] Psalm 105 is a hymn that praises YHWH for fidelity and acts on behalf of Israel, beginning with the ancestors, Abraham, Isaac, Jacob, and Joseph, and continuing with Moses and Aaron at the Exodus and the wilderness period. Verses 1-15 appear in 1 Chr 16:8-22 as part of the liturgy for bringing the Ark to Jerusalem.

Finally, Ps 106 concludes Book IV with a hymn that celebrates YHWH's goodness and fidelity. It acknowledges wrongdoing on behalf of the people, such as the golden calf at Horeb (Exod 32–34), the protests of the spies (Num 13–14), the apostasy at Baal Peor (Num 25), the rebellion at the waters at Meribah (Num 20), and the failure to destroy the nations in the land of Israel (Judg 1–2). These shortcomings form the basis for the assertion that YHWH saved the people in their various crises despite these problems. Such a portrayal reinforces the concept of divine fidelity, presence, and righteousness that informs Book IV, and thereby undergirds the final appeal for divine deliverance in v. 47. Portions of this psalm appear in 1 Chr 16 as part of the liturgy for bringing the Ark into Jerusalem (for example, Ps 106:47-48 appears in 1 Chr 16:35-36).

Book IV concludes with the blessing formula in Ps 106:48.

Book V

Book V completes the book of Psalms with Pss 107–150.[40] With 44 psalms, it is the largest of the five books. Like Book IV, it gives greatest emphasis to the hymns, with thirteen examples, although it also includes some eleven individual and community laments. Otherwise, Book V includes three thanksgiving songs, three royal psalms, one Zion psalm, one liturgical song, one mixed royal and liturgical song, five wisdom songs, and seven of unique or mixed character. The fifteen Songs of Ascent in Pss 120–134 form a distinct collection within this book that includes examples from the various genres just listed. Fifteen of the Psalms in Book V, including four of the Songs of Ascent are ascribed to David, and one, itself a Song of Ascent, is ascribed to Solomon.

The book of Psalms is intended to give voice to the questions of divine power, righteousness, presence, and fidelity on behalf of the people, but the book is also intended to provide a basis for reflection that will lead to answers to those questions. Thus Book V, with its emphasis on the hymns, serves that purpose by pointing to divine fidelity at the outset and emphasizing the celebration of YHWH's power, righteousness, and presence throughout. The book contains a relatively large number of wisdom songs as well, compositions that encourage reflection on the questions posed by the laments, both those found within Book V and those found throughout the other books. By encouraging such reflection and suggesting meditation on the tradition as the means to resolve the problems posed, the book of Psalms engages in the dialog initiated by the problems of the people by providing the means to discern divine response.

Psalm 107, a mixed genre composed of instructional and thanksgiving elements, opens Book V with calls to praise YHWH for divine goodness and fidelity and a lengthy meditation on YHWH's beneficent acts on Israel's behalf during the wilderness period and beyond. The psalm points to suffering as a means to humble the hearts of human beings. The conclusion of the psalm call upon the wise to take note of YHWH's beneficent acts as a means to understand YHWH's fidelity.

Psalm 108, a community lament ascribed to David, overlaps with elements of Ps 57:8-12 in vv. 2-6 and Ps 60:7-14 in vv. 7-14. It begins with the psalmist's declarations of praise and fidelity to YHWH, but it also points to G-d's rejection of the people and failure to live up to promises. Psalm 109, a lament ascribed to David, calls upon G-d to cease remaining aloof as the wicked are now closing in around the psalmist. It concludes with appeals to G-d to act on the psalmist's behalf.[41]

Psalm 110 is a royal psalm ascribed to David in which G-d declares divine support for the presumably Davidic king based in Zion, and declares him a priest of the order of Melchizedek, identified in Gen 14:8 as the king in Jerusalem (Salem) during the time of Abram. The psalm points to YHWH's fidelity in relation to the Davidic king.

Psalm 111 begins a brief sequence of Hallelujah (Praise YHWH) songs in Pss 111–113. Psalm 111 is an acrostic hymn that praises YHWH for a host of positive qualities, such as splendid deeds, beneficence, compassion, truth and justice, redemption of the people, and so on, and it cites the maxim from Prov 1:7, "the fear of YHWH is the beginning of wisdom; all who practice it gain sound understanding." Psalm 112 is an acrostic wisdom song that begins with the call to praise YHWH, and then turns to the wisdom theme of happiness for those who fear YHWH, observe divine commandments, acts graciously, lend generously, give to the poor, and so on.

Psalm 113 introduces the Egyptian Hallel in Pss 113–118, which are recited as part of the Passover Seder and are so-named because of their reference to the Exodus in Ps 114:1.[42] Psalm 113 is an acrostic hymn that again begins with a call to praise YHWH as a ruler recognized throughout the world and who takes care of the poor and destitute, most notably childless women. Psalm 114 is a hymn that celebrates YHWH's acts on behalf of Israel at the Red Sea and in the wilderness. Psalm 115 is a liturgical psalm that asserts YHWH's power and mindfulness of Israel over against the claims of foreign nations who maintain that YHWH is not present in the world. The lengthy polemic concerning idols is reminiscent of Isa 44:9-20. Psalm 116 is a thanksgiving song in which the psalmist declares love for YHWH because of YHWH's actions to save him from death and sorrow, prompting the psalmist to declare that he will serve YHWH with thank offerings and vows. Psalm 117 is a very brief hymn that calls upon the nations to praise YHWH for divine fidelity. Psalm 118 is a hymn that praises YHWH for divine fidelity and goodness. It includes a lengthy recounting of YHWH's beneficent acts on behalf the psalmist. The priestly perspective of the psalm is evident in the role that the house of Aaron will play in declaring YHWH's praise as people enter the house/Temple of YHWH.

Psalm 119, the longest psalm in the book of Psalms, is an acrostically formulated wisdom psalm that reflects at great length on the need to recognize YHWH, observe divine decrees, recognize YHWH's role as creator, do righteousness and justice in relation to YHWH's teachings, and so on, and it concludes with appeals for deliverance as the psalmist has observed YHWH and YHWH's requirements with a whole heart.[43]

The Songs of Ascent in Pss 120–134 were apparently sung on festival occasions as the people journeyed to the Temple to celebrate the festival in question.[44] One theory is that they were sung as people moved up the ramps that led from the south side of the Temple up to the Temple platform where the courtyards would have been located.

Psalm 120 begins the Songs of Ascent in Pss 120–134 with a lament in which the psalmist expresses his distress concerning the deceit of his enemies. Psalm 121 follows with a unique genre, sometimes identified as a hymn, in which the psalmist looks to the mountains from which divine deliverance will come. Psalm 122, ascribed to David, is a Zion song that rejoices over and prays for the city of Jerusalem as the site of YHWH's Temple. Psalm 123 is a community lament in which the singers turn their eyes to YHWH to ask for divine favor in the face of the contempt of enemies. Psalm 124, ascribed to David, is a unique form with thanksgiving elements that thanks and blesses YHWH for deliverance from unspecified assailants. Psalm 125 has a unique form, sometimes identified as a hymn, that calls upon YHWH to do good for the righteous and to overturn the wicked. Psalm 126 is a unique form, sometimes identified with thanksgiving elements, which appeals to YHWH to restore the fortunes of the people just as YHWH restores the fortunes of Jerusalem. Psalm 127, ascribed to Solomon, is a wisdom psalm which notes that YHWH is ultimately responsible for beneficence, such as the birth of sons, enjoyed in life. Psalm 128 is a wisdom psalm which declares that those who fear YHWH are happy; it then calls upon YHWH to bless them.[45] Psalm 129 is a community lament in which the psalmist recalls assailants from the time of his youth as he calls for the defeat of those who hate Zion. Psalm 130 is a lament in which the psalmist cries out for YHWH from the depths as he then calls on Israel to wait for YHWH. Psalm 131, ascribed to David, is a unique form with hymnic elements which counsels humility while waiting for YHWH. Psalm 132 is a combination of royal and liturgical psalm which recalls David's efforts to find a resting place for the Ark of the Covenant. It reiterates YHWH's conditional promises of an eternal house of David while calling for celebration at the foundation of the site for YHWH's resting place, that is, the site of the Temple. Psalm 133, ascribed to David, is a wisdom psalm that celebrates how god

and how pleasant it is for brothers to dwell together. Finally, Ps 134 closes the
Songs of Ascent with a brief hymn that calls upon the servants of YHWH to bless
YHWH so that YHWH might bless them from Zion.

Following the Songs of Ascent, Ps 135 returns to a Hallelujah psalm with a
hymn that calls for praise of YHWH in the Temple. The reasons for praise
include YHWH's goodness, the choice of Jacob, acts of creation, the Exodus from
Egypt, and care in the wilderness. Psalm 136, the Great Hallel recited as part of
the Passover Seder, follows with a hymn that again calls for praise of YHWH, but
this example employs the repeated refrain, "for his fidelity (Hebrew, *hesed*) is
forever," following each attribute of YHWH. Attributes include YHWH's role
as highest of gods, creation and wisdom, the Exodus from Egypt, the journey
through the wilderness, the granting of the land of Israel, rescue from enemies,
and sustenance for the world.

Psalm 137 is a community lament, clearly written in the aftermath of the
destruction of Jerusalem, that depicts the exiles weeping in Babylon. The psalmist
calls for the remembrance of Zion as well as the destruction of the Edomites who
helped to make the fall of Jerusalem possible. The references to the babies dashed
against the rocks reflect memories of the deaths of Jewish babies murdered by the
Babylonians at the time of the conquest of Jerusalem.

Psalm 138 is a thanksgiving song attributed to David in which the psalmist
thanks YHWH for answering his pleas for help against enemies. Psalm 139 is a
unique type attributed to David and sometimes labeled a meditation. It reflects on
YHWH's knowledge of all, particularly the innermost thoughts of human beings,
as it asks for G-d to examine his being in order better to provide guidance.

Psalm 140 is a lament attributed to David that appeals to YHWH for deliverance from arrogant and wicked foes, and concludes with expressions of confidence that YHWH will do so. Psalm 141 is a lament attributed to David that
appeals to YHWH for assistance in guarding the psalmist's mouth against evil, as
well as against the traps laid by his foes. Psalm 142 is a lament, attributed to David
while he was in the cave (1 Sam 24), in which the psalmist appeals to YHWH to
grant refuge from enemies as he has nowhere else to turn. Psalm 143 is a lament,
ascribed to David, in which the psalmist pleads with YHWH not to judge him,
but instead asks for relief from enemies and guidance in doing YHWH's will.

Psalm 144 is an anthological royal psalm ascribed to David which draws on the
language of other psalms in an effort to bless YHWH and to reflect on divine
beneficence granted to mortal human beings.

Psalms 145–150 present the Daily Hallel, a sequence of hymns in praise of
YHWH that conclude the book and that is recited every day as part of the
morning synagogue service. Psalm 145 is an acrostic hymn ascribed to David that
extols YHWH as G-d and King for acts of beneficence, goodness, majestic glory,
support for those who stumble, watchfulness, and so on. Psalm 146 is a hymn that
calls for praise of YHWH, who will reign forever in Zion. Psalm 147 is a hymn
that calls for praise of YHWH, who will rebuild Jerusalem, gather the exiles,

provide rain, grant bounty to all creation, and issue commands to Jacob. Psalm 148 is a hymn that calls for praise of YHWH on behalf of all the elements of creation. Psalm 149 calls for praise for YHWH amongst the congregation of the faithful who will impose punishment on the doomed nations.

Finally, Ps 150 calls for praise of YHWH in the sanctuary for all of YHWH's mighty acts. Indeed, the doxology in Ps 150 concludes both Book V and the entire book of Psalms.

NOTES

[1] According to *b. Baba Batra* 14b, the book of Psalms follows Ruth, perhaps due to the fact that Ruth closes with the genealogy of David, who is credited with having authored the Psalms (see "Psalms, Book of," *EncJud* 13:1305).

[2] For methodological discussion of a dialogical reading of hymnic literature, such as the Psalms and Lamentations, see Carleen R. Mandolfo, *Daughter Zion Talks Back to the Prophets: A Dialogic Theology of the Book of Lamentations* (Semeia Studies 58; Atlanta: Society of Biblical Literature, 2007), 55–77; see also idem, *G-d in the Dock: Dialogic Tension in the Psalms of Lament* (JSOTSup 357; Sheffield: Sheffield Academic, 2002).

[3] On the motif of the hiddenness of G-d in the Psalms and elsewhere in the Bible, see Samuel E. Balentine, *The Hidden G-d: The Hiding of the Face of G-d in the Old Testament* (Oxford: Oxford University Press, 1983); Michael Emmendörfer, *Der ferne G-tt. Eine Untersuchung der alttestamentliche Volksklagelieder vor dem Hintergrund der mesopotamischen Literatur* (FAT 21; Tübingen: Mohr Siebeck, 1998).

[4] For introductory critical discussion of the book of Psalms, see especially James L. Crenshaw, *The Psalms: An Introduction* (Grand Rapids and Cambridge: Eerdmans, 2001). See also "Psalms, Book of," *EncJud* 13:1303–34; James Limburg, "Psalms, Book of," *ABD* 5:522–36.

[5] See Jon D. Levenson, "The Jerusalem Temple in Devotional and Visionary Experience," in *Jewish Spirituality*, Vol. 1, *From the Bible to the Middle Ages*, ed. A. Green (New York: Crossroad, 1988), 32–61.

[6] For discussion of the genres of Psalms, see especially Erhard S. Gerstenberger, *Psalms, Part 1, with an Introduction to Cultic Poetry* (FOTL 14; Grand Rapids: Eerdmans, 1988), 2–22; Limburg, "Psalms," 5:531–34; Crenshaw, *The Psalms*, 80–95; see also Hermann Gunkel, *An Introduction to the Psalms*, trans. J. D. Nogalski (Macon, GA: Mercer University Press, 1998). For discussion of the hymn, see Gunkel, *Introduction*, 22–65; Gerstenberger, *Psalms, Part 1*, 16–19; see also Frank Crüsemann, *Studien zur Formgeschichte von Hymnus und Danklied in Israel* (WMANT 32; Neukirchen–Vluyn: Neukirchener, 1969).

[7] For discussion of the lament psalms, see Gunkel, *Introduction*, 82–98, 121–98; Gerstenberger, *Psalms, Part 1*, 10–14; see also Mandolfo, *G-d in the Dock*.

[8] In addition to the studies of genre by Gerstenberger and Gunkel noted above, see Christine de Vos, *Klage als G-tteslob aus der Tiefe. Der Mensch vor G-tt in den indviduellen Klagepsalmen* (FAT 2/11; Tübingen: Mohr Siebeck, 2005), who examines the presuppositions and expectations of the human encounter with G-d in the Psalms. Cf. Claus Westermann, *Praise and Lament in the Psalms* (Atlanta: John Knox, 1981).

[9] For discussion of the Thanksgiving Psalm, see Gunkel, *Introduction*, 199–221; Gerstenberger, *Psalms, Part 1*, 14–16; see also Crüsemann, *Studien zur Formgeschichte von Hymnus und Danklied in Israel*.

[10] For discussion of the royal psalms, see Gunkel, *Introduction*, 99–120; Gerstenberger, *Psalms, Part 1*, 19; see also John H. Eaton, *Kingship and the Psalms* (SBT 2/32; London: SCM, 1976).

[11] See especially Limburg, "Psalms," 533.

[12] See especially Gunkel, *Introduction*, 293–305; Gerstenberger, *Psalms, Part 1*, 19–21; Crenshaw, *The Psalms*, 87–95.

[13] See Gunkel, *Introduction*, 313–19.

[14] For discussion of the Entrance Liturgy, see especially Klaus Koch, "Tempeleinlass Liturgien und Dekaloge," in *Studien zur Theologie der alttestamentlichen Überlieferungen (Fest. G. von Rad)*, ed. R. Rendtorff and K. Koch (Neukirchen–Vluyn: Neukirchener Verlag, 1961), 45–60.

[15] See, for example, Gunkel, *Introduction*, 306–9.

[16] For discussion of the structure and arrangement of the book of Psalms, see especially Gerald Henry Wilson, *The Editing of the Hebrew Psalter* (SBLDS 76; Chico: Scholars Press, 1981).

[17] For a diplomatic edition of 11QPsalms and discussion, see James A. Sanders, *The Psalms Scroll of Qumrân Cave 11 (11QPsa)* (DJD 4; Oxford: Clarendon, 1965).

[18] See Gerstenberger, *Psalms, Book 1*, 37–38.

[19] For discussion of the psalms attributed to David, see Crenshaw, *The Psalms*, 15–18.

[20] Crenshaw, *The Psalms*, 23–26; see also Michael D. Goulder, *The Psalms of Asaph and the Pentateuch* (JSOTSup 233; Sheffield: Sheffield Academic, 1996).

[21] See Crenshaw, *The Psalms*, 26–31; see also Michael D. Goulder, *The Psalms of the Sons of Korah* (JSOTSup 20; Sheffield: Sheffield Academic, 1982); Gunther Wanke, *Die Zionstheologie der Korachiten* (BZAW 97; Berlin: Töpelmann, 1966).

[22] Crenshaw, *The Psalms*, 18–22.

[23] See Gerstenberger, *Psalms, Part 1*, 40–50.

[24] Cf. Mandolfo, *G-d in the Dock*, 36–41.

[25] Gerstenberger, *Psalms, Part 1*, 72–76.

[26] Koch, "Tempeleinlass."

[27] See Jörg Jeremias, *Theophanie* (WMANT 10; Neukirchen–Vluyn: Neukirchener, 1977), 33–38.

[28] Koch, "Tempeleinlass."

[29] Cf. David R. Blumenthal, *Facing the Abusing G-d: A Theology of Protest* (Louisville: Westminster John Knox, 1993), 157–89, who reads this psalm in the aftermath of the experience of the Shoah as well as in relation to victims of child abuse in an effort to examine how the relationship between humans and the divine might be reconstructed in the aftermath of divine failure.

[30] See Gary A. Rendsburg, *Linguistic Evidence for the Northern Origin of Selected Psalms* (SBLMS 43; Atlanta: Scholars Press, 1990).

[31] Gerstenberger, *Psalms, Part 1*, 178–82.

[32] See Blumenthal, *Facing*, 85–110.

[33] Michael D. Goulder, *The Prayers of David (Psalms 51–72)* (JSOTSup 102; Sheffield: Sheffield Academic, 1990).

[34] Gerstenberger, *Psalms, Part 1*, 218–21.

[35] See Erhard Gerstenberger, *Psalms, Part 2, and Lamentations* (FOTL 15; Grand Rapids: Eerdmans, 2001), 34–46; see also Jeremias, *Theophanie*, 7–16.

[36] Contra Gerstenberger, *Psalms, Part 2*, 74.

[37] See Antony F. Campbell, "Psalm 78: A Contribution to the Theology of Tenth-Century Israel," *CBQ* 41 (1979): 51–79.

[38] Cf. Gerstenberger, *Psalms, Part 2*, 147, who notes the role that this psalm plays as the cornerstone that concludes Book III of the Psalms.

39 For discussion, see Gerstenberger, *Psalms, Part 2*, 221–30.

40 For discussion of Book V, see Michael D. Goulder, *The Psalms of Return (Book V: Psalms 107–150)* (JSOTSup 258; Sheffield: Sheffield Academic, 1998).

41 See also Blumenthal, *Facing*, 111–56.

42 Peter Knobel, "Hallel," in *The Oxford Dictionary of the Jewish Religion*, ed. R. I. Zwi Werblowsky and G. Wigoder (Oxford: Oxford University Press, 1997), 296.

43 Gerstenberger, *Psalms, Part 2*, 310–17.

44 For discussion of the Psalms of Ascent, see Crenshaw, *The Psalms*, 18–22.

45 Blumenthal, *Facing*, 67–83.

C. The Book of Proverbs

The book of Proverbs is the quintessential expression of the wisdom literature in the Tanak.[1] Its understanding of wisdom as the foundation of creation and social order is the benchmark against which works such as Job and Qoheleth take issue with their respective challenges concerning human suffering, divine justice, and the futility of human life. The major superscriptions of the book in Prov 1:1; 10:1; and 25:1 attribute Proverbs to King Solomon ben David of Israel and Judah. Talmudic tradition (*b. Baba Batra* 15a) maintains that the book as a whole was edited by Hezekiah's men as indicated by the superscription in Prov 25:1, although much of the material was actually composed by Solomon. Modern interpreters generally recognize the book as a later composition that grew by stages over time.[2] Royal courts were known throughout the ancient Near Eastern world as the major patrons of their respective wisdom traditions, insofar as wisdom literature is written and employed to train young men for public leadership in royal, priestly, administrative, and other roles.[3] Indeed, the portrayal of social and cosmic stability, the need for diligence and hard work for success, and the respect for authority throughout the book would prompt readers to see the Israelite or Judean royal court as the embodiment of the virtues of wisdom. The paucity of specific historical references precludes firm conclusions as to the specific historical setting of the book of proverbs, but the late Judean monarchy from the time of Hezekiah on is a likely candidate.

The basic literary genres of the book are the instruction or didactic speech and the *māšāl*, "proverb, parable." The instruction speech is a discursive genre in which an authority, such as a parent, a monarch, or a teacher, addresses a son, a subject, or a student, in order to give guidance, set forth values and rules of conduct, answer questions, and so on.[4] The *māšāl* is a short, often parallel or contrasting couplet that presents a maxim or didactic saying designed to impart a generally universal teaching concerning the world and life based on practical experience.[5] The teaching may be based on some metaphor, allegory, or simile that establishes a relationship between phenomena in the natural world and practices, events, or behavior in the human world to make its point. Proverbs is an empirically oriented work that calls upon its readers to observe and study the world carefully in order to discern its principles of order as the basis for a successful and productive life.

Modern interpreters of Proverbs pay particular attention to its diachronic dimensions, especially how its constituent collections of instruction speeches and individual proverbs emerged and were assembled together in the present form of the book. The first major collection of the book appears in Prov 1–9, introduced by the superscription in Prov 1:1, "the proverbs of Solomon ben David, King of Israel." Most interpreters consider this to be a late composition that employs the principle stated in Prov 1:7, "the fear of YHWH is the beginning of knowledge," to serve as an introduction to the book as a whole. The second collection in Prov 10:1—22:16, introduced by the superscription in Prov 10:1, "the proverbs of Solomon," is generally viewed as the oldest collection in the book due to its relatively simple style. This viewpoint is supported by the long-standing observations that Prov 22:17—24:22 constitutes a discrete collection in the book due to its introductory call to attention in Prov 10:17, "incline your ear and hear the words of the wise, that you may set your heart on my knowledge," and that it appears to be a reworked version of the well-known thirteenth-or twelfth-century BCE Egyptian wisdom composition, the Instruction of Amenemopet.[6] The superscription in Prov 24:23, "these too are from the wise," marks the short fourth collection in Prov 23:23-34. The fifth collection in Prov 25–29 is considered by most scholars to be later due to its superscription in Prov 25:1, which identifies the collection as "the proverbs of Solomon which the men of Hezekiah, King of Judah, transmitted." Two additional collections, usually considered as later appendices to the book, appear as "the words of Agur son of Jakeh, the oracle pronounced by the man of Ithiel, to Ithiel and Ucal" (Prov 30:1) in Prov 30, and as "the words of Lemuel, King of Massa, by which his mother instructed him" (Prov 31:1) in Prov 31. Agur and Lemuel must have been famed wisdom figures and perhaps rulers from ancient Near Eastern antiquity, but modern interpreters know nothing more about them.

Although many modern interpreters employ the diachronically defined collections listed above as the basis for understanding the structure of the book, a synchronic assessment of the literary structure of Proverbs must proceed along somewhat different lines. The diachronic structure indicated above facilitates understanding as to the compositional history of the book, but a synchronic structure facilitates understanding as to how the book functions.[7] The absence of a superscription in Prov 22:17 means that Prov 22:17—24:22 cannot constitute a discrete collection within the book. Instead, this text forms part of a larger collection together with Prov 10:1—22:16. Likewise, the introductory conjunction *gam*, "too, also," in Prov 24:23 and 25:1 means that both Prov 24:23-34 and 25:1—29:27 must be treated as sub-units within the larger unit in Prov 10:1—29:27. The result is a four-part superstructure for the book in which each component presents a distinctive collection of materials that expresses the basic teachings of the book.

The goal of the book is to prompt the reader to observe and study the world and to learn from such observation and study in order to lead a successful and well-ordered life in accordance with the will of YHWH.

The macrostructure of Proverbs presents a relatively simple sequence of collections, but closer analysis of each sub-unit within that macrostructure points to the hermeneutical perspectives and didactic functions of the book that posits a stable, discernable, and moral world order laid out by YHWH, the creator of heaven and earth. Insofar as the ideal monarch rules as the divinely designated agent of YHWH, the book of Proverbs likewise posits a stable, discernable, and moral social order overseen by the king of Israel (or perhaps a foreign monarch accepted as legitimate, for example, the Persian monarchy) and his surrogates.

The formal literary structure of the book of Proverbs appears as follows:[8]

The first major sub-unit of the book in Prov 1–9 presents the hermeneutical premises that inform the reading of the book. It begins with the superscription in Prov 1:1, which introduces both the book as a whole and Prov 1–9 due to its placement at the head of the book. The unit then proceeds with the prolog in Prov 1:2-7, which identifies the book's basic purposes and perspectives, viz., the imparting of wisdom, discipline, righteousness, and so on, in an effort to teach the reader that "the fear of YHWH is the beginning of knowledge." Although interpreters frequently translate the Hebrew expression, *yir'at yhwh*, as "the fear of YHWH," the Hebrew noun *yir'â* more commonly conveys "awe," "respect," and reverence" for YHWH.[9]

Proverbs 1:8—9:18 comprises eleven lectures or discourses on various topics formulated as speeches by a father to a son. Each speech typically includes three basic elements, viz., (1) a call to attention, (2) a lesson on the topic at hand, and (3) a conclusion which states the general principle of the lesson. Proverbs 1:8—9:18 also includes four interludes interspersed among the lectures which metaphorically portray wisdom as a woman who imparts her teachings as basic principles in the world of creation.[10] Given the focus on the feminine figure of wisdom, it would appear that the interludes interspersed among the discourses spoken by the father are intended to represent interjections by the mother who also participates in the instruction of the son. The first lecture, Prov 1:8-19, addressed by a father to "my son," admonishes the son to avoid sinners who engage in violence and robbery lest they bring the son to ruin. The first interlude in Prov 1:20-33 portrays the personified Lady Wisdom's condemnation of those who are evil and reject "awe of YHWH," together with her promise of security to those who listen to her.

The second lecture, Prov 2:1-22, again addressed to "my son," exhorts the son to allow reverence for YHWH to guide him on the proper path of wisdom. Proper wisdom here includes personal integrity or uprightness, loyalty to YHWH, and avoidance of strange women who maintain no fidelity with anyone. Lecture three, Prov 3:1-12, addressed to "my son," calls upon the son to honor YHWH continually and to accept divine discipline or correction as the basis for wisdom. Interlude two in Prov 3:13-20 portrays the man who finds Lady Wisdom as happy, and most importantly states a basic premise of the book, viz., "YHWH founded the earth by wisdom" in vv. 19-20. Such a statement presupposes that divine moral order is built into the very structure of the world of creation and that the human being must learn to live in accordance with such moral structure in order to attain success in creation.

Lecture four, Prov 3:21-35, addressed to "my son," calls upon the son to act with integrity, generosity, and straightforwardness toward others and to avoid plotting against or attempting to undermine others. Lecture five in Prov 4:1-9, addressed to an unstated number of "sons," calls upon the sons to acquire wisdom from the father as a guide for life just as the father learned from his own father. The personification of wisdom as a woman to be loved and embraced brings to expression images of family stability as cosmic and social stability. Lecture six in Prov 4:10-19, addressed to "my son," contrasts the path of wisdom with that of wickedness. In this respect, it promotes self-discipline, Hebrew, *mûsār*, often understood as a term for "ethics" in post-biblical Jewish literature,[11] as a foundation for success in life. Lecture seven in Prov 4:20-27, addressed to "my son," calls upon the son to employ honest speech in dealings with others and to train the mind against temptation to swerve from the path of honesty. Lecture eight in Prov 5:1-23, addressed to "my son" and later to "sons," calls upon the sons to adhere to their own wives and to avoid strange women. The father makes it clear that such affairs with strange women will only lead to disaster insofar as one's efforts will be sapped by others.

Lecture nine in Prov 6:1-19 is sometimes treated as an interlude because it differs from the typical lecture form, but it is addressed to "my son," and it employs four epigrams to provide examples of righteous and wicked behavior and their respective results and consequences.[12] The first epigram, in vv. 1-5, counsels avoidance of giving surety for another's loan. The second, in vv. 6-11, warns against laziness. The third, in vv. 12-15, warns against involvement with scoundrels who live by deception. The fourth, in vv. 16-19, enumerates the seven things that YHWH hates, such as arrogance, dishonesty, shedding innocent blood, and incitement to conflict.

Lecture ten in Prov 6:20-35, addressed to "my son," warns the son against adultery with another man's wife. Such an act will only lead to self-destruction, most certainly at the hands of the husband when he learns what has happened.

Lecture eleven in Prov 7:1-27, addressed to "my son," warns against accepting the overtures of a seductive woman who would lead him from his wife. Such a man is characterized as "an ox going to slaughter" (v. 22) and as "a bird rushing into a trap" (v. 23). Interlude three in Prov 8:1-36, addressed to sons" (v. 32), again personifies wisdom as a woman whom YHWH created first and consulted at the outset of creation so that she would set the basic principles by which the world functions. Finally, interlude four in Prov 9:1-18 calls on readers to accept the banquet invitation of Lady Wisdom and not that of the stupid woman. In doing so, it reiterates the principle that "the awe of YHWH is the beginning of knowledge"

The main block of material in the book appears in Prov 10–29, which is initially identified in Prov 10:1 as "the proverbs of Solomon." It comprises three sub-units in Prov 10:1—24:22, the words of the wise in Prov 24:23-34, and the proverbs of Solomon transmitted by the men of Hezekiah in Prov 25–29.

Proverbs 10:1—24:22 is the largest collection of the classical proverb style in the book. This style is employed to address a range of topics for proper behavior in the world, viz., contrasts between the rewards and punishment of the righteous and the wicked; proper and honest speech versus deceit; the contrasting rewards and consequences of a disciplined and industrious life versus laziness, sloth, and stupidity; proper control of anger and the use of forethought rather than impulse in dealings with others; loyalty and faithfulness to G-d, king, and others in all of one's dealings; honesty in all affairs; the need to seek out and heed wise advice; sobriety and moderation versus drunkenness and gluttony; respect for parents; proper behavior before the king; avoidance of envy; and others. The principle of reverence for YHWH is articulated throughout this sub-unit.

The literary structure of Prov 10:1—24:22 is notoriously difficult to establish insofar as there are few literary sign-posts, such as superscriptions or address forms, to guide the reader through this material.[13] Nevertheless, several subtle signals appear throughout the text. The first signal is the form of the super-scription in Prov 10:1aα, which labels the whole as "the proverbs of Solomon." As a superscription, this half-verse stands apart from, introduces, and characterizes the following material in Prov 10:1aβ—24:22.

The second signal is the form of the material in Prov 10:1aβ—15:33, which comprises a lengthy collection of individual proverbs written in a two-part antithetical style. In each proverb, the initial saying presents a thesis statement on the topic at hand which is then followed by a second thesis statement that contrasts with the first. The combined statement thereby presents two interrelated statements that present the two primary dimensions of the topic at hand, viz., "negligent hands cause poverty, but diligent hands enrich" (Prov 10:4). The proverbs within these chapters focus on the contrast between a variety of qualities in which the desirable quality is shown to be superior to its antithesis. Such qualities include wisdom versus ignorance, righteousness versus wickedness, diligence versus sloth, self-discipline versus lack of self-control, integrity versus deviousness, piety versus impiety, truthfulness versus deceit, patience versus tempestuousness, joyfulness versus despondency, farsightedness versus a failure to plan, and consultation with others versus isolation. There is no clear order to the topics that appear within this section, although readers will note that these qualities are applied both to men and women and that reference to adherence to YHWH appears throughout. The latter conveys the notion that YHWH stands as the foundation of social and moral order of the world, and human beings are best advised to conform their behavior and outlooks to YHWH's norms and expectations. Altogether, the collection of antithetical proverbs in Prov 10:1aβ—15:33 focuses on the qualities necessary for success in the world.

The third structural signal is the form of the material in Prov 16:1—22:16. This sub-collection continues to employ the form of the two-part antithetical proverb evident in the preceding collection, but the contents of this sub-collection differ insofar as they emphasize the contrast between the righteous and the wicked, as well as the consequences or outcomes of action. Again, this sub-collection is permeated with statements exhorting piety and trust in YHWH as a basis for human conduct so that it reinforces the notion that YHWH's righteousness stands as the moral foundation for the moral and social order of the world. Whereas the preceding section focuses on the qualities necessary for success in the world, Prov 16:1—22:16 focuses on the principles of conduct necessary for success in the world.

The fourth structural signal is the form of the material in Prov 22:17—24:22. Whereas the previous two sub-collections were constituted by antithetical proverbs, Prov 22:17—24:22 employs the language of second person masculine singular direct address. Indeed, the sub-collection begins with the initial address in Prov 22:17, "incline your ear and hear the words of the wise, and your heart you shall direct to my knowledge." Many observe that this statement functions as a sort of a superscription and have therefore labeled this unit "the words of the wise," but the statement is not formally a superscription; it merely functions as an introductory instruction for the following discourse. The addressee of this material is not stated at the outset, but Prov 23:15, 19; 24:13, 21 make it clear that the addressee is "my son," and Prov 23:22 indicates that the speaker is the father of the addressee. In this respect, the address form of Prov 22:17—24:22 corresponds to the address form of the lectures in Prov 1–9. Interpreters have also noted that Prov 22:17—23:11 corresponds closely to the Egyptian "Instructions of Amenemophet," but this is a diachronic observation relevant to understanding the compositional history of the text. The synchronic form of text provides no overt indication or awareness of this dependence, and the instructional address form continues through Prov 24:22 to the close of the unit. A synchronic reading must therefore consider the entirety of Prov 22:17—24:22 to constitute the unit at hand, even if part of it is derived from an Egyptian antecedent. The discourse is dominated by two-part instructions that once again focus on the proper conduct and perspectives necessary for success in life. As before, this sub-collection advises piety and adherence to YHWH, but it also aligns the king with YHWH. Indeed, it culminates in the statement in Prov 24:21-22, "Show respect to YHWH, my son, and the king, and with dissenters do not mix, for suddenly their disaster arises, and who will know the misfortune of both of them?" By aligning the king with YHWH, the text makes it clear that the king represents YHWH's social and moral order in creation.

The formal literary structure of Prov 10:1—24:22 emerges as these features are considered. The entire unit is introduced by the superscription in Prov 10:1aα, which identifies the following material as "the proverbs of Solomon." The two collections of antithetical proverbs in Prov 10:1aβ—22:16 appears as a single, two-part sub-unit that presents "proverbial statements of the qualities and conduct necessary for success in life. Within this sub-unit, Prov 10:1aβ—15:33 focuses on the qualities necessary for success, and Prov 16:1—22:16 focuses on the conduct necessary for success. Proverbs 22:17—24:22 constitutes an instruction speech by the father that calls upon the son to embrace and apply these principles for a successful life. Altogether, Prov 10:1—24:22 emerges as "the proverbs of Solomon, which instruct the son in the principles and conduct necessary for a successful life."

The second, brief sub-unit concerning the words of the wise in Prov 24:23-34 is introduced by the superscription, "these also are words for the wise," which aligns this sub-unit with the preceding material in Prov 10:1—24:22, but nevertheless allows Prov 24:23-34 to stand as a discrete sub-unit following the larger text. Proverbs 24:23-34 calls for honesty in jurisprudence and diligence rather than laziness. This sub-unit continues the second person masculine singular instructional form of the preceding material, but it adds first person illustrations of the points made. It continues the interest in conduct necessary for success in life, but it focuses especially on the principles employed by someone with the authority to make decisions that will have an impact on others. Such a person could be a king, but this passage easily envisions other types of government or religious officials as well.

The third sub-unit in Prov 25–29 is introduced by the superscription, "These also are the Proverbs of Solomon which the men of King Hezekiah of Judah copied," which aligns this sub-unit structurally with Prov 10:1—24:22 and 24:23-34. Although this unit was likely an independent composition, within its present literary framework Prov 25–29 builds on the earlier material by emphasizing the role and responsibility of royal officials in discerning wisdom in order to provide guidance in the world. The identification of the addressee as a royal official is evident from Prov 25:6, "Do not exalt yourself before the king, and in the place of nobles do not stand." Following the superscription in Prov 25:1, the balance of this sub-unit in Prov 25:2—29:27 displays a very distinctive style that employs a framework of imperative instruction and second person masculine address forms together with short aphorisms and comparisons, especially with events and features of the natural world, and to convey its basic teachings. This section emphasizes the proper qualities for a royal official, including the need for proper speech to persuade others, prudent interaction with neighbors, feeding the hungry, righteous action, avoidance of dullards and self-aggrandizement, the need to discern dishonest speech, avoidance of jealousy, fidelity to friends throughout generations, diligence in work, avoidance of greed, trust in YHWH, avoidance of harlots, discipline for sons, and other teachings.

The third collection in Prov 30 is identified by its superscription in Prov 30:1 as "the words of Agur son of Jakkeh, the Oracle, the utterance of the man to Ittiel, to Ithiel and Ucal." The reference to Massa is frequently taken as a tribal name on analogy to the mention of Lemuel as King of Massa in Prov 31:1.[14] But in the present context, Massa appears to function as the Hebrew term *māśśā'*, "pronouncement, saying," which is well known from the context of oracular prophecy (see also, *ně'um*, "utterance"). Here, it refers to the teachings spoken by this otherwise unknown sage. The brief instruction begins in vv. 2-6 with a discourse in which Agur dismisses his own wisdom and ascribes all knowledge to G-d. He asks little for himself, but does request in vv. 7-10 that lies be kept far from him and that he not be given riches. His teachings in vv. 11-33 emphasize threats to society, such as the debilitating effects of need and poverty, the unapologetic actions of an adulteress, the upending of social order when those who are low or stupid replace those who are high or in positions of authority. Models for emulation include the ants, who, despite their small size are wise, well-prepared, organized, and spiders, who are small but found in royal palaces. Agur looks to animals such as the lion and the greyhound as models for the king, who must act to avoid strife. Insofar as Prov 1–29 are ascribed to Solomon, the words of Agur must be viewed as a supplement that counsels humility, scrutiny of the natural world, and attention to the moral character of others.

The final collection in Prov 31 begins with the superscription in Prov 31:1, "The words of Lemuel, King of Massa, with which his mother disciplined him." The collection appears as the mother's instruction to the son in keeping with earlier admonitions to heed the instruction of the mother together with that of the father (see Prov 6:20). In contrast to the earlier admonitions to remain humble before G-d and to be attentive in making decisions, Lemuel's mother focuses on personal conduct and care for those in need. She counsels him not to waste his strength with women and wine, and instead to strive for righteous rule which looks to the welfare of the poor and needy. Following the instructions proper in vv. 2-9, vv. 10-33 presents a hymn concerning the capable wife, whose wisdom, industry, charity, and righteousness ensures the standing of her husband and the welfare of her family. Such a hymn serves the larger interest in Proverbs of a man's adherence to his wife, but by default it also reinforces the book's interest in a man's attention to the instruction of his mother.

The theological viewpoint of the book of Proverbs envisions a secure, stable, and moral world order. Such order is established from the outset of creation by YHWH, who first creates the feminine figure of *ḥokmâ*, "wisdom," as the foundational figure of creation who was present throughout the entire process of creation as YHWH's confidant or consultant proceeded. Rabbinic tradition codifies this viewpoint in Targum Yerushalmi to Gen 1:1 by translating, "in the beginning, with wisdom, YHWH created the heavens and the earth." Thus, Wisdom is embedded in creation itself, and she thereby personifies the basic principles by which the world and all in it operate. Wisdom and order in creation are readily discerned and understood by those who wisely and diligently observe the world and draw conclusions as to how to act in relation to the natural order of the created world. Insofar as *Genesis Rabbah* 1:2, 5 identify Torah with Wisdom, Rabbinic tradition maintains that Torah can be learned by observing and studying the world as Proverbs contends. The revelation of Torah at Sinai was undertaken as a means to facilitate the learning of Torah throughout the world. Reverence for YHWH, hard work, a temperate appetite, respect for parents and other forms of authority, and loyalty to wife and friends are rewarded with success and security in life. Such concerns come to expression as the foundation of the Rabbinic concept of *derek 'ereṣ*, "the way of the earth," which envisions a combination of moral and cultural practice that stands as the foundations for human norms of behavior.[15] Proverbs thereby stands together with Torah as the foundation of the ethical tradition of Judaism, particularly the Musar (*mûsār*, generally understood as "ethics" in Rabbinic Judaism) movement that originated in the eighteenth- and nineteenth-century Yeshivahs of Lithuania as a counterpoint to Hasidism.[16]

Proverbs' theological worldview both presupposes and promotes stability in the world of creation and human events. Because it calls upon its readers to study the world to gain wisdom, it imparts a sense of investment in the natural, moral, social and political order of the world created by YHWH that will prove necessary for those who would succeed in life. Thus, the images of parents and kings are key indicators here, because Proverbs inculcates not only reverence for YHWH, but reverence for the wisdom imparted by fathers and mothers and the exercise of wisdom in the rulings of kings as well. Proverbs is therefore very conservative in its theological and moral viewpoints because it strives to protect the avenues of moral, social, and political insight and power from the past by calling upon its readers to learn from past experience and to apply such experience and the models from which is derived in the present. It presumes the righteousness of G-d, parents, kings, and others entrusted in authority based on long experience.

But it would be a mistake to presume that Proverbs is irretrievably committed to the preservation of such paragons of institutional and social authority. Proverbs celebrates the human intellect and its capacity to discern wisdom in the world, and thereby the correct courses by which human beings should conduct their lives. Indeed, Eve provides the paradigm for human discernment in Gen 3 when she hears competing narratives concerning YHWH's expectations of her and Adam. Lacking full information, she must ultimately rely on her own intellect to make a decision—and to accept responsibility for that decision when it proves

to be wrong. Proverbs recognizes that human beings may go astray to act fool-
ishly or counterproductively. In such instances, it would serve as a benchmark to
measure the conduct of those in power. Should a parent or king fail to exercise
wisdom, Proverbs stands as a basis by which to call such persons to account.
Nevertheless, readers do not see direct critique of parents, kings, or even G-d in
the book of Proverbs. Such critique comes from elsewhere in the biblical literature. Thus, it is no accident that the pentateuchal, historical, and the prophetic
traditions rely so heavily on wisdom concepts, such as the observation of nature
and of human conduct, as the basis for their own critiques of kings and society
when they are perceived to be wrong. Joseph's long process of maturation in Gen
37–50 comes from his own experience of learning the principles of wisdom and
applying them in life. David's grave misconduct as king, husband and father in
2 Samuel serves as a basis for teaching readers the expectations of human conduct
and the consequences of misconduct. The prophets, especially Amos, Hosea,
Isaiah, Micah, Jeremiah, Habakkuk, and others, so frequently employ the norms
of wisdom literature as the basis for their critiques of the kings and people of
Israel and Judah. And finally, wisdom books such as Job and Qoheleth raise
critical questions concerning G-d and the futility of human life when they fail to
embody the norms taught by Proverbs.

    Altogether, Proverbs calls upon human beings to employ their intellect to
discern the principles of wisdom embodied in creation. Although it presumes the
morality and stability of the world in which we live and it expects reverence for
G-d, it also provides the foundations to call that world into account when it does
not meet the standards articulated throughout the book. But even when employed
for purposes of critique, the book of Proverbs envisions a process of learning and
self-discipline so that its readers may learn from mistakes, apply the lessons
learned from misconduct, and ultimately learn to live in accordance with the
moral and theological norms set out by YHWH at creation.

NOTES

[1] For introductory discussion of Proverbs, see especially Crenshaw, *Old Testament Wisdom*,
55–88; Michael V. Fox, *Proverbs 1–9* (AB 18A; Garden City: Doubleday, 2000), 1–27; Leo G.
Perdue, *The Sword and the Stylus: An Introduction to Wisdom in the Age of Empire* (Grand
Rapids: Eerdmans, 2008), 85–116; Richard J. Clifford, *Proverbs: A Commentary* (OTL; Louisville: Westminster John Knox, 1999), 1–33.
[2] For a survey of modern research on Proverbs, see R. N. Whybray, *The Book of Proverbs: A
Survey of Modern Study* (Leiden: Brill, 1995).
[3] See Perdue, *The Sword and the Stylus*, 1–84. For discussion of the role of wisdom literature in
the systems of education in the ancient world, see especially David M. Carr, *Writing on the
Tablet of the Heart: Origins of Scripture and Literature* (Oxford: Oxford University Press,
2004).
[4] Roland E. Murphy, *Wisdom Literature: Job, Proverbs, Ruth, Canticles, Ecclesiastes, Esther*
(FOTL 13; Grand Rapids: Eerdmans, 1981), 176–77.

[5] For discussion of the *māšāl* or "saying" as a fundamental genre of wisdom literature, see Murphy, *Wisdom Literature*, 4–6.

[6] For example, Crenshaw, *Old Testament Wisdom*, 62; for a partial translation of the Wisdom of Amenemope, see *ANET*, 421–25.

[7] See my "Form Criticism," in *Dictionary of the Old Testament: Wisdom, Poetry, and Writings*, ed. T. Longman and P. Enns (Downer Grove, IL: InterVarsity, 2008), 227–41.

[8] Contra Murphy, *Wisdom Literature*, 49, who employs a diachronic model for his assessment of the structure of Proverbs.

[9] See Clifford, *Proverbs*, 35–36.

[10] For discussion of the sequence of lectures in Prov 1–9, cf. Fox, *Proverbs 1–9*, especially 44–49 and passim. For discussion of feminine imagery in Proverbs, see Claudia V. Camp, *Wisdom and the Feminine in the Book of Proverbs* (Decatur, GA: Almond, 1985).

[11] See R. Alcalay, *The Complete Hebrew–English Dictionary* (Ramat-Gan: Massada, n.d.), 1234; cf. M. Jastrow, *A Dictionary of the Targumim, the Talmud Babli and Yerushalmi, and the Midrashic Literature* (Brooklyn, NY: Shalom, 1967), 745.

[12] See Clifford, *Proverbs*, 72–73.

[13] Clifford, *Proverbs*, 108–9.

[14] See Clifford, *Proverbs*, 259, 260.

[15] Shmuel Himmelstein, "Derekh Erets," in *The Oxford Dictionary of the Jewish Religion*, ed. R. J. Z. Werblowsky and G. Wigoder (Oxford: Oxford University Press, 1997), 197–98.

[16] H. H. Ben-Sasson, "Musar Movement," *EncJud* 12:534–37.

D. THE BOOK OF JOB

The book of Job is a book of wisdom—or perhaps more properly theology—that critically examines the questions of human suffering and divine righteousness.[1] Indeed, these are the very questions that stand behind the laments of the book of Psalms. Job's present position immediately following Psalms in the Ketuvim thereby enables the Tanak to probe the critical questions of human suffering and divine righteousness that so frequently appear in Psalms. At the same time, Job's ultimate portrayal of the Presence of G-d at the end of the book provides a basis for the frequent assertions of praise and confidence in G-d.

The book of Job portrays Job as a pious, righteous, and prosperous family man who lives in the land of Uz, commonly identified with Edom, in antiquity during the ancestral period of ancient Israel. He is cited by Ezekiel together with Noah and Daniel (Ezek 14:12-20) as one of the wise heroes of antiquity. Rabbinic tradition (*b. Baba Batra* 14b–16b) views Job as a righteous Gentile whose righteousness is greater than that of Abraham. Most rabbinic authorities place Job in the time of Moses, but a variety of other possibilities is given—for example, Job is just a literary character who never existed; he lived in the time of Abraham; he married Dinah bat Jacob; he lived in the time of the Judges, he lived in the time of the Queen of Sheba; he lived in the time of Ahasuerus, and others. Together with Balaam and Jethro, *b. Sota* 11a identifies Job as one of the three counselors of Pharaoh who was silent, and therefore was sentenced to the suffering that he endures in the book of Job.[2]

Job is severely tested by G-d, who inflicts upon Job the loss of his property, the death of his ten children, and an illness that produces painful sores all over his body, in an effort to demonstrate to Satan that this man who "fears G-d and shuns evil" will maintain his righteousness and piety even in the face of suffering. Job does not understand the reasons for his suffering, which is particularly striking in relation to the Torah, the Prophetic literature, and Proverbs, in which the righteous are supposed to flourish for observing G-d's will and the wicked are to suffer for their failure to do so. As Job appeals to G-d for an explanation for his suffering—and repeatedly states his willingness to accept his suffering as punishment if in fact he has committed some wrongdoing—he is visited by his three friends, Eliphaz the Temanite, Bildad the Shuhite, and Zophar the Naamathite who come to comfort him and engage him in a lengthy debate concerning the causes and meaning of his suffering. When Job remains unconvinced by his friends that he has committed some wrong that would justify his suffering, a fourth figure named Elihu enters the scene to summarize the terms of the debate and to declare to Job that he should accept his suffering as a form of divine discipline. At the end of the book, G-d finally appears to answer Job's pleas for an explanation, but instead of explaining Job's suffering, G-d questions Job on the basis by which he would challenge the creator of the universe, declares that Job was right to do so, and declares that his friends have sinned in contending that Job must have committed some wrong to deserve the punishment inflicted upon him. G-d prompts Job to intercede on behalf of his friends, spares their lives, restores Job's lost property, and grants Job ten more children to replace those who had been lost. In the end, Job lives happily ever after.

Interpreters have long recognized Job's preoccupation with the meaning of human suffering and the question of divine righteousness, but have been unable to discern clear answers to the moral and theological questions that the book poses.[3] Indeed, G-d appears to act arbitrarily in the book. The divine decision to afflict Job comes as a result of a discussion between G-d and the Satan figure, here understood not as the demonic figure of Judaism, Christianity, and Islam, but as the opponent or antagonist who so frequently challenges and attempts to undermine human figures such as David (1 Chr 21:1), Solomon (1 Kgs 11:14), and the high priest Joshua ben Jehozadak at the time of his ordination to serve in the restored Jerusalem Temple (Zech 3:1-2). The role of the Satan figure in biblical literature is based on the informants sent by the Babylonian and Persian empires to gather information from lands subject to the empire and to inform the king of any seditious or rebellious activities with which the king would then have to deal.[4] In the present case, G-d points out to Satan the model piety and moral righteousness of Job, but the Satan figure contends that Job's piety and righteousness is only a product of his wealth and security. If G-d were to take away Job's wealth and well-being, Job would curse G-d. But when Job's wealth and property are lost, Job continues to bless G-d with pious statements, such as "Naked I came from my mother's womb, and naked shall I return; blessed be the name of YHWH" (Job 1:21). When Satan proposes that illness and personal suffering would prompt Job to curse G-d, G-d permits Job to suffer illness, although G-d is careful to command that Satan is not able to threaten Job's life. Once again, Job responds with piety, "Should we accept only good from G-d and not evil?" (Job 2:10). This last statement prepares the scene for the introduction of Job's friends, who will then debate with him the meaning of his suffering and the righteousness of G-d.

Modern interpreters tend to focus on questions of philological interpretation and the compositional history of the book.[5] The questions of philological interpretation and compositional history are absolutely necessary. The philological issues stem from the fact that so much of Job's language is obscure and in need of clarification, and questions concerning the history of composition stem from the fact that two very different pictures of Job seem to emerge, viz., the patient Job of the narrative framework in Job 1–2; 38–42, and the Job who demands an audience with G-d and who responds vigorously to the arguments of his friends in Job 3–37. Most interpreters recognize that the philological evidence points to the sixth through fourth centuries BCE as the general period in which the book was composed. The book appears to have a compositional history as well. The narrative materials in Job 1:1—3:1 and 42:7-14 appear to have been composed as a narrative framework for the speeches of Job and his three friends in Job 3:2—31:40 and G-d's speeches in Job 38:1—42:6. The Elihu speeches in Job 32–37 and the wisdom poem in Job 28 appear to be discrete compositions that were later added to the book to provide further reflection on issues beyond those addressed in the basic cycle of speeches by Job and his friends.

Although the historical, philological, and compositional issues are important to the interpretation of the book, the theological issues addressed by Job and his friends must remain the major focus of interpretation.[6] Interpreters from antiquity through the present have attempted to point to wrongdoing or blasphemy on Job's part in an effort to justify his suffering at the hands of G-d.[7] But such efforts to find fault with Job as a means to explain the theological issues posed by the book miss the point. The book of Job deliberately presents the model of a righteous man who suffers with no apparent moral justification in an effort to force critical reflection on the issue. The arguments posed by Job's friends concerning the meaning of human suffering and their assertions of divine righteousness even in the face of evil and Job's responses to each of them are in fact the key issues of the book. The book of Job is intended to question the standard theological premises of the Torah and the Prophets, viz., is it really the case that observance of the divine will leads to success and peace in life? Is it really the case that the wicked suffer—and not the righteous? Is it really the case that G-d is just? Indeed, the final episode in which G-d affirms Job's demands for an explanation for his suffering—even though G-d never provides such explanation—indicates that such a critical agenda is in fact the purpose of the book. In the end, the book of Job affirms divine presence and it appears to affirm divine righteousness, but the book also affirms the right and obligation of human beings to ask such questions of G-d. In this respect, Job points to and affirms a model of a human being in critical dialog with G-d.

The literary structure of the book of Job is based on a narrative presentation of dialog between Job and his friends, between Job and Elihu, and between Job and G-d.[8] It begins with a narrative presentation in Job 1:1—2:13 of the circumstances that prompt the dialog, viz., G-d's own dialog with the Satan figure about Job and the decisions made to afflict Job in an effort to demonstrate his piety and righteousness. The dialog between Job and his three friends then follows in Job 3:1—31:40 in three cycles in which each of the friends speaks successively and Job responds to each discourse. Following the debate between Job and his friends, a fourth figure by the name of Elihu appears in Job 32:1—37:24 and engages in a lengthy discourse that urges Job to submit to divine judgment. G-d finally appears in Job 38:1—42:6, but rather than answer Job's questions, G-d challenges his right to question the creator of the universe. When Job submits to G-d, the narrative concludes with G-d's restoration of Job's fortunes. The literary structure of the book of Job may be presented as follows:

The Account of Job's Debate with his Friends and with G-d Concerning Divine Righteousness and Human Suffering

I. Introductory Account of Job's Suffering without Moral Cause at the Hands of G-d   1:1—2:13
II. Account of Job's Dialog with his Three Friends: Eliphaz, Bildad, and Zophar   3:1—31:40
   A. Job's initial speech: curse day of birth and question suffering   3:1-26
   B. Eliphaz's statement and Job's response concerning whether the righteous are punished   4:1—7:21
   C. Bildad's statement and Job's response concerning G-d's protection of the righteous   8:1—10:22
   D. Zophar's statement and Job's response concerning whether Job is able to question G-d's understanding   11:1—14:22
   E. Eliphaz's second speech and Job's response concerning Job's sinfulness in questioning G-d   15:1—17:16
   F. Bildad's second speech and Job's response concerning the futility of Job's questioning of G-d   18:1—19:29
   G. Zophar's second speech and Job's response concerning whether suffering is the lot of human beings   20:1—21:34
   H. Eliphaz's third speech and Job's response concerning whether humans can correct G-d   22:1—24:25
   I. Bildad's third speech and Job's response concerning whether humans can challenge G-d's power   25:1—26:14
   J. Job's speech concerning the hidden nature of wisdom   27:1—28:28
   K. Job's concluding speech asking for a hearing from G-d   29:1—31:40
III. Account of Elihu's Four Discourses to Job Concerning His Need to Submit to G-d's Judgment   32:1—37:24
IV. Account of G-d's Debate with Job Concerning the Futility of Job's Challenge and His Righteousness in Making It   38:1—42:6
V. Narrative Resolution: Job Restored   42:7-17

Close examination of each sub-unit of the book of Job indicates the major issues discussed.

The narrative introduction of the book presents an account of Job's suffering at the hand of G-d without moral justification. Job appears to be a patient figure in this portion of the book. This portrayal of his character is crucial to the rhetorical and theological agenda of the book insofar as it demonstrates G-d's capriciousness in allowing Job to suffer and Job's piety in the face of suffering. As noted above, G-d allows Job to suffer as a response to the Satan's charges that Job would curse G-d if he lost his property and wealth. But Job's initial responses to his suffering aid in establishing his character as a righteous and pious man, and thereby provide the foundations for the challenges that he poses to G-d concerning his new lot in life. Only a man with an impeccable reputation, such as that demonstrated in the narrative introduction to Job, could address G-d in such a way. Although the narrative may be viewed as a later literary framework for the dialog, its portrayal of Job actually makes the dialog possible. If the reader has any doubts about Job's righteousness and faithfulness, the following dialog would make absolutely no sense as Job's character would be easily impugned by readers who could dismiss him as a flawed figure and thereby ignore his argument. By establishing Job's credibility, the narrative thereby enables the debate to take place, and it enables the reader to take the debate seriously.

Job 3:1—31:40 then constitutes the major block of the book as an account of the dialog between Job and his friends, Eliphaz, Bildad, and Zophar. The segment begins with Job's initial speech in Job 3:1-26, in which he curses the day of his birth and lays out the questions of human suffering. Interpreters have noted parallels between this speech and the lament by Jeremiah in Jer 20:7-18, in which the prophet concludes his lament at having been overcome by G-d by stating his desire never to have been born.[9] In both cases, such a stance points to the severity of the suffering endured by Job and Jeremiah. In the case of Job, it provides a counter-point to the preceding narrative portrayal of his piety and righteousness. It thereby provides a further foundation for the debate that follows by pointing to the severity of his situation, particularly since Job has lost all of his children as well as his wealth and his own health. At this point, there is little more to take from him other than his life.

Three sets of exchanges then follow between Job and his friends. Eliphaz speaks first and Job replies in Job 4:1—7:21 on the question of whether or not the righteous are punished. Eliphaz's fundamental contention in Job 4:1—5:27 is that innocent people do not suffer. Only the guilty suffer, and therefore in his experience of the matter, anyone who suffers must therefore be guilty of some sin that prompted the suffering in the first place. But Eliphaz makes a further point that those who repent from wrongdoing are heard by G-d and restored. He therefore urges Job to repent of his sins so that G-d may forgive him and relieve him of his suffering. Job's response in Job 6:1—7:21 focuses on his insistence that he knows sin and suffering when he sees it and cannot fathom what he has done to deserve such a lot. In the end, Job demands to know what he has done to deserve such punishment and why G-d does not pardon him.

Bildad then follows with Job's response in Job 8:1—10:22 on the question of G-d's protection of the righteous. Bildad's speech in Job 8:1-22 focuses on the assertion that G-d is righteous and that human beings cannot live without the support of the righteous G-d. Following upon Eliphaz, Bildad emphasizes that G-d will grant Job happiness in life, but Job must first live a righteous life to merit such favor. Job's response in Job 9:1—10:22 begins with an acknowledgment of

G-d's power and the inability of human beings to challenge G-d. Again, Job demands to know what wrong he has done to deserve his suffering, but he continues by asking what benefit G-d might gain by tormenting him so. Again, he asserts that it would have been better for him to die at birth than to live such a life.

Zophar then speaks, followed by Job's response in Job 11:1—14:22 on the question as to whether or not Job even has the right to question G-d. Zophar's brief speech in Job 11:1-20 emphasizes the point that Job as a human being is incapable of understanding G-d, but that G-d understands Job and Job's iniquity. Like his colleagues, Zophar calls upon Job to turn to G-d in repentance so that he can be relieved of his suffering during the all-too-brief span of human life. Job's response in Job 12:1—14:22 rather testily points out that he is as wise as Zophar, and as everyone knows, the fate of human beings is determined by G-d. Job charges Zophar with deceit in his defense of divine justice, and argues that, since Job is a pious man, G-d will in fact hear his case. In Job's view G-d is just, and he therefore demands that G-d state to him the wrongs that he has done that have prompted his suffering. Indeed, Job counts on divine righteousness as his last defense. He points to the limits of his own life and to the possibility of his recovery like a tree that renews itself after it has been cut down.

The second cycle of debate then begins with Eliphaz's second speech and Job's response in Job 15:1—17:16 on the topic of Job's sinfulness in questioning G-d. Eliphaz's speech in Job 15:1-35 charges Job with sin in his willingness to question G-d. He asserts that Job is hardly the first human to exist and therefore has no basis in wisdom or knowledge from which he might call G-d to account. He therefore returns to his original contention that if Job suffers, it must be because he has committed some sin to deserve it. Job's response in Job 16:-17:16 again presumes divine righteousness insofar as he demands that G-d arbitrate his case. He maintains that his blood is visible on the ground, viz., his suffering is evident, and that G-d as supreme judge in creation must come to investigate the matter. At this point, Job is willing to take his chances with G-d as judge to vindicate him of wrongdoing. On the other hand, he makes it clear that he has little confidence in his friends.

Bildad's second speech with Job's response appears in Job 18:1—19:29 on the topic of the futility of Job's challenge of G-d. Bildad retorts angrily in Job 18:1-21 that Job must shut his mouth and cease regarding him and his colleagues as idiots. The wicked have no possibility of success in such a challenge against G-d, and in Bildad's view Job's challenge of G-d marks him as wicked with no hope of success. Job's response in Job 19:1-29 responds in kind—one wonders if these men can truly be regarded as friends! Job concedes once again that if he has committed some wrongdoing, he will take responsibility for it, but he reiterates his case that he can find no wrong that he has committed. At this point, Job asserts that G-d has wronged him, and that everyone has abandoned him. He then pleads with his friends to show pity to him and to cease tormenting him.

Yet, even in his anger and despair he continues to express confidence that G-d will vindicate him if G-d takes the trouble to examine the facts.

Zophar's second speech followed by Job's response appears in Job 20:1—21:34 on the question of whether suffering is the lot of human beings. Zophar's speech in Job 20:1-29 emphasizes that human beings are born to suffering. He asserts no moral basis for suffering, but simply asserts his contention as the existential fact of human existence. Although he does not state his case, his implication is that Job must accept his suffering as a fact of life. Job's response in Job 21:1-34 asserts that his case is with G-d, whom Job presumes does have moral perspective. He questions why the wicked live and prosper without any reprimand or punishment from G-d. Ultimately, the wicked and the righteous suffer the same fate—death. Job challenges Zophar to go into the world and make inquiries, and he will then see that Job's contention is correct.

A third cycle then begins with Eliphaz's statement and Job's response in Job 22:1—24:25 on the question of whether or not human beings can correct G-d. Eliphaz's speech in Job 22:1-30 begins with assertions that G-d does not benefit from a wise man, and follows through with charges that Job has committed numerous trespasses. Following his contentions that G-d knows all and gives all, he calls upon Job to return to G-d and reap the benefits. Job's response in Job 23:1—24:25 reiterates his demands for an audience with G-d so that he might know the cause of his afflictions, but he observes that he is unable to find G-d to make such a claim. Job states his fear and awe of G-d's power, but he then observes the numerous cases of injustice committed by human beings that go unpunished by G-d before calling upon G-d to act against such persons rather than to protect them.

Bildad's speech is followed by Job's response in Job 25:1—26:14 on the question of whether humans can challenge G-d's power. Bildad's very brief speech in Job 25:1-6 simply asserts that G-d is powerful and that human beings have no basis to challenge G-d's righteousness. Job's response in Job 26:1-14 is assigned by some to Bildad's speech or even to Zophar. The speech is a statement of divine power that would be easily assigned to Bildad. In Job's mouth, it provides further testimony of Job's awe of G-d even while pressing his case for a hearing.

Instead of Zophar's expected third speech, Job 27:1—28:28 appears as a speech by Job in which he discusses the hidden nature of wisdom. This speech is a key element of the book insofar as it takes up an intertextual debate with the book of Proverbs concerning the degree to which human beings can perceive wisdom in the world.[10] Job insists on his own integrity before G-d and asserts that the wicked deserve the punishment that they would reap from G-d. Beginning in Job 28:1, Job turns to the question of the difficulty of discerning wisdom in the world, which he likens to precious metals hidden deep within the earth. The metaphor provides him with a means to state the difficulty of finding wisdom when he asserts that only G-d understands the way to wisdom—such knowledge is not available to human beings or to other entities within creation. The discourse ends in Job 28:28 with the assertion drawn from Prov 1:7, "The fear of YHWH is wisdom, to shun evil is understanding." The intertextual allusion to Proverbs heightens the contrast between Job and Proverbs.[11] Although Proverbs points to some difficulty or effort in the quest to obtain wisdom, Proverbs by and large presents a model in which human beings may learn wisdom by studying elements and aspects of creation insofar as G-d created the world on the basis of wisdom (see Prov 8). Job by contrast maintains that such knowledge is not available to human observation and reflection.

Job 29:1—31:40 then closes the unit with Job's speech, in which he reiterates his demands for a hearing from G-d. Job's speech functions much like a concluding courtroom argument. He reflects on his past life when G-d watched over him and his life was good. But now he is mocked and derided by those whom he considers to be his inferiors in wisdom. He claims that he cries out to G-d, but G-d does not answer. He claims that G-d has turned against him and brought him to death. He then makes a final plea for a hearing before G-d, and reiterates his willingness to accept his punishment if in fact he is in the wrong. This assertion is especially important insofar as it expresses his confidence that G-d will in fact ultimately do justice if Job's case is heard.

The third major block appears in Job 32:1—37:24, a block in which Elihu ben Barachel appears to deliver four discourses to Job concerning Job's need to submit to divine judgment. The narrative introduction in Job 32:1-5 provides little basis to identify Elihu. His name means, "he is my G-d," which would suggest a reference to YHWH. His identity as a Buzite suggests that he is contemptible, but his identity as a member of the family of Ram suggests exalted status. The reader is never informed as to how Elihu happened to be present. He seems to be a bystander or observer. Elihu clearly aligns himself with G-d. In four speeches, Job 32–33, 34, 35, and 36–37, he berates Job for his failure to submit to G-d. In the first speech in Job 32:6—33:33, Elihu identifies himself as a younger man who has waited for his elders to speak before raising his own voice to assert that their speeches have been inadequate. Elihu attempts to refute Job's claims of innocence by claims that G-d is greater than any human being and that G-d speaks repeatedly to humans in dreams, visions, acts of discipline, and protection from death. Elihu invites Job's response, but he urges Job to remain silent if he is unable to answer this argument. Elihu's second speech in Job 34:1-37 attempts to counter Job's claims that humans gain nothing by turning to G-d. Elihu asserts that G-d is hardly wicked, but as creator of the universe must be recognized as just. He asserts that G-d knows all and that G-d acts either for or against human beings with deliberate justice based on knowledge of all that G-d observes in the world. Elihu's third speech in Job 35:1-15 challenges Job's assertions that he has gained nothing by refraining from sin. He asserts that Job's sins cannot adversely affect G-d, and he reiterates that G-d observes all. Elihu calls upon Job to wait for G-d's response, which will come at a time that G-d alone will determine. Elihu's last speech in Job 36:1—37:24 calls upon Job to acknowledge G-d's power and justice.

He points to G-d's marvels in the world of creation, and he reiterates the inability of humankind to stand beside G-d as equals or to say anything that would challenge G-d's actions.

The fourth major block of the book appears in Job 38:1—42:6, which presents G-d's speeches in answer to Job and brief accounts of Job's responses. The first speech in Job 38:1—39:30 challenges Job's ability to question G-d at all by asserting that Job did not create the universe and therefore lacks the wisdom to mount any case against the creator of the universe. The second speech in Job 40:1-2 simply demands Job's response. Job responds in Job 40:4-5 by stating that he has already spoken his piece and will say nothing more before YHWH. G-d then takes up a second major speech in Job 40:6—41:26 in which G-d challenges Job's right to impugn divine justice. The speech continues like the first with a focus on divine power which Job has no hope to match. Job's response in Job 42:1-6 acknowledges that power, and declines to challenge G-d further. At this point, Job withdraws his complaint, Job having seen G-d with his own eyes.

Finally, the concluding segment of the book appears in Job 42:7-17. It is here that Job's fortunes are restored. G-d begins with a condemnation of Job's friends for failing to speak the truth about G-d as Job has done. G-d proposes that the friends bring offerings to Job so that Job may appeal to G-d on their behalf and save their lives. G-d then restores the fortunes of Job, giving him double of everything he had possessed before. The narrative concludes with the restoration of Job's friends and family. Job then lives a wonderful life, filled with wealth and children, including seven new sons and three daughters to replace those who had been lost.

Clearly, the book of Job is formulated as an account of a debate between Job, his friends, and G-d, on the topics of human suffering and divine righteousness.[12] Such an observation is not simply a matter of form since it has important implications in a theological assessment of the book. The dialog format derives from the settings of wisdom and law in which a matter is examined and weighed in an effort to come to a decision concerning the problem or issue at hand. Indeed, the dialog format becomes a key basis for the discussion of halakhah and interpretation of the tradition in the later rabbinic period. In the present context, the dialog format allows for the articulation of the various perspectives of the participants in the dialog. Eliphaz emerges as the primary figure who holds to a standard theology of blessing for righteousness and punishment for wrongdoing, which is in keeping with the pentateuchal and prophetic literature, but he also affirms a positive divine response to human repentance. Bildad steadfastly affirms the righteousness of G-d together with the human responsibility to affirm divine righteousness and to live in accordance with divine expectations. Zophar maintains that as a human being created by G-d, Job has no right, knowledge, or standing to challenge his own creator. Indeed, human beings must accept suffering as their lot in the order of creation. Elihu basically reiterates and summarizes the terms of the debate and adds nothing substantially new to the positions articulated by Eliphaz, Bildad, and Zophar.

Throughout the debate, it is striking that Job actually agrees with the fundamental theological positions of each of his friends. He accepts Eliphaz's premise that the righteous should be blessed and the wicked punished—and he is willing to accept his punishment if he has sinned—but he has not been able to determine what wickedness on his part earned the suffering inflicted on him by G-d. He presumes Bildad's principle throughout the debate that G-d is righteous, and in his demands for G-d to look into his case he maintains that G-d will rescind his suffering when the true facts of his situation come to light. Job likewise presupposes Zophar's principle throughout the debate that as a human he has no right or wisdom to challenge G-d, but he does so nevertheless in the full confidence that G-d's righteousness will either prompt relief from his suffering or provide him with the explanation that he so desperately seeks. Although many interpreters point to the contrast between the patient Job of the narrative introduction and the challenging Job of the poetic dialogs,[13] Job remains a pious man devoted to G-d and to the principles of divine justice throughout the debate even as he demands an explanation from G-d for his suffering. It is not a sin to question G-d, as is exemplified by the experiences of Abraham at Sodom and Gomorrah (Gen 18), Moses in the Wilderness (Exod 32; Num 14), Amos at Beth El (Amos 7), and Jeremiah in his laments (Jer 20). It is a sin to abandon G-d, but Job never does this.[14] Such a position then highlights both the urgency and the necessity of the questions posed to G-d by Job, and indeed at the end of the book G-d affirms Job's righteousness in asking them while rebuking his friends for their erroneous representation of the divine (Job 42).

Yet, whereas the book of Job affirms the right and responsibility to pose such questions, it provides little in the way of answers. This position should come as no surprise in a book that asserts the near impossibility of human efforts to discern true wisdom (Job 28). There is a conflict in the book between an ontological understanding of moral action—that is, an act should be righteous in and of itself—and a teleological understanding of moral action—that is, an act should lead to a righteous result. The open-ended response of G-d to Job's questions highlights this issue. G-d does not and cannot explain to Job why his suffering must be considered a moral judgment upon him. He has done nothing to deserve such suffering that would enable G-d to explain it in moral terms. Such a position presupposes an ontological understanding of moral action that neither G-d nor the book of Job can explain or defend. Instead, G-d challenges Job's right and power as a human being to ask such questions, and G-d is right in this regard, that is, Job was not present at creation and can hardly be considered a god himself—how could he possibly understand? In the end, G-d affirms Job's right to raise such questions, restores his lost property and family, preserves the lives of his friends at his intercession, and sees to it that Job leads a long and happy life in the end. Ultimately, the book of Job must be considered a teleologically oriented book insofar as it points to Job's later life of blessing as a means to resolve the moral issues posed within. Of course such an outcome cannot resolve the moral issues posed by the book, because the ontological and teleological characters of these issues are mutually exclusive; the two positions cannot be reconciled. As presented in the book of Job, they remain mutually exclusive.

Furthermore, this moral ambiguity comes to a head near the conclusion of Job's audience with G-d in Job 2:1-6 when he purportedly submits to G-d, stating, "I had heard You with my ears, but now I see You with my eyes; therefore, I recant and relent, being but dust and ashes" (NJPS). The use of the Hebrew verb, 'em'as, "I recant," is an interesting choice in v. 6, insofar as the Hebrew verb root m's normally carries the connotation of rejection, refusal, and even contempt. Although it also carries a connotation of withdrawal or a refusal to continue pressing demands,[15] the ambiguity of the term suggests that Job is not satisfied with the nature of G-d's response even as he accepts G-d's contention that he is in no position to challenge his own creator.[16] Job has already accepted his limitations before his creator as expressed repeatedly throughout the debate. Nevertheless, such a standpoint on Job's part highlights the unsatisfactory nature of Job's restoration at the end of the book. G-d grants him twice what he had before his trial began, and G-d provides him with ten new children. Does such a double reward compensate him for his suffering? The issue is especially acute when one considers that even ten new children can hardly compensate for the loss of the first ten, especially when one considers Job's love for his children, as expressed in the narrative of Job 1.[17]

Indeed, the ambiguity of G-d's position is highlighted by G-d's anger at Job's friends, who "have not spoken the truth about Me as did My servant Job" (Job 42:7, 8 NJPS). Although modern translations such as the NJPS tend to emphasize the issue of truth spoken about G-d, a closer look at the Hebrew indicates that the issue must actually be construed as speaking what is right to G-d, that is, Hebrew, kî lō' dibbartem 'ēlî nĕkônâ kĕ'abdî 'îyôb, "for you have not spoken to me what is right like My servant Job."[18] G-d maintains that, as a human, Job cannot challenge G-d, but nevertheless G-d both affirms and expects Job's efforts to do so. It is Job's responsibility to ask such questions of G-d; failure to do so as exemplified by Eliphaz, Bildad, and Zophar, constitutes an act of sin by omission that leaves them subject to capital punishment in the eyes of G-d.

The issues of ambiguity at the end of the book both regard G-d's answers to Job and Job's response to G-d's answers, point to a further dimension. The debate between Job, his friends, and G-d is concluded at the end of the book with its narrative resolution. The dialogical character of the book takes in not only its major characters, but also the reader, who has been privy to the morally ambiguous circumstances that led to Job's suffering as well as to the debate itself.[19] The reader comes to the end of the book with a sense of dissatisfaction as well: Job's questions have not been adequately answered, and the issues of human suffering and divine righteousness have been left unresolved. As a participant in the debate, even if only by listening in, the reader is in a position to debate with the positions articulated throughout the book and to engage further in the debate beyond the terms offered on Job's pages. The book of Job presents a dialog between Job, his friends, and G-d, but it is also in dialog with other biblical literature, such as the Pentateuch and the Prophets, and with the reader as well. Indeed, the open-ended nature of the debate points to a far more active role for the reader beyond that of merely being a listener. The reader is enjoined to engage in the debate him- or herself and to continue the debate well beyond the confines of the book of Job. The book of Job is designed to stimulate discussion. It does not presume to answer the questions posed by Job, but it does that the answers may eventually be learned even though the process of such discovery will be arduous and nearly impossible. Nevertheless, the book of Job requires its readers to engage in such study and debate, just as Job and his friends have done in their efforts to understand G-d and the nature of the world of creation in which we live. Such a task in fact lies at the basis of Jewish life, study, worship, and practice.

NOTES

[1] For introductions to Job, see James L. Crenshaw, *Old Testament Wisdom: An Introduction* (Louisville: Westminster John Knox, 1998), 89–115; Roland E. Murphy, *The Tree of Life: An Exploration of Biblical Wisdom Literature* (Winona Lake, IN: Eisenbrauns, 2002), 33–48; Leo G. Perdue, *The Sword and the Stylus: An Introduction to Wisdom in the Age of Empire* (Grand Rapids: Eerdmans, 2008), 117–51. For commentaries on Job, see Édouard Dhorme, *A Commentary on the Book of Job*, trans. H. Knight (Nashville: Thomas Nelson, 1984); Marvin H. Pope, *Job* (AB 15; Garden City: Doubleday, 1973); Norman C. Habel, *The Book of Job: A Commentary* (OTL; Philadelphia: Westminster, 1985); Carol Newsom, "The Book of Job," in *The New Interpreter's Bible*, ed. L. E. Keck et al. (Nashville: Abingdon, 1996), 4:319–637. See also Leo G. Perdue, *Wisdom and Creation: The Theology of the Wisdom Literature* (Nashville: Abingdon, 1994); Carol A. Newsom, *The Book of Job: A Contest of Moral Imaginations* (Oxford: Oxford University Press, 2003).
[2] See Judith R. Baskin, *Pharaoh's Counselors: Job, Jethro, and Balaam in Rabbinic and Patristic Tradition* (BJS 47; Chico: Scholars Press, 1983), 7–43.
[3] See Crenshaw, *Old Testament Wisdom Literature*, 108–9. For readings of Job in relation to the theological questions prompted by the Shoah, see my *Reading the Hebrew Bible after the Shoah: Engaging Holocaust Theology* (Minneapolis: Fortress Press, 2008), 195–200; Richard L. Rubenstein, "Job and Auschwitz," in *Strange Fire: Reading the Bible after the Holocaust*, ed. T. Linafelt (Sheffield: Sheffield Academic, 2000), 233–51; Stephen Kepnes, "Job and Post-Holocaust Theodicy," in Linafelt, ed., *Strange Fire*, 252–66.
[4] A. Leo Oppenheim, "The Eyes of the L-rd," *JAOS* 88 (1968): 173–80.
[5] James L. Crenshaw, "Job, Book of," *ABD* 3:858–68.
[6] See especially Perdue, *Wisdom and Creation*, 123–92.
[7] See, for example, *b. Baba Batra* 16a, which presents a listing of Job's blasphemous statements against G-d.
[8] For discussion of the formal literary structure and generic character of Job, see especially Murphy, *Wisdom Literature*, 15–20.
[9] For example, Habel, *Job*, 109–10; Perdue, *Wisdom and Creation*, 123.
[10] For a full intertextual study of Job 28, see especially Newsom, *The Book of Job*, 169–82.

[11] See my *Reading the Hebrew Bible after the Shoah*, 198–99.

[12] For full discussion of the dialogical character of the book of Job, see Newsom, *The Book of Job*, passim.

[13] See especially Pope, *Job*, xxiii–xxx.

[14] Cf. Elie Wiesel, *Souls on Fire: Portraits and Legends of Hasidic Masters* (New York: Summit, 1972), 111, who states: "Man's inner liberation is G-d's justification. It all depends on where the rebel chooses to stand. From inside his community, he (man) may say everything."

[15] See Habel, *Job*, 576.

[16] I am indebted to Antony F. Campbell, S.J., for this observation, although he is not to be held responsible for the views expressed here.

[17] For discussion of Job's ten lost children, see Emil L. Fackenheim, *The Jewish Bible after the Holocaust: A Rereading* (Bloomington: Indiana University Press, 1990), 71–99, especially 92–99.

[18] Contra Dhorme, *Job*, 648.

[19] Cf. Newsom, *The Book of Job*, passim.

E. The Five Megillot

1. Overview

The Five Megillot or Scrolls (Hebrew, *ḥāmēš měgillôt*) designate five short books of the Ketuvim—Song of Songs, Ruth, Lamentations, Qoheleth, and Esther—that are read as part of the synagogue service on major Jewish holidays; Song of Songs is read on Passover; Ruth on Shavuot; Lamentations on Tisha b'Av; Qoheleth on Sukkot; and Esther on Purim.[1] The custom of reading these books on the holidays was apparently not yet fully instituted by the time when the Babylonian Talmud was completed (ca. 600 CE). Esther was already read on Purim during the Second Temple period, and the reading of Lamentations on Tisha b'Av is mentioned in *Ta'anit* 30a. The reading of Ruth, Song of Songs, and Qoheleth on their respective holidays must have originated at some point following the Talmudic period. Consequently, *b. Baba Batra* 14b does not treat the Five Megillot as a unit in the canonical order of the Ketuvim, but instead arranges the Ketuvim according to their chronological order, viz., Ruth, Psalms, Job, Proverbs, Qoheleth, Song of Songs, Lamentations, Daniel, Esther, Ezra–Nehemiah, and Chronicles. They are generally treated as a unit in the manuscript tradition of the Bible, for example, the Leningrad Codex arranges them as a unit according to their chronological order, viz., Ruth, Qoheleth, Song of Songs, Lamentations, and Esther. In printed editions of the Tanak, the Five Megillot are arranged as a unit according to the sequence of the festivals during the Jewish year, viz., Song of Songs, Ruth, Lamentations, Qoheleth, and Esther.

2. The Song of Songs

Song of Songs is read on Shabbat during the celebration of Passover, which commemorates the beginning of the grain harvest in the land of Israel as well as the Exodus from Egypt. It is both a highly innovative and controversial book because of its graphic portrayals of sensuality and sexuality in the relationship between the female and male lovers who appear as the main characters in the book.[2] G-d is nowhere mentioned in Song of Songs. Based in part on the traditions in the Prophets, which depict the relationship between YHWH and Israel or Jerusalem as a marital relationship between groom and bride (see Isa 54; Jer 2; Ezek 16; Hos 1–3; Zeph 3:14-20), Jewish tradition reads Song of Songs allegorically as a presentation of the marital relationship between YHWH and the people of Israel. The relationship between the two lovers thereby symbolizes the relationship between YHWH and Israel at the time of the Exodus from Egypt. Ironically, the identification of YHWH and Israel with either of the primary characters is never clear. YHWH could be the woman waiting for the man, much as G-d waits in the Holy of Holies of the Temple for Israel to come for worship, or G-d could be the male who comes to the woman in the poetic narrative but creates a crisis when he disappears without explanation.

The inclusion of Song of Songs in the Bible was challenged in the Mishnah by R. Judah, R. Jose (who noted that there was controversy), and Simon ben Azzai (who cited a tradition going back to R. Eleazar ben Azariah), perhaps because of its sexual motifs and perhaps because of its mystical associations. But Rabbi Akiba defended the inclusion of Song of Songs in the Bible by declaring it to be "the holy of holies" of Jewish scripture, thereby employing the terminology used to describe the inner sanctum of the Temple of Jerusalem. R. Johanan ben Joshua reports that the matter was then decided by taking into account the words of Shimon ben Azzai (*m. Yadaim* 3:5).[3] The Amoraic-period (ca. 200–260 CE) *Midrash Song of Songs Rabbah*, also known as *Midrash Hazita*, reads the Song of Songs as an allegorical text that portrays the marital relationship between YHWH and Israel in which G-d's love for Israel is apparent in the revelation of Torah from Sinai and the redemption from Egyptian bondage, and Israel's love for G-d is apparent in the acceptance of Torah and the readiness to endure martyrdom on behalf of G-d. *Song of Songs Rabbah* endorses the Solomonic authorship of the book by stating that Song of Songs was composed during Solomon's youth when he would be preoccupied with matters of sexuality, Proverbs was composed during his adulthood when he would be preoccupied with the practical concerns of living in the world, and Qoheleth was composed in his old age when he would reflect on the meaning of life.

Modern scholarship does not accept the claim made in Song 1:1 that Solomon is the author of the book. The book appears instead to have been composed at some time during the Second Temple period.[4] Linguistic features point to the Persian period or possibly the Hellenistic period as the time for the book's composition. The Hebrew term *pardēs*, "garden" (Song 4:13), is an Avestan term (*pairidaēza*) that originally referred to a "rampart," but it was employed in the late Babylonian period (*pardēsu*) as a term for a marvelous garden and in Achaemenid Persian times as a term to describe the domain of the king.[5] The Hebrew term *'appiryôn*, "sedan, palanquin" (Song 3:9), is a term known from

Jewish Aramaic, but it is derived from a Greek loan word, *phorein*, with the same meaning.[6] Although Song of Songs appears to have been written in a relatively late period, its concern with the portrayal of love and sensuality may be traced back to distant antiquity.[7] Many scholars point to the Egyptian love poetry of the fourteenth through twelfth centuries BCE as the model for a key literary device employed in the Song of Songs known as the *waṣf*, which metaphorically describes the physical form of the body of the lover (for example, Song 4:1-8; 5:10-16).[8] Others point to the Sumerian love poetry that portrays the love relationship between Inanna, the goddess of wisdom, order, and stability in creation, and Dumuzi, the god of fertility, that was employed in the ritual celebration of sacred marriage at the time of the Sumerian New Year.[9] The above-noted portrayal of YHWH and Israel or Jerusalem in a marriage relationship may have played a role in Israelite liturgy at some point during the Israelite ancestral or monarchic periods. The portrayal of the dancing maidens at the Shiloh Temple who are taken as brides by the men of Benjamin at the festival of Sukkot (Judg 21:19-24) would suggest some role for a marriage tradition in Israelite worship. Unfortunately, no further examples are known.

Although some interpreters contend that Song of Songs was written for the purposes of entertainment, the use of allegory, metaphor, and simile is typical in biblical and ancient Near Eastern wisdom literature. Such devices aid in establishing an analogy between one set of images or terms and another in an effort to point to some issue or image beyond the immediate portrayal of the text. In the ancient world, images of fruit, crops, flowers, plants, animals, and even sexuality are employed to point to the reality and power of deities who both create the world and are active within it. Indeed, ancient goddesses, such as Inanna, Ishtar, Anat, Asherah, Maat, may be symbolized by trees, stars, and fruit in their respective cultures. They are known both for their sexual natures and their capacities for childbirth, as well as for their roles as wisdom figures who represent the stability and order of creation and its capacity to create new life. In biblical literature, Proverbs portrays a world of creation that is founded by G-d and permeated by wisdom. This is done by means of a feminine figure who was the first of G-d's creations (see Prov 8). Proverbs counsels diligent study of the world of creation and human relations within it as a means to acquire the wisdom necessary for life in the world. Proverbs is far more subtle than Song of Songs in its consideration of human sexuality, but its advice to avoid the temptations of a strange woman and to adhere to one's own wife attests to the interrelationship between wisdom and sexuality. Likewise, human sexuality is intertwined with the creation of Adam and Eve in Gen 2–3, particularly after Eve introduces the knowledge of good and evil as a component of human experience that is bound up in her sexual relationship with Adam. And finally, the above-noted marriage tradition between YHWH and Israel served as a metaphor for the state of the relationship between the deity and the nation.

The wisdom characteristic of Song of Songs indicates an interest in pointing beyond the surface meaning of its text to greater concerns with the questions of divine absence and the role of human beings as agents of creation. Analysis of the book illustrates these concerns.

The superscription of the book in Song 1:1 ascribes the Song of Songs to King Solomon. The basis for this ascription is never made clear in the superscription, but interpreters surmise that this ascription is based on Solomon's own reputation as a lover of women, having some seven hundred wives and three hundred concubines (1 Kgs 11:1-3), as well as his reputation for wisdom and the composition of songs (1 Kgs 5:9-14).

Interpreters continue to disagree concerning the literary form of the book, but Trible's analysis points to a way forward insofar as it takes account of the roles of the major characters of the book and their relation to the dramatic presentation of the text to discern a literary structure of five major movements.[10] The primary characters are the female and male lovers, but Trible also points to a group of women identified as "the daughter of Jerusalem," whose voices appear in four formulaic variations of the phrase, "I adjure you, O Daughters of Jerusalem," that mark the conclusions of four major episodes in Song 2:7; 3:5; 5:8; and 8:4. Following the superscription in Song 1:1, the body of the book in Song 1:2—8:14 presents a sequence of five movements in the dramatic narrative action of the Song which portray five successive episodes as the lovers approach each other and consummate their love. The first movement in Song 1:2—2:7 focuses on the woman's expression of her desire for her lover and her anticipation of their meeting. The second episode in Song 2:8—3:5 focuses on the approach of the male lover, metaphorically described as a gazelle or stag bounding over the mountains, together with the woman's search throughout the city to find him. The third episode in Song 3:6—5:8 employs the *wasf* form to describe the physical charms of both the woman and the man, but when the woman opens to the man near the end of this episode, he is gone. The man's disappearance provides an opportunity for dramatic tension in the plot of the Song as the woman expresses her distress at the loss of her lover. The fourth movement in Song 5:9—8:4 again employs the *wasf* to describe the two lovers as they are ultimately reunited. The fifth and concluding movement in Song 8:5-14 relates the consummation of the relationship and opines that love is stronger than death and that passion is as mighty as Sheol. The formal structure of the Song of Songs appears as follows:

Allegorical Dramatization of Relationship between Two Lovers

I.	Superscription: Solomon's Song of Songs	1:1
II.	Dramatization in Five Episodes	1:2—8:14
	A. Woman expresses desire for her male lover	1:2—2:7
	B. Approach of the male lover	2:8—3:5
	C. Loss of the male lover	3:6—5:8
	D. Reunion of the two lovers	5:9—8:4
	E. Consummation	8:5-14

The formal dramatic structure of the Song of Songs conveys its basic thesis, viz., that the love expressed by the two lovers overcomes death. Yet, the corollary of the Song's focus on the two human lovers is the absence of G-d in this text. Allegorical interpretations of the Song have posited that G-d may well be hidden behind the text, viz., some interpreters argue that the Hebrew term *šalhebetyâ*, "blazing flame," in Song 8:6 points to the hidden presence of G-d in the Song insofar as the last syllable of the Hebrew term constitutes an abbreviated form of the divine name, though this element of the term simply conveys the intensity of the flame.[11] Interpreters might speculate that G-d is to be found in the intimacy of the passion of the couple, but such an interpretative stance sidesteps the crucial theological issue in the Song of Songs, that is, the absence or hiddenness of G-d.

The absence or hidden nature of G-d in the Song of Songs very strikingly allows the human characters of the Song full play as actors and powers in creation. The drama celebrates their sexuality,[12] which in biblical tradition is a function of knowledge or wisdom like that gained by Eve in the Garden of Eden (Gen 3). Although Eve and Adam are condemned by G-d for their acquisition—like G-d—of the knowledge of good and evil, their newly gained sexuality enables them to create a new relationship with each other as well as new life that stems from that relationship.[13] Their sexuality enables them to stand as creators on a par with G-d. The celebration of human sexuality in the Song of Songs thus ultimately points to the roles of human beings as creators and agents of action in the world of creation.

The question of divine absence or impotence then emerges as a key theological element in the interpretation of the Song of Songs. Yet, the question of human responsibility to act in the world when G-d is absent or hidden must also be recognized as a central theological concern. Although Song of Songs clearly celebrates human love, the realities of the threat of death or evil in the world of creation must also be considered, viz., to what extent does Song of Songs call upon human beings to use their capacities to act and to create in the world to overcome the threats or realities of death or evil? Song of Songs points directly to that responsibility, viz., human beings cannot always wait for G-d to act in the world. In the absence of G-d, human beings must act as creators like G-d to create relationship, to create life, and to overcome death, evil, and the absence of G-d in the world of creation. In this regard, Song of Songs is akin to Esther, which addresses analogous theological questions, but sets them in relation to a deliberate attempt by a foreign government to exterminate its Jewish population.

3. The Book of Ruth

The book of Ruth is read as part of the liturgy for the festival of Shavuot or Weeks. It presents an account of a Moabite woman named Ruth, who, following the death of her Judean husband, returned to the city of Beth Lehem with her mother-in-law, Naomi. In keeping with her loyalty to her late husband, Ruth declares her desire to become a part of Israel. Following Levirate law, in which a widow marries a male kinsman of her late husband in order to preserve his name and lineage (Deut 25:5-10), Ruth marries Boaz, a Judean kinsman of her late husband. Ruth therefore is recognized as a convert to Judaism. Because of its celebration of the revelation of Torah at Mt. Sinai, Shavuot also celebrates conversion to Judaism in which a Gentile formally becomes part of the Jewish people by choosing to accept divine Torah.[14]

The book of Ruth presents itself as a historical account of the experiences of Ruth and Naomi during the period of the Judges, but modern critical interpretation has correctly recognized that Ruth as a novella, a type of didactic narrative that is designed to make a point or teach a lesson.[15] Most interpreters correctly understand the lesson to be that Ruth is an ideal convert to Judaism who ultimately becomes the ancestor of the royal house of David. Such a lesson challenges the prohibition in Deut 23:4-7 against admitting an Ammonite or a Moabite to the congregation of Israel. Many also incorrectly believe that Ruth challenges Ezra's and Nehemiah's prohibitions of marriage to Gentile women (Ezra 9–10; Neh 13:13-31).

Analysis of the literary form of Ruth facilitates an understanding of its theological outlook. The formal structure of the narrative is relatively simple insofar as it includes four basic episodes that stand as sub-units within the larger structure of the text.[16] Ruth 1:1-22 constitutes the first episode in this text which relates the return of Naomi and Ruth to Judah following the deaths of their husbands in Moab. The sub-unit includes Ruth's emphatic statement in Ruth 1:16-17 that she will become a part of Naomi's people, accept her G-d, and live out the rest of her life with Naomi. Ruth's statement thereby confirms her intention to become a part of Israel by converting to Judaism and living as a Jew in the land of Israel. Ruth 2:1-23 constitutes the second episode, which relates Ruth's initial encounter with Boaz while gleaning in his fields with the other poor of the land. Ruth 3:1-18 is the third episodic sub-unit, which portrays her evolving relationship with Boaz in which she spends the night with him. Ruth 4:1-22 constitutes the final episode, which recounts the marriage of Ruth and Boaz and the birth of their son, Obed, the father of Jesse and the grandfather of David. The concluding element of the narrative indicates that Ruth's conversion to Judaism and her parentage of the Davidic line are key concerns of the book. The formal structure of the book may be portrayed as follows:

Account of Ruth's Conversion to Judaism by Marriage to Boaz
   I.   Episode One: Ruth's Declaration of Intent to Become
        Part of Israel   1:1-22
  II.   Episode Two: Ruth's Initial Encounter with Boaz   2:1-23
 III.   Episode Three: Ruth's Relationship with Boaz   3:1-18
  IV.   Episode Four: Ruth's Marriage to Boaz and Birth of Obed   4:1-22

Ruth's conversion to Judaism and her acceptance by the people of Beth Lehem are key elements of the narrative, but the role that Ruth plays in the inner-biblical debate concerning marriage to foreigners and conversion to Judaism must be taken into consideration. Interpreters recognize Ruth's intertextual relationship with Gen 38, which recounts Tamar's successful attempt to produce a son by her father-in-law, Judah, following the deaths of his three half-Canaanite sons to whom Tamar was successively married.[17] The narrative does not say so, but many interpreters presume Tamar to be a Canaanite and argue that Gen 38 is concerned with the acceptance of foreign women in Judah.[18] Such a conclusion is unwarranted, however, insofar as the text is silent concerning Tamar's identity. The deaths of Judah's sons, born to his Canaanite wife, point to an interest in establishing an Israelite/Judean line for Judah, much as the narratives in Gen 12; 20; 26; and 34 point to a concern with the potential roles of foreigners, such as Egyptians, Philistines, and Canaanites, as ancestors of the people of Israel. The marriage of Tamar, first to Judah's older sons and then to Judah himself, resolves the narrative tension of the text by ensuring that Judah's line is not Canaanite. Ruth, on the other hand, reworks the basic motifs of the Tamar narrative and the ambiguity of Tamar's status to state unequivocally that Ruth is a foreigner and to affirm both her conversion to Judaism and her acceptance in Judah. Ruth thereby enters into intertextual dialog with Gen 38 to shift the concern from the question of the integrity of Judah's—and therefore David's—ancestral line to a concern with the acceptance of a foreign woman as a bona fide convert among the Jewish people. If Tamar's status is ambiguous, Ruth's is not, and Ruth is accepted despite her foreign and Moabite origins.

The interest in Ruth's status as a foreign and specifically Moabite convert to Judaism is evident in its textual interrelationship with Deut 23:4-7, which prohibits the acceptance of Moabites and Ammonites as a part of Israel and justifies the ban by pointing to their hostility to Israel during the wilderness period, and Ezra 9–10 and Neh 13, which relate the rejection by Ezra and Nehemiah of foreign women in the post-exilic Jewish community. Other relevant texts include Deut 7:1-6, which bans intermarriage with the Canaanite nations; Num 25:1-9, which relates Israel's apostasy with Moabite and Midianite women at Baal Peor; and Isa 56:1-8, which allows foreigners to become a part of Israel if they will observe the covenant, most notably Shabbat.

Many contemporary interpreters argue that Ruth was written to counter the hostility to foreigners allegedly expressed in these texts, contending instead that Israel should accept foreigners in keeping with the teachings of Deutero-Isaiah, who calls for Israel to be a light to the nations.[19] Such a contention is in keeping with Christianity's own sense of mission, which calls for active proselytizing among all the nations of the world to bring them to Christ. Standing in the background is the long-standing anti-Semitic charge that Jews are hostile to Gentiles, a change which originated in Egypt during the Greco-Roman period when Jews declined to abandon their distinctive traditions and observances to assimilate into the larger gentile world.[20] The charge was reinforced by the failure of the Jewish revolts against Rome in 66–74, 114–117, and 132–135 CE, events which prompted tremendous Roman backlash against Jews as hostile to the empire. Such charges continued to be characteristic of Christian Europe from late antiquity, throughout the Middle Ages, and well into modern times, with Christian authorities appealing to them as rationales for laws restricting Jewish religious, economic, and social activities (including intermarriage between Christians and Jews and the conversion of Christians to Judaism).[21]

The underlying charge of Jewish hostility to Gentiles plays an important role in such interpretations of Ruth, but the issue is far more nuanced than a single-minded preoccupation with marriage to Gentiles would suggest. The inclusion of Ruth in the Tanak together with Deuteronomy and Ezra–Nehemiah indicates that an inter-textual dialog must take place between these books, whether or not they were written with such dialog in mind. Ruth's unequivocal acceptance of YHWH as her G-d and her willingness to become a full member of the people of Judah (or Israel) must emerge as a key concern in this dialog. When read in relation to Deut 23:4-7 and Ezra 9–10; Neh 13, two facets of this dialog become clear.

It is clear that Ruth challenges the position of Deut 23:4-7 concerning the ban against admitting Moabites (and perhaps also Ammonites) to the Jewish community. And yet it is not clear that Deuteronomy calls for the programmatic prohibition of foreigners. Deuteronomy 23:8-9 permits the admission of Edomites and Egyptians after three generations. Throughout the book, Deuteronomy maintains that foreigners or gērîm are permitted to live in Israel and accorded proper justice and mercy (for example, Deut 10:18-19; 14:29; 24:17). Deuteronomy 7:1-6 prohibits intermarriage between Jews and the seven Canaanite nations because they will become a source of idolatry in Israel, although Deuteronomy never makes clear whether such marriages are permitted to such foreigners who became a part of Israel. The above example indicates that Edomites and Egyptians could become a part of Israel, and Deut 21:10-14 specifies the procedure by which a foreign woman who was captured by Israel in war could become the wife of an Israelite and therefore a part of Israel. A fully developed notion of conversion to Judaism does not appear in Deuteronomy, but the treatment of gērîm, "foreigners," in Deuteronomy and elsewhere in biblical literature points to the fact that foreigners could become a part of Israel. Examples of such a notion include the stipulations that one law applies to both indigenous Israelites and gērîm (for example, Exod 12:48-49; Num 9:14; Ezek 14:7); the example of Rahab, the woman from Jericho who together with her family became a part of Israel (Josh 6:25); or Isa 56:1-8, which makes it clear that foreigners and eunuchs who would join YHWH are expected to abide by the terms of the covenant, particularly observance of Shabbat. In such cases, recognition of YHWH as G-d would be an important part of the conditions by which such acceptance would be possible. The book of Ruth portrays the means by which such an early form of conversion would take place.

When Ruth is read in relation to the prohibition of intermarriages to foreigners in Ezra 9–10 and Neh 13, a similar set of considerations comes into play. The reference to Nehemiah's opposition to marriages with foreign women in Neh 13:23-28 makes it clear that such women retained their foreign identities, viz., they continued to adhere to their own languages and traditions; they did not accept the G-d of Israel nor did they become a part of Israel. The passage cites both the above-cited prohibition in Deut 7:1-6 against marrying foreigners from the seven Canaanite nations, as well as the example of Solomon, whose marriages to foreign women prompted him to turn away from YHWH (1 Kgs 11:1-13). In both of these cases, the adherence of the foreigners to their own gods and the threat that they would then lead Israel into idolatry become the paramount concern behind the prohibitions of Ezra and Nehemiah against intermarriage. Although Ezra–Nehemiah stipulates no procedure for conversion of a foreigner to Judaism, there is no indication in the book that foreigners who adhere to YHWH were an issue. Again, the book of Ruth steps in to fill the gap by specifying how a foreigner would become a part of Israel, specifically by swearing adherence to YHWH and living as part of the nation of Israel as Ruth does in Ruth 1:16-18. Furthermore, Ruth is also in dialog with Num 25:1-9, which portrays the apostasy of the men of Israel with the women of Moab. Rather than viewing Moabite women monolithically as a source of apostasy, Ruth counters the image of Num 25:1-9 by stipulating that Moabite women can adhere to YHWH.

In sum, the book of Ruth points to some key theological issues. It points to the principle of dialog in biblical literature, insofar as Ruth can challenge or support the views of other biblical writings. On the one hand, Ruth challenges the notions in Num 25:1-9 and Deut 23:4-7 that Moabites cannot become a part of Israel because of their inherent idolatry and their record of oppression of Israel. The Bible does not speak consistently on this issue, but presents its readers with disagreement among its constituent books. Such a model insures that readers see both sides of an issue which must be taken into account when making decisions on such matters. On the other hand, Ruth steps in to fill some of the gaps noted above in Deuteronomy and Ezra–Nehemiah on how foreigners, especially foreign women, become a part of Israel. In this respect, Ruth makes it clear that it is possible for a foreigner to become a part of Israel, and it specifies conditions, specifically adherence to YHWH and identification with the nation of Israel.

4. *The Book of Lamentations*

The book of Lamentations is read on the Jewish observance of Tisha b'Av or the Ninth of Av, the traditional day of mourning in the Jewish calendar. Tisha b'Av commemorates the fall of both Solomon's Temple and the Second Temple as well as other catastrophes in Jewish history, such as the expulsion of Jews from Spain in 1492 by King Ferdinand and Queen Isabella and the Chimielnitzki massacres in Poland and Ukraine in 1648.[22] According to Talmudic tradition, Jeremiah was the author of Lamentations (cf. 2 Chr 35:25; *b. Baba Batra* 15a).

Lamentations employs the dirge or Qinah (Hebrew, *qînâ*) form, which typically appears in literature of mourning.[23] The dirge is characterized by a metrical 3/2 pattern in which each bi-colon includes three heavy beats in the first half followed by two heavy beats in the second. Such a metrical pattern likely accompanied a limping dance or processional march that would have been employed at times of liturgical mourning for a dead fertility god, such as Tammuz, Baal, or others, in anticipation of his return from the underworld to the world of the living at the onset of the rainy season (see 1 Kgs 18). Ancient Judah and Israel would not have venerated pagan deities, but the Dirge could easily have played a role in mourning rituals during the weeks prior to Rosh ha-Shanah and Sukkot, which marked the onset of the rainy season. Since the destruction of the Second Temple, mourning for the loss of the Temple is observed during this period. Lamentations 1–4 also employs the acrostic form, an artistic device employed in Hebrew poetry, in which each stanza begins with a successive letter of the Hebrew alphabet. The dirges in Lam 1; 2; and 4 each begin with the exclamation, *'êkâ*, "alas!" "how!" which frequently gives expression to mourning or alarm (see 2 Kgs 6:15; Isa 1:21; Jer 48:17; cf. 2 Sam 1:19; Jer 2:21; 9:18; Mic 2:4; Qoh 2:16).

Modern scholars do not accept the claim that Jeremiah is the author of the book.[24] Lamentations itself would have originated in mourning rituals for the loss of Solomon's Temple in 587/6 BCE insofar as it appears to be based in part on the experience of those who were in the city of Jerusalem at the time of the Babylonian siege and destruction. Such rituals appear elsewhere in biblical literature. Jeremiah 41:5 indicates that eighty men came to Jerusalem from Samaria or Shechem with their beards shaved to mourn for the loss of the Temple immediately prior to the assassination of the Babylonian governor of Judah, Gedaliah ben Ahikam ben Shaphan in 582 BCE. Zechariah 7:5 also mentions fast days and laments for the loss of the Jerusalem Temple (cf. Zech 8:19). The writings of Second Isaiah appear to presuppose Lamentations. Lamentations 4:15 is cited in Isa 52:11; the Bat Zion or Daughter Zion figure is prominent in both; and the depiction of Zion's comforter in Isa 40:1; 49:13; 51:19; 51:12; and 54:11 appears to presuppose Lam 1.[25]

The macro-structure of Lamentations includes five dirges, which constitute the five chapters of the book. Each dirge emphasizes a particular character, including the city of Jerusalem personified as the woman Bat Zion or Daughter Zion in Lam 1 and 2; an anonymous man, perhaps based on a royal or priestly figure who speaks on behalf of the Judean or Jerusalemite community in Lam 3; and the community itself in Lam 4 and 5. The five dirges take the reader or the liturgy through the expression of mourning and suffering from the standpoint of the personified city of Jerusalem, through the expression of the city's representative, and finally through the people to culminate in appeals for restoration. The book may be characterized as a mourning liturgy for the restoration of the Temple. The macro-structure of the book would appear as follows:

Mourning Liturgy for the Restoration of the Temple

Lamentations 1 is a communal dirge over the suffering of the city of Jerusalem which focuses on the plight of the city and appeals to YHWH for relief.[26] It begins with the typical opening cry, *'êkâ*, "alas!" "how!," to introduce the pattern of mourning for the depiction of the abandoned and ravaged city. Following the opening cry, the dirge comprises two major sub-units. The first sub-unit in vv. 1-11a is a heart-rending description of Jerusalem's misery in which the narrator portrays Jerusalem as Bat Zion, Daughter Zion, a desolate widow who weeps over the exile of her children and the downfall of the city of Jerusalem. Verses 5 and 8 refer to her transgressions, which brought about the disaster. Verse 9b appeals to YHWH to see her misery so that YHWH may take action to deliver her, and v. 10b reminds YHWH directly how the foreign nations have invaded the Temple which YHWH had expressly denied. The second sub-unit in vv. 11b-22 portrays Jerusalem's own lament. The first segment in vv. 11b-16 constitutes Bat Zion's first-person address to YHWH and to passersby concerning her current condition. She appeals for YHWH to act against her enemies in v. 11b, and in v. 14 she refers to her offenses which have caused YHWH to punish her so. The second segment in v. 17 describes how Zion spreads out her hands in mourning while YHWH summons enemies against Jacob. The third segment in vv. 18-22 returns to Bat Zion's first-person address to YHWH in which she acknowledges her guilt in vv. 18, 20, and 22, but appeals to YHWH in vv. 20 and 22 to punish the enemies who have brought about her suffering.

The dirge in Lam 2 gives expression to communal mourning by reversing the typical portrayal of YHWH's actions on behalf of Israel to portray YHWH instead as the cause of Jerusalem's suffering.[27] Again, the dirge begins with the typical 'êkâ, "alas!" "how!," in v. 1. The dirge proceeds in four sub-units. The first, in vv. 1-10, begins with a third-person description of YHWH's actions against Jerusalem, again portrayed as the young woman, Bat Zion. Such a portrayal highlights Jerusalem's suffering as a victim of war. YHWH becomes the enemy, rejecting the altar and the sanctuary and handing over the city to the attackers as Bat Zion and the women of Jerusalem sit in silence on the ground in dejection and mourning. The poet employs a first-person perspective in the second sub-unit in vv. 11-16 to lament over the destruction of the city in a second-person address to Bat Zion that expresses pathos and identification with her suffering. The narrator then turns to a third-person affirmation of YHWH's actions followed by calls to Bat Zion to mourn in the third sub-unit in vv. 17-19, emphasizing how YHWH accomplished purposes decided upon long ago (cf. Deut 28:15-68, which expresses curses if Israel fails to observe YHWH's instructions). The last sub-unit in vv. 20-22 is a direct address by Bat Zion to YHWH in which she accuses YHWH of having brought about her destruction and suffering. She illustrates her accusations with depictions of women forced to eat their own babies, priests and prophets lying dead in the Temple, and dead old and young people lying about the city.

Lamentations 3 again expresses a communal dirge, but this time emphasizes the role of an anonymous man in giving expression to mourning.[28] Some interpreters argue that the man may be based on a royal figure,[29] but a priest would make a more likely representative of the people in their address to YHWH, particularly since Lam 4:20 refers to the capture of YHWH's anointed. Lamentations 3 lacks the introductory 'êkâ, "alas!" "how!," and proceeds instead to a four-part address that culminates in appeals for YHWH's assistance. The first sub-unit in vv. 1-20 is a first-person complaint uttered by the man, who identifies himself as one who has suffered affliction. He speaks of YHWH throughout in the third person as he describes in detail the suffering that he has endured at YHWH's hand. The second sub-unit in vv. 21-39 is once again a first-person expression by the man who expresses confidence in YHWH's righteousness and mercy. The man emphasizes his hope in YHWH's willingness to maintain ḥesed, "fidelity," to the relationship with Jerusalem. He acknowledges the sins of the city, but in keeping with Pentateuchal notions of covenant (for example, Deut 28–30) trusts in YHWH's forgiveness of those who turn to YHWH. The third sub-unit in vv. 40-48 therefore calls for the people to repent and subtly calls for YHWH's forgiveness by reminding YHWH that no forgiveness has yet been forthcoming. Verses 49-66 then conclude with a petition for help from YHWH, who has seen the atrocities and now acts to punish the culprits and deliver the city.

Lamentations 4 is a community dirge in which the people as a whole give expression to their suffering.[30] Again, the introductory 'êkâ, "alas!" "how!," opens the dirge, which then proceeds in four sub-units. The first sub-unit is a descriptive lament of the people over their suffering, although the first-person perspective of the sub-unit suggests that the anonymous man of Lam 3 may still be the speaker. Verses 11-16 describe YHWH's anger against the people in third-person language that does not identify speaker or addressee, but emphasizes the sins of the prophets and the priests as the cause of the city's downfall and suffering. A communal lament in vv. 17-20 in first person plural form expresses the people's suffering and hope in deliverance as well as the chase of the pursuers who ultimately captured the king. The dirge concludes in vv. 21-22 with appeals for Edom's punishment for sins which likely include complicity in Jerusalem's destruction (cf. Obadiah; Ps 137).

Finally, the last dirge in Lam 5 again constitutes a community complaint in which the people appeal to YHWH to take the people back.[31] Lamentations 5 lacks the introductory 'êkâ, "alas!" "how!," and instead presents a first person plural appeal for YHWH to remember the people, see their current suffering, and accept their return to YHWH. The final appeal for restoration emphasizes the permanence of YHWH's sovereignty in the world and recalls the days of the past when the relationship was first constituted.

Lamentations draws upon a long tradition of ancient Mesopotamian lament literature which aids in enabling interpreters to understand its function. It resembles the Sumerian laments over fallen cities, such as Ur, Nippur, Eridu, Uruk, Sumer, and so on, from the Isin-Larsa period (1950–1700 BCE), which functioned as apologia for the foundation of new ruling dynasties and capital cities in times of political transition.[32] Like Sumerian and later Mesopotamian mourning rituals that call for the restoration of Dumuzi or Tammuz in anticipation of the rainy season, Lamentations gives expression to suffering, but it anticipates restoration in the aftermath of suffering just as the Mesopotamian laments envision the restoration of the dead fertility god and the rise of a new dynasty following the collapse of the old.

Lamentations does not directly raise the question of theodicy, viz. the question of divine righteousness or power in the face of suffering. It does not challenge YHWH's righteousness for having brought the suffering about; it accepts the notion that Jerusalem suffered punishment as a consequence of wrongdoing against YHWH. But it focuses instead on the suffering of Bat Zion—and indeed, the people at large—in an effort to demand divine response to alleviate the misery of the victimized city and people. In this respect, it calls to mind YHWH's eternal covenant with Israel (for example, Gen 17; Exod 31), particularly the assertion that YHWH will restore Israel in the aftermath of punishment (Deut 30). By giving voice to such suffering and mourning, Lamentations lays the groundwork for the restoration of the Temple and the people of Jerusalem and Judah. Tod Linafelt argues that Lamentations is a form of survival literature that enables Judean readers to rebuild their identity as a nation in relationship with YHWH in the aftermath of the disaster.[33] Carleen Mandolfo points to the dialogical character of Lamentations by pointing to YHWH's abandonment of Jerusalem and demanding divine response.[34] Lamentations continues the dialog with YHWH—much like the complaint psalms in relation to disaster—and thereby provides a model for continuing the relationship between YHWH and the nation.

5. *The Book of Qoheleth*

The book of Qoheleth is read on Shabbat as part of the liturgy for the festival of Sukkot, "Tabernacles, Booths," which is celebrated in the autumn beginning on the fifteenth day of Nisan shortly after Rosh ha-Shanah and Yom Kippur. Sukkot commemorates the conclusion of the fruit harvest and the onset of the rainy season in the seasonal cycle of the land of Israel. It also commemorates the period of wilderness wandering following the Exodus from Egypt in relation to the historical memory of Judaism.[35] Sukkot (*sukkōt*) refers to the temporary dwellings that ancient Israelites lived in while out in the fields during the concluding fruit harvest of the agricultural year as well as to the temporary dwellings that the people would have used while journeying through the wilderness. Because the book of Qoheleth reflects on the transitory nature of life, it is associated with the festival named after the transitory life that Israel led at the concluding harvest and during the wilderness wanderings. The book of Qoheleth examines the question of human mortality and concludes that because all humans must ultimately come to the grave, human existence is ultimately futile. Life is best lived and enjoyed when it is available without concern for what is to come beyond the grave.

The superscription of Qoheleth in Qoh 1:1 identifies the work as "the words of Qohelet son of David, King in Jerusalem." The Hebrew term *qōhelet* is not a proper name. Instead, it is a feminine participle that refers to "one who gathers" or "one who assembles" a group, presumably as an audience for the discourses presented in the book or perhaps for some other instructional, liturgical, or public occasion. The term Ecclesiastes (*ekklēsiastēs*), by which the book is sometimes known, is a Greek translation of *qōhelet* employed in the Septuagint version of the book. The reason for the feminine form of the Hebrew term is uncertain, but Jewish tradition identifies Qoheleth as Solomon, due to the references to "the son of David" and "King in Jerusalem." Rabbinic tradition considers Qoheleth to be a presentation of Solomon's reflections on life in his old age (*b. Sanhedrin* 20b; *Song Rabbah* 1:1), although *b. Baba Batra* 15a attributes the book to Hezekiah and his colleagues, apparently indicating that they edited the book.

Modern critical scholarship has raised important issues in the diachronic and theological interpretation of the book.[36] Qoheleth is identified as an example of the royal testament or royal autobiography, a typical Egyptian and Mesopotamian wisdom genre, in which a king or other royal figure summarizes his reflections on his life as a legacy or testament to be passed on to his descendants, heirs, or successors.[37] Modern scholars do not ascribe Qoheleth to Solomon, and instead date the book to the Persian period in the sixth to fourth centuries BCE or to the Hellenistic period in the fourth through second centuries BCE.[38] Given Qoheleth's engagement with skeptical philosophy, the Hellenistic period appears to be the better choice.

Key issues in modern research on Qoheleth have been the identification of its formal literary structure and the articulation of its arguments and ideas. Scholars are divided concerning the literary structure of the book, which provides few clues concerning its organization.[39] Many follow variations of an initial proposal by Addison Wright, who points to the role of formulaic language, particularly catch phrases, such as "vanity and a striving after wind" that mark eight sub-units in Qoh 1:12—6:9; "not find out/who can find out," which marks four sub-units in Qoh 6:10—8:17; and "do not know/no knowledge," which marks six sub-units in Qoh 9:1—11:6.[40] Other features of the book include the superscription in Qoh 1:1; the motto in Qoh 1:2 and again in Qoh 12:8; an introductory reflection on human labor in Qoh 1:3-11; a concluding discourse concerning youth and old age in Qoh 11:7—12:7; and an epilog in Qoh 12:9-14. The formal literary structure appears as follows:[41]

The Royal Testament of Qoheleth: Discourses on the Meaning of Human Existence

I.	Superscription: Words of Qoheleth ben David, King in Jerusalem	1:1
II.	Presentation of Qoheleth's Discourses	1:2—12:14
	A. Motto: Vanity of Vanities	1:2
	B. Qoheleth's discourses	1:3—12:7
	1. introductory reflection on the futility of human labor	1:3-11
	2. examination of life	1:12—6:9
	a. Qoheleth's situation and task	1:12-18
	b. reflection on pleasure	2:1-11
	c. reflection on wisdom and folly	2:12-17
	d. reflection on human labor	2:18-26
	e. reflections on labor and time	3:1—4:6
	f. reflection concerning "two"	4:7-16
	g. summary instruction and reflection	4:17—6:9
	3. conclusions concerning life	6:10—11:6
	a. introduction concerning divine causality and human impotence	6:10-12
	b. inability of humans to find out what is good	7:1—8:17
	1) instruction to enjoy the good	7:1-14
	2) instruction concerning illusive nature of right and wrong	7:15-24
	3) instruction concerning women	7:25-29
	4) instruction concerning the wise man	8:1-17
	c. inability of humans to know wisdom	9:1—11:6
	1) introductory reflection on human inability to know wisdom	9:1-6
	2) instruction concerning enjoyment of life	9:7-10

The formal structure of Qoheleth points to several important dimensions of the teachings conveyed in the book. First, the two variations of the motto of the book, "'vanity of vanities,' said Qoheleth, '(vanity of vanities,) all is vanity,'" appear at both the beginning of Qoheleth's discourses in Qoh 1:2 and immediately following the conclusion of his discourses in Qoh 12:8. The motto expresses Qoheleth's basic conclusion concerning the futility of human endeavor given the ultimate reality of death and therefore the existential context in which human life and effort must exist. The discourses themselves in Qoh 1:3—12:7 present a detailed examination of life that illustrates the motto of the book as well as Qoheleth's conclusions and instructions about how to live life in light of this reality. Interpreters universally acknowledge that Qoheleth calls upon its readers to seize the opportunity to live and enjoy life to its fullest. Qoholeth also calls upon readers to do so responsibly with an eye to justice and avoidance of that which is wrong or counterproductive, because life, particularly youth, is fleeting and old age comes upon one all to quickly in the passage of time. Based upon the presentation of Qoheleth's discourse, the epilog calls upon readers to emulate Qoheleth's pursuit of wisdom despite the ultimate futility of life and to fear G-d while doing so.

Although Qoheleth gives full play to intellectual skepticism concerning the meaning of human life, its conclusions are ultimately in keeping with the teachings of both Proverbs and Job. Like Proverbs, Qoheleth posits divine order, justice, and righteousness in the world, and human beings would do well to understand that order and to live in relation to it. Like Job, Qoheleth posits that it is difficult for human beings to understand that order, and human beings are justified in employing their intellects to raise critical questions about it in their quest to understand. Also like Job, Qoheleth posits that human beings must accept their limitations in understanding G-d and the world, but it nevertheless calls upon human beings to live life in the expectation that it is not futile despite our inability to understand.

Qoheleth's examination of the futility of human life in the face of death clearly presents important insights concerning the human opportunity and obligation to engage life and the world in which we live. The experience of death and disaster in the world, whether at the personal or the national level, accentuates these teachings. Qoheleth's teachings concerning the transitory nature of life and the uncertainty resulting from the chances that life and security might end at any time point to the realized and continuing threats to morality and stability that exist in our world. In the end, Qoheleth demands that human beings take responsibility for their lives and actions in the world in a manner not unlike that presupposed throughout the Torah and the Prophets.

6. The Book of Esther

The book of Esther is read on the festival of Purim to celebrate the deliverance of the Jewish people from extermination by the Persian empire during the reign of King Ahasuerus or Xerxes I (486–465 BCE). The book relates the story of how Esther, a beautiful Jewish woman who was selected by King Ahasuerus to be his bride, together with her uncle Mordecai, saved the entire Jewish people from destruction in a plot devised by a Persian government officer, Haman the Aggagite.[42]

Esther has always been treated as a particularly controversial book in Judaism because it never mentions G-d.[43] Other grounds for controversy include Esther's intermarriage with a gentile monarch, the general absence of traditional Jewish observance, and the role of the Jewish community in the slaughter of some 75,000 members of Haman's family. Rabbinic tradition notes disagreement concerning the status of the book as sacred scripture. Rab Judah questioned whether the book should be accepted as sacred scripture, but he ultimately accepted it as sacred, although he maintained that it was composed to be recited and not written (b. Megillah 7a). Levi ben Samuel and R. Huna ben Hiyya likewise questioned the status of the book, but were reproved by Rab Judah (b. Sanhedrin 100a). Medieval Jewish exegetes went to great efforts to demonstrate G-d's involvement in the Esther narrative.[44] Modern interpreters point to problems that challenge the historical character of the book, for example, a Jewish woman could never have become queen of Persia, Ahasuerus was not the drunken fool portrayed in the book, and no record of Esther's predecessor Vashti, who was dismissed by Ahasuerus when she refused to present herself before Ahasuerus's drunken cronies, has ever been preserved. Because of its association with Purim and the general frivolity of the day, modern interpreters recognize Esther's literary character as a novella that is designed to entertain rather than as a historical work that is designed to record historical events.

Despite its novelistic character and its failure to mention G-d, Esther is a book of sacred scripture that demands serious theological interpretation. The modern experience of the Shoah points precisely to the theological importance of the book insofar as it depicts divine absence at a time when the Jewish people is threatened with extermination by the government of one of the most advanced and powerful nations of the time. In the face of the absence of G-d at a time of extreme crisis, Esther makes a key theological point, viz., human beings are obligated to defeat evil in the world when G-d fails to do so. Such responsibility for human action applies to everyone and anyone no matter what their status or level of religious observance might be. Neither Esther nor Mordecai appears to be particularly religious, and they do not seem to be major leaders within the Jewish community. Nevertheless, they illustrate an important point, viz., anyone, no matter how unlikely, might find themselves in a position to act at a time of great crisis in which everything is at stake, and everyone, no matter how unlikely, is obligated to do so. Esther and Mordecai could be anyone, and yet they were the only persons in a position to do something to stop the annihilation of the entire Jewish people.

The literary character of Esther as a novella, with its development of plot, characterization, and its exaggeration and hyperbole in the portrayal of events enables the book to convey its teachings.[45] Interpreters generally recognize that the literary structure of the book is constituted by its sequence of episodes. Nevertheless, there is little general agreement concerning the definition of the individual episodes within the narrative structure,[46] although the various temporal formulae in the book, including specific dates and more generalized temporal notations, appear to carry the episodic structure and plot of the book. The formal literary character of Esther appears as follow:

Novella Concerning Esther's and Mordecai's Deliverance
of the Jewish People from Destruction by the Persian Empire
I.	Narrative Introduction: Ahasuerus's Banquet to Display his Power	1:1-9
II.	The Deposing of Vashti as Queen for Defying the King's Command	1:10-22
III.	Esther's Selection as Queen in an Empire-wide Beauty Contest	2:1-20
IV.	Mordecai's Discovery of a Plot against the King	2:21-23
V.	Haman's Anger at Mordecai's Refusal to Bow to Him	3:1-6
VI.	Haman's Plot to Exterminate the Jews authorized by Ahasuerus	3:7-11
VII.	Mordecai Calls upon Esther to Act to Thwart Haman's Decree	3:12—4:17
VIII.	Esther's Audience with the King to Invite Him and Haman to a Banquet	5:1-14
IX.	Ahasuerus's Decision to Honor Mordecai	6:1-14
X.	Esther's Exposing of Haman's Plot at the Banquet	7:1-10
XI.	The King's Decree to Countermand Haman's Orders	8:1-17
XII.	Narrative Conclusion: The Deliverance of the Jews and the Institution of the Festival of Purim	9:1—10:3

The formal literary structure of Esther presents a plot that conveys Esther's and Mordecai's roles in the deliverance of the Jewish people from destruction in a plot engineered by the Persian government minister Haman. But the exaggerated portrayal of events throughout the plot of Esther also plays a key role in building the narrative tension and the resolution of the book. The narrative introduction in Esth 1:1-9 introduces Ahasuerus as the king of Persia who would display his absolute power by holding a banquet lasting 180 days. Nevertheless, Ahasuerus appears as a drunken fool throughout the narrative, which contradicts his image. The second scene in Esth 1:10-22 portrays a diminished king whose absolute power is employed to depose his wife Vashti, who refuses his request to appear before his drunken friends at the banquet. The third scene in Esth 2:1-20 portrays Esther's selection as the next queen in an unlikely national beauty contest which runs counter to the Persian royal practice of marrying only within a select group of Persian noble families. The fourth scene in Esth 2:21-23 emphasizes the important role of chance when Esther's uncle Mordecai overhears a plot against the king and saves Ahasuerus's life by reporting the matter to the authorities. The fifth scene in Esth 3:1-6 depicts Haman's self-destructive vanity when Mordecai refuses to bow to him, prompting Haman's plot to destroy the entire Jewish people. The sixth scene in Esth 3:7-11 details Ahasuerus's approval of Haman's plot to exterminate the Jews in the Persian empire, not as the result of any serious discussion of the effects or wisdom of such an act, but as a result of Haman's bribe. The seventh scene in Esth 3:12—4:17 portrays Mordecai's conversation with Esther in which he convinces her that she must act to save the Jewish people because she is the only person able to do so. The eighth scene in Esth 5:1-14 depicts Esther's audience with Ahasuerus, in which she invites the king and Haman to a banquet despite the fact that she could have been executed if the king refused to see her. The ninth scene in Esth 6:1-14 recounts Ahasuerus's decision to honor Mordecai for saving his life after a chance reading of the royal chronicles. The tenth scene in Esth 7:1-10 portrays Esther's exposing of Haman's plot to Ahasuerus. Rather than making his decision on any rational basis, Haman's accidental fall onto Esther's couch at the banquet convinces the king that Haman has attempted to assault his wife. The eleventh scene in Esth 8:1-17 presents the king's decree to countermand Haman's orders to destroy the Jewish people. Finally, the narrative conclusion to the book in Esth 9:1—10:3 portrays the deliverance of the Jewish people when they are granted the right to defend themselves against their enemies as well as the institution of the festival of Purim.

Although the plot of this narrative seems incredible and even ludicrous, the modern experience of the Shoah—and prior to that the history of persecution and government-sponsored assaults against the Jewish people from antiquity through modern times—has demonstrated that such a scenario is not as incredible as perhaps Esther's authors and readers might have imagined it to be.[47] Several key elements emerge during the course of the narrative presentation of the book.

The first element is Mordecai's statement to Esther in Esth 4:13-14 when she is reluctant to act, "Do not imagine that you, of all the Jews, will escape with your life by being in the king's palace. On the contrary, if you keep silent in this crisis, relief and deliverance will come to the Jews from another quarter, while you and your father's house will perish. And who knows, perhaps you have attained to royal position for just such a crisis." As an assimilated Jewish woman, Esther is an unlikely heroine, but she is in a position to act and like any human being therefore has the responsibility to do so.

The second element is the identity of the primary protagonists in the narrative, Esther, Mordecai, and Haman, who are crucial to the narrative's didactic purposes. Each of these figures is constructed to reprise the failure of King Saul, the first king of Israel, to obey G-d's instruction through the prophet Samuel to kill the Amalekite king Agag, and thereby to destroy an implacable enemy of Israel who would rise again and again in attempts to destroy the entire Jewish people (1 Sam 15). As a result of his failure, Saul lost his right to serve as king of Israel and later died as a suicide in 1 Sam 31 as his people were defeated by the Philistines. On introducing Mordecai, Esth 2:5 identifies him as "the son of Jair son of Shimei son of Kish a Benjaminite," which recalls the identity of King Saul son of Kish of the tribe of Benjamin in 1 Sam 9:1-2. As Mordecai's niece, Esther would share his ancestry and identification with King Saul. On introducing Haman to the narrative, Esth 3:1 identifies him as the son of Hammedatha the Agagite, which of course reprises the character of Agag the Amalekite king from 1 Sam 15. Exodus 17:8-15 and Deut 25:17-19 identify the Amalekites as a people who are cursed because they attacked Israel from the rear in the wilderness when they were faint and weary. Later Jewish tradition identifies Amalek as the quintessential enemy who will stop at nothing to destroy Israel and must themselves be destroyed before they succeed in doing so.[48] By identifying Mordecai and Esther with Saul and Haman with Agag in this manner, the book of Esther places its protagonists in the same positions occupied by Saul and Agag in 1 Sam 15. But this time there is a different result, viz., Mordecai and Esther take action against Haman and his plot and in doing so save the entire Jewish people from annihilation by a powerful gentile government.

Finally, the absence of G-d in the narrative must be recognized as the quintessential theological issue of the book. It is so often the case in the Shoah and other atrocities and disasters in human experience that the presence of G-d is difficult or impossible to discern. Indeed, the question of the absence or hiddenness of G-d is an issue that appears throughout the Bible, especially in books such as Isaiah, Psalms, Job, and the Song of Songs. In the face of divine absence, Esther teaches that human beings must take the responsibility to act when confronted with evil. Divine absence hardly portends divine judgment, particularly in Esther. Rather, divine absence or hiddenness functions as a call for humans to act as responsible partners with G-d in creation.

NOTES

[1] See, "The Five Scrolls," *EncJud* 14:1057–58.
[2] For discussion of the Song of Songs, see especially Roland E. Murphy, *Wisdom Literature: Job, Proverbs, Ruth, Canticles, Ecclesiastes, Esther* (FOTL 13; Grand Rapids: Eerdmans, 1981), 98–124; idem, *The Song of Songs* (Hermeneia; Minneapolis: Fortress Press, 1990); Marvin

Pope, *Song of Songs* (AB 19; Garden City: Doubleday, 1977); Tremper Longman III, *The Song of Songs* (NICOT; Grand Rapids: Eerdmans, 2001); J. Cheryl Exum, *Song of Songs: A Commentary* (OTL: Louisville: Westminster John Knox, 2005).

[3] See Herbert Danby, *The Mishnah* (Oxford: Oxford University Press, 1933), 781–82.

[4] For a recent survey of the discussion, see Exum, *Song of Songs*, 63–67.

[5] See *HALOT*, 963. The term is also known from Greek as *paradeisos*, "paradise."

[6] *HALOT*, 80.

[7] See Exum, *Song of Songs*, 47–63.

[8] Michael V. Fox, *Song of Songs and the Ancient Egyptian Love Songs* (Madison: University of Wisconsin Press, 1999).

[9] Yitschak Sefati, *Love Songs in Sumerian Literature: Critical Edition of the Dumuzi-Inanna Songs* (Ramat Gan: Bar Ilan University Press, 1998).

[10] Phyllis Trible, *G-d and the Rhetoric of Sexuality* (OBT; Philadelphia: Fortress Press, 1978), 144–65; for discussion of the literary structure of Song of Songs, see especially Exum, *Song of Songs*, 37–42.

[11] See Longman, *Song of Songs*, 212–13; Murphy, *Song of Songs*, 191–92.

[12] Cf. David M. Carr, *The Erotic Word: Sexuality, Spirituality, and the Bible* (Oxford: Oxford University Press, 2002), who argues that the Bible affirms the erotic as a primary expression of the human relationship with G-d and human vocation in the world.

[13] Cf. Trible, *G-d and the Rhetoric of Sexuality*, 144, who argues that Gen 2–3 provides the key for reading Song of Songs. Her analysis of Gen 2–3 appears on pp. 72–143.

[14] For discussion of the role of Ruth in Judaism, see especially Moshe Weinfeld and Alexander Rofé, "Ruth, Book of," *EncJud* 14:518–24.

[15] Kirsten Nielsen, *Ruth: A Commentary* (OTL; Louisville: Westminster John Knox, 1997), 5–8; Murphy, *Wisdom Literature*, 85–86; cf. Robert L. Hubbard, Jr., *The Book of Ruth* (NICOT; Grand Rapids: Eerdmans, 1988), 47–48; Jack M. Sasson, *Ruth: A New Translation with a Philological Commentary and Formalist-Folklorist Interpretation* (BibSem 10; Sheffield: Sheffield Academic, 1995), 197–216.

[16] Nielsen, *Ruth*, 1–5; contra Murphy, *Wisdom Literature*, 85.

[17] For example, Nielsen, *Ruth*, 8–17.

[18] For example, Nielsen, *Ruth*, 13–15.

[19] For example, Anna L. Grant-Henderson, *Inclusive Voices in Post-Exilic Judah* (Collegeville, MN: Liturgical, 2002).

[20] See Peter Schäfer, *Judeophobia: Attitudes toward the Jews in the Ancient World* (Cambridge, MA: Harvard University Press, 1997); Aryeh Kasher, *The Jews in Hellenistic and Roman Egypt: The Struggle for Equal Rights* (TSAJ 7; Tübingen: Mohr Siebeck, 1985) for discussion of the origins of anti-Semitism in Roman-period Egypt.

[21] For discussion of the history of anti-Semitism, see especially the essays published in Shmuel Almog, ed., *Antisemitism through the Ages* (Oxford: Pergamon, 1988); cf. Daniel Jonah Goldhagen, *A Moral Reckoning: The Role of the Catholic Church in the Holocaust and its Unfulfilled Duty of Repair* (New York: Knopf, 2002); James Carroll, *Constantine's Sword: The Church and the Jews: A History* (Boston: Houghton Mifflin, 2001).

[22] For discussion of the book of Lamentations, see Erhard S. Gerstenberger, *Psalms, Part 2, and Lamentations* (FOTL 15; Grand Rapids: Eerdmans, 2001), 465–76; Adele Berlin, *Lamentations: A Commentary* (OTL; Louisville: Westminster John Knox, 2002); Carleen Mandolfo, *Daughter Zion Talks Back to the Prophets* (Semeia Studies 58; Atlanta: Society of Biblical Literature, 2007); Tod Linafelt, *Surviving Lamentations: Catastrophe, Lament, and Protest in the Afterlife of a Biblical Book* (Chicago: University of Chicago, 2000).

[23] For discussion of the Dirge, see especially Erhard S. Gerstenberger, *Psalms, Part 1, with an Introduction to Cultic Poetry* (FOTL 14; Grand Rapids: Eerdmans, 1988), 10–11; idem, *Psalms, Part 2, and Lamentations*, 469–71. Note also the foundational study of dirge forms throughout the Hebrew Bible, Hedwig Jahnow, *Das hebräischen Leichenlied im Rahmen der Völkerdichtung* (BZAW 36; Giessen: Töpelmann, 1923). Jahnow, who wrote this work as a dissertation under the direction of Hermann Gunkel and later served on the faculty of Marburg University, was murdered by the Nazis at Theresienstadt because her father was Jewish.

[24] Berlin, *Lamentations*, 30–32.

[25] For discussion of Second Isaiah's intertextual relationship with Lamentations, see especially Patricia Tull Willey, *Remember the Former Things: The Recollection of Previous Texts in Second Isaiah* (SBLDS 161; Atlanta: Scholars Press, 1997).

[26] For discussion of Lam 1, see Gerstenberger, *Psalms, Part 2, and Lamentations*, 477–84.

[27] For discussion of Lam 2, see Gerstenberger, *Psalms, Part 2, and Lamentations*, 485–91.

[28] For discussion of Lam 3, see Gerstenberger, *Psalms, Part 2, and Lamentations*, 492–97.

[29] See Linafelt, *Surviving Lamentations*, 5–18, for discussion.

[30] See Gerstenberger, *Psalms, Part 2, and Lamentations*, 497–501.

[31] See Gerstenberger, *Psalms, Part 2, and Lamentations*, 501–5.

[32] For discussion of the relationship between Lamentations and the Sumerian City-Lament genre, see especially F. W. Dobbs-Allsopp, *Weep, O Daughter of Zion: A Study of the City-Lament Genre in the Hebrew Bible* (BibOr 44; Rome: Pontifical Biblical Institute, 1993), especially 30–96. See also Paul Wayne Ferris, Jr., *The Genre of Communal Lament in the Bible and the Ancient Near East* (SBLDS 127; Atlanta: Scholars Press, 1992).

[33] Linafelt, *Surviving Lamentations*, especially 1–34.

[34] Mandolfo, *Daughter Zion*, especially 55–77.

[35] For discussion of memory in Judaism and ancient Israel, see Yosef Hayim Yerushalmi, *Zakhor: Jewish History and Jewish Memory* (Seattle: University of Washington, 1982); Mark S. Smith, *The Memoirs of G-d: History, Memory, and the Experience of the Divine in Ancient Israel* (Minneapolis: Fortress Press, 2004).

[36] For discussion of Qoheleth, see James L. Crenshaw, *Old Testament Wisdom: An Introduction* (Louisville: Westminster John Knox, 1998), 116–39; idem, *Ecclesiastes: A Commentary* (OTL; Philadelphia: Westminster, 1987); Michael V. Fox, *A Time to Tear Down and a Time to Build Up: A Rereading of Ecclesiastes* (Grand Rapids: Eerdmans, 1999); Choon-Leong Seow, *Ecclesiastes* (AB 18C; Garden City: Doubleday, 1997); Thomas Krüger, *Qoheleth* (Hermeneia; Minneapolis: Fortress Press, 2004); Norbert L. Lohfink, *Qoheleth* (ContCom; Minneapolis: Fortress Press, 2003).

[37] Fox, *A Time to Tear Down*, 153–55; cf. the discussion of genre in Qoheleth by Murphy, *Wisdom Literature*, 129–31; Krüger, *Qoheleth*, 8–14.

[38] For discussion of the unity and authorship of Qoheleth, see especially Crenshaw, *Old Testament Wisdom*, 132–33; Krüger, *Qoheleth*, 14–27.

[39] For discussion of the form and literary structure of Qoheleth, see especially Fox, *A Time to Tear Down*, 147–53; Murphy, *Wisdom Literature*, 127–29; Crenshaw, *Old Testament Wisdom*, 128–32; Krüger, *Qoheleth*, 5–8.

[40] A. Wright, "The Riddle of the Sphinx: The Structure of the Book of Qoheleth," *CBQ* 30 (1968): 313–34; idem, "The Riddle of the Sphinx Revisited: Numerical Patterns in the Book of Qoheleth," *CBQ* 42 (1980): 38–51.

[41] See Murphy, *Wisdom Literature*, 128–29.

[42] For treatments of Esther, see especially Adele Berlin, *Esther* (JPS Bible Commentary; Philadelphia: Jewish Publication Society, 2001); Michael V. Fox, *Character and Ideology in the Book of Esther* (Grand Rapids: Eerdmans, 2001); Jon D. Levenson, *Esther: A Commentary* (OTL; Louisville: Westminster John Knox, 1997).

[43] For the following, see my "Absence of G-d and Human Responsibility in the Book of Esther," in *Reading the Hebrew Bible for a New Millennium: Form, Concept and Theological Perspective. Volume 2: Exegetical and Theological Studies*, ed. Wonil Kim et al. (SAC; Harrisburg: Trinity Press International, 2000), 264–75.

[44] See Barry Dov Wallfish, *Esther in Medieval Garb: Jewish Interpretation of the Book of Esther in the Middle Ages* (Albany: SUNY Press, 1993).

[45] For discussion of the genre of Esther, see W. Lee Humphreys, "A Life-Style for Diaspora: A Study of the Tales of Esther and Daniel," *JBL* 92 (1973): 211–23; idem, "The Story of Esther and Mordecai: An Early Jewish Novella," in *Saga, Legend, Tale, Novella, Fable: Narrative Forms in Old Testament Literature*, ed. George W. Coats (JSOTSup 35; Sheffield: Sheffield Academic, 1985), 97–113; cf. Fox, *Character and Ideology*, 141–42; Murphy, *Wisdom Literature*, 154–56.

[46] See Murphy, *Wisdom Literature*, 153, for a survey of opinion and his own proposal. For further discussion of Esther's literary character, plot, and narrative structure, see Fox, *Character and Ideology*, 153–63; Berlin, *Esther*, xv–xxxii; Levenson, *Esther*, 1–23.

[47] For discussion of anti-Semitism throughout history, see Almog, ed., *Antisemitism through the Ages*.

[48] For discussion of the issue of Amalek, see Zev Garber, "Deconstructing Theodicy and Amelekut: A Personal Apologia," in *Shoah: The Paradigmatic Genocide. Essay in Exegesis and Eisegesis* (Studies in the Shoah 7; Lanham, MD: University Press of America, 1994), 119–36.

F. DANIEL

The book of Daniel presents an eschatological scenario in which four major empires will emerge during the course of human history to threaten the righteous of the world. As part of its projected scenario, a figure called the Ancient of Days will arise to pass judgment against the wicked and establish eternal dominion on behalf of the righteous. Various Jewish sources consider Daniel to be a prophet, including Flavius Josephus (*Ant.* 10.11.7), the sectarians of the Judean Desert (4QFlor 2:4), and some rabbinic midrashic works (*Mekilta* 16; *Pesikta de Rab Kahana* 4:36b; *Seder Olam* 20). At the same time, Talmudic tradition views him as a righteous seer and sage (*b. Megillah* 3a; *b. Baba Batra* 94a) who forgot the "end" revealed to him (*Genesis Rabbah* 98:2) and who gave good counsel to Nebuchadnezzar, the Babylonian king who destroyed the Temple (*b. Baba Batra* 4a).[1] Daniel is therefore included in the Ketuvim or Writings of the Tanak.

Daniel is the only example of a full apocalyptic work in the Hebrew Bible.[2] It is concerned with revealing the hidden secrets of G-d or Heaven that will ultimately be revealed to all humankind. Other works, such as Isa 24–27; 34–35; Ezek 38–39; Joel; and Zech 9–14, are considered to be proto-apocalyptic, but they are part of larger prophetic books and have no standing as independent apocalyptic books in their own right.[3] Apocalyptic books differ from prophetic books by their vivid depictions of visionary experiences, angels or heavenly mediators, otherworldly journeys, the reading of signs from heaven, and divine encounters that lay out otherwise hidden knowledge concerning the course of human history and the divine plans for the world.

Although later Jewish tradition reads the sequence of Daniel's empires in relation to Rome, Islam, and other nations, modern critical scholarship has demonstrated that the book of Daniel was written in relation to the early second-century BCE Jewish revolt against the Seleucid Syrian monarch, Antiochus IV (176–163 BCE).[4] The sequence of empires includes the Babylonians, Medes, Persians, and the Greeks, including both the Ptolemaic Egyptian and Seleucid Syrian Hellenistic dynasties. Daniel's purpose was to encourage Jewish warriors, led by the Hasmonean priestly family, in their efforts to overthrow Seleucid Syria's control of Judah and to re-establish an independent Jewish state with the holy Temple in Jerusalem at its center. The revolt broke out in late 167 BCE under the leadership of the Hasmonean priest Mattathias and his five sons.[5] Following Mattathias' death, his son Judah the Maccabee defeated several Seleucid armies and recaptured and purified the Temple in December 164 BCE. The war continued for some 22 more years. Antiochus IV died in 163 BCE, and Judah the Maccabee was killed in 160 BCE. The revolt finally succeeded in 142 BCE when Simon, Judah's last surviving brother, was able to broker a peace with Seleucid Syria that recognized Judean independence under Hasmonean rule.

Modern interpreters argue that Daniel was composed at some point between the outbreak of the revolt in 167 BCE and the re-sanctification of the Temple in December 164 BCE. The basis for this view lies in Dan 10–12, which presents Daniel's vision of future events. Although the sequence of events corresponds closely to known historical events from the time of the Persian empire through the outbreak of the revolt, its presentation of events beyond the outbreak of the revolt does not correspond to events as they actually occurred.[6] The transition takes place in relation to the battle between the king of the south (Ptolemaic Egypt) and the king of the north (Seleucid Syria, that is, Antiochus IV) beginning in Dan 11:40. Although the revolt began in the aftermath of Antiochus' failed invasion of Ptolemaic Egypt, the battles and the cataclysmic end of Antiochus mentioned from Dan 11:40 never took place. Because Judah's recapture and purification of the Temple is not mentioned, scholars maintain that Daniel was completed prior to December 164 BCE.

Modern interpreters date the composition of Dan 7–12 to the Judean revolt against Antiochus IV in 167–164 BCE, but the book appears to be the product of a longer history of composition. The Court Tales of Dan 1–6 present a generically distinct block of narratives concerning G-d's efforts to protect pious Jews living in the Diaspora under gentile rule that appear to have nothing to do with the Hasmonean revolt. Furthermore, the bulk of these court tales in Dan 2:4b—6:29 and the throne vision of Dan 7:1-28 are written in Aramaic whereas the rest of the book is written in Hebrew. These observations suggest that Daniel was composed in stages. Many interpreters date the composition of Dan 1–6 to the third century BCE and posit that the Aramaic section in Dan 2:4b—7:28 is the product of redactional efforts to join two very distinctive components of the book.[7] Such a compositional model prompts many interpreters to argue that Daniel displays a two-part literary structure, including the court tales of Dan 1–6 and the visions of Dan 7–12.[8]

Close attention to the literary form of the book and its contents, however, indicates that the court tales are worked into the narrative literary framework of the visions. Although the court tales are written in third-person narrative form and the visions are written in first-person autobiographical form, they are bound together by third-person narrative tags in Dan 7:1 and 10:1. When read as a unity, the court tales prepare the reader for the visions by demonstrating G-d's fidelity to righteous Jews and by alluding to Antiochus' faults, such as his decrees that Jews must worship Greek gods (Dan 3), his reputation for madness (Dan 4), and his attempts to proscribe Judaism and Jewish practice (Dan 6). Indeed, the vision of the writing on the wall at Belshazzar's feast (Dan 5) points to the ultimate downfall of the Seleucid empire as predicted in Dan 10–12.⁹ The formal literary structure of Daniel then appears as follows:

Daniel's Depiction of Divine Judgment against the Empire
Exhortation to Righteous Jews

I.	Divine Protection of Daniel and Friends in Nebuchadnezzar's Court	1:1-21
II.	Nebuchadnezzar's Dream: Ultimate Downfall of the Fourth Empire	2:1-49
III.	Divine Protection of Daniel's Friends in the Fiery Furnace and Nebuchadnezzar's Madness	3:1—4:34
IV.	Belshazzar's Feast: Downfall of the Empire and Divine Protection of Daniel in the Lion's Den	5:1—6:29
V.	Daniel's Initial Visions concerning the Downfall of the Empire	7:1—9:27
	A. The throne vision of the Ancient of Days	7:1-28
	B. The vision of the ram and the goat	8:1-27
	C. Daniel's interpretation of Jeremiah's seventy years of exile	9:1-27
VI.	Daniel's Vision of the Downfall of the Empire and the Time of Divine Sovereignty	10:1—12:13

The book of Daniel begins in Dan 1 with the depiction of Daniel and his three friends, Hananiah, Mishael, and Azariah, in the third year of King Jehoiachin of Judah.¹⁰ The date for the narrative indicates a literary setting in the period following the exile of Jehoiachin in 597 but prior to the destruction of the Temple in 587/6 BCE. The four young men have been taken into exile to serve as scribes in the Babylonian royal court of King Nebuchadnezzar, and each is given a Babylonian name, Belteshazzar for Daniel, Shadrach for Hananiah, Meshach for Mishael, and Abed-nego for Azariah, in order to assimilate them into the Babylonian court and culture. Thus, the question of maintaining Jewish identity under Gentile rule is paramount at the outset of the narrative. By refusing to drink the wine or to eat the meat served to them in the Babylonian royal court, Daniel and his friends seek to protect their observance of the kosher dietary laws that are inherent to Jewish identity. When fed vegetables instead of non-kosher meat, the four young men prove to be healthier than their Gentile counterparts. The narrative thereby makes two important points at the outset of the book of Daniel, viz., G-d will protect those who maintain Jewish identity under Gentile rule, and the image of Nebuchadnezzar's court differs markedly from that of Antiochus IV who attempted to suppress Judaism.

Daniel 2 builds on the prior narrative by illustrating Daniel's wisdom and by indicating G-d's intention to bring down the Seleucid Syrian empire. Nebuchadnezzar had a dream that disturbed him, and he demanded interpretation from his court sorcerers, magicians, exorcists, and so on. In order to heighten the drama, he also demanded that they tell him what the dream was. Upon appearing before Nebuchadnezzar, Daniel told him the dream and its interpretation. Nebuchadnezzar had seen a statue, apparently a colossus which was common in

Hellenistic culture, with a gold head, silver breast and arms, bronze belly and thighs, iron legs, and mixed iron and clay feet. A stone cut out by non-human hands was thrown against the feet of the statue causing the whole to collapse. Daniel's interpretation points to the successive emergence of four major world empires that are all brought down by the G-d of Heaven. Although the empires are not named, they refer to Babylonia, Medea, Persia, Greece, and the two Hellenistic kingdoms of Ptolemaic Egypt and Seleucid Syria whose dynasties were produced by the intermarriage of Greek generals into native ruling families. From the standpoint of the ancient reader, this narrative encourages the Judean revolt against Antiochus IV by signaling the coming downfall of the Seleucid Syrian empire.

Daniel 3–4 presents two narratives concerning divine protection of Daniel's companions in the fiery furnace and Nebuchadnezzar's madness. They are linked by Nebuchadnezzar's first-person speech in Dan 4:1, which continues that of Dan 3:31.

Daniel 3 begins with Nebuchadnezzar's erection of a gold statue and his demand that this statue be worshipped throughout the empire. As observant Jews, Daniel's companions would hardly obey such a command to practice idolatry. Learning of their refusal to worship the statue, Nebuchadnezzar orders that Shadrach (Hananiah), Meshach (Mishael), and Abed-nego (Azariah) be thrown into a fiery furnace to be executed for defying the king's order. Upon giving the order, Nebuchadnezzar remarks "what god is there that can save you from my power?" (Dan 3:15), which of course sets the reader up for an answer to his question. When the three young men are thrown into the furnace, they are not harmed and their garments do not burn, even when the fires are heated to the maximum. Nebuchadnezzar recognizes G-d's power in the narrative and issues a decree forbidding blasphemy against the G-d of Heaven who had protected the three young Jews in the furnace. Nebuchadnezzar's actions reflect those of Antiochus IV, who set up an idol of Zeus for worship in the Jerusalem Temple and later demanded worship of himself as a manifest god (*epiphanes*) as well. But Nebuchadnezzar's recognition of G-d contrasts with Antiochus IV and encourages the Judean revolt against his reign.

Daniel 4 continues Nebuchadnezzar's speech from Dan 3:31-33. Nebuchadnezzar describes a vision of a fruitful tree that grew to heaven, but a Watcher, that is, a heavenly figure who protected the sanctity of heaven, decreed that the tree be cut down and that his (Nebuchadnezzar's) mind be altered from that of a man to that of a beast.[11] Daniel interprets the vision as a reference to Nebuchadnezzar's kingdom and G-d's power over that kingdom. The vision draws upon images of the tower built to heaven in Gen 11 and the depiction of the Assyrian king as a tree that is cut down in Isa 10. The vision also draws upon Antiochus's claim to be manifest god, naming himself Antiochus Epiphanes, Antiochus Manifest God, whereas many critics of his time and afterwards referred to him as Antiochus Epimanes, Antiochus the Mad.[12] Once again, it reinforces the Jewish revolt against Antiochus by pointing to G-d as the ultimate sovereign of the world and arbiter of power in that world.

The narratives in Dan 5–6 take up Belshazzar's feast and G-d's protection of Daniel in the lions' den. Although the narratives appear to be discrete, they are linked together by the introductory conjunction in Dan 6:1 that signals Darius the Mede as the successor of Belshazzar following his death in Dan 5:30. The conjunction of these narratives makes the point that judgment against Belshazzar takes place immediately.

Daniel 5 relates the events of Belshazzar's feast in which the days of his kingdom are numbered. The historical Belshazzar was the son of Nabonidus, the last Babylonian king prior to Babylon's fall to Persia, and Belshazzar only served as regent while his father resided in the Arabian Desert away from Babylon. While drinking with his guests, Belshazzar orders that the sacred vessels pillaged by the Babylonians from the Jerusalem Temple be used to serve wine, thereby desecrating them. As he and his guests drink and praise their gods, a hand appears and writes the Aramaic words, *mĕnē' mĕnē' tĕqēl ûparsîn*. When Daniel is brought to the court to interpret the writings, he declares that *mĕnē'*, Aramaic for "numbering," indicates that Belshazzar days are numbered; *tĕqēl*, Aramaic for "weighing," indicates that Belshazzar has been weighed or judged; and *ûparsîn*, Aramaic for "and scattering, dividing," indicates that Belshazzar's kingdom will be scattered or divided among the Persians and the Medes. Indeed, Babylon fell to King Cyrus of Persia during Belshazzar's regency on behalf of his father Nabonidus. The image of the fall of Babylon highlights once again G-d's power to bring about change in the world, particularly against a Gentile monarch who displays such disregard for G-d and the holy vessels of the Temple, and encourages the Jewish revolt against Antiochus who had shown similar disregard for G-d and the Temple.

Daniel 6 then relates G-d's protection of Daniel in the lion's den during the reign of Darius the Mede. Darius the Mede is unknown in history, although the Persian general Darius, who was married into the Achaemenid royal house of Persia and Medea, succeeded Cyrus's son Cambyses in 522 BCE. In the literary context of Daniel, the presence of Darius the Mede highlights Belshazzar's death in Dan 5. Once again, the narrative highlights the issue of fidelity to G-d and Jewish identity. Although Daniel is appointed to a high position in the court of Darius the Mede, his enemies conspire against him and prompt the king to issue a decree forbidding petitions to any god or human other than Darius himself. When Daniel continues to pray three times a day to G-d in accordance with Jewish religious practice, he is charged with violating the king's decree and sentenced to death by being thrown into the lions' den. Although Darius resists this action, he too must abide by the law of the land. Nevertheless, G-d protects Daniel by sending an angel to shut the lions' mouths. When Darius learns of Daniel's protection, Daniel is released, and Darius affirms G-d as the true sovereign of the world. Once again, the Daniel narratives affirm divine power and the observance of Jewish identity in the face of threats from the Gentile empire, thereby undermining Antiochus' claims to be a manifest god and encouraging the Judean revolt against the Seleucid Syrian empire.

The account of Daniel's initial visions concerning the downfall of the empire in Dan 7:1—9:27 is tied into the literary framework of the court tales in Dan 1–6 by the initial third-person narrative introduction in Dan 7:1-2aα which dates Daniel's statements concerning his throne vision in Dan 7:2aβ-28 to the first year of Belshazzar's purported reign. Although the following vision accounts in Dan 8 and 9 have their own chronological introductions, they are formulated in the same first-person speech form as Dan 7:2aβ-28. Consequently, the third-person chronological statement in Dan 7:1-2aα introduces three first-person vision accounts by Daniel, including the throne vision of the Ancient of Days in Dan 7:2aβ-28, the vision of the ram and the goat in Dan 8:1-27, and Daniel's interpretation of Jeremiah's seventy years of exile in Dan 9:1-27. Each of the three vision accounts in this block of material serves the theological perspective of the book by pointing to the ultimate realization of the downfall of the empire and the establishment of divine sovereignty on behalf of the Ancient of Days.

The account of Daniel's throne vision in Dan 7:2aβ-28 appears in Aramaic like the preceding material in Dan 2:4b—7:2aα. Interpreters speculate that the throne vision may have concluded an early version of the book, but the appearance of the Hebrew vision accounts in Dan 8; 9; and 10–12 indicates that it is now intended to be read in relation to a much broader literary context. The vision account begins with references to the four winds of heaven stirring up the great sea, which takes up imagery from the creation account in Gen 1 to portray the Ancient of Days as YHWH, the creator of heaven and earth. Such a mythological context points to the heavenly realm where the action depicted in the vision will have originated and to the setting of the Temple where YHWH is conceived to be enthroned in the Holy of Holies. The vision account clearly builds on themes from the preceding court narratives by presenting a sequence of four mythological creatures that emerge from the sea to represent the four successive empires depicted in Dan 2. Thus the lion with eagle's wings is Babylon, the bear with three fangs in Medea, the leopard with bird wings is Persia, and the fearsome beast with iron teeth is Greece. The ten horns represent the succession of Seleucid rulers, culminating in the depiction of Antiochus IV as the arrogant horn that uprooted three others to make a place for itself. The enthronement of the Ancient of Days represents the enthronement of YHWH in the Temple to pass judgment on the world, which would take place at the time of the New Year (Rosh ha-Shanah), Yom Kippur (the Day of Atonement), and Sukkot (the festival of Booths). The granting of dominion to one like a human being (Aramaic, *bar 'ĕnāš*, lit., "son of man"; cf. Hebrew, *ben 'ādām*, employed for Ezekiel throughout his book), takes up the language generally applied to the priest in the Temple. The granting of dominion to a priestly figure points to the role that the priest in the Temple would play as the agent and locus for YHWH's divine sovereignty on earth. It also points to the role that the Hasmonean priestly family assumed as the political rulers of Judea during the revolt and its aftermath when later Hasmonean high priests also claimed the title of king. With the vision's depiction of the downfall of the four beasts and ultimately the horn speaking great things, the vision portends the time when "the Holy Ones of the Most High," that is, those dedicated to YHWH under the leadership of the (Hasmonean) priests, would rule on YHWH's behalf.

The second vision in the sequence concerning the ram and the goat appears in Dan 8:1-27. This narrative appears in first-person form to depict Daniel as the speaker, in keeping with the format introduced in Dan 7:2aβ-28, although the narrative is written in Hebrew (rather than Aramaic). Daniel finds himself in the vision standing in the city of Shushan by the Ulai, which was the winter capital of the Persian Empire. His vision of the ram with two horns butting in all directions symbolizes the combined Medean–Persian Empire, which defeated and took control of Babylon in 539 BCE. Daniel also sees a goat with a great horn to represent the power of Alexander the Great. The goat breaks the horns of the ram and tramples it to symbolize Alexander's defeat of Persia, but the breaking of its horn at the peak of its power symbolizes Alexander's early death in 323 BCE. Although four horns or kings then struggle for power, representing the Diadochi wars in which Alexander's generals fought for control of the empire following his death, only a small horn survived to threaten the world and the holy Temple. Of course, the small horn is Antiochus IV, who turned the Jerusalem Temple into a pagan shrine and thereby defiled the Temple and its sacred offerings. When a holy being appears to explain the matter to Daniel, he tells Daniel that a 2,300-day period will be necessary to purify the Temple. When the angel Gabriel appears to explain matters further to Daniel, he tells Daniel that the vision refers to the time when this threat will end after great struggle against the impudent king and when divine rule will be re-established on earth with the purification of the Temple.

The third vision account in the sequence appears in Dan 9:1-27, which takes up Daniel's interpretation of Jeremiah's seventy years of exile. Daniel's first-person language appears once again (in Hebrew). The account focuses on the understanding of the prophet Jeremiah's statements in Jer 25:10-11 (see also Jer 29:10) that the period of exile would last for seventy years until YHWH would punish the king and land of Babylonia. Because Jeremiah's seventy years were long past and the threat against Jerusalem, the Temple, and Judah had arisen once again from Antiochus IV, the book of Daniel offers an interpretation of Jeremiah's seventy-year exile in an effort to portray the time of the ultimate downfall of Antiochus. Jeremiah 25:10-11 refers to "seventy years," that is, *šibʿîm šānâ*, but the consonants of the Hebrew word *šibʿîm* may be repointed with different vowels to read *šābuʿîm*, "weeks," which produces the reading of "seventy weeks of years" (Hebrew *šābuʿîm šibʿîm šānâ*) in Dan 9:24.[13] Again, the angel Gabriel explains the matter to Daniel. An initial seven weeks (of years) refers to the Babylon exile from 587/6 through the time of the return following Cyrus's decree in 538 BCE; 62 weeks (of years) refers to the time of the rebuilding of Jerusalem in the Persian and Hellenistic periods from 538 BCE through 104 BCE when the Hasmonean priest Aristobulus I declared himself king of Judea; and the final week relates to the time when "the anointed one," apparently Aristobulus I, died unexpectedly in 103 BCE and his brother, Alexander Jannaeus, married his widow, Alexandra Salome, and assumed the offices of high priest and king over an independent Judah. Such a chronology points to the time of the Hasmonean rule beyond the revolt against Antiochus IV and suggests the continued growth of the book of Daniel beyond the time of the revolt.

The concluding segment of the book in Dan 10:1—12:13 concerning Daniel's vision of the downfall of the empire and the time of divine sovereignty begins with a third-person chronological formula that places the vision in the third year of King Cyrus of Persia. The choice of the Persian king points forward to the time of the Greek King Alexander whose conquest of the ancient Near East sets in motion the events that lead to the final downfall of the Seleucid Empire and the rise of divine sovereignty in Judea. Daniel undergoes three weeks of fasting and self-denial in preparation for the vision and sees an angelic figure dressed in white linen like a priest who will guide him through the visionary experience of what will take place in the future. Daniel 10:14 employs the Hebrew term *bĕ'aḥărît hayyāmîm*, "in the later days," that is, "in the future," in reference to the coming events.[14] The angelic figure must return to fight against the kings of Persia with the assistance of the archangel Michael, but will reveal the future to Daniel. Once he departs, he claims that the prince of Greece, that is, Alexander, will come.

The angelic figure describes a scenario in which three more Persian kings will rule prior to the emergence of the warrior king, that is, Alexander, who will have an extensive dominion that will be broken up following his death. The figure then describes in detail the emergence of the king of the south, that is, Ptolemy I Soter, who established the Ptolemaic Egyptian dynasty, and the king of the north, that is, Seleucus I, who established the Seleucid Syrian dynasty in Mesopotamia. A detailed account of the interrelations and conflicts between the two dynasties then follows through Dan 11:21-39, which describes the arrogant and contemptible rule of Antiochus IV and Jewish efforts to revolt against him. Beginning in Dan 11:40, the vision describes events that contradict the known historical record, particularly the final war between the king of the south and the king of the north in which the king of the north will prevail only to meet his doom between the sea and the holy mountain (Dan 11:45). During the course of these conflicts, the angel Michael will appear to rescue those Jews who had died by resurrecting them to either eternal life or everlasting abhorrence. The vision concludes with enigmatic attempts to predict when the final end of this conflict, that is, *'ēt qēṣ*, "the end time,"[15] would come; it would be either in "a time, times, and half a time" (Dan 12:7), perhaps three and a half years, "one thousand two hundred and ninety days" (Dan 12:11), and finally, "one thousand three hundred and thirty-five days" (Dan 12:12). The downfall of the king of the north would be complete and the knowledgeable would be like the stars (perhaps a reference to their becoming angelic figures), leading many to righteousness.

Once again, such a scenario is designed to encourage those supporting the Judean revolt against Antiochus IV with a vision of final victory.

Although the book of Daniel makes extensive use of mythological language and heavenly imagery to portray the rise and downfall of four successive world empires beginning with Babylonia, its theological perspective is ultimately rooted in attempts to encourage the Judean revolt against the Seleucid Syrian monarch, Antiochus IV, in the period from the outbreak of the revolt in 167 BCE but prior to re-sanctification of the Jerusalem Temple by Judah the Maccabee and his followers in 164 BCE. Nevertheless, the language and imagery of the book lends itself to readings of Daniel in relation to later empires and figures, Rome, Islam, the Antichrist, and so on, as the book of Daniel continued to function as sacred scripture in both Judaism and Christianity.

NOTES

[1] For discussion of Daniel in Judaism, see "Daniel," *EncJud* 5:1274–77.

[2] For discussion of the genre, apocalyptic, see John J. Collins, *Daniel, with an Introduction to Apocalyptic Literature* (FOTL 20; Grand Rapids: Eerdmans, 1984), 1–24.

[3] For discussion of apocalyptic literature, see John J. Collins, *The Apocalyptic Imagination* (New York: Crossroad, 1984); Ithamar Gruenwald, *Apocalyptic and Merkavah Mysticism* (Leiden: Brill, 1980); Stephen L. Cook, *Prophecy and Apocalypticism: The Postexilic Social Setting* (Minneapolis: Fortress Press, 1995); Otto Ploeger, *Theocracy and Eschatology* (Oxford: Blackwell, 1968); Greg Carey, *Ultimate Things: An Introduction to Jewish and Christian Apocalyptic Literature* (St. Louis: Chalice, 2005).

[4] For discussion of Daniel in modern critical scholarship, see John J. Collins, "Daniel, Book of," *ABD* 2:29–37. For current discussion of Daniel, see especially John J. Collins, *Daniel* (Hermeneia; Minneapolis: Fortress Press, 1993); L. F. Hartman and A. A. Di Lella, *Daniel* (AB 23; Garden City: Doubleday, 1978); Daniel L. Smith-Christopher, "Daniel: Introduction, Commentary, and Reflections," in *The New Interpreter's Bible*, ed. L. E. Keck et al. (Nashville: Abingdon, 1996), 7:17–152.

[5] For discussion of the Ptolemaic and Seleucid empires and the Judean revolt against Antiochus IV, see Victor Tcherikover, *Hellenistic Civilization and the Jews* (New York: Atheneum, 1982); W. D. Davies and Louis Finkelstein, ed., *The Cambridge History of Judaism*. Vol. 2, *The Hellenistic Age* (Cambridge: Cambridge University Press, 1989); Emil Schürer, *The History of the Jewish People in the Age of Jesus Christ* (Edinburgh: T. & T. Clark, 1973), 1:125–99.

[6] See the discussion of Dan 10–12 in Collins, *Daniel* (Hermeneia), 361–404.

[7] See especially Lawrence M. Wills, *The Jew in the Court of the Foreign King: Ancient Jewish Court Legends* (Minneapolis: Fortress Press, 1990).

[8] For example, see Collins, *Daniel* (Hermeneia), 24–38.

[9] See my "The End of Eschatology in Daniel? Theological and Socio-Political Ramifications of the Changing Contexts of Interpretation," in *Form and Intertextuality in Prophetic and Apocalyptic Literature* (FAT 45; Tübingen: Mohr Siebeck, 2005), 248–61.

[10] For the following discussion of Daniel, see especially my "The End of Eschatology in Daniel?"

[11] For discussion of Dan 4, see also Mattthias Henze, *The Madness of King Nebuchadnezzar: The Ancient Near Eastern Origins and Early History of Interpretation of Daniel 4* (JSJSup 61; Leiden: Brill, 1999).

[12] Polybius 26.10; 31.3–4; Livy 41.19-20; Diodorus 29.32; 31.16.1-2.

[13] See Lawrence M. Wills, "Daniel," in *The Jewish Study Bible*, ed. A. Berlin and M. Z. Brettler (Oxford: Oxford University Press, 2003), 1660; contra Collins, *Daniel* (Hermeneia), 352–56.

[14] Simon J. DeVries, *From Old Revelation to New* (Grand Rapids: Eerdmans, 1995), 89–95.

[15] For this understanding of the term, 'ēt qēṣ, cf. Collins, *Daniel* (Hermeneia), 337–38.

G. The Book of Ezra–Nehemiah

The book of Ezra–Nehemiah recounts the restoration of Jerusalem from the initial decree of the Persian King Cyrus in 539 BCE, who allowed Jews to return to Jerusalem to rebuild the Temple. It continues with the rebuilding of the Temple under Zerubbabel ben Shealtiel and Joshua ben Jehoazadak during the reign of Darius I (542–486 BCE); the initial attempts during the reign of Artaxerxes I (465–424 BCE) by Ezra ben Seraiah, the priest and scribe, to restore the covenant based on divine Torah; and the efforts of Nehemiah ben Hacaliah as governor of Judah, again in the reigns of Artaxerxes I and Darius II (423–405 BCE), to rebuild and repopulate Jerusalem and together with Ezra to implement the observance of divine Torah. Although the superscription in Neh 1:1a indicates that Nehemiah may once have been a separate book, Jewish tradition reads Ezra–Nehemiah as a single work written by Ezra and Nehemiah.[1] Ezra–Nehemiah appears to be written as a continuation of Chronicles, insofar as it begins with the decree of Cyrus in Ezra 1:1-4, whereas an account of Cyrus' decree concludes Chronicles in 2 Chr 36:22-23. Nevertheless, Ezra–Nehemiah precedes Chronicles in most standard editions of the Tanak, although Talmudic tradition also holds that Chronicles begins the Ketuvim and Ezra–Nehemiah concludes the Ketuvim and therefore the Tanak as a whole. Insofar as Jerusalem remained unrestored as a Jewish city from the onset of the Rabbinic period following the Zealot and Bar Kochba revolts through modern times, Ezra–Nehemiah is read as a means to anticipate the full restoration of the city (and the land of Israel as a whole)—including the re-establishment of the Temple—under divine Torah in Jewish tradition.

The book of Ezra–Nehemiah is named after its two dominant personalities, Ezra and Nehemiah, each of whom appears to have contributed first-person memoirs to the book. Ezra ben Seraiah is the priest and scribe who is sent to Jerusalem by the Persian King Artaxerxes I in the seventh year of his reign to implement divine Torah as the law of the land under Persian authority. Because of his role in bringing Torah to Jerusalem, Rabbinic tradition identifies Ezra with Malachi, who charges Israel to observe divine Torah in Mal 3:22 (see *b. Megillah* 15a). Because of his zeal for Torah, Ezra would have received the Torah at Sinai were it not for Moses, who preceded him (*t. Sanhedrin* 4:7). Ezra reinstituted the observance of Torah in the early Second Temple period (see also *b. Sukkah* 20a), and instituted the regular practice of reading Torah on Mondays, Thursdays, and Shabbat (*b. Megillah* 31b; *y. Megillah* 4:1, 75a). He is also credited with writing the Torah in "Assyrian" letters, that is, the current Hebrew alphabet derived from the Aramaic square alphabet, thereby abandoning the older paleo-Hebrew alphabet (*b. Sanhedrin* 21b). Although his genealogy indicates a potential pedigree as high priest (Ezra 7:1-5), it is never clear in Ezra–Nehemiah that he functions as such insofar as he does not present the offerings at the Temple altar but restricts himself to teaching Torah as all priests are expected to do (see Lev 10:10-11). Rabbinic Judaism maintains that Ezra was a student of Baruch ben Neriah in Babylon, but delayed his departure for the land of Israel in order to avoid embarrassing the high priest Joshua ben Jehozadak who was less adept at the study of Torah (*Song of Songs Rabbah* 5:5). Ezra was then appointed as high priest only after his arrival in Jerusalem (*b. Baba Batra* 15a). Rabbinic tradition also credits him with writing the genealogies of Chronicles (*b. Baba Batra* 15a), portions of the book of Psalms (*Song of Songs Rabbah* 4:19), and portions of the Mishnah tractate *Kelim*.[2]

Nehemiah ben Hacaliah is a Jew who serves as the cup-bearer for the Persian king Artaxerxes I. The office of cup-bearer is an administrative post that requires the tasting of wine or food presented to the king; it is a role that gives the holder of the office tremendous influence due to his proximity to the king. It is in this capacity that Nehemiah requests permission to return to Jerusalem to serve as governor of Judah so that he might address the needs of his languishing people. As governor of Judah, Nehemiah rebuilds the city walls of Jerusalem, populates the city with one-tenth of the population of Judah, and together with Ezra implements the observance of divine Torah as the law of the land under Persian authority. Particularly noteworthy are his efforts to re-establish the Tithe in order to support the Temple, the prohibition against marriage to non-Jewish women, and the observance of Shabbat in the city of Jerusalem. Rabbinic tradition identifies Nehemiah with Zerubbabel (*b. Sanhedrin* 38a), which would explain Zerubbabel's disappearance from the narrative. The Rabbis were also critical of Nehemiah, apparently seeking to explain why his portion of the book was subordinated to that of Ezra (*b. Sanhedrin* 93b). Nehemiah spoke vainly of himself, apparently disparaging the work of his predecessors (Neh 5:15) and demanding from G-d credit for the work of others (Neh 5:19; 13:31). Nevertheless, Rabbinic tradition also credits him with completing the book of Chronicles, which was started by Ezra (*b. Baba Batra* 15a).

Modern scholarship has focused especially on the historical and literary problems presented by the book.[3] Although early critical scholarship maintained that Ezra–Nehemiah was a part of the larger Chronicler's work, more recent scholarship maintains that it is a distinct work with its own compositional history and theological outlook. Ezra–Nehemiah is clearly a composite work. The superscription in Neh 1:1a indicates that Nehemiah was originally a self-standing work, and the first-person memoirs identified with Ezra in Ezra 7:27—9:15 and Nehemiah in Neh 1:1b—7:72; 12:31-43; 13:4-31 likewise stand out in an otherwise third-person narrative as material that may well have had an earlier literary form. Another literary problem is the account of the building of the Temple in Ezra 1–6. Ezra 1:8 notes an initial release of funds for an attempt at reconstruction led by a figure named Sheshbazzar, prince of Judah, but provides no further information. Ezra 3 posits that Zerubbabel ben Shealtiel, elsewhere identified as the governor of Judah (Hag 1:1), was present for the dedication of the Temple altar and the laying of the Temple foundation, but the account of the dedication of the Temple in Ezra 6 makes no mention of him, fueling speculation as to the cause of his disappearance. The account of opposition to the building of the Temple in Ezra 4 includes references to events and documents from the reigns of Xerxes (486–465 BCE) and Artaxerxes I (465–424 BCE) that are sent to support the efforts to rebuild the Temple during the reign of Darius (522–486 BCE). Indeed, the letter written by Rehum the commissioner and Shimshai the scribe to Artaxerxes in Ezra 4:8-16 and Artaxerxes's response in Ezra 4:17-22 are written in Aramaic, as is as the narrative through Ezra 7:18, which provides further grounds for concluding that these segments of text presuppose later sources or some sort of redaction. The third-person narrative material in Neh 7:6—12:30, which contains lists of various individuals as well as the account of Ezra's reading of the Torah to the people, appears within the first-person memoir of Nehemiah and likewise indicates later sources and redactional work.

In attempting to read Ezra–Nehemiah, scholars note that the redactional formation of the book tends to telescope events, such as the building of the Temple, which is narrated in relation to the later reigns of Xerxes and Artaxerxes, as well as the careers of Ezra and Nehemiah which, apart from their roles in reading the Torah to the people in Neh 8–10, appear to have nothing to do with each other. Indeed, the chronological order of the careers of Ezra and Nehemiah has proved to be a major historical issue as well. Ezra 7:7-10 dates Ezra's arrival in Jerusalem to the seventh year of the reign of Artaxerxes which would be 458 BCE. Nehemiah 2:1 dates Nehemiah's request to journey to Jerusalem to the twentieth year of Artaxerxes which would be 445 BCE. Nehemiah 5:14 states that the initial term of Nehemiah's appointment as governor was for twelve years, from the twentieth to the thirty-second year of Artaxerxes, that is, 445–433 BCE, and Neh 13:6 indicates that after returning to Babylon in Artaxerxes's thirty-second year, he was granted a second term as governor, although the duration of the second term is never stated.

Some interpreters note that the present sequence of the narrative, in which Nehemiah follows Ezra in Jerusalem by some thirteen years, makes little sense.[4] Ezra and Nehemiah appear together in Neh 8–10 when Ezra reads the Torah to the people, but it makes little sense for Ezra, a priest and scribe who is zealous for the Torah, to wait thirteen years before reading the Torah to the people.

Furthermore, Nehemiah's actions to rebuild the city walls of Jerusalem seem to be the necessary prerequisite to provide the security required for the mission of Ezra. If Nehemiah comes after Ezra, then Nehemiah, a layman who is governor of Judah, becomes the figure who enforces the reforms of Ezra, the priest, whose efforts and authority as priest must then be deemed a failure. A number of modifications to the chronology have been proposed. Some propose that the text of Ezra 7:9 be emended to read that Ezra arrived in the thirty-seventh year of Artaxerxes, which would be 428 BCE, although there is no textual evidence for such a proposal.

A second proposal argues that Ezra's reading of the Torah took place during his first year in Jerusalem and that Nehemiah was later added to the narrative by a redactor—but, again, evidence is lacking. A third proposal holds that Ezra's return in the seventh year of Artaxerxes must be dated to the reign of Artaxerxes II (404–358 BCE), which would be 397 BCE. This last proposal might make some historical sense, although it would contradict the current presentation of Ezra–Nehemiah. Nevertheless, many contemporary scholars are hesitant to accept such a proposal. Perhaps Ezra did not succeed at first and needed the support of a sympathetic governor like Nehemiah, who volunteered to come to Jerusalem to do something about the wretched state of his people.

Although the diachronic issues have tended to dominate modern discussion of the book, the synchronic form of Ezra–Nehemiah must stand as the basis for any theological assessment of the book.[5] Despite the historical problems of the book, including the issue of historical telescoping, it is possible to discern a literary structure that presents a chronological sequence. Three major narrative blocks are visible, including an account of the construction of the Temple in Ezra 1–6, an account of Ezra's return to Jerusalem in Ezra 7–10, and an account of Nehemiah's return to Jerusalem and his efforts to implement Torah together with Ezra in Neh 1–13.

Each of these constituent blocks is demarcated by its own distinctive literary formulation and thematic content.[6]

Ezra 1–6 is demarcated by its introductory chronological formula in Ezra 1:1, "and in the first year of Cyrus, King of Persia, to fulfill the word of YHWH from the mouth of Jeremiah, YHWH awakened the spirit of Cyrus, King of Persia, and he issued a decree throughout his kingdom, and also in written form, saying. . . ." The introductory conjunction signals that the book is to be read in relation to another work, presumably the book of Chronicles. The formula itself sets in motion the chain of events, all presented in third-person narrative style, which will lead to the completion of the new Temple in Jerusalem, which reaches its culmination in Ezra 6. Following the initial presentation of Cyrus's decree in Ezra 1:1-4 that authorizes Jews to return to Jerusalem to rebuild the Temple, Ezra 1:5—6:22 relates the people's compliance with the royal decree. Five sub-units appear within Ezra 1:5—6:22, including an account of the preparations for return in Ezra 1:5-11; a list of returnees in Ezra 2:1-70; an account of the dedication of the Temple altar and the commencement of the building in Ezra 3:1-13; an account of the opposition to the building of the Temple by the people of the land in Ezra 4:1-24; and an account of the resumption and completion of the building in Ezra 5:1—6:22. The concluding statement of this block in Ezra 6:22 reads, "and they (the sons of Israel who returned from the exile) celebrated the festival of Matzot for seven days because YHWH had overjoyed them by turning the heart of the Assyrian king concerning them to strengthen their hands in the work of the house of G-d, G-d of Israel." By noting the celebration of Passover and the ongoing worship conducted at the Temple, this statement indicates that the actual building of the Temple hardly exhausts the process of its restoration. Insofar as the Temple is the site for the worship of YHWH, an ongoing process of inter-relationship between YHWH and the people is signaled in which the people must learn to act in accordance with divine instruction. Such a notice thereby paves the way for the subsequent block which is concerned with the process by which Torah will be implemented in Jerusalem and Judah so that the people may observe YHWH's instruction.

Ezra 7–10 is demarcated initially by the formula in Ezra 7:1-6, "and after these things in the reign of Artaxerxes, King of Persia, Ezra ben Seriah ben Azriah ben Hilkiah ben Shallum ben Ben Zadok ben Ahituv, ben Amariah ben Azariah ben Meraiot ben Zerahiah ben Uzzi ben Bukki ben Abishua ben Pinhas ben Elazar ben Aharon the chief priest, he, Ezra, a scribe skilled in the Torah of Moses which YHWH, the G-d of Israel, gave, went up from Babylon, and the king gave to him, according to the hand of YHWH his G-d, all that he requested." This lengthy formula introduces Ezra as the primary character of the narrative block, which recounts his return to Jerusalem and his efforts to implement Torah in the land so as to complete the restoration of the Temple. The initial conjunction indicates that Ezra 7–10 is intended to follow upon Ezra 1–6, and the lengthy introduction of Ezra states his qualifications, first as a priest of the Zadokite line descended from Seraiah, the last high priest in the Jerusalem Temple (see 2 Kgs 25:18; Jer 52:24), Zadok ben Ahituv, the founder of the Zadokite line that served in the Jerusalem Temple, and Aaron, the founder of the priesthood, and second as a scribe skilled in the Torah of Moses. The narrative block employs a combination of third- and first-person autobiographical narrative to relate Ezra's efforts to return to Jerusalem and to implement divine Torah. Four major sub-units appear within the narrative, including an account of Ezra's return to Jerusalem in Ezra 7:1-10; Artaxerxes's letter commissioning Ezra in Ezra 7:11-26; Ezra's memoir in Ezra 7:27—9:15 which relates his prayer (Ezra 7:27-28), a list of returnees (Ezra 8:1-14), his preparations for the journey (Ezra 8:15-31), his arrival in Jerusalem (Ezra 8:32-36), and the crisis concerning intermarriage (Ezra 9:1-15); and an account of Ezra's covenant which focuses on his efforts to terminate the inter-marriages in Ezra 10:1-44. Insofar as the narrative concludes with a list of priests who had married foreign women, summed up with the statement in Ezra 9:44, "all these had married foreign women, and among them were women who had born children," it points to the issue of intermarriage as an ongoing issue that has not yet been resolved at the conclusion of this narrative block.

Nehemiah 1–13 constitutes the third major narrative block of the book which recounts Nehemiah's return to Jerusalem and his efforts to implement Torah within the city together with Ezra. The block is demarcated initially by the superscription in Neh 1:1a, "the words of Nehemiah," which introduces the block as a whole. The lack of a conjunction suggests that this superscription may at some point have introduced Nehemiah as a self-standing book, but within the current literary context of Ezra–Nehemiah as a single book, it simply signals the beginning of a new narrative block within the whole. Nehemiah 1:1b—13:31 then constitutes the account proper, in both first-person autobiographical and third-person narrative form, of Nehemiah's efforts with a sequence of three major sub-units. Nehemiah 1:1b—7:72 recounts Nehemiah's efforts to rebuild the city walls of Jerusalem and to repopulate the city with one-tenth or a tithe of the people residing in the land of Judah. Nehemiah 8:1—10:40 recounts the reconstitution of the covenant by both Ezra and Nehemiah. This block comprises four major sub-units, including Ezra's reading of the Torah in Neh 8:1-12; the celebration of Sukkot in Neh 8:13-18; the public confession of sins in a ceremony that looks remarkably like Yom Kippur in Neh 9:1-37 (although it falls on the twenty-fourth day of the seventh month rather than the tenth day of the seventh month as required in Lev 23:26-28); and Nehemiah's covenant in Neh 10:1-40. This last segment comprises five sub-units, including an account of the people settled in Jerusalem, Judah, and Benjamin in Neh 11:1-36; an account of the priests settled in the Temple in Neh 12:1-26; an account of the dedication of the walls of Jerusalem in Neh 12:27-43; an account of the tithe to support the Temple in Neh 12:44-47; and an account of the resolution of halakhic (legal) issues following Nehemiah's return in Neh 13:1-31. Nehemiah's resolution of the halakhic issues is exemplified in Neh 13:28, in which he expels a son of Jehoiada ben Eliashev the priest for intermarriage, "and one of the sons of Jehoiada ben Eliashev the priest who was son-in-law of Sanballat the Horonite, I expelled him from my presence." He continues by summing up his actions in Neh 13:29-31, asking for condemnation by G-d of those who defiled the priesthood and recognition by G-d for his own efforts to purify the priesthood, "Remember them, O my G-d, concerning the defilement of the priesthood and the covenant of the priesthood and the Levites. And I purified them from all foreignness and I established the priestly and levitical watches, each according to its task. And for the offering of the wood in its appointed times and for the first fruit offerings, remember me, O my G-d, favorably."

The work as a whole may be characterized as an Account of the Restoration of Jerusalem. The literary structure of Ezra–Nehemiah may be represented as follows:[7]

Account of the Restoration of Jerusalem

This analysis of the formal structure and generic character of the book of Ezra–Nehemiah provides the foundation for a theological assessment of the book. A number of major issues emerge.

First and foremost is the book's interest in re-establishing Jerusalem as the holy center of Israel and creation at large, as well as the re-establishment of the holiness of the people of Israel. Interpreters have long recognized that the Jerusalem Temple functions as the sacred center of creation in ancient Jewish thought and that the people of Israel function as the chosen people who are tasked with bringing the sanctity of YHWH to creation at large.[8] The formal structure of the book points directly to these concerns, insofar as it is organized to emphasize the reconstruction of the Temple at the center of a restored city of Jerusalem and the efforts by both Ezra and Nehemiah in their respective capacities as a priest skilled in the interpretation of Torah and as a governor of Judah to reconstitute both the population of Jerusalem per se as well as the sanctity of that population by assigning one tenth of the people of Judah to live in the city as a form of demographic tithe and to implement divine Torah as the foundation for the people's lives in the holy city. Such a view of the sanctity of the city and the people is in keeping with the outlook of the Torah itself, which posits the establishment of the people of Israel and their life in the land of Israel under divine Torah and centered on the divine sanctuary as the culmination of the process of creation. It also corresponds to the general outlook of the prophetic literature, including both the Former and the Latter Prophets, who posit that the welfare of Israel and creation at large is dependent upon the people's observance of divine Torah and the maintenance of the holy sanctuary at the center of the nation.

The intertextual relationship between Ezra–Nehemiah and other elements of the Bible is clear from the outset. When Ezra 1:1-4 relates Cyrus's decree that Jews may return to Jerusalem to rebuild the Temple, the passage makes sure to note that Cyrus's decree must be recognized as a fulfillment of the word of YHWH as spoken by the prophet Jeremiah. Jeremiah's prophecy would include a number of major elements, such as the obligation of Israel to live in accordance with divine Torah (for example, Jer 7–10), the recognition that the Babylonian exile was brought about by YHWH as a judgment for the people's alleged failure to live according to divine Torah (for example, Jer 27–28), the limited nature of the exile that would only last for some seventy years (for example, Jer 25; 29), and the expectation of the restoration of the people to the land of Israel and to the city of Jerusalem (for example, Jer 30–33). But of course, Jeremiah is not the only intertextual link with Ezra–Nehemiah. Even though there are discrepancies, such as the observance of a day of repentance that might be recognized as Yom Kippur on the twenty-fourth day of the seventh month (see Neh 9), it is clear that the book envisions the covenant made between the people and YHWH by both Ezra and Nehemiah as a covenant based upon divine Torah (see Ezra 10; Neh 7–10). Indeed, the various injunctions emphasized in the book, such as the need to build the Temple (Exod 25–30; 35–40; 1 Kgs 6–8); the reading of the Torah before the people (Neh 8–10; cf. Exod 19; Deut 31:10-13; Josh 8:3-35; 2 Kgs 23:1-3); the need to tithe to support the Temple (Neh 11:1; 13:10-14; cf. Lev 27:30-33; Num 18:21-32; Deut 14:22-29; 1 Sam 8); the need to observe Shabbat in the city of Jerusalem (Neh 13:15-22; cf. Exod 20:8-11; Deut 5:12-15; Isa 56:1-8; Jer 17:21-24; Ezek 20); and the prohibition against intermarriage with non-Jewish men and women (Ezra 9; Neh 13:23-30; cf. Exod 34:10-16; Deut 7:1-6; cf. 1 Kgs 11), are all derived from the Torah and the Prophets. Even Ezra's return to Jerusalem from Babylon is modeled on (Second) Isaiah's vision of a new Exodus in which the people of Israel would return to Jerusalem from Babylonian exile through the desert to re-establish the city as the holy center for YHWH's sovereignty over all creation (Isa 40–48; cf. Ezra 9).[9]

In considering the character of the restored Jewish nation in Jerusalem and Judah, the above analysis should make it clear that building the Temple and restoring the city walls of Jerusalem are insufficient means in and of themselves to see to the re-establishment of Jerusalem as the holy center of creation and the people of Israel as the chosen people of YHWH. Without the observance of divine Torah, Ezra–Nehemiah views the building of the Temple and the city as meaningless. Instead, the book envisions a process in which YHWH instigates the restoration effort by prompting Cyrus to issue his decree at the outset of the book, the process of Temple construction and dedication then follows, and finally, both Ezra and Nehemiah do their share to see to the implementation of Torah in the city. Such a sequence presupposes a theological worldview in which the Jerusalem Temple, much like Mt. Sinai, serves as a source for the revelation of divine Torah to the people of Israel who are in turn expected to observe divine Torah and, in doing so, play its role in the sanctification of creation at large.

Furthermore, the halakhic observances emphasized within the book display an interest in both the sanctification of the world at large and the nation in particular, as well as the maintenance or sustenance of both the Temple/city and the people. The public reading of Torah by Ezra in Neh 8–10, with the Levites interpreting to the people, leads to the recognition of the need to observe the holy festivals, such as Shabbat and Sukkot, which entails the sanctification of time as envisioned in the Torah. Such observance does not only impact the people of Israel as understood by the Torah, but creation at large, particularly since the observance of Shabbat is built into the very fabric of creation at the outset (Gen 1:1—2:3; Exod 31:12-17) and the festivals then mark the sacred times of history and the agricultural seasons throughout the year (Exod 23:10-17; 34:17-26; Lev 23; Num 28–29; Deut 16:1-16). Not only do Shabbat and the festivals reinforce the identity of Israel as a people bound throughout history in a covenant with YHWH, they also see to the support of the Temple insofar as the people are obligated to bring their offerings of agricultural produce and animals to the Temple in order to provide the support necessary to sustain the Temple and its priesthood. As many have recognized, the offerings brought to the Temple are a form of income tax designed to thank YHWH for protecting them, bringing them to the land, and providing them with food (see Deut 26). Indeed, by requiring that one tenth of the people reside in Jerusalem (Neh 11:1), Nehemiah imposes a tithe on the people themselves as well as on their offerings to ensure the continuity and sustenance of the city of Jerusalem once the walls are rebuilt.

But it is not simply a matter of ensuring the numbers of the people; their character as a distinctive, holy people must also be addressed.[10] The prohibition against intermarriage is designed specifically to ensure that foreign gods—and thus foreign identities—are not introduced into the people. World history teaches that nations large and small lose their identities as they are assimilated into larger cultures, nations, and religions. Not only did Israel's smaller neighbors, such as the Philistines, Edomites, Moabites, and others lose their identities as they were absorbed into the Babylonian Empire, but even larger nations, such as Babylonia itself, Assyria, Persia, and Egypt saw substantial change in their identities as they were absorbed first into other empires and ultimately into Islam, much as Greece, Rome, and others lost their distinctive identities as they were absorbed into the Constantinian Christian Empire and its heirs. Nehemiah 13:23-24 makes it clear that the foreign wives did not speak the language of Judah or teach it to their children, which in turn plays a major role in the dissolution of cultural and religious identity. Biblical texts, such as Deut 21:10-14; Isa 56:1-8, and Ruth, indicate that foreigners can convert to Judaism and become part of the Jewish people, but that conversion to Judaism entails adopting the religious perspectives and practice and indeed the language of Judaism to become part of the Jewish culture. In Ezra's and Nehemiah's time, that means learning Hebrew and teaching one's children, observing Shabbat and the rest of the Jewish tradition, and recognizing only YHWH as G-d. Without these defining characteristics, the Jewish people dissolves.

Finally, Ezra the priest cannot undertake the task of sanctifying the people alone. He needs the help of Nehemiah, the governor of Judah. Judaism in the biblical period had worked on the basis of a combination of the priestly functions of the Levites and the political functions of the kings, judges, and other figures. Even figures such as Moses and Samuel combined their roles as priests with political functions, such as leadership in war and government administration. In the aftermath of the Babylonian exile, the restoration of the Davidic monarchy was out of the question as long as the Persian Empire was in power. Cyrus and his successors were known for a certain degree of beneficence insofar as they allowed subject peoples to govern themselves according to their own laws. They could be just as brutal as the Assyrians or the Babylonians in putting down revolt. It is noteworthy, then, that the vision of restoration in Ezra–Nehemiah does not include an independent Davidic monarch as many books of the Bible would presuppose (for example, the Former Prophets; Ezekiel; the Twelve Prophets). Ezra and Nehemiah are both Persian appointees, and Zerubbabel ben Shealtiel, the grandson of the last recognized Davidic king of Judah, Jehoiachin ben Jehoiakim, disappears from the scene without comment. Rather, Ezra–Nehemiah accepts Persian rule as the will of YHWH, much like the book of Isaiah and to a certain extent, the book of Jeremiah. In this respect, the book of Ezra–Nehemiah enters into a debate within the Bible as to whether or not Israel should be constituted as an independent nation or as a distinctive people under foreign rule. Whereas Ezra–Nehemiah points to Persian rule as the will of YHWH, the book of Esther warns of the dangers posed to the Jewish people when foreign rulers such as the Persians do not concern themselves with justice as required by YHWH.

Notes

[1] For a survey of the reading of Ezra–Nehemiah in Jewish scholarship, see Jacob M. Myers, "Ezra and Nehemiah, Book of," *EncJud* 6:1111–23; cf. Hindy Najman, "Ezra," "Nehemiah," in *The Jewish Study Bible*, ed., A. Berlin and M. Brettler (New York: Oxford University Press, 2003), 1666–87, 1688–711.

[2] See Masseketh Kelim, mishnah 3, in Adolph Jellinek, *Bet ha-Midrasch* (Jerusalem: Bamberger & Wahrmann, 1938), 2:88.

[3] For surveys of modern critical scholarship on Ezra–Nehemiah, see H. G. M. Williamson, *Ezra and Nehemiah* (OTG; Sheffield: Sheffield Academic, 1987); Ralph W. Klein, "Ezra–Nehemiah, Books of," *ABD* 2:731–42. For major commentaries on Ezra–Nehemiah, see H. G. M. Williamson, *Ezra–Nehemiah* (WBC 16; Waco: Word, 1985); Joseph Blenkinsopp, *Ezra–Nehemiah: A Commentary* (OTL; Philadelphia: Westminster, 1988).

[4] For discussion, see Williamson, *Ezra and Nehemiah*, 55–69; idem, *Ezra–Nehemiah*, xxxix-xliv.

[5] Blenkinsopp, *Ezra–Nehemiah*, 41.

[6] Cf. Williamson, *Ezra–Nehemiah*, xxiii–xxxiii.

[7] Cf. Tamara Cohn Eskenazi, *In an Age of Prose: A Literary Approach to Ezra–Nehemiah* (SBLMS 36; Atlanta: Scholars Press, 1988), especially 37–136.

[8] For example, Jon D. Levenson, *Sinai and Zion: An Entry into the Jewish Bible* (Minneapolis: Winston, 1985); idem, "The Temple and the World," *JR* 64 (1984): 275–98.

[9] Klaus Koch, "Ezra and the Origins of Judaism," *JSS* 19 (1974): 173–97.

[10] For a sustained discussion of the role played by Nehemiah in rebuilding and asserting the identity of Judaism in the early Second Temple period, see especially Jacob L. Wright, *Rebuilding Identity: The Nehemiah Memoir and its Earliest Readers* (BZAW 348; Berlin: de Gruyter, 2004).

H. THE BOOK OF CHRONICLES

The book of Chronicles recounts the history of Israel from the time of Adam until the end of the Babylonian Exile when the Persian king Cyrus decreed in 539 BCE that exiled Jews could return to Jerusalem to rebuild the Jerusalem Temple. Although it begins with Adam, the book focuses especially on the reign of the royal house of David in Jerusalem from the institution of the monarchy under David until the end of Davidic rule in Jerusalem under Zedekiah ben Josiah. There is tremendous overlap with the books of Samuel and Kings, but Chronicles frequently adds additional material, corrects problematic readings from the Samuel–Kings text, and at times presents a very different account of history to serve its own theological agenda.[1] Although some scholars maintain that Chronicles presents a messianic agenda with regard to the restoration of the house of David,[2] the concern with David is actually secondary. Chronicles' interest in David is based in its interest in the Jerusalem Temple. It recognizes David as the founder of the Jerusalem Temple and as the figure who set in place its priesthood and much of its liturgical practice, and it recognizes Solomon as the builder of the Temple. Although it notes the kings who ruled northern Israel from the reigns of Saul ben Kish and Jeroboam ben Nebat, it does not include detailed accounts of the reigns of the northern kings and mentions them only when it is necessary for the presentation of the reigns of the Davidic kings. Chronicles' presentation of the reigns of the Judean kings generally favors the house of David. Nevertheless, it is hardly idealized, insofar as it recognizes both their strengths and their weaknesses. Chronicles is fundamentally interested in the Temple, and its conclusion with Cyrus's decree points to the inauguration of a new era in which Israel will return to Jerusalem and the land of Israel at large. The role of the house of David in that future, however, must remain uncertain.

The name of the book, *dibrê hayyāmîm*, "accounts/annals of the days," simply indicates its function as a Chronicle of the Kings of Judah, or ideally of all Israel.[3] Rabbinic tradition views Chronicles as a single book. It was divided into two books in the Septuagint and Latin versions of the book employed in Christianity. Jewish Bibles only began to present it as two books, following the Christian practice, with the advent of Hebrew printing in the fifteenth century CE. Rabbinic

471

tradition views Chronicles as a single work with Ezra–Nehemiah, and it maintains that Ezra wrote the genealogies of Chronicles (1 Chr 1–9) whereas Nehemiah wrote the rest of the book (*b. Baba Batra* 15a). It is generally viewed as a supplement to Samuel and Kings; indeed, the Greek version of the book is named *paraleipomenōn*, "(the book) of things omitted," perhaps reflecting the viewpoint of the Hellenistic Jewish community which initially produced and read the Greek version of the work as sacred scripture. Because of its overlapping character with Samuel–Kings, Rabbinic tradition maintains that the book is "only to be expounded midrashically" (*Lev Rab* 1:3). Isaac Abravanel, a well-known medieval Jewish interpreter, states that he never read Chronicles until he began to write his commentary on Samuel. No full commentary on Chronicles was produced by the medieval interpreters; apparently their commentaries on Samuel and Kings were deemed sufficient for overlapping segments. Commentaries on Chronicles tended to focus on elements of the work that deviated from Samuel and Kings.

Chronicles appears at the end of the Ketuvim immediately following Ezra–Nehemiah in most biblical manuscripts and printed editions, although it appears at the beginning of the Ketuvim in some major manuscripts, such as the Aleppo and St. Petersburg codices of the Bible. Chronicles' position at the end of the Ketuvim—and therefore of the Bible as a whole—apparently reflects its uncertainty concerning the future of the Jewish community following Cyrus's decree, viz., will a new monarchy be established at some point following the restoration of the Temple? Its position at the head of the Ketuvim in some manuscripts likely reflects its historical priority, beginning with Adam and continuing through the decree of Cyrus, so that together with Ezra–Nehemiah, which begins with the decree of Cyrus, it forms a literary envelope for the Ketuvim.

From the initial work of Leopold Zunz in 1832,[4] modern scholarship has tended to follow the Rabbinic viewpoint that Chronicles and Ezra–Nehemiah are the product of the same authors. Factors in this decision included the overlapping references to Cyrus's decree at the end of Chronicles and the beginning of Ezra–Nehemiah, similar linguistic features, including vocabulary, syntax, and style, the narrative of 1 Esdras which draws upon 2 Chr 35–36, Ezra 1–10, and Neh 10, and similar historical and theological viewpoints rooted in concerns for the Temple and the priesthood. But more recent work by a number of scholars has pointed to the differences between the two works. Commentaries and studies by Japhet and Williamson point to distinctive linguistic style in Chronicles and Ezra–Nehemiah.[5] There are major thematic differences as well. Chronicles' concept of retribution appears to be lacking in Ezra–Nehemiah; the two works display differing attitudes toward the northern tribes of Israel insofar as Chronicles considers them to be a part of Israel whereas Ezra–Nehemiah does not; Chronicles is far more concerned with the house of David than Ezra–Nehemiah; Chronicles focuses on Jacob as the ancestor of Israel whereas Ezra–Nehemiah is more concerned with Abraham as the chosen of G-d and the Exodus as the defining moment in Israel's national identity; Chronicles is very concerned with the role of prophets in Israel's history whereas Ezra–Nehemiah is not so greatly concerned with prophets; the *nĕtînîm*, "Temple servants," of Ezra–Nehemiah do not appear in Chronicles; and Chronicles views Israel as comprising all twelve tribes whereas Ezra–Nehemiah views Israel as comprising Judah, Benjamin, and Levi.

Dates for the composition of Chronicles range from the late sixth through the fourth or third centuries BCE. Although many scholars now place the date for the composition of Chronicles in the fourth century BCE, its concern for the restoration of the Temple, its interest in the house of David, and its concern with Cyrus's decree might point to the late sixth century when the Temple was rebuilt and the possibility of the restoration of the house of David was considered in some circles, for example, Haggai. Nevertheless, Chronicles' ambiguous viewpoint on the restoration of the house of David—it does not specifically call for the restoration of the Davidic monarchy—leaves open the possibility of the later date. In priestly thought, the destruction of the old Temple and the restoration of the new Temple inaugurate a new creation in the world.[6] In that new creation, the Persian monarch may well be recognized as G-d's anointed monarch (see Isa 44:28; 45:1; Ezra–Nehemiah). Chronicles is interested in the house of David, but it ends by pointing to the role of Cyrus in rebuilding the Temple. Perhaps this final episode in Chronicles justifies the lack of interest in Judaism for the restoration of the house of David in the fifth through third centuries BCE. Such interest only re-emerges in the second century BCE as a result of widespread dissatisfaction with the Hasmonean dynasty, which at times turned on its own people and ultimately led Judah to submission to Rome. Other factors pointing to a later date include the fact that the genealogy of the sons of Jehoiachin (Jeconiah) in 1 Chr 3:17-24 allow only for six generations, which would place the line in the years 400 to 350 BCE; the mention of darics, a Persian coin minted in 515 BCE during the reign of Darius I, in 1 Chr 29:7 points to Persian-period composition; and the reference to "the eyes of YHWH run to and fro throughout the whole earth" from Zech 4:10 suggests a time after the composition of the book of Zechariah. Finally, Chronicles' interpretative intertextual relationship with Samuel and Kings indicates that it was composed at a later time. Insofar as the final form of Samuel–Kings points to the period of the Babylonian exile when Jehoiachin was released from prison by Merodach Baladan of Babylon (Amel Marduk, r. 562–560), Chronicles must date to a later period.

The literary form of the book of Chronicles is determined by its interest in the construction of the Jerusalem Temple by the house of David, its history during the reigns of the kings of Judah, its destruction as a result of pollution by the generation of 587–586 BCE, and its rebuilding as a result of the decree of Cyrus of Persia. Insofar as the Temple is conceived as the holy center of creation, it makes sense to begin the history with Adam himself, the first human being created at the outset of creation, and to conclude with the destruction of the Temple and the decree for the building of new Temple in the aftermath of the destruction of the first.

The first major unit of the book of Chronicles is the genealogical lists in 1 Chr 1–9. The unit begins in 1 Chr 1:1 with a genealogy beginning with Adam, the first human being, and it continues through 1 Chr 9:44 with the conclusion of a genealogy devoted to Gibeon. An entirely new narrative concerned with the death of Saul and his sons in battle with the Philistines begins in 1 Chr 10:1. Insofar as this narrative introduces a major new block concerned with the reign of King David, 1 Chr 1–9 emerges as a genealogy of Israel within the context of humankind prior to David.

The internal structure of 1 Chr 1–9 comprises a series of genealogical lists. The first appears in 1 Chr 1:1-53, which trace the development of humankind from Adam through the ancestors of Israel, including Abraham, Ishmael, Isaac, Esau, and Israel (Jacob), and the Edomites. A second genealogy then follows in 1 Chr 2:1-55, which traces the sons of Israel (Jacob) and their respective descendants. The third genealogy in 1 Chr 3:1-24 takes up the sons of David, including all of the kings of Judah as well as the descendants of Jeconiah (Jehoiachin), the last king of Judah who spent his life in Babylon following his deportation from Jerusalem in 597 BCE. The fourth genealogy in 1 Chr 4:1—5:41 takes up the sons of some of the tribes of Israel, beginning with Judah and continuing with Simeon, Reuben, Gad, the half tribe of Manasseh living in the Trans-Jordan, and the Levites. The focus of this section appears to lie in Judah at the center and the marginal tribes in the Trans-Jordan and the Philistine plain. First Chronicles 6:1-66 then presents a genealogy of the tribe of Levi that lays out the major priestly families of Gersom, Kohath, and Merari. First Chronicles 7:1-40 then presents genealogies of the major tribes situated in the land of Israel west of the Jordan River, including Issachar, Benjamin, Naphtali, Manasseh, Ephraim, and Asher. First Chronicles 8:1-40 returns to Benjamin with a far more detailed genealogy that focuses especially on the line of Saul, the first king of Israel prior to David. Finally, 1 Chr 9:1-44 presents a genealogy of those Israelites who settled in Judah following Judah's exile to Babylon.

The second major segment of the book of Chronicles appears in 1 Chr 10–29 which presents the reign of King David. The segment begins with an account in 1 Chr 10 of the death of Saul and his sons in battle with the Philistines at Mt. Gilboa and it concludes in 1 Chr 29 with an account of David's final announcement that his son Solomon would succeed him as king followed by his death and a summation of his reign. The account of Solomon's reign then follows, beginning in 2 Chr 1.

The first subunit of the account of David's reign appears in 1 Chr 10:1—12:41, which relate David's rise to kingship over all Israel. 1 Chronicles 10:1-14 which recounts Saul's death in battle at Mt. Gilboa and the subsequent transfer of royal power to David ben Jesse as a result of Saul's trespass. 1 Chronicles 11:1—12:41 then presents an account of David's accession to kingship over all Israel, including accounts of Israel's anointing David as king in 1 Chr 11:1-3, David's capture of Jerusalem to serve as his capital in 1 Chr 11:4-9, and lists of the warriors who supported David in his rise to kingship over Israel in 1 Chr 11:10—12:41.

The second sub-unit, 1 Chr 13:1—17:27, relates David's efforts to move the Ark of the Covenant from Kirath Jearim to Jerusalem and thereby establish Jerusalem as the location for the holy presence of YHWH. First Chronicles 13:1-14 recounts David's first attempt to bring the Ark of the Covenant to Jerusalem, which resulted in failure when G-d killed Uzza for touching the sacred Ark. First Chronicles 14:1-17 relates events of David's early reign, including Hiram's efforts to build a house for David, the names of David's children born to him in Jerusalem, and his defeat of the Philistines. First Chronicles 15:1—16:43 relates David's successful attempt to move the Ark of the Covenant to Jerusalem, including the transport of the ark to Jerusalem by the Levites in 1 Chr 15:1-29 and the worship service conducted in Jerusalem upon the entry of the ark into the city in 1 Chr 16:1-43. First Chronicles 17:1-27 relates G-d's promise of an eternal royal house for David following the refusal to accept David's plans to build a temple for G-d.

The third major sub-unit, 1 Chr 18:1—21:30, relates David's victories over his enemies. First Chronicles 18:1-17 recounts David's victories over his enemies and the extent of the Davidic empire. First Chronicles 19:1-19 recounts David's victories over the Aramaeans. First Chronicles 20:1-8 relates further victories over the Ammonites and the Philistines. First Chronicles 21:1-30 recounts David's attempt to take a census of Israel and the plague unleashed against Israel as a result of G-d's displeasure over the matter.

The fourth major sub-unit appears in 1 Chr 22:1—29:25, which relates David's actions to prepare for the building of the Temple in Jerusalem. First Chronicles 22:1-19 recounts David's initial preparations, including his declaration that the Temple would be built in Jerusalem, his assignment of work details to aliens living in the land, his designation of Solomon as the one who would actually build the Temple, and his orders to his officers to support Solomon. First Chronicles 23:1—27:34 relates David's appointment of the Levites to undertake construction and administration to the Temple. Included within this section are David's census of the Levites in 1 Chr 23:1-32, the assignment of the Levites to the 24 priestly watches for he Temple in 1 Chr 24:1-31, the establishment of the Levitical musicians in 1 Chr 25:1-30, the establishment of the Levitical gatekeepers in 1 Chr 26:1-32, the assignment of building tasks to the people of Israel in 1 Chr 27:1-34, and David's final assembly of all Israel in which he laid out his plans for the Temple and designated Solomon as his successor in 1 Chr 28:1—29:25.

The final segment of the account of David's reign, 1 Chr 29:26-30, presents the summation of David's reign.

The third major segment of Chronicles, 2 Chr 1:1—9:31, presents the account of Solomon's reign. The segment begins with an account of Solomon's consolidation of his rule in 2 Chr 1:1-17 and it concludes with a regnal summation in

2 Chr 9:29-31. The account of Rehoboam's reign then follows, beginning in 1 Chr 10:1.

The first sub-unit, 2 Chr 1:1-17, relates Solomon's efforts to consolidate his reign, including his assembly of the people at Gibeon in 2 Chr 1:1-6, his dream at Gibeon in which YHWH granted him wisdom in 2 Chr 1:7-13, and his trade in chariots and horses that made him and Israel rich in 2 Chr 1:14-17.

The second sub-unit, 2 Chr 1:18—2:17, relates Solomon's initial preparations for the building of the Temple, including his resolution to build the Temple in 2 Chr 1:18, his negotiations with King Huram of Tyre to provide materials and assistance in the building in 2 Chr 2:1-15, and his assignment of building task to the resident aliens of the land in 2 Chr 2:16—2:17.

The third sub-unit, 2 Chr 3:1—4:21, relates Solomon's efforts to build the Temple in Jerusalem, including his commencement of the project in 2 Chr 3:1-2, the dimensions, layout, and features of the Temple in 2 Chr 3:3-17, his building of the various fixtures around the Temple in 2 Chr 4:1-22, including the altar in 2 Chr 4:1, the molten sea in 2 Chr 4:2-5, the various installations in 2 Chr 4:6-10, and the various implements in 2 Chr 4:11-21.

The fourth sub-unit, 2 Chr 5:1—7:22, recounts Solomon's dedication ceremony for the Temple, including his deposit of David's valuables in the Temple in 2 Chr 5:1, his calling of the assembly in 2 Chr 5:2-6, the priests' deposit of the Ark of the Covenant in the sanctuary in 2 Chr 5:7-14, the account of Solomon's dedication speech in 2 Chr 6:1-42, the account of the initial offerings in 2 Chr 7:1-8, the account of Solomon's speech on the eighth day of the festival in 2 Chr 7:9-22 in which he reiterated Israel's relationship with YHWH, including the promise to the house of David.

The fifth sub-unit, 2 Chr 8:1—9:28, relates the other accomplishments of Solomon's reign, including his building activities in 2 Chr 8:1-11, his further efforts on behalf of the Temple in 2 Chr 8:12-16, his trade relations in 2 Chr 8:17-18, the visit of the Queen of Sheba in 2 Chr 9:1-12, his riches in 2 Chr 9:13-21, and his reputation in 2 Chr 9:22-28.

Finally, 2 Chr 9:29-31 presents the concluding regnal summary of Solomon's reign.

Segments four through twenty-three of the book of Chronicles present accounts of the reigns of the kings of Judah, each of which is demarcated by introductory or concluding regnal formulae, including Rehoboam in 2 Chr 10:1—12:15, Abijah in 2 Chr 13:1-23, Asa in 2 Chr 14:1—16:14, Jehoshaphat in 2 Chr 17:1—20:37, Jehoram in 2 Chr 21:1-20, Ahaziah in 2 Chr 22:1-9, Athaliah bat Omri/Ahab in 2 Chr 22:10—23:21, Jehoash in 2 Chr 24:1-27, Amaziah in 2 Chr 25:1-28, Uzziah in 2 Chr 26:1-23, Jotham in 2 Chr 27:1-9, Ahaz in 2 Chr 28:1-27, Hezekiah in 2 Chr 29:1—32:33, Manasseh in 2 Chr 33:1-20, Amon in 2 Chr 33:21-25, Josiah in 2 Chr 34:1—35:27, Jehoahaz in 2 Chr 36:1-4, Jehoiakim in 2 Chr 36:5-8, Jehoia-chin in 2 Chr 36:9-10, and Zedekiah in 2 Chr 36:11-21, which saw the destruction

of the Temple by the Babylonians, the destruction of Jerusalem, and the exile of
the people to Babylonia from the land of Israel.

Finally, segment twenty-four of the book, 2 Chr 36:22-23, relates the decree of
King Cyrus of Persia that YHWH has charged him to rebuild the Temple in
Jerusalem.

The structural diagram of Chronicles appears as follows:[7]

The fundamental theological concerns of the book of Chronicles are evident from a combination of factors, including the formal literary structure of the book of the book and its intertextual relationship with the Former Prophets. Chronicles is a rewritten history of Israel. It is based on the account of Israel's history as presented in the Former Prophets, particularly Samuel and Kings and perhaps even the Pentateuch, but it revises the earlier work in an effort to present a more comprehensive account of Israel's history in keeping with its own worldview and theological principles.

In many cases, Chronicles simply reworks difficult readings in the narratives, such as 2 Chr 10:2, which states that Jeroboam "returned" (Hebrew, *wayyāšāb*) from Egypt, whereas 1 Kgs 12:2 states that Jeroboam "settled" (Hebrew, *wayyēšeb*) in Egypt after fleeing from Solomon. The difference is not inconsequential. In Kings, Jeroboam is not directly involved in planning or instigating the revolt against Rehoboam. He is in Egypt at the outset of the revolt against Rehoboam, but only appears at Shechem in the following verse when he is summoned to join the assembly of Israel. In Chronicles, Jeroboam has already returned from Egypt at the outset of the revolt and thereby has a hand in planning and instigating the revolt, that is, he is culpable figure from the outset in Chronicles whereas his role is ambiguous in Kings.

In other cases, Chronicles presents a completely new account, such as the genealogies of human ancestors in 1 Chr 1–9 and the details of Temple organization in 1 Chr 22–29 that do not appear in the Former Prophets at all. These new segments present the establishment of the Temple as the culminating event of human history and portray King David of Israel as the decisive figure who founds and plans the Temple, leaving his son Solomon as the figure who merely carries out his father's plans. Alternatively, Chronicles extensively rewrites a known narrative from Samuel–Kings, such as the entry of the Ark of the Covenant in 1 Chr 15–16. Second Samuel 6 presents the entry of the Ark into Jerusalem as a cultic event that establishes Jerusalem as the holy city and as the occasion when David upbraids his wife Michal for criticizing his dancing before the women of Jerusalem by stating that he will never have relations with her again, thereby denying her the opportunity to continue her father Saul's royal line. In 2 Sam 6, David's act brings the house of Saul to an end and opens the opportunity for David to found his own dynasty by having sons with his other wives. First Chronicles 15–16 presents the bulk of the Michal narrative, but omits David's statements insofar as David has already been declared king in his own right in 1 Chr 10:14 as a result of the trespasses of Saul. Furthermore, the liturgical ceremony accompanying the entry of the Ark into Jerusalem appears in 1 Chr 16, including portions of Pss 96; 105; and 106 as sung by the Levites. This text provides one of the few instances in the Bible where readers may learn how the Psalms functioned in Israelite/Judean liturgies and demonstrates from the outset how the site of the Temple would function in relation to the Temple liturgy.

Chronicles is first and foremost concerned with the Jerusalem Temple as the holy center of creation.[8] The book presents an account of the history of humankind from Adam through the reigns of all the Davidic kings as well as the reign of King Cyrus of Persia in an effort to portray the history of the Jerusalem Temple. By beginning with Adam and tracing human history through the reign of Saul in 1 Chr 1–9, Chronicles signals its interest in the establishment of the Jerusalem Temple as a decisive event in human history that firmly establishes recognition of YHWH as the G-d of Israel and the author of all creation. Insofar as the Temple serves as the holy center for the recognition of YHWH's reign and role as a creator, the Temple also serves as the focal point for the holiness and stability of that created world, viz., so long as the Temple stands in Jerusalem, both Israel and the world of creation at large are fundamentally secure. This does not mean that threats to the security of the house of David, Israel, and the world will not materialize, but it does mean that the capacity to address such threats that would destabilize the world lies with the people of Israel and their priests who are expected to maintain the sanctity of the Temple as the means to maintain the sanctity and security of the world. It is only when the officers and priests of the people allow the Temple to become corrupted by committing trespasses like those of the nations in 2 Chr 36:14 that the Temple, Jerusalem, Israel, and the world will fall into chaos and exile.

The house of David is the patron and caretaker of the Jerusalem Temple. Whereas the northern kingdom of Israel plays a prominent role in Samuel–Kings as the sinful breakaway kingdom against which Judah is judged, Chronicles gives only perfunctory attention to the northern kings and only when it is necessary to illustrate some aspect of the Judean monarchs. The book of Chronicles is heavily invested in the history of the royal house of David, but it is interested in the house of David primarily because of its role in building and maintaining the Jerusalem

Temple. The book gives detailed attention to David's reign in 1 Chr 10–29 in an effort to delineate David's role as the founder of the Jerusalem Temple and the figure who sets in order its placement in the city of Jerusalem, its structure and plans, the mechanisms for building the Temple, its priesthood and its various functions, and its fundamental role as the holy center of Israel and creation. The book also gives detailed attention in 2 Chr 1–9 to Solomon's reign and role as builder of the Temple and as chief officiant at the ceremony of its dedication. Solomon of course is not a priest, but as the king of Israel who built the Temple, he plays the key role in overseeing and speaking at the dedication ceremonies.

The reigns of the remaining kings of the house of David are presented in order. Throughout the presentation, it is clear that the kings are judged as righteous or wicked much as they are in the book of Kings, and the text of Chronicles makes it clear that the kings' observance of YHWH's Torah is the primary criterion by which they are judged. Thus Rehoboam abandons YHWH's Torah in 2 Chr 10–12 (see especially 2 Chr 12:1) and he is punished for having done so by Pharaoh Shishak's invasion of the land of Israel. Asa does what is right in 2 Chr 14–16 (see especially 2 Chr 14:1) and was able to protect his people from foreign invasion. Indeed, the prophet Azariah ben Oded reinforced the link between observance of YHWH's expectations and the king's fortunes in an oracle that lays out the basic premises that observance of Torah leads to blessing and abandonment of Torah leads to punishment (see 2 Chr 15:1-7). Jehoshaphat establishes the judicial system in Israel in 2 Chr 17–20 (see especially 2 Chr 19:4-11) as a means to ensure the proper adjudication of divine Torah. Hezekiah purged and rededicated the Temple and then invited all Israel and Judah to celebrate Passover in 2 Chr 29–32 in an effort to unite the nation around its holy center and to purge the land of Israel at large of its various abominations.

Nevertheless, Chronicles displays a very different understanding of human wrongdoing and repentance than that found in the Former Prophets. King Manasseh of Judah is portrayed as the quintessentially evil monarch of the Former Prophets, and he is charged in 2 Kgs 21 as the one man responsible for YHWH's decision to destroy the Jerusalem Temple. Manasseh thereby becomes responsible for the punishment of the city of Jerusalem and the deaths and exile of its inhabitants some sixty years after his own lifetime. By contrast, King Manasseh is portrayed in 2 Chr 33:1-20 as a figure who repents of his wrongdoing after having been dragged in chains to Babylon.[9] Manasseh thereby becomes the primary example in Chronicles for an understanding of repentance which maintains that YHWH will forgive even the most hardened wrongdoers when genuine repentance is offered. Josiah, on the other hand, portrayed in 2 Kgs 22–23 as the quintessential righteous king of the house of David, celebrates Passover like Hezekiah before him but becomes responsible for his own death in 2 Chr 34–35 when he refuses to abide by YHWH's will (articulated by Pharaoh Necho in 2 Chr 35:20-24). Unlike the portrayal of the kings in the book of Kings, whose sins condemn all Israel and Judah even generations after they are committed,

Chronicles maintains that the sins of a monarch only condemn him and the generation of Israelites living during his lifetime. Chronicles further maintains that the Temple and the city of Jerusalem were not destroyed on account of the sins of earlier generations; 2 Chr 36:14 maintains that the disaster took place because all the officers of the priests and the people of the time committed trespasses that defiled the holy Temple, thereby necessitating its destruction. Much like Ezekiel (see Ezek 18), Chronicles holds to a view of collective or corporate punishment and repentance for a generation that reaps the results of its own actions in its own time.

Finally, there is no indication of a future for the house of David at the end of the narrative. Zedekiah's death is omitted in 2 Chr 36:11-21; he simply disappears from the scene as the text focuses on the destruction of the Temple and the exile of the people. Jehoiachin's release from prison, which concludes the Kings narrative in 2 Kgs 25:27-30 is likewise absent from the Chronicles narrative. According to 2 Chr 36:9-10, he is simply exiled and we hear no more about him, although 1 Chr 3:16-17 names his sons even though none of them ever sits on the throne in Jerusalem. Shealtiel's son Zerubbabel returns to Jerusalem, but he disappears before the Temple is completed and no one knows what his fate might have been. Altogether, the house of David ceases to be relevant with the destruction of the Temple, but Cyrus emerges instead in 2 Chr 36:22-23. By issue his decree that Jews may return to Jerusalem to rebuild the Temple, Cyrus emerges in place of David as the patron of the Second Temple, and the Persian monarchy thereby becomes the caretakers of the sanctuary in place of the house of David. Such a portrayal raises questions about the role of a Judean monarchy or state, viz., Chronicles authorizes Persian rule of Judah, but it says nothing of the resumption of Davidic or even of native Judean rule.

By revising history as presented in the Former Prophets, Chronicles enters into a dialog with the Former Prophets that represents reflection on the earlier work, including attempts to resolve problems presented therein or to present alternative perspectives to those of the Former Prophets. Chronicles thereby points to a fundamental interest in the Jewish Bible to consider a variety of viewpoints in the understanding divine purpose in Israel's history, the fundamental role of the Jerusalem Temple as the holy center of creation, human responsibility for both wrongdoing and repentance in relation to Israel's experience in history, and finally, even the role of the house of David in Israel's past and its future.

NOTES

[1] For overviews of modern scholarship on Chronicles, see Ralph W. Klein, "Chronicles, Book of 1–2," *ABD* 1:992–1002; Roddy L. Braun, "Martin Noth and the Chronicler's History," in *The History of Israel's Traditions: The Heritage of Martin Noth*, ed. S. L. McKenzie and M. P. Graham (JSOTSup 182; Sheffield: Sheffield Academic, 1994), 63–80. For commentaries, see especially H. G. M. Williamson, *1 and 2 Chronicles* (NCeB; Grand Rapids: Eerdmans, 1982);

Simon J. DeVries, *1 and 2 Chronicles* (FOTL 11; Grand Rapids: Eerdmans, 1989); Sara Japhet, *I and II Chronicles: A Commentary* (OTL; Louisville: Westminster John Knox, 1993); Gary N. Knoppers, *1 Chronicles 1–9* (AB 12; New York: Doubleday, 2003); idem, *1 Chronicles 10–29* (AB 12A; New York: Doubleday, 2004); Steven L. McKenzie, *1–2 Chronicles* (AOTC; Nashville: Abingdon, 2004); Ralph W. Klein, *1 Chronicles* (Hermeneia; Minneapolis: Fortress Press, 2006). See also Martin Noth, *The Chronicler's History* (JSOTSup 50; Sheffield: Sheffield Academic, 1987).

[2] For example, William M. Schniedewind, *The Word of G-d in Transition: From Prophet to Exegete in the Second Temple Period* (JSOTSup 197; Sheffield: Sheffield Academic, 1995).

[3] For an overview discussion of Chronicles in Judaism, see "Chronicles, Book of," *EncJud* 5:517–34.

[4] Leopold Zunz, *Die gottesdienstlichen Vorträge der Juden* (Hildesheim: Olms, 1966).

[5] See Williamson, *1 and 2 Chronicles*, 5–17; see also idem, *Israel in the Books of Chronicles* (Cambridge: Cambridge University Press, 1977); Japhet, *I and II Chronicles*, 3–8, see also idem, *The Ideology of the Book of Chronicles and its Place in Biblical Thought* (Frankfurt: Lang, 1989).

[6] Jon D. Levenson, "The Temple and the World," *JR* 64 (1984): 275–98.

[7] Contra DeVries, *1 and 2 Chronicles*, 7–20, 21–28, 95–115.

[8] Levenson, "The Temple and the World."

[9] See my "King Manasseh of Judah and the Problem of Theodicy in the Deuteronomistic History," in *Good Kings and Bad Kings*, ed. L. L. Grabbe (JSOTSup 393; London: T&T Clark International, 2005), 264–78, and *Reading the Hebrew Bible after the Shoah: Engaging Holocaust Theology* (Minneapolis: Fortress Press, 2008), 64–83.

Part V

Conclusion

Some Concluding Thoughts

The preceding study of the Tanak makes a number of key points.

First, this study contends that biblical theology is a valid means for Jews to employ in an effort to interpret the Tanak. Although biblical theology originated in Christianity and continues to function as a means by which Christians interpret the Old and New Testaments, a Jewish biblical theology provides Judaism with a means to engage the Tanak, to identify and examine its views concerning the nature and character of G-d, the people of Israel and Judah, and the world of creation at large, and to engage in dialog with those claims together with those of the larger Jewish tradition. By such engagement, Judaism is better able to understand the foundations of Jewish tradition and to employ the Tanak in dialog with the rest of the tradition to address contemporary issues in Jewish life and thought, such as the character of Judaism in the modern world, including both the Diaspora and modern Israel; the theological, social, and political challenges posed to Judaism by the Shoah, assimilation, and attempts to delegitimize and undermine the modern state of Israel; and the opportunities offered to develop Judaism by the freedom enjoyed by Jews in the modern Diaspora community of America as well as in the modern state of Israel.

Second, this study of the Tanak contends that the Tanak itself, the Jewish version of the Bible, must be recognized as a unique version that rightly stands as the foundation of Judaism and Jewish life, tradition, thought, and practice. The Tanak displays a distinctive canonical structure and Hebrew/Aramaic Masoretic text that cannot be simply equated with the Christian forms and readings of the Old Testament that may have originated as Jewish scripture but may no longer be identified or function as such. The distinctive three-part structure of the Tanak, viz., Torah or Instruction, Nevi'im or Prophets, and Ketuvim or Writings, indicates a concern with articulating and reflecting upon the ideal relationship between G-d and the Jewish people within the context of G-d's creation, the disruption of that relationship as a result of the Assyrian and Babylonian exiles, and the restoration of that ideal relationship in the aftermath of exile. In this respect, the Tanak displays concerns that have occupied Jews for millennia, viz., the question of Judaism's ideal and unique relationship with G-d in the modern world, the challenges posed by exile following the destruction of the Second Temple by the Romans and life in non-Jewish lands, and the challenges and expectations of restoring Jewish life in the land of Israel itself.

Third, the Jewish Bible as a whole does not represent a consistent viewpoint concerning G-d, the nature of Israel's or Judah's relationship with G-d, the character of the Jewish people, the role and understanding of the Temple and divine Torah, life in the land of Israel, and others. Whereas the Torah and the Prophets generally present G-d as the all-powerful and righteous author of creation, books such as Job and Esther raise questions concerning divine righteousness, presence, and the will and power to act. Whereas the first four books of the Torah present G-d's covenant with Israel as permanent, Deuteronomy points to conditional aspects of the covenant while simultaneously maintaining that it is permanent. Whereas Leviticus and Deuteronomy posit a central sanctuary for Israel, Kings and Chronicles end with the destruction of the Jerusalem Temple and the question of what will happen next. Whereas Samuel and Kings maintain that the sins of the ancestors prompt the punishment of their descendants, Chronicles maintains that a given generation suffers for its own sins. Whereas books such as Ezekiel and the Twelve Prophets uphold G-d's promises to support and protect the Davidic monarchy, books such as Isaiah and Ezra–Nehemiah envision Jewish life under Persian control. Whereas the prophets, such as Isaiah, Jeremiah, Ezekiel, and the Twelve assert divine justice, Lamentations calls that justice into question. Whereas the bulk of the Bible posits a public relationship with G-d through the Temple and its teachings or through history, Song of Songs maintains that the relationship is experienced through intimacy. There is continuous debate in the Psalms concerning G-d's actions on behalf of Israel and G-d's willingness and ability to protect the nation from threats. To be sure, Jews in modern times do not always agree among themselves, as is exemplified by the differing approaches to Judaism by the religious movements, of Orthodoxy, Conservative Judaism, Reform Judaism, and the Reconstructionist and Renewal movements, as well as the different approaches offered by modern Jewish Diaspora cultural movements and modern Zionism in all of its forms. And Judaism throughout its history has demonstrated a marked ability to produce different movements that met and continue to meet the needs of Jews throughout time: the Rabbinic movement, the writings of the philosophers and poets, the works and practices of the Kabbalists and Hasidim, and others. Judaism cannot be reduced to a single movement or understanding of G-d and the Jewish people, and neither is the Tanak reduced to a single principle. Just as Judaism has flourished throughout the centuries as a result of its diversity, so the Bible displays the very diversity that lies at the heart of Judaism itself. Recognition of this point will aid in recognizing the diversity and dialogical character of Judaism in the present as well as in the past.

Finally, just as Judaism is in dialog with itself among its various constituent movements and viewpoints, so is Judaism in dialog with non-Jewish religious movements, such as Christianity, Islam, Buddhism, Hinduism, and others. This is a particularly important point with regard to Christianity because the two traditions share a common basis in the Hebrew Bible even, even though both construct and read that Bible very differently. Recognition of the distinctive character of the Tanak in relation to Christian understandings of the Old Testament plays a crucial role in articulating Judaism's distinctive theological worldview in dialog with Christianity and collapsing the notion that the two traditions should arrive at a common understanding of their Bibles. Such recognition also plays a crucial role in articulating Judaism's distinctive theological worldview to other religious traditions. True inter-religious dialog comes not from the assertions that all religions—or any religions for that matter—are fundamentally the same; it comes from recognition of the differences between them and affirming the right to differ while holding to the integrity of one's own viewpoint. Indeed, that principle is articulated in Mic 4:1-5,

> And it shall come to pass in future days,
> that the mountain of the house of YHWH shall be established
> at the top of the mountains and it shall be lifted up above the hills.
> And many nations shall come and say,
> "Come, let us go up to the mountain of YHWH,
> And to the house of the G-d of Jacob,
> So that YHWH may teach us G-d's ways that we may walk in G-d's paths,
> For from Zion, Torah goes forth and the word of YHWH from Jerusalem.
> And YHWH will judge many peoples, and arbitrate for strong nations,
> And they shall beat their swords into plowshares and their spears into pruning hooks
> A nation shall not lift a sword against another nation, and they shall no longer learn war.
> And they shall sit, each under its vine and under its fig tree,
> and no one shall make them afraid
> for the mouth of YHWH Seba'ot has spoken
> For all the peoples will walk, each in the name of its own gods,
> but we shall walk in the name of YHWH, our G-d, forever and ever."

BIBLIOGRAPHY

Ackroyd, Peter R. "Isaiah 36–39: Structure and Function." Pages 105–20, 274–78 in *Studies in the Religious Tradition of the Old Testament*. London: SCM, 1987.

Ahlström, Gösta W. *Joel and the Temple Cult of Jerusalem*. VTSup 21. Leiden: Brill, 1971.

———. *The History of Ancient Palestine*. Minneapolis: Fortress Press, 1993.

Alcalay, R. *The Complete Hebrew–English Dictionary*. Ramat-Gan: Massada, n.d.

Almog, Shmuel, ed. *Antisemitism through the Ages*. Oxford: Pergamon, 1988.

Alt, Albrecht. "Die Heimat des Deuteronomiums." Pages 250–75 in *Kleine Schriften zur Geshichte des Volkes Israel II*. Munich: Beck, 1953.

———. "The Formation of the Israelite State in Palestine." Pages 223–309 in *Essays in Old Testament History and Religion*. Garden City: Doubleday, 1967.

———. "Judas Gaue under Josia." Pages 276–88 in *Kleine Schriften zur Geschichte des Volkes Israel II*. Munich: Beck, 1953.

———. "The Monarchy in the Kingdoms of Israel and Judah." Pages 311–35 in *Essays in Old Testament History and Religion*. Garden City: Doubleday, 1967.

———. "The Settlement of the Israelites in Palestine." Pages 173–221 in *Essays on Old Testament History and Religion*. Garden City: Doubleday, 1967.

Amit, Yairah. *The Book of Judges: The Art of Editing*. BibInt 38. Leiden: Brill, 1999.

———. "Hidden Polemics in the Conquest of Dan: Judges xvii–xviii." *VT* 40 (1990): 4–20.

———. *Judges*. Miqra leYisrael. Jerusalem: Magnes, 1999 (Hebrew).

———. "Literature in the Service of Politics: Studies in Judges 19–21." Pages 28–40 in *Politics and Theopolitics in the Bible and Postbiblical Literature*. Edited by H. Graf Reventlow and B. Uffenheimer. JSOTSup 171. Sheffield: Sheffield Academic, 1994.

Anderson, Bernhard W. "'G-d with Us'—in Judgment and in Mercy: The Editorial Structure of Isaiah 5–10(11)." Pages 230–45 in *Canon, Theology, and Old Testament Interpretation*. Edited by Gene M. Tucker et al. Philadelphia: Fortress Press, 1988.

Avigad, Nahman. *Hebrew Bullae from the Time of Jeremiah: Remnants of a Burnt Archive*. Jerusalem: Israel Exploration Society, 1986.

Bakhtin, Mikhail. *The Dialogic Imagination*. Austin: University of Texas, 1981.

Balentine, Samuel E. *The Hidden G-d: The Hiding of the Face of G-d in the Old Testament*. Oxford: Oxford University Press, 1983.

Barr, James. *The Concept of Biblical Theology: An Old Testament Perspective*. Minneapolis: Fortress Press, 1999.

Baskin, Judith. *Pharaoh's Counselors*. BJS 47. Chico, CA: Scholars Press, 1983.

Baumann, Gerlinde. *Love and Violence: Marriage as Metaphor for the Relationship between YHWH and Israel in the Prophetic Books*. Translated by L. Maloney. Collegeville: Liturgical, 2003.

Beckwith, Roger T. "Formation of the Hebrew Bible." Pages 39–86 in *Mikra: Text, Translation, Reading, and Interpretation of the Hebrew Bible in Ancient Judaism and Early Christianity*. Edited by M. J. Mulder et al. CRIANT 2. Philadelphia: Fortress Press, 1988.

———. *The Old Testament Canon of the New Testament Church*. Grand Rapids: Eerdmans, 1986.

Benoit, P. et al. *Les Grottes de Murabba'at*. DJD 2. Oxford: Clarendon, 1961.

Ben Zvi, Ehud. *A Historical-Critical Study of the Book of Obadiah*. BZAW 242. Berlin: de Gruyter, 1996.

———. *Signs of Jonah: Reading and Rereading Jonah in Ancient Yehud*. JSOTSup 367. London: Sheffield Academic, 2003.

———. "Twelve Prophetic Books or 'The Twelve': A Few Preliminary Considerations." Pages 125–56 in *Forming Prophetic Literature: Essays on Isaiah and the Twelve in Honor of J. D. W. Watts*. Edited by J. W. Watts and P. R. House. JSOTSup 235. Sheffield: Sheffield Academic, 1996.

Bergler, Siegfried. *Joel als Schriftinterpret*. BEATAJ 16. Frankfurt: Peter Lang, 1988.

Berkovits, Eliezer. *Faith after the Holocaust*. New York: Ktav, 1973.

———. *Man and G-d: Studies in Biblical Theology*. Detroit: Wayne State University Press, 1969.

Berlin, Adele. *Esther*. JPS Bible Commentary. Philadelphia: Jewish Publication Society, 2001.

———. *Lamentations: A Commentary*. OTL. Louisville: Westminster John Knox, 2002.

Biran, Avraham, and Joseph Naveh. "An Aramaic Stele Fragment from Tel Dan." *IEJ* 43 (1993): 81–98.

———. "The Tel Dan Inscription: A New Fragment." *IEJ* 45 (1995): 1–18.

Blenkinsopp, Joseph. *Ezra–Nehemiah: A Commentary*. OTL. Philadelphia: Westminster, 1988.

———. *Gibeon and Israel: The Role of Gibeon and the Gibeonites in the Political and Religious History of Israel*. SOTSMS 2. Cambridge: Cambridge University Press, 1972.

———. *A History of Prophecy in Israel*. Louisville: Westminster John Knox, 1996.

———. *Isaiah 56–66*. AB 19B. New York: Doubleday, 2003.

———. *The Pentateuch: An Introduction to the First Five Books of the Bible*. New York: Doubleday, 1992.

Blum, Erhard. *Die Komposition der Vätergeschichte*. WMANT 57. Neukirchen–Vluyn: Neukirchener Verlag, 1984.

———. *Studien zur Komposition des Pentateuch*. BZAW 189. Berlin: de Gruyter, 1990.

Blumenthal, David. *Facing the Abusing G-d: A Theology of Protest*. Louisville: Westminster John Knox, 1993.

Boecker, Hans Jochen. *Die Beurteilung der Anfänge des Königtums in den deuteronomistischen Abschnitten des 1. Samuelbuches*. WMANT 31. Neukirchen–Vluyn: Neukirchener Verlag, 1969.

Boling, Robert. *Judges*. AB 6A. Garden City: Doubleday, 1975.

Boling, Robert, and G. Ernest Wright. *Joshua*. AB 6. Garden City: Doubleday, 1982.

Braiterman, Zachary. *(G-d) After Auschwitz: Tradition and Change in Post-Holocaust Jewish Thought*. Princeton: Princeton University Press, 1998.

Braun, Roddy L. "Martin Noth and the Chronicler's History." Pages 63–80 in *The History of Israel's Traditions: The Heritage of Martin Noth*. Edited by S. L. McKenzie and M. P. Graham. JSOTSup 182. Sheffield: Sheffield Academic, 1994.

Brettler, Marc. "Biblical History and Jewish Biblical Theology." *JR* (1997): 563–83.

———. *The Book of Judges*. London: Routledge, 2002.

———. *How to Read the Bible*. Philadelphia: Jewish Publication Society, 2005.

Bronner, Leah L. *The Stories of Elijah and Elisha as Polemics against Baal Worship*. POS 6. Leiden: Brill, 1968.

Brueggemann, Walter. *Theology of the Old Testament: Testimony, Dispute, Advocacy*. Minneapolis: Fortress Press, 1997.

Buber, Martin, *The Eclipse of G-d: Studies in the Relation between Religion and Philosophy*. New York: Harper & Row, 1952.

———. *I and Thou*. New York: Charles Scribner's, 1970.

Buccellati, Giorgio. *Cities and Nations of Ancient Israel: An Essay on Political Institutions with Special Reference to the Israelite Kingdoms*. Rome: Istituto di Studi del Vicino Oriente, Università di Roma, 1967.

Calderone, Philip J. *Dynastic Oracle and Suzerainty Treaty. 2 Samuel 7, 8–16*. Manila: Manila University, 1966.

Camp, Claudia V. *Wisdom and the Feminine in the Book of Proverbs*. Decatur, GA: Almond, 1985.

Campbell, Antony F. SJ. *1 Samuel*. FOTL 7. Grand Rapids: Eerdmans, 2003.

———. *2 Samuel*. FOTL 8. Grand Rapids: Eerdmans, 2005.

———. *The Ark Narrative (1 Sam 4–6. 2 Sam 6): A Form-Critical and Traditio-Historical Study*. SBLDS 16. Missoula: Scholars Press, 1975.

———. *Joshua to Chronicles: An Introduction*. Louisville: Westminster John Knox, 2004.

———. *Of Prophets and Kings: A Late Ninth-Century Document*. CBQMS 17. Washington: Catholic Biblical Association, 1986.

———. "Psalm 78: A Contribution to the Theology of Tenth-Century Israel." *CBQ* 41 (1979): 51–79.

Campbell, Antony F., and Mark A. O'Brien. *Unfolding the Deuteronomistic History: Origins, Upgrades, Present Text*. Minneapolis: Fortress Press, 2000.

———. *Sources of the Pentateuch: Texts, Introductions, Annotations*. Minneapolis: Fortress Press, 1993.

Carr, David M. *The Erotic Word: Sexuality, Spirituality, and the Bible*. Oxford: Oxford University Press, 2002.

———. *Reading the Fractures in Genesis: Historical and Literary Approaches*. Louisville: Westminster John Knox, 1996.

———. *Writing on the Tablet of the Heart: Origins of Scripture and Literature*. Oxford: Oxford University Press, 2004.

Carey, Greg. *Ultimate Things: An Introduction to Jewish and Christian Apocalyptic Literature*. St. Louis: Chalice, 2005.

Carroll, James. *Constantine's Sword: The Church and the Jews: A History*. Boston and New York: Houghton Mifflin, 2001.

Childs, Brevard S. *Biblical Theology of the Old and New Testaments: Theological Reflection on the Christian Bible*. Minneapolis: Fortress Press, 1993.

Clements, Ronald E. *Abraham and David: Genesis 15 and its Meaning for Israelite Tradition*. SBT 2/5. London: SCM, 1967.

———. "Beyond Tradition-History: Deutero-Isaiah's Development of First Isaiah's Themes." *JSOT* 31 (1985): 95–113.

———. *Deuteronomy*. OTG. Sheffield: JSOT Press, 1989.

———. "Deuteronomy and the Jerusalem Cult Tradition." *VT* 15 (1965): 300–312.

———. *G-d and Temple: The Presence of G-d in Israel's Worship*. Philadelphia: Fortress Press, 1965.

———. "The Prophecies of Isaiah and the Fall of Jerusalem in 587 B.C." *VT* 30 (1980): 421–36.

———. "The Unity of the Book of Isaiah." *Int* 36 (1982): 117–29.

Clifford, Richard J. *Proverbs: A Commentary*. OTL. Louisville: Westminster John Knox, 1999.

Coats, George W. *Exodus 1–18*. FOTL 2A. Grand Rapids: Eerdmans, 1999.

———. *Rebellion in the Wilderness*. Nashville: Abingdon, 1968.

Cogan, Mordechai, *1 Kings*. AB 10. New York: Doubleday, 2001.

Cogan, Mordechai, and Haim Tadmor. *2 Kings*. AB 11. New York: Doubleday, 1988.

Cohn, Robert L. *2 Kings*. BO. Collegeville: Liturgical, 2000.

Collins, John J. *An Introduction to the Hebrew Bible*. Minneapolis: Fortress Press, 2004.

———. *The Apocalyptic Imagination*. New York: Crossroad, 1984.

———. *Daniel*. Hermeneia. Minneapolis: Fortress Press, 1993.

———. *Daniel, with an Introduction to Apocalyptic Literature*. FOTL 20. Grand Rapids: Eerdmans, 1984.

———. *Does the Bible Justify Violence?* Minneapolis: Fortress Press, 2004.

Conrad, Edgar W. *Zechariah*. Readings. Sheffield: Sheffield Academic, 1999.

Cook, Stephen L. *Prophecy and Apocalypticism: The Postexilic Social Setting*. Minneapolis: Fortress Press, 1995.

Cortese, Enzo. *Josua 13–21: Ein priesterschriftlicher Abschnitt im deuteronomistischen Geschichtswerk*. OBO 94. Freiburg: Universitätsverlag, 1990.

Crenshaw, James L. *Ecclesiastes: A Commentary*. OTL. Philadelphia: Westminster, 1987.

———. *Old Testament Wisdom: An Introduction*. Louisville: Westminster John Knox, 1998.

———. *Prophetic Conflict*. BZAW 124. Berlin: de Gruyter, 1971.

———. *The Psalms: An Introduction*. Grand Rapids: Eerdmans, 2001.

———. *Samson: A Secret Betrayed. A Vow Ignored*. Atlanta: John Knox, 1978.

Cross, Frank Moore, Jr. "The Priestly Work." Pages 293–325 in *Canaanite Myth and Hebrew Epic*. Cambridge, MA: Harvard University Press, 1973.

———. "The Themes of the Books of Kings and the Structure of the Deuteronomistic History." Pages 274–89 in *Canaanite Myth and Hebrew Epic*. Cambridge, MA: Harvard University Press, 1973.

Crüsemann, Frank. *Studien zur Formgeschichte von Hymnus und Danklied in Israel*. WMANT 32. Neukirchen–Vluyn: Neukirchener Verlag, 1969.

Danby, Herbert. *The Mishnah*. Oxford: Oxford University Press, 1933.

Darr, Katheryn Pfisterer. "Ezekiel." Pages 6:1110 in *The New Interpreter's Bible*. Edited by L. Keck et al. Nashville: Abingdon, 2001.

———. "Ezekiel Among the Critics." *CR:BS* 2 (1994): 9–24.

Davies, W. D., and Louis Finkelstein, ed. *The Cambridge History of Judaism*. Vol. 2, *The Hellenistic Age*. Cambridge: Cambridge University Press, 1989.

Dearman, Andrew, ed. *Studies in the Mesha Inscription and Moab*. SBLABS 2. Atlanta: Scholars Press, 1989.

Dearman, J. Andrew, and Gerald L. Mattingly. "Mesha Stele." *ABD* 4:708–9.

DeVries, Simon J. *1 and 2 Chronicles*. FOTL 11. Grand Rapids: Eerdmans, 1989.

———. *1 Kings*. WBC 12. Waco: Word, 1985.

———. *From Old Revelation to New*. Grand Rapids: Eerdmans, 1995.

———. *Prophet against Prophet*. Grand Rapids: Eerdmans, 1978.

Dhorme, Édouard. *A Commentary on the Book of Job*. Translated by H. Knight. Nashville: Thomas Nelson, 1984.

Di Vito, Robert A. "Lachish Letters." *ABD* 4:126–28.

Diamond, A. R. *The Confessions of Jeremiah in Context: Scenes of a Prophetic Drama.* JSOTSup 45. JSOT Press, 1987.

Dietrich, Walter. *Prophetie und Geschichte. Eine redaktionsgeschichtliche Untersuchung zum deuteronomistischen Geschichtswerk.* FRLANT 108. Göttingen: Vandenhoeck & Ruprecht, 1972.

Dobbs-Allsopp, F. W. *Weep, O Daughter of Zion: A Study of the City-Lament Genre in the Hebrew Bible.* BibOr 44. Rome: Pontifical Biblical Institute, 1993.

Dozeman, Thomas B., and Schmid, Konrad, eds. *A Farewell to the Y-hwist? The Composition of the Pentateuch in Recent European Interpretation.* SBLSymS 34. Atlanta: Society of Biblical Literature, 2006.

Driver, S. R. *Notes on the Hebrew Text and Topography of the Books of Samuel.* Oxford: Clarendon, 1913/1960.

Duhm, Bernhard. *Das Buch Jesaia.* HKAT 3/1. Göttingen: Vandenhoeck & Ruprecht, 1892.

Eaton, John H. *Kingship and the Psalms.* SBT 2/32. London: SCM, 1976.

Eichrodt, Walter. *Theology of the Old Testament.* OTL. 2 vols. Philadelphia: Westminster, 1961–67.

Eidevall, Göran. *Grapes in the Desert: Metaphors, Models, and Themes in Hosea 4–14.* ConBibOT 43. Stockholm: Almqvist & Wiksell, 1996.

Emmendörfer, Michael. *Der ferne G-tt. Eine Untersuchung der alltestamentliche Volksklagelieder vor dem Hintergrund der mesopotamischen Literatur.* FAT 21. Tübingen: Mohr Siebeck, 1998.

Eskenazi, Tamara Cohn. *In an Age of Prose: A Literary Approach to Ezra–Nehemiah.* SBLMS 36. Atlanta: Scholars Press, 1988.

Evans, Craig A. "On the Unity and Parallel Structure of Isaiah." *VT* 38 (1988): 129–47.

Exum, J. Cheryl. *Song of Songs: A Commentary.* OTL. Louisville: Westminster John Knox, 2005.

Fackenheim, Emil. *G-d's Presence in History: Jewish Affirmations and Philosophical Reflections.* New York: New York University Press, 1970.

———. *The Jewish Bible after the Holocaust: A Rereading.* Bloomington: Indiana University Press, 1990.

———. *To Mend the World: Foundations of Jewish Thought.* New York: Schocken, 1982.

Ferris, Paul Wayne, Jr. *The Genre of Communal Lament in the Bible and the Ancient Near East.* SBLDS 127. Atlanta: Scholars Press, 1992.

Finkelstein, Israel. *The Archaeology of the Israelite Settlement.* Jerusalem: Israel Exploration Society, 1988.

Fishbane, Michael. *Biblical Interpretation in Ancient Israel.* Oxford: Oxford University Press, 1985.

———. *Biblical Myth and Rabbinic Mythmaking.* Oxford: Oxford University Press, 2003.

———. "Composition and Structure in the Jacob Cycles (Gen 25:19–35:22)." Pages 40–62 in *Text and Texture: Close Readings of Selected Biblical Texts.* New York: Schocken, 1979.

———. *The Exegetical Imagination: On Jewish Thought and Theology.* Cambridge, MA: Harvard University Press, 1998.

———. "Genesis 1:1–2:4a: The Creation." Pages 1–16 in *Text and Texture: Selected Readings of Biblical Texts.* New York: Schocken, 1979.

———. *Haftarot: The JPS Bible Commentary.* Philadelphia: The Jewish Publication Society, 2002/5762.

———. *The Kiss of G-d: Spiritual and Mystical Death in Judaism.* Seattle: University of Washington Press, 1994.

Fox, Michael V. *Character and Ideology in the Book of Esther*. Grand Rapids: Eerdmans, 2001.
———. *Proverbs 1–9*. AB 18A. Garden City: Doubleday, 2000.
———. *Song of Songs and the Ancient Egyptian Love Songs*. Madison: University of Wisconsin, 1999.
———. *A Time to Tear Down and a Time to Build Up: A Rereading of Ecclesiastes*. Grand Rapids: Eerdmans, 1999.
Friedman, Richard. *The Exile and Biblical Narrative: The Formation of the Deuteronomistic and Priestly Works*. HSM 22. Chico, CA: Scholars Press, 1981.
Fritz, Volkmar. *1 and 2 Kings*. ContCom. Minneapolis: Fortress Press, 2003.
———. *Das Buch Josua*. HAT 1/7. Tübingen: Mohr Siebeck, 1994.
Frolov, Serge. *The Turn of the Cycle: 1 Samuel 1–8 in Synchronic and Diachronic Perspectives*. BZAW 342. Berlin: de Gruyter, 2004.
Fuchs, Esther. "The Emergence of Biblical Theologies." Pages 109–21 in *Jews, Christians, and the Theology of the Hebrew Scriptures*. Edited by A. O. Bellis and J. S. Kaminsky. SBLSymS 8. Atlanta: Society of Biblical Literature, 2000.
Gabler, Johann P. "An Oration on the Proper Distinction between Biblical and Dogmatic Theology and the Specific Objectives of Each." Pages 497–506 in *Old Testament Theology: Flowering and Future*. Edited by B. C. Ollenburger. SBTS 1. Winona Lake, IN: Eisenbrauns, 2004.
Galambush, Julie. *Jerusalem in the Book of Ezekiel: The City as YHWH's Wife*. SBLDS 130. Atlanta: Scholars Press, 1992.
Garber, Zev. "Reconstructing Theodicy and Amalekut: A Personal Apologia." Pages 119–36 in *Shoah: The Paradigmatic Genocide. Essays in Exegesis and Eisegesis*. Studies in the Shoah 8. Lanham: University Press of America, 1994.
Gerstenberger, Erhard S. *Psalms, Part 1, with an Introduction to Cultic Poetry*. FOTL 14. Grand Rapids: Eerdmans, 1988.
———. *Psalms, Part 2, and Lamentations*. FOTL 15. Grand Rapids: Eerdmans, 2001.
Gevirtz, Stanley. "Of Patriarchs and Puns: Joseph at the Fountain, Jacob at the Ford." *HUCA* 46 (1975): 33–54.
Ginsburg, Christian D. *Introduction to the Massoretico-Critical Edition of the Hebrew Bible*. New York: Ktav, 1966.
Goldhagen, Daniel Jonah. *A Moral Reckoning: The Role of the Catholic Church in the Holocaust and its Unfulfilled Duty of Repair*. New York: Knopf, 2002.
Goldman, Yohanan. *Prophétie et royauté au retour de l'exil*. OBO 118. Freiburg: Universitätsverlag. Göttingen: Vandenhoeck & Ruprecht, 1992.
Goshen-Gottstein, Moshe. "Christianity, Judaism, and Modern Study." Pages 69–88 in *Congress Volume: Edinburgh, 1974*. Edited by J. A. Emerton. VTSup 28. Leiden: Brill, 1975.
———. "Jewish Biblical Theology and the Science of the Bible," *Tarbiz* 50 (1980–81): 37–64 (Hebrew).
———. "Tanakh Theology: The Religion of the Old Testament and the Place of Jewish Biblical Theology." Pages 587–644 in *Ancient Israelite Religion: Essays in Honor of Frank Moore Cross, Jr*. Edited by P. D. Miller et al. Philadelphia: Fortress Press, 1987.
Goulder, Michael D. *The Prayers of David (Psalms 51–72)*. JSOTSup 102. Sheffield: Sheffield Academic, 1990.
———. *The Psalms of Asaph and the Pentateuch*. JSOTSup 233. Sheffield: Sheffield Academic, 1996.
———. *The Psalms of Return (Book V: Psalms 107–150)*. JSOTSup 258. Sheffield: Sheffield Academic, 1998.

———. *The Psalms of the Sons of Korah.* JSOTSup 20. Sheffield: Sheffield Academic, 1982.

Graffy, Adrian. *A Prophet Confronts his People.* AnBib 104. Rome: Pontifical Biblical Institute, 1984.

Grant-Henderson, Anna L. *Inclusive Voices in Post-Exilic Judah.* Collegeville, MN: Liturgical, 2002.

Gray, John. *I and II Kings: A Commentary.* OTL. Philadelphia: Westminster, 1970.

Green, Barbara. *Mikhail Bakhtin and Biblical Scholarship: An Introduction.* SemSt 38. Atlanta: Society of Biblical Literature, 2000.

Greenberg, Moshe. *Ezekiel 1–20.* AB 22. Garden City: Doubleday, 1983.

———. *Ezekiel 21–37.* AB 22A. New York: Doubleday, 1997.

———. "Reflections on Job's Theology." Pages 327–33 in *Studies in the Bible and Jewish Thought.* Philadelphia: Jewish Publication Society, 1995.

Greenspahn, Frederick. "Jewish Ambivalence towards the Bible." *HS* 49 (2007): 7–21.

Greenstein, Edward. "The Wrath of G-d in the Book of Lamentations." Pages 29–42 in *The Problem of Evil and its Symbols in Jewish and Christian Tradition.* Edited by H. Graf Reventlow and Y. Hoffman. JSOTSup 366. London: Continuum, 2004.

Grønbæk, Jakob H. *Die Geschichte vom Aufstieg Davids (1. Sam. 15–2. Sam. 5). Tradition und Komposition.* Copenhagn: Prostant apud Munksgaard, 1971.

Gruenwald, Ithamar. *Apocalyptic and Merkavah Mysticism.* Leiden: Brill, 1980.

Gunkel, Hermann. *An Introduction to the Psalms.* Translated by J. D. Nogalski. Macon, GA: Mercer University Press, 1998.

Haak, Robert D. *Habakkuk.* VTSup 44. Leiden: Brill, 1992.

Habel, Norman C. *The Book of Job: A Commentary.* OTL. Philadelphia: Westminster, 1985.

Halpern, Baruch. *David's Secret Demons: Messiah, Murderer, Traitor, King.* Grand Rapids: Eerdmans, 2001.

———. *The First Historians: The Hebrew Bible and History.* San Francisco: Harper & Row, 1988.

Halpern, Baruch, and David Vanderhooft. "The Editions of Kings in the 7th–6th Centuries." *HUCA* 62 (1991): 179–244.

Hals, Ronald M. *Ezekiel.* FOTL 19. Grand Rapids: Eerdmans, 1989.

Hartman, L. F., and A. A. Di Lella. *Daniel.* AB 23. Garden City: Doubleday, 1978.

Hasel, G. F. "Sabbath." *ABD* 5:849–56.

Hauser, Alan J. "YHWH versus Death: The Real Struggle in 1 Kings 17–19." Pages 9–89 in *From Carmel to Horeb: Elijah in Crisis.* By Alan J. Hauser and Russell Gregory. JSOTSup 85. Sheffield: Almond, 1990.

Haynes, Stephen R. *The Bonhoeffer Legacy: Post Holocaust Perspectives.* Minneapolis: Fortress Press, 2006.

Hayward, C. T. R. *The Jewish Temple: A Non-Biblical Sourcebook.* London: Routledge, 1996.

Henze, Matthias. *The Madness of King Nebuchadnezzar: The Ancient Near Eastern Origins and Early History of Interpretation of Daniel 4.* JSJSup 61. Leiden: Brill, 1999.

Hertzberg, Arthur. *The French Enlightenment and the Jews.* New York: Columbia University Press, 1968.

Heschel, Abraham Joshua. *Die Prophetie.* Krakow: Nakladem Polskiej Akademi Umiejetmpco, 1936. English ed. *The Prophets.* Philadelphia: Jewish Publication Society, 1962.

———. *G-d in Search of Man: A Philosophy of Judaism.* New York: Meridian & Jewish Publication Society, 1955.

———. *Israel: Echo of an Eternity.* New York: Farrar, Straus & Giroux, 1969.

———. *Man is Not Alone.* Philadelphia: Jewish Publication Society, 1951.

————. *The Sabbath: Its Meaning for Modern Man.* New York: Farrar, Straus & Giroux, 1951.

Hobbs, T. R. *2 Kings.* WBC 13. Waco: Word, 1985.

Hoffmann, Hans-Detleff. *Reform und Reformen. Untersuchungen zu einem Grundthema der deuteronomistischen Geschichtschreibung.* AThANT 66. Zürich: Theologischer Verlag, 1980.

Hoffman, Y. "Jeremiah 50–51 and the Concept of Divine Evil in the Hebrew Bible." Pages 14–28 *The Problem of Evil and its Symbols in Jewish and Christian Tradition.* Edited by H. Graf Reventlow and Y. Hoffman. JSOTSup 366. London: Continuum, 2004.

Holiday, John S. "Kom, Khirbet el-." *ABD* 4:97–99.

Horner, Thomas Marland. *Jonathan Loved David: Homosexuality in Biblical Times.* Louisville: Westminster John Knox, 1978.

Hubbard, Robert L. Jr. *The Book of Ruth.* NICOT. Grand Rapids: Eerdmans, 1988.

Humphreys, W. Lee. *The Character of G-d in the Book of Genesis: A Narrative Appraisal.* Louisville: Westminster John Knox, 2001.

————. "A Life-Style for Diaspora: A Study of the Tales of Esther and Daniel." *JBL* 92 (1973): 211–23.

————. "The Story of Esther and Mordecai: An Early Jewish Novella." Pages 97–113 in *Saga, Legend, Tale, Novella, Fable: Narrative Forms in Old Testament Literature.* Edited by George W. Coats. JSOTSup 35. Sheffield: Sheffield Academic, 1985.

Hurowitz, Victor. "Isaiah's Impure Lips and their Purification in Light of Akkadian Sources." *HUCA* 60 (1989): 39–89.

Hyatt, J. Philip. "The Beginning of Jeremiah's Prophecy." Pages 63–72 in *A Prophet to the Nations: Essays in Jeremiah Studies.* Edited by L. G. Perdue and B. W. Kovacs. Winona Lake, IN: Eisenbrauns, 1984.

Hylander, Ivar. *Der literarische Samuel-Saul-Komplex (1. Sam. 1–15). Traditionsgeschichtlich Untersucht.* Uppsala: Almqvist & Wiksell. Leipzig: Otto Harrassowitz, 1932.

Irvine, Stuart. *Isaiah, Ahaz, and the Syro-Ephraimitic Crisis.* SBLDS 123. Atlanta: Scholars Press, 1990.

Isaac, Jules. *The Teaching of Contempt: The Theological Roots of Anti-Semitism.* New York: Holt, Rinholt & Winston, 1964.

Ishida, Tomoo. *The Royal Dynasties in Ancient Israel.* BZAW 142. Berlin: de Gruyter, 1977.

Jahnow, Hedwig. *Das hebräischen Leichenlied im Rahmen der Völkerdichtung.* BZAW 36. Giessen: A. Töpelmann, 1923.

Janzen, J. Gerald. *Studies in the Text of Jeremiah.* HSM 6. Cambridge, MA: Harvard University Press, 1973.

Japhet, Sara. *I and II Chronicles: A Commentary.* OTL. Louisville: Westminster John Knox, 1993.

————. *The Ideology of the Book of Chronicles and its Place in Biblical Thought.* Frankfurt: Peter Lang, 1989.

Jastrow, M. *A Dictionary of the Targumim, the Talmud Babli and Yerushalmi, and the Midrashic Literature.* Brooklyn, NY: P. Shalom, 1967.

Jellinek, Adolph. *Bet ha-Midrasch.* Jerusalem: Bamberger & Wahrmann, 1938.

Jeremias, Jörg. *Theophanie.* WMANT 10. Neukirchen–Vluyn: Neukirchener Verlag, 1977.

Jones, Barry Alan. *The Formation of the Book of the Twelve: Study in Text and Canon.* SBLDS 149. Atlanta: Scholars Press, 1995.

Jones, Douglas R. *Jeremiah.* NCenB. London: Marshall Pickering. Grand Rapids: Eerdmans, 1992.

Jones, Gwillym H. *1 and 2 Kings.* NCenB. Grand Rapids: Eerdmans, 1984.

————. *The Nathan Narratives.* JSOTSup 80. Sheffield: JSOT Press, 1990.

Kalimi, Isaac. "History of Israelite Religion or Hebrew Bible/Old Testament Theology? Jewish Interest in Biblical Theology." Pages 107–34 in *Early Jewish Exegesis and Theological Controversies: Studies in Scripture in the Shadow of Internal and External Controversies.* Assen: Van Gorcum, 2002.

————. "Religionsgeschichte Israels oder Theologie des Alten Testaments." *JBibTh* 10 (1995): 45–68.

Kallai, Zecharia. *Historical Geography of the Bible.* Jerusalem: Magnes, 1986.

Kaminsky, Joel. *Yet I Loved Jacob: Reclaiming the Biblical Concept of Election.* Nashville: Abingdon, 2007.

Kaplan, Edward K. *Spiritual Radical: Abraham Joshua Heschel in America.* New Haven: Yale University Press, 2007.

Kaplan, Edward K., and Samuel H. Dresner. *Abraham Joshua Heschel: Prophetic Witness.* New Haven: Yale University Press, 1998.

Kasher, Aryeh. *The Jews in Hellenistic and Roman Egypt: The Struggle for Equal Rights.* TSAJ 7. Tübingen: Mohr Siebeck, 1985.

Katz, Steven T. *Post-Holocaust Dialogues: Critical Studies in Modern Jewish Thought.* New York: New York University Press, 1985.

Kaufmann, Yehezkel. *The Babylonian Captivity and Deutero-Isaiah: History of the Religion of Israel.* New York: Union of American Hebrew Congregations, 1970.

————. *A History of Israelite Religion from Antiquity to the End of the Second Temple.* 8 vols. Tel Aviv: Mosad Bialik, 1937–56 (Hebrew).

————. *The Religion of Israel from its Beginnings through the Babylonian Exile.* New York: Schocken, 1972.

Kellenbach, Katharina von. *Anti-Judaism in feminist Religious Writings.* Atlanta: Scholars Press, 1994.

Kenyon, Kathleen M. "Jericho: Tell Es-Sultan." *NEAEHL* 2:674–81.

Kepnes, Stephen. "Job and Post-Holocaust Theodicy." Pages 252–66 in *Strange Fire: Reading the Bible after the Holocaust.* Edited by T. Linafelt. Sheffield: Sheffield Academic, 2000.

Keys, Gillian. *The Wages of Sin: A Reappraisal of the "Succession Narrative".* JSOTSup 221. Sheffield: Sheffield Academic, 1996.

Klein, Ralph W. *1 Chronicles.* Hermeneia. Minneapolis: Fortress Press, 2006.

Knierim, Rolf P. "The Composition of the Pentateuch." Pages 351–79 in *The Task of Old Testament Theology: Substance, Method, and Cases.* Grand Rapids: Eerdmans, 1995.

————. "Cosmos and History in Israel's Theology." Pages 171–224 in *The Task of Old Testament Theology: Substance, Method, and Cases.* Grand Rapids: Eerdmans, 1995.

————. *Text and Concept in Leviticus 1:1–9.* FAT 2. Tübingen: Mohr Siebeck, 1992.

Knierim, Rolf P., and George W. Coats. *Numbers.* FOTL 4. Grand Rapids: Eerdmans, 2005.

Knohl, Israel. *The Divine Symphony: The Bible's Many Voices.* Philadelphia: Jewish Publication Society, 2003/5763.

————. *The Sanctuary of Silence: The Priestly Torah and the Holiness School.* Minneapolis: Fortress Press, 1995.

Knoppers, Gary N. *1 Chronicles 1–9.* AB 12. New York: Doubleday, 2003.

————. *1 Chronicles 10–29.* AB 12A. New York: Doubleday, 2004.

————. *Two Nations under G-d: The Deuteronomistic History of Solomon and the Dual Monarchies.* HSM 52–53. Atlanta: Scholars Press, 1993–94.

Koch, Klaus. "Ezra and the Origins of Judaism." *JSS* 19 (1974): 173–97.

————. "Tempeleinlass Liturgien und Dekaloge." Pages 45–60 in *Studien zur Theologie der alttestamentlichen Überlieferungen: Festschrift G. von Rad.* Edited by R. Rendtorff and K. Koch. Neukirchen–Vluyn: Neukirchener Verlag, 1961.

Köhler, Ludwig. *Old Testament Theology.* Philadelphia: Westminster, 1957.

Krapf, Thomas. *Die Priesterschrift und die vorexilische Zeit. Yehezkel Kaufmanns vernachlässigter Beitrag zu Geschichte der biblischen Religion.* OBO 119. Freiburg: Üniversitätsverlag, 1992.

————. *Yehezkel Kaufmann. Ein Lebens- und erkenntnisweg zur theologie der Hebräischen Bible.* Berlin: Insitut Kirche & Judentum, 1990.

Kraus, Hans-Joachim. *Die biblische Theologie. Ihre Geschichte und Problematik.* Neukirchen–Vluyn: Neukirchner, 1970.

Krüger, Thomas. *Qoheleth.* Hermeneia. Minneapolis: Fortress Press, 2004.

Kugel, James L. *In Potiphar's House: The Interpretive Life of Biblical Texts.* San Francisco: HarperSanFrancisco, 1990.

Kuhrt, Amélie. *The Ancient Near East, c. 3000–330 BC.* London: Routledge, 1998.

Lambert, W. G. "Enuma Elish." *ABD* 2:526–28.

Lambert, W. G., and A. R. Millard. *Atra Hasis: The Babylonian Story of the Flood.* Oxford: Clarendon, 1969.

Landy, Francis. *Hosea.* Readings. Sheffield: Sheffield Academic, 1995.

Lee, Won W. *Punishment and Forgiveness in Israel's Wilderness Campaign.* Grand Rapids: Eerdmans, 2003.

Leiman, Sid Z. *The Canonization of Hebrew Scripture: The Talmudic and Midrashic Evidence.* New Haven: Connecticut Academy of Arts and Sciences, 1976.

Levenson, Jon D. *Creation and the Persistence of Evil: The Jewish Drama of Divine Impotence.* Princeton: Princeton University Press, 1988.

————. *Death and the Resurrection of the Beloved Son: The Transformation of Child Sacrifice in Judaism and Christianity.* New Haven: Yale University Press, 1993.

————. *Esther: A Commentary.* OTL. Louisville: Westminster John Knox, 1997.

————. "The Jerusalem Temple in Devotional and Visionary Experience." Pages 32–61 in *Jewish Spirituality.* Vol. 1, *From the Bible to the Middle Ages.* Edited by A. Green. New York: Crossroad, 1988.

————. *Resurrection and the Restoration of Israel: The Ultimate Victory of the G-d of Life.* New Haven: Yale University Press, 2006.

————. *Sinai and Zion: An Entry into the Jewish Bible.* Minneapolis: Winston, 1985.

————. "The Temple and the World." *JR* 64 (1984): 275–98.

————. *Theology of the Program of Restoration in Ezekiel 40–48.* HSM 10. Missoula: Scholars Press, 1976.

————. "Why Jews are not Interested in Biblical Theology." Pages 287–307 in *Judaic Perspectives on Ancient Israel.* Edited by J. Neusner et al. Philadelphia: Fortress 1987. Reprinted in pages 33–61, 165–70 of Levenson, *The Hebrew Bible, the Old Testament, and Historical Criticism: Jews and Christians in Biblical Studies.* Louisville: Westminster John Knox, 1993.

Levenson, Jon D., and Baruch Halpern. "The Political Import of David's Marriages." *JBL* 99 (1980): 11–28.

Levin, Christoph. *Der J-hwist.* FRLANT 157. Göttingen: Vandenhoeck & Ruprecht, 1993.

Levine, Baruch. *Numbers 1–20.* AB 4. New York: Doubleday, 1993.

————. *Numbers 21–36.* AB 4A. New York: Doubleday, 2000.

Levinson, Bernard M. *Deuteronomy and the Hermeneutics of Legal Innovation.* Oxford: Oxford University Press, 1997.

Lewis, Jack P. "What do we Mean by Jabneh?" *JBL* 32 (1964): 125–32.

Linafelt, Tod. *Surviving Lamentations: Catastrophe, Lament, and Protest in the Afterlife of a Biblical Book.* Chicago: University of Chicago, 2000.

Lohfink, Norbert L. *Qoheleth.* ContCom. Minneapolis: Fortress Press, 2003.

Long, Burke. *1 Kings, with an Introduction to Historical Literature.* FOTL 9. Grand Rapids: Eerdmans, 1984.

———. *2 Kings.* FOTL 10. Grand Rapids: Eerdmans, 1989.

Longman, Tremper, III. *The Song of Songs.* NICOT. Grand Rapids: Eerdmans, 2001.

Lundbom, Jack R. *Jeremiah 1–20.* AB 21A. New York: Doubleday, 1999.

Lyke, Larry L. *King David with the Wise Woman of Tekoa: The Resonance of Tradition in Parabolic Narrative.* JSOTSup 255. Sheffield: Sheffield Academic, 1997.

McCarter, P. Kyle. *1 Samuel.* AB 8. Garden City: Doubleday, 1980.

———. *II Samuel.* AB 9. Garden City: Doubleday, 1984.

McKenzie, Steven L. *1–2 Chronicles.* AOTC. Nashville: Abingdon, 2004.

———. *King David: A Biography.* Oxford: Oxford University Press, 2000.

———. "The So-Called Succession Narrative in the Deuteronomistic History." Pages 123–35 in *Die sogenennte Thronfolgegeschichte Davids. Neue Einsichten und Anfragen.* OBO 176. Freiburg: Universitätsverlag, 2000.

———. *The Trouble with Kings: The Composition of the Books in the Deuteronomistic History.* VTSup 42. Leiden: Brill, 1991.

Mandolfo, Carleen R. *Daughter Zion Talks Back to the Prophets: A Dialogic Theology of the Book of Lamentations.* Semeia Studies 58. Atlanta: Society of Biblical Literature, 2007.

———. *G-d in the Dock: Dialogic Tension in the Psalms of Lament.* JSOTSup 357. Sheffield: Sheffield Academic, 2002.

Mason, Rex. *Preaching the Tradition: Homily and Hermeneutics after the Exile.* Cambridge: Cambridge University Press, 1990.

Matties Gordon H. *Ezekiel 18 and the Rhetoric of Moral Discourse.* SBLDS 126. Atlanta: Scholars Press, 1990.

Maybaum, Ignaz. *The Face of G-d after Auschwitz.* Amsterdam: Polak & Van Glennep, 1965.

Mazar, Amihai. *Archaeology of the Land of the Bible, 10,000–586 B.C.E.* New York: Doubleday, 1990.

Melugin, Roy F. "Figurative Speech and the Reading of Isaiah 1 as Scripture." Pages 282–305 in *New Visions of Isaiah.* Edited by R. F. Melugin and M. A. Sweeney. JSOTSup 214. Sheffield: Sheffield Academic, 1996.

———. *The Formation of Isaiah 40–55.* BZAW 141. Berlin: de Gruyter, 1976.

Melugin, Roy F., and Marvin A. Sweeney, eds. *New Visions of Isaiah.* JSOTSup 214. Sheffield: Sheffield Academic, 1996.

Mendelssohn, Moses. *Jerusalem, or On Religious Power and Judaism.* Hanover, NH: University Press of New England, 1983.

Meshel, Zev. "Kuntillat Ajrud." *ABD* 4:103–9.

Mettinger, T. N. D. *A Farewell to the Servant Songs: A Critical Examination of an Exegetical Axiom.* Lund: Gleerup, 1983.

Milgrom, Jacob. *Leviticus.* AB 3, 3A, 3B. 3 vols. Garden City: Doubleday, 1991–2001.

———. *Numbers.* JPS Torah Commentary. Philadelphia: Jewish Publication Society, 1990/5750.

Miller, J. Maxwell, and John H. Hayes. *A History of Ancient Israel and Judah*. Philadelphia: Westminster, 1986.

Montgomery, James A., and Henry Snyder Gehman. *The Books of Kings*. ICC. Edinburgh: T. & T. Clark, 1951.

Moran, William L. "The Ancient Near Eastern Background of the Love of G-d in Deuteronomy." *CBQ* 25 (1963): 77–87.

Morgan, Donn F. *Between Text and Community: The "Writings" in Canonical Interpretation*. Minneapolis: Fortress Press, 1990.

Morgan, Michael L. *Beyond Auschwitz: Post-Holocaust Jewish Thought in America*. Oxford: Oxford University Press, 2001.

Müller, W. W. "Pishon." *ABD* 5:374.

Murphy, Roland E. *The Song of Songs*. Hermeneia. Minneapolis: Fortress Press, 1990.

———. *The Tree of Life: An Exploration of Biblical Wisdom Literature*. Winona Lake, IN: Eisenbrauns, 2002.

———. *Wisdom Literature: Job, Proverbs, Ruth, Canticles, Ecclesiastes, Esther*. FOTL 13. Grand Rapids: Eerdmans, 1981.

Murray, Donald F. *Prerogative and Royal Pretension: Pragmatics, Poetics and Polemics in a Narrative Sequence about David (2 Samuel 5.17–7.29)*. JSOTSup 264. Sheffield: Sheffield Academic, 1998.

Na'aman, Nadav. "Amarna Letters." *ABD* 1:174–81.

Najman, Hindy. "Ezra." "Nehemiah." Pages 1666–87, 1688–711 in *The Jewish Study Bible*. Edited by A. Berlin and M. Brettler. New York: Oxford University Press, 2003.

Nelson, Richard D. *The Double Redaction of the Deuteronomistic History*. JSOTSup 18. Sheffield: JSOT Press, 1981.

———. *The Historical Books*. IBT. Nashville: Abingdon, 1998.

———. *Joshua: A Commentary*. OTL. Louisville: Westminster John Knox, 1997.

———. "Josiah in the Book of Joshua." *JBL* 100 (1981): 531–40.

Newsom, Carol. "The Book of Job." Pages 4:319–637 in *The New Interpreter's Bible*. Edited by L. E. Keck et al. Nashville: Abingdon, 1996.

———. *The Book of Job: A Contest of Moral Imaginations*. Oxford: Oxford University Press, 2003.

Nicholson, Ernst W. *Deuteronomy and Tradition: Literary and Historical Traditions in the Book of Deuteronomy*. Philadelphia: Fortress Press, 1967.

———. *The Pentateuch in the Twentieth Century: The Legacy of Julius Wellhausen*. Oxford: Oxford University Press, 1998.

———. *Preaching to the Exiles: A Study of the Prose Traditions in the Book of Jeremiah*. New York: Schocken, 1971.

Niditch, Susan. *Judges: A Commentary*. OTL. Louisville: Westminster John Knox, 2008.

Nielsen, Kirsten. *Ruth: A Commentary*. OTL. Louisville: Westminster John Knox, 1997.

Noth, Martin. "The Background of Judges 17–18." Pages 68–85 in *Israel's Prophetic Heritage*. Fs. J. Muilenburg. Edited by B. W. Anderson and W. Harrelson. London: SCM, 1962.

———. *The Chronicler's History*. JSOTSup 50. Sheffield: Sheffield Academic, 1987.

———. *Exodus: A Commentary*. OTL. Philadelphia: Westminster, 1962.

———. *Numbers: A Commentary*. OTL. Philadelphia: Westminster, 1968.

———. *Überlieferungsgeschichtliche Studien I*. Tübingen: Max Niemeyer, 1957. ET, *The Deuteronomistic History*. JSOTSup 15. Sheffield: JSOT Press, 1981.

O'Brien, Mark A. "The Book of Deuteronomy." *CR:BS* 3 (1995): 95–128.

———. *The Deuteronomistic History Hypothesis: A Reassessment.* OBO 92. Freiberg: Universitätsverlag, 1989.

O'Connell, Robert H. *The Rhetoric of the Book of Judges.* VTSup 63. Leiden: Brill, 1996.

O'Connor, Kathleen M. *The Confessions of Jeremiah: Their Interpretation and Role in Chapters 1–25.* SBLDS 94. Atlanta: Scholars Press, 1988.

Odell, Margaret S. "You Are What You Eat: Ezekiel and the Scroll." *JBL* 117 (1998): 229–48.

Olson, Dennis T. *The Death of the Old and the Birth of the New: The Framework of the Book of Numbers and the Pentateuch.* BJS 71. Chico, CA: Scholars Press, 1985.

Oppenheim, A. Leo. "The Eyes of the L-rd." *JAOS* 88 (1968): 173–80.

Orlinsky, Harry M. "The Biblical Concept of the Land of Israel: Cornerstone of the Covenant Between G-d and Israel." Pages 27–64 in *The Land of Israel: Jewish Perspectives.* Edited by L. Hoffman. Notre Dame: University of Notre Dame Press, 1986.

———. *Notes on the New Translation of the Torah.* Philadelphia: Jewish Publication Society, 1969.

Otto, Susan. *Jehu, Elia und Elisa.* BWANT 152. Stuttgart: W. Kohlhammer, 2001.

Parpola, S., and K. Watanabe. *Neo-Assyrian Treaties and Loyalty Oaths.* SAS 2. Helsinki: University of Helsinki Press, 1988.

Peckham, Brian. "The Significance of the Book of Joshua in Martin Noth's Theory of the Deuteronomistic History." Pages 213–34 in *The History of Israel's Traditions* Edited by S. McKenzie and M. P. Graham. JSOTSup 182. Sheffield: Sheffield Academic, 1994.

Perdue, Leo G. *Reconstructing Old Testament Theology: After the Collapse of History.* Minneapolis: Fortress Press, 2005.

———. *The Sword and the Stylus: An Introduction to Wisdom in the Age of Empires.* Grand Rapids: Eerdmans, 2008.

———. *Wisdom and Creation: The Theology of the Wisdom Literature.* Nashville: Abingdon, 1994.

Petersen, David L. *The Prophetic Literature: An Introduction.* Louisville: Westminster John Knox, 2002.

Ploeger, Otto. *Theocracy and Eschatology.* Oxford: Blackwell, 1968.

Polley, Max. *Amos and the Davidic Empire.* New York: Oxford University Press, 1989.

Pope, Marvin H. *Job.* AB 15. Garden City: Doubleday, 1973.

———. *Song of Songs.* AB 19. Garden City: Doubleday, 1977.

Pressler, Carolyn. *The View of Women Found in Deuteronomic Family Laws.* BZAW 216. Berlin: de Gruyter, 1993.

Propp, William H. C. *Exodus 1–18.* AB 2. Garden City. Doubleday, 1999.

Provan, Iain W. *Hezekiah and the Books of Kings.* BZAW 172. Berlin: de Gruyter, 1988.

de Pury, Albert, and Thomas Römer. "Le Pentateuch en question. Position du problem et brève historie de la recherché." Pages 9–80 in *Le Pentateuch en Question.* Edited by A. de Pury. Geneva: Labor et Fides, 1989.

Rad, Gerhard von. *Old Testament Theology.* 2 vols. New York: Harper & Row, 1962–65.

———. *Studies in Deuteronomy.* SBT 9. London: SCM, 1953.

Redford, Donald B. *Egypt, Canaan, and Israel in Ancient Times.* Princeton: Princeton University Press, 1992.

———. "Merenptah (Person)." *ABD* 4:700–701.

Rendsburg, Gary A. *Linguistic Evidence for the Northern Origin of Selected Psalms.* SBLMS 43. Atlanta: Scholars Press, 1990.

Rendtorff, Rolf. *Die "Bundesformel." Eine exegetisch-theologische Untersuchung.* SBS 160. Stuttgart: Katholisches Bibelwerk, 1995.

———. *The Canonical Hebrew Bible: A Theology of the Old Testament*. Leiden: DEO, 2005.

Richter, Wolfgang. *Die Bearbeitungen des "Retterbuches" in der deuteronomischen Epoche*. BBB 21. Bonn: P. Hanstein, 1964.

———. *Traditionsgeschichtliche Untersuchungen zum Richterbuch*. BBB 18. Bonn: P. Hanstein, 1963.

Rom Shiloni, Dalit. "Ezekiel as the Voice of the Exiles and Constructor of Exilic Identity." *HUCA* 76 (2005): 1–75.

———. "Facing Destruction and Exile: Inner-Biblical Exegesis in Jeremiah and Ezekiel." *ZAW* 117 (2002): 189–205.

Römer, Thomas. *The So-Called Deuteronomistic History: A Sociological, Historical, and Literary Introduction*. London: Continuum, 2007.

Römer, Thomas, and Albert de Pury. "L'historiographie deueronomiste (HD): Histoire de la recherché et enjeux du débat." Pages 9–120 in *Israël construit son histoire*. Edited by A. de Pury et al. Geneva: Labor et Fides, 1996.

Rose, Paul Lawrence. *Revolutionary Antisemitism in Germany from Kant to Wagner*. Princeton: Princeton University Press, 1990.

Rosenberg, A. R. *The Book of Kings*. Judaica Books of the Bible. 2 vols. New York: Judaica, 1998, 1993.

Rosenzweig, Franz. *The Star of Redemption*. Notre Dame, IN: University of Notre Dame Press, 1985.

Rost, Leonhard. *The Succession to the Throne of David*. Sheffield: Almond, 1982. German ed. 1926.

Rowlett, Lori. *Joshua and the Rhetoric of Violence: A New Historicist Analysis*. JSOTSup 226. Sheffield: Sheffield Academic, 1996.

Rubenstein, Richard. *After Auschwitz: Radical Theology and Contemporary Judaism*. Indianapolis: Bobbs-Merrill, 1966.

———. "Job and Auschwitz." Pages 233–51 in *Strange Fire: Reading the Bible after the Holocaust*. Edited by T. Linafelt. Sheffield: Sheffield Academic, 2000.

Ruether, Rosemary Radford. *Faith and Fratricide: The Theological Roots of Anti-Semitism*. Eugene, OR: Wipf & Stock, 1997.

Ruether, Rosemary Radford, with Hermann J. Ruether. *The Wrath of Jonah: The Crisis of Religious Nationalism in the Israeli-Palestinian Conflict*. New York: Harper & Row, 1989.

Sæbø, M. ed. *Hebrew Bible/Old Testament. The History of its Interpretation*. Vol. I/1: *Antiquity*. Göttingen: Vandenhoeck & Ruprecht, 1996.

Sanders, James A. "Hermeneutics in True and False Prophecy." Pages 21–41 in *Canon and Authority*. Edited by G. W. Coats and B. O. Long. Philadelphia: Fortress Press, 1977.

———. *The Psalms Scroll of Qumrân Cave 11 (11QPsa)*. DJD 4. Oxford: Clarendon, 1965.

Särkiö, Pekka. *Die Weisheit und Macht Salomos in der Israelitischen Historiographie*. Schriften der Finnischen Exegetischen Gesellschaft. Helsinki. Finnish Exegetical Society. Göttingen Vandenhoeck & Ruprecht, 1994.

Sarna, Nahum. *Exploring Exodus: The Heritage of Biblical Israel*. New York: Schocken, 1986.

———. *Genesis*. JPS Torah Commentary. Philadelphia: Jewish Publication Society, 1989/5749.

———. *Understanding Genesis: The Heritage of Biblical Israel*. New York: Schocken, 1970.

Sasson, Jack M. *Ruth: A New Translation with a Philological Commentary and Formalist-Folklorist Interpretation*. BibSem 10. Sheffield: Sheffield Academic, 1995.

Schäfer, Peter. *Judeophobia: Attitudes toward the Jews in the Ancient World*. Cambridge, MA: Harvard University Press, 1997.

Schmid, H. H. *Der sogenannte J-hwist. Beobachtungen und Fragen zur Pentateuchforschung.* Zurich: Theologischer Verlag, 1976.

Schneider, Tammi J. *Judges.* BO. Collegeville: Liturgical, 2000.

———. *Sarah: Mother of Nations.* London: Continuum, 2004.

Schniedewind, William M. *The Word of G-d in Transition: From Prophet to Exegete in the Second Temple Period.* JSOTSup 197. Sheffield: Sheffield Academic, 1995.

Schürer, Emil. *The History of the Jewish People in the Age of Jesus Christ.* Edinburgh: T. & T. Clark, 1973.

Seebass, Horst. *Numeri 10,11–30,1.* BKAT 4/1-3.3. Neukirchen–Vluyn: Neukirchener, 1993–2006.

Seely, Jo Ann H. "Succoth." *ABD* 6:217–18.

Sefati, Yitschak. *Love Songs in Sumerian Literature: Critical Edition of the Dumuzi-Inanna Songs.* Ramat Gan: Bar Ilan University Press, 1998.

Seitz, Christopher R. "The Prophet Moses and the Canonical Shape of Jeremiah." *ZAW* 101 (1989): 3–27.

———. *Theology in Conflict: Reactions to the Exile in the Book of Jeremiah.* BZAW 176. Berlin: de Gruyter, 1989.

Seow, Choon-Leong. *Ecclesiastes.* AnBib 18C. Garden City: Doubleday, 1997.

Shead, Andrew G. *The Open and the Sealed Book: Jeremiah 32 in its Hebrew and Greek Recensions.* JSOTSup 347. London: Sheffield Academic, 2002.

Shechter, Jack. *The Land of Israel: Its Theological Dimensions. A Study in the Promise and of a Land's Holiness.* Lanham: University Press of America, 2010.

Ska, Jean-Louis. *Introduction to Reading the Pentateuch.* Winona Lake, IN: Eisenbrauns, 2006.

Skinner, John. *Genesis.* ICC. Edinburgh: T. & T. Clark, 1969.

Smend, Rudolf. "Die Gesetz und Völker: Ein Beitrag zur deuteronomistischen Redaktions-geschichte." Pages 494–509 in *Probleme Biblischer Theologie. Festschrift G. von Rad.* Edited by H. W. Wolff. Munich: Kaiser, 1971.

Smith, Mark S. *The Laments of Jeremiah and their Contexts.* SBLMS 42. Atlanta: Scholars Press, 1990.

———. *The Memoirs of G-d: History, Memory, and the Experience of the Divine in Ancient Israel.* Minneapolis: Fortress Press, 2004.

Smith-Christopher, Daniel L. "Daniel: Introduction, Commentary, and Reflections." Pages 7:17–152 in *The New Interpreter's Bible.* Edited by L. E. Keck et al. Nashville: Abingdon, 1996.

Soggin, J. Alberto. *Judges: A Commentary.* OTL. Philadelphia: Westminster, 1981.

Sommer, Benjamin D. *The Bodies of G-d and the World of Ancient Israel.* Cambridge: Cambridge University Press, 2009.

———. "Dialogical Biblical Theology: A Jewish Approach to Reading Scripture Theologically." Pages 1–53 in *Biblical Theology: Introducing the Conversation.* Edited by L. G. Perdue et al. LBT. Nashville: Abingdon, 2009.

———. *A Prophet Reads Scripture: Allusion in Isaiah 40–66.* Stanford: Stanford University Press, 1998.

———. Revelation at Sinai in the Hebrew Bible and in Jewish Theology." *JR* 79 (1999): 422–51.

Speiser, Ephraim A. *Genesis.* AB 1. New York: Doubleday, 1964.

Stacey, David. *Prophetic Drama in the Old Testament.* London: Epworth, 1990.

Steck, Odil Hannes. *The Prophetic Books and their Theological Witness.* Translated by J. D. Nogalski. St. Louis: Chalice, 2000.

Stern, Ephraim. *Archaeology of the Land of the Bible*. Vol. 2, *The Assyrian, Babylonian, and Persian Periods (732–332 B.C.E.)*. New York: Doubleday, 2001.

Sternberg, Meir. *The Poetics of Biblical Narrative: Ideological Literature and the Drama of Reading*. Bloomington: Indiana University Press, 1987.

Steymans, Hans Ulrich. *Deuteronomium 28 und die adê zur Thronfolgeregelung Asarhaddons: Segen und Fluch im Alten Orient und in Israel*. OBO 145. Freiburg: Éditions universitaires, 1995.

Stoebe, Hans Joachim. *Das erste Buch Samuelis*. KAT 8/1. Gütersloh: Gerd Mohn, 1973.

———. *Das zweite Buch Samuelis*. KAT 8/2. Gütersloh: Gerd Mohn, 1994.

Sweeney, Marvin A. *1 and 2 Kings: A Commentary*. OTL. Louisville: Westminster John Knox, 2007.

———. "Absence of G-d and Human Responsibility in the Book of Esther." Pages 264–75 in *Reading the Hebrew Bible for a New Millennium: Form, Concept and Theological Perspective*. Vol. 2, *Exegetical and Theological Studies*. Edited by Wonil Kim et al. SAC. Harrisburg: Trinity Press International, 2000.

———. "The Assertion of Divine Power in Ezekiel 33:21–39:29." Pages 156–72 in *Form and Intertextuality in Prophetic and Apocalyptic Literatur*. FAT 45. Tübingen: Mohr Siebeck, 2005.

———. "Biblical Theology. I. Hebrew Bible/Old Testament." In *Encyclopaedia of the Bible and its Reception*, vol. 3. Edited by H. J. Klauck et al. Berlin: de Gruyter, forthcoming.

———. "The Book of Isaiah as Prophetic Torah." Pages 13–27 in *Form and Intertextuality in Prophetic and Apocalyptic Literature*. FAT 45. Tübingen: Mohr Siebeck, 2005.

———. "The Critique of Solomon in the Josianic Edition of the Deuteronomistic History." *JBL* 114 (1995): 607–22.

———. "Davidic Polemics in the Book of Judges." *VT* 47 (1997): 517–29.

———. "The Democratization of Messianism in Modern Jewish Theology." Pages 87–101 in *Biblical Interpretation: History, Context, and Reality*. Edited by C. Helmer. SBLSymS 26. Atlanta: Society of Biblical Literature, 2005.

———. "The Destruction of Jerusalem as Purification in Ezekiel 8–11." Pages 144–55 in *Form and Intertextuality in Prophetic and Apocalyptic Literature*. FAT 45. Tübingen: Mohr Siebeck, 2005.

———. "The Emerging Field of Jewish Biblical Theology." Pages 84–105 in *Academic Approaches to Teaching Jewish Studies*. Edited by Z. Garber. Lanham: University Press of America, 2000.

———. "The End of Eschatology in Daniel? Theological and Socio-Political Ramifications of the Changing Contexts of Interpretation." Pages 248–61 in *Form and Intertextuality in Prophetic and Apocalyptic Literature*. FAT 45. Tübingen: Mohr Siebeck, 2005.

———. "Ezekiel: Zadokite Priest and Visionary Prophet of the Exile." Pages 125–43 in *Form and Intertextuality in Prophetic and Apocalyptic Literature*. FAT 45. Tübingen: Mohr Siebeck, 2005.

———. "Ezekiel's Debate with Isaiah." Pages 555–74 in *Congress Volume, Ljubljana 2007*. Edited by A. Lemaire. VTSup 133. Leiden: Brill, 2010.

———. *Form and Intertextuality in Prophetic and Apocalyptic Literature*. FAT 45. Tübingen: Mohr Siebeck, 2005.

———. "Form Criticism." Pages 58–89 in *To Each its Own Meaning: Biblical Criticism and their Application*. Edited by S. L. McKenzie and S. R. Haynes. Louisville: Westminster John Knox, 1999.

———. "Form Criticism." Pages 227–41 in *Dictionary of the Old Testament: Wisdom, Poetry, and Writings*. Edited by T. Longman and P. Enns. Downer Grove, IL: InterVarsity Press, 2008.

———. "Form Criticism: The Question of the Endangered Matriarchs in Genesis." Pages 17–38 in *Method Matters: Essays on the Interpretation of the Hebrew Bible in Honor of David L. Petersen*. Edited by J. M. LeMon and K. H. Richards. ResBibSt 56. Atlanta: Society of Biblical Literature, 2009.

———. *Isaiah 1–39, with an Introduction to Prophetic Literature*. FOTL 16. Grand Rapids: Eerdmans, 1996.

———. "Isaiah and Theodicy after the Shoah." Pages 208–19 in *Strange Fire: Reading the Bible after the Holocaust*. Edited by T. Linafelt. Sheffield: Sheffield Academic, 2000.

———. "Jeremiah 30–31 and King Josiah's Program of National Restoration and Religious Reform." Pages 109–22 in *Form and Intertextuality in Prophetic and Apocalyptic Literature*. FAT 45. Tübingen: Mohr Siebeck, 2005.

———. "Jewish Biblical Theology." Pages 191–208 in *The Hebrew Bible: New Insights and Scholarship*. Edited by F. E. Greenspahn. New York: New York University Press, 2008.

———. "Jewish Biblical Theology and Christian Old Testament Theology." *ThLZ* 134, no. 4 (2009): 397–410.

———. *King Josiah of Judah: The Lost Messiah of Israel*. Oxford: Oxford University Press, 2001.

———. "King Manasseh of Judah and the Problem of Theodicy in the Deuteronomistic History." Pages 264–78 in *Good Kings, Bad Kings*. Edited by L. L. Grabbe. LHBOTS 393. London: T&T Clark International, 2005.

———. "Micah's Debate with Isaiah." Pages 210–21 in *Form and Intertextuality in Prophetic and Apocalyptic Literature*. FAT 45. Tübingen: Mohr Siebeck, 2005.

———. "On the Literary Function of the Notice concerning Hiel's Reestablishment of Jericho in 1 Kings 16.34." Pages 104–15 in *Seeing Signals, Reading Signs: The Art of Exegesis*. Edited by M. A. O'Brien and H. N. Wallace. JSOTSup 415. Sheffield: Sheffield Academic, 2004.

———. "The Priesthood and the Proto-apocalyptic Reading of Prophetic and Pentateuchal Texts." Pages 239–47 in *Form and Intertextuality in Prophetic and Apocalyptic Literature*. FAT 45. Tübingen: Mohr Siebeck, 2005.

———. "The Problem of Ezekiel in Rabbinic Literature." Pages 11–23 in *After Ezekiel: Essays on the Reception of a Difficult Prophet*. Edited by P. M. Joyce and A. Mein. LHBOTS 535. London and New York: T&T Clark International, 2011.

———. "Prophetic Exegesis in Isaiah 65–66." Pages 46–62 in *Form and Intertextuality in Prophetic and Apocalyptic Literature*. FAT 45. Tübingen: Mohr Siebeck, 2005.

———. *The Prophetic Literature*. IBT. Nashville: Abingdon, 2005.

———. "Puns, Politics, and Perushim in the Jacob Cycle: A Case Study in Teaching the English Hebrew Bible." *Shofar* 9 (1991): 103–18.

———. *Reading the Hebrew Bible after the Shoah: Engaging Holocaust Theology*. Minneapolis: Fortress Press, 2008.

———. "Reconceiving the Paradigms of Old Testament Theology in the Post-Shoah Period." *BibInt* 6 (1998): 141–61. Reprinted on pages 155–72 of *Jews, Christians, and the Theology of the Hebrew Scriptures*. Edited by A. O. Bellis and J. S. Kaminsky. SBLSymS 8. Atlanta: Society of Biblical Literature, 2000.

————. "The Reconceptualization of the Davidic Covenant in the Book of Isaiah." Pages 41–61 in *Studies in the Book of Isaiah: Festschrift Willem A. M. Beuken*. Edited by J. van Ruiten and M. Vervenne. BETL 132. Leuven: Leuven University Press and Peeters, 1997.

————. The Religions of Israel and Judah." In *The Cambridge History of Ancient Mediterranean Religions*. Edited by M. Salzman et al. Cambridge: Cambridge University Press, forthcoming.

————. "The Royal Oracle in Ezekiel 37:15–28: Ezekiel's Reflections on Josiah's Reform." Pages 239–53 in *Israel's Prophets and Israel's Past: Essays on the Relationship of Prophetic Texts and Israelite History in Honor of John H. Hayes*. Edited by B. E. Kelle and M. B. Moore. LHBOTS 446. New York: T&T Clark International, 2006.

————. "Sequence and Interpretation in the Book of the Twelve." Pages 49–64 in *Reading and Hearing the Book of the Twelve*. Edited by J. D. Nogalski and M. A. Sweeney. SBLSymS 15. Atlanta: Society of Biblical Literature, 2000.

————. "Structure and Redaction in Jeremiah 2–6." Pages 94–108 in *Form and Intertextuality in Prophetic and Apocalyptic Literature*. FAT 45. Tübingen: Mohr Siebeck, 2005.

————. "Synchronic and Diachronic Considerations in the Portrayal of the Demise of Solomon's Kingdom." Pages 1:175–89 in *Birkat Shalom: Studies in the Bible, Ancient Near Eastern Literature, and Post-Biblical Judaism Presented to Shalom Paul on the Occasion of his Seventieth Birthday*. Edited by C. Cohen et al. Winona Lake, IN: Eisenbrauns, 2008.

————. "Tanak versus Old Testament: Concerning the Foundation for a Jewish Theology of the Bible." Pages 353–72 in *Problems in Biblical Theology: Essays in Honor of Rolf Knierim*. Edited by H. T. C. Sun and K. L. Eades. Grand Rapids: Eerdmans, 1997.

————. "The Truth in True and False Prophecy." Pages 78–93 in *Form and Intertextuality in Prophetic and Apocalyptic Literature*. FAT 45. Tübingen: Mohr Siebeck, 2005.

————. *The Twelve Prophets*. BO. Collegeville: Liturgical, 2000.

————. "Why Jews are Interested in Biblical Theology: A Retrospective on the Work of Jon D. Levenson." *Jewish Book Annual* 55–56 (1997–99/5758–59): 134–68.

————. "Why Jews Should be Interested in Biblical Theology." *CCAR Journal* 44, no. 1 (1997): 67–75.

————. "The Wilderness Traditions of the Pentateuch: A Reassessment of their Function and Intent in Relation to Exodus 32–34." Pages 291–99 in *Society of Biblical Literature 1989 Seminar Papers*. Edited by D. J. Lull. Atlanta: Scholars Press, 1989.

————. *Zephaniah*. Hermeneia. Minneapolis: Fortress Press, 2003.

Tcherikover, Victor. *Hellenistic Civilization and the Jews*. New York: Atheneum, 1982.

Tengström, Sven. *Die Toledotformel und die literarische Struktur der priesterlichen Erweiterungsschicht im Pentateuch*. ConBibOT 17. Uppsala: Gleerup, 1981.

Thomas, Matthew. "These are the Generations: Identity, Promise, and the Toledoth Formulae." Ph.D. diss. Claremont Graduate University, 2006.

Thompson, Thomas L. *The Historicity of the Patriarchal Narratives: The Quest for the Historical Abraham*. BZAW 133. Berlin: de Gruyter, 1974.

Tov, Emanuel. "Jeremiah." Pages 145–207 in *Qumran Cave 4. X. The Prophets*. Edited by E. Ulrich et al. DJD 15. Oxford: Clarendon, 1997.

————. "Some Aspects of the Textual and Literary History of the Book of Jeremiah." Pages 145–67 in *Le livre d'Jérémie. Le prophète et son milieu. Les oracles et leur transmission*. Edited by P.-M. Bogaert. BETL 54. Leuven: Leuven University Press and Peeters, 1981.

————. *Textual Criticism of the Hebrew Bible*. 2d ed. Minneapolis: Fortress Press, 2001.

Tov, Emanuel et al. *The Greek Minor Prophets Scroll from Naḥal Ḥever (8ḤevXIIgr)*. DJD 8. Oxford: Clarendon, 1990.

Trible, Phyllis. *G-d and the Rhetoric of Sexuality.* OBT. Philadelphia: Fortress Press, 1978.

Tucker, Gene M. "Prophetic Superscriptions and the Growth of the Canon." Pages 56–70 in *Canon and Authority.* Edited by G. W. Coats and B. O. Long. Philadelphia: Fortress Press, 1977.

Tuell, Steven Shawn. *The Law of the Temple in Ezekiel 40–48.* HSM 49. Atlanta: Scholars Press, 1992.

Tull Willey, Patricia. *Remember the Former Things: The Recollection of Previous Texts in Second Isaiah.* SBLDS 161. Atlanta: Scholars Press, 1997.

———. "The Servant of YHWH and Daughter Zion: Alternating Visions of YHWH's Community." Pages 267–303 in *Society of Biblical Literature 1995 Seminar Papers.* Edited by Eugene H. Lovering, Jr. Atlanta: Society of Biblical Literature, 1995.

Tzevat, Mattitiahu. "Theology of the Old Testament: A Jewish View." *HBT* 8 (1986): 33–49.

Uffenheimer, Benjamin. "Isaiah's and Micah's Approaches to Policy and History." Pages 176–88 in *Politics and Theopolitics in the Bible and Postbiblical Literature.* Edited by H. Graf Reventlow et al. JSOTSup 27. Sheffield: Sheffield Academic, 1994.

Van Buren, Paul. "On Reading Someone Else's Mail: The Church and Israel's Scriptures." Pages 595–606 in *Die Hebräische Bibel und ihre Zweifache Nachgeschichte. Festschrift für Rolf Rendtorff.* Edited by E. Blum et al. Neukirchen–Vluyn: Neukirchener Verlag, 1990.

Van Seters, John. *Abraham in History and Tradition.* New Haven: Yale University Press, 1975.

———. *The Life of Moses: The Y-hwist as Historian in Exodus—Numbers.* Louisville: Westminster John Knox, 1994.

———. *Prologue to History: The Y-hwist as Historian in Genesis.* Louisville: Westminster John Knox, 1992.

Veijola, Timo. *Die ewige Dyastie: David und die Enstehung seiner Dynastie nach der deuteronomistischen Darstellung.* Helsinki: Suomalainen Tiedeakatemia, 1975.

———. *Das Königtum in der Beurteilung der deuteronomistischen Historiographie.* Helsinki: Suomalainen Tiedeakatemia, 1977.

de Vos, Christine. *Klage als G-tteslob aus der Tiefe. Der Mensch vor G-tt in den indviduellen Klagepsalmen.* FAT 2/11. Tübingen: Mohr Siebeck, 2005.

Wallfish, Barry Dov. *Esther in Medieval Garb: Jewish Interpretation of the Book of Esther in the Middle Ages.* Albany: SUNY Press, 1993.

Walsh, Jerome T. *1 Kings.* BO. Collegeville: Liturgical, 1996.

Wanke, Gunther. *Die Zionstheologie der Korachiten.* BZAW 97. Berlin: Töpelmann, 1966.

Wei, Tom F. "Pithom." *ABD* 5:376–77.

Weinfeld, Moshe. "The Covenant of Grant in the OT and in the Ancient Near East." *JAOS* 90 (1970): 184–203.

———. *Deuteronomy 1–11.* AB 5. Garden City: Doubleday, 1991.

———. "Deuteronomy, Book of." *ABD* 2:168–83.

———. *Deuteronomy and the Deuteronomic School.* Winona Lake, IN: Eisenbrauns, 1992.

———. "Judges 1.1–2.5: The Conquest under the Leadership of the House of Judah." Pages 388–400 in *Understanding Poets and Prophets.* Fs. G. W. Anderson. Edited by A. G. Auld. JSOTSup 152. Sheffield: JSOT Press, 1993.

———. "Sabbath, Temple, and the Enthronement of the L-rd: The Problem of the Sitz im Leben of Genesis 1:1–2:3." Pages 501–12 in *Mélanges bibliques et orientaux en l'honneur M. Henri Cazelles.* Edited by A. Caquot and M. Delcor. AOAT 212. Kevelaer: Butzon & Bercker. Neukirchen–Vluyn: Neukirchener Verlag, 1981.

———. *Social Justice in Ancient Israel and the Ancient Near East.* Jerusalem: Magnes, 1995.

———. "Zion and Jerusalem as Religious and Political Capital: Ideology and Utopia." Pages 75–115 in *The Poet and the Historian: Essays in Literary and Historical Biblical Criticism.* Edited by R. E. Friedman. HSS 26. Chico, CA: Scholars Press, 1983.

Weippert, Helga. "Die 'deuteronomistischen' Beurteilungen der Könige von Israel und Juda und das Problem der Redaktion der Königsbücher." *Bib* 53 (1972): 301–39.

Wellhausen, Julius. *Die Composition des Hexataeuch under Historischen Bücher des Alten Testaments.* Berlin: Reimer, 1889.

———. *Prolegomena to the History of Ancient Israel.* Gloucester, MA: Smith, 1973.

Westermann, Claus. *Genesis 1–11.* ContCom. Minneapolis: Augsburg, 1984.

———. *Praise and Lament in the Psalms.* Atlanta: John Knox, 1981.

———. *The Promises to the Fathers: Studies on the Patriarchal Narratives.* Philadelphia: Fortress Press, 1980.

Whedbee, J. William. *The Bible and the Comic Vision.* Cambridge: Cambridge University Press, 1998.

White, Marsha C. *The Elijah Legends and Jehu's Coup.* BJS 311. Atlanta: Scholars Press, 1997.

Whybray, R. N. *The Succession Narrative: A Study of II Sam. 9–20 and I Kings 1 and 2.* SBT 2/9. Naperville: Allenson, 1968.

———. *The Book of Proverbs: A Survey of Modern Study.* Leiden: Brill, 1995.

Wiesel, Elie. *Souls on Fire: Portraits and Legends of Hasidic Masters.* New York: Summit, 1972.

Wilcoxen, Jay. "The Political Background of Jeremiah's Temple Sermon." Pages 151–66 in *Scripture in History and Theology: Essays in Honor of J. Coert Rylaarsdam.* Edited by A. Merrill and T. Overholt. Pittsburgh: Pickwick, 1977.

Wildberger, Hans. *Isaiah 1–12: A Commentary.* ContCom. Minneapolis: Fortress Press, 1991.

Williamson, Clark. *A Guest in the House of Israel: Post-Holocaust Church Theology.* Louisville: Westminster John Knox, 1993.

Williamson, H. G. M. *1 and 2 Chronicles.* NCenB. Grand Rapids: Eerdmans. London: Marshall, Morgan & Scott, 1982.

———. *The Book Called Isaiah: Deutero-Isaiah's Role in Composition and Redaction.* Oxford: Clarendon, 1994.

———. *Ezra–Nehemiah.* WBC 16. Waco: Word, 1985.

———. *Ezra and Nehemiah.* OTG. Sheffield: Sheffield Academic, 1987.

———. *Israel in the Books of Chronicles.* Cambridge: Cambridge University Press, 1977.

Wills, Lawrence M. "Daniel." Pages 1640–65 in *The Jewish Study Bible.* Edited by A. Berlin and M. Z. Brettler. Oxford: Oxford University Press, 2003.

———. *The Jew in the Court of the Foreign King: Ancient Jewish Court Legends.* Minneapolis: Fortress Press, 1990.

Wilson, Gerald Henry. *The Editing of the Hebrew Psalter.* SBLDS 76. Chico, CA: Scholars Press, 1981.

Wiseman, D. J. *The Vassal Treaties of Esarhaddon.* London: British School of Archaeology in Iraq, 1958.

Wolff, Hans Walter. *Amos the Prophet: The Man and his Background.* Translated by F. McCurley. Philadelphia: Fortress Press, 1973.

———. "The Kerygma of the Deuteronomic Historical Work." Pages 83–100 in *The Vitality of the Old Testament Traditions.* Edited by W. Brueggemann and H. W. Wolff. Atlanta: John Knox, 1975.

———. *Obadiah and Jonah.* Translated by M. Kohl. ContCom. Minneapolis: Fortress Press, 1986.

Wright, A. "The Riddle of the Sphinx: The Structure of the Book of Qoheleth." *CBQ* 30 (1968): 313–34.

———. "The Riddle of the Sphinx Revisited: Numerical Patterns in the Book of Qoheleth." *CBQ* 42 (1980): 38–51.

Wright, David P. "Holiness (OT)." *ABD* 3:237–49.

———. "Priestly ("P") Source." *ABD* 5:454–61.

Wright, David P., and Richard N. Jones. "Leprosy." *ABD* 4:277–82.

Wright, J. Edward. *Baruch Ben Neriah: From Biblical Scribe to Apocalyptic Seer.* Columbia: University of South Carolina Press, 2003.

Wright, Jacob L. *Rebuilding Identity: The Nehemiah Memoir and its Earliest Readers.* BZAW 348. Berlin: de Gruyter, 2004.

Yee, Gale. "Ideological Criticism: Judges 17–21 and the Dismembered Body." Pages 146–70 in *Judges and Method: New Approaches in Biblical Studies.* Minneapolis: Fortress Press, 1995.

Yerushalmi, Yosef Hayim. *Zakhor: Jewish History and Jewish Memory.* Seattle: University of Washington, 1982.

Zenger, Erich. *Das erste Testament. Die jüdische Bibel und die Christen.* Düsseldorf: Patmos, 1993.

Zevit, Ziony. "Jewish Biblical Theology: Whence? Why? And Whither?" *HUCA* 49 (2005): 289–340.

Zimmerli, Walter. *Ezekiel 1: A Commentary on the Book of the Prophet Ezekiel 1–24.* Translated by R. E. Clements. Hermeneia. Philadelphia: Fortress Press, 1979.

———. *Ezekiel 2: A Commentary on the Book of the Prophet Ezekiel Chapters 25–48.* Translated by J. D. Martin. Hermeneia. Philadelphia: Fortress Press, 1983.

———. "I am YHWH." Pages 1–28 in *I am YHWH.* Atlanta: John Knox, 1982.

Zunz, Leopold. *Die Gottesdienstlichen Vorträge der Juden.* Hildesheim: Olms, 1966.

INDEX OF AUTHORS
CITED IN THE TEXT

INDEX OF SUBJECTS

185, 189, 194–95,
203, 223, 225,
241, 244, 247–49,
256–60, 265, 267,
364, 371, 373,
468, 479, 481–82
Gad   70, 73–75, 124,
126, 132, 136,
142, 180, 188,
193, 199–200,
203, 231, 474, 477
Garden of Eden   16, 58, 60, 107,
242, 261, 287,
334, 339, 429
Gath   183, 218–19, 357,
386
Gaza   183, 352
G-d   3, 6–17, 19–27,
29–30, 32–40, 51,
55–68, 71, 73, 79,
81-83, 85-88, 90–
99, 105, 107–8,
111–12, 116–18,
123, 129–30, 133,
150–52, 162, 165,
167, 174, 178,
185, 189, 194,
198, 208, 210,
223, 232, 237,
243, 246–47,
251–52, 267–68,
275, 280, 285,
287, 291, 317,
319, 322, 324,
349, 351, 356,
371–73, 375–77,
380–90, 392,
394–96, 402, 404,
407–9, 411–23,
426–27, 429–30,
432–33, 440–42,
444–47, 449–53,
460, 463–64, 468,
472–73, 475, 480,
483, 487–89,
491–95, 497–503,
505–6, 509

Gedaliah ben Ahikam   294, 310–11, 314,
434
Gemariah ben Shaphan   310
Gematria   30
Gerizim   154, 163
Gershom   87, 95, 124, 128,
132, 140, 142, 320
Gibeah   23, 195–97, 201,
213, 348
Gibeon   179–84, 187,
189–90, 202,
221–22, 229, 233,
241, 474, 476–78,
492
Gideon   143, 185, 193–94,
199–202
Gilead   73–74, 142, 196,
199–201, 203,
212–14, 221, 237,
250, 253, 349
Gilgal   180–81, 223, 348
Gog   337–38
Golden Calf   52, 102–3, 127,
135, 194–95, 328,
348, 391
Goliath   216–18, 230
Gomer   345–47
Gomorrah   55, 67, 283, 348,
353, 420
Greek   21, 29–30, 40, 52,
183, 295, 316,
363, 427, 438,
445, 450, 452,
456, 472, 505, 508
Guilt Offering   108, 111, 328
Habakkuk   265, 343–44,
360–61, 367, 409,
497
Habiru   90, 173, 183, 185
Haftarah   371
Haftarot   17, 39, 495
Hagar   67–68, 70, 82,
122, 210
Haggai   265, 343–44,
361–62, 368, 473
Haggit   241
Halakhah   3, 32, 419
Hallel   371, 392, 394, 397

Hallelujah	392, 394		494–500, 504–8,
Haman	24, 95, 441–44		510
Hamsin	89, 92	Hebrew Bible	7, 9–11, 18, 19,
Hananiah	299, 307–8, 451–52		26, 28, 36–37, 39,
			40, 53, 57, 82-83,
Hanina ben Hezekiah	319		106, 167, 191,
Hannah	61, 82, 90, 128,		261, 291–92, 328,
	186, 210, 247		341, 373, 422–23,
Hasidism	3, 12, 408		446–47, 449, 483,
Hathor	60		489, 492, 494–
ḥaṭṭa't	108–13, 115, 130,		500, 504–8
	135, 328	Hebron	69, 74, 143, 187,
Hazor	179–81, 183–84,		221–22, 225,
	187, 189–90, 194,		240–41
	199, 202	*Heilsgeschichte*	8, 32
Heaven	45–47, 49, 55, 58,	Heman the Erahite	387, 389
	62, 64, 112, 199,	Hermeneutics	8, 17–18, 30, 39–
	242, 251, 350,		40, 166, 316–17,
	366, 401, 449,		341, 501, 504
	452, 454	*ḥesed*	27, 394, 436
Hebrew	7, 9–14, 18–19,	Hezekiah	81, 120, 138, 174,
	21, 26, 28–31,		176–78, 204, 235,
	35–40, 45, 52–53,		237–38, 256–57,
	57–59, 64, 71–73,		266, 269–72, 275,
	82-83, 87-88, 90,		277, 279–80,
	105–6, 114, 118,		283–84, 298, 307,
	143–44, 152, 167,		319, 328, 345,
	171, 174, 178,		357, 385, 399–
	183, 190–91, 193,		400, 402, 404,
	205, 214, 218,		406, 438, 476,
	231, 242, 246,		479, 481, 503
	250, 261, 265,	Hidden face of G-d	14
	279, 281–82, 287,	Hiram	132, 222, 236,
	289–92, 295, 301,		241–42, 244, 475
	305, 316, 322,	Hobab	124, 133
	328, 339, 341,	Holiness	11–13, 15–16, 19,
	346, 350, 365,		27, 40, 49, 56–57,
	371, 373, 379,		62, 88, 97, 109,
	381, 383, 385,		113, 115, 117,
	394, 396, 402–3,		120–22, 146, 155,
	407, 410, 421–23,		167, 278, 319,
	425–26, 429, 434,		323–24, 332–33,
	438, 446–47,		338–41, 465, 480,
	449–50, 454–56,		499, 505, 511
	460, 468, 471,	Holiness code	19, 49, 115, 120,
	479, 483, 487,		122, 323, 332–33
	489, 491–92,	Holocaust	8–9, 12–13, 36,
			38–39, 82, 106,

Prophets	3, 6, 8, 12, 18–25, 28–29, 31–32, 34, 37, 39–40, 89, 105, 147, 156, 158–59, 165, 169, 171–79, 182, 185–86, 189, 194–95, 203, 206, 223, 225, 232, 241, 244, 247–50, 252, 256–60, 263, 265–69, 275, 293, 302, 306, 313–14, 317, 319, 330, 333, 338, 341, 343, 347, 349, 354, 364–68, 371–73, 375, 395, 409, 413, 422, 426, 436–37, 441, 445, 466, 468, 473, 479, 481–82, 487–88, 493, 497, 501, 508–9		438–41, 446, 500–501, 510–11
		Queen of Sheba	236, 244, 411, 476, 478
		Qumran	29–30, 40, 152, 379, 508
		R. Akiba	28
		R. David Kimhi	270, 338
		Rabbis	12, 32–33, 265–66, 371, 460
		Rachel	3, 21, 70–74, 78, 157, 210, 285, 288, 349
		Rahab	56, 179, 181–82, 190, 287, 432
		Rameses II	90
		Rashi	16, 31, 56, 338
		Rebekah	21, 68, 70–72, 122
		Rechabites	309–10
		Red sea	100, 105, 134, 244, 287, 315, 350, 392
		Reed sea	47, 49, 76, 92–93, 181, 349
Protestant Christianity	4, 51	Rehoboam	229, 236, 241, 245–46, 248, 476, 478–79, 481
Proverbs	9, 24, 32, 35, 371–73, 376, 399–402, 404–11, 417–18, 425–27, 440, 444, 493–94, 496, 502, 510	Remez	30
		Repentance	162–64, 167, 185, 198, 250, 256, 258, 289, 302, 305, 330–31, 336, 346, 348, 352, 355–56, 364, 377, 416, 419, 435, 466, 481–82
Psalms	15, 24, 28, 35, 103, 294, 303–4, 317, 350, 371–73, 375–87, 389–97, 411, 425, 438, 444–46, 460, 480, 488, 494–97, 501, 503–4, 510	Restoration	17–18, 23–24, 38, 68, 75, 104, 119, 127, 140, 147, 154, 162–64, 166–67, 173, 175, 204, 235, 237, 253, 258–59, 266–67, 270–75, 277, 280–81, 283–90, 293–94, 296–301, 305, 307–9, 315, 317, 319–21, 324–25,
Ptolemaic (Empire)	449, 450, 452, 456, 457		
Ptolemy	456		
Purim	24, 371, 373, 379, 425, 441–43		
Qere'/Ketiv	29		
Qinah	332, 334–35, 434		
Qoheleth	24, 371, 373, 376, 399, 409, 425–26,		